DATE DUE

DEMCO 38-296

NO '87

CRITICAL SURVEY
OF
POETRY

CRITICAL SURVEY
OF
POETRY

Supplement

Edited by
FRANK N. MAGILL

SALEM PRESS

Pasadena, California   Englewood Cliffs, New Jersey

Library of Congress Cataloging-in-Publication Data
Critical survey of poetry. Supplement.
    Bibliography: p.
    Includes index.
    Poetry—History and criticism—Dictionaries. 2.
Poetry—Bio-bibliography. 3. Poets—Biography. I.
Magill, Frank Northen, 1907-   .
PN1021.C7 1984   Suppl.   809.1'003   87-13139
ISBN 0-89356-349-8

PUBLISHER'S NOTE

The present volume is a supplement to the *Critical Survey of Poetry*, English Language Series (1982) and Foreign Language Series (1984). It is being published in conjunction with comparable supplements to the other sets in Magill's Salem Press genre series, which together constitute a forty-five-volume, worldwide study of the major figures in the fields of short fiction, poetry, long fiction, and drama.

The primary purpose of this supplement is to extend coverage to significant poets who were not included in the earlier volumes—particularly contemporary poets, who could be covered only very selectively in the original survey. Of the forty-nine poets included in the supplement (ten of whom are women), all but four are from the twentieth century, and about half are still active. Slightly less than half of the poets included are from the United States; in all, eighteen countries are represented on the list, which includes poets from England, Scotland, and Ireland, South Africa and Australia, Eastern and Western Europe, the Soviet Union and the Middle East, Brazil, Turkey, and Japan.

This geographical range is matched by the wide variety of poetic traditions represented in the supplement: from the classical Persian verse of Firdusi, Hafiz, and Jalal al-Din Rumi to the haiku of Issa; from the open forms of Charles Olson and Muriel Rukeyser to the sonnets of Tony Harrison. Two of the poets included are Nobel laureates: Harry Martinson of Sweden, who shared the 1974 prize with his countryman Eyvind Johnson, and Jaroslav Seifert of Czechoslovakia, who received the prize in 1984.

While the list includes such well-established figures as Olson and Rukeyser, A. R. Ammons, Stanley Kunitz, and Yvor Winters, it also includes relatively neglected figures such as Lorine Niedecker, whose work is receiving long-overdue critical recognition. Younger writers such as Susan Howe and Australia's Les A. Murray, who have added distinctive voices to contemporary poetry, are also represented here.

The format of the individual articles in this volume is consistent with that of the earlier volumes. Pertinent top matter is followed by a listing of the poet's principal collections, with dates of first publication, a brief survey of work in literary forms other than poetry, a summary of the subject's professional achievements, a biographical sketch, and a critical analysis of the subject's canon, which is the body of the essay. Following these critical overviews is a list of major publications other than poetry and a bibliography of significant criticism.

In addition, the supplement updates information provided in the *Critical Survey of Poetry*. For poets who were living when those earlier volumes were published, the supplement provides a record of subsequent publications and awards and, when applicable, a death date. These listings appear in a separate section following the articles on individual poets.

A comprehensive Index to the volume supplements the original *Critical Survey of Poetry* index, listing all major poets, titles, and terms discussed. Entries for poets who appear in the volume are in boldface type, followed by an alphabetical listing of those of their works which are analyzed in the text.

CONTRIBUTORS

Peter Baker

J. R. Broadus

David Bromige

John Carpenter

Patricia Clark

Robert P. Ellis

Massud Farzan

Kenneth E. Gadomski

Lois Gordon

William H. Green

R. S. Gwynn

Steven L. Hale

Paul Kane

Leon Lewis

Michael Loudon

Janet McCann

Arthur E. McGuinness

Joseph Maltby

Anne Laura Mattrella

Laurence W. Mazzeno

Jane Ann Miller

Leslie Norris

George O'Brien

James O'Brien

Mahmoud Omidsalar

Coílín Owens

Charles A. Perrone

John Povey

Charles H. Pullen

Jed Rasula

David Rigsbee

Sven H. Rossel

Mark Sanders

Tuula Stark

Shelby Stephenson

Shelley Thrasher

Klaus Weissenberger

Bruce Wiebe

Patricia A. R. Williams

LIST OF AUTHORS

CRITICAL SURVEY OF POETRY

CRITICAL SURVEY
OF
POETRY

YEHUDA AMICHAI

Born: Würzburg, Germany; May 3, 1924

Principal poems and collections

Akhshav u-ve-yamin aherim, 1955; *Be-Merhak Shteitikvot*, 1958; *Shirim, 1948-1962*, 1962; *Akhshav ba-Ra'ash*, 1968; *Ve-lo 'almenat lizkor*, 1971; *Selected Poems*, 1971; *Me-ahore kol zel mistater osher gadol*, 1974; *Ha-zeman*, 1978 (*Time*, 1979); *Shalyah gedolah*, 1980 (*A Great Tranquillity: Questions and Answers*, 1980); *Love Poems*, 1981; *She'at ha-hessed*, 1983; *Me'adam ve-el adam tashav*, 1985; *The Selected Poetry of Yehuda Amichai*, 1986.

Other literary forms

Yehuda Amichai has written three volumes of fiction. *Lo me-akhshav, lo mi-kan* (*Not of This Time, Not of This Place*), a novel, was published in Hebrew in Tel Aviv in 1963 and translated into English in 1968. A collection of short stories, *Ba-ruah ha-nora'ah ha-zot*, was published in Tel Aviv in 1961; a translation of about half the stories appeared in English in 1984 under the title *The World Is a Room and Other Stories*. Amichai has also written a play for the radio, titled *Pa'amonim ve-rakavot* (1968; pr. as *Bells and Trains*, 1966).

Achievements

With Amir Gilboa, Abba Kovner, and Dan Pagis, Amichai is a leading member of the first generation of Israeli poets. They were born in Europe and Hebrew was not their mother tongue, yet they came to Palestine and soon wrote in Hebrew.

A continuous tradition of secular Hebrew poetry existed since A.D. 1000, flourishing first in Spain, Portugal, Provence, Italy, and the Netherlands, migrating in the nineteenth century to Central and Eastern Europe. No one spoke the language that the poets used; their Hebrew was largely derived from sacred texts. Amichai and his contemporaries were the first literary generation to use Hebrew as a vernacular. The new generation felt the need to break with the preceding poetic traditions, yet the new spoken language alone did not suffice as a literary instrument. It was this first generation that provided different models and showed how an everyday language might be transformed into poetry.

Amichai has been one of the leaders of this generation, and the various forms, tonalities, and influences which he has introduced into Hebrew literature will have a lasting effect. As the critic Gabriel Josipovici has written, Amichai and his colleagues were European Jews first and Israelis second; the dreadful history of Europe and the Middle East in their lifetime forced them to contemplate their relationship to both Judaism and the State of Israel. Amichai's generation has been unique in Hebrew literature, and of this group it is perhaps Amichai who has explored the broadest range of poetic forms.

His poetry and prose have been awarded the Shlonsky Prize and two Acum prizes. His radio play *Bells and Trains* won the first prize in Kol, the country's competition for original radio plays.

Biography

Yehuda Amichai was born in Würzburg in 1924. He grew up in an Orthodox Jewish home; his father was a shopkeeper, his grandfather a farmer. His mother tongue was German; although he entered the government-sponsored Israelitische Volkschule at the age of six and learned to read and to write Hebrew, he did not begin to speak Hebrew until 1935, when he moved to Palestine with his parents and settled in Jerusalem. His outlook was influenced by the Socialist youth movement, to which most Jewish adolescents belonged in the Palestine of the 1930's and early 1940's. He fought with the British army in World War II, then with the Palmakh in the Israeli War of Independence of 1948. He also fought with the Israeli army in 1956 and 1973.

For most of his life, Amichai has made his living as a schoolteacher. His poetry has always been very popular in Israel, and since the publication of his first book in 1955, his writing has been an important source of revenue. Although there are fewer than three million readers of Hebrew in Israel, the collection of his early work, *Shirim, 1948-1962* (poems, 1948-1962), several times reprinted, has sold fifty thousand copies.

Amichai was a visiting poet at the University of California at Berkeley in 1971. He has a son by his first wife and lives with his second wife, Chana, his second son, David, and his daughter, Emanuella, in Jerusalem. Amichai frequently travels abroad and gives poetry readings.

Analysis

Yehuda Amichai is not a poet of a single major theme, and a variety of approaches to his work are open to the reader and critic. He is—perhaps above all—an autobiographical poet, yet it is also possible to consider him as a national poet whose personal concerns overlap those of his country. Amichai is one of the few poets of the late twentieth century who can be called genuinely "popular," and it is important to consider the nature of his relationship to his audience. Other important features of Amichai's poetry are the apparent effortlessness of his poems, with their agile, attractive speaking voice and complex tone; his use of conceits (his early poetry especially has been called "metaphysical") and his consistent success in finding striking, original metaphors; the rich variety of forms he has tried, from quasi-Shakespearean sonnets to mock-heroic couplets and free verse; his emphasis on the concrete, palpable events of everyday life, as opposed to the abstract phraseology of ideologies and philosophers; and, finally, his love poetry, the major theme of his work from the 1950's and 1960's.

The autobiographical nature of Amichai's poetry has been the cause of some attacks on his work. Spontaneous reference to his own experiences characterizes his entire oeuvre. The other, equally important, impulses are also present: the desire to describe what is real, immediate, and concrete, and the need to reach out to his surroundings. In his second collection of poems, he wrote about his thirty-second birthday: "Thirty-two times I have put on the world/ and still it doesn't fit me./ It weighs me down,/ unlike the coat that now takes the shape of my body."

His references to himself are usually self-demeaning and rueful. He does not have the "beautiful soul" held up for admiration by many contemporary American poets. The persona of his poems is always complex. Clearly there is no barrier between the speaker and his surroundings. Amichai's self—his autobiography—proves to be remarkably synoptic and inclusive. Amichai describes himself at home in Jerusalem in his poem "Travels of the Last Benjamin of Tudela" thus:

> I've been patched together
> from many things, I've been gathered in different times,
> I've been assembled from spare parts, from disintegrating
> materials, from decomposing words. And already now,
> in the middle of my life, I'm beginning to return them gradually.

The speaker of such a passage is intimate, his mind agile and far-reaching, never confined. The critic Robert Alter has stressed that archaeology has always been one of Amichai's primary metaphors for his perception of the human condition; he sees both the individual self and history as an elaborate depositing of layers in which nothing is entirely buried from sight. There is also an uncanny overlapping between his own life and that of the country of Israel. He writes in the poem titled "When I Was Young, the Whole Country Was Young":

> When I first fell in love, they proclaimed
> her independence, and when my hair
> fluttered in the breeze, so did her flags.
> When I fought in the war, she fought, when I got up
> she got up too, and when I sank
> she began to sink with me.

The combination of the two themes seems spontaneous and unstudied, always accompanied by humor, irony, and the special effortlessness that by the mid-1970's had become one of the most distinctive features of Amichai's poetry.

Since 1980, Amichai has fused the two themes to the point of self-parody. In "You Mustn't Show Weakness" he writes: "This is the way things stand now:/ if I pull out the stopper/ after pampering myself in the bath,/ I'm afraid that all of Jerusalem, and with it the whole world,/ will drain out into the huge darkness." Although such a thought might have actually occurred to him while taking a bath, it is doubtful whether the passage could be called autobiographical; Amichai is building a different, much more synoptic persona than the "I" of the earlier poems. This development is confirmed by a passage such as this: "If I'm a hedgehog, I'm a hedgehog in reverse,/ the spikes grow inward and stab./ And if I'm the prophet Ezekiel, I see/ in the Vision of the Chariot/ only the dung-spattered feet of oxen and the muddy wheels." After 1980, it is no longer possible to speak of Amichai's poetry as autobiographical. He has achieved an inclusive view of the world in which the speaker's observations and his use of a first-person pronoun are strictly vehicles at the service of other concepts: of society and time, of reality, and of the world.

Looking back from the vantage point of Amichai's mature style of the 1980's, it is clear that he always appreciated the reality of concrete, individual experience, and of the personalities of other people. For example, some poems were excellent portraits of women, especially "You Are So Small and Slight in the Rain," "The Sweet Breakdowns of Abigail," and the devastating and sensual "A Bride Without a Dowry," which ends:

> And she's got a will of iron inside
> that soft, self-indulgent flesh.
> What a terrible bloodbath
> she's preparing for herself.
> What a Roman arena streaming with blood.

In another poem he writes that as a child, when he banged his head on the door, he did not scream "Mama" or "God," but simply, "my head, my head," and " door, door." The meaning is clear: He always preferred solid, palpable reality to subjective notions.

In this context, the problem of Amichai's tone, of the speaking voice in his poems, becomes particularly acute. Is it a personal or autobiographical tone? When he writes, "I'm like an ambulance/ on two legs, hauling the patient inside me to Last Aid/ with the wailing cry of a siren,/ and people think it's ordinary speech," the rhythms of the tone become the subject of the poem itself. Indeed this is not "ordinary speech," nor is it merely a wail of pain; Amichai is warning his readers that it is a construct. Gabriel Josipovici has written that, "like much postwar East European poetry, Amichai's is poetry which can travel"; that is, it is easily translated. His fluctuating tone, the humor, irony, and playfulness with words are extremely subtle, however, and much is lost, in both style and content, in translation.

An example is the ending of "When a Man's Far Away from His Country," a wry, bitter poem whose subject is the quality of language. Not only in style but also in theme the tone and spoken rhythms are all-important. One translation, by Chana Bloch, ends:

> In my words
> is the soul's garbage, the trash of lust,
> and dust and sweat. In this dry land even the water I drink
> between screams and mumblings of desire
> is urine,
> recycled back to me by a twisted route.

As English translation by Amichai himself reads:

> In my words there is garbage of soul
> and refuse of lust and dust and sweat.
> Even the water I drink in this dry land,
> between screams and memories of love,
> is urine recycled back to me
> through complicated circuits.

Amichai's version has one line less (like the original), a different system of emphases, stresses, and tonalities. In the first translation, it would be difficult for the reader to divine that the "twisted route" could refer to the theme of memory, while the humorous "complicated circuits" clearly recalls the theme—and process—of memory. The stress on excretion in the first translation is far too heavy-handed and destroys the meaning.

Much is lost in translation. The English-speaking reader should always keep this in mind when reading the English versions. As Robert Alter writes, "His Hebrew is often rich in soundplay, wordplay, allusion, and other traits of virtuosity that are not readily evident in translation, and his language is a shifting mixture of colloquial and literary." Colloquial, spoken tone is important, and Amichai has been influenced by W. H. Auden: When he was a soldier in the British army, he accidentally found a Faber and Faber anthology of contemporary British and American poetry. Perhaps the best way for an English-speaking reader to have a sense of Amichai's verbal textures is to read the selections in *The Modern Hebrew Poem Itself* (1965), edited by Stanley Burnshaw, and the *Penguin Book of Hebrew Verse* (1981), edited by T. Carmi. These provide literal translations and full commentaries that give the English speaker an idea of the density of Amichai's style in the original Hebrew.

One feature of Amichai's style much easier to translate is the use of metaphor. From the very beginning, Amichai has been a virtuoso of metaphor. He seemed to produce them effortlessly—perhaps too effortlessly, as some early poems were metaphorical tours de force. He could write about Jerusalem as "the Venice of God," or, in another context, as "An operation that was left open." A fig tree is "that brothel where ripe figs/ couple with wasps and are split to death." Sometimes they seem simply witty, as in "Jerusalem's a place where everyone remembers/ he's forgotten something/ but doesn't remember what it is" or "tears/ remain longer than whatever caused them." Yet the wit often is turned into profound meaning, as in this stanza:

> There are candles that remember for a full twenty-four hours,
> that's what the label says. And candles that remember
> for eight hours, and eternal candles
> that guarantee a man will be remembered by his children.

One of the vices of Amichai's poetry was that often he was willing to settle for easy metaphors. This might have been partly a result of his respect for solidity, for reality; as a young poet his posture was of assent, of necessary yet ironic acceptance. His concept of life was basically linear: "Our lives were stamped *To the last stop: one way.*" He makes a similar statement in another volume of poems: "I am always Cain:/ a fugitive and a vagabond before the deed that I won't do,/ or after the deed that/ can't be undone." This had its pious side; although he could be irreverent about God (Amichai ceased to believe in a deity at the age of fifteen), there was another, greater loyalty to his community: "When I was a child I sang in the synagogue choir,/ . . . and I'll go on singing/ till my heart breaks, first heart and second heart./ A Psalm." It required some time, perhaps two decades, for him to pass through the stage in which he thought of himself primarily as a vehicle—a head "like the heads of those senseless weeds" through which fate passes like wind from one place to another—to his later and far more dynamic, nonlinear version of history and life.

It is in Amichai's earlier volumes that he is primarily a love poet. When he was in his twenties and thirties, it seemed as if the love of woman, and especially one woman, was to be his overriding theme. Some of these poems express wonder at a woman's beauty and a concentrated dedication to sensual, heterosexual love that resembles poems by Jaroslav Seifert, the Czech poet and 1984 winner of the Nobel Prize for Literature. Woman's sexual beauty was one of Seifert's abiding concerns: "But when I first saw/ the picture of a nude woman/ I began to believe in miracles." In the 1960's, it seemed that for Amichai, too, woman's sexual beauty might become his major devotion. He wrote: "I tried to go out into my times, and to know,/ but I didn't get further/ than the woman's body beside me."

Many of Amichai's love poems are very moving, and they are frequently anthologized. A bilingual collection of *Love Poems* was selected from his different volumes by Amichai himself and published in 1981. He is a fine love poet: His commitment to a woman, to sensual love, seemed almost total. The poems are sensual, savage, nothing seems to be held back, and they run the range of a broad spectrum of emotions. "Six Songs for Tamar" and "Songs for a Woman" are especially beautiful. The note of wonder Amichai expresses can be very moving: "If you open your coat/ my love must widen." In many poems, however, there is a note not only of deep sadness but also of self-pity, as in the much-admired poem "A Pity. We Were Such a Good Invention," which ends:

> A pity. We were such a good
> and loving invention.
> An airplane made from a man and a wife.
> Wings and everything.
> We hovered a little above the earth.
>
> We even flew a little.

Although the clipped, elegiac mood is obviously ironic, it spread from poem to poem and became obsessive, threatening to swamp Amichai's other concerns. Yet he grew. He added new themes.

The result is that today Amichai is recognized as the author of a body of work extremely varied, rich, and inventive in form. One of Amichai's most remarkable traits is that his poems continue to surprise.

Other major works

NOVEL: *Lo me-akhshav, lo mi-kan*, 1963 (*Not of This Time, Not of This Place*, 1968).

SHORT FICTION: *Ba-ruah ha-nora'ah ha-zot*, 1961; *The World Is a Room and Other Stories*, 1984.

RADIO PLAY: *Pa'amonim ve-rakavot*, 1968 (pr. as *Bells and Trains*, 1966).

Bibliography

Alter, Robert. "Israel's Master Poet," in *The New York Times Sunday Magazine*. June 8, 1986.

Burnshaw, Stanley, T. Carmi, and Ezra Spicehandler, eds. *The Modern Hebrew Poem Itself*, 1965.

Hamburger, Michael. Introduction to *Selected Poems*, 1971.

Josipovici, Gabriel. "Translating the World," in *The Times Literary Supplement*. October 17, 1986, p. 1158.

Sachs, Arieh. "The Poetry of Yehuda Amichai," in *Judaism*. XIV, no. 4 (1965).

John Carpenter

A. R. AMMONS

Born: Near Whiteville, North Carolina; February 18, 1926

Principal poems and collections
Ommateum, with Doxology, 1955; *Expressions of Sea Level*, 1964; *Corsons Inlet*, 1965; *Tape for the Turn of the Year*, 1965; *Northfield Poems*, 1966; *Selected Poems*, 1968; *Uplands*, 1970; *Briefings: Poems Small and Easy*, 1971; *Collected Poems, 1951-1971*, 1972; *Sphere: The Form of a Motion*, 1974; *Diversifications*, 1975; *The Snow Poems*, 1977; *The Selected Poems 1951-1977*, 1977; *Selected Longer Poems*, 1980; *A Coast of Trees*, 1981; *Worldly Hopes*, 1982; *Lake Effect Country*, 1983; *Selected Poems: Expanded Edition*, 1987; *Sumerian Vistas*, 1987.

Other literary forms
Although A. R. Ammons is known primarily for his poetry, he has also published reviews and essays. Central to an understanding of his work are "A Poem Is a Walk" and his short autobiographical reflection "I Couldn't Wait to Say the Word." Ammons' several published interviews give additional insight into his poetics, especially that by Cynthia Haythe.

Achievements
Through a distinguished and prolific career, Ammons has always succeeded in seeing the particulars of the world within a longing for a sense of unity. He immerses himself in the flow of things, celebrating the world and the self that sees and probes it.

Ammons' work can be seen within the Emersonian tradition: He writes out of his life without any set poetic form. Yet more than any other poet since Ralph Waldo Emerson, he has developed a transcendentalism rooted in science and in a poetic which includes himself in the work. His epigrams, his short to moderate-length nature lyrics, and his long verse-essays are popular reading among poets.

His many awards include the Bread Loaf Writers' Conference Scholarship (1961), a Guggenheim Fellowship (1966), an American Academy of Arts and Letters Traveling Fellowship (1967), a National Endowment for the Arts grant (1969-1970), a Levinson Prize (1970), a National Book Award for *Collected Poems, 1951-1971* (1973), an honorary Litt.D. from Wake Forest University (1973), a Bollingen Prize for *Sphere: The Form of a Motion* (1974-1975), a National Book Critics Circle Award for *A Coast of Trees* (1981), a John D. and Catherine T. MacArthur Foundation Award (1981), and the North Carolina Award for Literature (1986). Ammons' place in the poetry of the twentieth century is, clearly, recognized as one of major significance.

Biography

Archie Randolph Ammons was born on February 18, 1926, near White-ville, North Carolina, in a house bought by his grandfather and situated on the family farm. The main book in the house was the Bible. Ammons' early experiences on the farm, working the land, helped shape his imagination. The self in his poems appears most frequently in relation to the natural world he knew as a child.

He was his parents' fourth child. Three sisters were born before him and two brothers after; one sister lived for only two weeks, and both brothers died, one in infancy and the other stillborn. Ammons remembers the deaths of his brothers, saying that they account in part for the undercurrent of loss and loneliness in his work.

Upon graduation from high school in 1943, Ammons took a job in the shipyard in Wilmington, North Carolina. In 1944, he joined the navy, spend-ing nineteen months in service, including time in the South Pacific, where he began writing poems. Returning home after the war, Ammons attended Wake Forest College (his tuition paid for by the government under the terms of the G.I. Bill) and was graduated with a B.S. in 1949. That year he married Phyllis Plumbo and took a job as principal of an elementary school in the remote coastal community of Hatteras, North Carolina. From 1950 to 1952, he studied English at the University of California at Berkeley. In 1952, he took a position with a New Jersey medical glassware firm, a job he held for twelve years. He began to send poems to literary magazines, and in 1953 *The Hudson Review* took two of his poems. His first book of poetry, *Ommateum, with Doxology*, appeared in 1955. Nine years later, *Expressions of Sea Level* appeared. That same year, 1964, he began teaching at Cornell University. Other books of poems followed, and in 1972 most of his poems were pub-lished as *Collected Poems, 1951-1971*. *Sphere: The Form of a Motion*, his poem of more than two thousand lines, published in 1974, gained for him the Bollingen Prize for Poetry for 1974-1975. Whitmanesque in its tendency toward a democratic feeling, *Sphere* presents Ammons' aesthetic of continual motion and the musical affirmation of the interworking of relationships in the energy of all life.

Ammons is Goldwin Smith Professor of Poetry at Cornell University. He lives in Ithaca, New York, with his wife and son, John. Ammons makes fre-quent trips to eastern North Carolina, a place which figures prominently in his poems.

Analysis

In one of A. R. Ammons' early poems, "So I Said I Am Ezra," from *Ommateum, with Doxology*, the speaker is whipped over the landscape, driven, moved by the natural elements. He is at once ordered and dis-ordered, close and far, balanced and unbalanced, and he exclaims: "So I

Ezra went out into the night/ like a drift of sand." The line is representative
of Ammons' entire body of work, for it searches through language for an attempt to mean and to be clear, and, failing to succeed completely in such
clarity, ends by affirming a presence of radiance.

Ammons' poems have a tendency, like most contemporary poems, to take
their own process, their own making, as a theme. Wanting to express something changeless and eternal, he is constrained by his own intricate mortality.
So in the title poem of *Expressions of Sea Level*, he presents the ocean as
permanent and impermanent, as form and formlessness. He is interested in
what man can and cannot know, giving full sway and expression to the
ocean's activity: "see the dry casting of the beach worm/ dissolve at the delicate rising touch."

Ammons attempts always to render visual details accurately. Some of the
most moving poems in this regard are the poems inspired by his background
in Columbus County, North Carolina. "Nelly Meyers" praises and celebrates
a woman who lived on the farm where Ammons grew up; "Silver" records
Ammons' love for and rapport with a mule he used to work. "Hardweed
Path Going" tells of his life as a boy, doing chores on the farm, his playtime
with a pet bird (a jo-reet) and a hog named Sparkle. Almost all memory,
these poems represent Ammons' past, particularly his boyhood, which he
renders in astonishingly realistic details.

Ammons infuses the natural world with his own attuned sensibilities,
acknowledging in the title poem of *Corsons Inlet* that "Overall is beyond
me." The form of the poem is a walk over the dunes. What lives beyond his
perception reassures, although he knows "that there is no finality of vision."
Bafflement is a feeling in the poem which may be studied for what it says
about the relationship between logic and reason, imposed order and discovered order, art and life, reality and illusion, being and becoming. "Corsons
Inlet" concludes the walk/quest on the note that "tomorrow a new walk is a
new walk." Ammons' desire to say something clearly, therefore, is not so
much a search for the Word as it is an attempt to find original ways to make
and shape poetry.

With *Tape for the Turn of the Year*, Ammons writes a long, narrow poem
on adding-machine paper. The poet improvises and spontaneously records
his thoughts and moods in what resembles a poetic diary. In one place, he
praises how writing gets done, suggesting that doing it is almost its own practical reward, as the speaker acknowledges in another poem, "Identity," "it is
wonderful how things work."

By the mid-1960's, Ammons' major themes had emerged, his sensibility
oscillating between extremes: formlessness-form, center-periphery, high-low,
motion-stasis, order-disorder, one-many. One of his most constant themes
has been the self in the work and in the world. He is concerned not only with
the form of natural fact but also with form in the abstract sense, that is, with

physical laws that govern the way individual entities act and behave. Ammons reaffirms the resonance of his subject, as in "The Eternal City," in which destruction must "accept into itself piece by piece all the old/ perfect human visions, all the old perfect loves."

Motion within diversity is perhaps Ammons' major theme. In "Saliences," from *Northfield Poems*, he discovers continuity in change. In "Snow Log," from *Uplands*, recognizing that nature's intentions cannot be known, he responds simply as an individual to what he sees in the winter scene: "I take it on myself:/ especially the fallen tree/ the snow picks/ out in the woods to show." In "The City Limits," from *Briefings*, a poem whose urban subject removes the speaker from nature, Ammons celebrates the "gold-skeined wings of flies swarming the dumped/ guts of a natural slaughter or the coil of shit."

Awarded the National Book Award for Poetry in 1973, *Collected Poems, 1951-1971* comprises most of Ammons' first six volumes, except for *Tape for the Turn of the Year* and three long verse-essays—"Extremes and Moderations," "Hibernaculum," and "Essay on Poetics." In these poems, Ammons is a seer, lamenting man's abuse of the earth and appreciating the immediacy of a world that takes care of itself. "Essay on Poetics" considers the structural advantages and disadvantages of poetry. One reads this essay to appreciate more fully Ammons' views on writing.

In perhaps his major work, the book-length poem *Sphere: The Form of a Motion*, Ammons explores motion and shape in a set form: sentences with no full stops, 155 sections of four tercets each. He relies on colons, perhaps suggesting a democratization and a flow. Shifting freely, sometimes abruptly, within a given stanza, phrase, or word, Ammons says, "I do not smooth into groups." Thus the book explores the nature of its own poetics, the poet searching everywhere for a language of clarity. In one place, he says that he is "sick of good poems." Wanting the smooth and raw together, Ammons reminds the reader that his prejudice against neat, traditional structures in poetry relates to the natural world where "the shapes nearest shapelessness awe us most, suggest the god." He regards a log, "rigid with shape," as "trivial." Ammons, therefore, makes his case for the poem of the open form as opposed to strong, traditional verses.

Ammons demythologizes poetics and language, while testifying to an Emersonian faith in the universe as flowing freely and spontaneously. At the same time, there is a counter feeling always working. He refers often to clarity and wants his poems to arrive and move forward "by a controlling motion, design, symmetry."

While he is writing the poem, commenting on it, writing himself into it, he shows his instinct for playfulness, for spoofing. This aspect of his work—the clowning humor—adds an inherent drama to his work, as Jerald Bullis has written:

The tone of the poem or, I should say, of the voices of its "parts," ranges and range from
that of the high and hard lyric, the crystalline and *as if* final saying, through a talky and
often latinate professorial stance, to permutations of low tone: "bad" puns, catalogues
that seem to have been lifted from a catalogue, and, in the example below, the high-pres-
sure pitch-man tone of How-To scams: "Now, first of all, the way to write poems is just to
start: it's like learning to walk or swim or ride the bicycle, you just go after it."

The poem goes on, praising the ability of man to write and to appreciate
being alive.

Reverence for creation runs throughout *Sphere*, investing the work with a
vision beyond and through the details of the poet's aesthetic. This religious
strain has its source in Ammons' absolute reverence for the natural world. A
religious vocabulary, then, is no surprise in his work and connects with his
childhood, when church services and hymn-sings were dominant parts of his
life. As in *Sphere*, he questions what is "true service," saying "it must be a
service that is celebration, for we would celebrate even if we do not know
what or how, and for He is bountiful if/ slow to protect and recalcitrant to
keep." Ammons goes on to say: "What we can celebrate is the condition we
are in, or we can renounce the condition/ we are in and celebrate a condition
we might be in or ought/ to be in." Ammons fuses and plays on the relationship between creation and imagination, hoping and trying to discover "joy's
surviving radiance." In the presence of this radiance—the hues and bends of
Ammons' music—exist the crux of his aesthetic, his art and his being: the
solitary man never surrendering as he is being imposed on and whipped
about, as he writes in one of his earliest poems, "So I Said I am Ezra/ and the
wind whipped my throat/ gaming for the sounds of my voice." Yet the self is
not dwarfed by the world. Ammons understands his moral and aesthetic
convictions and will not cease to assert them. Such desire allows the visionary
in Ammons to discover constantly new ways to see and understand his life. In
this regard, key words crop up often: "salience," "recalcitrant," "suasion,"
"periphery," "possibility," tentative words that tend to illuminate or seek the
proper blend in experience. So *Sphere* ends as it began, clear and free of all
encumbrances except the spoken voice: "we're ourselves: we're sailing." The
ending is right for the "form of a motion," the sense of wonder and uncertainty going on beyond the finality of the poem. Past, present, and future are
one, and the poem and its end recall Walt Whitman's absorption into the dirt
in "Song of Myself."

In *The Snow Poems*, Ammons continues his experimental attempt to
arrange a poetic journal, recounting in lyrical splendor the concerns of daily
life, including details about weather, sex, and the poet's attempt to write and
to experience a dialogue between the specific and the general.

Ammons' work since the mid-1970's marks a return to his more visionary
tendencies contained in his earlier terse, fierce lyrics of short or moderate
length. "Progress Report" is an epigram from *Worldly Hopes*:

> Now I'm
> into things
>
> so small
> when I
>
> say boo
> I disappear

The words flow in natural motion.

Lake Effect Country, continues Ammons' love of form and motion. The whole book represents one body, a place of water, a bed of lively recreation. In "Meeting Place," for example, "The water nearing the ledge leans down with/ grooved speed at the spill then,/ quickly groundless in air." His vision comes from the coming together of the natural elements in the poem, rising and falling, moving and forming the disembodied voices that are the real characters in his poems: "When I call out to them/ as to the flowing bones in my naked self, is my/ address attribution's burden and abuse." "Meeting Place" goes out "to summon/ the deep-lying fathers from myself,/ the spirits, feelings howling, appearing there."

A major contemporary poem is "Easter Morning," from *A Coast of Trees*. Based on the death in infancy of the poet's younger brother, the poem is filled with reverence for the natural world, Ammons' memory ever enlarging with religious and natural resonances. "I have a life that did not become,/ that turned aside and stopped,/ astonished." The poem carries the contradictory mysteries of the human condition—death, hope, and memory—working together in a concrete and specific aesthetic. Presented in the form of a walk, "Easter Morning" reveals the speaker caught in the motion, as two birds "from the South" fly around, circle, change their ways, and go on. The poem affirms, with the speaker in another poem called "Working with Tools," "I understand/ and won't give assertion up." Like Ezra going out "into the night/ like a drift of sand," the poet celebrates "a dance sacred as the sap in/ the trees . . . fresh as this particular/ flood of burn breaking across us now/ from the sun." Though the dance is completed in a moment, it can never be destroyed, because it has been re-created as the imagination's grand dance.

The range and flow in Ammons' poetry, his search for balance, move him to create his philosophical music, using a vocabulary drawn largely from everyday speech. He celebrates the need in every human being to discover a common experience in the least particular thing.

Bibliography

Bloom, Harold. "Dark and Radiant Peripheries: Mark Strand and A. R. Ammons," in *The Southern Review*. VIII (1972), pp. 133-149.

_____ . "The New Transcendentalists: The Visionary Strain in Merwin, Ashbery, and Ammons," in *Chicago Review*. XXIV (Winter, 1973), pp. 25-43.

_____ , ed. *A. R. Ammons*, 1986.

Diacritics. III (Winter, 1973). Special Ammons issue.

Elder, John. *Imagining the Earth: Poetry and the Vision of Nature*, 1985.

Haythe, Cynthia. "An Interview with A. R. Ammons," in *Contemporary Literature*. XXI (Spring, 1980), pp. 173-190.

Holder, Alan. *A. R. Ammons*, 1978.

Pembroke Magazine. XVIII (1986). Special Ammons issue.

Waggoner, Hyatt H. "The Poetry of A. R. Ammons: Some Notes and Reflections," in *Salmagundi*. Nos. 22/23 (Spring/Summer, 1973), pp. 285-293.

Shelby Stephenson

ROSE AUSLÄNDER

Born: Czernowitz, Bukovina; May 11, 1901

Principal poems and collections
Der Regenbogen, 1939; *Blinder Sommer*, 1965; *36 Gerechte*, 1967; *Inventar*, 1972; *Ohne Visum*, 1974; *Andere Zeichen*, 1975; *Gesammelte Gedichte*, first edition 1976, second expanded edition 1977; *Noch ist Raum*, 1976; *Doppelspiel*, 1977; *Es ist alles anders*, 1977; *Selected Poems*, 1977; *Es bleibt noch viel zu sagen*, 1978; *Aschensommer*, 1978; *Mutterland*, 1978; *Ein Stück weiter*, 1979; *Einverständnis*, 1980; *Mein Atem heisst jetzt*, 1981; *Im Atemhaus wohnen*, 1981; *Einen Drachen reiten*, 1981; *Schatten im Spiegel*, 1981 (in Hebrew); *Mein Venedig versinkt nicht*, 1982; *Südlich wartet ein wärmeres Land*, 1982; *So sicher atmet nur Tod*, 1983; *Gesammelte Werke in sieben Bänden*, 1984-1985; *Ich zähl die Sterne meiner Worte*, 1985; *Festtage in Manhattan*, 1985.

Other literary forms
Rose Ausländer's reputation is based solely on her poetry. Volume 3 of her collected works, containing her writings from 1966 to 1975, includes several short prose pieces; volume 4, containing her writings from the year 1976, comprises, aside from her poetry, only one short autobiographical piece.

Achievements
Ausländer did not become recognized as a major poet until the late 1960's and early 1970's, when volumes of her poetry appeared in rapid succession. At the same time, various German newspapers and magazines printed some of her poems, and her work appeared in anthologies as well. Because of the outbreak of World War II and her Jewish background, her early writings had never reached a sizable audience beyond her hometown. Not until her visit to Paul Celan in 1957, when she became acquainted with his elliptic hermetic style and that of his European contemporaries, did she adopt the curt, laconic manner of her mature poetry. In this style she vividly expressed the horrors of the Nazi persecution and her total desolation and despair, which continued even after the war in her exile in the United States, and later in Germany. Although the trauma of her persecution and exile was not diminished, she was able to transcend the pain of these experiences to reach a level beyond despair, a new affirmation of life and its riches—each object of which becomes the motif for a poem. Perhaps her hard-won message of consolation and redemption explains the increasing recognition of Rose Ausländer's achievements.

In 1957, Marianne Moore, herself a highly acclaimed poet, awarded

Ausländer the poetry prize of the Wagner College in New York. In 1967, Ausländer received the Meersburger Droste Prize; in 1977, the Ida Dehmel Prize and the Andreas Gryphius Prize; in 1978, the prize of the Federation of German Industry; and in 1980, the Roswitha Medal of the city of Bad Gandersheim.

Biography

Rose Ausländer was born Rosalie Beatrice Ruth Scherzer on May 11, 1901, to Jewish parents in Czernowitz, the capital of Bukovina. Her mother's name was Etie Binder and her father's, Sigmund Scherzer. Originally her father was supposed to become a rabbi, but later he decided to become a businessman. Until 1918, Bukovina was the easternmost part of the Habsburg Empire. The population of Czernowitz was around 110,000 and consisted of Germans, Romanians, Ukranians, Poles, and a large proportion of Jews. The Jewish population had assumed the role of preserving the German culture and being an intermediary between it and the Slavic culture. As a child, Ausländer was educated in the German-Austrian school system, but she also learned Hebrew and Yiddish. Through her schooling she became acquainted with the German literary classics, especially those by Johann Wolfgang von Goethe, Friedrich Schiller, and Heinrich Heine. She enjoyed a harmonious childhood, which was filled with love toward her parents and her native country. With the advent of World War I and the Russian occupation of Czernowitz, however, this peaceful existence was abruptly terminated. Rose's family fled first to Bucharest and later to Vienna. There they led a life full of suffering and misery. As a result of the Versailles treaty, Bukovina became a part of Romania. The Scherzer family returned to their hometown, where Rose finished her secondary education and subsequently attended the University of Czernowitz, majoring in literature and philosophy. At the university, she became especially interested in Plato, Spinoza, and Constantin Brunner, a follower of Spinoza who lived in Berlin at that time. Later the teachings of Brunner were to become an integral part of her poetry.

Her studies and her active membership in literary circles exposed her to the poetry of Friedrich Hölderlin, Franz Kafka, Georg Trakl, Rainer Maria Rilke, Else Lasker-Schüler, and Gottfried Benn. Despite their distance from Vienna, the Jewish literary circles in Czernowitz had adopted the Viennese Karl Kraus as mentor. With the publication of the journal *Die Fackel* (the torch), Kraus had assumed the role of the "high priest of truth," the herald of an ethical humanism and poetry against nationalist chauvinism and the corruption of bureaucracy and politics.

In 1921, as a result of the worsening of the family's already dire financial situation following her father's death, Ausländer decided to emigrate to the United States. She emigrated with her childhood friend Ignaz Ausländer. After failing to establish themselves in Minneapolis–St. Paul, they settled in

New York City, where they were married in 1923. Ausländer had a position in a bank, and her husband worked as a mechanic. The marriage was not to last; they separated in 1926 and were finally divorced in 1930. In 1924, Rose met Alfred Margul-Sperber, who later became the major sponsor of her poetry after her return to Czernowitz. In 1926, she became an American citizen and in 1927 visited Constantin Brunner in Berlin. She returned to New York in 1928, where she lived with Helios Hecht, a graphologist, writer, and editor of several periodicals. She published her first poems in the *Westlicher Herold-Kalender*, a Minneapolis publication, and later published a few poems in the *New Yorker Volkszeitung*. In 1931, she returned to Czernowitz with Helios Hecht and remained there to care for her ailing mother. After her prolonged absence from the United States, her American citizenship was revoked in 1934. Eventually she and Helios Hecht separated.

Between 1931 and the outbreak of World War II, Ausländer published poems in various periodicals. Alfred Margul-Sperber arranged for the publication of her first volume of poetry, *Der Regenbogen* (the rainbow), despite the Romanian government's policy of suppressing non-Romanian literature. In 1941, the Germans occupied Czernowitz, forced the Jews to return to the old ghetto and periodically deported groups to concentration camps in Transnistria. Ausländer and her mother escaped almost certain death by hiding from the Gestapo in basements where friends supplied them with food and clothes. The experience of persecution and underground existence was to become the motivating force behind her later poetry. In secret poetry-reading groups she met Paul Antschel, who later changed his name to Paul Celan. It was during this time that she came to believe in the existential function of poetry to preserve her own identity in a hostile world.

When the Soviet Union seized Bukovina after World War II, Ausländer, together with her mother and her brother's family, left Czernowitz for Bucharest. With the help of friends in the United States, she was able to obtain an immigration visa, but only for herself; her family had to stay behind. In the fall of 1946 she arrived again in New York and found work as a translator and foreign-language secretary for a large shipping company. All of her attempts to obtain an immigration visa for her mother proved futile. The news of her mother's death in 1947 caused a psychological breakdown, after which for some time she wrote poetry only in English.

Although Ausländer became naturalized again in 1948, she never felt at home in New York. The American life-style remained alien to her. During a visit to Europe in 1957, she again saw Paul Celan, who had emigrated to Paris. He introduced her to contemporary European poetry, which resulted in the rebirth of her poetry in German. The new poems, however, were stripped of all harmonizing prosodic elements.

In 1961, in failing health, Ausländer could not continue her job and was forced to live on her Social Security income. In 1966, she received additional support from the West German government. By that time, she had once again returned to Europe, where she attempted unsuccessfully to settle in Vienna, which was to her the cultural center of the former Habsburg Empire. Finally she moved to Düsseldorf, West Germany, in 1965. The year 1965 was not only the date of the publication of her second volume of poetry, twenty-six years after her first one, but also the year of her belated reintroduction to a German audience. Although she could not return to her native country, she returned to her mother tongue, the only medium through which she could express her poetic message and establish a dialogue with an audience. In 1970, she moved into Nelly-Sachs-Haus, a Jewish home for the aged, which she made her permanent home.

Analysis

The titles of Rose Ausländer's collections, such as *Blinder Sommer* (blind summer), *Ohne Visum* (without a visa), and *Aschensommer* (ash summer), like the images and motifs in the poems themselves, such as "ash," "smoke," and "dust," clearly reveal that Ausländer's poetry is directly linked to the Holocaust. She deeply identified with the suffering of her people. Even her first volume of poetry in 1939, however, reflected a troubled outlook on life. Here, nature, homeland, and love provide a refuge from a threatening reality, as the danger of national socialism loomed on the horizon. Despite their harmonizing prosodic elements, these early poems are characterized by a beginning awareness of the general crisis during these years. This awareness is put into the cosmogonic perspective of the world's fall from its original godlike state. Poetry became to Ausländer the only means of renewing this divine state. This concept is in direct accordance with Spinoza's philosophical theory of harmonizing microcosm and macrocosm. As acceptable as the harmonizing prosodic elements may be in this idealized conception, however, they are self-contradictory in the poems from the underground, appropriately titled *Ghettomotifs*. They first became available to a wider audience in volume 1 of *Gesammelte Werke*, containing the poetry from 1927 to 1956. The English poems written from 1948 to 1956 in the United States continue in this style, which Ausländer abandoned when she was confronted with the modern development of poetry during her 1957 visit to Europe.

Aside from the departure from rhyme and classical meters, her change in style can best be seen in the inclusion of the Holocaust into the cosmogonic process and in the reduction of the imagery to key words or constellations. The images of sun, stars, and earth lose all of their divine characteristics, and references to the Holocaust are so explicit that they evoke the absolute perversion and denaturalization of the human calling. "Ashsummer," "ashrain" or "smoke is pouring out of the eyes of the cannibals" are only a few examples. The trauma of persecution is carried into the depiction of her experience of exile in the United States. The escape to freedom across the

Atlantic resembles the never-ending search of the Flying Dutchman for a final resting place; the Nazi persecution is reenacted in America: "Men in Ku Klux Klan hoods, with swastikas and guns as weapons, surround you, the room smokes with danger"; the "ghetto-garb has not been discarded" despite a "fragrant" table full of food. This threat overshadows all personal relationships: "Can it be/ that I will see you again/ in April/ free of ashes?" The exile only reinforces the expulsion from paradise; the house turns into a prison, New York into a jungle, the subway into a funeral procession of war victims, and the summer heat of one hundred degrees evokes the image of the cremations in the concentration camps. Even more significant, the technology and modern civilization in New York are seen as symbols of the absolute denial of God.

Against this background of persecution and exile, Ausländer's native country takes on the qualities of a fairy tale—it is a "once-upon-a-time home" representing a "once-upon-a-time existence"—or is mythologized as filled with the presence of God: "the Jordan river emptied into the Pruth" (the Pruth being the main river of Bukovina, the country of beech trees). Although political reality does not allow a physical return to her homeland, Ausländer's "always back to the Pruth" can only be a spiritual return to the full awareness of her cultural, religious, and family roots, to her beginnings; in its "u-topian" fulfillment it would signify the unity of beginning and ending. The poet calls this state "the dwelling," in conscious or subconscious reference to the Cabalistic *schechina*, which symbolizes the dwelling place for God's bride, or the lowest level of the sefiroth tree. She laments, "Flying on the air swing/ Europe America Europe// I do not dwell/ I only live"; her settling in Germany becomes merely another stage in her continuous exile.

The poet's desire to return to her homeland corresponds to that of the Jewish people to reestablish their homeland in Israel: "Phoenix/ my people/ cremated// risen/ among cypress and/ orange trees." To these "wandering brethren," to "Ahasver, the wandering Jew," she offers the Jewish greeting "Le Cháim": "We/ risen/ from the void/ . . . we are talking/ softly/ with risen/ brethren." Despite that bond, her social and national identity has been lost forever: "born without a visa to this world/ she never looks the other way/ people like us are always/ suspicious." For that reason poetry itself takes over the function of reestablishing a dwelling place that secures Ausländer's spiritual identity.

Yet the creative poetic process had to build upon the foundation of annihilation and exile before any redemption and transfiguration could occur. As late as 1979, Ausländer maintained, in a poem: "I do not forget// my family roots/ mother's voice/ the first kiss/ the mountains of Bukovina/ the escape in World War I/ the suffering in Vienna/ the bombs in World War II/ the invasion of the Nazis/ the anguish in the basement/ the doctor who saved our lives/ the bitter sweet America// Hölderlin Trakl Celan// my agony to write/ the compulsion to write/ still." In the strictest consistency with her fate, the redemptive process begins, "retracing my steps/ in the urn of memory," and culminates in a paradoxical statement that combines trauma and bliss: "Nothing is lost/ in the urn/ the ash is breathing." The ambiguity of this statement is heightened by the middle line being grammatically linked to both the first and the third lines. This grammatical linking is employed again in these lines: "how beautiful/ ash can blossom/ in the blood." Only by "losing herself in the jungle of words" can Ausländer "find herself again in the miracle of the word," ultimately God's Word, "my word/ born out of despair// out of the desperate hope/ that poetry/ is still possible." Only poetry can grant this renewed existence: "mother tongue is putting me together// mosaic of people" in a space "free of ashes/ among verses." Poetry offers renewed life, the divine breath of life that links past and future in a timeless present: "The past/ has composed me/ I have/ inherited the future// My breath is called/ NOW."

Such stances became more frequent in Ausländer's old age, possibly because the poet, being bedridden, had only poetry left as a means of self-affirmation: "My fatherland is dead/ they have buried it/ in fire// I live/ in my motherland/ the word"—an obvious play on the word "mother tongue," which has taken on the extreme existential function of being the only guarantor of Rose Ausländer's identity. Even then, this process does not entail an escape from reality but rather builds upon "professing to the earth and its dangerous secrets . . . to man I profess myself with all the words that create me." It is a reciprocal act which grants poetic identity by giving meaning to both man and life. For that reason, Ausländer can arrive at an otherwise unbelievable statement affirming the poetic process out of the annihilation of man: "Magnificent despite all/ dust of flesh// This light-birth/ in an eyelash womb/ Lips/ yes/ much remains/ to be said."

Ausländer has called the specific mode of this poetic process "this dual play/ flower words/ war stammering." It is a play of mediation or reconciliation between language and reality that might result in simplistic affirmation if the never forgotten point of departure were not to forbid such a reduction. On the contrary, this play takes on mystical proportions, striving for the redemption of the world by making it transparent to manifest its divine destiny. This interdependence between language and reality culminates in the image of the crystal, in which microcosm and macrocosm meet, in reverence to Spinoza, who was a lensmaker as well as a philosopher: "My saint/ is called Benedict// He has/ polished/ the universe// Infinite crystal/ out of whose heart/ the light radiates."

Although the later poems, especially those after 1981, reduce the poetic process to such a degree that they can become manneristic, Ausländer's total poetic production clearly shows her to be among the most significant post–World War II poets. She has been able to find meaning in life despite the traumas she has experienced. Her "self-portrait" lists all the conditions that denied her the status of a regular member of society and at the same time testifies to poetry's power to transcend personal tragedy: "Jewish gypsy/ raised/ in the German language/ under the black and yellow flag// Borders pushed me/ to Latins Slavs/ Americans Germanic people// Europe/ in your womb/ I dream/ my next birth."

Bibliography

Baumann, Gerhart. "Rose Ausländer: Aufbruch in das 'Land Anfang,' " in *Neue Rundschau*. XCII (1981).

Glenn, Jerry. "Blumenworte/Kriegsgestammel: The Poetry of Rose Ausländer," in *Modern Austrian Literature*. XII, nos. 3/4 (1979).

Klaus Weissenberger

MARY BARNARD

Born: Vancouver, Washington; December 6, 1909

Principal poems and collections

Cool Country in *Five Young American Poets*, 1940; *A Few Poems*, 1952; *Collected Poems*, 1979; *Time and the White Tigress*, 1986.

Other literary forms

While Mary Barnard's principal genre is poetry, she has also worked with translations from the Greek, most notably in her well-known *Sappho: A New Translation* (1958). The bulk of her fiction, published in widely read periodicals in the 1950's, is as yet uncollected, though *Three Fables* appeared in 1983. Her essays from her research into Sappho, *The Mythmakers* (1966), also inform her poetry collection *Time and the White Tigress*. Perhaps her best-known work, aside from the poetry, is the autobiography *Assault on Mount Helicon* (1984), which features portraits of many of the chief figures in modern American literature but especially of Ezra Pound and William Carlos Williams.

Achievements

Barnard's work shows the influence of the modernists transposed to a minor key. While it lacks the cosmopolitan effusiveness of Ezra Pound, or the cultural skeet-shooting of T. S. Eliot, or the secret ambition of William Carlos Williams, it nevertheless sets forth a legitimate agenda and succeeds in convincing its readers that while it is small as an oeuvre, it is by no means slight. Moreover, the scope belies the small size. If one believes with Samuel Taylor Coleridge that one of the distinguishing characteristics of high art is its ability to pack maximum content into minimum space, then the miniatures of Mary Barnard offer more aesthetic satisfaction than their collective heft would suggest. By invoking the mythical within the ordinary and the everyday within the mythical, she has created a resonant parallel device for treating the subjects of her choice: childhood, the meaning of change, the pervasiveness of limits, man's relation to nature and to his past, and the fate of women.

While she has written essays and fiction as well as translating from the Greek, these endeavors provide—to use one of her favorite images—a spring from which to enlarge and refresh her poetry. In its classical approach to hidden truths about human nature, it bears resemblance to such earlier writers as Leonie Adams and Louise Bogan. Her translations of Sappho show what can be done to breathe life into revered but seldom-read classics, and the autobiographical *Assault on Mount Helicon* is an important and engaging document of literary history and literary survival from one who wrote from "the far shore" but was nevertheless in the midst of one of the great cultural revolutions of modern times.

Biography

Born of parents who moved west from Indiana, a move inspired in part by the Lewis and Clark Exposition of 1905, Mary Barnard was born on December 6, 1909, in Vancouver, Washington. Her father ran a lumber mill, and Barnard was able to grow up happily in congenial surroundings. Her parents encouraged her early interest in poetry, and Barnard—unusual for her time—attended Reed College, where she took creative writing courses and was graduated in 1932.

Twice during the 1930's, Barnard took up summer residencies at Yaddo in upstate New York and met a number of writers, including Muriel Rukeyser, Kenneth Fearing, Eleanor Clark, and Delmore Schwartz. It was during this decade that she also began corresponding with Ezra Pound and William Carlos Williams, who further encouraged her. In 1935, she won the Levinson Prize from *Poetry* magazine, and her poems were first collected in New Directions' *Five Young American Poets* in 1940. From 1939 to 1943, she worked as curator of the poetry collection at the University of Buffalo, and from 1943 to 1950, she worked as a research assistant to Carl Van Doren and wrote fiction that appeared in such periodicals as *The Saturday Review of Literature*, *The Kenyon Review*, and *Harper's Bazaar*. A Few Poems appeared from Reed College in 1952, and in the mid-1950's she worked on her translations of Sappho. In 1957, simultaneously with their acceptance, she moved back to the West Coast and settled in Portland, Oregon. Her collection of essays, *The Mythmakers*, appeared in 1966. The 1979 publication of her *Collected Poems* brought Barnard's poetry to the attention of a new generation of readers. Both this book and her memoir, *Assault on Mount Helicon*, were widely reviewed and warmly received. *Time and the White Tigress* won the 1986 Western States Book Award for Poetry and prompted the jury to cite it as "an impressive achievement from a distinguished writer, and an admirable new American poem."

Analysis

Mary Barnard's poetic output, while quite slim, nevertheless spans and reflects more than half a century of involvement in the art. Her brief, solicitous early lyrics delineate the natural world of the Pacific Northwest with quiet precision, while her later poems reveal her increasing interest in mythological models. Devoid of gimmick and rhetoric, they are as unassuming and well-made as Shaker furniture. The world described in the earlier poems is a world in transition—mostly gone, a remote place of springs and rivers, of meadows and deer, where railroads provide the transfusions of people and goods necessary for a human population to flourish. The later poems cease to reflect a period aspect and, with increasing awareness and confidence in her powers, rely more heavily on invention than recollection. The dominant elements throughout are water and earth rather than air or fire.

Collected Poems opens in childhood, not a childhood toggled to personal memory, but a childhood that any adult might imagine as belonging to a young girl. In "Playroom," there is

> mournfulness of muddy playgrounds,
> raw smell of rubbers and wrapped lunches
> when little girls stand in a circle singing
> of windows and of lovers.

The lives within the playground sing of the life beyond their experience and place, just as the mature poet sings of her "beyond," the past:

> Hearing them, no one could tell
> why they sing sadly, but there is in their voices
> the pathos of all handed-down garments
> hanging loosely on small bodies.

The poem suggests that life itself is a process of outgrowing "garments," that the provisional is the domain of the living. Thus, the girls "sing sadly," not because they understand this condition but because, literally, they embody it.

If the girls have to content themselves with hand-me-downs, a young girl in "The Fitting" must contend with a "trio of hags . . . with cold hands" who roam over her young body and "compress withered lips upon pins" in order to produce a dress for her. They are the three Fates, who determine the quality and duration of life. As they fit the girl, "The knocking of hammers comes/ from beyond the still window curtain. . . ." Some portion of the future, pertinent to others, is being constructed, but her hands will make nothing: "Her life is confined here, in this depth/ in the well of the mirrors." The poem ends with the soft snipping of scissors and pulled threads—also not to be hers—lying on the carpet. The tiny separations imparted by the scissors suggest many more consequential leavetakings to come.

The understanding of limitations of which the young may only have vague intimations, and their delineation, drawn from images in the natural world, are the subjects of many of Barnard's poems. To define a limit, to put a form to what is already form, is to pay it authentic homage. One of the most elemental limits and the source of centuries of solemn meditation from Homer to Wallace Stevens is the seashore. The sea, as a self-sufficient, obverse universe, confronts people both with their otherness, with respect to their mutually incompatible biologies, and with their own "shores," beyond which begins the vast Not-me, a country about which they are impelled to educate themselves, education being the development of commerce between the two realms. Yet their bodies feel a distant affinity to that otherness not easily accessible to language. As the Metaphysical poet Thomas Traherne noted, humanity is "both with moons and tides."

In "Shoreline," one of Barnard's longer poems (and her first published poem), the poet states flatly, "Sand is the beginning and the end/ of our dominion." Yet "The way to the dunes is easy," as children, who have not yet transformed the sea and land, water and earth, into concepts, instinctively know: "their bodies glow/ in the cold wash of the beach." When they return from the beach, "They are unmoved by fears/ that breed in darkening kitchens at sundown/ following storm. . . ." Barnard asserts of the shoreline: "This, then, is the country of our choice." The operative word here is "choice," for one would have thought that limitation was, on the contrary, merely the country of necessity. By choice, however, one stands by the shore "and long[s] for islands"; thus, in some measure, one equally and consciously partakes of one's limitations as well. As one gets older, on the other hand, and one's choices dwindle in the face of increased experience, "We lose the childish avarice of horizons." The poem ends with the refrain, "sand/ is the beginning and the end/ of our dominion," though with a different line break, as if to suggest its shifting against "our dominion." One hears a gentle corrective here both to the infinitude of William Blake's sand and, prophetically, to the sonorous "dominion" of which death shall have none in Dylan Thomas. Barnard's poem seems more thoughtfully located in the actual experiences of people, less in the seductive undertow of language.

Those childhoods, suspended in the ancestral and the domestic, however unique they may seem to the individual and web-spun consciousness of children, carry with them the evidence of their lineages. This evidence, which bespeaks of generations of labor needed to produce the child into its time, is present everywhere but especially in those objects that address the body, as in "Beds": "The carved oak headboards of ancestral beds tilt/ like foundered decks from fog at the mouth of the river." The lovely image of care and protection is addressed specifically to the body, whose vulnerability reaches its apex at night. Fear—of being abducted (into the night, into the future, into death)—alternates with remembered or implied assurances of protection:

> Lulla, lulla, will there be, will there
> always be a place to sleep when smoke gathers in the rafters?
> ....
> Lulla, lulla. Flood after flood. When the beds float
> downstream, will there be a place to sleep, Matthew, Mark?

Unlike the children's playground, the sanctuary of the bed is permanent, even obligingly providing, albeit somewhat transformed, humanity's last "resting place." Consequently, the bones' sanctuary posture is the horizontal, and it is through this "angle" that one can see that the eternal nature of the forms links people from biology to biography to history, from their bodies to those of their ancestors and of all humankind:

> The feathers of my grandmothers' beds melted into earlier darkness
> as, bone to earth, I lay down. A trail that leads out, leads back.
> Leads back, anyway, one night or another, bone to earth.

Limits, which provide Barnard with so much of her subject matter, are not inert barriers but, because they are "our choice," are rather actively engaged in transformations. In "The Rapids," the poet focuses on the distinction between the boundary as limit and as transformer: "No country is so gracious to us/ as that which kept its contours while we forgot them. . . ." The precisely placed "gracious" suggests how accommodating a contour a boundary can manage to be to satisfy one's need for orientation and security. At the same time, it is an agency of change: "The water we saw broken upon the rapids/ has dragged silt through marshland/ and mingled with the embittered streams of the sea." In the last stanza of this three-stanza poem, Barnard telescopes the stationary and the moving into a single image of "ungatherable blossoms floating by the . . . rock." These "have flung light in my face, have made promises/ in unceasing undertone." The promises are guarantees made subliminally that one will be at home in the world, or at least that one can recover his home. "Alienation"—one of the most self-incriminating buzzwords of the century—and all the philosophical ramifications tangled up with it, are, after all, of human manufacture, and while the mind can surely suffer from alienation, it can also break out of it in an instant. Such an instant constitutes the poetic moment of this and other of Barnard's poems.

Being at home in the world means also adjusting to its cyclic nature, which involves death. Usually, human beings do all they can to insulate themselves from its blows, and when the time comes when they can no longer do that, they remember, if they still can, the traditional loophole, lamentation, channeling their sorrow, paying homage, and letting off the steam of outrage and fear all at once. The ability and courage to confront death (of others and one's own) is inversely proportional to the amount of insulation one has accumulated (in this century, quite a lot). In "Winter Evening," Barnard examines the mythical place of death, for mythological treatment tends to "naturalize" death and so render it less psychically damaging by treating it as an equal partner in the scheme of things. On the other hand, modern middle-class living has tried, in countless ways and to its detriment, to dust its hands of the unflattering fact of terminal being:

> In the mountains, it is said,
> the deer are dying by hundreds.
> We know nothing of that
> in the suburbs.

Doubtless, suburban life has what passes for myths, too, but these are not "ancestral myth," the myth of origins. Rather, "our century/ clings to the novel./ Coffee and novels." Only the train whistles "howl against death/ ... like Lear in his heartbreak,/ savage as a new myth." Lear, in his vanity, also upset a primordial set of precedents and suffered madness and death for his trouble. The odd juxtaposition of Lear (though, appropriately, Lear is a winter king) and the suburbans clearly boosts the latter into a mythical realm of danger, for the forces involved are huge and indifferent to human willfulness. The leveling snow that is the immediate cause of the animals' deaths goes on quietly covering all the houses in the town.

While Barnard has clearly absorbed the image-based tenets of Pound and Williams, she most clearly follows the homegrown variety of Williams. In the slyly self-referential "The Spring," Barnard follows the course—one is tempted to say "career"—of a spring, "a mere trickle," as it "whispers" out from under a boulder and fills, first, a pond, then travels (somehow keeping its integrity as a separate spring as it does so) over a spillway, fills another pond, and then falls between trees "to find its fate in the river." The poet concludes,

> Nameless, it has two little ponds
> to its credit, like a poet
> with two small collections of verse.
>
> For this I celebrate it.

Executed in Williams-style tercets, the poem concerns the question of poetic identity, as the simile makes clear. It is also a self-celebration, for the spring is a decidedly naturalistic image and so in Barnard's canon gets a *de facto* seal of approval. From the boulder of obscurity to the river of judgment, the stream has avoided dilution, just as a poet with two small collections will, one hopes, have avoided assimilation. To the untrained eye, however, the spring's continuity, its purposefulness, will be invisible: At the point that it is a pond, it *is* a pond; at the river, the river. Guiding her own stream between the "tall cottonwoods" of Pound and Williams (as one would imagine) becomes a matter of integrity that she does not need to spell out, just as it is an act of homage in form and feeling.

Barnard's revival ("arrival" might more accurately indicate the tone of her reception) in the late 1970's was to a considerable degree enhanced by her feminist principles. "Inheritance" addresses the theme of the woman's largely uncommemorated contribution to the settling of America:

> Spoon clink fell to axe-chink
> falling along the Ohio. Those women
> made their beds, God bless them,
> in the wandering, dreamed, hoped-for

> Hesperides, their graves
> in permanent places.

The poet admits that, indeed, she was left no tangible inheritance, only pride, and not even pride, but the memory of it, which she identifies as "armor/ . . . against time and men and women." The final placement of women in the list of the enemies of women is a fine idea, and the poem, armored, ends on that note. Barnard obviously believes that one of the chief battles of feminism must be fought on the field of memory, and indeed much of feminist work has been in rectifying the obscured and mystified history of the sex and in transferring future custodianship to women.

Barnard's reading of the classics, from which emerged her translations of Sappho, shows up in poems such as "Persephone." Here, the poet disposes of the hierarchical view of the surface as implicitly preferable to the underworld:

> I loved like a mole. There were
> subterranean flat stone stairways
> to columns supporting the earth and its
> daffodils. Or shall we say, to the façade
> of the hiding place of earth's treasure?

Nostalgia has no place in the erection of hell: "Homesickness here/ is for the raw working and scars of the surface. . . ." Persephone will make do with what is at hand and will not be enticed into living by "hunger—to which/ . . . surrender is death." She will return to the surface, but not by giving in to her hunger for it. Rather, she will have her pride, and presumably the memory of it, to strengthen her for her return:

> How many times it is said to the living,
> Conquer hunger! If you
> want to go back, up, up where the sun falls
> warm on flowering rock and make garlands again.

Barnard puts an effective feminist spin on Persephone's self-denial: Neither the hunger for the world nor the conquering of it is tinged with the desire to return to men (they are conspicuously absent from the poem); rather, Persephone's desire is "to make garlands again."

The image of another "buried" woman appears in "Ondine." Here, the speaker has invited the mermaid into her house to eat, but instead of eating, she sits weeping and blames the speaker for stealing driftwood to burn, a charge the speaker denies. At this, the mermaid stands up and wrings her hair "so that the water made a sudden splash/ on the round rug by the door" and leaves to return to the sea. The speaker throws the knot of wood where the mermaid had sat into the fire ("I beat it out with a poker/ in the soft ash"). At length, she comes to regret her fit of anger:

> Now I am frightened on the shore at night,
> and all the phosphorescent swells that rise
> come towards me with the threat of her dark eyes
> with a cold firelight in them . . .

Her sense of self-reproach at her inability to establish any but the most cursory of relationships with the strange creature gives way to anxiety and guilt. The poem ends with an apocalyptic image that hints at the psychological forces involved in her failure:

> Should she return and bring her sisters with her,
> the withdrawing tide
> would leave a long pool in my bed.
> There would be nothing more of me this side
>
> the melting foamline of the latest wave.

It is in her mythological voice that Barnard most comfortably addresses the larger themes. In one of these, "Fable from the Cayoosh Country," the subject is the power and influence of language. The poet and an unnamed companion lie beside a lake in a pastoral setting. Aware of the nature surrounding them, their thought "pushed forward into the margins of silence/ . . . the boundaries of an inarticulate world." Falling asleep, she dreams of being a missionary of language to the beasts:

> I preached the blessing of the noun and verb,
> but all was lost in the furred ear of the bear,
> in the expressive ear of the young doe.
> What the doe said with her ear, I understood.
> What I said, she obviously did not.

Exasperated, she hurls her grammar books into a pool that immediately begins to address her. It relates the story of a time when all nature could speak with the eloquence that men have, but found it was a curse, not a blessing:

> . . . The blade of this tool, useless for digging, chopping,
> shearing, they used against each other with such zeal
> they all but accomplished their own extermination.

The creatures of nature therefore "abandoned speech" yet "retained cries expressive of emotion,/ as rage,/ or love." The pool adds, "They have never seen any cause to repent their decision." The speaker then dreams that the lake has risen over them and confesses, "My consternation was that of a poet, whose love/ if not his living was gravely endangered." She wakes and, finding the lake in place as before, wonders whether it is not a pity that it had not, in fact, flooded over them. As a visionary poem, "Fable from the Cayoosh Country" locates in language not the tool that binds human beings together in a mutually satisfying quest for articulation, but a tempting means to allow oneself to become separate from nature and from one's self. Unfortunately, language cannot police its abuses. In fact, it is not usually aware of them until the harm has been done. Obviously, the poem is a retelling of the Fall, and the striving after language (not in the sense of naming but in the proud rise to eloquence) becomes an activity inappropriate to either Paradise or redemption, the beasts having already fallen and redeemed their natures through a return to the inarticulate. The triumph and burden of language being the human lot, however, the wish to do as the beasts do becomes moot, as language is, for humankind, an irreversible phenomenon.

Another fine poem that speculates on erasure (and mentioned approvingly by Ezra Pound) considers the return to the *tabula rasa* of the soul recycled and made ready for reincarnation by the waters of Lethe. The soul in "Lethe" pauses over the waters and ponders the enormous human loss necessary to prepare the soul for return to earth:

> Will a few drops on the tongue
> like a whirling flood submerge cities,
> like a sea, grind pillars to sand?
> Will it wash the color from the lips and the eyes
> beloved? It were a thousand pities
> thus to dissolve
> the delicate sculpture of a lifted hand. . . .

The cost of such forgetting, is, for a poet, unbearable, even as it is inevitable. Oblivion is the exact enemy of art, just as Satan is the enemy of virtue, and the poet, "hesitant, unwilling to drink," is ennobled by her resistance.

Following the publication of her *Collected Poems*, Barnard issued another collection of poems, *Time and the White Tigress*, a series of verse essays (she refers to it as a single long poem) about the celestial and natural cycles and their impact on human understanding of its place in the cosmos. Harking back to her classical studies and the archaeological arcana of *The Myth-makers*, the poems present, complete with contextual notes, a rationale for the capture and implementation of time as a series of demarcations suitable to the use of custom, since there is "no society without customs. . . ." Hence, the possession of knowledge about time is power inasmuch as it gives its possessor(s) knowledge of the cycles through which one conducts one's life:

> A rhythm established by moon after moon,
> tide after tide, and year after year
> has formed the framework for all our cultures,
> a pattern of custom that echoes the pattern
> woven by time in the heavens.

Principally, it is to the ancient astronomers, whose priestly function it was to observe and mime the activities of the sky, that beginnings of mythology can be traced: the Twins (dark and light), the signs of the Zodiac, the gods and goddesses of the ancient religions. Yet far from pushing mythology deeper into the mists, Barnard shows that the sky watchers were pragmatic sages who interpreted the heavens in ingenious and economic ways and set the stage for the growth of civilization, from the role of priests and kings to the use and democratization of time to the techniques of mythologizing as a form of advancing out of the darkness. Miming her own subjects, she writes,

> We are following here the spoor
> of a White Tigress who prowled
> Time's hinterlands. . . .
> ....
> Her teats, dripping a moon-milk,
> suckled the Twins. The savor,
> still on our tongues, is fading.
>
> Here, a pug-mark in the path.
> There, bent grass where she crouched.
> From this I construct a tigress?
>
> A mythical one?
> Perhaps. Why
> should we cease to make myths?

One of Barnard's achievements will be seen to be a conscious invention and perpetuation of myths, which are the "necessary fictions" by which human beings try to invoke principles of memory and harmony in their otherwise partial and painful existence through time's indifferent hallways.

Other major works

SHORT FICTION: *Three Fables*, 1983.

NONFICTION: *The Mythmakers*, 1966; *Assault on Mount Helicon*, 1984 (autobiography).

TRANSLATION: *Sappho: A New Translation*, 1958.

Bibliography
American Literature. Review of *Assault on Mount Helicon*. LVII (March, 1985), p. 169.
Antioch Review. Review of *Collected Poems*. XXXVIII (Spring, 1980), p. 246.
Barnard, Mary. "Ragged Robin," in *The New York Times Book Review*. LXXXIX (May 20, 1984), p. 47.
Raffel, Burton. "Mary Barnard's Sappho," in *The Hudson Review*. XVIII (Summer, 1965).

Sewanee Review. Review of *Assault on Mount Helicon*. XCIII (April, 1985),
    p. R30.
World Literature Today. Review of *Assault on Mount Helicon*. LIX (Sum-
    mer, 1985), p. 434.

David Rigsbee

EAVAN BOLAND

Born: Dublin, Ireland; September 24, 1944

Principal collections

23 Poems, 1962; *New Territory*, 1967; *The War Horse*, 1975; *In Her Own Image*, 1980; *Introducing Eavan Boland*, 1981; *Night Feed*, 1982; *The Journey*, 1983.

Other literary forms

Eavan Boland collaborated with Michael MacLiammoir on the critical study *W. B. Yeats and His World* (1971). Boland has contributed essays in journals such as the *American Poetry Review*; she also reviews regularly for the *Irish Times*.

Achievements

Ireland has produced a generation of distinguished poets since 1960, and all of them have been men. Seamus Heaney is the best known of this group of poets to American audiences, but the reputations of Thomas Kinsella, Derek Mahon, Michael Longley, Paul Muldoon, and Tom Paulin continue to grow. Poetry by contemporary Irishwomen is also a significant part of the Irish literary scene. Boland is one of a group of notable women poets including Medbh McGuckian, Eithne Strong, and Eilean Ni Chuilleanain. In an essay published in 1987, "The Woman Poet: Her Dilemma," Boland indicates her particular concern with the special problems of being a woman and a poet. Male stereotypes about the role of women in society continue to be very strong in Ireland and make Irishwomen less confident about their creative abilities. Women must contend as well with another potentially depersonalizing pressure, that of feminist ideology, which urges women toward another sort of conformity. Boland and the other poets mentioned above have managed to overcome both obstacles and develop personal voices.

Biography

Eavan Boland was born on September 24, 1944, in Dublin, Ireland. Her parents were Frederick Boland and Frances Kelly Boland. Her father was a distinguished Irish diplomat who served as Irish ambassador to Great Britain (1950-1956) and to the United States (1956-1964). Her mother was a painter who had studied in Paris in the 1930's. Boland's interest in painting as a subject for poetry can be traced to her mother's encouragement. Because of her father's diplomatic career, Boland was educated in Dublin, London, and New York. From 1962 to 1966, she attended Trinity College, Dublin; beginning in 1967, she taught at Trinity College for a year. In 1968, she received the Macauley Fellowship for poetry. She is married to Kevin Casey, the novelist, and has two children, Sarah, born in 1975, and Eavan, born in 1978.

Boland began writing poetry in Dublin in the early 1960's. She recalls this early period: "... scribbling poems in boarding school, reading Yeats after lights out, revelling in the poetry on the course.... Dublin was a coherent space then, a small circumference in which to ... become a poet.... The last European city. The last literary smallholding." After her marriage, Boland left academe and moved out of Dublin and into the suburbs to become "wife, mother and housewife." *In Her Own Image* and *Night Feed* focus on Boland's domestic life in the suburbs and especially on her sense of womanhood.

Analysis

Hearth and history provide a context for the poetry of Eavan Boland. She is inspired by both the domestic and the cultural. Her subjects are the alienating suburban places which encourage one to forget one's cultural roots, her children with their typically Irish names, demystified horses in Dublin streets that can still evoke the old glories from time to time, and the old Irish stories themselves, which may at times be vivid and evocative and at times mere nostalgia. Boland's distinctly female perspective is achieved in several poems about painting which note the dominance of male painters in the history of art from the Renaissance to the Impressionists, painters such as Jan van Eyck, Edgar Degas, Jean Auguste Dominique Ingres, and Auguste Renoir. Women were painted by these artists in traditional domestic or agrarian postures. Boland perceives woman as far less sanitized and submissive. Her collection *In Her Own Image* introduces such shocking and taboo subjects as anorexia, mastectomy, masturbation, and menstruation.

Two of Boland's most recent volumes, *In Her Own Image* and *Night Feed*, deal exclusively with the subject of woman. *Night Feed* for the most part treats suburban woman and chronicles the daily routine of a Dublin housewife in a quite positive way. The book has poems about babies' diapers, about washing machines, about feeding babies. The cover has an idyllic drawing of a mother feeding a child. The other volume, however, *In Her Own Image*, published two years before *Night Feed*, seems written by a different person. Its candid and detailed treatment of taboo subjects contrasts sharply with the idyllic world of *Night Feed*. Boland's ability to present both worlds testifies to her poetic maturity.

The need for connection is a major theme in Boland's poetry. Aware of traditional connections in Irish and classical myths, she longs for an earlier period when such ties came instinctively. Her sense of loss with respect to these traditional connections extends beyond mythology to Irish history as well, even to Irish history in this century. Modern-day Dubliners have been cut off from the sustaining power of myth and history. Their lives, therefore, seem empty and superficial. Surrounded with the shards of a lost culture, they cannot piece together these shards into a coherent system.

The alienation of the modern urban Irish from their cultural roots is the subject of Boland's poem "The New Pastoral." She considers alienation from a woman's perspective. Aware of the myths which have traditionally sustained males, Boland desires equivalent myths for females. She longs for a "new pastoral" which will celebrate women's ideals, but she finds none. She encounters many domestic "signs," but they do not "signify" for her. She has a vague sense of once having participated in a coherent ritual, of having "danced once / on a frieze." Now, however, she has no access to the myth. Men seem to have easier access to their cultural roots than women do. The legends of the cavemen contain flint, fire, and wheel, which allowed man "to read his world." Later in history, men had pastoral poems to define and celebrate their place in the world. A woman has no similar defining and consoling rituals and possesses no equivalent cultural signs. She seems a "displaced person / in a pastoral chaos," unable to create a "new pastoral." Surrounded with domestic signs, "lamb's knuckle," "the washer," "a stink / of nappies," "the greasy / bacon flitch," she still has no access to myth. Hints of connection do not provide a unified myth. "I feel / there was a past, / there was a pastoral / and these / chance sights—/ what are they all / but late amnesias / of a rite / I danced once / on a frieze?" The final image of the dancer on the frieze echoes both John Keats's Grecian urn and William Butler Yeats's dancers and golden bird. The contemporary poet, however, has lost contact. Paradoxically, the poem constitutes the "new pastoral" which it claims beyond its reach. The final allusion to the dancer on the frieze transforms the mundane objects of domestic life into something more significant, something sacred.

Boland seems in conflict over whether women should simply conform to male stereotypes for women or should resist these pressures to lead "lesser lives," to attend to "hearth not history." Many poems in *Night Feed* accept this "lesser" destiny, poems such as "Night Feed," "Hymn," and "In the Garden." The several poems in this volume which deal with paintings, "Domestic Interior," "Fruit on a Straight-Sided Tray," "Degas's Laundresses," "Woman Posing (After Ingres)," "On Renoir's 'The Grape-Pickers,'" all deal with paintings by male painters which portray women in traditional domestic or rural roles. The women in these paintings appear content with their "lesser lives." Poems such as "It's a Woman's World" seem less accepting, however, more in the spirit of *In Her Own Image*, which vigorously rejects basing one's identity on male stereotypes. "It's a Woman's World" complements "The New Pastoral" in its desire for a balance between hearth and history.

> as far as history goes
> we were never
> on the scene of the crime. . . .

> And still no page
> scores the low music
> of our outrage.

Women have had no important roles in history, Boland asserts. They produce "low music," rather than heroic music. Nevertheless, women can have an intuitive connection with their own "starry mystery," their own cosmic identity. The women in those paintings apparently pursuing their "lesser lives," may have a sense of "greater lives." The male world (including male artists) must be kept in the dark about this, must keep believing that nothing mythic is being experienced.

> That woman there,
> craned to the starry mystery
> is merely getting a breath
> of evening air,
> while this one here—
> her mouth
> a burning plume—
> she's no fire-eater,
> just my frosty neighbour
> coming home.

The "woman's world" and the "starry mysteries" are presented far less romantically in Boland's volume *In Her Own Image*. The poems in this volume refuse to conform to male stereotypes of woman as happy domestic partner. They explore male/female conflicts in the deepest and most intimate psychic places. The title *In Her Own Image* indicates the volume's concern with the problem of "identity." Boland wishes to be an individual, free to determine her own life, but other forces seek to control her, to make her conform to female stereotypes. A woman should be perfect, unchanging, youthful, pure, in short, should be ideal. Male-dominated society does not wish women to explore their own deepest desires. Women transform these social messages into the voice of their own consciences, or, in Sigmund Freud's terms, their own superegos: "Thou shalt not get fat!" "Thou shalt not get old!" "Thou shalt not get curious."

These naysaying inner voices dominate the first three poems of *In Her Own Image*: "Tirade for the Mimic Muse," "In Her Own Image," and "In His Own Image." The "mimic muse" in the first poem urges the speaker to "make up," to conceal aging with cosmetics. The illustration for this poem shows a chunky and unkempt woman gazing into a mirror and seeing a perfect version of herself, thin, unwrinkled, physically fit. The phrase "her own image" in the second poem refers to another idealization, the "image" of perfection which the speaker carries around inside herself. She finally frees herself of this psychic burden by planting it outside in the garden. The illustration shows a naked woman bending over a small coffin. The third poem, "In His Own Image," considers the pressures of a husband's expectations on a wife's sense of self. The speaker in this third poem does not try to reshape her features with makeup. She is battered into a new shape by a drunken husband. No illustration appears with this poem.

The speaker's "tirade" in "Tirade for the Mimic Muse" begins at once and establishes the intensely hostile tone of much of *In Her Own Image*: "I've caught you out. You slut. You fat trout." She despises the impulse in herself to conform to a stereotype, to disguise the physical signs of time passing: "the lizarding of eyelids," "the whiskering of nipples," "the slow betrayals of our bedroom mirrors." In the final section of the poem, the authentic self has suppressed those conforming impulses: "I, who mazed my way to woman-hood/ Through all your halls of mirrors, making faces." Now the mirror's glass is cracked. The speaker promises a true vision of the world, but the vision will not be idyllic: "I will show you true reflections, terrors." Terrors preoccupy Boland for much of this book.

"In Her Own Image" and "In His Own Image" deal with different aspects of the "perfect woman." The first poem has a much less hostile tone than does "Tirade for the Mimic Muse." The speaker seems less threatened by the self-image from which she wishes to distance herself. Images of gold and amethyst and jasmine run through the poem. Despite the less hostile tone, Boland regards this "image" as a burdensome idealization which must be purged for psychic health: "She is not myself/ anymore." The speaker plants this "image" in the garden outside: "I will bed her,/ She will bloom there," safely removed from consciousness. The poem "In His Own Image" is full of anxiety. The speaker cannot find her center, her identity. Potential signs of identity lie all around her, but she cannot interpret them: "Celery feath-ers, . . ./ bacon flitch, . . ./ kettle's paunch, . . ./ these were all I had to go on, . . ./ meagre proofs of myself." A drunken husband responds to his wife's identity crisis by pounding her into his own desired "shape."

> He splits my lip with his fist,
> shadows my eye with a blow,
> knuckles my neck to its proper angle.
> What a perfectionist!
> His are a sculptor's hands:
> they summon
> form from the void,
> they bring
> me to myself again.
> I am a new woman.

How different are these two methods of coping with psychic conflict. In "In Her Own Image," the speaker plants her old self lovingly in the garden. In "In His Own Image," the drunken husband reshapes his wife's features with violent hands. The wife in the second poem says that she is now a "new woman." If one reads this volume as a single poem, as Boland evidently intends that one should (all the illustrations have the same person as their subject), one understands that the desperate tone of other poems in the book derives from the suffering of this reshaped "new woman," victim of male exploitation.

The next four poems of *In Her Own Image* deal with very private subjects familiar to women but not often treated in published poems, anorexia, mastectomy surgery, masturbation, and menstruation. Both poems and Constance Hart's drawings are startlingly frank. The poet wants readers to experience "woman" in a more complete way, to realize the dark side of being female. The poems further illustrate Boland's sense of alienation from cultural myths or myths of identity. She desires connections, but she knows that she is unlikely to have them. She is therefore left with images which signify chaos rather than coherence, absence rather than presence, emptiness rather than fullness.

Two of the four poems, "Anorexia" and "Mastectomy," read like field reports from the battle of the sexes. The other two poems, "Solitary" and "Menses," have a female perspective but are also full of conflict. In the illustrations for "Anorexia," a very determined, extremely thin, naked woman, arms folded, looks disapprovingly at a fat woman lolling on a couch. An anorexic woman continues to believe that she is fat, despite the fact that she is a virtual skeleton. Boland introduces a religious level in the first three lines: "Flesh is heretic./ My body is a witch./ I am burning it." The conviction that her body is a witch runs through the whole poem. Here, in an extreme form, is the traditional Roman Catholic view that soul and body are separate. The body must be punished because, since the Fall, it has been the dwelling place of the devil. The soul must suppress the body in order for the soul to be saved. This tradition provides the anorexic with a religious reason for starving herself. In this poem, she revels in the opportunity to "torch" her body: "Now the bitch is burning." A presence even more disturbing than the witch is introduced in the second half of the poem, a ghostly male presence whom the anorexic speaker desires to please. To please this unnamed male presence, the speaker must become thin, so thin that she can somehow return to the womb imagined here paradoxically as male: "I will slip/ back into him again/ as if I had never been away." This return to the male womb will atone for the sin of being born a woman, with "hips and breasts/ and lips and heat/ and sweat and fat and greed."

In "Mastectomy," male-female conflict predominates. Male surgeons, envious of a woman's breasts (an effective transformation of the male-centered Freudian paradigm), cut off a breast and carry it away with them. The shocking drawing shows one gowned male surgeon passing the breast on a serving dish to another gowned male surgeon. The woman who has experienced this physical and psychological violation cries despairingly "I flatten to their looting." The sympathetic words of the surgeon before the operation belie the sinister act of removing the breast. It can now become part of male fantasy, as a symbol of primal nourishment and primal home: "So they have taken off/ what slaked them first,/ what they have hated since:/ blue-veined/ white-domed/ home/ of wonder/ and the wetness/ of their dreams."

The next two poems, "Solitary" and "Menses," deal with equally private aspects of a woman's life, autoeroticism and menstruation. "Solitary" has a celebratory attitude toward self-arousal. The drawing shows a relaxed naked female figure lying on her stomach. Religious imagery is used in this poem as it is in "Anorexia," but here the body is worshiped rather than feared. The only negative aspect of "Solitary" is its solitude. The female speaker is unconnected with another person. Solitary pleasures are intense but less so than the pleasures of intercourse. The reader is taken on a journey from arousal to orgasm to postorgasmic tranquillity. The religious language at first seems gratuitous but then perfectly appropriate. The speaker affirms the holiness of her body: "An oratory of dark,/ a chapel of unreason." She has a few moments of panic as the old words of warning flash into her mind: "You could die for this./ The gods could make you blind." These warnings do not deter her, however, from this sacred rite:

> how my cry
> blasphemes
> light and dark,
> screams
> land from sea,
> makes word flesh
> that now makes me
> animal.

During this period of arousal and climax, her "flesh summers," but then it returns again to winter: "I winter/ into sleep." "Menses" deals with the private act of menstruation. A cosmic female voice addresses the speaker as menstruation begins, attempting to focus her attention solely on the natural powers working in her body. The speaker resists this effort. She feels simultaneously "sick of it" and drawn to this process. She struggles to retain her freedom. "Only my mind is free," she says. Her body is taken over by tidal forces. "I am bloated with her waters./ I am barren with her blood." At the end of the poem, the speaker seems more accepting of this natural cycle. She reflects on two other cycles which she has experienced, childbirth and intercourse. All three cycles, she begins to see, make her a new person: "I am bright and original."

The final three poems of *In Her Own Image*, "Witching," "Exhibitionist," and "Making-up," return to the theme that "Myths/ are made by men"

("Making-up"). Much of a woman's life is spent reacting to male stereotypes. In "Witching," Boland further explores the idea of woman-as-witch, which was introduced in "Anorexia." Historically, women accused by men of being witches were doomed. The charges were usually either trumped-up or trivial. Boland's witch fantasizes about turning the table on her male persecutors and burning them first: "I will/ reserve/ their arson,/ make/ a pyre/ of my haunch . . . the stench/ of my crotch"—it is a grim but fitting fate for these male witch-burners. Another male stereotype, woman-as-stripper, is treated in the poem "Exhibitionist." This poem has the last accompanying drawing, a vulnerable young woman pulling her dress up over her head and naked to those watching her, perhaps as Boland feels naked toward those who have read through this volume. The male observers in "Exhibitionist" have in mind only gratifying their lusts. The speaker detests this exploitation and hopes to have a deeper impact on these leering males, hopes to touch them spiritually with her shining flesh: "my dark plan:/ Into the gutter/ of their lusts/ I burn/ the shine/ of my flesh." The final poem, "Making-up," returns to the theme of "Tirade for the Mimic Muse," that women must alter their appearances to please men, but that men have no such demands. The poem rehearses a litany of transformations of the speaker's "naked face." "Myths/ are made by men," this poem asserts. The goddesses men imagine can never be completely captured by that "naked face." A woman's natural appearance inevitably has flaws; it is not perfect like that of a goddess. Women are encouraged by men to disguise these flaws to make themselves look perfect. From these "rouge pots," a goddess comes forth, at least in men's eyes. Women should really know better.

> Mine are the rouge pots,
> the hot pinks, . . .
> out of which
> I dawn.

Eavan Boland is determined to make poetry out of her domestic life. *In Her Own Image* and *Night Feed* indicate that she has turned to the very ordinary subjects of hearth, rather than to the larger subjects of history, which she explored in her earlier volumes *New Territory* and *The War Horse*. In "The Woman Poet: Her Dilemma," Boland admits to uncertainty about this new orientation. She is encouraged especially, however, by the example of French and Dutch genre painters, whose work she calls "unglamorous, work-aday, authentic," possessing both ordinariness and vision: "The hare in its muslin bag, the crusty loaf, the women fixed between menial tasks and human dreams." In her own equally ordinary domestic life, she believes that she has found a personal voice.

Other major work

NONFICTION: *W. B. Yeats and His World*, 1971 (with Michael MacLiammoir).

Bibliography

Frazier, Adrian. "Nationalism and Obsession in Contemporary Irish Poetry: Interview with Eavan Boland," in *Literary Review*. XXII (Winter, 1979), pp. 237-257.

Arthur E. McGuinness

YVES BONNEFOY

Born: Tours, France; June 24, 1923

Principal collections

Traité du pianiste, 1946; *Anti-Platon*, 1947; *Du mouvement et de l'immo-
bilité de Douve*, 1953 (*On the Motion and Immobility of Douve*, 1968); *Hier
régnant désert*, 1958; *Pierre écrite*, 1965 (*Words in Stone*, 1976); *Selected Poems*, 1968; *L'Ordalie*, 1975; *Dans le leurre du seuil*, 1975 (*The Lure of the
Threshold*, 1985); *Rue traversière*, 1977; *Trois remarques sur la couleur*, 1977;
Poèmes, 1978; *Poems, 1959-1975*, 1985.

Other literary forms

Yves Bonnefoy has distinguished himself highly in other written forms in
addition to his poetry, particularly in the fields of art criticism and literary
criticism. His essays on art span the entire range from Byzantine to contemporary, with particular attention to the Renaissance and Baroque periods.
Bonnefoy is not simply an academic critic; some of his most moving prose
writing is that which ties the experience of the artist to the interior experience of the imaginative writer. In *L'Arrière-pays* (1972), for example, he
combines insightful discussions of classical Renaissance paintings with meditations on the sources of inspiration he draws from his own childhood. The
title's *arrière-pays* (which brings to mind *arrière-plan*, the background in a
painting, and which means, roughly, "backcountry") allows for an extended
meditation on the figures in the backgrounds of classic paintings and the feeling of well-being which Bonnefoy has experienced in his childhood and in his
many travels.

This interior experience is Bonnefoy's major focus in his literary criticism
as well, from the essays in *L'Improbable et autres essais* (1959, 1980), to the
monograph *Rimbaud par lui-même* (1961); *Rimbaud*, 1973), to the collections *Le Nuage rouge* (1977) and *La Présence et l'image* (1983). Bonnefoy returns again and again to the idea that the images a poet uses, while in some
sense unreal, are able to lead the reader to what he calls the "true place" of
poetry. Thus the line "Ô Saisons, ô châteaux" (Oh Seasons, oh castles),
which begins the famous poem by Rimbaud, becomes for Bonnefoy both a
utopian dream and a reality which can be reached through language.

The philosophical issues that the poet locates in his artistic and literary
researches are, in turn, fed back into his poetry, with the result that the poetry and the critical works come to mirror each other's concerns.

Achievements

Bonnefoy is one of the most highly admired poets to reach maturity in

France in the post–World War II period. His early work had the character of being challenging and even hermetic, but it struck a chord with a whole generation of readers and poets. His poetry has always maintained the quality of being highly meditated and serious to its purpose. While his preoccupations are philosophical—death, the existence of the loved one, the place of truth—his poetic language is highly imaged and moves equally in the realms of beauty and truth.

The close association Bonnefoy has always maintained with visual artists who are his contemporaries has given him a high prominence in the art world as well. Though he maintains a teaching position in literature, he has tended more and more in his later career to pursue his interests in art and the theory of culture. His writings on art are prized both for what they say about individual artists and for the high level of reflection they bring to the subject of creativity.

Bonnefoy's nomination to the Chair of Comparative Studies of the Poetic Function at the Collège de France in 1981 confirmed his position as one of France's leading poets and intellectual figures. A regular affiliation with Yale University and visiting professorships at other American universities have helped to ensure Bonnefoy's prominence among American academic circles as well. In France, his unique position as a poet and a theorist has made him someone to listen to for a wide range of the literate public.

Biography

Yves Bonnefoy was born on June 24, 1923, in Tours, France, to a family of workers and, more distantly, peasants and shepherds. His early life was divided between the working-class surroundings of Tours and the rural home of his maternal grandfather, which in many ways Bonnefoy considered his true home. He studied in Tours and at the University of Poitiers, primarily chemistry and mathematics.

Bonnefoy moved to Paris in 1943 to continue his scientific studies, but once there he found that his interests moved more toward poetry and philosophy. He sought out what remained of the Surrealist group and, though his formal association with it was brief, he formed many important friendships with young artists and poets. He married, edited a review, and studied widely different subjects, eventually taking a degree by writing a thesis on Charles Baudelaire and Søren Kierkegaard. This combined interest in poetry and philosophy has remained with him during his entire career.

Bonnefoy has earned a living teaching at lycées and universities, both in France and in the United States. In 1981, at the inauguration ceremony of his being named a department chair at the Collège de France, his highly publicized lecture "La Présence et l'image" (presence and the image) became a major statement for his particular style of intermixing philosophy and literature. Throughout his working career, Bonnefoy has traveled widely, especially in pursuing his growing interest in art, art history, and the theory of culture. He is widely recognized as one of the most important poets of his generation.

Analysis

From the beginning of his poetic career, Yves Bonnefoy's work has sounded the note of a serious pursuit of the truths which language reveals. His early divergence from the later figures of the Surrealist movement in France seems to have been provoked by what he perceived as a lack of purpose in their pursuits. For Bonnefoy, poetic language, above all, is a place or a function which grants access to the truths of existence. The path to those truths may of necessity be a difficult one, but once one is on that path, there can be no turning back. Bonnefoy is a highly original and engaging writer of criticism in which he explores these issues, but it has always been in his poetry that he has sought to discover their ground.

The early works *Anti-Platon* and *On the Motion and Immobility of Douve* introduce his poetry of high seriousness and announce a break from Surrealist practice. If Bonnefoy declares early his stance "against Plato," as the title of the first collection states, it is to restore the real dimension of experience, this object here and now, over against any sort of Platonic ideal. By extension, the importance of this real object leads Bonnefoy to examine the importance of this real life, here and now, in its affective dimension. Perhaps paradoxically, the importance of life emerges fully only when one confronts the actual death of someone. The poems in the second collection take up this theme; they are also the poems which established Bonnefoy as one of the most important poets of his generation.

The figure of Douve in Bonnefoy's second collection is based on a young girl of his acquaintance who died a sudden and tragic death. (He gives her name only in a later collection; see below.) As the form in the poems alternates between highly organized quatrains and looser prose-poem utterances, so the investigation in the poems moves between the image of the dead young woman and Death in general. As the sequence progresses, the speaker seeks to discover his own destiny based on an identification with the words of the young woman. In this work, death is present in the form of a person who is no longer there. She is troubling, however, because she poses the question of existence, of essence, of Being. It is by means of this questioning that the poet discovers his own means of expression. More even than the torment of mourning, there seems to emerge the injunction to silence as the most accurate means of representing death.

There is a progression, then, in the poems of this collection as far as the identification of the poet with the figure of the dead woman by means of her speech. When she speaks in the first part of the collection, it is in the past tense, and she speaks of natural forces, wind and cold. The poet-speaker sees her, however, and as a result there is a separation, the separation of death. The only way to overcome this separation is by the identification involved in speaking. Changing to the present tense, the speaker says, "Douve je parle en toi" (Douve, I speak in you):

> Et si grand soit le froid qui monte de ton être,
> Si brûlant soit le gel de notre intimité,
> Douve, je parle en toi; et je t'enserre
> Dans l'acte de connaître et de nommer.

> (And though great cold rises in your being,
> However burning the frost of our intimacy
> Douve, I speak in you; and I enshroud you
> In the act of knowing and of naming.)

This is one of the strong moments of identification and the beginning of poetic creation, as Bonnefoy describes it in his essay "The Act and the Place of Poetry": "So Dante who has lost her, will *name* Beatrice." Over against the natural forces that are imaged here as present because of her death, the act of naming and of knowing restores a certain presence to the lost loved one. Even so, this is a first stage: Far from being consoling, it leads the poet to the point of anguish.

The central part of the collection, "Douve parle" (Douve speaks), begins with this identification in speaking, "ce cri sur moi vient de moi" (this cry above me comes from me). Paradoxically, in the series of poems bearing the title "Douve speaks," she finishes by saying: "Que le verbe s'éteigne" (Let the verb be extinguished). That which one must recognize in oneself as death surpasses the function of speech. The poet enters this region of contradiction when he says: "Je parle dans ton sang" (I speak in your blood).

This progression reaches its completion in the injunction, which the figure of the woman makes to the speaker, to remain silent. The poem which begins "Mais que se taise" (But that one be silent) requires silence above all of the one "Qui parle pour moi" (Who speaks for me). In the following poems, she is even more direct, saying simply, "Tais-toi" (remain silent; shut up). The speaker finds himself in a place of radical transformations, during a time of anguish and of struggle: "Quand la lumière enfin s'est faite vent et nuit" (When the light at last has become wind and night). The figure of the dead woman has led the speaker to a privileged place of being, where the poet not only recognizes himself in his own expression but also is faced with his own anguish, his authentic attitude toward death.

The collected edition of Bonnefoy's poetry, *Poèmes*, adds three important collections to the earlier work, *Hier régnant désert* (yesterday the desert reigning), *Words in Stone*, and *The Lure of the Threshold*. These collections continue to explore the areas mapped out by Bonnefoy's earlier work. The tone is serious and the subject matter highly philosophical. Death is a constant presence and is confronted continually for what it tells about existence. In the first of these later collections, *Hier régnant désert*, Bonnefoy returns again to the Douve figure, although here, at least in one poem, she is named—Kathleen Ferrier. The same contradictions between a conflicted natural universe and a tragic sense of human destiny are confronted again in the elemental terms: face, voice. Whereas to see an image of the dead young woman leads to separation, an identification with her voice allows for the poet to discover his own utterance. As he says in "À la voix de Kathleen Ferrier" (to the voice of Kathleen Ferrier):

> Je célèbre la voix mêlée de couleur grise
> Qui hésite aux lointains du chant qui s'est perdu
> Comme si au delà de toute forme pure
> Tremblât un autre chant et le seul absolu.

> (I celebrate the voice mixed with grey color
> Which hesitates in the sung distances of what is lost
> As if beyond every pure form
> Trembled another song and the only absolute.)

This poem is more insistently philosophical than any examined hereto. The voice that is celebrated seems to have lost all contact with the merely human as it moves toward the realms of pure being.

Even the poems ostensibly concerned with inanimate objects bear their burden of existence, as does this short poem from *Words in Stone*, "Une Pierre" (a stone):

> Il désirait, sans connaître,
> Il a péri, sans avoir.
> Arbres, fumées,
> Toutes lignes de vent et de déception
> Furent son gîte.
> Infiniment
> Il n'a étreint que sa mort.

> (It desired, without knowing
> It perished, without having.
> Trees, smoke,
> All lines of wind and of deception
> Were its shelter
> Infinitely
> It only grasped its death.)

This deceptively simple poem about a stone carries a weight of thought and image balanced off in a skillful suspension. It may or may not carry direct reference to Jean-Paul Sartre's existential philosophy, which affirmed the stone's interiority and self-identity over time while denying these same inherent qualities to the human subject. Bonnefoy's turn on the idea here is to introject the tragic sense into the simple being of the stone. Bereft of the human qualities of knowing or having, it was at one with nature and alone to face death.

Bonnefoy's later poems in the collected volume trace a dialectic between the tragic sense of human destiny, as presented in Douve's words, and the introjected tragedy of nature just examined in the poem from *Words in Stone*. The difference in the later works is in their form. From the short, often highly formal, verse of his early career, Bonnefoy here moves to a more expanded utterance. Though the poems are longer, however, there is a greater degree of fragmentation. It is as though the silence which was so important thematically in the speech of Douve has been refigured in the form of the poem itself. From the highly wrought, lapidary form of the early work has emerged a laconic style, hinting at what the speaker cannot say.

Into the atmosphere of charged philosophical speculation—in effect, a dialogue between being and nonbeing—Bonnefoy brings a new element of disjunction and, ultimately, of mystery, as in these lines from "Deux Barques" (two boats): "Étoiles, répandues./ Le ciel, un lit défait, une naissance." (Stars, spread out./ The sky, an unmade bed, a birth.) The traditional analysis of metaphor in terms of "tenor" and "vehicle" becomes very difficult with lines such as these. How is one to decide what is the content of the statement and what is the rhetorical trapping? Here the stars could be the vehicle for an image having as its content the beginning of human life. In like manner, the heavens could be the content and the bed an image to describe the appearance of stars, with birth as an added metaphorical element. As this example makes clear, Bonnefoy's long meditations on the power of language to investigate the central issues of existence remain as intense in his later work as in his earlier poetry.

In all of Bonnefoy's work, an extremely restricted vocabulary is used to describe the conflicts between nature and human existence. Words such as "stone" and "fire," "wind" and "star," take on an elemental sense rather than being merely descriptive. These word elements are placed in the context of laconic statements, each statement offering but a hint of the overall movement in the poem. This overall movement in turn is established through the cumulative force of these elemental images placed into disjunctive and often contradictory sequences. Almost always, a mood of high seriousness is the result. The simplest language thus becomes a language of tragic dimensions. The elemental forces at work in the poem's image sequences reflect directly on the human dimension of existence. Bonnefoy places hard demands on the conceptual capabilities of his readers. He is clearly uninterested in easy sentiment or pleasing verses. His poetry presents a continual invitation to join in the struggle out of which the truths of existence emerge.

In the final poem of his collected edition, "L'Épars, l'indivisible" (the sparse, the indivisible), an anaphoric repetition is utilized, with the first word of most stanzas being "Oui" (yes). Under the general structuring principle of affirmation, the seemingly most opposite elements are joined. One section reads simply: "Oui, par la mort,/ Oui, par la vie sans fin" (Yes, through death,/ Yes, through life without end). Affirming opposites in this manner runs the risk of affirming nothing, but again the cumulative effect of the con- tradictions is to lead to a synthesis of values. Two sections later, the speaker states: "Oui, par même l'erreur,/ Qui va,// Oui, par le bonheur simple, la voix brisée." (Yes, even through error,/ Which passes,// Yes, through simple happiness, the broken voice.) Bonnefoy does not seek easy resolution or unexamined pleasures. When he speaks of happiness in the same breath with a broken voice, however, the force of the image goes beyond the conceptual setting up of paradoxes. Happiness which leads to a broken voice is happi- ness that carries with it a strong emotion and the force of personal history. These deceptively simple images are weighted with complex and achieved emotion.

The figure of Yves Bonnefoy the poet is closely allied to that of Bonnefoy the thinker. His researches into art, literature, and the sources of creativity in life history have always been motivated by a search for truth which can then find form and be expressed in his poetry. This is not to say that reading Bonnefoy's poetry is the equivalent of reading his essays and criticism or that the philosophical underpinnings of the works are presented in a predigested or easily digestible form. His highly imaged poems show a consistent concern for poetic image and emotion. As a result, the reality they possess is one which adds to experience. The highly wrought, imaginatively charged poems of Yves Bonnefoy reveal the common origins of thinking and of poetry. By posing the central questions of existence, they are timeless. They are also of a pressing timeliness in that they recall the reader to being in the present.

Other major works

NONFICTION: *Peintures murales de la France gothique*, 1954; *L'Improbable et autres essais*, 1959, 1980; *La Seconde Simplicité*, 1961; *Rimbaud par lui- même*, 1961 (*Rimbaud*, 1973); *Un Rêve fait à Mantoue*, 1967; *Rome 1630: L'Horizon du premier baroque*, 1970; *L'Arrière-pays*, 1972; *Le Nuage rouge*, 1977; *Entretiens sur la poésie*, 1981; *La Présence et l'image*, 1983.

TRANSLATIONS: *1 Henri IV*, *Jules César*, *Hamlet*, *Le Conte d'hiver*, *Vénus et Adonis*, *Le Viol de Lucrèce*, 1957-1960 (as a series of translations of William Shakespeare's works); *Le Roi Lear*, 1965 (of Shakespeare's play); *Roméo et Juliette*, 1968 (of Shakespeare's play).

Bibliography
Albert, Walter. "Bonnefoy and the Architecture of Poetry," in *Modern Lan-*

  guage Notes. LXXXII (1967), pp. 165-173.

Caws, Mary Ann. *Yves Bonnefoy*, 1984.

Jackson, John E. *La Question du moi: Un Aspet de la modernité poétique européenne—T. S. Eliot, Paul Celan, Yves Bonnefoy*, 1978.

Maurin, Mario. "On Bonnefoy's Poetry," in *Yale French Studies.* No. 21 (1958), pp. 16-22

Naughton, John T. *The Poetics of Yves Bonnefoy*, 1984.

Thélot, Jérôme. *La Poétique d'Yves Bonnefoy*, 1983.

Vernier, Richard. *Yves Bonnefoy: Ou, Les Mots comme le ciel*, 1985.

Peter Baker

BREYTEN BREYTENBACH

Born: Bonnievale, South Africa; September 16, 1939.

Principal poems and collections

Die ysterkoei moet sweet, 1964; *Die huis van die dowe*, 1967; *Kouevuur*, 1969; *Lotus*, 1970; *Oorblyfsels*, 1970; *Skryt*, 1972; *Met ander woorde*, 1973; *Voetskrif*, 1976; *Sinking Ship Blues*, 1977; *And Death as White as Words: An Anthology of the Poetry of Breyten Breytenbach*, 1978 (edited by A. J. Coetzee); *In Africa Even the Flies Are Happy: Selected Poems, 1964-1977*, 1978 (translated by Denis Hershon).

Other literary forms

In addition to his poetry, Breyten Breytenbach has written the short stories *Katastrofes* (1964; catastrophes), and *De boom achter de maan* (1974; the tree behind the moon), the biographical *'n Seisoen in die Paradys* (1976; *A Season in Paradise*, 1980), and *The True Confessions of an Albino Terrorist*, (1983), a record of his prison experiences. This last, his best-known work, describes his decision to return to South Africa with the intention of establishing a revolutionary organization. The ideas are presented indirectly: Instead of the simple diary chronology that might be anticipated, he devises a complex literary structure. A series of interrogations and confessions, made to an impersonal, elusive, but threatening figure, Mr. Interrogator, are interrupted by "inserts," which act as a kind of chorus providing lyrical speculation and philosophic debate among the evidence of the persecution he was suffering. Breytenbach makes his most defiant challenge to the regime with subtle literary technique rather than blatant accusation.

Achievements

Breytenbach's distinction occurs at two levels. The fact that he writes his poetry in Afrikaans has limited his audience outside South Africa. His immense reputation within that country derives from the same fact. He was part of the so-called Sestiger movement of the 1960's, which revolutionized Afrikaans literature. For the first time, Afrikaans was made to describe radical attitudes that horrified the Afrikaner establishment, whose puritanism and reactionary beliefs had until then controlled all literary expression. Understandably, conventional social attitudes made his work highly controversial. The old with anger, the young with excitement, saw Breytenbach as a literary iconoclast who broke the controls that had traditionally restricted both form and subject of Afrikaans poetry and who linked Afrikaner concerns with the dangerously experimental, outspoken and often-censored writings being published in English, the language of those who had traditionally sought to extirpate the culture of the Afrikaner "volk." All of his work has provoked bitter attack and equally violent counterattack. For every critic who denounced the blasphemy and radicalism of his work, others praised his originality that liberated the Afrikaans language from a narrow and bigoted orthodoxy. Internationally, his poetry is known in translation, but he is far more renowned as a political figure, as a fighter against apartheid. His prison memoirs, *The True Confessions of an Albino Terrorist*, have been accepted as an important addition to the literary condemnations of the Pretoria regime.

Biography

Breyten Breytenbach was born in a conservative small town, Bonnievale, on the western side of Cape Town. He entered the then-unsegregated Cape Town University to study painting. The opportunity, for him, was revolutionary. For the first time, Breytenbach met Africans as equals, mixed with left-wing student groups, and delighted in his intellectual freedom and his escape from the narrowness and racism of his upbringing. He became a member of the radical African National Congress. At twenty-one, he left for Paris, completing his liberation, or revolt, from his family and race. He married a Vietnamese woman (illegal under his country's race acts). "It was . . . against the moral principles of the Christian Community that two human beings of different skin colour should lie together." He had no choice but to remain in Paris, where he worked as an artist. He was prevented from returning with his wife even to accept the national prizes that were being awarded his work. A brief visit was arranged in 1972, during which his wife stayed across the border in independent and unsegregated Swaziland. This discrimination and rejection fostered his resentment. In 1975, he decided on active involvement and made plans almost as bizarre in practice as they were optimistic in intention. He returned on a forged French passport to set up a revolutionary organization for whites called Okhela, which would use sabotage and guerrilla action to overthrow the government. There is still some confusion about his true motives and expectations. Given his wide fame, his attempt at disguise was ludicrous. He was arrested, and charged under the Terrorism Act. His unexpected apologies to the court allowed him to escape a potential death penalty, but he was sentenced to nine years imprisonment for terrorism. Frequent international appeals effected his release in 1982, and he returned to Paris, where he still lives.

Analysis

The poetry of Breyten Breytenbach is both highly personal and highly public. This paradox is explained by his intense emotional involvement with the society in which he was born, a society that is condemned universally for its racism and bigotry. His sensitivity to this relationship readily leads self-expression into public posture. He was constantly antagonistic to apartheid, yet he realized that he was inevitably a part of it. The consequent dilemma may begin to explain the moods of near suicidal despair and depression that are found in his more intimate poems. Brought up among cosmic cruelties, it must have seemed to him that the opportunity for any individual to find separate solace was as delusive as it was reprehensible. That admission contains within it one of the reasons for the constant emotional tension encountered in his revealing verse.

Another way in which Breytenbach's work may be considered personal is the close link it has with his actual experience. The sequence of his poems follows the events that were occurring in his life as an exile and a political prisoner. By exploring and confronting the anxieties he faces as a human being, he indicates that his responses are based upon political conviction but have a deeper psychological origin than radical activism. Breytenbach defies and rejects apartheid in his writing through introspective self-analysis, rather than through a more open and formal stand. There is an almost a neurotic emotion that commands the efflorescence of extraordinarily violent language and metaphor, but it affects only the poetic surface. By implication, as much as by direct statement, there clearly remains an underlying political stance in Breytenbach's poetry. Breytenbach denounces the regime with an anger that derives some of its intensity from his own sense of personal affront as well as his predetermined and principled political beliefs. The man is the poet and the poet is a political activist. The paradox provokes a revealing duality of aims between poet as artist and poet as spokesman. This divergence has preoccupied both writers and critics in the twentieth century. The essential elements of the controversy have never been convincingly resolved. What is the proper role of a poet who exists under an oppressive regime? Does the urge toward declamatory affirmation make poetry mere propaganda? Jean-Paul Sartre's famous essay "What is Literature?" explores this issue with typical acuity. Does moral and political commitment minimize the expression of the more universal human truths which many believe constitute the ultimate reason for poetry? Breytenbach's work both explores and exemplifies this dilemma. These are the issues that must be considered as one examines the volumes of poetry that have come from his pen. Across a period of twenty years, these ideas have confirmed his development as a writer and signaled his commitment to revolution.

Breytenbach's earliest poetry, collected in *Die ysterkoei moet sweet* (the iron cow must sweat) gives immediate early evidence of his capacity for a striking vigor of imagery. His language is extravagant and unexpected. Expressions such as "blood like peaches in syrup," "people are biting at each other's gullets," "spiky Jesus stands out on a cross," from a single poem, exhibit his evocative originality. At the center of his use of language is a vividly confident assurance remarkable in so youthful a poet. His effusive self-confidence is particularly apparent in comparison to the formality and polished moderation of the poets of the Afrikaner establishment. In spite of this verbal virility, the mood that Breytenbach's brilliant language expresses is curiously negative. There are hints of suicide. "I am not yet ready/ for I must still learn how to die." He emphasizes death often enough to suggest that some psychological imbalance, almost a neurosis, exists within the poet even in his earlier years. There is fear, also, as if he realized the conclusions of his combative attitudes. "But keep Pain far from Me o Lord/ That others may bear it/ Be taken away into custody,/ Shattered/ Stoned/ Suspended/ Lashed. . . ."

Yet all is not gloom; there is also a gentle deprecatory irony: "Ladies and gentlemen allow me to introduce you to Breyten Breytenbach," begins one poem which concludes with a comment so infinitely more poignant, given our knowledge of his future: "Look he is harmless, have mercy upon him." Perhaps he was not. Certainly, no one did.

The later poems in this volume are written from Paris after his departure from South Africa, occasioned partly by political constraints, but more by his desire to explore the cosmopolitan world beyond the margins of Cape Town. Quickly there is an awareness of disillusion, albeit he proclaimed his satisfaction. "I can't complain." "I'm happy here." Away from his country, freed from its constant social tensions that rapidly became his own, he has a new freedom of choice. It is precisely that luxury, however, that requires him to determine what he will do with such a dramatic opportunity. For a South African, the relief of exile is always attended by some guilt. The decision can be interpreted as cowardly escape or as bold defiance. In this new context of liberation, Breytenbach must ask himself those unanswerable questions: "What were your grand resolutions?/ or is your existence only a matter of compromise?/ what are you looking for here/ without the excuse of being young . . . and what are you planning to do?" South Africa refuses to be wished away. The recognition of distance more acutely induces memory. In contrast to Paris, "somewhere the aloes are shining/ somewhere some are smelling fresh guavas." (Aloes are the floral symbol of South Africa.) The mood is sad and fretful. Escape does not constitute solution "because other worlds and other possibilities exist you know."

Only in some of the later poems dedicated to his new wife does any happier note appear: "I press my nose in the bouquet of your neck/ how ripe how intoxicating its fragrance the smell of life/ you live." Even so intense an intimacy is laced with an insistent bitterness of spirit. "You are a butterfly of trembling light/ and inside you already your carcase is nibbling."

Similarly, the second collection, *Die huis van die dowe* (the house of the deaf), though intended to celebrate love, expresses his persistent self-doubt: "Pain bruises us all to a more intimate shade—/ . . . which can never heal, the dreams." The bitterness of the words suggests that the freedom that Breytenbach so eagerly sought by departure has proved geographic rather than spiritual. "No restful eye/ and no rest or surrender or cellars or the cool of sleep." His agitation is both personal and professional. There are insistent expressions of concern about his poetry; inspiration seems to be weakening without the violent indignation that the daily experience of South Africa provided. He realizes that there has begun to be a separation between his life and his work. He observes that "My fire has slaked/ I must stand to one side." More vulgarly, "My arsehole is full of myself," a crudely worded but significant condemnation since, unlike more circumspect poets, he deplores an introspective style. The intention to escape from the constrictions of self was to determine his decision to play a public role as an activist, rather than as a poet-spokesman.

He soon began to achieve some international recognition, but this publicity did not fulfill him, since it seemed totally remote from his indigenous commitment to South Africa. Success only increased his sense of painful isolation. "I'm a globe-trotter... as thirsty as ever" and "from a lot of travelling/ the heart grows mute and waterlogged." No political condemnation of his country will drive away his exile's longing. Of his own city, Cape Town, he writes, "that's how I love you/ as I have dreamed of you.../ my cape, godcape, lovecape, capeheart... Fairest cape in all the world."

His urge toward verse remains strong, though its effect seems constantly tainted even while he uses it to sustain his personal and ardent life. "Give me a pen/ so that I can sing/ that life is not in vain." Perhaps he presents his own reflection in a poem he dedicated to Yousef Omar, and recognizes the same emotions and the same fate: "His heart is a clot of fear/ the man is not a hero/ he knows he'll have to hang/ for he is stupid/ and wanted to believe." One might hope that Breytenbach's disillusionment is not so comprehensive, but his doubts persist in his private life. He yearns for love: "Give me a love/ like the love I want to give to you," while suggesting that desire is equivocal.

Breytenbach explores his anxieties further in his *Kouevuur* (coldfire-gangrene). Some of these poems show the beginnings of disintegration in both form and statement. Burning with an inner bitterness, he finds himself giving others the advice he should have taken to his own heart: "Above all watch out for the slimy black paw paw/ of bitterness, black child—/ he that eats of it dies on bayonets." He might well have deliberated upon this truth. In this collection, passionate lyric poems are matched by violent expressions of self-condemnation. His political work distracts him from poetry and yet at the same time its obligations tease him with the more shocking thought that writing may no longer be considered an adequate response to South African circumstances. He is increasingly aware of how separated he has become from his country. "You ask me how it is living in exile, my friend/ What can I say?/ that I'm too young for bitter protest/ and too old for wisdom and acceptance/ of my destiny." Acceptance of destiny was gradually invading Breytenbach's thoughts, but his unexpected reversal of the anticipated attitudes of youth and age display the convolutions of his present moods. Return was legally forbidden with a "non-European" wife, and therefore his marriage required that he express his gradual recognition of the permanence of exile (which he somewhat casually chose as a young man) and its painful results: "Yes, but that I now also know the rooms of loneliness/ the desecration of dreams, the remains of memories." The "if" in the following line indicates both admission and anxiety: "I've been thinking if I ever come back." He realizes that there are the outward changes, that he will appear, "wearing a top hat/ a smart suit . . . new Italian shoes for the occasion," garb that defines his new European citizenship. He can only hope that "ma knows it's me all the same." He can still write lyrically of his love, of the happiness that it has brought. "I love you—you lead me through gardens/ through all the mansions of the sun . . ./ love is sweeter than figs." Or even more tenderly, "sleep my little love/ sleep well sleep dark/ wet as sugar in coffee/ be happy in your dreams." Love is a pleasure that provides no resolution of his confusion. Old age is seen not as a conclusion but as a period of harmony and calm. It provides comfort in allowing escape from the obligations of action that he and others had imposed, and permits abdication from oppressive responsibility: "That's the answer, to be an old man, a naked/ treedweller, too old to climb down."

The *Lotus* collection is specifically addressed to his wife. There are lines of unusual exhilaration and intensity. "For my love travels along with you/ my love must stay with you like an angel." Yet such elevated emotions are not entirely convincing. More typical is the ambivalent self-flagellation of the following lines: "I'm in love with my loneliness/ because I'm alone/ . . . Two things I have to say:/ I'm alone, but I love you."

In *Oorblyfsels*, Breytenbach's increasing emotional disgust spills over. His psychological dismay urges him toward greater political assertiveness. He describes himself with shame as "I, a white African featherless fowl." He turns upon his entire race, equating whiteness with evil, blaming whites for his own cursed Afrikaner inheritance: "whitedom." "The white man knows only the sun/ knows nothing of black or man." This judgment exacerbates his ferocious inner conflicts. It requires that he accept connection with the atrocity he perceives and condemns, but from which he cannot free himself. No matter his protestations of racial neutrality, he is one of them. His admission of this is more angry than sad, "I am German/ I am cruel/ I am white, I steal." It becomes an inverse communion with his soul. It is a kind of litany of social condemnation in which, in color terms, he must include himself.

By the time the even more belligerent *Skryt* (write) was written, the political accusations are more apparent than the introspective anxieties which provide their source. It is South Africa that Breytenbach has in mind when he describes, from a different coast, how "the ocean washes like blood against the land/ I stand on my knees where the hearts are laid down/ sand in my throat like grievances that cannot be stomached." His inspection is factual; his response has become pathological. He contemplates with increased aware- ness what Africa has suffered, comprehending that in his own country "to live black is a political crime." He also contemplates how Africa might sur- vive. "Africa so often pillaged, purified, burnt!/ Africa stands in the sign of fire and flame." His hatred for his country intensifies. He excoriates it merci- lessly as "this is hell with God." He roundly condemns its people, seeing them as villains "lugging an attache case with shares and gold in one hand/ and a sjambok [whip] in the other." It would be far simpler if such denegra- tion could remain purely political, but inevitably he incorporates the same scathing attitudes into his more intimate analyses. The fact that the regime survives increases his sense of incompetence and inadequacy. Gloomily he re- ports on his present state: "You grow less agile, more compliant/ . . . yet death walks in your body . . . and by the time you want to smash the day with your fist/ and say: look my people are rising up! . . . you've forgotten the silences of the language." He expresses his failure as a poet, a lover, and as a revolutionary: "I fold the dead of that/ which we/ called love/ in chalk dark words/ bury it here/ within this paper/ that a God should fill the gaps." It is clear that only some defiant and unequivocal action will satisfy his needs, but that action would not cure his heart's malaise.

Ironically, South Africa's liberation would not affect Breytenbach's own. It is this despairing admission that permeates the 1973 collection *Met ander woorde* (in other words). Poetry can provide no adequate means of resolving the racial and social impasse of South Africa. In this book he more openly announces his intention for more explicit assaults on the system. "Now that death/ begins to seek out the eyes/ a single burning purpose remains/ to grow stronger towards the end/ you feel you are bound to yourself/ by an underground movement." Yet is he, the poet-artist, the person capable of carrying out such deliberate service? Can an intellectual become a function- ing revolutionary? In a self-deprecatory way, Breytenbach offers himself some disguised advice in a wry and comic metaphor: "When the canopy of sky tears/ then all the stars fall out:/ you know you can't let a drunk man work on the roof." In spite of this warning, his determination to transmute his art and philosophy into action drove him to the deeds that resulted in arrest, trial, and conviction. His incarceration did not free his spirit from his recognition of racial guilt. The fact that he had so demonstrably and publicly suffered in the cause of revolution did not purge him of his association from Afrikaner history. Given what he was, or more accurately, what he thought himself to be, there were no acts he could perform that would satisfy him nor assuage his inner despair. Even Afrikaans, the language which he had done so much to vivify, seems to be the vehicle in which the oppression is ex- pressed. "We ourselves are aged./ Our language is a grey reservist a hundred years old and more." The Afrikaans language defines the racist system, "For we are Christ's executioners./ . . . We bring you the grammar of violence/ and the syntax of destruction." A few poems survived his incarceration, though many were lost and stolen. Some are personal, for the painful imposition of extended solitary confinement necessitated an introspection which opened up vistas of self-awareness impossible during the cosmopolitan distractions of his Paris exile. Part of this discovery is expressed in purely physical terms. "I feel the apples of decay in my chest/ and in my wrists the jolt of trains./ Now—after how many months of solitary confinement?"

At the conclusion of *The True Confessions of an Albino Terrorist* are thirteen poems that record his last days in jail and his liberation. He tries to write but thinks little of his efforts: "A man has made himself a poem/ for his birthday the sixteenth of the ninth—/ o, no not a fancy affair with room and rhyme/ and rhythm and iambs and stuff. . . ." He can rejoice in the memories that fill the long hours of his confinement. They are sometimes recalled with irony: "Do you remember when we were dogs/ you and I?" Other moments are recollected more poignantly, "He will remember—/ mornings before daybreak." Memory is reinforced by the arrival of a letter, "word from outside." He tells, "I fled to your letter, to read/ that the small orange tree is a mass of white blossoms." This ordinary world becomes richer and more exotic when set against the one he inhabits where, "in the middle of the night/ the voice of those/ to be hanged within days/ rise up already sounding thin."

Finally, there is the bliss of release. "I arrive on this first day already glistening bright/ among angel choirs." Then the return to the haven of Paris, where he writes one of the few expressions of unalloyed delight to be found in his poetry: "Listen to that same wind calling/ through the old old Paris streets/ you're the one I love and I'm feeling so good." The final couplet has a fine ring, so positive in contrast to his earlier anxieties. He still speaks of death, but his attitude is now devil-may-care: " Burn, burn with me love—to hell with decay to live is to live, and while alive to die anyway."

Other major works

NOVEL: *Mouroir: Mirrornotes of a Novel*, 1984.

SHORT FICTION: *Katastrofes*, 1964; *De boom achter de maan*, 1974.

NONFICTION: *'n Seisoen in die Paradys*, 1976 (*A Season in Paradise*, 1980); *The True Confessions of an Albino Terrorist*, 1983; *End Papers*, 1986.

Bibliography

Cope, Jack. *The Adversary Within: Dissident Writers in Afrikaans*, 1982.

Des Pres, Terrence. "Rimbaud's Nephew," in *Parnassus*. XI (Fall/Winter, 1983, Spring/Summer, 1984), pp. 83-102.

Moore, Gerald. "The Martian Descends: The Poetry of Breyten Breytenbach" in *Ariel: A Review of International English Literature*. XVI (April, 1985), pp. 3-12.

Roberts, Sheila. "South African Prison Literature," in *Ariel: A Review of International English Literature*. XVI (April, 1985), pp. 61-73.

van der Merwe, P. P. "Breyten Breytenbach and the Poet Revolutionary," in *Theoria*. LVI (May, 1981), pp. 51-72.

John Povey

TURNER CASSITY

Born: Jackson, Mississippi; January 12, 1929

Principal poems and collections

Watchboy, What of the Night?, 1966; "The Airship Boys in Africa," 1970; *Steeplejacks in Babel*, 1973; *Silver Out of Shanghai: A Scenario for Josef von Sternberg, Featuring Wicked Nobles, a Depraved Religious, Wayfoong, Princess Ida, the China Clipper, and Resurrection Lily, with a Supporting Cast of Old Hands, Merchant Seamen, Sikhs, Imperial Marines, and Persons in Blue*, 1973; *Yellow for Peril, Black for Beautiful: Poems and a Play*, 1975; *The Defense of the Sugar Islands: A Recruiting Poster*, 1979; *Keys to Mayerling*, 1983; *Hurricane Lamp*, 1986.

Other literary forms

While primarily a poet, Turner Cassity has also written several uncollected short stories, a poetic drama (*Men of the Great Man*, contained in *Yellow for Peril, Black for Beautiful*) and an essay on the cataloging of periodicals, "Gutenberg as Card Shark," published in *The Academic Library: Essays in Honor of Guy R. Lyle* (1974).

Achievements

Perhaps because of its traditional form, Cassity's poetry has received less attention than it deserves. Cassity has won the Blumenthal-Leviton-Blonder Prize for poetry in 1966 and has gained an increasingly large group of supporters, but he seems to have had little influence on the course of contemporary writing. Detractors, and occasionally even champions, argue that while technically polished, the poems are often unrewardingly distant or difficult, and that although the poet's formal talent is considerable, his range is somewhat limited. A closer reading of Cassity's work as a whole, however, reveals the complexity to be a necessary outgrowth of the poet's vision—not merely cleverness for its own sake—and the limited scope to be a false modesty. The wealth of allusion never makes the writing pedantic or pretentious; instead it reflects the poet's refusal to adopt a single, narrow perspective as his guide. Conscious of his heritage, the poet is able to distance himself ironically from that past and to discover his present. Further attention to Cassity's work should continue to reveal both the significance of his refusal to write a less traditional, more accessible type of poetry, and the importance of his unique and challenging view, a view that rewards even as it frustrates the reader's expectations of what contemporary poetry should be.

Biography

Turner Cassity was born in Jackson, Mississippi, on January 12, 1929. His father, who died when Cassity was four, was in the sawmill business; his mother was a violinist and his grandmother a pianist in silent film theaters. The family moved to Forrest, Mississippi, in 1933 and later back to Jackson, where Cassity attended Bailey Junior High School and was graduated from Central High School. Cassity was graduated from Millsaps College with a B.A. in 1951 and from Stanford University with an M.A. in English in 1952; at Stanford he studied poetry with Yvor Winters in a program that he likens to "the strict technical training a musician would get at a good conservatory." He was drafted in 1952 during the Korean War and spent the two years of his duty in Puerto Rico, an experience that provides the basis for his sequence *The Defense of the Sugar Islands.* He received an M.S. in library science from Columbia University in 1956 and served as an assistant librarian at the Jackson Municipal Library for 1957-1958 and for part of 1961. From 1959 to 1961, Cassity was an assistant librarian for the Transvaal Provincial Library in Pretoria, South Africa. Observations from his stay in Pretoria and Johannesburg frequently appear in his poems. In 1962, Cassity accepted a job at the Emory University Library in Atlanta, where he works as Librarian in the Original Cataloging Department.

Cassity travels regularly, mainly to the desert or the tropics, having little interest in Europe, and has spent much time in California. Both his job as librarian and his love of exotic locations are reflected in his poems, particularly in their sense of history and of place. Cassity has referred to his poems as "tropical pastorals," but this description conceals the sense of amusement and horror with which many of his speakers perceive the past. Cassity also describes himself as "a burgher" in temperament and conviction, and this label is also somewhat misleading, for his poems seldom reveal a complacent attitude; his scrutiny of colonialism, while not obviously polemical, often reveals more the flaws inherent in the underlying psychology of the colonist than do more tendentious poems. Cassity writes at a regular pace, publishing in *Poetry*, *The Kenyon Review*, *The Southern Review*, and *Chicago Review*, and many other journals and magazines; for him writing is a profession, not a hobby.

Analysis

Ever since his first volume of poetry, *Watchboy, What of the Night?*, Turner Cassity has continued to write terse, elliptical poems in unfashionably strict metrical form. For Cassity, the discipline of writing in meter and rhyme is prerequisite to his creative process: "without it, nothing comes into my head." Yet, while traditional, his verse avoids monotony and is typically supple and lively. His poems often include exotic settings or historical figures, juxtaposing them to the tawdriness of the familiar modern world. The combination of this irony with the restrained meter and diction yields a body of poetry that is formal and wittily aloof; the polish and urbanity, however, do not conceal the poet's ongoing search for a deliverance from decay and loss. Ultimately, the poet returns to his medium, language, and to his craftsmanship to find this deliverance, and in this sense Cassity is truly modern—in contrast to many contemporary poets, who, though severing ties with traditional form, fail to understand the relationship of past to present and their role in defining that relationship.

Clearly, Cassity is to some extent an heir of earlier modern poets writing in traditional modes, especially of Yvor Winters, with whom Cassity studied; many have also noted similarities between Cassity's work and that of W. H. Auden, Wallace Stevens, and Robert Frost. Equally evident, though, is the deft, colloquial irony of French post-Symbolists such as Jules Laforgue; and the formal control, epigrammatic wit, and social concern of eighteenth century poetry, particularly that of Alexander Pope, are, for some readers, evident in many of Cassity's poems. Still, the density of Cassity's allusions and the complexity of his contrasts—past and present, great and trivial, historical and personal—distinguish his writing from that of the traditional poet.

The fact that Turner Cassity frequently juxtaposes the noteworthy with the mundane may in part account for his being labeled a satirist. Such a strategy, however, is a means more of evaluating the past than of ridiculing the present, a means of understanding change and loss. The poem "Seven Destinations of Mayerling," for example, imaginarily relocates the castle of a German baron's suicide/murder to seven sites: Arizona (across from the London Bridge, which was actually relocated there), Orlando (another Disneyworld), Dallas (the Budapest Hymnbook Depository), Nashville (an attraction at the Grand Ol' Opry), Milwaukee (a beer hall), Tokyo (a brothel), and Montana (a hunting lodge). Cassity's purpose here, in spite of his witty and acerbic parodies, is not to lament the banality of modern culture, for the castle, like Europe itself, is no holy relic to be venerated. Rather, by juxtaposing the contrasting and even conflicting worlds, the poet simultaneously depicts the difficulty of living outside time and change, and the capacity of the imagination, wit, poetic language, and form to create an amusement, which itself becomes the sought-after haven, the refuge.

A key to Cassity's attitude toward the past may be found in his essay "Gutenberg as Card Shark," an essay primarily about the cataloging of periodicals. Cassity criticizes the tendency of librarians to efface the traces of a periodical's original state (such as deleting the advertisements from magazines); he finds these indexes of the ephemeral nature of the publication often more revealing of the time than the verbal text itself, and points out that an emphasis on the more academic nature of the publication simplifies and hence falsifies the text's reality. Behind this priority lies the preference for the genuine though ephemeral artifact (which may in fact be genuine because it is ephemeral) over the self-consciously didactic and hence derivative and unreal artwork. The article concludes: "The Gutenberg Bible was no doubt a towering achievement, but if we could retrieve entire the cultural environment of those printed playing cards which preceded it, who would not trade Scripture away?"

Cassity's first collection, *Watchboy, What of the Night?*, like most of his works, is divided into several sections. The first section, "Rudiments of Tropics," consists primarily of scenes and recollections from such places as Indochina and Haiti. These poems reflect on change and chance and loss, as in "La Petite Tonkinoise," a monologue by a Vietnamese prostitute who is an object of exploitation but also the force that controls the colonizer: "Yet I and wheel, meek where your glance is hurled,/ Combined, were Fortune, Empress of the World." The second section, "Oom-Pah for Oom Paul," extends the analysis of imperialism to South Africa. In "Johannesburg Requiem," the blacks lament a social, linguistic, and economic structure that is not theirs but which they must serve.

The section "In the Laagers of Burgherdom" celebrates with deft irony the comforts of kitsch: Café musicians complain of having to play the same tunes repeatedly (though they do have steady employment), heaven is depicted as a Hollywood production number, lovers are compared to the Katzenjammer kids, and elderly ladies find "Grace at the Atlanta Fox" (an art-deco film theater in the style of a Turkish mosque).

The forty-page poem "The Airship Boys in Africa: A Serial in Twelve Chapters," published in *Poetry* in 1970, is dedicated "To the Crabbes: George and Buster" (a reference to the eccentric early nineteenth century poet who described simple village life in eighteenth century couplets and to the swimmer/actor hero of Tarzan films and films such as *Mars Attacks the World*). Here again Cassity relies on an urbane mixture of kitsch and culture, in this instance to convey the failure that results when one culture attempts to impose itself on another for mere gain; the story depicts the doomed flight of a German Zeppelin in World War I to secure territory in Africa. Interweaving past with present, reality with mirage, the poet presents a wry but frightening vision. The heroism of the German crew, like their airship, is finally deflated, their mission pointless. The first chapter describes a Namibian who, talking and thinking in clicks, watches the airship crash; the poem then, in the *in medias res* fashion of epics, reverts to the beginning of the story and follows the crew on their mission. The final chapter describes the survivors searching for the last remaining German stronghold, one of them falling back and clicking his tongue against his teeth. This unexpected union of conqueror with conquered is repeated in the epitaph, a conclusion with nightmarish overtones of the Flying Dutchman legend:

> Full throttle low above the high savannah;
> Game running into, out of pointed shadow.
> Herr, between drummed earth and silent heaven,
> We pursue a shade which is ourselves.

Cassity's preoccupation with kitsch, as represented here and in other works, signifies neither an amused cynicism nor a predilection for form over content, but an awareness of the liberating power of coming to terms with one's own culture. While admiring its technical virtuosity, Donald Davie has criticized "The Airship Boys in Africa" for what he calls a tendency toward campiness, in which the poet seeks "to always astonish, outsmart, upstage any conceivable reader." Though characterized by cleverness and wit, Cassity's poems do not lack a seriousness or a sincerity, nor are they marred by what Davie calls a lack of shapeliness; rather, they assume a shape that, while unexpected or startling, is in fact the only shape that can convey the poet's meaning. The reference to Buster Crabbe, for example, reminds the reader of the naïve and ethnocentric assumptions of the Hollywood film about civilization and savagery, progress and technology. Yet whereas the naïveté of the Hollywood production obscures one's awareness of reality, so can culture—the failed Parsifal myth, the Germanic heroic code—stifle with its insistence on the reenactment of the past. In a later poem in *Hurricane Lamp*, "Advice to King Lear," the poet describes a San Antonio theater with seats on one side of a river and a stage on the other side. During a production of *King Lear*, as the weather onstage grows more and more threatening (thanks to the arbitrary aid of wind machines) and as Lear's situation becomes increasingly tragic, a boat passes between the stage and the audience, and the speaker admonishes the protagonist "Get on the boat, Old Man, and go to summer." The very tackiness of the theatrical setup allows the audience to free itself from its dependence on illusion and from its slavery to the single prescribed ending. In "The Airship Boys in Africa," the poet's exposing of the tawdriness of the Teutonic myth undermines the repressive nature not only of Fascism but also of the unquestioning allegiance to myth and culture.

Even more than "The Airship Boys in Africa," Cassity's narrative poem *Silver Out of Shanghai: A Scenario for Josef von Sternberg, Featuring Wicked Nobles, a Depraved Religious, Wayfoong, Princess Ida, the China Clipper, and Resurrection Lily, with a Supporting Cast of Old Hands, Merchant Seamen, Sikhs, Imperial Marines, and Persons in Blue*, as its full title indicates, builds a poetic world out of the soundstage exoticism of such films as *Shanghai Express*. Ostensibly the story describes the attempt of a wealthy British merchant, Sir V. M. Grayburn, to smuggle silver out of Shanghai without causing a drop in silver prices; he hires a South African engineer to suggest that the ship carries gold instead, but his rivals have the ship sunk, and a last-minute salvage effort by the engineer saves the day, or at least the silver. While overtly mocking the heroics of the adventure genre, with its exaggerated characterizations, its moral chiaroscuro, and its contrived resolution, *Silver Out of Shanghai* also attacks the attempt of the colonialist to create through manipulation a world without change. As a character remarks to Grayburn,

"Oh, V., you've missed the point. It's *temporary*.
Daddy thought the Boxer Wars would end it;
Then the Straits.

. . . .
                                        The rest of us
Know better. Take that Afrikaaner boy.
He knows a country has to be reconquered
Day by day.

Yet while the narrative of *Silver Out of Shanghai*, if not its purpose, is clear, the form of *Steeplejacks in Babel* is much more perplexing, primarily because of the elliptical nature of the diction and the allusions. Here, as elsewhere, the poet dissects the Fascist and colonialist mentalities, but in several poems, he treats more sympathetically the colonialist as displaced person, particularly in "Two Hymns" ("The Afrikaaner in the Argentine" and "Confederates in Brazil"). Technically, the poems of *Steeplejacks in Babel* are among Cassity's tersest and densest; as Richard Johnson has observed, the poet has removed "all but the essentials." The strictures of brevity, along with the formal discipline exacted by the rhymed couplets of iambic pentameter, creates a poetry whose knowledge comes from its form, and not the reverse. The first and last poems, "What the Sirens Sang" and "Cartography Is an Inexact Science," underscore this characteristic truth.

The Defense of the Sugar Islands marks a significant change in Cassity's writing; these poems, based on his experience as a soldier in Puerto Rico during the Korean War, are first-person accounts of events and memories (though in a sense these poems are no more or less autobiographical than is any other of his poems, and one need not know the poet's life to understand the poems). From musing on his past, the speaker comes to realize and rejoice in his own fragility: "Those airs, without their scouring sand, seem more,/ Not less, sand's vessel set to measure time." In "A Walk with a Zombie" (another reference to a kitsch Hollywood film), the speaker contrasts himself as rememberer with a mummified Pharaoh: "If in my eyes the light is less,/ Yours, Pharaoh, have not looked on loss/ As mine have looked"; through memory and imagination, he can "sustain/ One blood unmummied: living wound/ Of armless mills that mock the wind,/ Of crystal words I cannot say,/ Of bladed cane I cannot see."

Hurricane Lamp returns to the less obviously reflective style of the earlier works, but it, too, is a progression forward, albeit a subtle one. The disciplined meters and richly textured allusions again contrast with the wit and ironic distance of the speaker. Here, however, the speaker begins to adopt a more colloquial diction and a less reserved stance, particularly in such poems as "Berolina Demodee" and "A Dialogue with the Bride of Godzilla."

In the mid-1980's, Cassity began to move away from the terse formality of his short lyrics in a series of medium-length poems (about a hundred lines long), conversational poems which are more relaxed in meter and tone than longer narratives but equally rich in juxtaposition of past and present. "Mainstreaming" and "Soldiers of Orange" are, with *The Defense of the Sugar Islands*, among Cassity's few directly autobiographical poems: "Mainstreaming" recounts the experience of soldiers assigned to work with a unit of mentally defective draftees; "Soldiers of Orange" blends memories of a meeting with a former girlfriend and her daughter, including an encounter with Dutch colonial soldiers, with present-day observations of a drive through a Louisiana which has been colonized by Vietnamese refugees.

The growing acceptance of Cassity's terse, restrained style has led to a greater appreciation of his poetry; still, the work of Turner Cassity has yet to receive a full, comprehensive critical account. Perhaps only when the historicity of what is now called contemporary poetry becomes clear will it be possible to understand the unique merit of Cassity's contribution. In the meantime, his poetry may gradually become for the general reader less of a curiosity and more of a hallmark of a complex and significant response to the modern age.

Bibliography
Davie, Donald. "On Turner Cassity," in *Chicago Review*. XXXIV, no. 1 (1983), pp. 22-29.
Griffin, John Jones. "[Interview with] Turner Cassity," in *Mississippi Writers Talking*. Vol. 2, 1983.
Johnson, Richard. "Actions Outdone," in *Parnassus*. III, no. 1 (Fall/Winter, 1974), pp. 192-203.
Steele, Timothy. "Curving to Foreign Harbors: Turner Cassity's *Defense of the Sugar Islands*," in *The Southern Review*. XVII, no. 1 (January, 1981), pp. 205-213.

Steven L. Hale

AUSTIN CLARKE

Born: Dublin, Ireland; May 9, 1896
Died: Dublin, Ireland; March 19, 1974

Principal poems and collections

The Vengeance of Fionn, 1917 (based on the Irish Saga "Pursuit of Diarmid and Grainne"); *The Fires of Baal*, 1921; *The Sword of the West*, 1921; *The Cattledrive in Connaught and Other Poems*, 1925 (based on the prologue to *Tain bo Cuailnge*); *Pilgrimage and Other Poems*, 1929; *The Collected Poems of Austin Clarke*, 1936; *Night and Morning*, 1938; *Ancient Lights*, 1955; *Too Great a Vine: Poems and Satires*, 1957; *The Horse-Eaters: Poems and Satires*, 1960; *Collected Later Poems*, 1961; *Forget-Me-Not*, 1962; *Flight to Africa and Other Poems*, 1963; *Mnemosyne Lay in Dust*, 1966; *Old-Fashioned Pilgrimage and Other Poems*, 1967; *The Echo at Coole and Other Poems*, 1968; *Orphide and Other Poems*, 1970; *Tiresias: A Poem*, 1971; *The Wooing of Becfolay*, 1973; *Collected Poems*, 1974; *The Selected Poetry of Austin Clarke*, 1976.

Other literary forms

Besides his epic, narrative, and lyric poetry, Austin Clarke published three novels, two volumes of autobiography, some twenty verse plays, and a large volume of journalistic essays and literary reviews for newspaper and radio. He also delivered a number of radio lectures on literary topics and gave interviews on his own life and work on Irish radio and television.

Achievements

In a poetic career that spanned more than fifty years, Clarke was a leading figure in the "second generation" of the Irish Literary Revival. Most of his career can be understood as a response to the aims of that movement: to celebrate the heroic legends of ancient Ireland, to bring the compositional technique of the bardic poets into modern English verse, and to bring poetry and humor together in a socially liberating way on the modern stage.

Clarke's earliest efforts to write epic poems on pre-Christian Ireland were not generally successful, although his first poems do have passages of startling color and lyric beauty which presage his later work. When, in the 1930's, he turned to early medieval ("Celtic Romanesque") Ireland, he found his métier, both in poetry and in fiction. To the celebration of the myth of a vigorous indigenous culture in which Christian ascetic and pagan hedonist coexisted, he bent his own disciplined efforts. Unlike William Butler Yeats and most of the leading writers of the Revival, Clarke had direct access to the language of the ancient literature and worked to reproduce its rich

assonantal effects in modern English. In this effort he was uniquely successful among modern Irish poets.

In his later years, Clarke turned to satirizing the domestic scene, living to
see cultural changes remedy many of his complaints about Irish life. Although writing in obscurity through most of his career, in his later life Clarke
was belatedly recognized by several institutions: He was awarded an honorary D.Litt. in 1966 from Trinity College, received the Gregory Medal in
1968 from the Irish Academy of Letters, and was the "Writer in Profile" on
Radio Telifís Éireann in 1968.

Biography

Austin Clarke was born into a large, middle-class, Catholic, Dublin family
on May 9, 1896. He was educated by the Jesuits at Belvedere College and
took a B.A. and an M.A. in English Literature from University College,
Dublin, in 1916 and 1917, and he was appointed assistant lecturer there in
1917. In his formative years, he was heavily impressed by the Irish Literary
Revival, especially Douglas Hyde's Gaelic League and Yeats's Abbey Theatre, and his political imagination was fired by the Easter Rising of 1916. In
1920, following a brief civil marriage to Geraldine Cummins, he was dismissed from his university post; shortly thereafter, he emigrated to London
and began to write his epic poems on heroic subjects drawn from the ancient
literature of Ireland.

In 1930, Clarke married Nora Walker, with whom he had three sons, and
between 1929 and 1938 he wrote a number of verse plays and two novels—
both banned in Ireland—before returning permanently to Ireland in 1937.
Since in his creative career and national literary allegiance he was from the
beginning a disciple of Yeats, he was sorely disappointed to be omitted from
The Oxford Book of Modern Verse which Yeats edited in 1936. Nevertheless,
with the publication of *Night and Morning*, Clarke began a new and public
phase in his creative career: The following year, he began his regular broadcasts on poetry on Radio Éireann and started to write book reviews for *The
Irish Times*. Between 1939 and 1942, he was president of Irish PEN and
cofounder (with Robert Farren) of the Dublin Verse-Speaking Society and
the Lyric Theatre Company. Subsequently, his verse plays were produced at
the Abbey and on Radio Éireann.

Clarke's prolonged creative silence in the early 1950's seems, in retrospect,
oddly appropriate to the depressed state of Ireland, where heavy emigration
and strict censorship seemed to conspire in lowering public morale. Yet, as if
he were anticipating the economic revival, he published *Ancient Lights* in
1955. Here began a new phase in his poetic career, that of a waspish commentator on contemporary events, composing dozens of occasional poems,
some of which can lay claim to a reader's attention beyond their particular
origins. Between 1955 and his death, a collection of these pieces appeared

every two or three years, as well as two volumes of autobiography. His public profile was maintained through his radio broadcasts, his regular reviews in *The Irish Times*, his attendance at many PEN conferences, and visits to the United States and the Soviet Union. In 1972, he was nominated for the Nobel Prize for Literature. He died on March 19, 1974, shortly after the publication of his *Collected Poems*.

Analysis

The first phase of Austin Clarke's poetic career, 1917-1925, produced four epic poems which are little more than apprentice work. Drawing on Celtic and biblical texts, they betray too easily the influences of Yeats, Sir Samuel Ferguson, and other pioneers of the Revival. Considerably overwritten and psychologically unsure, only in patches do they reveal Clarke's real talent: his close understanding of the original text and a penchant for erotic humor and evocative lyrical descriptions of nature. The major preoccupations of his permanent work did not appear until he assimilated these earliest influences.

Clarke's difficulties with religious faith, rejection of Catholic doctrine, and an unfulfilled need for spiritual consolation provide the theme and tension in the poems from *Pilgrimage and Other Poems* and *Night and Morning*. These poems arise from the conflicts between the mores of modern Irish Catholicism and Clarke's desire for emotional and sexual fulfillment. These poems, therefore, mark a departure from his earlier work in that they are personal and contemporary in theme. Yet they are also designedly Irish, in setting and technique.

In searching for a vehicle to express his personal religious conflicts while keeping faith with his commitment to the Irish Literary Revival, Clarke found an alternative to Yeats's heroic, pre-Christian age: the "Celtic Romanesque," the medieval period in Irish history, when the Christian Church founded by Saint Patrick was renowned for its asceticism, its indigenous monastic tradition, its scholastic discipline, its missionary zeal, and the brilliance of its art (metalwork, illuminated manuscripts, sculpture, and devotional and nature poetry). Although this civilization contained within it many of the same tensions which bedeviled Clarke's world—those between the Christian ideal and the claims of the flesh, between Christian faith and pagan hedonism—it appealed to his imagination because of his perception of its independence from Roman authority, the separation of ecclesiastical and secular spheres, and its respect for artistic excellence. This view of the period is selective and romanticized but is sufficient in that it serves his artistic purposes.

Clarke's poetry is Irish also in a particular, technical sense: in its emulation of the complex sound patterns of Gaelic verse, called *rime riche*. In this endeavor, he was following the example set by Douglas Hyde in his translations of folk songs and by the poems of Thomas MacDonagh. This technique employs a variety of rhyming and assonantal devices so that a pattern of rhymes echoes through the middles and ends of lines, playing off unaccented as well as accented syllables. Relatively easy to manage in Gaelic poetry because of the sound structure of the language, *rime riche* requires considerable dexterity in English. Yet Clarke diligently embraced this challenge, sometimes producing results which were little more than technical exercises or impenetrably obscure, but often producing works of unusual virtuosity and limpid beauty. Clarke summed up his approach in his answer to Robert Frost's inquiry about the kind of verse he wrote: "I load myself with chains and I try to get out of them." To which came the shocked reply: "Good Lord! You can't have many readers."

Indeed, Clarke is neither a popular nor an easy poet. Despite his considerable output (his *Collected Poems* runs to some 550 pages), his reputation stands firmly on a select number of these. Of his early narrative poems, adaptations of Celtic epic tales, only a few passages transcend the prevailing verbal clutter. With the publication of *Pilgrimage and Other Poems*, however, the focus narrowed, and the subjects are realized with startling clarity. Perhaps the most representative and accomplished poem in this volume is the lyric "Celibacy." This treatment of a hermit's struggle with lust combines Clarke's personal conflicts with the Catholic Church's sexual teachings and his sympathy with the hermit's spiritual calling in a finely controlled, ironic commentary on the contemporary Irish suspicion of sex. Clarke achieves this irony through a series of images which juxtapose the monk's self-conscious heroism to his unconscious self-indulgence. The rhyming and assonantal patterns in this poem are an early example of the successful use of the sound patterns borrowed from Gaelic models that became one of the distinctive characteristics of his work.

With the publication of *Night and Morning*, there is a considerable consolidation of power. In this collection of sterling consistency, Clarke succeeds in harnessing the historical elements to his personal voice and vision. In the exposition of the central theme of the drama of racial conscience, he shows himself to be basically a religious poet. The central problems faced here are the burden to the contemporary generation of a body of truth received from the centuries of suffering and refinement, the limitations of religious faith in an age of sexual and spiritual freedom, and the conflicts arising from a sympathy with and a criticism of the ordinary citizen. Clarke's own position is always ambivalent. While he seems to throw down the gauntlet to the dogmatic Church, his challenge is never wholehearted: He is too unsure of his position outside the institution he ostensibly abjures. This ambivalence is borne out in the fine title poem in this volume, in the implications of the Christian imagery of the Passion, the candle, the celebration of the Mass, the Incarnation, and the double lightning of faith and reason. A confessional poem, "Night and Morning" protests the difficulties in maintaining an adult faith in the Christian message in a skeptical age. While it criticizes the lack of an intellectual stiffening in modern Irish Catholicism and ostensibly yearns for the medieval age when faith and reason were reconciled, the poem's passion implies an allegiance to the Church that is more emotional than intellectual. These ambiguities are deftly conveyed by the title, design, tone, and imagery of the poem.

Almost every poem in this volume shows Clarke at his best, especially "Martha Blake," "The Straying Student," and "The Jewels." In "Martha Blake," a portrait of a devout daily communicant, Clarke manages multiple points of view with lucidity and ease. From one perspective, Martha's blind faith is depicted as heroic and personally valid; from another, Martha is not very aware of the beauty of the natural world around her, although she experiences it vicariously through the ardor of her religious feelings; from a third, as in the superb final stanza, the poet shares with his readers a simultaneous double perspective which balances outer and inner visions, natural and supernatural grace. The ambiguity and irony which permeate this last stanza are handled with a sensitivity that, considering the anguish and anger of so much of his religious verse, reveals a startling degree of sympathy for ordinary, sincere Christians. He sees that a passionate nature may be concealed, and may be fulfilling itself, beneath the appearances of a simple devotion.

When, after a long silence, *Ancient Lights* appeared in 1955, Clarke had turned from his earlier historical and personal mode to a public and satirical posture. These poems comment wittily on current issues controversial in the Ireland of the early 1950's: the mediocrity and piety of public life, "scandalous" women's fashions, the domination of Irish public opinion by the Catholic Church, the "rhythm" method of birth control, and the incipient public health program. Many of these poems may appear quaint and require annotations even for a post–Vatican II Irish audience. The lead poem, "Celebrations," for example, in criticizing the smug piety of postrevolutionary Ireland, focuses on the Eucharistic Congress held in Dublin in 1932. The poem is studded with references to the Easter Rising of 1916, its heroic antecedents and its promise for the new nation. These are set in ironic contrast with the jobbing latter-day politicians who have made too easy an accommodation with the Church and have thus replaced the British with a native oppression. Clarke vehemently excoriates the manner in which the public purse is made to subscribe to Church-mandated institutions. Despite its highly compressed content, this poem succeeds in making a direct statement on an important public issue. Unfortunately, the same is not true of many of Clarke's subsequent satires, which degenerate into bickering over inconsequential subjects, turn on cheap puns, or lapse into doubtful taste.

This cannot be said, however, of the title poem of this volume, one of Clarke's best achievements. Autobiographical and literally confessional, it can be profitably read in conjunction with his memoir, *Twice Around the*

Black Church: Early Memories of Ireland and England (1962), especially pages 138-139. It begins with the familiar Clarke landscape of Catholic Dublin and the conflict between adolescent sex and conscience. Having made a less than full confession, the persona guiltily skulks outside, pursued by a superstitious fear of retribution.

Emerging into the light like an uncaged bird, in a moment reminiscent of that experienced by James Joyce's Stephen Daedalus on the beach, the protagonist experiences an epiphany of natural grace which sweeps his sexual guilt away. The Church-induced phobias accumulated over the centuries drop away in a moment of creative self-assertion. This experience is confirmed in nature's own manner: Driven by a heavy shower into the doorway of the Protestant Black church (for the full significance of the breaking of this sectarian taboo, see again his memoir), he experiences a spiritual catharsis as he observes the furious downpour channeled, contained, and disposed by roof, pipe, and sewer. With the sun's reappearance, he is born again in a moment of triumphant, articulate joy.

The narrative direction, tonal variety, and especially the virtuosity of the final stanza establish this poem as one of Clarke's finest creations. It weaves nostalgia, humor, horror, vision, and euphoria into a series of epiphanies which prepare the reader for the powerful conclusion. This last stanza combines the images of penance with baptism in a flood of images which are precisely observed and fraught with the spiritual significance for which the reader has been prepared. It should be noted, however, that even here Clarke's resolution is consciously qualified: The cowlings and downpipes are ecclesiastical, and the flood's roar announces the removal of but "half our heavens." Nevertheless, in the control and energy of its images and sound patterns, the poem realizes many of Clarke's objectives in undertaking to write poetry that dramatizes the proverbial tensions between art, religion, and nature in the national conscience.

In the nineteen years following the publication of *Ancient Lights*, Clarke produced a continuous stream of satires upon occasional issues, few of which rise above their origins. They are often hasty in judgment, turgid almost beyond retrieval, or purely formal exercises. These later volumes express a feeling of alienation from modern Ireland, in its particular mix of piety and materialism. Always mindful of the myths lying behind Irish life, his critique begins to lose its currency and sound quixotically conservative. Then in the early 1960's, with the arrival of industrialization in Ireland, relative prosperity, and the Church reforms following Vatican II, many of Clarke's criticisms of Irish life become inapplicable and his latter-day eroticism sounds excessively self-conscious and often in poor taste. Nevertheless, some of his later lyrics, such as "Japanese Print," and translations from the Irish are quite successful: lightly ironic, relaxed, matching the spirit of their originals.

The most impressive personal poem of this last phase in his career is the confessional *Mnemosyne Lay in Dust*. Based on his experiences during a lengthy stay at a mental institution some forty years before, it recrosses the battleground between his inherited Jansenism and his personal brand of secular humanism. In harrowing, cacophonic verse, the poem describes the tortured hallucinations, the electric shock treatment, the amnesia, the pain of rejection by "Margaret" (his first wife), the contemplated suicide, and the eventual rejection of religious taboos for a life directed to the development of reason and human feeling. For all of its extraordinary energy, however, this poem lacks the consistency and finish of his shorter treatments of the same dilemma.

The last phase of Clarke's poetic career produced a group of poems on erotic subjects which affirm, once again, his belief in the full right to indulge in life's pleasures. The best of these—such as "Anacreontic" and "The Healing of Mis"—are remarkably forthright and witty and are not marred by the residual guilt of his earlier forays into this subject.

Austin Clarke's oeuvre, then, is by turns brilliant and gauche. Learned and cranky, tortured and tender, his work moves with extraordinary commitment within a narrow range of concerns. His quarrels with Irish Catholicism and the new Irish state, his preoccupation with problems of sexuality, with Irish myth and history, and his technical emulation of Irish-language models set him firmly at the center of Irish poetry after Yeats. These considerations place him outside the modernist movement. In Ireland, he has been more highly rated by literary historians than by the younger generation of poets. Recognition abroad is coming late: In about twenty poems, he has escaped from his largely self-imposed chains to gain the attention of the world at large.

Other major works

NOVELS: *The Bright Temptation*, 1932; *The Singing Men at Cashel*, 1936; *The Sun Dances at Easter*, 1952.

PLAYS: *Collected Plays*, 1963.

NONFICTION: *Poetry in Modern Ireland*, 1951; *Twice Around the Black Church: Early Memories of Ireland and England*, 1962; *A Penny in the Clouds: More Memories of Ireland and England*, 1968; *The Celtic Twilight and the Nineties*, 1969.

Bibliography

Halpern, Susan. *Austin Clarke: His Life and Works*, 1974.
Irish University Review. IV (Spring, 1974). Special Clarke issue.
Schirmer, Gregory. *The Poetry of Austin Clarke*, 1983.
Tapping, G. Craig. *Austin Clarke: A Study of His Writings*, 1981.

Cóilín Owens

J. V. CUNNINGHAM

Born: Cumberland, Maryland; August 23, 1911
Died: Marlboro, Massachusetts; March 30, 1985

Principal collections

The Helmsman, 1942; *The Judge Is Fury*, 1947; *Doctor Drink*, 1950; *Trivial, Vulgar, and Exalted: Epigrams*, 1957; *The Exclusions of a Rhyme: Poems and Epigrams*, 1960; *To What Strangers, What Welcome: A Sequence of Short Poems*, 1964; *Some Salt: Poems and Epigrams . . .* , 1967; *The Collected Poems and Epigrams of J. V. Cunningham*, 1971; *Selected Poems*, 1971.

Other literary forms

J. V. Cunningham wrote scholarly and critical essays on Statius, Geoffrey Chaucer, William Shakespeare, and Wallace Stevens, as well as on a number of other poets and aspects of poetry. He edited a literary anthology, *The Renaissance in England* (1966), and wrote commentaries on his own poetry under the titles *The Quest of the Opal: A Commentary on "The Helmsman"* (1950) and *The Journal of John Cardan: Together with The Quest of the Opal and The Problem of Form* (1964). The volume into which his prose was collected is extremely valuable in the study of his poetry, not only for his penetrating essays on style and form but also for his scholarly discussions of literary modes and periods, which cast light on his own poetic practice.

Achievements

During the early 1930's, when Cunningham was composing the first of the poems which he later considered worth printing, T. S. Eliot and Ezra Pound were exerting a powerful influence on modern poetry. In many respects a literary maverick, Cunningham objected particularly to the growing disregard of poetic meter and to Archibald MacLeish's dictum that "A poem should not mean/ But be." While pursuing degrees at Stanford University and beginning his career as an English instructor, Cunningham wrote uncompromisingly metrical poems which always meant something. Although he taught in several leading universities, he achieved prominence as scholar and poet only upon his appointment as chair of the English department at the young Brandeis University in Waltham, Massachusetts, in 1953; thereafter, he gained many honors: Guggenheim Fellowships in 1959 and 1967, a National Institute of Arts and Letters grant in 1965 and a grant from the National Endowment for the Arts the following year, as well as designation as only the second University Professor at Brandeis in 1966. He was awarded an Academy of American Poets Fellowship in 1976.

His highly disciplined, concise, and intellectual poetry won acknowledgment from literary scholars such as Yvor Winters and Denis Donoghue, as well as from the makers of many poetry anthologies. In addition, Cunningham's teaching influenced a younger generation of poets, particularly Alan Shapiro.

Biography

Although born in Cumberland, Maryland, in 1911, James Vincent Cunningham's earliest recollections were of Billings, Montana, where the family settled when he was about four years old. After growing up in Montana and in Denver, Colorado, and briefly attending St. Mary's College in Kansas, he earned his A.B. and Ph.D. at Stanford University, where he also taught English.

From 1945, when he achieved his doctorate, until 1953, he taught at the Universities of Hawaii, Chicago, and Virginia, publishing two books of poetry and a book on Shakespearean tragedy during this period. Recognition followed at Brandeis University, where Cunningham taught from 1953 until his retirement in 1982.

Married and divorced twice earlier, Cunningham was married to Jessie MacGregor Campbell in 1950. Following his appointment to Brandeis, the Cunninghams settled in Sudbury, Massachusetts, between Waltham and Worcester, where she taught English at Clark University. Retiring in 1982, he died on March 30, 1985, at the age of seventy-three.

Analysis

J. V. Cunningham's small but distinguished corpus of poetry (he preferred to call it verse) challenges many modern assumptions. In an age dominated by freer forms, he devoted himself to meter, fixed stanzas, and—more often than not—rhyme. His poems are taut, plain, and philosophical, with the feeling tightly controlled. The proportion of general statement to sensory detail is high, as is that of abstract words to concrete and imagistic language. Although he eschewed the self as the focus of lyric, he had a highly proprietary attitude toward his poems, insisting that they belonged essentially to him rather than to his readers. He appeared quite content to reach a relatively select readership capable of appreciating the subtlety and precision of his work. In both theory and practice, he went his own way, often in contradistinction to, sometimes in defiance of, the norms of twentieth century lyric.

As a scholar trained in the Greek and Latin classics and in English Renaissance poetry, he brought the predilections of his favorite literary periods to his own verse. His classicism emerges in a number of ways. Cunningham's favorite form, the epigram, was perfected in Latin by Martial in the first century A.D. and in English by Ben Jonson early in the seventeenth century. More than half the poems in *The Collected Poems and Epigrams of J. V. Cunningham* are termed epigrams, while a number of others have epigrammatic qualities. Although he called only one of his poems an ode, a number

of others fall within the tradition of the Horatian ode. He frequently imitates—or rather seeks English equivalents for—Latin stanzas and meters. It
is no accident that his favorite stanzas, like those of Horace in his odes, are
quatrains, sometimes with the contours and movement of the Roman poet's
alcaic meter, and couplets, which were Martial's and Ben Jonson's preferred
way of rendering the terse and witty statements of epigram.

Another aspect of his classicism is his fondness for Latin titles such as
"Agnosco Veteris Vestigia Flammae" (I recognize the traces of an old
flame), "Timor Dei" (the fear of God), and "Lector Aere Perennior." The
last of these illustrates his penchant for allusion, as it appropriates a famous
Horatian phrase about poetry being a monument more lasting than bronze
and applies it to the *lector*, the reader of the poetry. Wittily manipulating a
Latin commonplace about the fame of poets, some basic concepts of medieval Scholasticism, and Pythagoras' theory of the transmigration of souls,
Cunningham argues that the poet's immortality inheres not in the poet, who,
except as a name, is forgotten, but in the reader—in each successive reader
for whom the poem comes to life again. Adapting phrases from Horace is
one of his favorite ploys. Horace wrote *odi profanum vulgus* (I hate the common crowd), Cunningham, "I like the trivial, vulgar, and exalted." He also
appropriates the old but relatively rare Latinate word *haecceity*, meaning
"thisness," to express Cunningham's own theory that the preoccupation with
any particular "this" is evil.

Often, he takes advantage of Latin roots to extend meaning. One of his
lines in "All Choice Is Error"—"Radical change, the root of human woe!"—
reminds the reader that "radical" means root. His poem "Passion" requires
for its full effect an awareness that *patior* (whose past participle, *passus*, provides the basis of the English word) means "suffer," that *patior* is a passive
verb (he calls passion "love's passive form"), and that the medieval derivation
passio was used not only in theological discourse, referring to Christ's suffering, but also in philosophical discourse, to indicate that which is passive or
acted upon. Sometimes his employment of etymology is very sly, as in his
phrase "mere conservative," where, clued by his awareness that "conservative" is an honorific to Cunningham, the reader benefits from knowing
that *merus* means "pure," a fact now obscured by the English adjective's having changed from meaning "nothing less than" to "nothing more than."

Classical poets also manipulated syntax for emphasis in ways which are not
always available to English poets, but Cunningham plays the sentence against
the line variously, using enjambments in such poems as "Think" and "Monday Morning" to throw into striking relief words that might otherwise be obscured. He is fond of classical syntactical figures such as chiasmus. "So he
may discover/ As Scholar truth, sincerity as lover" exhibits this reversal of
word order in otherwise parallel phrases. It might be noted that Cunningham
shares with many free-verse poets a liking for visually arresting enjambments

and displacements; he differs primarily in adjusting them to the formal demands of meter.

What might be called Jonsonian neoclassicism favors poets such as Horace and Martial, who treat of their subjects in a cool and somewhat impersonal tone, carefully regulating—though not abjuring—feeling and striving for the general import of their subjects. Readers of Jonson's lyrics will recall his poem "On My First Son," which illustrates these traits well, though dealing with a heart-rending experience, the death of a young son. Jonson generates not only a quiet but unmistakable sense of grief and resentment but also a corrective admonition against the moral dangers of selfishness and presumption in lamenting such a common occurrence too much. Cunningham's "Consolatio Nova" (new consolation), on the death of his publisher and champion, Alan Swallow, exhibits many of the same virtues. It generalizes, and no feeling overflows, but the careful reader sees that the loss is a specific and deeply felt one. A similarly quiet tone and controlled feeling marks "Obsequies for a Poetess."

A scholar himself, Jonson would have appreciated "To a Friend, on Her Examination for the Doctorate in English" and, except for the feminine pronoun and the latter-day degree, would have recognized in the title a perfectly appropriate theme for a poem, for in both classical and neoclassical Renaissance poetry, friendship rivaled love as a theme. "The Aged Lover Discourses in the Flat Style" is also Jonsonian from its title onward, Cunningham even adapting to his own sparer person some of Jonson's physical description in "My Picture Left in Scotland." The modern poet's fine "To My Wife," though more paradoxical than Jonson was as a rule, illustrates well the classical restraint in dealing with love. It is a poem of four quatrains in cross-rhymed tetrameter, the first two presenting images of landscape and the seasons, the last two modulating to quiet statement dominated by abstractions: terror, delight, regret, anger, love, time, grace.

Two more reputed classical virtues are simplicity and brevity. At first glance, Cunningham's poems do not seem unfailingly simple, for although the language itself is not notably difficult, the thought is often complex and usually highly compressed. Cunningham displays no urge to embellish or amplify, however, and his assessment of his own style as plain or "flat" is accurate. Brevity can test the reader's comprehension, and brevity is the very essence of Cunningham's poetic. Of the 175 original poems and epigrams in his collected verse, the longest is thirty-six lines, and many are much shorter. It is a small book for a man who wrote poetry for more than forty years. The classical model here is perhaps Vergil, traditionally thought to be happy with a daily output of an acceptable line or two. For Cunningham, the perfection of a lyric outshines any number of diamonds in the rough.

Although Cunningham's classically inspired challenge to modern poetry was thoroughgoing and persistent, he did modify it over his career. He disapproved vigorously of poetry that merely recounts experience or indulges in emotion, and his early poems in particular concentrate on interpreting experience and subduing emotion. An early poem, "All Choice Is Error," sets forth a conviction that because choice signifies not merely the preference of one thing for another but also the rejection of all other possibilities, choice must be seen as evil, even if it is necessary evil. Choices restrict life, and the habit of favoring particularities in verse—a habit of twentieth century poets, in Cunningham's view—is an especially lamentable habit. This poem develops the theme with reference to lovers' traditional fondness for carving their initials on such surfaces as tree trunks provide. Since there can be few people who have not reflected on the folly of thus publicizing a choice that all too soon may look silly or embarrassing, it is a clever motif to illustrate his point about the folly of particularity. The poem celebrates time and the elements, which smooth the lovers' initials. What remains is recognizable as love, but the specificity of the lovers is happily lost.

"Haecceity" carries this theme further. It is a more philosophical poem, based on the argument that the actualization of any possibility is the denial of all other possibilities. Cunningham knows that people must make choices and that morally it may be better to choose one thing over another, but, at the same time, choice is inherently evil because of the exclusions it necessitates. A consequence of this conviction that to restrict any general possibility to one manifestation constitutes evil is that any particular poem setting forth this idea is evil, a paradox that Cunningham does not hesitate to admit.

Since man has a fundamental urge to carry out choices, to achieve particularity, and since all choices are equally denials of the remaining possibilities, on what basis is choice to be made? Cunningham, struck by the arbitrary and even despairing nature of many human choices, reasoned that carefully considered judgments would assure the best, or least damaging, decisions. He came to doubt reason's capacity to best emotion, however, particularly since the latter is more likely to enlist the assistance of religion. (Cunningham was reared a Roman Catholic and gave up all religious beliefs in his maturity, but he realized that his early religious training continued to influence his imagination, and references to Catholic doctrine appear in some of his mature poems.) In his commentary *The Quest of the Opal*, Cunningham discusses the poems he wrote in his attempts to escape the consequences of his theory of the evil of particularity. Although his intellectual search bore little fruit, some interesting poems, including "Summer Idyll," "Autumn," and "The Wandering Scholar," resulted.

Meanwhile, Cunningham was discovering a more satisfying way of dealing with experience in "The Helmsman: An Ode." He had been much interested in Horace's Ode 1.9, in which the poet describes Mount Soracte under its cap of snow and then modulates to his frequent theme of *carpe diem*, "seize the day," embodied in a celebration of young love. Cunningham hoped to imitate the way Horace's images delicately implied the theme rather than merely exemplifying it. "The Helmsman," a poem about "the voyage of the soul . . . / Through age to wisdom," imitated Horace procedurally as well as formally. It builds on memories and disappointments along the way, asserting the need to strike out on one's own, ever alert lest he slip and drown like Vergil's Palinurus in the fifth book of the *Aeneid* (c. 29-19 B.C.). Wisdom "comes like the ripening gleam of wheat" to this voyager, "flashing like snakes underneath the haze." In the second half of the poem, the imagery imitates that of another Horatian ode, 1.7, in which Teucer, an ancient king of Troy, prepares festively for a dangerous voyage with his cohorts. Security is only an illusion: The wheat may not ripen, the voyage may come to naught. The voyager must acknowledge the possibility of defeat but not flag in his pursuit.

By his own admission, Cunningham's poetry was becoming more autobiographical, although hardly in the manner of, for example, Robert Lowell. The closing poem of the second group in *The Collected Poems and Epigrams of J. V. Cunningham* draws on recollections of the landscape of his childhood. "Montana Pastoral" is a good example of Cunningham's ability to revive old modes by unexpected departures from convention. Over the centuries, poets have rung many changes on pastoral, turning Theocritus' and Vergil's shepherds into other rural types, into pastors in the ecclesiastical sense (John Milton's "Lycidas") or even into denizens of Lewis Carroll's *Alice's Adventures in Wonderland* (1865), as William Empson has suggested in *Some Versions of Pastoral* (1935). Cunningham's speaker can find no evidence of the supposed pastoral virtues in the wild and bleak Montana landscape. More precisely, the poem is an antipastoral, gaining its effect by holding out in its title the perennially attractive promise of the simpler, more wholesome life but then detailing briskly and briefly the harshness of the land.

Cunningham found other ways of being new. He experimented with meters, including syllabic ones freer than most free verse in all but line lengths. "Think," for example, uses a seven-syllable line with three variously placed stresses per line, while "Monday Morning" uses a nine-syllable line with four stresses per line. In his essay "How Shall a Poem Be Written?" Cunningham cites precedents for such types of syllabic lines, albeit chiefly ten-syllable ones, in Thomas Wyatt, John Donne, and Philip Sidney. In the eighth poem of his *To What Strangers, What Welcome* sequence, he tries blank-verse tetrameter, extremely rare in English poetry.

It is tempting to read this sequence autobiographically. The earlier of the fifteen short poems take a traveler westward in the United States. Along the white lines of highways and barbed-wire fences, past tumbleweed and locoweed, the speaker wends his way. He stops in Las Vegas, takes in gaming and shows unenthusiastically, and finally passes through desert to the land of redwood trees and the Pacific surf. In the eleventh poem, the speaker turns back toward the East and, after more desert, prairie, and "stonewalled road," is found at the end relaxing in New England. The poems also allude to a love affair, although rather obscurely. While the nominal subject of the sequence is a transcontinental automobile trip, it may perhaps be read also as a telescopic account of Cunningham's career. Born in Maryland, he went west to Montana and Colorado with his family, received most of his higher education at Stanford University (not far from the redwoods and closer yet to the surf), and, after teaching mostly at points intermediate, gravitated to New England, specifically to Brandeis University in Massachusetts, where he received the swift academic preferment that had been denied him everywhere else and where he remained for the duration of his working life. The title of the sequence—an ironic twist on the western "welcome, stranger"—becomes more ironic if one reads into it a kind of career résumé, since by far the heartiest welcome Cunningham ever received was in that urban, New England university under Jewish auspices. It must be noted, however, that the sequence does not end triumphantly but in a series of questions about identity, as if "what welcome?" remains a query without an answer.

There is much more description and concrete detail than in Cunningham's earlier poetry. He seems more inclined to imply, rather than state, his theme. The "I" of the sequence is more like the first person in the work of his autobiographical or confessional contemporaries in verse, more often found in the midst of specific, yet offhand, experiences: "I drive Westward," "I write here," "I go moseying about." It is impossible to find, difficult to imagine, Cunningham "moseying" in his earlier poetry. The footloose sequence raises a series of questions about love, fulfillment, identity. While it does not appear to answer any of them, the tone is that of a modern man responding dryly and sarcastically to Walt Whitman, the ingenuous traveler of the open road, who reveled not only in the redwoods but even in their destruction by men determined to rival them in grandeur. Cunningham's road, with its boundaries of interminable white lines and barbed wire, speaks of a land whose greatness remains but whose inhospitability looms, and man no longer seems commensurate with it, save in degree of unfriendliness.

To What Strangers, What Welcome confirms what careful readers of Cunningham's verse had surely already recognized: that he was very much a man of his own time, a man whom poetic theory was in no danger of turning into a pale imitation of a Roman of the Empire or an Englishman of the age of Elizabeth I. Not only in subject matter but also in form, he seemed to be edging closer to the prevailing poetry of his time. His verse in the sequence is measured but flexible and untrammeled.

Despite his sometimes intransigent defiance of the poets in Whitman's train, Cunningham objected to *vers libre* far less than to the assumption, unfortunately still common among its advocates, that meter is passé and that free forms constitute the only defensible mode of poetry in the later twenti-

eth century. Despite the strictness of so much of his practice, he conceded
that much modern verse is also metrical, for it departs from, often returns to,
and inevitably is measured against, meter as a norm. His attitude in this
respect does not differ greatly from that of another strict metrist, Robert
Frost, who also loved classical poetry, found the limitations of traditional
forms an irresistible challenge, and even suspected free-verse poets of unac-
knowledged but nevertheless recurrent iambic tendencies.

The epigrams, which are found at the end of his collection of original poetry, are more regular. They represent poems both early and late in his career
and are the best exemplars of his fondness for wit, brevity, and a cool and often satirical tone. That they are also twentieth century poems is evident from
the titles that some of them bear: "With a Detective Story," "History of
Ideas," "For a College Yearbook," "New York: 5 March 1957," "Towards
Tucson." In short, they are full of subjects, concepts, and attitudes unimag-
inable to Martial, Ben Jonson, or Walter Savage Landor. There are some for
which Latin equivalents might have been composed two thousand years ago,
but only because they are about universal types and habits.

The epigrams are about love, drink, music, grief, wisdom, illusion, calculus, Freudianism, and many other things. They vary considerably in tone:
reflective, cynical, sardonic, risqué, indecent, smug, earnest. They contain
lapses in taste and judgment, but virtually all of them display an alert intelligence. Writing in an age little interested in the epigram, Cunningham
proves its durability and his right to be considered with the masters of this
ancient form. A free-verse epigram would be a contradiction in terms; thus,
to deny the legitimacy of Cunningham's art is to deny the possibility of the
contemporary epigram.

The Collected Poems and Epigrams of J. V. Cunningham concludes with
twenty-one translations of classical, medieval, and Renaissance Latin poems.
Like the epigrams, these poems were written over many years. The most rol-
licking is his translation of "The Confession of Bishop Golias," attributed to
the Archpoet of Cologne, a twelfth century figure. The finest, however, are
of classical Latin poetry.

One might suppose that by the twentieth century, no one would be able to
find a new way to render Catullus' famous couplet "Odi et amo," but Cunningham succeeded in finding a new equivalent for its final word, *excrucior.*
This poem about the lover who does not know why he both hates and loves
his girl but feels it and is "tormented" or "tortured," as translators usually
have it, Cunningham concludes with "I feel it and am torn." His choice,
simpler and yet more graphic, is certainly justified, for the cross (*crux,* from
which *excrucior* derives) tore the flesh of the crucified as the conflicting emotions tear Catullus' lover's psyche.

Cunningham also translated the Mount Soracte ode of Horace, whose procedure he found so instructive. Somewhat more formal and literal than other

modern versions, his translation avoids the casual, even flippant, effect of those who bend over backward to avoid sounding archaic and bookish and, as a result, answers to the dignity of Horace's theme:

> Tomorrow may no man divine.
> This day that Fortune gives set down
> As profit, nor while young still
> Scorn the rewards of sweet dancing love,
>
> So long as from your flowering days
> Crabbed age delays.

Why Cunningham did not choose to translate more of Horace for publication is a nagging question; surely few writers have been as well qualified to do this poet justice.

In one of his most valuable critical essays, Cunningham discusses his translation of Statius' poem on sleep. By reviving a comparison first made in the late nineteenth century by the great Latin scholar J. W. Mackail between the Latin poem and William Wordsworth's sonnet "To Sleep," Cunningham establishes six points of contrast between the poetry of Horace, Vergil, Statius, and many modern poets, on the one hand, and William Wordsworth, along with many medieval and Tudor lyric poets, on the other. The first has to do with the relative complexity of the meter that was used by the earlier group, the second with the playing off of syntax against meter, which the medieval-Tudor group seldom did. The earlier group determined the length of the poem relatively freely, while the later group worked with a fixed idea of length. The earlier group did not match thought units to formal divisions, whereas the later group did. The paraphrasable meaning of the early group is implicit, of the later group explicit. Conceptually, the earlier group's poems exhibit continuity and degree, while the later group's are more likely to show discontinuity, identity, and contradiction. The reader must consult the essay "Classical and Medieval: Statius on Sleep" for clarification and exemplification of these differences.

What is important to see is that the group referred to above as the earlier includes not only Roman poets of antiquity but also much modern poetry. According to Cunningham, the tendency of the English lyric over the centuries has been from the medieval-Tudor practice to that best exemplified by Horace, Vergil, and Statius. Far from carrying on warfare with these modern poets, whom Cunningham does not name but who surely include T. S. Eliot, Wallace Stevens, and presumably even William Carlos Williams, together with their followers in contemporary poetry, Cunningham in effect finds these moderns to be classical in a number of important ways. In his own translation of Statius' poem, he employs the now unfashionable form of blank verse, but he has clearly attempted to achieve the six qualities which he has designated as at once classical and modern. The translation ends:

If this long night some lover
In his girl's arms should willingly repel thee,
Thence come, sweet Sleep! Nor with all thy power
Pour through my eyes—so may they ask, the many,
More happy—: touch me with thy wand's last tip,
Enough, or lightly pass with hovering step.

He has not declared a truce with modern poetry, and his diction will not impress many readers as typically modern, but in at least some respects, his verse and that of his contemporaries attain peaceful coexistence.

Other major works

NONFICTION: *The Quest of the Opal: A Commentary on "The Helmsman,"* 1950; *Woe or Wonder: The Emotional Effect of Shakespearean Tragedy*, 1951; *Tradition and Poetic Structure: Essays in Literary History and Criticism*, 1960; *The Journal of John Cardan: Together with The Quest of the Opal and The Problem of Form*, 1964; *The Collected Essays of J. V. Cunningham*, 1976.

ANTHOLOGIES: *The Renaissance in England*, 1966; *The Problem of Style*, 1966; *In Shakespeare's Day*, 1970.

Bibliography

Chicago Review. XXXV, no.1 (1985). Special Cunningham issue.

Donoghue, Denis. *Connoisseurs of Chaos*, 1965.

Hooley, Daniel M. "Some Notes on Translation: Martial and J. V. Cunningham," in *Classical and Modern Literature*. III (Summer, 1983), pp. 181-191.

Shapiro, Alan. " 'Far Lamps at Night': The Poetry of J. V. Cunningham," in *Critical Inquiry*. IX (March, 1983), pp. 611-629.

Steele, Timothy. "Interview with J. V. Cunningham," in *Iowa Review*. XV (Fall, 1985), pp. 1-24.

Stein, Robert A. Review of *The Collected Poems and Epigrams of J. V. Cunningham* in *Western Humanities Review*. XXVII (1973), pp. 1-12.

Winters, Yvor. *The Poetry of J. V. Cunningham*, 1961.

Robert P. Ellis

DONALD DAVIE

Born: Barnsley, England; July 17, 1922

Principal collections

Brides of Reason, 1955; *A Winter Talent and Other Poems*, 1957; *The Forests of Lithuania*, 1959; *A Sequence for Francis Parkman*, 1961; *New and Selected Poems*, 1961; *Events and Wisdoms: Poems, 1957-1963*, 1964; *Essex Poems 1963-1967*, 1969; *Six Epistles to Eva Hesse*, 1970; *Collected Poems, 1950-1970*, 1972; *The Shires*, 1974; *In the Stopping Train and Other Poems*, 1977; *Three for Water-Music, and The Shires*, 1981; *The Battered Wife and Other Poems*, 1982; *Collected Poems, 1970-1983*, 1983.

Other literary forms

Donald Davie is a highly respected man of many letters. In addition to his poetry, he has published numerous works of literary theory and criticism, including important books on Ezra Pound and Thomas Hardy, and an abundance of material on various British, American, and European authors. He has also written several cultural histories that discuss the impact of religious dissent on culture and literature and has edited a number of anthologies of Augustan and Russian poetry; he has, in addition, published biographical essays and translated Russian poetry.

Achievements

In both his poetry and his critical commentary, Davie advocates a poetry of formal structure and prose syntax, along with restrained metaphor and feeling. He urges repeatedly that art communicate rational statement and moral purpose in technically disciplined forms. His work, usually highly compressed, erudite, and formally elegant, is sometimes criticized for its lack of feeling and for tending toward the overly academic—in short, for the notable absence of the personal element. Davie, nevertheless, stands firm in his position that the poet is responsible primarily to the community in which he writes for purifying and thus correcting the spoken language: "The central act, of poetry as of music, is the creation of syntax, of meaningful arrangement." The poet thus helps one understand his feelings; he improves the very process of one's thinking, and hence one's subsequent actions; ultimately, the poet helps correct the moral behavior of the community at large.

Biography

Donald Davie was born July 17, 1922, into a lower-middle-class Baptist family, the son of a shopkeeper and the grandson of domestic servants. He grew up amid the slag heaps of industrial West Riding. His mother frequently recited poetry, and, according to Davie, "Robin Hood . . . surely did more than any other single text to make me a compulsive reader for ever after." His father, a lively and emotionally expressive man, encouraged the young boy to take piano lessons. Even as a child, however, Davie rankled at the pretensions and philistinism of his more well-to-do neighbors.

In 1940, Davie began his studies of seventeenth century religious oratory and architecture at St. Catharine's College, Cambridge. He joined the Royal Navy in 1941, and between 1942 and 1943 was stationed in northern Russia, where he studied the poetry of Boris Pasternak, who was to become an important and lasting influence. He married Doreen John, from Plymouth, in 1945; they have three children. Davie returned to Cambridge in 1946, and studied under F. R. Leavis; he earned his B.A. in 1946, his M.A. in 1949, and his Ph.D. in 1951. Between 1950 and 1957, he taught at Trinity College, Dublin, where he met the writers and poets Joseph Hone, Austin Clarke, and Padraic Fallon. He spent 1957-1958 as visiting professor at the University of California, Santa Barbara, where he was introduced to Yvor Winters, Thom Gunn, and Hugh Kenner (whose teaching post he actually filled for the year); it was during this period that he joined the "Reactionary Generation" of poets. In 1958, he returned to Cambridge as a lecturer in English at Gonville and Caius colleges, "worried" about how the "sentimental Left occupied all the same positions." Commenting further on his isolation during this time, he has said: "The politics of envy. . . [and] self-pity had sapped independence, self-help and self-respect." In 1964, he cofounded and became professor at the University of Essex (he later became pro-vice-chancellor there). Then, only four years later, feeling utter disillusionment with a declining British society and the philistinism of even his fellow poets, and also feeling totally alienated from his university colleagues, he moved to the United States and joined the faculty of Stanford University, where he remained until 1978. Since 1978, he has been Andrew W. Mellon Professor of Humanities at Vanderbilt University. His high reputation in the United States is apparent in the many awards and other academic appointments he has received, including a Guggenheim Fellowship, membership in the American Academy of Arts and Sciences, and honorary appointments and degrees from Vanderbilt University and the Universities of Southern California and Cincinnati; Davie has received honorary degrees from St. Catharine's College, Cambridge University, and Trinity College, Dublin.

Analysis

Donald Davie's poetry, frequently labeled "neo-Augustan," is characterized by formal elegance, classical restraint, urbane wit, meticulous syntax, and plain diction. A widely respected poet, Davie is dedicated to a chaste and austere art in which he treats the contemporary need for personal moderation and restraint in verse forms that reinforce his vision. For Davie, it is the word itself—indeed the very instrument of language—that requires purification, for if the poet can purify the speech of the tribe, perhaps the values of propriety and control—those moral values that inspire integrity and courage—might return to his diminished England and the decadent world at large. Man might better understand his personal and perhaps even metaphysical place in the scheme of things. It is the absolute responsibility of the poet, Davie frequently comments, to improve the spoken language of his society in an effort to expand, stretch, or restore civilization to its greatest potential for creative moral and social betterment. Again and again, Davie has said: "The abandonment of syntax testifies to . . . a loss of confidence in the intelligible structure of the conscious mind, and the validity of its activity.

In his earliest work, Davie was associated with the *New Lines* anthology and the "Movement" of the 1950's. His name was linked with John Wain, Kingsley Amis, Philip Larkin, Thom Gunn, Robert Conquest, D. J. Enright, Elizabeth Jennings, and John Holloway, along with the other reactionary poets who stood against the romantic excesses (as Davie put it, the "tawdry amoralism") and imagism and symbolism of the British poets of the 1940's, such as Dylan Thomas, T. S. Eliot, and Ezra Pound. The Movement argued for a return to conventional prose syntax in poetry and a more formal poetry that utilized the conservative metaphors of the eighteenth century Augustans. These poets, who shared a similar class background, as well as similar educational and professional goals, were, in addition, linked to various "Reactionary Generation" Americans such as Yvor Winters, Louise Bogan, the Fugitives, and even Hart Crane, and to those poets who were pursuing concrete poetry, such as H. D. and Pound. For Davie and the Movement, a decorous diction was to be selected according to subject or genre; so, too, structure was to be logical rather than musical.

Davie's early volume *Brides of Reason*, in traditional meter, is specifically directed to the "logic" in man, so that "poets may astonish you/ With what is not, but should be, true,/ And shackle on a moral shape." ("Hypochondriac Logic"). The frequent obscurities and ambiguities of this volume reflect the influence of William Empson and Leavis, although more noteworthy now is Davie's debt to the Augustans William Cowper, Oliver Goldsmith, Samuel Johnson, and Christopher Smart. "Homage to William Cowper," which proposes that "Most poets let the morbid fancy roam," goes on to insist that "Horror starts, like Charity, at home." Davie, admitting that he is "a pasticheur of late-Augustan styles," will work with rhetoric of the eighteenth century and attempt a rational structure through absolute clarity of premeditated logic ("Zip!"):

> I'd have the spark that leaps upon the gun
> By one short fuse, electrically clear;
> And all be done before you've well begun.
> (It is reverberations that you hear.)

"On Bertrand Russell's 'Portraits from Memory,'" begins with a familiar Davie verse:

> Those Cambridge generations, Russell's, Keynes' . . .
> And mine? Oh mine was Wittgenstein's, no doubt:
> Sweet pastoral, too, when some-one else explains,
> Although my memories leave the eclogues out.

Davie's early poetry was frequently compared to Charles Tomlinson's because of their mutual equation of form and morality. Poise, control, and clarity of statement, both poets maintained, reflect moral imperatives and contribute toward the establishment of a society of common sense, human decency, and high moral principle. Nevertheless, with his admittedly high moral stance, Davie began a long isolation from his more fashionable contemporaries—from the early Dylan Thomas to the confessional poetry of Theodore Roethke, Sylvia Plath, and Robert Lowell. Throughout his career, Davie has remained aloof from even the great W. B. Yeats and T. S. Eliot, in whose vast mythmaking he sensed a distancing from the human condition. For Davie, the poet must speak directly to his reader and take on the role of "spokesman of a social [not mythic] tradition"; the poet is responsible for the rescue of culture from decline by "making poetry out of moral commonplace." Interestingly, although Davie's aims have not been entirely unlike Yeats's and Eliot's—to inspire action and change in a philistine and unimaginative contemporary world—he would accomplish his ends not through imaginative participation in myth, but rather through conscious control of language, and thus thought, and, finally, action. Responding to Davie's example of proper rhythm, meter, and syntax, for example, one might feel himself affirming the proper values of a more stable and civilized past. In "Vying," Davie writes:

> There I, the sexton, battle
> Earth that will overturn
> Headstones, and rifle tombs,
> And spill the tilted urn.

Over the years, Davie has gradually moved toward shorter and brisker lines, as well as a less obscure poetry. There has also been an increasing display of emotion and a greater revelation of self—a closer relationship between the speaker to his landscape, history, and metaphor. The specific and general have been more closely integrated. His rejection of a poetry consumed with the "messy ego," nevertheless, has remained absolute, like his insistence that language remain the starting point of moral betterment. As such, he has continued to reject accepted modern usage: "the stumbling, the moving voices," "the Beat and post-Beat poets,/ The illiterate apostles" ("Pentecost"). What is needed instead is a "neutral tone" ("Remembering the 'Thirties"), reasonableness, and common values.

"A Sequence for Francis Parkman" reveals Davie's fascination with the openness of North America with its empty and uncluttered spaces that lack the detritus of a long history of human failure. The continent functions not unlike a grand *tabula rasa* on which the poet can project his meditations. He writes in "A Letter to Curtis Bradford": "But I only guess,/ I guess at it out of my Englishness/ And envy you out of England. Man with man/ Is all our history; American,/ You met with spirits. Neither white nor red/ The melancholy, disinherited/ Spirit of mid-America, but this,/ The manifest copiousness, the bounties." *A Sequence for Francis Parkman*, Davie's response following his first visit to North America during 1957-1958, contains brief profiles of Sieur de La Salle, the Comte de Frontenac, Louis Joseph de Montcalm, Pontiac, and Louis Antoine de Bouganville, as Davie adapts them from the historiographer Francis Parkman.

The volume *Events and Wisdoms*, while retaining Davie's witty, epigrammatic style, also introduces a more sensual imagery in its precise descriptions of nature. In "Low Lands," for example, Davie describes a river delta "Like a snake it is, its serpentine iridescence/ Of slow light spilt and wheeling over calm/ Inundations, and a snake's still menace/ Hooding with bruised sky belfry and lonely farm./ The grasses wave on meadows fat with foison." Both *Events and Wisdoms* and *Essex Poems 1963-1967* illustrate Davie's pastoral-elegiac mode ("I smell a smell of death," "July, 1964"). He focuses on death and emptiness, moving away from the more self-conscious literary subject matter of the Movement poetry. In the well-known "Winter Landscapes," he writes: "Danger, danger of dying/ Gives life in its shadows such riches./ Once I saw or I dreamed/ A sunless and urbanized fenland/ One Sunday, and swans flying/ Among electric cables." The sense of exile both within and outside his native country is also pronounced in poems such as "Rodez" and "The North Sea." Davie once again projects a concrete geography upon which to elaborate his meditations on human history and personal conduct. There is even an immersion in the external world of human event and interaction. Like Pound, who exerted a complex influence upon him, Davie wanders through the traditions of history, reexamining and restating human values worthy of restoration. "Rodez" admits "Goodbye to the Middle Ages! Although some/ Think that I enter them, those centuries/ Of monkish superstition, here I leave them/ With their true garlands, and their honest masks." Davie also accepts Pound's regard for nonhuman nature in its purposive indifference and essential *quidditas*. The poems in this volume, many composed in his most direct and sparsest language thus far, retain Davie's essential urbanity, what Eliot called "the perfection of a common language"—impersonal, distinguished, and well mannered—a language sometimes called by Davie's detractors uninspiredly chaste, versified prose, an academic and excessively moralistic statement removed from sense experience. Nevertheless, "The practise of an art," he insists, "is to convert all terms/ into the terms of art" ("July, 1964").

Six Epistles to Eva Hesse again reflects Pound's rich influence on Davie. Like Pound, Davie incorporates the influences of numerous older and foreign literary traditions; he remains, like Pound, the traveler through history—the connoisseur of historical value, time, place, and event. Yet Davie retains his rage against disorder and freewheeling individuality, along with a rejection of Pound's experimental dislocations of traditional syntax. *Six Epistles to Eva Hesse*, addressed to Pound's German translator, is, in fact, Davie's "Essay on Criticism." He asks rhetorically "Is it time/ For self-congratulating rhyme/ To honour as established fact/ The value of the artefact?/ Stoutly to trumpet Art is all/ We have, or need, to disenthrall/ Any of us from the chains/ History loads us with?" Again utilizing the verse epistle form and experimenting with a mixture of didactic narrative, satire, and a fluid octosyllabic couplet structure, Davie continues to return to the past in order to contemplate old and new values:

> Confound it, history. . . we transcend it
> Not when we agree to bend it
> To this cat's cradle or that theme
> But when, I take it, we redeem
> This man or that one.

Thus Davie establishes a connection between the virtues of common sense, proportion, and compassion; linear and empirical history; and specific, fixed verse forms.

One associates most of Davie's subjects with England, and *Collected Poems, 1950-1970* recapitulates his proclamation of "faith that there are still distinctively English—rather than Anglo-American or 'international'—ways of responding imaginatively to the terms of life in the twentieth century." One is particularly reminded of Davie's Baptist roots and the severities of his faith. "Dissentient Voice," with its clear reference to Dylan Thomas' "Fern Hill," reminds one of the severities of Davie's childhood: "When some were happy as the grass was green/ I was as happy as a glass was dark." "England" recalls the bitterness of expatriation: On his way back from the United States to Great Britain, Davie confesses: "I dwell, intensely dwell/ on my flying shadow/ over the Canadian barrens,/ and come to nothing else/ .../ Napoleon was right:/ A nation of purveyors./ Now we purvey ourselves/ ... [with] brutal manners, brutal/ simplifications as/ we drag it all down."

To be sure, many of Davie's poems focus on England, and many compare the Mediterranean and Northern worlds. "The Forests of Lithuania," written earlier (1959), however, was based on Adam Mickiewicz's romantic epic *Pan Tadeusz* (1834; English translation, 1917) and dealt with Lithuania during its 1811-1812 Russian Occupation. In this experimental poem, Davie utilized

novelistic techniques, explaining that his goal was to deal with "common human experiences in the way they are commonly perceived, as slowly and
gradually evolving amid a wealth of familiar and particular images" in the effort to "win back some of this territory from the novelist." One sequence,
"The Forest," for example, builds upon a series of lush and classical descriptions, as the poet conveys the sensual, as well as visual and tactile, richness of
the landscape:

> Currants wave their hop-crowned tresses,
> Quickbeams blush like shepherdesses,
> The hazel in a maenad's shape
> Crowned with her nuts as with the grape
> Twirls a green thyrsus, and below
> The striplings of the forest grow—

Davie's tour de force, entirely about England, is *The Shires*. It consists of
forty poems, one for each county in England, arranged in alphabetical order
from Bedfordshire to Yorkshire. *The Shires* contains, primarily, reveries
about the English landscape, culture, and history, and as Davie laments the
unfulfilled potential of entire communities, as well as of individuals, he
reveals the influence of Thomas Hardy. Also, in a voice that ranges from the
formal to the informal, Davie fills the landscapes with autobiographical
information and personal notations. He writes of major and minor events, of
the tragic and of the trivial. At times, he is serious and even bitter about the
problems of the modern world; at other times, he is resigned, wry, and even
witty. These are poems of dissent and praise, as they treat his own experience
and contemporary and historical England. Their subject, however, is primarily human and social neglect, and the waste brought on by the indifference to
precise language and thought.

In "Suffolk," Davie writes: "My education gave me this bad habit/ Of reading history for a hidden plot/ And finding it; invariably the same one,/ Its
fraudulent title always, 'Something Gone.'" The poems are filled with
historical and literary figures such as Lord Nelson, John Calvin, Sir Francis
Drake, Jane Austen, William Wordsworth, A. E. Housman, W. H. Auden,
and John Fowles. Mankind is described in terms of one's relationship with his
past: "We run through a maze of tunnels for our meat/ As rats might . . ./
Drake,/ This is the freedom that you sailed from shore/ To save us for?"
("Devonshire"). Once again, Davie blends the particular and the abstract.
Each shire reveals its own lesson. "Essex," where Davie taught, speaks of
how language—our means of experiencing order of the self and society—is
corrupted: "Names and things named don't match/ Ever." "Cornwall"
describes the decline of imagination and intelligence: We live, says the poet,
with "black patches on both eyes." "Devonshire" treats the corruption of
community, and in "Staffordshire," the unrealized potential of the past has

blighted the future. The "Dorset" sequence, of particular interest, is organized in the manner of Pound's *The Pisan Cantos* (1948), with reveries and
shifts of perspective and multileveled allusions to scholarship, history, culture, and autobiography. In "Sussex," however, one truly hears the poet's elegiac sadness for the general vacancy and lovelessness that has blanketed all
the shires and which extends into the future. He writes:

> The most poeticized
> Of English counties . . .
>
> "Brain-drain" one hears no more of,
> And that's no loss. There is
> Another emigration:
> Draining away of love.

Throughout, the modern world is characterized by empty ceremony, diminished political acumen, and imprecise language. Davie also portrays a physically vast, industrialized, polluted, and drab landscape.

The extraordinary "Trevenen" is a verse biography, a narrative tragedy,
about the late–eighteenth century Cornish naval officer who, after a heroic
career, was used, abused, and driven mad by those he served. Trevenen lived
in "an age much like our own;/ As lax, as vulgar, as confused;/ Its freedoms
just as much abused;/ . . . Where personalities were made,/ And makers of
them plied a trade/ Profitable and esteemed;/ Where that which was and that
which seemed/ Were priced the same, where men were duped/ And knew
they were." Davie's portrayal of Trevenen's heroic life, basic naïveté, and final death are among his most moving lines:

> Aware man's born to err,
> Inclined to bear and forbear.
> Pretense to more is vain.
> Chastened have they been.
> Hope was the tempter, hope.
> Ambition has its scope
> (Vast: the world's esteem);
> Hope is a sickly dream.

In his poems since the mid-1970's, Davie has moved toward a more open
and personal statement, although his commitment to perfect language and
syntax has remained, he has said, less for the purpose of strengthening social
and moral law than as a means of coming to terms with his personal life,
which, he has also confessed, is "the man going mad inside me." The title
piece of *In the Stopping Train and Other Poems*, for example, is clearly less
obscure and more emotionally expansive than has been his custom; it portrays a divided sensibility, an "I" and a "him." Davie admits that the poem "is

an expression of a mood of profound depression and uncertainty about what it has meant for me personally, and for people close to me, that for so many years I have devoted myself to this curious activity we call poetry." The poet boards a slow train in a journey of personal and historical reverie that moves through time and engages him in the difficult struggle to understand himself and define poetry. Not unlike the confessional poets, moreover (from whom he had always separated himself), he indicts himself: "This journey will punish the bastard," and "torment him with his hatreds . . . with his false loves." "The man going mad inside me" is rendered mad by history and must mount "a slow/ and stopping train through places/ whose names used to have virtue." Like *The Shires*, "In the Stopping Train" integrates the abstract and particular and accomplishes a tighter relationship between the personal, social, and abstract. Its complex narrator is closely integrated into the vast experience of common humanity.

In "To Thom Gunn in Los Altos, California," Davie admits the joys and terrors of the poet-exile and of the fear that accompanies the search for meaning: "What am I doing, I who am scared of edges?" Poetry, nevertheless, remains for him the means of approaching the inscrutable and of carving out one's space in the vast unknowable, although, he writes, "Most poems, or the best/ Describe their own birth, and this/ Is what they are—a space/ Cleared to walk around in" ("Ars Poetica"). *Three for Water-Music*, which contains noticeably sensuous and colorful images, also reminds one of Eliot's *Four Quartets* (1943), with its use of multiple allusions and formal divisions. The poet contemplates specific places, dates, his personal life, and philosophical issues, typically, against the backdrop of various landscapes. There are "epiphanies all around us/ Always perhaps," he remarks, and his personal recollections and even mythic evocations merge within a broad variety of styles.

Many of the poems in *The Battered Wife and Other Poems* recall Davie's early life—playing the piano, living in Dublin, and, especially, being "martyred to words." Particularly effective is the title poem, an unusually simple, straightforward narrative about hopeless love, and "Screech-Owl," in which the poet admits that "Nightingales sang to me/ Once, and I never knew." In "Artifex in Extremis," Davie writes, "Let him rehearse the gifts reserved for age/ Much as the poet Eliot did," and then proceeds to explore the consciousness of the dying poet. He measures his success "to confess" that "The work that would . . . speak for itself/ Has not, [and this awareness] comes hard." The poems have an unusual intimacy about them, and the reader can sense a lament for the time and passion that have passed and forever been lost.

As a critic, Davie's remarks shed an interesting perspective on his poetry and reinforce his continuing concerns. For example, in *Purity of Diction in English Verse* (1952), he reaffirms that the strength of statement is found most often in a chaste or pure diction, because it goes together with economy in metaphor; and such economy is a feature of such a diction. It is achieved by judgment and taste, and it preserves the tone of the centre, a sort of urbanity. It purifies the spoken tongue.

This sentiment continues through *The Poet in the Imaginary Museum: Essays of Two Decades* (1977), a collection of essays whose title refers to the artist's obligation to wander through history to absorb and utilize art in all of its forms. Speaking of Pound, for example, Davie again reiterates the poet's responsibility to link poetics and politics: "One could almost say. . . that to dislocate syntax is to threaten the rule of law in the community."

Other major works

NONFICTION: *Purity of Diction in English Verse*, 1952; *Articulate Energy: An Enquiry into the Syntax of English Poetry*, 1955; *The Language of Science and the Language of Literature, 1700-1740*, 1963; *Ezra Pound: Poet as Sculptor*, 1964; *Thomas Hardy and British Poetry*, 1972; *Pound*, 1975; *A Gathered Church: The Literature of the English Dissenting Interest, 1700-1930*, 1976; *The Poet in the Imaginary Museum: Essays of Two Decades*, 1977 (edited by Barry Alpert); *Trying to Explain*, 1979; *Kenneth Allott and the Thirties*, 1980; *English Hymnology in the Eighteenth Century: Papers Read at a Clark Library Seminar, 5 March 1977*, 1980; *Dissentient Voice: The Ward and Phillips Lectures for 1980 with Some Related Pieces*, 1982; *These the Companions: Reflections*, 1982; *Czeslaw Milosz and the Insufficiency of Lyric*, 1986.

TRANSLATION: *The Poems of Doctor Zhivago, by Boris Pasternak*, 1965.

ANTHOLOGIES: *The Late Augustans: Longer Poems of the Eighteenth Century*, 1958; *Pasternak: Modern Judgements*, 1969 (with Angela Livingstone); *Augustan Lyric*, 1974; *The New Oxford Book of Christian Verse*, 1982.

Bibliography
Agenda. XIV (Summer, 1976). Special Davie issue.
Bedient, Calvin. "On Donald Davie," in *Iowa Review*. II (Spring, 1971), pp. 66-88.
Dekker, George, ed. *Donald Davie and the Responsibilities of Literature*, 1984.
Greene, Donald. "A Breakthrough into Spaciousness," in *Queen's Quarterly*. LXXX (Winter, 1973), pp. 601-616.
Kermode, Frank, ed. *Ezra Pound/Donald Davie*, 1976.

Lois Gordon

CARLOS DRUMMOND DE ANDRADE

Born: Itabira, Brazil; October 31, 1902

Principal collections

Alguma poesia, 1930; *Brejo das almas*, 1934; *Sentimento do mundo*, 1940; *Poesias*, 1942; *A rosa do povo*, 1945; *Poesia até agora*, 1947; *Claro enigma*, 1951; *Fazendeiro do ar*, 1953; *Poemas*, 1959; *Lição de coisas*, 1962; *In the Middle of the Road*, 1965; *Boitempo*, 1968; *A falta que ama*, 1968; *Menino antigo*, 1973; *Esquecer para lembrar*, 1979; *A paixão medida*, 1980; *The Minus Sign: Selected Poems*, 1980; *Travelling in the Family*, 1986.

Other literary forms

In addition to many books of poetry, Carlos Drummond de Andrade has published three volumes of stories, nine collections of *crônicas* (journalistic "chronicles," or short prose pieces which may take the form of anecdotal narratives or commentary on current events or behavior), and numerous Portuguese translations of works of French literature. The language of many of his prose-narrative poems is closely related to that of his *crônicas*.

Achievements

In a distinguished career spanning six decades, Drummond—as he is called in Brazil—has produced a formidable body of poetry and prose. Appealing to connoisseurs of literature and the broader public alike, he is Brazil's most beloved modern writer. With a vast poetic repertory of considerable thematic and stylistic variety, Drummond is widely regarded as the leading Brazilian poet of the twentieth century; many consider him to be the most important lyrical voice in that nation's entire literary history. He rightly stands alongside the great Portuguese-language poets, the classic Luís de Camões and the modern Fernando Pessoa, as well as the major contemporary Latin American poets Pablo Neruda, César Vallejo, and Octavio Paz.

Brazilian *Modernismo* of the 1920's and 1930's sought to free poetry from the lingering constraints of Parnassian and Symbolist verse. Iconoclast writers combated conservative tradition, infusing poetry with New World awareness and revitalizing lyric through application of avant-garde techniques. Perhaps more than any other poet of *Modernismo*, Drummond was capable of crystallizing the aims of the movement to institute newness and give value to the national variety of the Portuguese language, while forging an intensely personal style with universal scope.

Drummond has received numerous literary prizes in Brazil for individual works and overall contribution, including those of the PEN Club of Brazil and the Union of Brazilian Writers. He was twice nominated for the Neustadt International Prize for Literature awarded by *World Literature Today* (formerly *Books Abroad*). In his modest way, Drummond has refused many other prizes and declined to seek a chair in the Brazilian Academy of Letters. His work has had a tremendous impact on successive generations of Brazilian artists, influencing emerging lyric poets since the 1930's. On another front, more than seventy musical settings of his poems have been made. Composers inspired by Drummond include the renowned Heitor Villa-Lobos (who set Drummond's poems to music as early as 1926) and the contemporary popular vocalist Milton Nascimento. Academic studies of Drummond's work abound; hundreds of articles and more than a dozen book-length analyses of his poetry have appeared in Brazil.

Biography

Carlos Drummond de Andrade was born in a small town in the interior of Brazil, the ninth son of a rancher with strict traditional values. His rural origins and family life were to be constant sources of inspiration for his poetry. As a rebellious youth, he studied in Belo Horizonte, the capital city of the state, where the family moved in 1920. The young Drummond had already published several items when, in 1922, he became aware of the Modern Art Week in São Paulo, an event which officially launched *Modernismo* as a program of artistic renovation and nationalist spirit. In 1924, two leaders of the movement from São Paulo, Oswald de Andrade and Mário de Andrade (no relation), took Swiss-French poet Blaise Cendrars on a tour of Brazil; Drummond met them in Belo Horizonte. The young poet from Minas corresponded with Mário de Andrade, one of Brazil's most influential men of culture, until the death of the latter. Still in his home state, Drummond was a cofounder, in 1925, of *A revista* (the review), a modernist organ which lasted through three issues. In the same year, Drummond received a degree in pharmacy, a profession which he never practiced. Instead, he began to earn his living in journalism. In 1928, Oswald de Andrade's radical literary journal *Revista de antropofagia* (review of anthropophagy) published a neoteric poem by Drummond which generated much controversy and some early notoriety for the author. His first two books of verse were published in 1930 and in 1934, the year Drummond moved to Rio de Janeiro, the political and cultural capital of the nation.

In Rio, the writer from Minas served as chief of staff for the minister of health and education and collaborated on magazines and literary reviews. By 1942, he had been contracted by a major publishing house which would regularly publish cumulative editions of the poet's work, affording renewed exposure to poetry which had originally appeared in limited first editions of narrow circulation. Drummond lost his position in the ministry when the government fell in 1945. For a brief period, he was part of the editorial board of the tribune of the Communist Party. Later in that same year, he found work with the directorship of the National Artistic and Historical Patrimony, a bureaucratic position he held until his retirement in 1962. During his years of public service, Drummond kept up a prolific pace as a journalist, narrator, and poet of diverse talents. In 1954, he obtained a permanent column in a major Rio daily to publish his *crônicas*; he maintained this activity until the early 1980's. Throughout these four decades, the author periodically joined the best of his journalistic prose pieces with other original writings for publication in volumes. Parallel to these endeavors, to which a significant part of his wide-ranging recognition and popularity can be attributed, Drummond's reputation as poet steadily grew. His work has been translated into Spanish, German, French, Swedish, Bulgarian, Czech, Russian, and English.

Analysis

In 1962, Carlos Drummond de Andrade edited an anthology of his own poetry. Rather than follow a standard chronological sequence or order selections according to the book in which they originally appeared, the author chose poems from each of his collections and organized them into nine representative thematic divisions. This self-characterization reflects, in very general terms, the main preoccupations of Drummond's poetry before and after the publication of the anthology. Each of what the poet calls his "points of departure" or "materials" corresponds to a titled subdivision: the individual ("Um eu todo retorcido," a totally twisted self); the homeland ("Uma província: Esta," a province: this one); the family ("A família que medei," the family I gave myself); friends ("Cantar de amigos," singing of friends); social impact ("Amar-amaro," better-bitter love); knowledge of love ("Uma, duas argolinhas," one, two jousts); lyric itself ("Poesia contemplada," contemplated poetry); playful exercises ("Na praça de conuites," in the square of invitations); and a vision, or attempt, of existence ("Tentativa de exploração e de interpretação do estar-no-mundo," efforts at exploration and interpretation of being-in-the-world).

These are, as the author himself notes, imprecise and overlapping sections. Indeed, any effort at classificatory or chronological categorization of Drummond's poetry, like that of any complex and prolific verse-maker, is subject to inconsistencies and inaccuracies. In addition to the wide thematic concerns enumerated above, several stylistic constants run through the whole of Drummond's work. Certain traits of form and content fade and reappear, other aspects merit consideration from a cumulative point of view, and there is much transitional overlap between the broadly defined phases of his production. With these caveats in mind, the general lines of Drummond's poetic trajectory can be traced. His earliest production, in the 1930's, following the antinormative paths of *Modernismo*, is direct, colloquial, and circumstantial. Sarcastic tones abound within a somewhat individualistic focus. Broader perspective is evident in the next stage, in the 1940's, as the poet explores the physical and human world around him. Existential questions are raised within the context of community; social and historical events move the poet, whose own anguish is a reflection of a generalized crisis of consciousness. A third phase, in the 1950's, incorporates personal and social concerns into an all-encompassing consideration of man and his environment from a philosophical standpoint. A certain formal rigidity accompanies this more contemplative and speculative poetry. The development of Drummond's verse from the 1930's to the 1950's reveals, in broad strokes, a process of opening and expansion. This unfolding can be described with a tripartite metaphor of sight and attitude. The dominant voice of the early poetry is ironic yet timid; the poet *observes* but the lyric vision is uninvolved, hardly surpassing the limits of self. As the poet begins to confront the surrounding world, he *looks* more intently at the faces of reality. Existential meditations lead to a project of encounter; the struggles of others are seen and internalized. In his most mature stage, the poet not only observes and looks but also *contemplates* objects and subjects in an effort to see essences or the roots of contradictions. Having developed this broader vision, Drummond returns, in a cycle of books beginning in 1968, to examine his provincial origins. These latest works—in a reflection of the predominance of paradigms over temporal progression in Drummond's work—are permeated with the vigorous irony that characterized his earliest verse.

A thoroughly modern poet, Drummond can be inspired by and use effectively almost any source for his poetry. Much of his raw material is quotidian; the molding of everyday reality into poetic frameworks may be anecdotal or manifest utopian aspirations. One of his notable strengths is the ability to strike a balance between the light, vulgar, direct, or colloquial and the heavy, elevated, evocative, or contemplative. He is at home with the concrete and the abstract, finding the structures of language most adequate for a particular situation. His is a poetry of discovery, whether of a provincial past in its psychic and mythical dimensions or of the relationships and values that form modern society. Drummond's literary discoveries are not presented as truths or absolutes. His poetry is informed by a fundamental skepticism. Yet bouts with relativism and anguish do not result in nihilism or cynicism. His lyric universe is fundamentally secular; his speculative and metaphysical considerations of essences and human experience rarely involve concepts of god or divinity. Throughout, there operates a dialectic of inner examination and outward projection, of introspection and denunciation of social problems. Expressions of anguish and impotence unveil emblematic poetic selves threatened by technology and a hostile world. The poet seeks to apprehend the profound sense of unresolved differences and change for the individual, the family and affective relationships, society at large, his nation, and the community of mankind. When he bares himself and his personal psychic states, well-tuned devices filter or block the potential for self-indulgence or confessionalism. The revelation of oppressive senses of reality is related to a view of the human condition, to the crises of modern man and civilization. T. S. Eliot said that great poets writing about themselves are writing about their times. A clear sign of Drummond's greatness is his linkage of substances of private, public, and transcendent planes.

A particularly important aspect of Drummond's poetry is the explicit preoccupation with words and expressive means. At the outset, the poet expressed his disquiet through attacks on worn values and stale traditions. As his impulsive impressionism evolved, he undertook an ever-expanding search for nuances, key words, the secrets of language and its virtualities. Words themselves and the making of poetry are the themes of some of Drummond's most important poems. In such works, the necessity of expression may be played against incommunicability or the imperfections of language. There is no tendency or approach in his poetry without a corresponding questioning of linguistic instruments or the sense of poetry. The modernist period, in Western culture in general, has been characterized as the age of criticism. Drummond's poetry is marked by self-consciousness; he is a constant critic of his own art. After *Modernismo* had effectively dissolved as a movement in Brazil, only its most complete poet would be able to write: "And how boring it's become to be modern/ Now I will be eternal."

Drummond's prime linguistic concern is with meaning. In his poetry, conceptual dimensions are generally more important than visuality or sonorousness. Occurrence, idea, and conceit dominate over imagery or symbolism. He seeks to use words in unusual and provocative combinations. Drummond's verse, moreover, is not very musical, in the sense of melodious and harmonious formation of words. There is notable formal variety in the poet's repertory, which incorporates everything from minimalist epigrams to long prose poems, both lyrical and narrative. Much of the poetry seems direct or simple. In the fashion of an Ernest Hemingway character who can "know that it's complicated and write it simple," Drummond, in the realm of poetry, has an uncanny ability to sculpt seemingly spontaneous airs. The simplicity of the poet is deceptive or even duplicitous. While Drummond's customary approach is free verse, he has written in consecrated forms such as the sonnet. He has cultivated the ode, the ballad, and the elegy as well.

Drummond's earliest work is written under the sign of *Modernismo* and demonstrates a combative frame of mind with respect to conservative and preceptive notions of belles lettres associated with Parnassian and Symbolist traditions, long surpassed in Europe but slow to die in South America. Following the Brazilian modernists who preceded him in the 1920's, Drummond sought, once and for all, to pierce the "sacred air" of poetry by abandoning the idea of "noble" thematics and insisting on a more colloquial approach. In 1930, *Modernismo* had already conquered some ground. Thus, Drummond's poetry could not constitute rebellion alone. He was presented with the challenges that liberation presents and had to forge an iconoclasm of the second degree. Drummond succeeded in delivering the *coup de grâce* on propriety, academic language, and mandatory stylization of diction. Humor and irony, never perverse, permeate the early poems, several of which can be called, in the Brazilian fashion, "joke-poems."

Two memorable selections from Drummond's first book, modestly titled *Alguma poesia* (some poetry), illustrate the poet's characteristically daring and provocative attitudes. In the ten lines of the poem "No meio do caminho" ("In the Middle of the Road"), the speaker simply announces, in a starkly unadorned and repetitive fashion, that he, with "fatigued retinas," will never forget that "there was a stone in the middle of the road." Readers wondered whether the poem was sheer mockery or designed to baffle. Conservative critics laughed at the author, some even suggesting that the poem demonstrated a state of schizophrenia or psychosis. The extent of the controversy enabled Drummond, many years later, to edit a book consisting solely of commentaries and critiques of the neoteric set of verses. On the positive side, the poem can be read as a drama of obsession with ideas or as an expression of a monotonous human condition. It can also represent confrontation with impediments of any kind, be they personal, related to self-fulfillment, or literary (that is, ingrained norms). "In the Middle of the Road" can further be considered as a premonition of the hermetic mode in which Drummond would operate in subsequent poetry.

Another symptomatic modernist work is the seemingly disjunct "Poema de sete faces" ("Poem of Seven Faces"). The opening lines—"When I was born, a crooked angel/ one of those who live in shadows/ said: Go on, Carlos! be *gauche* in life."—embody senses of repudiation, marginality, and awkwardness that inform the poet's early work and never completely disappear. This is the first presentation of the "twisted self" that inhabits Drummond's poetic world. The penultimate group of verses of the heptagonal poem alludes to a neoclassical poem, well-known by Brazilian readers, to present aspects of a new poetics: "World world oh vast world/ If I were called Earl'd/ it would be a rhyme, it wouldn't be a solution." Here Drummond attacks the canons of rhyme and meter as external formalities that restrict expressive plenitude. This aggressive insistence on artistic freedom is again formulated with reference to rhyme in "Considera ção do poema" (consideration of the poem), in which the poet writes that he will not rhyme *sono* (slumber) with "the uncorresponding word" *outono* (autumn) but rather with "the word flesh/ or any other for all are good for me." Such statements should not be misconstrued, for Drummond has utilized delicately all manners of rhyme (verse-initial, verse-final, horizontal, vertical, diagonal, internal), especially in his middle years. The question is not rhyme per se but the adaptation of form to the exigencies of particular poetic situations. In the early years of modernist enthusiasm, free verse indeed dominates Drummond's output.

As for the nationalistic concerns of *Modernismo*, the young Drummond did present a series of poetic snapshots of Brazil, focused on his home state of Minas Gerais, but these poems were not strictly regionalist. Even the validation of national reality did not escape the ironic provocations of the young poet. In a poem entitled "Também já fui brasileiro" (I have been Brazilian too), he writes: "... I learned that nationalism is a virtue/ But there comes a time when bars close/ and all virtues are denied." Unwillingness to be restricted by the imposition of new values can also be read between lines such as "A garden, hardly Brazilian ... but so lovely." Drummond's all-encompassing irony is crystalline in a poem called "Hino naçional" (national anthem), which begins, in typical Brazilian modernist fashion "We must discover Brazil!" only to declare, toward the conclusion of this exercise in skepticism, "We must, we must forget Brazil!" This distancing effect is a good measure of the poet's independence and unyielding search for revelations beyond given and constituted frames of reference, above and below evident surfaces.

The social phase of Drummond's poetry is identifiable not so much by formal development but rather by attitudinal and ideological shifts. The titles of his third and fourth collections, *Sentimento do mundo* (feeling of the world) and *A rosa do povo* (the people's rose, his most popular work), clearly indicate in what directions the poet moved. Personal and family preoccupations are linked to the surrounding world, as the poet explores the consequences of pragmatism, mechanization, and the reification of man. The disquiet of the ironic Self gives way to concerns with the Other and with more far-reaching societal problems. Within this orientation, one of Drummond's masterpieces is "Canto ao homem do povo Charlie Chaplin" ("Song to the Man of the People C. C."). Harry Levin has written that Chaplin was one of the greatest modernists for his brilliant renderings of the frustrations and incongruities of modern urban life. Drummond, master of Brazilian *Modernismo*, pays homage to that cinematographic genius and incorporates reverberations of his work into a long (226-line) Whitmanesque piece which speaks for the "abandoned, pariahs, failures, downtrodden." In general, Drummond's poetry of this period gives rise to an existential *raison d'être* that is determined via interaction and giving. Individuality is encompassed by new perspectives: ethics, solidarity with the oppressed and the international community. The symptomatic poem "Os ombros suportam o mundo" ("Shoulders Bear the World") establishes a vital perspective—"Just life without mystifications"— alongside "Mãos dadas" ("Hand in Hand"), which presents the poetic voice of commitment: "I am shackled to life and I see my companions/ They may be taciturn but they nourish great hopes/ It is among them that I consider the enormity of reality." The 1940's were marked by the ravages of world war, and events touched Drummond the poet. The effects of the war in Europe are reflected, for example, in his "Congresso internacional do medo" (international congress of fear). Anti-Fascist positions and Socialist sympathies are evident in such representative poems as "Carta a Stalingrado" (letter to Stalingrad) and "Con o russo em Berlin" (with the Russians in Berlin).

In the midst of this social and historical commotion, Drummond wrote two of his most enduring poems, "Resíduo" ("Residue"), an instigating inventory of emotive and objective presences, and "Procura da poesia" ("Search for Poetry"), which voices an ideal poetics. Here the persona speaks against making poetry of events, feelings, memories, or thoughts. Instead, he advises one to "penetrate quietly the kingdom of words" and contemplate the "thousands of secret faces under the neutral face" of each word. This advice might seem to point out inner contradictions, for much of Drummond's poetry itself derives from the sources he seems to reject. Without discounting a touch of ironic self-commentary, a less literal reading would not hold occurrences, sentiment, recollection, and ideas to be, in themselves, ill-advised for poets. Indeed, unmediated experience will not yield poetry; the true search is for a linguistic craft capable of reformulating experience into viable art.

Formal and thematic properties alike permit establishing a third phase in Drummond's poetic career, beginning in the 1950's and continuing into the next decade. The free-verse and colloquial emphases of his eminently modernist and *engagé* poetry give way to somewhat neoclassical methods. The poet rediscovers the sonnet (and other measured forms) and withdraws from events into a philosophical mode. Reflection on the self, the world, and words takes place at the level of abstract expression. Drummond's confrontation with issues of metaphysics and transcendence signify an interpretative poetry, which becomes somewhat hermetic. The book titles *Claro enigma* (clear enigma) and *Fazendeiro do ar* (farmer of the air) are suggestive of the evolution of the poet's endeavors, as are the names of specific poems such as "Ser" ("Being"), "Entre o ser e as coisas" ("Between Being and Things"), "Aspiração" ("Aspiration"), "Dissolução" ("Dissolution"), and "Contemplação no banco" ("Contemplation on a Bench"). In this more "pure" poetry, love (carnal and psychic) may constitute a means of sublimation. Consideration of family and of the past may evoke wonder about immortality or heredity as a cognitive category. What Drummond calls in the most representative poem of this period, "A máquina do mundo" ("The Machine of the World"), is not to be understood in terms of personal accommodation or social structure but as phenomenological totality with mythical and archetypal dimensions. The poet reports an awakening:

> the machine of the world half-opened
> for whom its breaking was avoiding
> and at the very thought of it moaning . . .
>
> the whole of a reality that transcends
> the outline of its own image drawn
> in the face of mystery, in abysms. . . .

Such poetry of paradox and enigma is also present in *Poemas*, but narrative procedures and concrete referents are reminiscent at times of the more "realistic" poetry of earlier years. The title of the poem "Especulações emtorno da palavra homem" ("Speculations Around the Word Man") suggests its philosophical stance, but rather than affirmations the poem is made up entirely of questions. In this way, one is reminded of the celebrated poem "José," which portrayed disillusionment and the potential for resignation through a series of questions. "A um hotel em demolição" ("To a Hotel Under Demolition") is a long, digressive work which was inspired by an actual event and has prosaic moments. The wandering poem is anchored at the end of the metaphor of the hotel, as the speaker, who has "lived and unlived" in the "Great Hotel of the World without management," finds himself to be "a secret guest of himself." Here Drummond balances narrative and lyrical impulses, private and social dimensions, as well as observation and contemplation.

The two most important selections of *Lição de coisas* (lesson of things), which represents fully the author's mixed style, operate within strict binomial structures. Philosophical speculation is tempered in (by) "A bomba" (the bomb), an extended series of reactions to and statements about atomic explosive devices, the most humbling and frightening invention of modern technology. Each line begins with "the bomb," except the last, in which "man" appears with the hope that he "will destroy the bomb." The realism of this lyric contrasts, but ultimately links, with the experimental "Isso é aquilo" (this is that). This second work is measured and balanced, consisting of ten numbered sets of ten, two-item lines. The pairs of words or neologisms in each line are determined by free lexical, morphological, or semantic associations, for example, "The facile the fossil/ the missile the fissile . . . the atom the atone . . . the chastity the castigate . . ." The final two lines have but one item—"the bombix/ the pytx"—and connect the playful linguistic exercise to the thematic of destruction. These two poems reflect how philosophical, humanitarian, and poetically inventive concerns can interpenetrate and synthesize in Drummond's poetry.

The publication of *Boitempo* (oxtime) begins a homonymous trilogy which incorporates hundreds of poems. This production constitutes a detailed return to historical roots and rural origins. The poet sets out to explore memories, incidents, and personages of his childhood and adolescence in Minas Gerais, much as he did in the 1930's. Inherent in this project is the potential for self-indulgence, cathartic sentimentalism, or autobiographical nostalgia. Yet Drummond undertakes this effort with all the perspective of his varied poetic activities—modernist struggles, committed verse, metaphysical divagations, metapoetics—and makes poetic distance of the chronological distance that separates him from his material. His moods are serene, and a generalized irony tempers the tenderness of memory. The poet is sufficiently detached to employ light, humorous tones in his review of a parochial (and paternalistic) past. There are certainly literarily self-conscious moments in the flow of Drummond's *Boitempo*. Passages which might appear to be dialogues with what was lived long ago are actually evocations of a literary oeuvre. There are returns to the birth of the "totally twisted self" as well as dramatizations of the genesis of nonconformity and rebelliousness. The poetry's comic character signifies a turning away from problematic relations as the center of poetic concern. Only about a tenth of the first set of the *Boitempo* poems are suggestive of Drummond's philosophical muses. The continuation of that mode is to be found in *A falta que ama* (loving lack) and in parts of the brief *A paixão medida* (measured passion).

The contributions of Carlos Drummond de Andrade to the modern art of poetry can be measured in regional, national, continental, and international terms. His regional role in *Modernismo* developed into Brazil's most powerful body of poetry. His reformulation of academic verse as idiomatic lyricism was unique in the diversity of tones, depth of psychological probing, and complexity of thought. With its linguistic flexibility, Drummond's poetry has the eminent capacity to represent metamorphoses, the mobility of sentiment, and the multiplicity of being. In his craft, he achieves a balance of emotion, intelligence, ethical senses, and irony. While Drummond's poetry has been a vehicle for expressions of social awareness, self-discovery, and transcendent inquiry, none of these is more fundamental than the poet's disquiet with the instrument of language itself. Drummond's truest vocation is not the profession of a literary creed or promulgation of any set of ideas but the very uncovering and shaping of words and verbal structures to reflect and explore multiple moods and attitudes.

Other major works

SHORT FICTION: *Contos de aprendiz*, 1951; *70 historinhas*, 1978.

NONFICTION: *Confissões de Minas*, 1944; *Fala, amendoeira*, 1957; *Cadeira de balanço*, 1966; *O poder ultra jovem*, 1972.

Bibliography

Foster, David W., and Virginia R. Foster, eds. *Modern Latin American Literature*, 1975.

Martins, Wilson. "Carlos Drummond de Andrade and the Heritage of *Modernismo*," in *World Literature Today*. LIII, no. 1 (1979), pp. 16-18.

Nist, John. *The Modernist Movement in Brazil*, 1967.

Sternberg, Ricardo. *The Unquiet Self: The Poetry of Carlos Drummond de Andrade*, 1986.

Charles A. Perrone

NORMAN DUBIE

Born: Barre, Vermont; April 10, 1945

Principal collections
The Horsehair Sofa, 1969; *Alehouse Sonnets*, 1971; *The Prayers of the North American Martyrs*, 1975; *Popham of the New Song and Other Poems*, 1975; *In the Dead of the Night*, 1975; *The Illustrations*, 1977; *A Thousand Little Things and Other Poems*, 1978; *The City of the Olesha Fruit*, 1979; *Odalisque in White*, 1979; *The Everlastings*, 1980; *The Window in the Field*, 1981; *Selected and New Poems*, 1983; *The Springhouse*, 1986.

Other literary forms
Norman Dubie has contributed several critical pieces to such journals as *American Poetry Review*, *Poetry*, and *Iowa Review*, but he is known primarily for his poetry.

Achievements
Dubie is one of America's most important and innovative contemporary poets. Since the publication of his first volume of verse when he was twenty-three, Dubie has, on average, published one book every two years, accumulating an impressive body of work. At a time when American poetry has been both praised and criticized for its preoccupation with intimate personal experience, Dubie has sought to see the world through the eyes of historical figures from many different times and places—painters, fellow writers, individuals of all sorts, whose distinctive perspective he adopts for the duration of a poem.

In 1976, Dubie won the Bess Hokin Award from *Poetry* and the Modern Poetry Association for "The Negress, Her Monologue of Dark Crepe." He has also been the recipient of creative writing fellowships from the National Endowment for the Arts and the Guggenheim Foundation. In honor of Dubie's literary achievements, the University of Iowa, where he received his M.F.A., houses the Norman Dubie Collection in its library.

Biography
Norman Evans Dubie, Jr., was born on April 10, 1945, in Barre, Vermont. His father, Norman Evans Dubie, Sr., was a clergyman, and his mother, Doris, was a registered nurse. Dubie was educated in Vermont and received his undergraduate degree at Goddard College in Plainfield, being graduated from there in 1969. In 1968, while a student at Goddard, Dubie married the first of his wives, Francesca Stafford. This marriage would produce Dubie's only child, Hannah.

Leaving Vermont after his graduation, Dubie studied creative writing in the M.F.A. program of the Iowa Writers Workshop at the University of Iowa. He received his degree in 1971 and began lecturing in the Workshop afterward. From 1971 through 1972, Dubie was the poetry editor of *Iowa Review*; from 1973 through 1974, he edited *Now*. During this period, his first marriage ended in divorce.

When Dubie left the University of Iowa, he became an assistant professor of English at Ohio University in Athens. He retained this position from 1974 through 1975; during this period, Dubie published three volumes of poetry: *The Prayers of the North American Martyrs*, *Popham of the New Song and Other Poems*, and *In the Dead of the Night*. Following the publication of these collections, Dubie left Ohio University and accepted a position at Arizona State University.

Dubie was writer-in-residence at Arizona State from 1975 until 1976. He was a lecturer there from 1976 until 1983 and was then promoted to the rank of full professor of English. He has been the director of Arizona State's graduate writing program since 1976.

In 1975, Dubie was remarried, to Pamela Stewart, a poet and a teacher. Five years later, this marriage also ended in divorce. In 1981, Dubie remarried again, this time to Jeannine Savard, also a poet.

Analysis

In his introduction to Norman Dubie's *The Illustrations*, poet Richard Howard says that Dubie's poetry centers on "the experience which has the root of *peril* in it, the ripple of danger which enlivens the seemingly lovely surfaces, the 'ordinary' existence." That perilous quality is evident in nearly all of Dubie's work; it is the very thing that guarantees its success. Still, "the ripple of danger" creates a difficult poetry, too, embracing experience in exciting, innovative ways. The ordinary becomes extraordinary. As Howard puts it, "Dubie identifies that experience, by reciting it, with his own life to a hallucinatory degree: we are not to know what is given and what is taken, what is 'real' and what 'made up.'"

The juxtaposition of "real" and "fiction" is particularly engaging in much of Dubie's early work. In *Alehouse Sonnets* and *The Illustrations*, Dubie wrote historically based poems in the form of dramatic monologues. Perhaps it is this for which Dubie is best known; not only do these monologues create a space in which the poet can move outside himself and the time in which he lives, but also they allow him the intellectual advantage of innovation as well as imagistic and allusive complexity. The result is an engaging, demanding verse. The reader must work to understand; he must either clarify the obscurity or resign himself to the "hallucinatory"; he must not relent in his reading if he is to discover the value of such complexity. These are imperatives; the reader has no choice.

Still, one reader will find Dubie's work elegant and beautiful; the next will find it distant and foreign, purposely ignoring accessibility. Both appraisals may be justified. Dubie's demands upon his poetry and upon his readers, however, set him apart from nearly all other contemporary poets. His is an original, fanciful voice, and often the distinction he makes between reality and fancy is fuzzy. This creates a sometimes lethargic, somnambulant effect, quite like walking along some foggy, hazed-over street under white lights, dreamy, disembodied, and more than a little disenchanted. The reader is much like the character in "Hazlitt Down from the Lecture Table" (*Alehouse Sonnets*) who " . . . just/ sat out the stupor in a corner."

This seems to be Dubie's exact intention, though. Dubie's imagination draws him—and the reader—away from the mundane, real world and intensifies that "stupor" by displacing him to a paradoxical, mundane, exotic world. The lives of Dubie's characters, their triumphs and their failures, are no more special than are those of his readers—and no more worse. The difficulty, then, is the importance readers may attribute to the allusive figures or to the thick, ambiguous imagery. One assumes that the allusion *means* something essential, or that knowledge of the allusion will clarify the poem. The reader may puzzle an interminable time, trying to unravel an obscure image. Each of these, however, is a failed reading; such scrutiny may aid comprehension, but it will not guarantee tidy answers. The man who "sat out the stupor" knows and accepts this.

While some of Dubie's critics find his work incomprehensible, still others accuse him of being too impersonal. This is especially so in Dubie's early writing. *Alehouse Sonnets*, for example, is characterized by a detached, unidentified persona. All one knows of the persona is his affinity to William Hazlitt, the nineteenth century English critic, whom he addresses throughout the book. One can imagine, after reading *Alehouse Sonnets*, a companionship made between men of two different centuries and, likely, two different life-styles. Time and place cannot erase mankind's disappointments, however, for the characters in the poems share those experiences universally. In order to juxtapose the contraries of time and place, Dubie approaches his subjects and his characters with calculated distance. The poet hovers over the characters, sometimes coming in, intruding, but usually standing not far off, aloof and watchful.

To fault this as being impersonal is also a misreading of Dubie's work. As Lorrie Goldensohn has written of Dubie, "What mostly gets left out is the explicitly autobiographical self. The self, that darling of contemporary poetry, here has little to do; it appears to be just another dreamer, usually present as disembodied voice rummaging around . . . interchangeable with others." Contemporary poetry is excessively burdened with poems of "self," and Dubie's poems offer a refreshing break from that tendency. The fanciful mind discovers commonality of experience, how the persona's life, Hazlitt's, the poet's, and the reader's are much the same. The verse does not need to be autobiographical, because Dubie is writing everyone's biography. The poem cannot be personal; as Dubie wrote in "Address to the Populous Winter Youths," "Nearness exasperates."

In the several collections which immediately followed *Alehouse Sonnets*, Dubie continued to experiment with deliberate distancing. Rather than addressing only one allusive figure—Hazlitt, for example—Dubie would address numerous historical personages or speak through them. *In the Dead of the Night* and *The Illustrations* are most notably characterized by a profusion of allusions to artists. A quick listing of Dubie's titles presents many: "The Suicide of Hedda Gabler," "Charles Baudelaire," "Seurat," "El Greco," "Sun and Moon Flowers: Paul Klee, 1879-1940," "The Czar's Last Christmas Letter: A Barn in the Urals," and "Horace." In particular, *The Illustrations* handles these monologues with mastery.

Quite literally, one can approach the poems of this volume as "illustrations." Dubie, himself, is the illustrator, the artist whose own perceptiveness becomes the voices of his characters. The illustrations are of any number of stories, and the reader involves himself in as many ways as his experience will allow. For,

> In a world that
>
> Belongs to a system of things
> Which presents a dark humus with everything
>
> Living

(an excerpt from "These Untitled Little Verses . . ." in *The Illustrations*), the reader discovers, as Dubie knows, vital connections.

As his career has progressed, however, Dubie has discovered the limitations of his dramatic monologues. *Selected and New Poems*, while including a generous selection from earlier volumes, introduced a noticeable change in Dubie's manner. The emotional excessiveness of his earlier work was toned down, and many of the new poems eschewed the dramatic monologue for a more personal voice. David Wojahn, reviewing this book in *Western Humanities Review*, remarked that while the new poems "do not match the ambition of some of the earlier poems . . . they are often better crafted and more genuine." That Dubie's style changed is indicative of his desire to move ahead. It also puts Dubie into a certain degree of peril: His writing is turning inward, becoming personal, and—if more lyrical—more conventional.

The Springhouse is a promising extension of the new material found in *Selected and New Poems*. What makes *The Springhouse* remarkable is Dubie's ability to move away from the style and subjects that brought him acclaim while still reveling in his mastery of rich verbal textures. The result is a collection of thirty highly intimate lyrics—poems of youth, religious belief,

and love. The new note of intimacy in *The Springhouse* is unmistakable:
Readers who found themselves fighting through the earlier dramatic monologues will find the poems of *The Springhouse* similarly dramatic but infinitely more delicate and accessible.

Consider, for example, "Hummingbirds," which suggests that the world is
hostile to its fragile creatures:

> They have made a new statement
> About our world—a clerk in Memphis
> Has confessed to laying out feeders
> Filled with sulphuric acid. She says
>
> God asked for these deaths . . . like God
> They are insignificant, and have visited us
>
> Who are wretched.

What is the "new statement"? That we are wretched because we find hummingbirds and God insignificant; we are poorer because of it. This is hardly
the Norman Dubie of the earlier collections, the one who distanced himself
from his subjects and his readers, who disdained closeness. Similarly, "Old
Night and Sleep," dedicated to Dubie's grandfather, moves the reader:

> A cold rain falls through empty nests, a cold rain
> Falls over the canvas
> Of some big beast with four stomachs
> Who eats beneath a white tree
> In which only a dozen dry pods are left . . .
>
> Some new sense of days being counted.

The poem is a lamentation, an emptiness of soul accounted for visually in
sensuous imagery. Things are drizzly, vague, empty; loss of a loved one
makes one feel this way, makes one aware of one's own temporal existence.

The importance of Dubie's contribution to the poetics of his time is evident. More than most of his contemporaries, Dubie has risked much to offer
an unusual, resonant voice. Granted, his poems are difficult, evasive at
times, incomprehensible at other times, yet his imagination addresses very
real issues. That Dubie expects his reader to work is really no fault inherent
in his poetry; already, too many other poets write easy, disposable verse.
Dubie's poetry is not disposable. It will not let its readers let it loose.

Bibliography

Goldensohn, Lorrie. "Not in the Browning Shade," in *Parnassus: Poetry in
    Review*. VIII, no. 2 (1980), pp. 152-175.
Raab, Lawrence. "Illustrations and Illuminations: On Norman Dubie," in

The American Poetry Review. VII, no. 4 (1978), pp. 12-14.
St. John, David. "A Generous Salvation: The Poetry of Norman Dubie," in
   The American Poetry Review. XIII, no. 5 (1984), pp. 17-21.
Stitt, Peter. "The Circle of the Meditative Moment," in *Georgia Review*.
   XXXVIII (Summer, 1984), pp. 402-414.
Wojahn, David. Review in *Western Humanities Review*. XXXVIII (Autumn,
   1984), pp. 269-273.

Mark Sanders

PAUL LAURENCE DUNBAR

Born: Dayton, Ohio; June 27, 1872
Died: Dayton, Ohio; February 9, 1906

Principal poems and collections
Oak and Ivy, 1893; *Majors and Minors*, 1895; *Lyrics of Lowly Life*, 1896; *Lyrics of the Hearthside*, 1899; *Lyrics of Love and Laughter*, 1903; *Lyrics of Sunshine and Shadow*, 1905; *Complete Poems*, 1913.

Other literary forms
Though Paul Laurence Dunbar is best known for his poetry, he was a fiction writer as well. His achievements in fiction include four volumes of short stories and four novels. Recent criticism of Dunbar's short fiction suggests that the stories contained in *Folks from Dixie* (1898) represent his best accomplishment in this literary form. His novels *The Uncalled* (1898) and *The Sport of the Gods* (1902) acquired more critical acclaim than his other two novels, *The Love of Landry* (1900) and *The Fanatics* (1901).

In addition to his work in these more traditional literary forms, Dunbar wrote an assortment of lyrics and libretti for a variety of theatrical productions. He also wrote essays for newspapers and attempted to establish a periodical of his own.

Achievements
Dunbar's literary career was brilliant, extending roughly across two decades. He can be credited with several first-time accomplishments: He was the first to use dialect poetry as a medium for the true interpretation of Negro character and psychology, and he was the first Afro-American writer to earn national prominence. In range of style and form, Dunbar remains the most versatile of Afro-American writers.

Biography
Paul Laurence Dunbar was born to former slaves Joshua and Matilda J. Murphy Dunbar on June 27, 1872. He spent his early childhood in Dayton, Ohio, where he attended Central High School. Dunbar began to write at age sixteen and gained early patronage for his work, and he was introduced to the Western Association of Writers in 1892.

The next few years of his life found him in the presence of great black leaders. He met Frederick Douglass, Mary Church Terrell, and Ida B. Wells at the World's Columbian Exposition in Chicago in 1893. He met W. E. B. Du Bois in 1896 and Booker T. Washington in 1897. These encounters influenced Dunbar's literary tone and perspective significantly. He blended the creative perspective of Booker T. Washington with the social philosophy of

Du Bois in order to present a valid scenario of Afro-Americans after the Civil War.

Major James B. Pond, a Dunbar enthusiast, sponsored a trip to England for the writer which extended from February to August of 1897. Upon his return to the United States, Dunbar married Alice Moore and decided to earn his living as a writer. Between 1898 and 1903, Dunbar wrote essays for newspapers and periodicals, primarily addressing the issues of racial equality and social justice in America. He attempted to establish his own journalistic voice through a periodical which he named the *Dayton Tattler* in 1890. This effort failed.

During the latter years of his life, Dunbar wrote lyrics, including those for the school song for Tuskegee Institute. Dunbar died in Dayton, Ohio, on February 9, 1906.

Analysis

The body of poetry produced by Paul Laurence Dunbar illustrates some of the best qualities found in lyrical verse. It is obvious that the poet concentrated on a creation of mood and that he was an innovator who experimented with form, meter, and rhyme. Equally apparent is the fact that Dunbar's creative style was influenced by the great British poetic innovators of the seventeenth and nineteenth centuries. Dunbar's commitment to speak to his people through his verse is reflected in his dialect poetry. Writing in all the major lyrical forms—idyll, hymn, sonnet, song, ballad, ode, and elegy—Dunbar established himself as one of the most versatile poets in American literature.

The more than four hundred poems written by Dunbar are varied in style and effect. It is clear, however, that his dominant aim was to create an empathetic poetic mood resulting from combinations of elements such as meter, rhyme, diction, sentence structure, characterization, repetition, imagery, and symbolism. His most memorable poems display the influence of such masters as William Wordsworth; Robert Herrick; Alfred, Lord Tennyson; John Donne; Robert Browning, and John Keats.

Such an array of influences would ordinarily render one's genius suspect. There are common threads, however, which organically characterize the poetic expressions of Paul Laurence Dunbar. The undergirding strain in his poetry is his allegiance to lyrical qualities. He carries mood through sound patterns; he creates images which carry philosophical import; he shapes dramatic events in the pattern of movement in his syntactic forms; and he develops a rhythmic pattern which is quite effective in recitation. These lyrical qualities predominate in the best of Dunbar's poetry. Indeed, one might easily classify Dunbar's poetry in typical Romantic lyrical categories: The bulk of his poems can be classified as love lyrics, reflective lyrics, melancholic lyrics, or nature lyrics. Sometimes these moods overlap in a single poem.

Consequently, an analysis of the features in Dunbar's poetry is necessarily complex, placing his lyrical qualities in the poetic traditions which shape them.

Dunbar's lyricism is substantially displayed in his love poetry. In "A Bridal Measure," from *Lyrics of the Hearthside*, the poet's persona beckons maidens to the bridal throne. His invitation is spirited and triumphant yet controlled, reminiscent of the tradition in love poetry established by Ben Jonson. The tone, however, more closely approximates the *carpe diem* attitude of Robert Herrick.

> Come, essay a sprightly measure,
> Tuned to some light song of pleasure.
> Maidens, let your brows be crowned
> As we foot this merry round.

The rhyming couplets carry the mood and punctuate the invitation. The urgency of the moment is extended further in the direct address: "Phyllis, Phyllis, why be waiting?/ In the woods the birds are mating." The poem continues in this tone, while adopting a pastoral simplicity.

> When the year, itself renewing,
> All the world with flowers is strewing,
>   Then through Youth's Arcadian land,
>   Love and song go hand in hand.

The accentuation in the syntactic flow of these lines underlines the poet's intentions. Though the meter is irregular, with some iambs and some anapests, the force of the poet's exhortation remains apparent.

Dunbar frequently personifies abstractions. In "Love and Grief," also from *Lyrics of the Hearthside*, Dunbar espouses a morbid yet redemptive view of love. While the reflective scenario presented in this poem recalls Tennyson's meditations on death and loss, the poetic event echoes Wordsworth's faith in the indestructibility of joy. Utilizing the heroic couplet, Dunbar makes an opening pronouncement:

> Out of my heart, one treach'rous winter's day,
> I locked young Love and threw the key away.
> Grief, wandering widely, found the key,
> And hastened with it, straightway, back to me.

The drama of grief-stricken love is thus established. The poet carefully clarifies his position through an emphatic personification of Grief's behavior: "He unlocked the door/ and bade Love enter with him there and stay." Being a lyric poet of redemptive sensibility, Dunbar cannot conclude the poem on this note. The "table must turn," as it does for Wordsworth in such situations. Love then becomes bold and asks of Grief: "What right hast thou/ To part or parcel of this heart?" In order to justify the redemptive quality he presents, Dunbar attributes the human frailty of pride to Love, a failing which invites Grief. In so doing, the poet's philosophical intuitiveness emerges with a measure of moral decorum. Through the movement in the syntactic patterns, the intensity of the drama is heightened as the poem moves to resolution. Dunbar utilizes a variety of metrical patterns, the most significant of which is the spondee. This poetic foot of two accented syllables allows the poet to proclaim emphatically: "And Love, pride purged, was chastened all his life." Thus, the principal emotion in the poem is redeemed.

The brief, compact lyrical verse, as found in Browning, is among Dunbar's typical forms. "Love's Humility," in *Lyrics of the Hearthside* is an example:

> As some rapt gazer on the lowly earth,
>   Looks up to radiant planets, ranging far,
> So I, whose soul doth know thy wondrous worth
>   Look longing up to thee as to a star.

This skillfully concentrated simile elevates love to celestial heights. The descriptive detail enhances the power of the feeling the poet captures and empowers the lyrical qualities of the poem with greater pathos.

Dunbar's *Lyrics of Love and Laughter* is not the best of his collections, but it contains some remarkable dialect verse. "A Plea" provides an example of this aspect of his reputation. Speaking of the unsettling feelings experienced by one overcome with love, Dunbar exhorts a lover's love object to "treat him nice."

> I ain't done a t'ing to shame,
> Lovahs all ac's jes de same:
> Don't you know we ain't to blame?
>   Treat me nice!

Rendering a common experience in the Afro-American idiom, Dunbar typifies the emotionally enraptured lover as one who has no control over his behavior.

> Whut a pusson gwine to do,
> W'en he come a-cou'tin' you
> All a-tremblin' thoo and thoo?
>   Please be nice.

The diction in this poem is not pure dialect. Only those portions which describe the emotions and behavior of the lover are stated in dialect, highlighting the primary emotions and enhancing the pathetic mood, which is apparently Dunbar's principal intent. Typical of Dunbar's love lyrics, "A Plea" is rooted in the experience of a particular culture yet remains universal in its themes. Through his use of diction, meter, and stanzaic form, Dunbar captures fundamental human emotions and renders them with intensity and lyrical compassion.

Reflective lyrics form a large segment of Dunbar's poetry. Some of his best poems of this type are found in *Lyrics of Lowly Life*, including the long stanzaic poem "Ere Sleep Comes Down to Soothe the Weary Eyes." This poem utilizes one sensory impression as a focal point for the lyrical evolution in the style of Keats. The sleep motif provides an avenue through which the persona's imagination enters the realm of reflection.

Through sleep's dream the persona is able to "make the waking world a world of lies—/ of lies most palpable, uncouth, forlorn." In this state of subconscious reflection, past pains are revisited as they "come thronging through the chambers of the brain." As the poem progresses, it becomes apparent that the repetitive echo of "ere sleep comes down to soothe the weary eyes" has some significance. This refrain begins and ends each stanza of the poem except the last. In addition to serving as a mood-setting device, this expression provides the channel of thought for the literary journey, which is compared with the "spirit's journeying." Dunbar's audience is thus constantly reminded of the source of his revelations.

Dunbar reveals his poetic thesis in the last stanza. He uses images from the subconscious state of life, sleep, to make a point about death. Prior to making this point, Dunbar takes the reader to the realm of reflective introspection: "So, trembling with the shock of sad surprise,/ The soul doth view its awful self alone." There is an introspective confrontation of the soul with itself, and it resolves:

> When sleep comes down to seal the weary eyes,
> . . . .
> Ah, then, no more we heed
> the sad world's cries,
> Or seek to probe th' eternal mystery,
> Or fret our souls at long-withheld replies.

The escape from pain and misery is death; there is no intermediary state which will eradicate that fact of life. Dunbar presents this notion with sympathy and sincerity. His metaphorical extensions, particularly those relative to the soul, are filled with compassion. The soul is torn with the world's deceit; it cries with "pangs of vague inexplicable pain." The spirit, an embodiment of the soul, forges ahead to seek truth as far as Fancy will lead. Questioning begins then, and the inner sense confronts the inner being until Truth emerges. Dunbar's presentation of the resolution is tender and gentle.

Dunbar wrote reflective lyrics in the vernacular as well. Espousing the philosophy of Divine intention, Dunbar wrote "Accountability," a poem also found in *Lyrics of Lowly Life*. In this poem, the beliefs and attitudes of the persona are revealed in familiar language.

> Folks ain't got no right to
>   censuah othah
>   folks about dey habits;
> . . . .
> We is all constructed diff'ent,
>   d'ain't no two of
>   us de same;
> . . . .
> But we all fits into places dat
>   no othah ones
>   could fill.

Each stanza in this poem presents a thesis and develops that point. The illustrations from the natural world support a creationist viewpoint. The persona obviously accepts the notion that everything has a purpose. The Creator gave the animals their members shaped as they are for a reason and so, "Him dat giv' de squr'ls de bushtails made de bobtails fu' de rabbits." The variations in nature are by design: "Him dat built de gread big mountains hollered out de little valleys"; "Him dat made de streets an' driveways wasn't shamed to make de alley." The poet establishes these notions in three quatrains, concluding in the fourth quatrain: "When you come to think about it, how it's all planned out it's splendid./ Nuthin's done er evah happens, dout hit's somefin' dat's intended." The persona's position that Divine intention rules the world is thereby sealed.

Introspection is a feature of Dunbar's reflective lyrics. In "The Lesson," the persona engages in character revelation, interacts with the audience toward establishment of appropriate resolution, and participates in the action of the poem. These qualities are reminiscent of Browning's dramatic monologues. As the principal speaker sits by a window in his cottage, reflecting, he reports:

> And I thought of myself so sad and lone,
> And my life's cold winter that knew no spring;
> Of my mind so weary and sick and wild,
>   Of my heart too sad to sing.

The inner conflict facing the persona is revealed in these lines and the perspective of self-examination is established. The persona must confront his sadness and move toward resolution. The movement toward resolution presents the dramatic occasion in the poem: "A thought stole into my saddened heart,/ And I said, 'I can cheer some other soul/ By a carol's simple art.'" Reflective introspection typically leads to improved character, a fundamental tenet in the Victorian viewpoint. Sustained by his new conviction and outlook, the persona "sang a lay for a brother's ear/ In a strain to soothe his bleeding heart."

The lyrical quality of "The Lesson" is strengthened by the movement in the poet's syntactic patterns. Feelings of initial despair and resulting joy and hope are conveyed through the poet's syntax. The sequential conjoining of ideas as if in a rushing stream of thought is particularly effective. The latter sections of the poem are noteworthy in this regard. This pattern gives the action more force, thereby intensifying the feeling. Dunbar presents an emphatic idea—"and he smiled . . ."—and juxtaposes it to an exception—"Though mine was a feeble art." He presents a responsive result—"But at his smile I smiled in turn"—connected to a culminating effect—"And into my soul there came a ray." With this pronouncement, the drama comes full circle from inner conflict through conversion to changed philosophical outlook. Dunbar captures each moment with appropriate vigor.

The subjects of love and death are treated in Dunbar's lyrics of melancholy, the third major mood found in the poet's lyrical verse. "Yesterday and To-morrow," in *Lyrics of Sunshine and Shadow*, is an example of Dunbar's lyric of melancholy. The mood of this poem is in the tradition of the British Romantic poets, particularly that of Wordsworth. Dunbar treats the melancholy feeling in this poem with tenderness and simplicity. The persona expresses disappointment with the untimeliness of life's events and the uncertainties of love. This scenario intimates a bleak future.

"Yesterday and To-morrow" is developed in three compact quatrains. Each quatrain envelops a primary emotion. The first stanza unfolds yesterday's contentment in love. The lover remembers the tender and blessed emotion of closeness with his lover: "And its gentle yieldingness/ From my soul I blessed it." The second stanza is reminiscent of the metaphysical questionings and imagery of Donne: "Must our gold forever know/ Flames for the refining?" The lovers' emotions are compared with precious metal undergoing the fire of refinement; their feelings of sadness are released in this cynical question.

In the third quatrain, Dunbar feeds the sad heart with more cynicism. Returning to the feelings of disappointment and uncertainty, the persona concludes: "Life was all a lyric song/ Set to tricksy meter." The persona escapes in cynicism, but the poem still ends on a hopeless note.

"Communion," which is collected in *Lyrics of the Hearthside*, is another of Dunbar's melancholy lyrics and focuses the theme of love and death. The situation in the poem again evokes a cynical attitude, again reminiscent of Donne. The poem presents a struggle between life's memories and death. Life's memories are primarily of the existence of the love relationship, and death symbolizes its demise. This circumstance unfolds in a dramatic narrative in the style of Browning. The first two stanzas of the poem introduce the situation and the mood begins to evolve in stanza three. The poet uses images from nature to create the somber mood. The "breeze of Death," for example, sweeps his lover's soul "Out into the unsounded deeps." On one hand, the Romantic theme of dominance of nature and man's helplessness in the face of it creeps through; on the other hand, faith in love as the superior experience resounds. The conflict between conquering Death, symbolized in Nature, and Love creates tension in the poem. Consequently, though the breeze of Death has swept his bride away, the persona announces that "Wind nor sea may keep me from/ Soft communing with my bride." As these quatrains of iambic pentameter unfold, the poem becomes somewhat elegiac in tone.

The persona solemnly enters into reflective reminiscence in the fifth stanza and proclaims: "I shall rest my head on thee/ As I did long days of yore." Continuing in stanza 6, he announces: "I shall take thy hand in mine,/ And live o'er the olden days." Leading up to the grief-stricken pledge of eternal love, the melancholic feeling is intensified. The mourner details his impression as follows:

> Tho' the grave-door shut between,
> Still their love lights o'er me steal.
>
> I can see thee thro' my tears,
> As thro' rain we see the sun.

The comfort which comes from such memories brings a ray of light; the lover concludes;

> I shall see thee still and be
> Thy true lover evermore,
> And thy face shall be to me
> Dear and helpful as before.

The drama cannot end unless the persona interacts with his audience. The audience is therefore included in the philosophical conclusion: "Death may vaunt and Death may boast,/ But we laugh his pow'r to scorn." Dunbar illustrates an ability to overcome the causes of melancholy in his lyrics of this mood. He works with contrasting feelings, cynicism, and determinism to achieve this goal. His melancholic mood is therefore less gloomy than one might expect.

Since he was greatly influenced by the British Romantic writers, it is not surprising that Dunbar also wrote nature lyrics. "In Summer," from *Lyrics of the Hearthside*, and "The Old Apple-Tree," from *Lyrics of Lowly Life*, are representative of his nature lyrics. "In Summer" captures a mood of merriment which is stimulated by nature. The common man is used as a model of one who possesses the capacity to experience this natural joy. Summer is a bright, sunny time; it is also a time for ease, as presented in the second stanza. Introducing the character of the farmer boy in stanza 3, Dunbar presents a model embodiment of the ease and merriment of summer. Amid the blades of green grass and as the breezes cool his brow, the farmer boy sings as he plows. He sings "to the dewy morn" and "to the joys of life." This behavior leads to some moralizing, to which the last three stanzas of the poem are devoted. The poet's point is made through a contrast:

> O ye who toil in the town,
>   And ye who moil in the mart,
> Hear the artless song, and your faith made strong
>   Shall renew your joy of heart.

Dunbar admonishes the reader to examine the behavior of the farm boy. Elevation of the simple, rustic life is prevalent in the writings of early British Romantic poets and postbellum Afro-American writers alike. The admonition to reflect on the rustic life, for example, is the same advice Wordsworth gives in "The Old Cumberland Beggar." Both groups of writers agree that there are lessons to be learned through an examination of the virtues of the rustic life. In this vein, Dunbar advises: "Oh, poor were the worth of the world/ If never a song were heard." He goes further by advising all to "taunt old Care with a merry air."

The emphasis on the rustic life is also pervasive in "The Old Apple-Tree." The primary lyrical quality of the poem is that the poetic message evolves from the poet's memory and imagination. Image creation is the medium through which Dunbar works here: His predominant image, dancing in flames of ruddy light, is an orchard "wrapped in autumn's purple haze."

Dunbar proceeds to create a nature scene which provides a setting for the immortalization of the apple tree. Memory takes the persona to the scene, but imagination re-creates events and feelings. The speaker in the poem admits that it probably appears ugly "When you look the tree all over/ Unadorned by memory's glow." The tree has become old and crooked, and it bears inferior fruit. Thus, without the nostalgic recall, the tree does not appear special at all.

Utilizing the imaginative frame, the speaker designs features of the simple rustic life, features which are typically British Romantic and peculiarly Wordsworthian. The "quiet, sweet seclusion" realized as one hides under the shelter of the tree and the idle dreaming in which one engages dangling in a swing from the tree are primary among these thoughts. Most memorable to the speaker is the solitary contentment he and his sweetheart found as they courted beneath the old apple tree.

> Now my gray old wife is Hallie,
>   An I'm grayer still than she,
> But I'll not forget our courtin'
>   'Neath the old apple-tree.

The poet's ultimate purpose, to immortalize the apple tree, is fulfilled in the last stanza. The old apple tree will never lose its place in nature or its significance, for the speaker asks:

> But when death does come a-callin',
> This my last request shall be,—
> That they'll bury me an' Hallie
> 'Neath the old apple-tree.

The union of man and nature at the culmination of physical life approaches a notion expressed in Wordsworth's poetry. This tree has symbolized the ultimate in goodness and universal harmony; it symbolizes the peace, contentment, and joy in the speaker's life. Here Dunbar's indebtedness to the Romantic traditions that inform his entire oeuvre is most profoundly felt.

Other major works

NOVELS: *The Uncalled*, 1898; *The Love of Landry*, 1900; *The Fanatics*, 1901; *The Sport of the Gods*, 1902.

SHORT FICTION: *Folks from Dixie*, 1898; *The Strength of Gideon and Other Stories*, 1900; *In Old Plantation Days*, 1903; *The Heart of Happy Hollow*, 1904.

Bibliography

Brawley, Benjamin. *Paul Laurence Dunbar, Poet of His People*, 1936.
Cunningham, Virginia. *Paul Laurence Dunbar and His Song*, 1947.
Martin, Jay, ed. *A Singer in the Dawn: Reinterpretations of Paul Laurence Dunbar*, 1975.
Revell, Peter. *Paul Laurence Dunbar*, 1979.

Patricia A. R. Williams

FIRDUSI

Born: Near Tús, in Iran; between A.D. 932 and 941
Died: Near Tús, in Iran; between A.D. 1020 and 1025

Principal poem
Shahnamah, c. 1010.

Other literary forms
Although the only surviving work by Firdusi is the *Shahnamah* (the book of kings), another long poem entitled *Yusuf u Zulaikha* (Joseph and Zulaikha), detailing the story of the biblical character Joseph and Potiphar's wife, has been attributed to Firdusi. This poem, however, is not Firdusi's and belongs to a much later period. Other verses scattered in various anthologies of the classical period have been ascribed to the poet, but none of these fragments can be assigned to him with certainty. These fragments have been collected and studied by H. Ethé in his *Firdûsî als Lyriker* (1872-1873).

Achievements
The national saga of Iran, which constitutes an ethnic history of the Iranians, existed in written form long before the time of Firdusi. Sagas of this type formed a genre of classical Persian literature, both in verse and in prose, which were known by the generic name *Shahnamah*. Firdusi chose an existing prose *Shahnamah* to versify during his long poetic career. He included in his narrative other relevant tales from the oral tradition, creating a coherent narrative detailing the national saga of Iran in verse. His masterful verse gradually replaced the original prose work, and in time the term *Shahnamah* came to be applied exclusively to his poem. Thus, the names of Firdusi and his *Shahnamah* became synonymous with the national epic of Iran. With the birth of the discipline of Orientalism, this book was brought to the West through translations and in turn influenced Western authors such as Matthew Arnold, who based his "Sohrab and Rustum" on it. Thus, Firdusi's poem was established as an important work in world literature.

Biography
Little factual information is available concerning Firdusi's life. The character of the poet is overgrown by a thicket of tales which sprang up around him shortly after his death. His first name was Ḥasan, or Aḥmad, or Manṣūr, the latter being more commonly used. He was born in or around the city of Tús in northeastern Iran, possibly in a village called Bāzh. His date of birth is given as any year between A.D. 932 and 941. His father was a country gentleman of the *dihqān* class, the rural landowners. Firdusi's youth was spent in circumstances of financial ease. When still young, he versified individual he-

roic tales, but it was not until the age of thirty-five or forty that he systematically attempted the versification of one of the existing prose *Shahnamahs* of his time, spending between twenty and thirty-five years of his life on this project. During this time, he completed at least two redactions of his work, one in A.D. 994-995, and the other in A.D. 1009-1010.

Apparently Firdusi was hoping to offer his great epic to a king whom he considered worthy of it. Thus, when he finished the first redaction, he kept it for nearly twenty years before finally offering it to King Maḥmūd of Ghazna in the hope of receiving some reward. During this time, the poet had grown old and destitute. It would be incorrect to assume that Firdusi began his project with the intention of offering the finished product to King Maḥmūd or even for the sake of financial gain: From references to the project scattered throughout the epic, it is clear that he began the work at least twenty years before Maḥmūd ascended the throne. That the poet was relatively young and financially secure when he began his versification of individual stories is evident from the introduction to the story of Bīzhan and Manīzha, in which he paints a picture of himself as a young and affluent country gentleman.

In the middle of his great project, however, his life had already changed for the worse. He was old, tired, and poor. When he submitted his poem, completed in A.D. 1010 or 1011, the court disregarded his great effort.

It is known from references within his poem that Firdusi lost a son, who was about thirty-seven years old at the time of his death and probably not very loving toward his father. The classical Persian sources refer to a daughter of the poet as well, but Firdusi himself mentions nothing about her. Firdusi lived some ten or fifteen years after his disappointment with the court of Maḥmūd, busying himself with making corrections to and insertions in the text of his poem, and finally dying in A.D. 1020 or 1025.

Whereas dependable historical data about Firdusi's life are difficult to unearth, a wealth of folklore concerning him exists in the classical accounts of his life. This folk biography of the poet exists not only in the living oral tradition but also within the classical Persian texts. The contents of the classical Persian sources recounting the biography of the poet demonstrate standard folk motifs. They further disregard historical facts by telling of Firdusi's meeting with famous persons long dead when the poet was born. These texts seem to be largely retellings, in courtly prose, of the stories circulating about the poet in the oral tradition of the period of their composition.

According to these sources, the poet began the versification of the *Shahnamah* so that he could supply his daughter with an adequate dowry out of the reward he expected to obtain for it. When he finished the work, he had it transcribed in seven volumes and took it to the court of King Maḥmūd. There, with the help of a great minister, he presented it and it was accepted by the king, who promised the poet sixty thousand gold coins, or one coin per verse. Yet the monarch paid Firdusi only twenty thousand silver coins in the end. The reason for this change of heart on the part of the king was that Firdusi was accused of heresy by those who wished him ill. Firdusi, bitterly disappointed, went to the bath, and on coming out, bought a drink of sherbet and divided the money between the bath man and the sherbet seller. Knowing, however, that he had thus insulted the king, he fled the capital, taking his poem with him. Firdusi sought refuge with a noble Iranian prince, and in his palace he composed a satire of one hundred or more couplets on King Maḥmūd, which he inserted as a preface to the *Shahnamah*. When he recited this satire to his host, the prince, a prudent man, told him: "Maḥmūd is my liege-lord, sell me these one hundred satirical verses for one thousand coins each." The poet agreed, and the prince took possession of the verses and destroyed them. Of the one hundred verses, it is said, only six remain. This account, however, is inconsistent with the fact that the entire text, showing every sign of authenticity, remains.

After this episode, Firdusi retired to his native city of Tús, where he lived his last years in the company of his daughter. Meanwhile, the king had a change of heart and decided to send the poet his just reward. As the camels bearing the royal reward were entering the city through one gate, however, the corpse of Firdusi was being borne forth through another. Such is the account of the classical Persian texts.

Analysis

The *Shahnamah* is a long epic poem which in the great majority of manuscripts comprises between forty-eight thousand and fifty-two thousand distichs. In some later manuscripts the number of distichs reaches fifty-five thousand or more. The *Shahnamah* is composed in the meter of *mutaqarib*, which is made of a line of eight feet in two hemistichs. Whereas the hemistichs of each line have end rhyme, successive lines do not rhyme with one another. As in the case of all other classical Persian poetry, a regular caesura exists between hemistichs. The *mutaqarib* meter, although used in the work of pre-Firdusian poets in different kinds of narrative poetry, came to be almost exclusively reserved for epic poems after Firdusi. The *Shahnamah* has been repeatedly published in Iran, Europe, and India, and has been translated either in whole or abridged form into many languages.

The narrative of the *Shahnamah* can be divided into three parts. The first, a mythological section, begins with the reign of the first king, Kayūmars, and deals with a dynasty of primordial rulers, or demigods, who function as creative kings or culture heroes. They either invent some useful item or teach men a new craft. This group of kings, possibly based on an ancient class of old Iranian gods, are called the *Pīshdādīs* (the ancient creators).

The second part of the epic deals with a series of kings called the *Kayāniyān*. The rule of this group constitutes the purely legendary section of the *Shahnamah*. As all creative activities have already been dealt with by the *Pīshdādīs*, the *Kayāniyān* dynasts mark the beginning of the legendary and the heroic section. Their reign is filled with great wars and lofty deeds of heroes and kings. In this section, men become the main figures of the tales. Although the men encountered in these stories are heroic, or idealized, they are nevertheless completely human, lacking the creative powers of the demigods of the previous section. While they may be sorcerors, makers of illusions, they are not divine.

The third part of the *Shahnamah* is the semihistorical section, which narrates an idealized version of the reign of historical monarchs who ruled Iran from roughly the sixth century B.C. to the Arab conquest in the seventh century A.D. Incorporating a version of the medieval Alexander romances, of which Alexander of Macedonia is the central figure, this semihistorical section is comparatively lacking in action and includes much didactic verse. Recounting the tales which sprang up around the characters of certain historical monarchs of this period, it ends with an account of the fall of the Sasanid Empire (A.D. 224-641) and the Moslem conquest of Iran.

One gets the impression that in composing the narrative of the first two parts, the mythical and the heroic/legendary section, the poet exercised his imagination to a greater extent than when working with the semihistorial section. Scholars such as W. L. Hanaway have suggested that this feature of the *Shahnamah* results from a greater availability of detailed material relating to the historical monarchs of Iran at the time of its composition. The availability of this detailed material limited the extent to which the poet could exercise his imagination. Firdusi repeatedly states that he tried to remain faithful to the sources from which he was working. As a result of his faithfulness to these sources, Hanaway observes, he became more of a historian than an epic poet. In one instance at the end of a long episode in the reign of King Anūshīravān and his grand vizier Būzarjumihr, just before he began to compose the legend of the invention of the game of chess, Firdusi writes:

> Thanks be to the lord of the sun and of the moon
> That I was finally rescued from Būzarjumihr and the king.
> Now that this boring task has come to an end
> Let us begin to relate the tale of Chess.

Thus, the poet seems to have been restricted by a text, one which bored him, but to which he remained faithful.

Amin Banani has observed that Firdusi is in a sense the historian of his race. Firdusi often specifies the source from which he obtained his information, a habit which enables scholars to distinguish between the tales which have an oral origin and those which are based on written sources. The *Shahnamah* narrates, in chronological order, the progression and the evolution of the concept of kingship in the context of the Iranian legendary history. Individual kings may fall, but the line of kings continues uninterrupted. In the course of the steady progression of the institution, kings evolve from divine priest-kings/culture heroes (such as Jamshīd) to monarchs who rule by divine grace through their royal glory (called *farr* in the epic).

A motif that runs through the poem is that of the royal person who is recognized and restored to his rightful place. Sometimes it is a hero who helps establish the new king. The central hero of the epic, Rustam, is one such protector of king and crown. At other times, the king is restored through the efforts of more obscure persons, such as shepherds or blacksmiths. Yet as G. M. Wickens observes, "at no point in the vast cavalcade are we in any serious doubt that the true line of kingship, as distinct from individual kings, will survive." Exploits of individual heroes, such as Rustam's mortal battle with his son Suhrāb, his battles with demons, and the tale of his seven trials, are couched in the overriding motif of the protection of the crown.

Similarly, there is a recurring dramatic tension between good and evil, legitimacy and illegitimacy, and Iranian and non-Iranian. It is in this context that the tale of the perpetuation of the institution of kingship is told. This dramatic tension in the epic is heightened by a skillful use of characterization. There are, as Banani has pointed out, no archetypes in the *Shahnamah*. Every character is so minutely developed that he ceases to be a hero in the abstract and develops instead into an individual with a well-defined pattern of behavior. Through this characterization, "the goodness of the best is possible and the evil of the most wretched is not incredible." Thus, there is no fairy-tale world of black and white, or absolute good and absolute evil, in Firdusi's poem.

Because of its size, the *Shahnamah* is not easily manageable as an object of literary criticism. It should be remembered that the two great classical epics of the Western world, the *Iliad* (c. 800 B.C.) and the *Odyssey* (c. 800 B.C.), together comprise no more than approximately twenty-seven thousand lines. The *Shahnamah's* great length, as well as its relative linguistic inaccessibility, have made it a poor candidate for literary criticism. Thus, Firdusi's poem still remains virtually virgin territory for critical analysis.

Bibliography
Banani, Amin. "Ferdowsi and the Art of Tragic Epic," in *Islam and Its Cultural Divergence*, 1971. Edited by G. L. Tikku.
Ethé, H. *Firdûsî als Lyriker*, 1872-1873.
Hanaway, W. L. "The Iranian Epics," in *Heroic Epic and Saga*, 1978. Edited by F. J. Oinas.
Nöldeke, Theodor. *The Iranian National Epic*, 1930. Translated by Leonid Bogdanov.
Rypka, Jan. *History of Iranian Literature*, 1968. Translated by P. van Popta-Hope.

Wickens, G. M. "The Imperial Epic of Iran: A Literary Approach," in *Iranian Civilization and Culture*, 1971. Edited by C. J. Adam.
Yohannan, J. D. *Persian Poetry in England and America: A Two-hundred-year History*, 1977.

Mahmoud Omidsalar

JEAN FOLLAIN

Born: Canisy, France; August 29, 1903
Died: Quai des Tuileries, France; March 10, 1971

Principal collections

La Main chaude, 1933; *Chants terrestres*, 1937; *Ici-bàs*, 1941; *Usage du temps*, 1943; *Exister*, 1947; *Les Choses données*, 1952; *Territoires*, 1953; *Objects*, 1955; *Des Heures*, 1960; *Appareil de la terre*, 1964; *D'Après tout*, 1967 (*Après Tout: Poems by Jean Follain*, 1981); *Transparence of the World*, 1969; *Espaces d'instants*, 1971; *Présent Jour*, 1978.

Other literary forms

In addition to his poetry, Jean Follain wrote several nonfiction works, notable among which are *Collège* (1973), an account of his secondary-school experiences in the years immediately following World War I, and a history of Peru, *Pérou* (1964).

Achievements

Follain has been hailed as one of the great secret voices of the twentieth century. He addressed man's search for a total union between the known surroundings of his fleeting earthly life and the unknown, absolute finalities of death, space, and time. He succeeded in integrating a world of directly observable facts with the complexities of experiences and powers beyond man's control. His ability to communicate this message by choosing the proper words and by realizing their full semantic value and power in their proper placement in a sentence constitutes his greatest poetic achievement.

Follain was the recipient of several awards for his poetic achievements, including the Mallarmé (1939), the Blumenthal (1941), the Capri (1958), and the Grand Prix de Poésie of the French Academy (1970). He was also made a Chevalier in the French Legion of Honor.

Biography

Jean René Follain was born in Canisy, Normandy, France, on August 29, 1903. His maternal grandfather was a notary and his paternal grandfather was a schoolteacher. His father was a professor at the Collège de Saint-Lô, located in a neighboring town. Follain was to study at this institution, where he was awarded a prize for excellence in philosophy, and subsequently wrote one of his finest prose works, *Collège*, about his experiences there.

In 1921, Jean Follain began his law studies at the law school at Caen and was graduated with honors. As a student, he was also interested in the history of the nineteenth century. In 1923, he went to Paris on a probationary basis with a lawyer and in 1927 became a member of the Paris bar and practiced law until 1952.

Meanwhile, Follain became a part of the group of poets and painters that formed around the review *Sagesse*, founded by Fernand Marc, where he published his first poems. There he met André Salmon, Pierre Reverdy, Pierre MacOrlan, Léon-Paul Fargue, Guegen, Armen Lubin, Max Jacob, Pierre Minet, Madeleine Israel, Georges Duveaux, and Alfred Gaspart. In 1932, he collaborated with several of these writers to publish in literary journals such as *Dernier Carre*, *Feuillets inutiles*, and *Montparnasse*. His first poems were published in the *Nouvelle Revue française*, *Commerce*, *Europe*, and *Cahiers du sud*. Jean Follain married Madeleine Denis, a painter, in 1934.

In 1952, Follain quit the bar to become a court magistrate in Charleville, where he remained until 1961. Between 1957 and 1967, he traveled quite extensively all over the world to countries such as Thailand, Japan, Brazil, Peru, the United States, the Ivory Coast, and Senegal. In 1969, he made a film for educational television called *Canisy, vu par Jean Follain* (Canisy, as seen by Jean Follain), directed by Michel Nicoletti.

Jean Follain was killed accidentally by a car on March 10, 1971, on the Tuileries quay. He had enjoyed an active and distinguished literary career, serving as president of the Friends of Rimbaud; president of the selection committees for the Cazes Prize, the Max Jacob Prize, and the Deux Magots Prize; and Assistant Secretary General of the French PEN Club.

Analysis

Three major collections of Jean Follain's poetry will be discussed: *La Main chaude* (the hot hand), *Chants terrestres* (terrestrial songs), and *Exister* (to exist). Each of these three collections introduces a theme or a stylistic component which is essential to the understanding of Follain's art and is repeated in later works. *La Main chaude* introduced Follain's concept of poetry as a continuum of incongruous events, the role of memory, and the ever present village of Normandy where he spent his youth. *Chants terrestres* presents Follain's preoccupation with words: word choice, syntax, the play of sound, and the power of evocation. *Exister* introduces stylistic patterns that were established for the first time in Follain's poetry and that persisted in later volumes.

La Main chaude is composed of poems whose titles are rather surprising and completely unrelated to one another. They include "Poème glorieux" (glorious poem), "L'Épicier" (the grocer), "Mets" (food), "La Digestion aux cannons" (the digestion of cannons), "La Place publique en été" (the public square in summer), "Ode à l'amour juvenile" (ode to young love), "À la dame du temps de Borgia" (to the lady of Borgia's time), "Milords" (milords), "Les Belles Noyées" (the beautiful drowned ones), "Combat singulier de seigneurs dans la campagne" (the singular combat of lords in the country), and "Appel aux soldats roux" ("Appeal to the Red-haired Soldiers"). At first glance each poem seems to be a disparate fragment sharing no unity of leitmotif or style with the other poems.

The objective of this collection is to conjure the sense of specific recollections of places, occasions, and objects. Although the poems refer to simple evocations, the familiar is suddenly juxtaposed to unexpected or incongruous words or happenings which shatter known and assumed relationships. The harmony of the collection, then, is achieved from the unity of contrasting spectacles.

Follain's intention in constructing the poems in this manner is not to distort language but to convey the message that the world as perceived and the world of visions are one. He creates a web with simple words whose meanings are unclear. He then compares the web he has created to the Normandy countryside of his youth, where echoes can be discerned from unclear depths and where lights shining on objects create an impression of uncertainty as to whether the lights are illuminating the objects or the grouping of the objects is creating the lights.

Memory has a special role in these poems. It is not simply a link between the past and the present. According to Follain, memory is distinct from the past on which it draws, and is what makes the past a key to the mystery that stays with us and does not change: the present. The different evocations presented in the various poems of this collection concern the mystery of the present. They recall the concrete details of his youth in Normandy and give them their form, both luminous and removed at the same time. Simultaneously, the form gives the evocations the aura of a ceremony, another of Follain's preoccupations. He compares the evocations of this poetry collection to an unchanging ceremony heralding some inexorable splendor. For Follain, it is a fulfillment not only of a need for ceremony but also of a fondness for the ceremonious, in which each isolated detail is an evocation of the procession of an immeasurable continuum.

The collection *Chants terrestres* takes its name from the poem "Chants terrestres" in the collection *La Main chaude*. As in the earlier collection, the poems in *Chants terrestres* bear titles that seem unrelated to one another. They include "La Dame à crieurs de pâtés" (the lady at the pâté-vendor's), "L'Adieu du diplomate" (the diplomat's farewell), and "Le Gant rouge" (the red glove). Again, it is not possible to speak of a unifying thread among the individual poems with regard to a structural plan, a rhythmical pattern, or conventional poetic themes such as nostalgia, death, or regret.

These poems, however, are a testimony to Follain's preoccupation with words. As always, the evocations in the poems reflect his tendency to recall the beloved memories of his native village of Canisy in Normandy. He constructs a world with seemingly simple words which encompass the most minute instances of his life, perpetually in search of the elusive reality of things. Nature and humanity in their most universally accepted forms are seized in sentences in which their substance and truth defy classification or definition. Objects become stratified, and the precision of the lines of verse gives life to inert words so that they, too, become objects. Human life becomes stratified as well. Follain constructs it layer by layer, piece by piece, in such a way that the reader is never really able to distinguish the importance of the events discussed because the most obscure, abandoned, and minute details surface to haunt him in these poems.

In the collection *Exister*, thematic and structural patterns begin to emerge for the first time. In these poems, Follain shows that the emotions experienced in the activities of daily life give rise to complexities or contradictions and can be transcended through disengaged contemplation.

The themes are few and recurring: daily life (especially from Follain's childhood) in contact with the power of time, and the possibility of overcoming its restrictions—work, illness, and violence—through the transcendental forces of love, religion, and contemplation. The style is stark, austere, and simple. Rhetorical devices are seldom used. The depth and power of the text depends on the reader's ability to become an active participant and interpreter of its message on many levels. This is consistent with the goal of modern poetry since Arthur Rimbaud.

Two major and several minor structural patterns emerge. The first major structural pattern deals with emotion and can be presented as follows: emotional response, reversal of emotion, suppression of emotion. For example, in "L'Amirauté" (the admiralty), the first section presents a world which excludes the observer: The windows do not give light, the weather is bad, the town is alien, the building is seen from the exterior. The second section is a complete reversal of the darkness and pessimism of the first part: The building is a place of shelter; it is attractively furnished and comes to be associated with the heart. The second part, then, cancels the initial emotion, and the rest of the poem avoids further emotional reactions. The third section of the poem presages death. The emphasis, however, is on the time of passage into death and not on the physical or mental destruction of the person. The vocabulary is abstract, and there is no evocation of suffering. The fourth part of the poem moves to a totally intellectual level.

This pattern recurs in many other poems of this collection and other subsequent collections. For example, in "L'Amitié" (friendship), pride and human contact are replaced by the frustration of departure and then by detached observation of the external world. In "L'Enfant au tambour" (the child with the drum), the threat of death and the oppressiveness of the garden are succeeded by a contempt for war and by a return to the original scene from an intellectual perspective. In "L'Appel du chevalier" (the call of the chevalier), the boy's tedious work gives way to the heroism of the past and then to a suppression of emotion and consciousness in sleep. This irrelevance of emotion is later evidenced in the poem "Postures" (situations), from the collection *Des Heures*.

The second major structural pattern which emerges in Follain's poetry is as follows: immediate, nonimmediate, conflict, solitude, harmony, essential, partial harmony. The manifestations of this pattern, however, vary from poem to poem. In the poem "L'Amirauté," it is constructed in the following way: The first section presents a self-contained world which can be easily comprehended by the reader. The second section shows this immediate perception to be only partially valid, and the interplay of elements beyond the observable plays an important role in this section. The poem ends with a shift to the sphere of the timeless and unconditional truth which is beyond the perceived world, in this case, religion. The opposing elements become reconciled. Examples of the shift from the immediate include the introduction of the elemental forces of wind and night in "L'Appel du chevalier"; the inscription of the hours in the wearing out of the damask in "Paysage des deux ouvriers" (landscape of two laborers); and the wild nature surrounding the enclosure in "Amis d'Austerlitz" (friends from Austerlitz). Another variation is the sudden interruption of one human activity by another one—for example, work after love in "Indifference du bricoleur" (the handyman's indifference), "Chanson de la maîtresse du boulanger" (song of the baker's mistress), "La Brodeuse d'abeilles" (the embroiderer of the bees); or the inverse, love after work, as in "L'Empailleur d'oiseaux" (the taxidermist of birds), and "L'Anecdote" (the anecdote). Yet another technique is the intrusion of psychological elements after establishing an introduction based on the tangible and the concrete, as in "Métaphysique" (metaphysics), and "L'Histoire" (the story). Conflict and solitude appear in many forms. They include the violence of passion and conflict in the kisses of "Les Portraits" (the portraits); solitude in "L'Ennui" (boredom) and "L'Enfant de l'amour" (the love child); torture in "La Matière" ("Matter"); separation in "L'Empailleur d'oiseaux"; the destruction of the flower in "Domaine d'ombre" (the domain of shadow); the duel in "Le Vin du soir" (evening wine); and abandonment in "La Créature" (the creature).

These examples bear witness to the inadequacy of man's attempts to live in harmony with the rest of mankind. Harmony or unity may be achieved in a variety of ways. They include love in "Des Hommes" (men); gentleness in "Le Pain" (the loaf); beauty in "La Pyramide" ("The Pyramid"); familiarity in "Parler seul" ("Speech Alone"); benevolence in "La Vie domestique" ("Domestic Life"); reciprocal influence in "L'Existence" ("Existence"); and a communion between nature and the senses in "La Bête" ("The Beast"). Other variations, however, may occur. At times, the reference to harmony is indirect. For example, in "L'Asie" ("Asia"), the man is eating soup. At first glance, this does not seem to be a universal portrayal of harmony, but it must be noted that in Follain's poetry, food and drink are synonymous with peaceful human interaction. In other cases, conflict and harmony may appear in the same poem—for example, the moans of passion and the soft sounds in "Les Jardins" (the gardens); the conflict between darkness and flames and the harmony which arises from the unity of friends in "Les Amis d'Austerlitz." In still other cases, conflict and solitude are present in the same poem, such as in "Le Vin du soir," as is partial harmony and total harmony (such as compassion and marriage) in "Les Devoirs" (duties), or the loyalty and cooperation between the father and the daughter and the union between the daughter and the leaf (in "Aux Choses lentes," to slow things). The essential is often represented by references to death (as in "Existence"), which is then linked to the world or universe (as in "Les Portraits," "Le Vin du soir," and "Ineffable de la fin," ineffable to the end), or to religion (as in "Balances," balances, and "Le Pas," the step), or to eternity (as in "Natures mortes," still lifes, and "Les Journaliers," the day laborers), or to timelessness (as in "Le Secret," "The Secret"). This structural pattern directly reflects Follain's sensitivity to man's need to integrate his earthly surroundings with the absolutes of death, religion, space, and time.

Again, there is a certain variation and flexibility among the elements of the pattern. For example, in the poem "La Brodeuse d'abeilles," the introductory lines present the theme of physical love. The succeeding lines then place the theme of solitude alongside the theme of passion. Follain's intention here is to show the multidimensional aspect of life, represented by people or objects. In this case, it is clearly communicated that the reader cannot perceive this person in a solely physical context. The poem appeals to his sensitivity and depth of perception and comprehension as well as his ability to integrate the deeper meanings of the relationship between two opposing concepts. In this poem, the ability to shift the perspective of the relationship leads to a coherent conclusion of the text. It is suggested that a union or harmony may be attained on an aesthetic level between the brodeuse and the physical world represented here by her clothing, her jewelry, and other outward manifestations. This can be realized, however, only when the element of passion or direct physical contact is eliminated entirely.

There are also different rates of progress among the various elements which constitute the pattern. For example, the poem "Enfantement" (childbirth) shows some deviation from the order and progress of the pattern. It begins with the contact with the inaccessible and then moves to the tangible, accessible environment of the city. The person is introduced first and then the description of the city is given. Also, the reversal of emotion precedes rather than coincides with the shift from the immediate. Another example occurs in the poem "Le Sapeur" (the sapper). The progression begins normally from calm observation to the agitation of the fish, which reverses the emotional tone. Next, there is a shift to the remote in terms of the fish being nonhuman and being caught. The next element to be introduced, however, has nothing to do with union or harmony. It shifts back to concrete details, which then leads to the nonimmediate, as represented by the sound of the church bells.

Other, simpler patterns also exist. They appear less uniformly but still serve to indicate general tendencies.

The first pattern traces the development from the depiction of the exterior world as a setting for mankind to the presentation of a single person and then to the intangible represented by the soul or God. This pattern occurs in "L'Amirauté," "Domaine d'ombre," and "L'Haine en été" (hate in summer). The development of this pattern is often linked to another one: the introduction of a woman who allows the escape from the immediate, the reference to the soul allowing the reduction of emotional tone and the introduction of the dimension of unity. The latter element of this pattern is especially important because it allows the extension of the poem beyond a point which might otherwise have been final. An example of this occurs in "Apparition de la vieille" (the appearance of the old woman). The harmony brought about by the return of the old woman from the childhood stories seems sufficient to conclude the poem, but a more satisfying conclusion is created by the shift to the intangible—memory—as a culmination of the movement from the person to the objects associated with her. The same occurs in "Les Uns et les autres" (the ones and the others). The expected conclusion was one which would have preserved the severity of the last lines of verse. Instead, however, it ends with a reference to love, after depicting nature, people, and objects. The effect of this tendency is quite compatible with other aspects of Follain's writing—that is, to show a decrease of man's involvement with the exterior world.

The second pattern which emerges is that the poems tend to move from a restrictive view of the world to one which permits penetration into the normally inaccessible, thereby reducing the incommunicability with the world. For example, in "L'Ennui," the poet penetrates into the interior of the body with the song; the body underneath the clothes in "La Mémoire" (the memory) and "Aux Choses lentes"; the invisible heart in "L'Amirauté"; and the knowledge of secrets in "Paysage des deux ouvriers."

The third observation to be made is that the poems tend to move from the temporal to the atemporal, which bridges the past and the present.

Finally, the senses alluded to appear in an order of decreasing materialism: touch, sound, sight, scent. At times, this order motivates the harmonious conclusion of the poem—for example, the intense stare in "Aux Choses lentes" or the peaceful visual conclusion of "Pathétique" in contrast to the noise presented in the introduction. Scent is especially associated with the intangible and the essential, as in "Métaphysique" and "La Journée en feu" (the day on fire).

Follain aims at recording the flow of life rather than imposing a form on it.

His writing reflects his perception of the duality of life. There is a double in-clination to address the known objects of the world and then to subject them to a more abstract vision, thereby giving the reader access to the essential and intangible, which allows him to reconcile these two tendencies. Stylisti-cally, the reader must realize that the patterns underlying Follain's poetry do not impose absolute constraints of any kind. The reader is not able to predict accurately what the succeeding line of verse will say. That is because the im-ages and concepts which constitute the text cannot be construed as examples of a single topic. Follain's poetry overflows with semantic excess; the meaning of the lines is not exhausted by their structural relationships. This allows space within the poem for the unpredictable and the spontaneous, thus free-ing language and experience from automatization and compelling the reader to take an active part in the creation of meaning.

Other major works
NONFICTION: *Paris*, 1935; *L'Épicerie d'enfance*, 1938; *Canisy*, 1942 (English translation, 1981); *Chef-lieu*, 1950; *Pérou*, 1964; *Collège*, 1973; *Selected Prose*, 1985.

Bibliography
Dhôtel, A. *Jean Follain*, 1956.
Gavronsky, Serge, ed. Introduction to *Poems and Texts*, 1969.
Marks, Elaine. *French Poetry from Baudelaire to the Present*, 1965.
York, R. A. "Some Semantic Structures in the Verse of Jean Follain," in *Europe*. No. 53, pp. 384-398.

Anne Laura Mattrella

LOUISE GLÜCK

Born: New York, New York; April 22, 1943

Principal poems and collections
Firstborn, 1968; *The House on Marshland*, 1975; *The Garden*, 1976; *Teh*, 1976; *Descending Figure*, 1980; *The Triumph of Achilles*, 1985.

Other literary forms
Although known primarily for her poetry, Louise Glück occasionally publishes essays about her work and about other poets. Of most interest is "The Dreamer and the Watcher," published in *Singular Voices: American Poetry Today* (1985, edited by Stephen Berg), in which Glück writes quite personally about her poem "Night Song" and about her writing process. Discussing T. S. Eliot in a piece in *The Southern Review* entitled "Fear and the Absent 'Other,'" Glück further identifies her literary affinities.

Achievements
In her career, Glück has consistently written with a spare tautness that has gained for her much respect among her contemporaries and among an older generation of poets and critics. With each book, Glück has deepened her range and her vision; each volume has gained for her additional recognition.

Among her awards are Columbia University's Academy of American Poets Prize (1967), a Rockefeller Foundation grant (1968), a National Endowment for the Arts grant (1969-1970), the Eunice Tietjens Memorial Award (1971), and a Guggenheim Fellowship (1975-1976).

Upon publication of her fourth book, *The Triumph of Achilles*, Glück received the 1986 Poetry Society of America's Melville Cane Award and the National Book Critics Circle Award for poetry. As her work receives continued attention, Glück's importance, and her readership, grows. She is frequently mentioned as one of the best younger American poets.

Biography
Louise Elisabeth Glück was born on April 22, 1943, in New York City, into an upper-middle-class family. She attended Sarah Lawrence College and Columbia University. Married to John Dranow, a professor, Glück has a child, Noah, from a previous marriage. She lives in Vermont with her family and teaches at Williams College.

Analysis
Louise Glück's poetry has been remarkably consistent, both in its controlled, spare, laconic language and in its thematic interests. The universe, as

portrayed in a poem such as "The Racer's Widow," is a violent assault, in which "spasms of violets rise above the mud," and the poet faces loss and estrangement in every human relationship. For consolation there is myth, art, language, and—occasionally—love between a man and a woman. With these consolations, however, there often comes either an oppressive permanence or an admission of terrible impermanence.

Another consistency seen in Glück's work is the refusal to romanticize one's predicament. There is a relentless vision in Glück's four books as well as a gradual loosening of her tight syntactical grip. By the fourth book, Glück can be relentless, sparse, and (newly) vulnerable. The door to emotion has been set ajar. "Birth, not death, is the hard loss," Glück says in her first book. That remains true in the fourth book as well, but the poet has learned how to transform loss into art.

Firstborn, Glück's first book, was published when the author was only twenty-five. The book is arranged in three sections: "The Egg," "The Edge," and "Cottonmouth Country." The titles of the book's sections give little clue to the book's subject matter: the squalor of both city and suburb, domestic and family tension, the coldness between people, and the bitter disappointment of marriage. Fully three-quarters of the volume consists of formal poems, often sonnetlike, which employ a tight, albeit "slant," rhyme scheme.

Typical of the first section is the opening poem, "The Chicago Train," which details the shocking sight of a couple with a child on a commuter train. The writer here spares no detail as she practically recoils from the smell and sight in recollection: "just Mister with his barren/ Skull across the arm-rest while the kid/ Got his head between his mama's legs and slept." The air is "poison," and the couple appear riveted in place, "as though paralysis preceding death/ Had nailed them there." Glück uses colloquial language to heighten the shock: "I saw her pulsing crotch . . . the lice rooted in that baby's hair."

Again and again the speaker is the onlooker, watching with a detachment that is both ironic and bitter. In "Thanksgiving" Glück details the holiday atmosphere in the suburbs where the speaker's sister is circled by "a name-/ less Southern boy from Yale" much the way a cat prowls the driveway outside, "seeking waste." Hardly festive, the day wears on toward "that vast consoling meal." The mother is seen with "skewers in her hands," and the turkey itself is a vision of "pronged death." Glück's vision here is relentlessly dark, the images those of waste and destruction. For this, by implication, the speaker is supposed to give thanks.

The second section, "The Edge," consists entirely of dramatic monologues spoken by various personae. The speaker might be a bride, a cripple, a nun, a child's nurse, or a man speaking about spring. Most powerful here (as well as typical) are "The Edge" and "The Racer's Widow." The former poem foreshadows much that is to come in Glück's work, especially the alienation of the female speaker from her husband. The speaker's heart is tied "to that headboard," and her "quilted cries/ Harden against his hand." The tension between them is palpable; the buried violence threatens to overwhelm the poem: "Over Mother's lace I watch him drive into the gored/ Roasts, deal slivers in his mercy." The speaker is trapped, "crippled with this house."

Also typical is the obsession with the physical body which gives "The Racer's Widow" much of its power. The speaker must face the loss of her husband, and she sees around her the ironic return of spring. Though she claims, "It is not painful to discuss/ His death," the poem's details belie her indifference. The widow states that "his face assaults/ Me, I can hear that car careen again." For consolation, she does not turn to a remembrance of love but to sharp observation and wry comment. Her last view of him was as he lay "draining there." No one can take him from her now, not even his adoring crowds: "And see/ How even he did not get to keep that lovely body." *Firstborn* shows the influence of Robert Lowell, John Berryman, and Sylvia Plath, and it has an obsessiveness that is both interesting and unnatural.

Louise Glück's second book, *The House on Marshland*, is considered by many critics to mark quite an advance over her first book. A slim volume, the book is divided into two sections. Like the poems in *Firstborn*, the poems here are quite short, but the attention to formal qualities of rhyme and meter is now gone. The poems retain a spareness in language and imagery that continues to command respect. The book's subject is the twin loss of paradise and of innocence. The second section, "The Apple Trees," describes a journey away—physically and psychically—from a loved one.

The use of fairy tale and myth in *The House on Marshland* informs some of the book's strongest poems. In "For My Mother," for example, the speaker appears to be able to remember being in the womb, and this myth of Platonic oneness provides the poet with a reason to mourn, now, separateness and division: "It was better when we were/ together in one body." The father arrives, like a prince, and closes the mother's eyelids "with/ two kisses." What is there to mourn? The "absolute/ knowledge of the unborn" and the knowledge that there is no way back.

"Gretel in Darkness" uses a fairy tale to evoke its terror. The poet's method is not simply to retell the tale; the reader feels, and is meant to feel, that a personal story lies behind the retelling. The images here are straight out of Grimm: oven, witch, moonlight, and sugar. "This is the world we wanted," is the haunting first line. Lost in this horrifying world "far from women's arms/ and memory of women," the speaker is comforted by the presence of her brother, Hansel. Sadly, Gretel must admit, "But I killed for you." The end of Gretel seems to be a paranoiac madness from which she reaches futilely for Hansel. The nightmares recur: "We are there still and it is real, real,/ that black forest and the fire in earnest."

One change from *Firstborn* is the predominance of pastoral images in *The*

House on Marshland. These images work well with the theme of the loss of Eden. Such images occur in "The School Children," in which "children go forward with their little satchels." The world the children face, however, is not a pastoral one. They hang their coats on "nails" and the fruit trees bear "little ammunition."

The journey that part 2 of *The House on Marshland* appears to describe begins, appropriately, with a poem titled "The Undertaking." The biblical images here, typical of Glück's work, provide the means for the speaker's escape. The first line, darkly ironic, makes this statement: "The darkness lifts, imagine, in your lifetime." The irony and darkness are discarded as the poem progresses and there seems to be hope, at last, in movement: "Extend yourself—/ it is the Nile, the sun is shining,/ everywhere you turn is luck." The hope, however, is short-lived. The speaker's journey is a lonely one; she must first don a widow's clothes and mourn the lost relationship. Her sole consolation is insight: "I think now it is better to love no one/ than to love you."

It is with her third book, *Descending Figure*, that Glück begins to consider possible ways of redemption. The images and themes, even the method, of *Descending Figure* are by now familiar: images of a garden, a lost world, the body, and lovers. The mood is one of cold appraisal. One must not mourn too easily; one must look around and find what it will take to go on. Glück here begins to use a new structure, a poem in several sections. Actually, she had used this structure in both earlier books, but now it is used more frequently and at what appear to be critical moments. "The Garden," "The Mirror," and "Lamentations" are the three sections of *Descending Figure*.

In the long title poem of the book's first section, "The Garden," the poet insists on further detailing the moments of being cast out of the biblical and mythical "garden." If the speaker can do nothing to prevent these losses, she will accurately detail what she sees—again, the impulse of the onlooker (the artist), who finds consolation in the recording of grief. The titles of the five sections of "The Garden" are "The Fear of Birth," "The Garden," "The Fear of Love," "Origins," and "The Fear of Burial." "The Fear of Birth" harks back to "For My Mother" in *The House on Marshland*, but there is the added resignation of these lines: "And then the losses,/ one after another,/ all supportable." The poet refuses to overdramatize her situation: Loss must be bearable; it will be borne.

Opening with "Epithalamium," the book's second section at first seems to contain poems with the most hope. The poems here bespeak a new beginning: marriage and new love. Almost immediately, however, the darkness intrudes. After the ceremony, there "begins/ the terrible charity of marriage"; the rightness of the word "charity" and its coldness keep the Glück tradition of spareness and relentless vision. The speaker's happiness is tinged with the sadness of former loves when her new husband must reassure her: "*Here is my hand that will not harm you.*"

The second section ends with a poem called "Happiness," in which two lovers lie in bed together. The speaker watches from a distance, watches how the "sunlight/ pools in their throats." The "I" here seems to be the alter ego of the female lover; when she opens her eyes, the "I" inhabits her rather than being outside her. This split between the conscious and unconscious self is another theme in Glück's work. There is also an interesting gentleness that the poems in *Descending Figure* begin to show. Perhaps the universe is not as hostile as formerly seen, the reader begins to think. "Happiness" ends with an image of the sun "the burning wheel/ passes gently over us."

Whatever hope the second section appeared to pose, the poet seems to find herself back in a world of loss and estrangement in the third section, appropriately titled "Lamentations." Here the poet begins to propose as possibilities for redemption both art and myth. She says as much in "Autumnal," which describes the harvest of fallen leaves and how they are carted off or burned: "So waste is elevated/ into beauty." There is also a bitter consolation to be found in the woman's role: "you give and give, you empty yourself/ into a child. And you survive/ the automatic loss." It is the woman who bends, accommodates, shapes herself to others: "At the grave,/ it is the woman, isn't it, who bends,/ the spear useless beside her." The descending figure of the book's title is, in one sense, God—who may take pity on those sorrowing down below. The poet longs for that vision, that distance from her suffering: "How beautiful it must have been,/ the earth, that first time/ seen from the air."

With her fourth volume, *The Triumph of Achilles*, Louise Glück reached a maturity of style and voice that is unusual for a poet of her age. Her vision of the world has remained constant in many ways, but there is a change in the poet's attitude toward herself and thus toward her readers. The poems proceed with much the same method—using myth and art to discuss one's life—but in this book the passion seems more evident, the loss more immediate, the stakes more critically viewed. If the previous volume has a cool tone, this volume is still hot from the artistic forge. There are three epigraphs at the beginning of *The Triumph of Achilles*: one is unidentified, one is from Saint Ignatius and focuses on being a prisoner to suffering, and the third is from Bruno Bettelheim and focuses on knowing good from evil. Clearly these identify the book's predominant themes.

"Mock Orange," the book's first poem, is the harrowing lament of a woman who finds the sex act to be humiliating and unsettling. Sex is an indignity which she hates, "the man's mouth/ sealing my mouth, the man's paralyzing body— . . ." Once again, the poet is preoccupied with the body and with the inevitable alienation she feels from the lover. Yes, the lovers are momentarily "fused," but only by the "premise of union"; the "tired antagonisms" remain.

"Metamorphosis," another important poem, shows the poet's interest in finding, again, redemption. Perhaps suffering can be the means to a metamorphosis, in this case the suffering felt at watching a parent die. The poet's tenderness is reined in, by now something to be expected in Glück's work, but her restraint is more evident than in previous poems and books. The poem's third section, "For My Father," is surely meant to recall the piece to the mother in *Firstborn*. The remarkably parallel statement here is to the father: "I'm going to live without you/ as I learned once/ to live without my mother." The directness of Glück's utterance is newfound and hard-won; it shows in the rest of the poems as well.

The references to Greek myths are frequent and important. Glück alludes to Apollo, to Hyacinth, and to Patroclus and Achilles. The poems in which these references are made are some of the volume's finest: Glück is using the myths, the gods, to tell her stories and simultaneously is turning her suffering into its own "myth." For Glück, what is triumphant, finally, about Achilles is his feeling for another, a feeling which is both his doom and his "triumph": "he was a man already dead, a victim/ of the part that loved,/ the part that was mortal."

Finally, however, it is Glück's long poem "Marathon" which is the crowning achievement of *The Triumph of Achilles*. It provides the book's focus; it shows the speaker being made mortal by suffering as Achilles was made mortal. Glück's vision is still relentless, but here her focus is turned on herself in the most personal of ways. The poems are not confessional—few personal details are given—yet they are deeply felt. For all of their distance, they seem torn from the heart. The process begins with "Last Letter" (section 1): "When I tried to stand again, I couldn't move,/ . . . Does grief change you like that?" The speaker longs to believe in such a transformation, but fears it is transitory, illusory, as is so much else: "What happens afterward/ occurs far from the world, at a depth/ where only the dream matters/ and the bond with any one soul/ is meaningless; you throw it away."

Such poems have come a long way from the wrenched syntax of the "sonnets" of *Firstborn*. Glück has reached a sophistication of theme and method that enables her to turn her vision to events of daily life and render them, truly, into art. What in *Firstborn* Glück struggled to say, in *The Triumph of Achilles* she writes of with grace and power. The intervening books show her progress toward this achievement.

The work of Louise Glück has shown a steady unfolding. Its attention to language and theme has been consistent, as has its view of the world. As her work has become more open, more lyrical, nothing of its austerity and perseverance has been lost. As Glück herself notes in "Song of Invisible Boundaries" (section 8 of "Marathon"): "Finally, this is what we craved,/ this lying in the bright light without distinction—/ we who would leave behind/ exact records."

Bibliography

Bedient, Calvin. "Birth, Not Death, Is the Hard Loss," in *Parnassus*. IX (Spring/Summer, 1981), pp. 168-186.

——————. "Four American Poets," in *Sewanee Review*. LXXXIV (Winter, 1976), pp. 351-364.

Glück, Louise. "Fear and the Absent 'Other,'" in *The Southern Review*. XXI (Autumn, 1985), pp. 1139-1163.

Hirsch, Edward. "The Watcher," in *The American Poetry Review*. XV (November/December, 1986), pp. 33-36.

Stitt, Peter. "Contemporary American Poems: Exclusive and Inclusive," in *The Georgia Review*. XXXIX (Winter, 1985), pp. 849-863.

Vendler, Helen. "Sociable Comets," in *The New York Review of Books*. XXVIII (July 16, 1981), p. 24.

Patricia Clark

PAAVO HAAVIKKO

Born: Helsinki, Finland; January 25, 1931

Principal poems and collections

Tiet etäisyyksiin, 1951; Tuuliöinä, 1953; Synnyinmaa, 1955; Lehdet lehtiä, 1958; Talvipalatsi, 1959 (The Winter Palace, 1968); Puut, kaikki heidän vihreytensä, 1966; Selected Poems, 1968; Neljätoista hallitsijaa, 1970; Runoja matkalta salmen ylitse, 1973; Kaksikymmentä ja yksi, 1974; Runot 1949-1974, 1975; Runoelmat, 1975; Viiniä, kirjoitusta, 1976; Rauta-aika, 1982 (The Age of Iron, 1982); Kullervon tarina, 1983; Sillat: Valitut Runot, 1984.

Other literary forms

Paavo Haavikko is one of the most prolific Finnish writers; he has published more than fifty books in his native language and has written equally masterfully in every literary genre. He made his debut in the 1950's with collections of lyrical poems, and in the following decades he published novels, short stories, epic poems, and plays, in addition to which he has written two opera librettos, based on his plays: Ratsumies (1974; The Horseman, 1974) and Kuningas lähtee Ranskaan (1984; The King Goes Forth to France, 1984). The music for both operas was composed by Aulis Sallinen, and they were first performed at the Savonlinna Opera Festival in Finland. They have since been staged in West Germany, New Mexico, and London's Covent Garden. History has provided some of the major themes for Haavikko's poetry and plays, and he has also published nonfiction in that field. His literary work includes collections of aphorisms, scripts for films, and radio and television plays. Some of Haavikko's work has been translated into English, French, German, and Swedish.

Achievements

From the very start of his literary career, Haavikko has never sought favor with the reading public; in fact, he has rebelled against the thought that art and literature should be "pretty" or popular; for him, a poet's greatest achievement is the writing itself. His unique contributions in the forefront of post–World War II literature were early recognized, and consequently he was awarded the Finnish Government Literature Prizes for his work in the years 1958, 1960, 1962, 1964, 1966, 1969, 1970, and 1974. In 1966, Haavikko received the Aleksis Kivi Prize (which is named after the writer of the first Finnish-language novel, published in 1870), and in 1969 he was awarded the Finnish Government Drama Prize and an honorary doctorate from the University of Helsinki. A symposium was held in 1976 in Joensuu, Finland, at which the participants, who represented the academic disciplines of literature, history, political science, and economics, analyzed and examined Haavikko's work. In 1978, he received the Order of the White Rose of Finland for his literary achievements. Haavikko's four-part television drama, *Rauta-aika* (based on his poem), which has also been published in book form, won for him the Prix d'Italia as best European television series of the year 1982. Only a sampling of Haavikko's poetry, plays, and other literary work has been translated into other languages, largely because Finnish is sometimes considered an "exotic" language, since it does not belong to the Indo-European language group. As Philip Binham, one of the English-language translators of Haavikko's work, has pointed out, it is particularly difficult to render in translation the subtlety and rhythm of Haavikko's language; indeed, Haavikko's poetic expression has often posed problems even to native Finnish readers. In the 1960's, however, some of Haavikko's work began to appear in translations, and based on these, he was awarded the Neustadt International Prize for Literature in 1984.

Biography

Paavo Juhani Haavikko was born on January 25, 1931, in Helsinki, the capital city of Finland, a city in which the poet has lived all of his life and which he has always found attractive and exciting, and about which he also has written a book. Haavikko's father was a businessman, and after his high school graduation in 1951 and customary service in the Finnish Army, Haavikko also entered the business world, working as a real estate agent. Like many Finnish modern poets, Haavikko has consistently maintained a second profession alongside his literary career; in fact, he believes that an author who is solely occupied by writing loses touch with the realities of life. Indeed, in his poetry Haavikko never seems to be an observer on the sidelines; he appears to be in the middle of the events and freely uses concepts and imagery from commerce and the business world in his creative writing, most of which he has done on weekends. From the late 1960's, Haavikko has been the literary editor for a major Finnish publishing company and a literary consultant to several printing presses.

In 1955, Haavikko married poet and writer Marja-Liisa Vartio; she died in 1966. Haavikko and literary historian Ritva Rainio Hanhineva were married in 1971.

Haavikko has always, in his work, shown a great skepticism toward any political or philosophical ideology: "If the philosophy is wrong, all deeds become crimes." Varying political ideologies are much the same in Haavikko's eyes: "Socialism! so that capitalism could begin to materialize./ Capitalism! the Big Money!/ They spend their evenings in a small circle,/ hand in hand, fingers linked in fingers, and like to remember their youth." Haavikko's stand is that of an anti-utopian realist, to whom an individual's uniqueness and freedom are the highest values; in his view, man has "perhaps a two percent margin" in the maze of corporations, institutions, and governments and their bureaucracies, or simply in the complexity of life and in facing fate. To Haavikko, the most positive aspects of life are nature, the biological world, and the human mind.

In his own country, Haavikko is generally seen as a conservative and patriotic poet, who paradoxically has often through his work questioned some of his society's most cherished myths and values.

Analysis

Paavo Haavikko belongs to the generation of Finns who experienced World War II as children, growing into maturity in the immediate postwar years, a period which in many ways constituted a watershed for the Finnish society, in which a major, still ongoing culture change began in the 1950's. The largely rural society (seventy percent of the population lived in the countryside until the postwar years) had been a major source of literary themes for the prewar writers and poets. Finnish as a creative literary language was still relatively new, Finland having been part of the Swedish kingdom for six hundred years and of the Russian empire for one hundred years, during which time Swedish was the language of culture and education. In the nineteenth century, a smoldering nationalistic movement gained impetus, under the influence of the ideas of the German philosopher Johann Gottfried von Herder, and, in 1863, the Finnish language was granted equal status with Swedish. The following decades produced an abundance of writers of Finnish-language literature, which reflected Continental European trends and the "national neo-Romanticism." The latter was partly a product and a culmination of the struggle for the country's independence, which was gained in 1917.

World War II broke the continuity of Finnish literature. The war experience and the resulting circumstances and conditions caused a reevaluation of prewar ideas and ideology. It was a time of careful assessments of history and of the present possibilities for the country's political, economic, and cultural survival. New influences from the Anglo-Saxon world, especially in the form of translated literature, reached Finland, and in the late 1940's a new generation of poets entered the literary scene.

Many of the representatives of the new poetry experimented with a number of styles, not immediately finding one distinctly their own. Not so with Haavikko. His first poetry collection, *Tiet etäisyyksiin* (the roads to far away), published in 1951, when the writer was twenty years old, showed him following his own instincts and philosophy about the nature of poetry and of language, mankind, and the world. The poets of the new era of modernism strove for fresh forms of expression, rejecting the preexisting poetic structures and in their themes avoiding any sort of ideology or sentimental self-analysis. Haavikko took these aims further than anybody else. He constructed his poems in nonrhyming, rhythmical language, attempting to get as close as possible to the spoken idiom. He set out to examine the "eternal issues" of love, death, the identities of man and woman and their relationship to each other, and the possibilities for the individual human being in an ever-changing world, in which the human character, man's psyche and behavior, and his actions and passions stay the same. Haavikko also set out to find linguistic expressions which would most clearly and honestly define and depict all these phenomena. Haavikko sees language as restricting man's perception of human processes and thoughts, even causing his estrangement from the realities of life. In an early poem, he speaks of the limitations of his native language: "Finnish isn't a language, it's a local custom/ of sitting on a bench with hair over your ears,/ it's continual talking about the rain and the wind." In another poem, he speaks of his own role as a poet in improving the existing modes of expression: "I'm on a journey into the language/ of this people." On the other hand, Haavikko has also realized the advantages of his mother tongue, whose structure allows a compactness and a poetic construction in which "the relations between one thing and another, the world picture, are the most important elements." Haavikko's last observation pertains to Finnish folk poetry, a rich warehouse of themes and frames for his work; Haavikko set out to clear from literary expression all empty rhetoric and pathos, taking words, which he perceives as "treacherous symbols," and using them to find the truth. In this never-ending search for truth—for ultimately there are no answers—Haavikko creates poetry in fluid combinations of images and concepts, taken from nature, everyday urban surroundings, mythology and tales, and classical antiquity as well as more recent history.

The structures of Haavikko's poems are complex, multifaceted, and multilayered. His lyrics have been compared to rich tapestries, to top rough-edged crystals, and to modern Finnish objets d'art. All these descriptions are fitting, and perhaps one more could be added, a concept taken from nature: Haavikko's poems could be seen as many items frozen in a block of ice; the block may melt, the ice become water and part of the continuous life cycle, and the pieces encased may become recognizable and identifiable, or the iceblock may remain an enigmatic, opaque object, beautiful to contemplate but giving no answers to the viewer. Haavikko's poetry has also been likened to music, its sound obviously being most resonant in the original language. In the end, the responsibility for an interpretation and an understanding of the poet's ideas is left to each individual reader.

In an interview, Haavikko has stated that, when composing poems, he always lets the entire poem take shape in his mind, before writing it down, for fear that the words will take over and begin to lead a life of their own. He may use concrete images or paradoxes, weave the thread of human experience through several time periods, illuminating the present through the past and speaking about the future at the same time:

The Greeks populated Mycenae,
the poets of Rome in their turn
filled Greece with shadowless beings,

there is no night when no one wrote
someone's writing into these rooms too,
poem-dressed lovers, when we are not saying

The room is not free but full of breathing
and embraces, light sleeping, hush,
be still, so we don't wake, someone's writing
into the night.

For Haavikko, there is no separation of time and space; man's existence, his behavior, his interactions, and in the end his fate, remain the same.

The collections of poems published by Haavikko in the 1950's firmly established him as the most original and brilliant representative of the modernist group. The nine-poem collection *The Winter Palace* is a synthesis of all the themes which had preoccupied Haavikko in his previous work. The collection derived its name from the imperial Russian palace in St. Petersburg, and within this frame of a center for historical events, the poet examines the nature of art, poetry, love and death, and political power. The first poem begins: "Chased into silver,/ side by side:/ The images./ To have them tell you." The poet warns the reader to be alert, to enter this experience with an open mind, and through personal perception to organize the kaleidoscope, which will follow, into a comprehensible whole.

As an eighteen-year-old high school student, Haavikko had read T. S. Eliot, who without doubt pointed him the way "into the unknown." At about that time, Haavikko wrote a poem which served as a declaration of his intentions: "Bridges are taken by crossing them/ Each return is a defeat." From then on Haavikko continued crossing bridges, and *The Winter Palace* has been mentioned as the Finnish *Waste Land*:

This poem wants to be a description,
And I want poems to have
only the faintest of tastes.
Myself I see as a creature, hopeful
As the grass.

These lines are almost improbable
This is a journey through familiar speech
Towards the region that is no place.

After *The Winter Palace*, Haavikko turned to writing prose. He had already in his earlier collections of lyrical poetry, particularly in *Synnyinmaa* (native land) and *Lehdet lehtiä* (leaves, pages), dealt with the issues of the politics of the day, especially examining the events during the war and its aftermath, illuminating and assessing, through similar historical events, the actions and reasoning of the principal Finnish statesmen, as well as probing the Finnish national identity and attitudes. Historical themes in general increased in Haavikko's work considerably in the next two decades; seventeen of his plays are within a historical framework. Haavikko continued questioning the essence of power, the motives and aims of those wielding it, and how they influence the world, in particular the fate of the individual, who is tied to a historical situation. Most of Haavikko's novels and plays deal with social problems and issues involving the state, the church, the judiciary and taxation systems, diplomacy, commerce, and the family unit. In these contexts, the writer examines the problem of communication, how different social roles are manifested in the speech act, and the ways in which language is used and manipulated by various interest groups and individuals. For Haavikko, nonverbal communication is much less dangerous than verbal communication; generally, everything bad derives from words: "And so out of words grow war/ and war becomes real/ it eats men, horses, corn,/ fire devours houses, years gnaw on man." An individual's odds for survival, however, are increased if he is aware of and can master the largest possible body of the various ways of communicating and knows the requirements that certain social roles impose on speech. Women's language is different from that of men: "It is pleasant to listen to, difficult to speak,/ impossible to understand." One of Haavikko's themes is that of a woman's greater strength, compared with that of a man; men desire power, they plan and develop; women have more common sense and keep everything together, and they steer life along healthier lines. Haavikko's writing implies that the cruelties and injustices of the world usually derive from men's actions. There is a deep, underlying pessimism in his prose, but it is lightened by a special brand of humor, the Finnish "gallows humor," which is a mixture of absurdity and irony and which, alongside more classical satire, is embedded in all the poet's work.

In 1966, Haavikko published his only collection of lyrical poems of that decade, *Puut, kaikki heidän vihreytensä* (trees in all their verdure), which in its direct and clear simplicity remains one of his major works, alongside the collections of 1973 and 1976, when he returned briefly to lyrical poetry, dealing with new and different subject matter. Haavikko's interest was turning increasingly toward economics and history, particularly Finnish history and toward Byzantium, both of which provided him with a background against which to examine the fate of rulers, political factions and their intrigues, and man's quest for power and riches. In short, Haavikko could study the entire world in microcosm. The world as expressed in Haavikko's poetry is illogical, it is a paradox, and it is merciless; once an individual comes to terms with this understanding of the world, however, "looking it into the eyes every moment," it is possible for him to live without fear and, characteristic of Haavikko, without hope.

Haavikko's epic poem *Neljätoista hallitsijaa* (fourteen rulers) consists of fifteen cantos, based on the events described in the chronicle of Michael Psellus, a tenth century Byzantine court historian. The first four songs are the poet's first-person prologue, after which he merges with Psellus, through whose eyes he draws the Byzantine worldview. The main themes are, as in much of Haavikko's work, the position of the individual, who cannot escape his fate though he himself also shapes that fate, and history repeating itself over and over again, the historical process devouring the individual, who searches for permanence but finds it an illusion. In this cyclical world, however, in which everything is in flux, an individual must, in some way, influence the outcome of the events, and he must try to combat evil, which Haavikko includes in his term "fascism." The word represents to the poet, among some other aspects, all accumulated stupidity, in which an initially small, annoying amount may become dangerous. In Haavikko's terminology, the opposite of fascism is pragmatic caution in all human endeavor, perceiving realities, being prepared for the worst, all the while maintaining the ability to function and staying alive.

Haavikko's stylistic and thematic concerns and his preoccupation with human cognitive processes are expressed in the following lines: "Every house is built by many people/ and is never through,/ history and myth are told and told again/ contradicting halls lead to understanding." These concerns led the poet to begin telling old Finnish myths anew, by rewriting one of the central cycles of the *Kalevala*, a compilation of folk poetry which was collected and edited by Elias Lönnrot and first published in 1835. This compilation became the national epos and had a great impact on the national culture, inspiring writers, painters, and composers, such as Jean Sibelius. Haavikko's version of the Sampo cycle (which in folk tradition centers on a mythical talisman which brings good fortune), *Kaksikymmentä ja yksi* (twenty and one), takes place in Byzantium, where, according to the poet, Finnish Vikings went in search of a coin-minting machine, which they hoped to plunder. Haavikko continued following a partially economic point of view in his subsequent recreations of the world of the folk poetry, which he inhabited with antiheroes, people modeled after those of modern times, while at the same time depicting the archetypal man. The poet has acknowledged his indebtedness to his native oral traditions, which have provided him with an inheritance of the world of the epic, and he has interpreted that world in the language and with the techniques of the twentieth century.

As Kai Laitinen and others have pointed out, Haavikko's writing is deeply rooted in a cultural and geographic area and its social and historical processes; the poet's perspectives are those of a European and of a citizen of a small European nation. At times, the author's work reflects not only an individual's loneliness and feeling of being different but also an entire nation's sense of isolation and separateness. Besides that, Haavikko has had much to say about the most central and universal issues of human existence—the identity of an individual, the relativity of values, and the difficulty of living—and about the concepts of society, history, and literature. He has said it through complex anachronisms, analogies, and "precise ambiguities," all the while refining and defining language, which in his work, especially in the operettos and the aphorisms, has become increasingly sparse and intense. He has moved freely between literary genres, letting the subject matter determine the form of his writing. From the early metaphysical lyrical poetry through the plays, opera librettos, epic poetry, aphorisms, and historical analyses, Haavikko's work has continued to create lively debate, providing new perspectives and new insights through its oracle-like visions and presentation of world structures. In the meantime, Haavikko continues to search for "himself, woman, god, tribe, old age and the grave" and the uniqueness of things, "not wanting generalizations, either, but trying to make things concrete." For Haavikko, one who generalizes is a fool, and in his work the poet never pontificates. He merely invites the reader onto new paths, to which he has opened the way.

Other major works

PLAYS: *Münchhausen, Nuket,* 1960; *Lyhytaikaiset lainat,* 1966; *Audun ja jääkarhu,* 1966; *Freijan pelto,* 1967; *Ylilääkäri,* 1968 (*The Superintendent,* 1978); *Agricola ja kettu,* 1968; *Sulka,* 1973; *Harald Pitkäikäinen,* 1974; *Ratsumies,* 1974 (libretto, music by Aulis Sallinen; *The Horseman,* 1974); *Agricolan linja,* 1975; *Näytelmät,* 1978; *Viisi pientä draamallista tekstiä,* 1981; *Kuningas lähtee Ranskaan,* 1984 (libretto, music by Sallinen; *The King Goes Forth to France,* 1984).

TELEPLAY: *Rauta-aika,* 1982 (adaptation of his poem).

NONFICTION: *Puhua, vastata, opettaa,* 1972; *Ihmisen ääni,* 1977; *Kansakunnan linja,* 1977; *Ikuisen rauhan aika,* 1981; *Pimeys,* 1984;

MISCELLANEOUS: *Romaanit ja novellit,* 1981 (novels and short fiction).

Bibliography
Binham, Philip. "Dream Each Within Each: The Finnish Poet Paavo Haavikko," in *Books Abroad.* L, no. 2 (1976), pp. 337-341.
_____. "A Poet's Playground: The Collected Plays of Paavo Haavikko," in *World Literature Today.* LIII, no. 2 (1979), pp. 244-245.
Dauenhauer, Richard. "The View from the Aspen Grove: Paavo Haavikko in National and International Context," in *Snow in May: An Anthology of Finnish Writing, 1945-1972,* 1978. Edited by Philip Binham and Richard Dauenhauer.
Haavikko, Paavo. "What Has the Kalevala Given Me?" in *Books from Finland.* I (1985), pp. 65.
Hart, Maija-Liisa. "Paavo Haavikko Takes a Walk in Helsinki," in *Look at Finland.* I (1986), pp. 36-43.

Kinnunen, Aarne. *Syvä nauru: Tutkimus Paavo Haavikon dramatiikasta*, 1980.

Laitinen, Kai. *Literature of Finland: An Outline*, 1985.

Sihvo, Hannes. *Soutu Bysanttiin: Paavo Haavikon metodin ja maailmanku- van tarkastelua*, 1977.

Viksten, Vilho. "Analogian ja relaation mestari," in *Parnasso*. V (1965), pp. 244-255.

Tuula Stark

HAFIZ

Born: Shiraz, Persia; c. 1320
Died: Shiraz, Persia; 1389 or 1390

Principal poem

The *Divan* was composed and edited by Hafiz, possibly as early as 1368; it contains much of the poetry that can safely be assigned to Hafiz. There are existing manuscript copies of his poems from the first quarter of the fifteenth century. The first printed collection in Persian appeared in 1791. The first English translations of individual poems were performed by Sir William Jones, in *A Grammar of the Persian Language* (1771), and other works published in 1797 and 1799. Other translators published selections from Hafiz's works in 1774, 1787, 1795, 1800, and in subsequent years. The first English-language compilation laying any claim to completeness, *The Dīvān*, was published by H. Wilberforce Clarke in 1891.

Other literary forms

Apart from manuscripts he is known to have copied, the only existing works for which Hafiz's authorship has been established are poetry. Other Persian writers have referred to prose works by the author, but no such writings are extant.

Achievements

In the hands of Hafiz, the lyric poem, or *ghazal*, reached its highest level of development as the author combined technical virtuosity with sublime poetic inspiration. With subtle, meticulous craftsmanship, this literary form, which otherwise could be reproached as stilted and artificial, reached under Hafiz the zenith of its expressive qualities. The author's spiritual and romantic quests are evoked in delicate tones that are admirably suited to the Persian metric forms. The exquisite aspects hidden in everyday experience merge with elements of the author's larger vision, which is tinged with mystical yearnings in places as well. It is a measure also of Hafiz's unexpected depth that simple odes, with their seemingly transparent imagery, upon closer examination reveal multiple patterns of meaning that reflect the timeless qualities of daily joys and sorrows. At its finest, the poetical raiment of Hafiz's work displays meticulous, seemingly effortless construction as the diverse, multicolored threads of thought and feeling are interwoven in bright and perennially appealing designs.

In addition to the odes, or lyric poetry, Hafiz wrote elegies (*qasa'id*), of which two are included in his collected verse; he also wrote a certain number of shorter works (*qita'*) and at least forty-two quatrains (*rubai'yat*). These forms, with their own harmonic and metrical requirements, demonstrate the author's attainments with other kinds of poetry. Although outwardly the entire corpus of Hafiz's known work does not exemplify a single unitary or holistic theme, the various elements of his poetical canon combine patterns and topics that are in keeping with the standards of versification upheld by classical Persian prosody.

During his lifetime, Hafiz earned the title *khwajah*, or learned man. It would appear that he was honored, as well as tolerated, by some of the rulers of his day. The claims of some writers that, possibly with the support of the shah, he was at one time a professor of Koranic exegesis at an institution of religious learning have not been confirmed. Hafiz never obtained an appointment as a court poet; while he gained some renown during his lifetime, the honor with which his name is held was conferred largely by subsequent generations of poets and literary men.

Biography

Little is known with exactitude about the life of the great poet, born Shams al-Din Muhammed. Even the outlines of his biography are uncertain, and rather few details may safely be accepted from the historical works and literary studies that deal with his age. Hafiz's own work has been examined for hints and allusions that would reveal more about his personal circumstances or his station in society. Some poems contain dedications, which would indicate some of the political figures to whom they were addressed; some works conclude with chronograms, by which numerical values assigned to characters yield certain dates. Nevertheless, such evidence may be gleaned only from some writings, mainly from the middle period of the author's life. The entire problem has been exacerbated by the incompleteness of existing manuscript texts, the earliest of which were transcribed possibly twenty years after the poet's death; other texts date from thirty to sixty years or more after Hafiz's own time. In its turn, the lack of a single accepted body of work limits the usefulness of biographical research based on Hafiz's own writings. Tantalizing suggestions, which can be neither proved nor disproved, add an aura of the legendary to the rather sparse data that have been established beyond doubt.

It would seem that the poet's father was a merchant who moved from Isfahan to Shiraz under conditions suggesting family circumstances of relative poverty. The author was probably born about 1320, the date most often mentioned by the pertinent authorities, though some works cite 1317 and others suggest 1325 or 1326. When he was quite young, his father died; nevertheless, he evidently received a thoroughgoing education. To his given name, Shams al-Din Muhammad, was added the epithet Hafiz, which is bestowed upon those who have learned the Koran by heart. There are enough learned references in his poetry, to Arabic theology and Persian literature, to suggest that he gained familiarity with classical subjects relatively early in life.

During his youth, Hafiz is reputed to have served as a dough maker in a baker's shop and as a manuscript copyist. Some of Hafiz's poems were dedicated to Qiwam al-Din Hasan (died 1353), who served at times as vizier to a local ruler who had arisen during the waning years of the Mongol period of Persia's history. While Hafiz thus wrote some of his most important works by about the age of thirty, political upheaval, and the struggle between rival dynasties for the control of Shiraz, probably complicated the poet's life. During the reign of Mubariz al-Din Muhammad (died 1358), religious differences arose between the Sunni ruler and the Shi'ite citizenry; Hafiz still may have enjoyed protection from one of the shah's ministers.

The most important creative period for the author evidently occurred early in the reign of Jalal al-Din Shah Shuja' (died 1384); it would seem that Hafiz's renown spread across Persia, into the Arab lands, and as far as India. There is some evidence that he was invited to serve other rulers, though he declined, as he was notoriously reluctant to leave his native city. He may well have been married; one poem from 1362 or 1363 seems to have been meant as a eulogy for a deceased son.

It is thought that Hafiz lost favor at the Shah's court, and remained in some disgrace from 1366 to 1376; though the grounds remain obscure, it has been alleged that the author's exuberant celebration of the joys of wine and love disquieted those in political power. He may have spent a year or two in other Persian cities, such as Isfahan or Yazd. One account, which is generally deemed apocryphal, has the poet undertaking a journey to India, only to turn back at Hormuz, on the Persian Gulf, from fear of the open sea. Much of the rest of Hafiz's life, so far as is known, was spent in Shiraz. He may have regained some favor with patrons in the government; whether he held any academic position is unclear. There are no records, in any event, of his appointment to any educational institutions in Shiraz. Moreover, it is quite possible that the recurrent complaints about personal poverty, which appear at intervals throughout the *Divan*, actually did reflect the poet's own situation to some extent.

The last years of the author's life occurred during the unsettled period that followed Timur's invasion of Persia. While Hafiz may have been assisted sporadically by members of the earlier government who remained in Shiraz, by some accounts, which historical research has actually tended to confirm, he met with the great conqueror in 1387 and half-seriously set forth his justification for placing love's attractions above the control of provinces and nations. Hafiz died in 1389 or 1390, and subsequently his tomb became one of the most celebrated monuments in Shiraz, at which later generations of literary aficionados would gather.

Analysis
While Hafiz's lyrics have widely been considered the most nearly perfect

examples of this genre, his poetry has an ineffable quality which seemingly eludes exact analysis. For that matter, specialists have contested whether cohesiveness may be found in specific poems, and whether shifting levels of meaning may account for abrupt transitions in topical content. In a technical sense, however, the felicitous union of diction, metric length, emphasis, and rhyme is everywhere in evidence. Hafiz's appeal is veritably universal: Romantic, often lighthearted, and alive to the joys of this world, his poems reveal sublime attributes in the experiences and perceptions felt on this earth. It is from this point of departure that metaphysical or theological speculation may begin, but while concerns of this sort are taken up in the author's writings, they are far from obtrusive. Indeed, in some connections they may appear inscrutable. The poet's philosophical interests, though immanent, do not impede the measured, melodious currents that guide his thoughts across specific series of lines.

In some quarters Hafiz was reproached as a hedonist and a libertine; he has been charged as well with the use of blasphemous motifs, both in his attitude toward the clergy and for poetic symbolism suggesting affinities with mystical schools of thought. The cast of mind revealed in his verse is effulgent, and slightly irreverent; in calling for the wine bowl or in depicting woman's beauty, however, he shows little that is immoderate or overly indulgent. He may seem bedazzled, but he is not really helpless, in the face of love's charms or the lure of the tavern; at least the precision with which his verses are delivered would suggest controlled self-awareness. There are some rhetorical flights of fancy which most readers probably will tolerate. The features of women conjured forth in Hafiz's poems point to an idealized romantic conception, the embodiments of which would appear now and again before the writer.

The poet seems wistfully conscious that this life is fleeting; but unburdened by fatalism he has resolved to accept the world's pleasures where they may be found. Literary and theological references crop up here and there; they suggest the author's familiarity with learned works even as his own views on life's deeper issues are recorded. When they make their appearances, reflections on death and ultimate designs to this existence reveal a thoughtful, broadly tolerant outlook that, for all of its mystical, seemingly heterodox inspiration, complements and affirms the positive values the author has proclaimed elsewhere in his verse.

The enduring qualities of Hafiz's poetry are maintained in the first instance through his consummate use of imagery; indeed, memorable lines and passages are recalled specifically from these associations. Although classical Persian poetry to an extent depended upon specific, fixed points of reference— the roses and nightingales that make their appearances in Hafiz's works originated in prototypes handed down by generations of versifiers—his poetic vision placed these stock images in fresh and distinctively personal literary settings. The allegorical and the actual merge gracefully in the gardens where many of his poetic encounters take place; directly and through allusions, visions of orchards, meadows, and rose gardens are summoned forth. These settings, almost certainly taken from those in and around the author's own city, are typically flanked by box trees, cypresses, pines, and willows. The wind, likened sometimes to the breeze of paradise, wafts scents of ambergris, musk, and other perfumed fragrances; at times there is jasmine in the air.

Roses also figure prominently in many of Hafiz's lines, often as buds, blossoms, and petals; at other times hyacinths, lilies, violets, and tulips appear. The narcissus seems to have its own self-answering connotation. The nightingale, which at places alights upon the roses, provides musical accompaniment to the poet's fonder thoughts; at some junctures swallows or birds of paradise enter the poet's landscape. Celestial bodies often mark transitions to metaphorical passages: the Pleiades sparkle but sometimes provoke tears; at times Venus or Saturn is in the ascendant. The moon mirrors and hurls back images of the beloved's features.

Archetypal visions of women enter many of the lyrics, though generally by hints and partial references. Seemingly bemused by the eyebrows, the pupils of the eyes, the hair, the neck, or the moonlike visage of the loved one, the author must have readily conceived a host of similes. Tresses resemble a tree's leafy growth; lips recall roses in the fullness of their blossom. Perfumed winds mingle with the lover's soft voice. Hafiz seems to have been particularly entranced by the mole, or beauty spot (*khal*), to be found on the cheeks of some women. This fascination, and his willingness to place love above riches and power, led him to compose some of the most celebrated lines in all poetry: "If that beauteous Turk of Shiraz would take my heart in hand,/ I would barter for her dark mole Bukhara and Samarqand."

In other moods the author wrote from the standpoint of a *rind*, or vagabond; in this frame of mind the cares of this world are gently shunted aside for the tavern and the bowl of wine. Many such lyrics at the outset are addressed to the *saqi*, or cupbearer; sad tidings and glad are greeted with the thought that the rosy glow of drink will set matters in perspective. The intrinsic pleasures of fellowship around the bowl are evoked; at times there are melancholy images as well, as when the poet's heart-blood, or the ruby lips of an absent lover, are contrasted with the tawny drink before him. Poverty and the vicissitudes of romantic encounters could seemingly be offset by the mellowing reflections good wine could bring. There are occasions as well when the bowl suggests another quest, when the pursuit of enigmatic romance might be superseded by concern with the ultimate questions. Another image is introduced here and there, that of the cup of Jamshid from old Persian lore, which was supposed to provide magical visions of the universe. Another very famous ode begins with the lines

> Long years my heart had made request
> Of me, a stranger, hopefully
> (Not knowing that itself possessed
> The treasure that it sought of me),
> That Jamshid's chalice I should win
> And it would see the world therein.

This poem ends with speculation on the views of divinity propounded by thinkers and groups from various persuasions that were out of favor in the Persia of Hafiz's day.

The religious themes developed in Hafiz's verse betray heterodox influences coupled with a broadly tolerant point of view. Some references merely bear the outward stamp of mystic ways of life: the dervish's cloak (*khirqah*) and the dusty, stony path of the spiritually inclined mendicant are featured in some notable lyrics; there are odd juxtapositions of the religious search and the meditations of the wine bibber. Although in some passages the author suggests that his innate liberality and profligacy precluded any commitments to the religious life, he seems nevertheless to have been struck by the free and open spiritual journeys of the peripatetic dervish, or *qalandar*. The impious, slightly scandalous regard with which Hafiz was held in some quarters was given added weight by his references to religious views that went beyond those officially upheld by the authorities.

Mystical currents in Islamic thought had been disseminated under the general rubric of Sufism; such habits of mind eluded the strict doctrinal categories of more orthodox thinkers. Sufi interpretations of philosophical and religious questions still had found adherents among important men of letters in Persia; the evidence from Hafiz's works suggests a more than casual acquaintanceship with mystical teachings. Indeed, though without conferring his entire approval, the poet refers to the distinctive spiritual orientation of the Sufis in many places. More controversial were his quotations from al-Husayn ibn Mansur al-Hallaj, who was executed in Iraq in 922 for his alleged personal identification with God. Hafiz apparently found some inspiration in the celebrated martyr's beliefs in love and manifestations of the divine all around in the world. Moreover, in keeping with the multiple sources of Sufism, where elements of several religious doctrines could be acknowledged in the continuing quest for spiritual guidance, Hafiz's lyrics also point to vital truths in Christianity and in Magian (Zoroastrian) traditions. Elsewhere the author quotes from the Koran, generally where matters of love and tolerance embracing diverse ways of life are involved.

Conflicting interpretations have been advanced on another level, however; it has been contended that hidden meanings lie within the outwardly simple and straightforward compositions of Hafiz. It has been averred, for example, that the vocabulary of mystical sects appears with enough regularity that two, or several, connotations were intended in many of the author's verses. This approach, which can be applied to certain Persian expressions, as well as to loan words from Arabic, assumes great depth in lyrics whose nominal subject matter already is handled through direct and metaphorical means. In this light, mentions of roses may be taken, specifically and obliquely, as references to love, but also (in Sufi usage) may denote initiates in a religious order. The common term *sihr* (magic), originally from Arabic, acquires numerous connotations where contexts involving both romantic and mystical-theological concerns arise. No single pattern of such underlying meanings, beyond those to be found in a literary language that is rich in poetic and theological usage, has been uncovered that may be used uniformly throughout Hafiz's works. On the other hand, it may well have been the case that the poet at certain junctures freely adopted semantic forms that would reflect the several concerns that at various times bemused him.

Political concerns across the range of Hafiz's works may be considered briefly under two headings. In the first place there are a certain number of frankly panegyric poems, which openly were meant to gain or retain the benevolent attention of rulers during his age. Such works are useful largely in that they cast some light on the poet's position in society and may readily be assigned dates; most are from the 1350's and 1360's. Flattery here is couched in terms that to some extent recall the images from other verse. Other poems, however, disclaim interest in political controversies, and indeed regard power as one of the less desirable ends in this life. In some notable lines the reader is advised to practice kindness with friends and courtesy toward enemies; beyond this point the author evidently had little interest in the polemical issues of political philosophy.

By inference and from direct references it may be learned that two of the most important literary predecessors of Hafiz were Nizami Ganjavi (c. 1140– c. 1202) and Sa'di, from the thirteenth century. By his own time the *ghazal* had long been established as a major vehicle of poetic expression. It had become a standard form by which a certain number of distichs, or *bayt*, could be set to a single rhyme; the hemistichs also are made to rhyme. The final distich often contains the author's identifying name; in these lines Hafiz often addressed himself in self-congratulatory tones or in wry and self-effacing expressions. A set number of line feet are used in the verses of a single poem; emphasis follows a pattern that is strictly consistent throughout. To be sure, some variations may be observed among separate compositions. The number of lines may vary, generally between five and twelve; syllables may be emphasized in different patterns from one poem to the next. A notable feature in many of Hafiz's lyrics is the conclusion of each line with the same word; this practice, as a further demonstration of his virtuosity, lends added impact to many poems. Specific standards of emphasis and metric construction may also be found in other poetic forms, such as the elegies and quatrains Hafiz wrote; these works, while expressing some of the same concerns as the lyrics, are of interest largely as illustrating other facets of the author's poetic craftsmanship.

The troubled question of unity was raised by early critics, possibly including some readers from the poet's own lifetime. In discussing the works of the Persian author, Hafiz's first English translator, Sir William Jones, described his verse as "like orient pearls at random strung." One of the British scholar's contemporaries contended that Hafiz's works were utterly incoherent, although he nevertheless managed to produce Latin translations of some poems. Later writers have reached decidedly mixed conclusions on this vexed issue, which has also preoccupied leading Iranists of the twentieth century. Even when allowance is made for the diversity of themes and subjects in works composed possibly over a number of years, there are outward and rather conspicuous signs of inconsistency in individual compositions. Separate lyrics often enough will deal abruptly with two or more topics; sometimes transitions are not clearly made. This trait has given added credibility to theories of multiple mystical meanings in Hafiz's works, but even in this sense internal discrepancies arise. Although metaphorical usage may be considered to conjoin elements in the frankly romantic lyrics, in some poems the setting is transferred from the garden to the tavern with no specific mode of passage. Other lyrics, after the contemplation of worldly cares and joys, shift rather sharply to essentially philosophical or religious concerns. Apart from the poetic conventions of metric length, emphasis, and rhythm that unite the lines within specific compositions, some passages would not be incongruous if affixed or transposed to other works. At the same time, it should be noted that allegations of disunity have been made against only a certain number of poems; it may be argued that in the author's works as a whole, continuity of themes and outlook may readily be discerned. Moreover, where combined meanings are concerned, suggesting both a symbolic and an actual realization of the author's design, it may be contended that conceptual integrity is preserved where imagery and allusion are interwoven about issues of major concern to the poet.

The influence of Hafiz has been very great. In Persia, though the example he set probably precluded yet further summits in the development of the classical *ghazal*, many later writers derived inspiration from his works; the most notable from the great early age of Persian poetry probably was Jami (1414-1492). A number of commentaries and transcribed manuscripts, as well as poetry composed along similar lines, attest the reception of Hafiz in the lands of the Ottoman Empire. Although it was several centuries before Hafiz's works were printed, translations eventually did much to acquaint important creative thinkers with the poems of the Persian author. Among writers in the English language, there are notable references to Hafiz in the works of Alfred, Lord Tennyson, and Ralph Waldo Emerson; even given the vagaries of translation and comparative availability, it has been maintained that among classical Persian authors only Omar Khayyám made a more definite impression in England and America. In continental Europe Hafiz's renown was spread particularly with the publication of a German translation of the *Divan* in 1812-1813, by the Austrian Orientalist Joseph von Hammer-Purgstall. Johann Wolfgang von Goethe utilized this work in according Hafiz pride of place in his *West-östlicher Divan* (1819; *West-eastern divan*, 1877). Later translations of Hafiz, eventually into a number of languages, assisted both in the scholarly assessment and the public availability of his works. In Russia a number of poets were notably influenced by Hafiz's lyrics, beginning probably with Afanasii Afanas'evich Fet (Shenshin) in the middle of the nineteenth century. It may be added as well that the modern Islamic world has also drawn inspiration from the Persian poet's works; here Sir Muhammad Iqbal, of Pakistan, might be mentioned in particular. In Iran itself, a spate of articles, studies, and scholarly editions of Hafiz's poetry have maintained his high reputation during the twentieth century.

Bibliography
Bashiri, Iraj. "Hafiz and the Sufic Ghazal," in *Studies in Islam*. XVI, no. 1 (1979), pp. 34-67.
_____. "Hafiz' Shirazi Turk: A Structuralist's Point of View," in *Muslim World*. LXIX, nos. 3/4 (1979), pp. 178-197, 248-268.
Broms, Henri. *Two Studies in the Relations of Hafiz and the West*, 1968.
Hillmann, Michael C. *Unity in the Ghazals of Hafez*, 1976.
Meisami, Julie Scott. "The World's Pleasance: Hafiz's Allegorical Gardens," in *Comparative Criticism*. V (1983), pp. 153-185.
Rehder, Robert M. "The Unity of the Ghazals of Hafiz," in *Der Islam*. LI, no. 1 (1974), pp. 55-96.
Schimmel, Annemarie. "Hafiz and His Critics," in *Studies in Islam*. XVI, no. 1 (1979), pp. 1-33.
Skalmowski, Wojciech. "The 'Blasphemous' Motif in Hafiz," in *Orientalia Lovaniensia periodica*. XII (1981), pp. 273-281.
_____. "Old Iranian Motifs in the *Divan* of Hafiz," in *Orientalia J. Duchesne-Guillemin emerito oblata*. Acta Iranica, 2d series, IX (1984), pp. 473-478.
Yousofi, Gholam Hosein. "The Image of the *Rind* in the Poetry of Hafiz," in *Bulletin of the British Association of Orientalists*. N.s. IX (1977), pp. 22-29.

J. R. Broadus

MICHAEL S. HARPER

Born: Brooklyn, New York; March 18, 1938

Principal collections

Dear John, Dear Coltrane, 1970; *History Is Your Own Heartbeat*, 1971; *Photographs: Negatives: History as Apple Tree*, 1972; *Song: I Want a Witness*, 1972; *Debridement*, 1973; *Nightmare Begins Responsibility*, 1974; *Images of Kin: New and Selected Poems*, 1977; *Rhode Island: Eight Poems*, 1981; *Healing Song for the Inner Ear*, 1984.

Other literary forms

Michael Harper works almost exclusively as a poet, but, in collaboration with Robert B. Stepto, he has edited one of the most influential anthologies of Afro-American letters since Alain Locke's anthology from the Harlem Renaissance, *The New Negro: An Interpretation* (1925). Like Locke's anthology, *Chant of Saints: A Gathering of Afro-American Literature, Art, and Scholarship* (1979) represents a substantial accomplishment in defining the importance of Afro-American artists and writers to American culture. Unlike Locke, whose task was to gather enough material, Harper and Stepto had to select from a diverse multitude of texts and works in several aesthetic disciplines. The resulting anthology, from the dual perspectives of poet and critic, documents amply the growth and complexity of Afro-American art since Locke's time, including poetry, fiction, visual art, music, criticism, cultural history, and interviews by not only representative Afro-Americans but also African and West Indian writers and artists. With a focus on ethically committed concerns, the anthology emphatically resists the discourse of social science, stressing instead the cultural authenticity of blackness as an international consciousness that grounds itself in the historical kinship of various artistic disciplines and illuminates the work of both acknowledged masters such as Chinua Achebe and Ralph Ellison and gifted but relatively neglected writers such as Derek Walcott and James Alan MacPherson.

In addition to his poetry and the anthology, Harper has published an essay, "My Poetic Technique and the Humanization of the American Audience," in *Black American Literature and Humanism*, and three interviews which provide useful insights into his poetry. His coediting, with John Wright, of *The Carleton Miscellany: A Ralph Ellison Festival* (1980) also attests Harper's roles as teacher, historian, and critic of black American literature.

Achievements

Harper's nine books of poems within two decades have established his stature as a significant voice in contemporary poetry. As an Afro-American poet, Harper explores the historical and contemporary duality of consciousness that was first expressed by Frederick Douglass in the nineteenth century and W. E. B. Du Bois in the early twentieth century: what it means to be both black and American, and how one survives as both. While using to a limited extent a narrative frame, Harper's lyricism pays homage to the heroic endurance of family members, unsung musicians, and historical activists through a consciously developed technique that affirms the Afro-American literary tradition, grounded in the oral tradition of storytelling and the musical heritage of the spirituals, blues, and jazz. Avoiding the sometimes strident, polemical tones of black poetry in the 1960's and 1970's, Harper nevertheless fashions an ethically powerful voice, marked not only by a passion in exposing the tragedy of black history in America but also by a compassion for the individuals who have sought to endure and to create out of the cauldron of racism. His distinctive voice and all-embracing vision have evoked praise from both black and white reviewers and critics.

Formal recognition of Harper's poetry has thus been consistent from the publication of his first collection of poems, *Dear John, Dear Coltrane*, which was nominated for the National Book Award in 1971. After *History Is Your Own Heartbeat*, his second collection, received the Poetry Award of the Black Academy of Arts and Letters in 1972, other grants and awards followed: a National Institute of Arts and Letters Creative Writing Award (1972), a Guggenheim Fellowship (1976), a National Endowment for the Arts grant (1977), and the Massachusetts Council of Creative Writing Award (1977). In 1977, Harper's seventh book, *Images of Kin*, received the Melville Cane Award and was nominated in 1978 for the National Book Award.

Beyond his awards for publishing, Harper is also an excellent reader of his own work and, accordingly, has been invited to read in the bicentenary exchange with England in 1976, at the Library of Congress in 1975 and 1976, and, receiving an American Special Grant in 1977, in several African countries—Senegal, Ghana, Gambia, Zaire, Zambia, Tanzania, Botswana, and South Africa—as well as at numerous American universities.

While Harper has been honored with visiting professorships at Harvard and Yale and distinguished professorships at Carleton College and the University of Cincinnati, he has been employed at Brown University since 1970. Promoted to full professor at the age of thirty-six in 1974, Harper received the endowed chair of the Israel J. Kapstein Professorship in 1983.

Biography

Michael Steven Harper was born on March 18, 1938, in Brooklyn, New York, and his birth brought with it particular pressures to succeed: He was the first male born on either side of the family, and he was delivered at his parents' home by his grandfather, Roland R. Johnson. His father, Walter Harper, was a postal worker and supervisor; his mother, Katherine Johnson, worked as a medical stenographer. While not wealthy, the Harper family did enjoy a middle-class income that permitted the acquisition of a good record collection, interesting the young Harper in music and serving as a source for his later development as a poet.

At thirteen, Harper and his family, including his younger brother Jonathan and his sister Katherine, moved to a predominantly white neighborhood in West Los Angeles, an area in which several black families were to have their houses bombed in the early 1950's. Enrolling shortly thereafter in Susan Miller Dorsey High School, Harper was assigned to an industrial arts course of study rather than to an academic one, presumably because he was black, and only his father's intervention with a counselor reversed the institutional assumptions about his abilities. Suffering from extreme asthma in 1951, Harper spent the summer confined to the house and, also because of his asthma, later refused to undress for gym class, for which he failed the class and was kept off the honor roll. Always having been encouraged to study medicine in the tradition of his grandfather and his great-grandfather Dr. John Albert Johnson, an African Methodist Episcopal Church bishop and missionary in South Africa from 1907 to 1916, Harper used the incident to escape the family's pressures and to turn his attention from the classroom and his interests in medicine, literature, and history to the ordinary life in the streets and neighborhoods around him. While not a disciplined student, he was a good test-taker, and he was graduated from high school in 1955.

From 1956 to 1961, Harper pursued a premedical course at Los Angeles State College (now California State University at Los Angeles) while at the same time working full-time as a postal worker. In college, a zoology professor discouraged his study of medicine, assuming that blacks were incapable of sustaining the rigors of medical school. On the job, Harper encountered well-educated blacks who were unable to advance—not because they lacked merit, but because they were black. Together, the two experiences of racism at first hand helped shape his sense that American society was essentially schizophrenic: It celebrated free competition based on merit, but it barred blacks from an equal chance to participate in the culture—color was too often more consequential than character.

While Harper was in college, two books in particular, *The Letters of John Keats* (1958) and Ralph Ellison's *Invisible Man* (1952), and a course, "The Epic of Search," which offered a historical view of the human quest for self-assertion from *The Odyssey* (c. ninth century B.C.) to *Invisible Man*, rekindled his desire to write. In high school, he had experimented with poetry, short fiction, and drama, but he had abandoned those early attempts. Deprived of encouragement to study medicine, Harper enrolled in the Iowa Writers Workshop in 1961. Restricted to segregated housing, he became increasingly aware of the fragmentation in American cultural life. As the only black enrolled in both poetry and fiction classes, Harper began to write poetry seriously, receiving encouragement from the writer Ralph Dickey and the painter Oliver Lee Jackson. In 1962, turning his attention to teaching, Harper left Iowa to student teach at Pasadena City College, armed at twenty-four with a long-standing knowledge of black music and a newly developing expertise in black history, writing, and painting—all of which would come to inform his new commitment to his principal mode of expression: poetry.

The following year, 1963, Harper returned to Iowa and, although he had been in the Creative Writers Program, he passed the comprehensive examinations in English, receiving his master's degree. He taught then at Contra Costa College, San Pablo, California, from 1964 to 1968. After teaching the following year at Reed College and Lewis and Clark College in Oregon, he taught as associate professor of English at California State College at Haywood in 1969-1970. Although receiving a tenured appointment as an associate professor at Brown University in 1970, Harper spent 1970-1971 at the University of Illinois, pursuing a postdoctoral fellowship at the Center for Advanced Studies. Since then, Harper has taught at several universities as a visiting professor while employed at Brown University, where he served as director of the Graduate Creative Writing Program from 1974 to 1983. He was appointed to an endowed chair at Brown in 1983.

Analysis

In an interview with Abraham Chapman, Michael Harper identifies the poetic technique of much of his work as "modality," an abstract musical concept that he uses as a metaphor for his ethical vision as well as for his subjective principle of composition. Many of Harper's poems lend themselves to performance; they are meant to be read aloud. In hearing them, one hears, through a range of idiom, dialect, and individual voices, the past fused with the contemporary, the individual speaking forth from communal experience and the black American's kinship, simultaneously tragic and heroic, to the whole of American cultural values. Rooted in classic jazz patterns from such musicians as Duke Ellington, Charlie Parker, and John Coltrane, modality is "about relationships" and "about energy, energy irreducible and true only unto itself." As a philosophical, ethical perspective, modality is a "particular frequency" for expressing and articulating "the special nature of the Black man and his condition and his contributions" to the American synthesis of cultural values. As such, modality refutes "the Western orientation of division between denotative/connotative, body/mind, life/spirit, soul/body, mind/ heart" and affirms a unity of being and experience: "*modality is always about unity*." Consequently, Harper's poetry gathers fragments from private and public experience, past and present, and seeks to rejuvenate spiritual forces historically suppressed by bringing them to the surface in a poetry of "tensions resolved through a morality worked out between people."

In the early poems of *Dear John, Dear Coltrane*, Harper's modal experiments succeed in a variety of forms that nevertheless remain unified in the power of his particular voice. In "Brother John," Harper eulogizes Charlie Parker, the "Bird/ baddest nightdreamer/ on sax in the ornithology-world," Miles Davis, "bug-eyed, unspeakable,/ Miles, sweet Mute,/ sweat Miles, black Miles," and John Coltrane, who serves as a mythic center for the poem and the volume as well as several later poems. Typical of Harper's multiple allusions in naming, however, both the poem and the volume also eulogize John O. Stewart, a friend and fiction writer; nor is Coltrane merely a mythic figure, for Harper maintained a personal friendship with him until his death in 1967; in addition, the name "John" also conjures echoes from Harper's great-grandfather, who spent several years in South Africa, and, further, evokes John Brown, who figures prominently in later poems by Harper. Thus, from early in his work, Harper uses modality to reconcile past and present, myth and history, and private and public; personal mourning becomes part of a universal experience and a communal celebration. Drawing inspiration from both the suffering and the achievement of jazz artists in this poem and in subsequent poems in his career, Harper establishes the modal wordplay that affirms his philosophical stance as an activist of the conscience, "I'm a black man; I am;/ black; I am; I'm a black/ man; I am; I am," and his own cry of being, refusing any limiting universality of humanness that is blind to ethnic heritage and experience: "I am; I'm a black man;/ I am."

In other poems from that first volume, Harper links past and present as well as private and public by exploring larger patterns of history. In "American History," Harper asserts the invisibility of black suffering to mainstream America by juxtaposing "Those four black girls blown up/ in that Alabama church" with "five hundred/ middle passage blacks,/ in a net, under water. . . so *redcoats* wouldn't find them." Concluding in an ironic but colloquial idiom, he asks: "Can't find what you can't see/ can you?" In "Reuben, Reuben," Harper uses the death of his own son to overcome his pain in the transcendence of creative energy, just as blues singers have always done when faced with the horror of loss: "I reach from pain/ to music great enough/ to bring me back . . . we've lost a son/ the music, *jazz*, comes in."

Harper's early poems test the possibilities of modality, and, in such techniques as concrete imaging, literary allusions, sprung syntax, enjambment, blues refrains, idioms, variable line lengths, and innovative cadences, he discovers in modality a formalism strong enough to bear diverse experiments in free-verse forms and yet a visionary field large enough to draw from virtually any relationship, however intimate or distant, however painful or joyful, for individual affirmation. In his second collection, *History Is Your Own Heartbeat*, Harper uses modality to reconstruct personal history, integrating it with a mythic sense of spiritual unity. Divided into three sections, the book begins with a twenty-poem sequence, "Ruth's Blues," which employs his white mother-in-law's physical deterioration as an extended metaphor for the denial of black and white kinship. In tribute to Ruth's endurance in her quest for physical and psychological health, Harper shows the potential for a unified American sensibility, one which respects cultural differences yet realizes from the pain of division that American experience "is all a well-knit family;/ *a love supreme*," if one chooses to affirm multiple origins. The following two sections, "History as Personality" and "High Modes," pay homage, respectively, to influential personalities such as Martin Luther King, Jr., and Gwendolyn Brooks and, in the latter, to the painter Oliver Lee Jackson. Throughout these sections, Harper emphasizes the unity of a historical and cultural continuum that reaches back to Africa and comes forward to his own family, claiming his own past and an American history that is freed of its delusions, confronting its origins in the slavery of Africans and the genocide of Native Americans, to whom Harper also unearths literal kinship. In several ways, then, this volume, as the title suggests, builds from literal links of kinship with a diversity of races and cultures to a holistic view of American values, in contrast to the exclusive emphasis on European origins characteristic of traditional American history. By healing himself of narrow stereotypes, Harper offers "a love supreme" to his fellow citizens, asserting kinship even where citizenship has been denied and is diminished by racism.

Subsequent books extend Harper's sense of kinship and develop the aesthetic of modality. In *Song: I Want a Witness*, he explores the black American religious heritage, using the metaphor of testifying, and conceptualizes the literary process as essentially one of an ethical affirmation of heroic character. Tracing American culture back both to Native America, by a link with a great-great-grandmother who was Chippewa, and to the Puritan legacies of Roger Williams and John Winthrop, by a link to the spirit of place where he lives, Harper, in "History as Appletree," develops an organic metaphor that embodies history and family while also bringing the negative, through an extended photographic metaphor of those ignored by history, to present light and image. In this vision, the fruit of the tree, American culture itself, blossoms with the fertility of long-forgotten bones whose dust nurtures the root system.

The collection *Debridement*, a medical term for cutting away the dead flesh of a wound so that it will not infect the healthy body and a metaphor for revising stereotyped versions of American history, honors the heroic actions of John Brown, Richard Wright, and the fictional John Henry Louis. Together, the three sections, each revolving around its respective persona, correct the myth that Americans who have fought against racism were insane, zealous, hysterical. Instead, Harper argues through the modality of these poems, they were—and are—themselves the victims of racism, surviving because they have pursued a truth that has for the most part been hidden from them.

In *Nightmare Begins Responsibility*, the poet extends a logic that runs through the previous two books. Once one realizes that the pejorative American myth is false, then one must act to overcome the cultural insensitivity of racism and the apathy toward the land, both as physical and cultural environment. Alienation and isolation yield only to courageous, often unpopular action, and the American Dream and Manifest Destiny are concepts of death riddled with literal exploitation and genocide unless one replaces them with the values of kinship and acts to establish historical knowledge and contemporary intimacy as the basis for defining oneself as an American.

Harper's insistence that one accept both unity and diversity, both pain and love, continues in *Images of Kin*, which reverses the chronological order of the selections which represent an anthology of his earlier poetry. By beginning with new poems and working back to the earlier ones, Harper testifies to the imperative for reconstructing American myth and history. *Healing Song for the Inner Ear* expands the modality of celebrating friends, family, musicians, and poets by bringing them into Harper's constantly expansive vision of history. Functioning much like his first book, this collection moves both backward and forward, but it also moves toward a more international perspective than that found in any of his earlier collections. From the American perspective of "Goin' to the Territory," which salutes the influence of Ralph Ellison and witnesses his aesthetic endurance, and "The Pen," which gives voice to an oral tradition become literary artifact, embodying values inherent in both black American and Native American lives, a modality in which "patterns of the word fling out into destiny/ as a prairie used to when the Indians/ were called Kiowa, Crow, Dakota, Cheyenne," to a series of poems set in South Africa, Harper explores the complexity of image and story embedded in history and the enduring truth of experience excavated in modal expression.

In the poem "The Militance of a Photograph in the Passbook of a Bantu Under Detention," Harper meditates on the history behind the photograph that identifies a black South African from Soweto, and he asserts "This is no simple mug shot/ of a runaway boy in a training/ film. . . ." Harper senses his own history here; the runaway might have been a nineteenth century slave, the training film could well serve as a powerful tool for the suppression of historical facts, and the mug shot suggests that color itself (since only blacks must carry passbooks) is the crime. Personally, Harper must also unite his great-grandfather's experience in South Africa with the present strategies of apartheid, and, in uniting the past personal association with the contemporary public policies of racism, Harper affirms the courage of the oppressed: "The Zulu lullaby/ I cannot sing in Bantu/ is this song in the body/ of a passbook/ and the book passes/ into a shirt/ and the back that wears it." Perhaps the modality of such a link between Americans and South Africans, between forgotten language and forgotten people, serves as the celebration of Harper's enduring theme, as in the epigraph to the poem: "Peace is the active presence of Justice."

Other major works

ANTHOLOGIES: *Chant of Saints: A Gathering of Afro-American Literature, Art, and Scholarship*, 1979 (with Robert B. Stepto); *The Carleton Miscellany: A Ralph Ellison Festival*, 1980 (with John Wright).

Bibliography

Callahan, John F. "The Testifying Voice in Michael Harper's *Images of Kin*," in *Black American Literature Forum*. XIII (Fall, 1979), pp. 89-92.

Chapman, Abraham. "An Interview with Michael S. Harper," in *Arts in Society*. II (Fall/Winter, 1974), pp. 463-471.

Fussell, Edwin. "Double-Conscious Poet in the Veil (for Michael S. Harper)," in *Parnassus*. IV (Fall/Winter, 1975), pp. 5-28.

Harper, Michael. "My Poetic Technique and the Humanization of the American Audience," in *Black American Literature and Humanism*, 1981. Edited by R. Baxter Miller.

Lieberman, Laurence. "Derek Walcott and Michael S. Harper: The Muses of History," in *Yale Review*. LXII (October, 1973), pp. 284-296.

O'Brien, John. "Michael Harper," in *Interviews with Black Writers*, 1973.

Rampersand, Arnold. "The Poetics of Michael S. Harper," in *Poetry Miscellany*. VI (1976), pp. 43-50.

Randall, James. "An Interview with Michael Harper," in *Ploughshares*. VII, no. 1 (1981), pp. 11-27.

Stepto, Robert B. "Michael Harper's Extended Tree: John Coltrane and Sterling Brown," in *The Hollins Critic*. XIII (June, 1976), pp. 2-16.

——————. "Michael S. Harper, Poet as Kinsman: The Family Sequences," in *Massachusetts Review*. XVII (Autumn, 1976), pp. 477-502.

Michael Loudon

TONY HARRISON

Born: Leeds, England; April 30, 1937

Principal collections
Earthworks, 1964; *The Loiners*, 1970; *From 'The School of Eloquence' and Other Poems*, 1978; *Continuous: Fifty Sonnets from 'The School of Eloquence,'* 1981; *Selected Poems*, 1984; *The Fire-Gap*, 1985.

Other literary forms
Tony Harrison has strong, continuing connections with the theater and opera. His version of Molière's *Le Misanthrope* (1666; *The Misanthrope*, 1709) was produced by Great Britain's National Theatre in 1973, and his radical adaptation of Jean Racine's *Phèdre* (1677; *Phaedra*, 1701) whose title, *Phaedra Brittanica*, suggests how far he took it away from its source, appeared in 1975. His translation of Aeschylus' *Oresteia* (458 B.C.) came in 1981. He has also worked in opera, both as a librettist (with Harrison Birtwistle in *Bow Down* in 1977) and as a regular translator and adaptor for the Metropolitan Opera in New York. He provided the English lyrics for Mikis Theodorakis' songs for the film *The Blue Bird* (1976).

Harrison has a wide range of interests as a translator, and the occasional translation often shows up in his volumes of poetry, but he also addresses himself to more substantial translation projects. While a lecturer in English in Nigeria, he collaborated with James Simmons on a translation of Aristophanes' *Lysistratē* (411 B.C.; *Lysistrata*) into the Pidgin English of a native tribe. He is also the translator of the work of the fourth century A.D. Greek epigrammatist Palladas, and the selection, *Poems*, came out in 1975.

Achievements
Unusual in actually being able to make a living as a poet, albeit by adapting his talents to the theater, Harrison is a major spokesman for that peculiarly British phenomenon, the educated, working-class intellectual, nostalgically loyal to the class from which he came while committed without hypocrisy to the primarily middle-to-upper-middle-class world of the arts with all of its comforts and civilities.

In 1969, Harrison won the Cholmondeley Award for Poetry, and in the same year the UNESCO Fellowship in Poetry allowed him to travel as a representative of the international world of poetry to South America and Africa. Those journeys, through several countries, were to be used as subjects of several poems in his later publications. In 1972, *The Loiners*, his first full-length collection, won the Geoffrey Faber Memorial Prize.

Biography
Tony Harrison was born in Leeds (Yorkshire) to a working-class family, and his primary education was in the Cross Flatts County Primary School. A promising student, he moved from there to the Leeds Grammar School. (At the secondary school level, English education clearly differentiates between students with academic inclinations and talents and students likely to terminate their education in their teens, a separation which often has serious class implications.) Harrison went on to Leeds University, where he took a degree in classics and a diploma in linguistics.

Harrison was married in 1962 and has one daughter and one son. He also began his first career that year as an itinerant university lecturer, teaching for four years in Nigeria, and in Prague, Czechoslovakia, for one year. In 1967, he became the first Northern Arts Fellow in Poetry at the Universities of Newcastle-upon-Tyne and Durham. Between 1973 and 1978, he had close connections as a translator and adaptor of European dramas with Great Britain's National Theatre and served as Resident Dramatist with them in 1977-1978. He also developed a continuing relationship as translator and librettist with the Metropolitan Opera, while maintaining his personal connections with northern England by living in Newcastle. He has traveled extensively, particularly in Third World countries under the sponsorship of UNESCO, and is widely known as a poet and commentator upon poetry in countries as far apart as Cuba, Brazil, Senegal, and Gambia.

Analysis
It is generally accepted that Tony Harrison is not quite like his contemporaries in English poetry. That is true in more ways than one, although at the same time, seen from another angle, he is clearly aligned with many of the poets of postwar Great Britain. On the obvious level, he can be distinguished because of his use of his poetic gifts in the service of the theater. The role of translator and adapter is difficult to assess and is often unheralded. Indeed, it might be argued that the least obvious intrusion of the translator is the best indication of how successful that act of necessary manipulation of another's text is, since what is desired is a mirror image (in another language) of the original act of creation. Harrison, however, has not always confined himself to such gentle tumbling of art into another language, and it is of some value, when speaking of him as a writer, to look at a work such as *Phaedra Britannica* in order to see just how "creative" he can be in the face of a foreign text, using a flexible, almost unhinged couplet to turn Racine's *Phèdre* into a play about the English and their personal and political involvement in India. The result is not Racine, and it would be silly to suggest that it is, but it is an interesting example of how a late twentieth century poet can make verse drama despite its unfashionableness, and make it without ascending to fulsome, pumped-up afflatus, which would be risible, at the least, and pomp-

ously inappropriate in an age of deliberately flattened rhetoric.

It is not, however, simply a matter of Harrison's ability to turn his poetic gifts to the theater which is meant in distinguishing him from other poets. There is, for various reasons, a tendency in British poets to confine themselves, with some considerable success, to a narrow thematic line. This is not always true, and it should not be taken as necessarily debasing the quality of their work. Harrison, on the other hand, perhaps partly because of his travels as an educator, itinerant poet, and theatrical journeyman, has a very wide range of interests in his poems. *The Loiners*, his first collected volume, is the best example of that breadth and includes poems not only about his native north of England but also about Africa, America, South America, Europe, and the Iron Curtain countries, and in those poems his liberal-leftist political inclinations are joined to his mischievous enthusiasm for sexual high jinks in poems which set out to smash the linguistic and political barriers with some considerable sophistication and impropriety. The poem "The Bedbug" puts it succinctly:

> Comrade, with your finger on the playback switch,
> Listen carefully to each love-moan,
> And enter in the file which cry is real, and which
> A mere performance for your microphone.

Along the way, in a manner consistent with his education in the classics and linguistics, he plants elegant, teasingly relaxed translations of European poets from the classical period forward; he surprises with the economy with which he intrudes metaphysical tendencies into poems, seemingly without effort. In "The Nuptial Torches," men burning at the stake are seen thus: "Their souls/ Splut through their pores like porridge holes./ They wear their skins like cast-offs. Their skin grows/ Puckered round the knees like rumpled hose."

The high-spirited cleverness of such imagery and the wit and sophistication with which Harrison interpolates allusions of intellectual (and technical) complexity into *The Loiners* brings him closer to American poets than one might expect of a writer who comes from the working class of Yorkshire, and at his deliberately flashy, improper best (see "Flying Down to Rio: A Ballad of Beverly Hills" in *From 'The School of Eloquence' and Other Poems*), there are touches of James Merrill. Harrison knows that he has this sweet tooth for being naughty, and he sometimes makes poetry out of it. In *Continuous*, the poem "Bringing Up" allows him to talk of his mother's reaction to some of the poetry in *The Loiners*: He ruefully remembers, at her death, his desire to put a copy of his poems in her hands before her cremation. "You'd've been embarrassed though to meet your God/ clutching those poems of mine that you'd like banned." He retrieves himself for a moment with the wry idea that they could both have their way: "I thought you could hold my *Loiners*, and both burn!" The poem continues, with Harrison determined to follow the idea with metaphysical doggedness in which he mingles (as he often does) wit with tenderness:

> And there together in the well wrought urn
> what's left of you, the poems of your child,
> devoured by one flame, unreconciled,
> like soots on washing, black on bone-ash white.
>
> May be you see them in a better light!
>
> But I still see you weeping, your hurt looks:
>
> *You weren't brought up to write such mucky books!*

Perhaps something ought to be said about this word "metaphysical," which is usually applied to a group of late sixteenth and early seventeenth century poets including John Donne and Andrew Marvell, and is taken to mean that style of poetry, sometimes of philosophical theme (hence the word "metaphysical"), in which metaphors, images, and ideas, while often deliberately inappropriate, not only are used but also are explored rigorously in order to wring every association out of them, sometimes to a wildly ridiculous extent. There is a touch of swagger, of showing off, about this kind of poetry, even when it is tonally serious and thematically profound; when it is neither, it can still be aesthetically exciting. Harrison often attaches metaphysical structures to the most innocent metaphors, and his "riding" them with relentless enthusiasm is seen as informally connecting him to the "Martian" group (if it can even be called that), whose most obvious and successful practitioner is the British poet Craig Raine.

Harrison is, however, much more formidable than such improvisatory zest for the startling image might suggest, and it is in his "The School of Eloquence" series that much of his best work has been done, and indeed may continue to appear, since the concept is open-ended. Appropriating a prosodic oddity which had previously been employed by George Meredith in his *Modern Love* (1862), a sonnet consisting of sixteen rhyming pentameter lines, Harrison has provided himself with a flexible form (with which he often deliberately tampers, committing "errors" to achieve spontaneity and tonal densities), and which serves as an ideal vehicle for his worldly-wise comments on modern society. Most important, the form provides him with a supple shape in which he can explore the dilemma of his worldly success with considerable range of feeling. Caught between his working-class background (which is still a potent force in British society), for which he has considerable affection, and his enviable position as an educated traveling man with reputation and connections in the glamorous world of the arts and the theater, he believes that he has, albeit innocently, betrayed his family. Educated out of his "clothed-capped" background and possessing artistic gifts far beyond the ambitions which his parents had for him, he uses these sonnets to try to make sense of what happened:

> The mams, pig-sick of oilstains in their wash,
> wished for their sons a better class of gear,
>   wear their own clothes into work 'but not go posh,
> go up a rung or two but settle near.

The poems come together, a few at a time, and develop into a small auto-biographical novel, ranging from memories of childhood to rueful anecdotes about his fragile relationship with his parents before their deaths. Sometimes the poems deal with the difficult times of the parents' last illnesses, attempting to discover why so much love was so ineptly expressed. Despite his determination to write simply and to use working-class and regional dialect when appropriate, the poems are not simplistic. The last verse of "Breaking the Chain," from which the quotation above was drawn, deals with the expensive draftsman's instruments which his father bought for him, hoping that he might end up close at hand: "This meant the 'drawing office' to the dads,/ same place of work, but not blue-collar, white." It ends in a way which ought to remind the reader of Harrison's metaphysical bent, and perhaps of John Donne's use of the compass image in "A Valediction: Forbidding Mourning." Harrison uses the idea with the lightest touch so that the smartness will not breach the plangent feeling:

> Looking at it now still breaks my heart!
> The gap his gift acknowledged then 's wide as
> eternity, but I still can't bear to part
> with these never passed on, never used, dividers.

There is some danger in this fusion of metaphysical imagery and deep feeling, the former threatening to fall into "cuteness," as it does occasionally (disastrously so in "Guava Libre," *From 'The School of Eloquence' and Other Poems*), and the latter always a possible danger in the sonnets dealing with his family. Usually he knows how far to go, and his good taste allows him to decide what the mix of high intelligence, clever allusions, deliberate technical awkwardisms, and native dialect ought to be and how far he can dare take them. The danger is most apparent when the poems get into the area of private feeling, where he chooses to divest himself of sophistication for simple tale-telling, where the flatness of the language and the lines teeters on the edge of sentimental excess:

> James Cagney was the one up both our streets
> His was the only art we ever shared.
> A gangster film and choc ice were the treats
> that showed about as much love as he dared.

That "choc ice" (from the poem "Continuous") may be a bit too cunning, a bit too much total recall of the language of the cinema house of his childhood. Yet a poem such as "Marked with D" gets much of its power from the way in which he strides into danger, taking his father's past job as a baker and indecorously describing his father's cremation in metaphysical images and puns baldly related to the baking of a loaf of bread:

> The baker's man that no-one will see rise
> and England made to feel like some dull oaf
> is smoke, enough to sting one person's eyes
> and ash (not unlike flour) for one small loaf.

In context, this kind of impropriety works not so much because it is so outrageously smart, but because, in a peculiar way, its enforces the simplicity of this working-class life, a world in which only the sparseness, the paucity of aspiration, exists in the crudest metaphor: The poetry comes out of its unpoetic rejection of appropriately sonorous language.

The family poems allow Harrison to enter into the continuing problems of the British working classes, the continuing limitations and disappointments of stunted lives, seemingly destined to be similarly confined in the future as the country goes on its inexorably threadbare way. The intrusion of the black and brown Commonwealth refugees into the working-class neighborhoods, already run-down and overcrowded, is the subject of a series of poems in which the wariness, the sense of the despair and helplessness of the lower class, seeing themselves as the victims of other people's problems, at and on the edge of racial prejudice that they hardly understand, is expressed through the eyes of his father. In these poems, Harrison can be most clearly identified as a working-class poet.

He is, however, always more than one kind of poet, and he often uses the sonnet form to explore his continuing fascination with language and how it can be used, misused, and sometimes betray, not simply within a community but also on the wider scale of political chicanery and indifference. He is a poet of considerable range; the open-ended nature of "The School of Eloquence" series, both thematically and tonally, allows for personal intimacies, political comment, scholarly puzzles, and arcane jokes about high and louche lowlife. Harrison is a cosmopolitan poet in the very best and widest sense of that word: intelligent, lettered, witty, skeptical, and, sometimes, cheerfully rude.

Finally, it is interesting to see him reacting to America, not only in his obviously satiric poems about urban excess but also in his pastoral mode, which was not strongly represented in his work until the early 1980's. Harrison has two lovely long poems, set in the rural fastness of central Florida, "The Fire-Gap: A poem with Two Tails" and "Cypress and Cedar," which extend his range into thoughtful apprehension of man's relation to the natural world in ways which are reminiscent of Samuel Taylor Coleridge's conversation poems on one hand and haunting reminders of Robert Frost on the other.

Other major works

PLAYS: *Aikin Mata*, 1965 (with James Simmons, adaptation of Aristophanes' play *Lysistratē*); *The Misanthrope*, 1973 (adaptation of Moliere's play *Le Misanthrope*); *Phaedra Britannica*, 1975 (adaptation of Jean Racine's play *Phèdre*); *Bow Down*, 1977 (libretto, music by Harrison Birtwistle); *The Passion*, 1977 (adaptation of the York Mystery Plays); *The Bartered Bride*, 1978 (libretto, adaptation of Karel Sabina's opera, music by Bedřich Smetana); *The Oresteia*, 1981 (libretto, music by Birtwistle, adaptation of Aeschylus' play); *Dramatic Verse, 1973-1985*, 1985.

TELEPLAY: *The Big H*, 1984 (libretto, music by Dominic Muldowney).

TRANSLATION: *Poems*, 1975 (by Palladas of Alexandria).

Bibliography

Robson, Jeremy. *Corgi Modern Poets in Focus 4*, 1971.
Simmons, James. *The Honest Ulsterman*, 1970.
Thwaite, Anthony. *Poetry Today: A Critical Guide to British Poetry, 1960-1984*, 1985.

Charles H. Pullen

NAZİM HİKMET

Born: Salonika, the Ottoman Empire; January 20, 1902
Died: Moscow, U.S.S.R.; June 3, 1963

Principal poems and collections

Güneşi içenlerin türküsü, 1928; *835 satır*, 1929; *Jokond ile Si-Ya-U*, 1929; *Varan 3*, 1930; *1 + 1 = bir*, 1930; *Sesini kaybeden şehir*, 1931; *Gece gelen telgraf*, 1932; *Benerci kendini niçin öldürdü?*, 1932; *Portreler*, 1935; *Taranta Babu'ya mektuplar*, 1935; *Simavne Kadısı oğlu Şeyh Bedreddin destanı*, 1936 (*The Epic of Sheik Bedreddin*, 1977); *Moskova senfonisi*, 1952 (*The Moscow Symphony*, 1970); *Piraye için yazılmış saat 21-22 şiirleri*, 1965; *Şu 1941 yılında*, 1965; *Kurtuluş Savaşı destanı*, 1965 (expanded as *Kuvayı Milliye*, 1968); *Dört hapisaneden*, 1966; *Rubailer*, 1966 (*Rubaiyat*, 1985); *Yeni şiirler*, 1966; *Memleketimden insan manzaraları*, 1966-1967 (five volumes; *Human Landscapes*, 1982); *Son şiirler*, 1970; *Kerem gibi*, 1976. A comprehensive anthology, which includes Hikmet's collected poetry as well as prose works, was published in Bulgaria as *Bütün eserleri* (1967-1972, eight volumes), and another collection, under the same title, began to appear in Istanbul in 1968. Collections in English translation have tended to draw from various of the author's publications; among these are *Poems by Nazim Hikmet*, 1954; *Selected Poems*, 1967; *The Day Before Tomorrow*, 1972; *Things I Didn't Know I Loved: Selected Poems of Nazim Hikmet*, 1975; and *Selected Poetry*, 1986. Other collections in English translation include *The Moscow Symphony and Other Poems*, 1970, and *The Epic of Sheik Bedreddin and Other Poems*, 1977.

Other literary forms

Although he is remembered primarily for his poetry, Nazim Hikmet also became known early in his career for his plays; among the most notable of these are *Kafatası* (1931; the skull) and *Unutulan adam* (1935; the forgotten man), which deal with the practice of psychology and the conflict between worldly recognition and inner dissatisfaction. Other works in this genre, however, have been criticized for a facile identification of personages with political and social standpoints which they were meant to represent. Hikmet subsequently moved in other directions in his dramatic writing, first with works such as *Bir aşk masalı* (1945; a love story), which attempted a modern interpretation of traditional Middle Eastern characters; other plays involved experiments with old and new technical forms, as a part of the author's effort to adapt classical literary themes to contemporary concerns. Among later plays, by far the most widely known was *İvan İvanoviç var mıydı yok muydu?* (was there or was there not an Ivan Ivanovich?), which was written in exile and was first published in a Russian translation in 1956. In this contribution to the literary "thaw" in the Soviet Union, the author took issue with the personality cult and rigid, unswerving norms of criticism that had dominated creative writing under dictator Joseph Stalin.

Hikmet's narrative fiction is rather uneven; there is some moving and effective writing in *Sevdalı bulut* (1968; the cloud in love), which brings together short pieces, including children's stories, written over many years. His novels tend to display his ideological concerns; of these perhaps the most interesting is *Yeşil elmalar* (1965; green apples), which deals with crime, corruption, and penal detention. Also of interest as a semiautobiographical effort is *Yaşamak güzel şey bekardeşim* (1967; *The Romantics*, 1987). Works of political commentary furnish direct statements of the author's views on leading issues of his time; his treatises on Soviet democracy and on German Fascism, both originally published in 1936, are particularly revealing in this regard. Other insights into the writer's thought may be gathered from his collected newspaper columns and compilations of his personal letters.

Achievements

Throughout his creative lifetime, Hikmet was regarded as a politically controversial figure whose poetry expressed ideological concerns that situated him well to the left among Turkish writers of his generation. Although officially he was almost invariably out of favor in his own country—indeed, much of his adult life in Turkey was spent in prison, and work from his later years was composed under the shadow of Soviet cultural standard-bearers—his experiments with versification produced poetic forms that, more than any other works, announced the introduction of modern techniques into Turkish writing in this genre. During the last years of the Ottoman Empire, major innovations had been attempted by leading literary figures; language reform movements proceeded alongside the development of literary vehicles suitable for wider circles of readers among the masses. Enlarging upon the earlier efforts of Mehmet Tevfik Fikret and other important writers, Nazim Hikmet devised new and strikingly resonant verse patterns that in their turn pointed to the possibilities that could be achieved with the use of free verse. Moreover, while admittedly experimental, his verse was distinctive in the unusual confluence of models chosen: Hikmet's poems show the influence of Soviet postsymbolists while, in some notable works, recalling classical Islamic traditions in modern, reworked guises. Hikmet's poetry is alternately strident in its political declamations and intensely personal in its evocations of the writer's sufferings and innermost wants. Many of his prose works, while never really descending to the level of Socialist Realism, are somewhat more narrowly symptomatic of the ideological persuasions that guided him.

Apart from his literary fame, Hikmet became well-known from the political charges for which he served an aggregate of seventeen years in Turkish prisons. In 1949, an international committee was formed in Paris to press for his release; among others, Jean-Paul Sartre, Pablo Picasso, Louis Aragon, and Paul Robeson petitioned for the reopening of the Turkish government's case against him. In 1950, the Soviet Union conferred its World Peace Prize upon Nazim Hikmet, an award he shared with Pablo Neruda. During the last years of Hikmet's life, he made a number of public appearances in Moscow, Warsaw, and capitals of other Soviet Bloc countries. After his death, his work became the subject of lively discussion, much of it favorable, in his native Turkey, and important writings once more were published. Students of and specialists in Turkish literature have widely acknowledged his leading position among modern poets.

Biography
   On January 20, 1902, Nazim Hikmet was born in Salonika, the port city in Thrace which was then part of the Ottoman Empire. His father was a physician who had held government appointments; his mother was a painter, and his grandfather, Nazim Paşa, was a poet and critic of some note. As a boy, Hikmet was introduced to local literary circles. His first poems were written when he was about seventeen. He was educated in Istanbul, at the French-language Galatasaray Lycée and at the Turkish Naval Academy. Although poor health precluded a military career, he went on to Moscow during the early period of Soviet-Turkish friendship; between 1922 and 1924 he studied at the University of the Workers of the East. He derived inspiration from the events of the Russian Revolution and probably was influenced as well by the bold new literary ventures of Soviet poets such as Sergei Aleksandrovich Esenin and Vladimir Vladimirovich Maiakovskii. Upon his return to his native country, Hikmet joined the Turkish Communist Party, which by then had been forced into a clandestine existence; in Izmir he worked for a left-wing publication and was sentenced to fifteen years in prison. He fled to the Soviet Union and returned only after a general amnesty was proclaimed in 1928. By that time his first book-length collection of poems had been published in Soviet Azerbaijan. In Turkey the Communist Party had been formally outlawed, and Hikmet was arrested forthwith. Nevertheless, Turkish publishers brought out verse collections such as *835 satır* (835 lines) and others; his works were deemed inflammatory by the authorities, who claimed that they incited workers against the government. He was imprisoned twice, and later was able to find work mainly as a proofreader, translator, and scriptwriter. Indeed, some of his early poems refer to the tedious routine of his daily work, to which he was effectively restricted because of his political convictions. Although his plays won critical recognition, and some acclaim, for their introduction of new, unconventional dramatic forms—here Hikmet may in some ways have followed the technical innovations of Bertolt Brecht—political writings and newspaper columns had to be published under a pseudonym. He turned to historical topics, which nevertheless allowed range for his left

populist outlook: The last work published in Turkey during his lifetime was *The Epic of Sheik Bedreddin*, a long poem narrating events surrounding the life and death of the leader of a fifteenth century peasant revolt.

In January, 1938, new charges were brought against Hikmet; because copies of his poems were found in the possession of military cadets, he was arraigned for inciting unrest in the armed forces. A military court found him guilty, though the original sentence of thirty-five years was reduced to twenty-eight. During his imprisonment in Bursa, Hikmet embarked upon his poetic magnum opus, *Human Landscapes*, which was to be published only after his death, in a five-volume edition of 1966-1967. This monumental, and sometimes disjointed, work was circulated in parts among the poet's friends, family, and confidants; some portions of it were confiscated by the Turkish police or otherwise disappeared. Much of the writing Hikmet produced in prison has a musing, poignant, indeed bittersweet quality that was not so pronounced in his earlier works. On the other hand, some poems alight upon world events of which he had heard in passing: Germany's invasion of the Soviet Union, in 1941, and the United States' use of an atom bomb against Hiroshima, at the end of World War II, are discussed in his verse from this period. In 1949, in spite of having suffered a heart attack, Hikmet undertook a hunger strike that lasted seventeen days. In response to international pressure, the Turkish government released him from prison in 1950, but shortly thereafter, in order to curb the expression of his political views, he was made liable for conscripted military service. The following year, Hikmet fled the country alone in a small fishing boat; he was taken on board a Romanian ship in the Black Sea and eventually made his way to Moscow.

During his years in exile, the last period of his life, Hikmet lived for some time in the Soviet capital and in Warsaw; he took out a Polish passport under the name Borzęcki, after a family to which he had traced some of his ancestors. Sometimes he also used the added surname Ran. He traveled widely and attended literary congresses in other Soviet bloc countries; he also spent much time in Paris. He visited China, Cuba, and Tanganyika. Once he was refused a visa to enter the United States. Although he was not a literary conformist, he continued to uphold Soviet positions on international security. Some of his works from this period did him little credit, though they dealt with issues similar to those of his earlier activist poems. He suffered from angina pectoris, which had developed during his longest prison term, and other chronic health complaints arose later as well. While he lived in Turkey he had married three times; his imprisonment had made settled family life impossible. In Moscow he took up residence with a fetching young "straw blonde," Vera Tuliakova. Some of his later poems wistfully call back images of the women in his life or point to the hopes he still cherished in spite of his advancing age and his problematical physical state. After a final heart attack, Nazim Hikmet died in Moscow on June 3, 1963. Homage was rendered him from leading literary figures in many countries. Since his death his reputation among Turkish writers has grown apace.

Analysis

According to some estimates, the poetry of Nazim Hikmet has been translated into at least fifty languages. Perhaps more than any other Turkish writer, his work transcended the bounds of stylized Ottoman versification; at their best, his poems call to mind settings the author knew well while extending a universal appeal on behalf of his social beliefs. Lyrical and rhetorical passages occur alternately in some of his major works; his epics exhibit narrative powers which in some segments are used to depict events from the distant past or to evoke those from the author's lifetime. Moreover, though early in his career he came to be known as much for his outspoken ideological positions as for his literary achievements, Hikmet's poetry conveys the sudden dramatic impact of historical occurrences; social issues are depicted in ways that can be felt beyond the strict limits of party politics. On a more personal level, romantic yearnings, whimsical observations of street scenes and travel, and indeed nature and the weather are discussed in simple yet deeply felt lines that complement Hikmet's more directly expressed political concerns. Some of his poems communicate the loneliness and anxiety he felt as a political prisoner, without indulging particularly in self-pity. On the whole, he cannot be classified purely as a rationalist or a romantic; rather, his works combine elements of both inclinations.

From the outset, Hikmet's poetry was brash, vibrant, and politically engaged; defiantly casting aside traditional poetic styles, the author's work exuberantly mixed ideology and amorous inclinations in lines that at first glance resemble dismembered declarative sentences punctuated by crisp, staccato repetitions of phrases and nouns. Statements begun on one line are carried forward, with indentations, to the next, and sometimes further indentations are inserted before the thought is concluded. Question marks and exclamation points enliven stirring passages in which the author seems to be carrying on a dialogue with himself, if not with nature or society. The vowel harmony characteristic of the Turkish language is used to impart added force and velocity to some passages; moreover, the author's writing drew from folk songs, time-honored national sagas, and other sources in eclectic and distinctive combinations. Colloquial expressions, lower-class idioms, and outright vulgarisms appear from time to time. This approach, which seems ever fresh and lively in the hands of a talented practitioner, is notably well suited to Hikmet's subject matter. One early poem, evidently composed in a devil-may-care mood, contrasts the author's straitened and difficult circumstances—his many monotonous hours as a lowly proofreader were rewarded with a pittance—and the effervescent sensations of springtime, with Cupid urging him after a comely girl.

Considerable powers of creative imagination were called upon in early poetry of a political character. In the long poem *Jokond ile Si-Ya-U* (the
Gioconda and Si-Ya-U), various narrative transitions are conjoined with
abrupt changes of setting, from Paris to the open sea to Shanghai under the
white terror; eventually the author's summary is presented from his vantage
point in Europe. Some of Hikmet's experiences during his travels—he had
met Chinese revolutionaries during a visit to France—appear in an ultimately
fictional and somewhat fantastic form. The author, who is bored and chafing
at what he regards as hidebound aesthetic classicism in the Louvre, comes
upon a modern Gioconda in a most unusual guise. Her modern incarnation is
exotic and remote, but deeply concerned about mass upheaval that aims at
the transformation of traditional Asian society. Still inscrutable, she is made
to stand by as the soldiers of nationalist leader Chiang Kai-shek execute a
Chinese Communist spokesman. Ultimately the Gioconda is tried and found
guilty by a French military court; hers is a fate quite different from spending
centuries on canvas as a creation of Leonardo da Vinci. Other works express
Hikmet's proletarian views of art: Beethoven's sonatas, he maintains, should
be played out on wood and metal in the workplace. The raw power of the
industrial age is reflected in his taut descriptive lines about iron suspension
bridges and concrete skyscrapers. Yet the workers in his native Turkey were
invariably badly off: They were bound to an unthinking routine and could
afford only the lowest quality of goods.

One early composition took up the cause of striking transportation workers in Istanbul in 1929. At times Hikmet considered events that were not too
far removed from his own experience; his sojourns in Russia during the early
years of the Soviet government probably furnished impressions recaptured in
verses about the revolutionary events of 1917. Poems collected in *Taranta
Babu'ya mektuplar* (letters to Tarantu Babu) raised another problem in
world politics; they are letters in verse purportedly written by a young Italian
to a native woman caught up in the Ethiopian war launched under Benito
Mussolini. The author's commentary on the brutal excesses of Fascism
reveals a measure of political prescience as well as an expanded sense of solidarity with like-minded people in many nations.

Historical dimensions of class struggle are explored in *The Epic of Sheik
Bedreddin*. Although government pressure by this time had restricted his
choice of subject matter, making it almost impossible for him to publish work
on contemporary issues, the author turned to more remote ages with the
avowed intent of rescuing major events from the antiquarian dust that had
gathered around them. This epic, based upon a book he had read during one
of his early prison terms, was given added intensity by the author's experience of seeing a man hanged outside the window of his cell. While set in the
early fifteenth century, Hikmet's work underscores the solidarity that brought
together Turkish peasants, Greek fishermen, and Jewish merchants; in places

he suggests that though historical works had depicted this era as the prelude to an age of imperial greatness, it in fact was rife with social unrest and discontent provoked by inequality and injustice. Ten thousand common people took up arms to oppose the Sultan before the rebellion was finally put down. The eventual execution of his protagonist, one of the insurgents' leaders, was a grim, bloody business that Hikmet recounts in unsparing detail but with impassioned sensitivity. This long poem, one of the most celebrated in Turkish literature of the twentieth century, is also notable for the author's broadening concern with different verse techniques, which reached fruition with his works combining modern usage with classical Persian meters.

During Hikmet's longest period of imprisonment, between 1938 and 1950, works displaying other facets of his poetic consciousness were composed; his outlook seemed to become more deeply personal, though perhaps not so brash and self-assertive as in some of his first poems. His meditations on the springtime reveal a sense of yearning and melancholy that was previously absent. For a time he was held in solitary confinement. He wrote of singing to himself, and watching shadows on the wall; simple things began to matter more to him. There are a number of touching passages in prison poems that he addressed to Piraye, his second wife; brief, bittersweet phrases recall their shared joys together, aspects of her appearance, and simple pleasures that mattered most to him. The long period of his incarceration led to some brooding reflections on the transitory and changeless issues of this life. In some poems there is speculation on the seasons that have come and gone, children who have been conceived and grown since he entered prison; mountains in the distance, however, remain fixed points separated by specific spatial intervals. There are also some ironic musings on the fates of common criminals from among his fellow prisoners: One of them was held for murder but was paroled after seven and one-half years; after a second, much shorter, sentence for smuggling, he was released for good and eventually married. The couple's child would be born while much of Hikmet's term, as a political prisoner, still remained to be served. Angina pectoris, followed by a heart attack, aroused uncertainty about the author's physical condition. He wrote poems reaffirming the necessity to go on living, particularly with half his heart devoted anyway to social concerns in Turkey, on the outside, or to political struggles in Greece and China. Some works that begin by marking the passage of time in prison contain brief but intense reactions to events of World War II, including bombing raids, the liberation of concentration camps at Dachau, and the dawn of the nuclear age.

One collection of poems, *Rubaiyat*, written in 1945 but published posthumously in 1966, reveals the author's search for further literary forms that would express the ideological and philosophical content of his thought. Beginning with the example of the Sufi poet and religious thinker Jalal al-Din Rumi (1207-1273), Hikmet took up the position in effect that mysticism is merely a veiled means of approaching material and social reality. Hikmet purposely adopted the quatrain, on a pattern similar to that used by Omar Khayyám, specifically to take issue with the Persian poet's supposed hedonism. In some lines, counsel to take wine and be joyful is contrasted with the harsh, inescapable routines of working-class life. Elsewhere the philosophical idealism of classical writers is challenged by Hikmet's own commitment to dialectical materialism; in poems dedicated to Piraye, the poet asks whether the images he retains of her correspond to the material reality he remembers. On a technical level, this work is notable as well for the author's provocative insertion of colloquial language in passages that otherwise conform to time-honored standards of versification.

Contemporary history on a panoramic scale is taken up in *Human Landscapes*, which was written during the author's prison years but was only published several years after his death. Beginning with the project for an epic study of Turkish history during the twentieth century, at intervals the poet's narrative also turns to major events in adjoining regions, notably naval action of World War II in the Mediterranean and the work of Soviet forces against Nazi invaders.His commentary on the Turkish War of Independence (1919-1922) stands in stark contrast to the heroic national themes repeatedly invoked by other writers of that period. In Hikmet's view, it would seem that the people as a whole contributed to final victory, but only through an inchoate mass rising that did not also lead to a social revolution. Indeed, many passages suggest that class differences remained acute but were altered by Turkey's changed status in the world economy. There are a number of brief sketches of individual lives, both from the wealthy and from the lower orders, often to state unpleasant truths about the people's living situation. Some characters, it is recorded, died of disease at early ages; farmers retained their land but lost all means of production. Many of the personages are war veterans from one conflict or another. There is much attention to dates, but not in the sense of commemorating events with patriotic connotations; important occurrences in individual lives are accorded the same emphasis as major developments in the nation's history. There is also a fair amount of random, seemingly senseless violence: Family quarrels lead to murder; after a man kills his wife, children use the head as a ball in a macabre game. A wrenching, gripping scene records the lynching of a Turk who had collaborated with the British occupation forces. There are some sardonic religious references which call to mind folk superstitions; in some later passages, Turks of a pro-German inclination speculate about whether Adolf Hitler could be a Muslim. Leading Turkish statesmen and thinkers figure as portraits on the walls of business offices; the memories associated with them are quirky bits of characterization that are far from flattering.

The work as a whole darts about and circumambulates historical epochs as they affected different, indeed opposing, social classes. After nearly fifteen years of national independence, homeless and desperately hungry men are to be found outside a newspaper office; if wealthy businessmen cannot turn a profit in some branches of the export trade, because of government restrictions, they move readily to other sectors where their fortunes can be augmented. Some of them end up dealing with both the Allies and the Axis powers during World War II. The incidence of suicide on either side of the class divide is fairly high; among the poor, childbirth is difficult, painful, and sometimes ends in tragedy. Although this exercise in historical realism, based on the author's own observations of Turkish life, does not seem to hold out any immediate hopes for a better future, the poet's descriptions of nature and simple joys serve to leaven an otherwise grim and unsentimental saga. Some later segments of this work are essentially similar to portions of *The Moscow Symphony*, an imaginative lyrical reconstruction of German-Soviet fighting which in the first instance was probably based upon news stories that Hikmet received in prison. After allowance for the different languages, it may be argued that some passages would do credit to a Soviet wartime poet: the anxiety of the war's first year, the vast human drama of armies locked in combat, and the camaraderie of soldiers brought together in common struggle are evoked in brisk, telling lines. Hikmet's own allegiances are discussed in another section, which depicts the execution of an eighteen-year-old Russian girl for partisan action against the Nazis. He wrote, "Tanya,/ I have your picture here in front of me in Bursa Prison," and, before returning to the Turkish settings where his epic had commenced, he added:

> Tanya,
> I love my country
> as much as you loved yours.

Nazim Hikmet's last poems in some ways chronicled the tribulations of exile; many works had to do with his travels about the Communist world, as well as into Switzerland and to Paris. The impression arises that he considered many of his destinations as way stations; hotel balconies, train depots, arrivals and departures are recorded repeatedly and almost mechanically. His political works from this period, albeit written in countries that were openly receptive to his views, were lacking perhaps in the combative spirit that had distinguished the poems written in Turkey. Among such productions there may be found some caustic observations in verse on the Korean War—he deplored Turkey's participation in that conflict—as well as more positive and uplifting efforts composed for May Day celebrations or in response to the Cuban revolution. One poem was meant to commemorate the fortieth anniversary of the foundation of the Turkish Communist Party. His personal concerns, perhaps, were handled more effectively in his later works. One poem describes his meeting with a young blonde woman in an express train; as the sights pass by outside afterimages of her hair and eyelashes, and of her long black coat, repeatedly appear before his eyes. Some poems expressed his desire to be reunited with his lover, Vera Tuliakova, after journeys about various East European countries. In other works there are somewhat sour comments on his physical condition, which continued to deteriorate during his years in exile. Although he continued to cherish the values of this existence, some passages became dour and premonitory. Toward the end of his life he speculated:

> Will my funeral start out from our courtyard?
> How will you take me down from the third floor?
> The coffin won't fit in the elevator,
> and the stairs are awfully narrow.

For many years, Nazim Hikmet was regarded as Turkey's best-known Communist; his conspicuously partisan poetry on behalf of the working classes created more controversy than the pronouncements of many political figures. His importance as a poet, however, may be measured by the extent to which his works have been read even as interest in his ideological agitation, the long-standing scandal of his imprisonment, and his life in exile have become past concerns. While it is possible to distinguish major phases in his career as a poet—and arguably within those periods he was subject to variable moods—there are also elements of continuity which in their turn point to the enduring features of his work. Although some of his efforts may have aged more gracefully than others, his concerns with social justice, and with the struggle against Fascism in Europe, certainly would find sympathy with many subsequent readers. He maintained that Marxism interested him largely for its literary possibilities and that his work was involved largely in the basic human issues of his time. His poems are quite possibly the most readily recognized of those from any Turkish writer of the twentieth century. Aside from his political fame, or notoriety, it may be contended not only that he had discovered forms by which modern free verse might be composed in Turkish but also that he had come upon themes and techniques which have been found to be intrinsically appealing on a much wider level.

Other major works

NOVELS: *Kan konuşmaz*, 1965; *Yeşil elmalar*, 1965; *Yaşamak güzel şey bekardeşim*, 1967 (*The Romantics*, 1987).

SHORT FICTION: *Sevdalı bulut*, 1968.

PLAYS: *Ocak başında*, 1920; *Kafatası*, 1931; *Bir ölü evi yahut merhumun hanesi*, 1932; *Unutulan adam*, 1935; *Bir aşk masalı*, 1945; *İvan İvanoviç var mıydı yok muydu?*, in Russian 1956, in Turkish 1971; *Enayi*, 1958; *İnek*, 1958; *İstasyon*, 1958; *Yusuf ve Zeliha*, 1963; *Sabahat*, 1966; *Yolcu*, 1966; *Damokles'in kılıcı*, 1971; *Fatma, Ali ve başkaları*, 1971; *Her şeye rağmen*, 1971.

NONFICTION: *Sovyet demokrasisi*, 1936; *Alman faşizmi ve ırkçılığı*, 1936; *İt ürür kervan yürür*, 1965; *Cezaevinden Mehmet Fuat'a mektuplar*, 1968; *Kemal Tahir'e mahpusaneden mektuplar*, 1968; *Oğlum, canım evladim, Memedim*, 1968; *Bursa cezaevinden Va-Nu'lara mektuplar*, 1970; *Nazim ile Piraye*, 1975.

Bibliography

Baybars, Taner. "Nazim Hikmet: Poems," in *Delos*. IV (1970), pp. 185-192.

Blasing, Mutlu Konuk. "Translating Poetry: Texts and Contexts of Nazim Hikmet," in *Translation Review*. V (1980), pp. 43-45.

Des Pres, Terrence. "Poetry and Politics: The Example of Nazim Hikmet," in *Parnassus: Poetry in Review*. VI, no. 2 (1978), pp. 7-25.

Halman, Talat Sait. "Nazim Hikmet: Lyricist as Iconoclast," in *Books Abroad*. XLIII, no. 1 (1969), pp. 59-64.

J. R. Broadus

A. D. HOPE

Born: Cooma, Australia; July 21, 1907

Principal poem and collections

The Wandering Islands, 1955; *Poems*, 1960; *A. D. Hope*, 1963; *Collected Poems, 1930-1965*, 1966; *New Poems, 1965-1969*, 1969; *Dunciad Minor: An Heroick Poem*, 1970; *Collected Poems, 1930-1970*, 1972; *Selected Poems*, 1973; *The Damnation of Byron*, 1973; *A Late Picking: Poems, 1965-1974*, 1975; *A Book of Answers*, 1978; *The Age of Reason*, 1985; *Selected Poems*, 1986.

Other literary forms

A. D. Hope has distinguished himself as poet, critic, and editor. His collections of lectures, essays, and reviews include *Australian Literature, 1950-1962* (1963), *The Cave and the Spring: Essays on Poetry* (1965), *A Midsummer Eve's Dream: Variations on a Theme by William Dunbar* (1970), *Native Companions: Essays and Comments on Australian Literature, 1936-1966* (1974), and *The Pack of Autolycus* (1979). In addition, he has published a critical study of a contemporary Australian poet, *Judith Wright* (1975), and a collection of "notes on the craft of poetry," *The New Cratylus* (1979). He has also edited an anthology, *Australian Poetry, 1960*, and, with Leonie Kramer, a selection of poems, prose, and letters by Henry Kendall, the nineteenth century Australian colonial poet.

Achievements

While Australia has yet produced no poet who has had a lasting influence on world literature, Hope has perhaps come closest to attaining an international reputation. Since the publication of his first collection in 1955, he has emerged as the dominant figure in Australian poetry.

Hope stands outside the mainstream of much modern poetry in his rigid formalism and outspoken disdain for much of the poetry and critical theories of his contemporaries, or what he calls in *The New Cratylus* "Heresies of the Age." In his carefully balanced wit and in the lucidity of his use of such neo-classical forms as the heroic couplet, he seems much closer in his attitudes and manner to Alexander Pope than to T. S. Eliot. While early compared to W. H. Auden in his sometimes scathing denunciations of twentieth century life, Hope possesses a distinctive voice with a wide range; his satirical poems have been no less admired than his passionate love poetry. In all of his work, the notion of poetry as a learned craft is preeminent. Unlike many of his contemporaries, he has remained content to express his vision in the traditional patterns of accentual-syllabic meter and rhyme. His poetic conservatism and use of classical learning make him unique among living poets.

Hope's first collection was published when he was nearly fifty; since then, his reputation has grown rapidly. He has been the recipient of numerous awards, including the Arts Council of Great Britain award for poetry (1965), the Ingram Merrill Award for Literature (1969), the Levinson Prize (1969), and the Robert Frost Award (1976). In 1972, he was named Officer, Order of the British Empire, and in 1985, he was elected Ashby Visiting Fellow of Clare Hall, Cambridge, and Honorary Fellow of University College, Oxford. He has traveled and lectured extensively, especially in the United States.

Biography

Alec Derwent Hope was born in Cooma, New South Wales, Australia, on July 21, 1907, the firstborn of the family. His father, Percival Hope, a Presbyterian minister, moved the family to Tasmania when Hope was four years old. In the rural area where Hope's father's new congregation was located, school was rudimentary at best, often being held in the local sheepshearing shed. Hope, like many middle-class children, received much of his primary instruction at home. His mother, who had been a schoolteacher, taught him to read and write, and his father later instructed him in Latin. The family library was large, and the parents took turns reading classics of English literature aloud to the five children. Hope began to write poems in ballad stanzas when he was seven or eight, and by the time he was in his early teens, he had published his first poem, a translation of Catullus' *Phasellus ille quem videstis, hospites*.

When Hope was fourteen, he was sent to the Australian mainland for his secondary education, first at Bathurst High School and later at Fort Street High School, one of the best schools in Sydney. Upon graduation, he was awarded a scholarship designated for sons of Presbyterian clergymen and matriculated at St. Andrew's College of the University of Sydney. He had originally intended to study medicine, but low science marks forced him to read for an arts degree instead. During his undergraduate years, he published poems in university magazines and in the Sydney *Bulletin*. He was graduated in 1928. Hope distinguished himself in his undergraduate work in philosophy and English and won a scholarship for further study in England.

He entered University College, Oxford, in the fall of 1928, shortly after the graduation of Auden, Louis MacNeice, and Stephen Spender. Poor and underprepared, Hope had difficulty with the tedious Oxford English curriculum, which at that time leaned heavily toward philological studies: Despite his admiration for such notable scholars as C. S. Lewis, he managed no better than a third-class degree, which he completed in 1930.

He returned to Sydney just as the Depression was deepening and became a public-school teacher and vocational psychologist for several years before obtaining a position as a lecturer in education at Sydney Teachers' College in 1937. In 1938, he married Penelope Robinson and was appointed lecturer in

English at Sydney, where he remained until 1944. In 1945, he became the Senior Lecturer in English at the University of Melbourne, where he taught courses in English and European literature. In 1951, he became the first Professor of English at Canberra University College (now the Australian National University), a chair which he held until 1969, after which he was Library Fellow for three years and, later, Professor Emeritus.

Analysis

In his introduction to a selection of his poems published in 1963 as part of the Australian Poets series, A. D. Hope stated that "all theories about poetry are inadequate and that good poetry has been written on many assumptions which actually appear to be incompatible with one another." That claim notwithstanding, Hope does admit to several "comfortable prejudices" which allow him to ignore poetical practices with which he has no sympathy. "The chief of these," he says, "is a heresy of our time which holds that by excluding those things which poetry has in common with prose, narrative, argument, description, exhortation and exposition, and that, depending entirely on lyric impulse or the evocative power of massed imagery one can arrive at the pure essence of poetry." This remark is central to any understanding of Hope's work, for he consistently laments the impoverishment of twentieth century poetry when it is compared to the "great variety of forms practised in the past." The remark also reveals the strong influence of Latin studies on Hope's work, for his list includes most of the common topics of classical rhetoric. Of those he mentions, narrative and argumentation are important techniques that he consistently employs in his best poems.

Hope's second complaint is with "the notion that poetry can be improved or its range extended by breaking down the traditional structure of English verse by replacing its rhythms by those of prose." Hope, who studied at Oxford with C. L. Wrenn, editor of *Beowulf*, has written learnedly on the origins of English poetic meter, particularly on the transition from accentual meters to accentual-syllabics that took place in the century after Geoffrey Chaucer's death and on the metrical practices of John Dryden and Pope. Like Robert Frost, Hope credits the tension between meter and sentence rhythm as the key to the successful iambic pentameter line, of which Hope is a master. Indeed, he is perhaps more knowledgeable about meter than any other living poet and, thus, has little patience with theories of "open form" or "projective verse" that have been forwarded in defense of free verse.

According to Hope, another of these modern "heresies" stems from "that irritable personalism which is partly a heritage of the Romantics, the view that poetry is primarily self-expression." Even though Hope has stated his disagreement with the poetical theories of Edgar Allan Poe, he would seem to agree with the primacy of a poem's effect on its audience: "The poem is not a feeling, it is a structure of words designed, among other things, to arouse a certain state of feeling." Similarly, Hope would seem to agree with T. S. Eliot ("a poet whose poetry I cannot bring myself to like at all") in the need for a poet to find "an 'objective correlative' for the transmission of the poet's state of heart and mind to his readers." It should be apparent from these comments that Hope has little sympathy for the confessionalist tendencies of much contemporary poetry, which have provided many poets with "an adoring cannibal audience waiting for the next effusion of soul meat." He adds that the emotions in poems should not necessarily be equated with the emotions of poets: "The delight of creation and invention is their proper emotion and this must be in control of all other feelings."

Finally, Hope comments on his personal preferences in the language of poetry, which he prefers "to be plain, lucid, coherent, logically connected, syntactically exact, and firmly based in current idiom and usage." To a large degree, Hope has remained true to this dictum; his poetry is remarkable for its avoidance of needless obscurity and ambiguity. As he says, "A poem which can be parsed and analysed is not necessarily a good poem, but a poem which cannot is almost certainly bad." He does, however, allow himself the option of a certain elevation of language, what has been disparagingly called "poetic diction" in this century. With William Wordsworth, Hope agrees that "a poet should certainly be a man speaking to men in a language common to all," but that does not mean that the debased vocabulary of conversational speech should be his sole resource. For Hope, whose learning is catholic, the "word-hoard" of the poet should be ample enough to include terms from a great range of interests which, in his own case, include numerous historical and literary references, classical allusions, and scientific terms.

Australian literature, like all colonial literatures, including that of the United States, has been throughout much of its short history in search of an identity. During the nineteenth century, Australian poets fell into two general classes: those who imitated the poetic styles of the English Romantics and Victorians and those who carried on a lively body of "bush poetry," largely anonymous balladry derived from the folk traditions of Great Britain. Of this first group, Oscar Wilde, reviewing an 1888 anthology of Australian writing, could find "nothing but echoes without music, reflections without beauty, second-rate magazine verses, arid third-rate verse for Colonial newspapers, . . . artless Nature in her most irritating form." Hope makes two revealing comments regarding the situation of the Australian writer of his generation: The first is that his father's library, while amply supplied with the classics of English literature, contained no Australian poets; the other is that, as late as the early 1950's, Hope had to struggle to obtain credit-status for the course in native literature that he instituted and taught at Canberra University College. Thus, the Australian poet is caught in an uncomfortable dilemma: He may wish to create a truly "national" poetry, but he lacks a tradition upon which to build it.

Hope has himself identified, in *Native Companions*, the three main stages of a colonial literature. In the first, the work of colonial writers is simply part of the literary tradition of the homeland. In the second, writers born in the new land but educated in the tradition of the mother country attempt to create a literature of their own. In the final stage, this self-consciousness disappears, and writers emerge who can influence the whole literary tradition, including that of the mother country. Though Hope believes that Australian literature still resides in the middle stage, one could argue, with the novelist Patrick White's winning of the Nobel Prize, the publication of Judith Wright's *The Moving Image* and James McAuley's *Under Aldeberan* in 1946, and the publication of Hope's first collection, *The Wandering Islands*, in 1955, that Australian writing has clearly moved into its maturity.

Though Hope had been publishing poetry and criticism since the late 1930's, *The Wandering Islands*, which appeared when he was forty-eight, was his first full collection. In a cultural climate that was still marked by parochialism and censorship, Hope's first book was something of a *succès de scandale*. The sexual explicitness of the title poem, his lightly worn learning, and his unsparing satire caused many critics to accuse him variously of academism, obscurity, misogyny, and even anti-Australian sentiments. Certainly, "Australia" would not have pleased the nationalistic poets of the Jindyworobak movement, at whose expense Hope had on occasion been mercilessly critical in his reviews. In this outwardly bitter poem, Hope sees his homeland as "without songs, architecture, history." Despite the fact that Hope later characterizes himself as one who turns "gladly home/ From the lush jungle of modern thought" to a country which has not yet been overwhelmed by "the chatter of cultured apes," the poem gave his early critics an abundant supply of ammunition with which to attack him.

In the book's title poem Hope also delineates another constant theme of his work: the attractions and disappointments of love. For Hope, "the wandering islands" are the isolations of individual sexual identities, which are always, like the sundered beast in Plato's analogy of the two sexes, frustrated in their attempts at complete union: "An instant of fury, a bursting mountain of spray,/ They rush together, their promontories lock,/ An instant the castaway hails the castaway,/ But the sounds perish in that earthquake shock." In these brief seconds of orgasmic loss of self lies "all that one mind ever knows of another,/ Or breaks the long isolation of the heart." Commenting on Hope's recurrent motifs in a review of *The Wandering Islands*, S. L. Goldberg notes that "the attitude from which his themes arise is Dionysian or tragic, disturbed, romantic, existentialist at least in its premises; on the other hand, the sense of tradition and order implicit in his art . . . is decidedly Apollonian or classical, and intellectual rather than freely organic." In this sense, Hope seems closest to the tradition of the English Metaphysical poets, John Donne in particular, who saw no divorce between passion and intellect, the "dissociated sensibility," to borrow Eliot's phrase.

A significant number of Hope's best poems deal with the sexual theme, by turns satirically and seriously. In "Conquistador" he sings "of the decline of Henry Clay/ . . . a small man in a little way," who is mashed flat in a sexual encounter with a "girl of uncommon size," who uses "him thereafter as a bedside mat." The poem, which is not without its darker side, bears comparison with Auden's "Ballad of Miss Gee." In "The Brides," Hope, in an impressive piece of social satire, works an extended conceit comparing the bridal and automotive "industries." The prospective groom, shopping for the smartest model in the sexual showroom, is lured to the altar by promises of "every comfort: the full set/ Of gadgets; knobs that answer to the touch/ For light or music; a place for his cigarette;/ Room for his knees; a honey of a clutch." That the majority of contemporary marriages last not much longer than a new car's extended warranty period is at least implicit in this witty poem.

In other poems Hope expands the sexual theme to include larger observations of nature and human history. "Imperial Adam," one of his most widely reprinted poems, retells the story of the Fall as a sexual fable. Having partaken of the "delicious pulp of the forbidden fruit," Adam and Eve immediately experience the first awakening of sexual desire:

Sly as the snake she loosed her sinuous thighs.

And waking, smiled up at him from the grass;
Her breasts rose softly and he heard her sigh—
From all the beasts whose pleasant task it was
In Eden to increase and multiply

Adam had learned the jolly deed of kind:
He took her in his arms and there and then,
Like the clean beasts, embracing from behind
Began in joy to found the breed of men.

In lines that are reminiscent of W. B. Yeats's "A shudder in the loins engenders there/ The broken wall, the burning roof and tower. . . ," Hope foreshadows the whole violent future of humanity in the "sexual lightning stroke" of that first embrace. The poem closes with Adam witnessing the consequences of his act:

Adam watching too
Saw how her dumb breasts at their ripening wept,
The great pod of her belly swelled and grew,

And saw its water break, and saw, in fear,
Its quaking muscles in the act of birth,
Between her legs a pigmy face appear,
And the first murderer lay upon the earth.

It is significant that Hope, in a later poem entitled "The Planctus," offers "another version of the Fall" in which Eve escapes the Garden and is provided with another helpmate, "While Adam, whose fellow God had not replaced,/ Lived on immortal, young, with virtue crowned,/ Sterile and impotent and justified." In Hope's view, a purely hermetic retreat from the moral perplexities of life is equivalent to a living death.

One other early poem comments, at first satirically, on those who see the "standardization" of the modern age as somehow unnatural, in particular the typical "Nature Poet" who "from his vegetable Sunday School/ Emerges with the neatly maudlin phrase" to protest the "endless duplication of lives and objects" which the American poet Theodore Roethke decried in "Dolor." Against this romantic assumption, Hope weighs the evidence of Earth herself, whose procreative fecundity "gathers and repeats/ The cast of a face, a million butterfly wings." Hope argues persuasively that such "standardization" is, in fact, the essence of the reproductive forces that rule nature and human life. As he says, it is love that "still pours into its ancient mould/ The lashing seed that grows to a man again."

Even in those poems which seem purely lyrical, Hope resists the romantic temptation to find in love any easy solutions. In one of his finest short poems, "As Well as They Can," he combines the twin demands of art and love in lines that ironically echo the conceit of Donne's "The Bait":

> As well as he can, the poet, blind, betrayed
> Distracted by the groaning mill, among
> The jostle of slaves, the clatter, the lash of
>   trade,
>   Taps the pure source of song.
>
> As well as I can, my heart in this bleak air,
> The empty days, the waste nights since you went,
> Recalls your warmth, your smile, the grace and
>   stir
>
>   That were its element.

Hope's poetry is founded on dialectical premises—between the sexes, between assertion and counterargument, between art and life, even between the living poet and his predecessors. In "Moschus Moschiferus," which is on first glance conventional in its subtitle, "A Song for St Cecilia's Day," he contrasts "the pure, bright drops of sound" of Tibetan hunters' flute music with the ends to which it is put, ensnaring the hapless mouse-deer of the title, hunted almost into extinction for their precious musk glands. As a footnote to a century which has seen, in Nazi Germany to cite only one example, the powers of music set to evil uses, Hope can offer the saint little more than a sardonic gift: "Divine Cecilia, there is no more to say!/ Of all who praised the power of music, few/ Knew of these things. In honor of your day/ Accept this song I too have made for you."

Similarly, in carrying on a continuing dialogue with the writers and literature of the past, Hope takes a revisionist view of personalities and characters that must now be seen from a contemporary perspective. In "Man Friday" he writes a sequel to Daniel Defoe's *Robinson Crusoe* (1719) in which Friday, having had his fill of life in a country where "More dreadful than ten thousand savages,/ In their strange clothes and monstrous mats of hair,/ The pale-eyed English swarm to joke and stare,/ With endless questions round him crowd and press/ Curious to see and touch his loneliness," makes his escape home by a last, suicidal swim. "Faustus," informed by the Devil that "Hell is more up-to-date than men suppose" and that his soul has long since been in hell, now "reorganized on the hire-purchase plan," avoids living further in his purely material world by killing both Helen and himself. Lord Byron, who boasted of thousands of seductions, in "The Damnation of Byron" is condemned to a "Hell of Women" where, at last satiated by endless "wet kisses and voluptuous legs agape// He longs for the companionship of men, their sexless friendliness." In all these poems, as well as in many others from *A Book of Answers* and *The Age of Reason*, Hope's collection of verse epistles and narratives concerning leading figures, both historical and fictional, from the Augustan Age, one is always aware of an intellect passionately involved in a debate with the past.

Even though Hope has stressed, perhaps ingenuously, that his own poems are "hardly ever 'confessions' and [are] usually written in a spirit of 'as if' highly misleading to any unwary commentator or putative biographer," it would be a mistake to assume that his poetry is impersonal in any sense. Eliot, who said that poetry should be "an escape from personality," went on to add that one must first have a personality to be able to escape from it. In "Hay Fever," a late poem which is one of the few clearly autobiographical works in Hope's oeuvre, the gentle memory of an Edwardian summer spent mowing hay in rural Tasmania moves the mature poet to speculate on the abundant harvest of a life's work:

> It is good for a man when he comes to the end
>   of his course
> In the barn of his brain to be able to romp
>   like a boy in the heap . . .
> To lie still in well-cured hay . . . to drift
>   into sleep.

A. D. Hope's voice, so distinctive in its ability to match the orchestra's full range, is truly remarkable.

Other major works

NONFICTION: *The Structure of Verse and Prose*, 1943; *The Study of English*, 1952 (lecture); *Australian Literature, 1950-1962*, 1963; *The Cave and the Spring: Essays on Poetry*, 1965; *The Literary Influence of Academies*, 1970 (lecture); *A Midsummer Eve's Dream: Variations on a Theme by William Dunbar*, 1970; *Henry Kendal: A Dialogue with the Past*, 1971; *Native Companions: Essays and Comments on Australian Literature, 1936-1966*, 1974; *Judith Wright*, 1975; *The Pack of Autolycus*, 1979; *The New Cratylus: Notes on the Craft of Poetry*, 1979; *Poetry and the Art of Archery*, 1980 (lecture).

Bibliography

Brooks, David. "Poets of My Country," in *New England Review*. IV, no. 4 (1982), pp. 510-529.

Goldberg, S. J. Review of *The Wandering Islands*, in *Meanjin Quarterly*. XVI (June, 1957), pp. 127-139.

Hollander, John. Review of *New Poems: 1965-1969*, in *Harper's Magazine*. CCXLI (September, 1970), p. 109.

Hooton, Joy. *Bibliography: A. D. Hope*, 1979.

Kalstone, David. Review of *Collected Poems, 1930-1965*, in *Partisan Review*. XXXIV (Fall, 1967), p. 619.

Kramer, Leonie. *Australian Writers and Their Work: A. D. Hope*, 1979.

_____, ed. *The Oxford History of Australian Literature*, 1981.

McGann, Jerome J. "Australian Felix," in *Poetry*. CXVIII (July, 1971), p. 223.

Morse, Ruth. Introduction to *Selected Poems*, 1986.

R. S. Gwynn

SUSAN HOWE

Born: Boston, Massachusetts; June 10, 1937

Principal collections
Hinge Picture, 1974; *The Western Borders*, 1976; *Cabbage Gardens*, 1979; *Secret History of the Dividing Line*, 1978; *The Liberties*, 1980; *Pythagorean Silence*, 1982; *Defenestration of Prague*, 1983; *Articulation of Sound Forms in Time*, 1987.

Other literary forms
Susan Howe has also published several reviews and *My Emily Dickinson* (1985). This last, a book-length consideration of Dickinson's work, elucidates the poetry not only of its subject but also of its author, and it is central to an understanding of her oeuvre.

Achievements
In the dozen years since she began to publish her poetry, Howe has established herself as a poet of profound engagement with the problematic of Being in the era she confronts. Her work also addresses the meaning of being American and being a woman, in order to strip away obsolete ideas concerning both America and Woman, the better to discover the realities of these conditions in the present.

Because her poetry is engendered both by a close attention to the minims of language and by a constant examination of the ground from which the language stems, Howe has come into association with the group known as the Language Realists, publishing in the magazines of that movement as well as in several anthologies predominantly or wholly of Language Realism: *The $L=A=N=G=U=A=G=E$ Book* (1984), *21 + 1 American Poets Today* (a bilingual edition, 1986), *In the American Tree* (1986), and *Language Poetry* (1987).

Howe has twice received the American Book Award of the Before Columbus Foundation, in 1982 for *Pythagorean Silence* and again in 1985 for *My Emily Dickinson*. In 1980, she received a Pushcart Prize for "The Art of Literary Publishing," an interview she conducted with James Laughlin, and in 1986, she was awarded a Writer's Fellowship by the New York State Arts Council. In 1985, she participated in the Colloquium on New Writing held by the Kootenay School for Writers in Vancouver, Canada, and in that same year was writer-in-residence at New College in San Francisco. In 1986, she spoke on Emily Dickinson to a Conference on H. D. and Emily Dickinson held at San Jose State University.

Biography

Susan Howe was born in Boston, Massachusetts, on June 10, 1937. With the exception of a relatively brief period in Buffalo, New York, her childhood and adolescence were spent in Boston and Cambridge, where she attended the Beaver Country Day School, from which she was graduated in 1955. Also in 1955, she began a year's study at the Gate Theater, Dublin, Ireland, acting and designing sets. From 1957 to 1961, she attended the Museum School of Fine Arts in Boston. She next took up residence in New York City, working as a painter and exhibiting her paintings at a number of galleries, including the Kornblee. In 1961 she married Harvey Quaytman, and their daughter Rebecca was born that same year. When her marriage ended in 1966, Howe began living with the sculptor David von Schlegell, and in 1967, their son Mark was born. The couple was married in 1976.

In 1971, Howe moved to Guilford, Connecticut, which she made her permanent residence. From 1975 to 1980, she produced the program "Poetry" for WBAI, New York City's Pacifica Radio station.

Analysis

Susan Howe's poetry challenges habitual assumptions on many levels, but the level the reader is most likely to notice first is the syntactic; what Howe says of Dickinson can with equal force be applied to herself: "In prose and poetry she explored the implications of breaking the law just short of breaking off communication with a reader." Generally, Howe's poems make much use of the page, where the white space is allowed to interrupt the sequence of print, so that a variety of statements may be derived from relatively few phrases, and the overall thrust of the syntax is continually thwarted. Denied easy access to an overarching meaning, the reader must work with smaller units (phrase, line, couplet) and can only gradually constitute the meaning of the whole. This process parallels the approach to Being advocated both explicitly and implicitly in Howe's work. The presumptions of categorical value which modern Western culture persists in advocating are resisted at every turn, for Howe sees (and reveals) just how damaging such presumptions and categories can be. Often, she labors to construct a fresh view of her subject, be it Esther Johnson (known to Jonathan Swift's readers as Stella), Emily Dickinson, or Jonathan Edwards. To this end, Howe employs the various devices of deconstruction, notably the fracturing of sentence, phrase, or even word.

Such a project inevitably must challenge received notions of the poetic. It is for this reason that traditional forms are absent from Howe's poetry. Such forms by their very ease of recognition would defeat her purpose. To arouse the critical faculties in her reader, Howe must abjure whatever constructions might encourage a reader to glide effortlessly onward: The work must be difficult, not only to reflect accurately the difficulty of living but also to remind the reader at each turn of his or her preconceptions concerning the nature of reality, art, and the very act of reading. For Howe, as for other poets wedded to this task, the question then becomes, What portion of the inherited conceptions of beauty, truth, and the good ought to be retained (as inherent to the art of poetry), and what portion uprooted and discarded (as inimical to a faithful representation of the present)? Language, derived from Being, comes then to govern Being; the reader projects back onto the world expectations previously drawn therefrom: Yet the world is always in process, always changing, always endangering our assumptions and rendering them obsolete. It is therefore to language itself, argue poets who share Howe's address, that the poet ought to draw attention; the reader must be kept aware of the ways in which language governs not only one's concepts but also one's perceptions, and it is for this reason that Howe through "parataxis and rupture" never lets her readers forget the effect of words and phrases on content. Content, in fact, always includes the agony of choice, whether it be the deliberations as to formal procedure or their counterparts in other modes of action.

"The lyric poet," Howe writes in *My Emily Dickinson*, "reads a past that is a huge imagination of one form," and while the labor of precursors in one sense is enormously beneficial, providing as it does countless elucidations of Being, in another sense it becomes a mighty burden, because of the irresistible nature of preexisting formulations, whether to the poet or to her audience, formulations which nevertheless demand to be resisted if one is to come to a personal definition of one's epoch. Howe, then, in her determination to "make it new," aligns herself with such high modernists as Ezra Pound, Gertrude Stein, and William Carlos Williams, although she must also—for the reasons given above—keep her project distinct from theirs. The world in the 1970's and 1980's is far from the world of the 1910's and 1920's; Howe is among those who see the poet's calling as a demand to make forms consonant with her own day.

The analysis provided during the 1960's and 1970's of dominant patriarchal elements in Western society is one example of this altered ideology to which Howe would be responsible. Therefore *The Liberties*, a book of poetry whose sufficient cause is the largely masculine-engendered version of Esther Johnson, known—and it is the commonality of this means of recognition Howe intends to attack—as Dean Swift's Stella. Howe would liberate from this patriarchal version another picture of this historical personage. As she writes in another context (in her analysis of the received idea we termed "Emily Dickinson"): "How do I, choosing messages from the code of others in order to participate in the universal theme of Language, pull SHE from all the myriad symbols and sightings of HE?" In *The Liberties*, Howe begins by providing a prose sketch, "Fragments of a Liquidation," whose import can best be summarized by repeating the last two sentences of its first paragraph:

"Jonathan Swift, who gave allegorical nicknames to the women he was romantically involved with, called her 'Stella.' By that name she was known to their close friends, and by that name she is known to history." The poems that follow spring from Howe's desire to liberate Esther from Stella and, by extension, Howe's own self from equally pernicious assumptions. In practice, it is not always possible to distinguish from each other these twin liberations, and so a composite woman, struggling to be freed from the roles provided for her by men and a male-dominated history, becomes the shadow heroine of Howe's pages.

If the method is to question in this manner, and to reconstitute a truer history, the technique that Howe develops and that is consonant with her method is to call meaning into question not only at the level of the sentence (these poems are so severely underpunctuated that the reader usually must decide the limits of the sentence) but also at the level of the phrase or even the word. One poem, for example, begins "and/ she/ had a man's dress mad/ e/ though her feet ble/ d/ skimming the surf/ ace," a series of ruptures which militates against any "skimming of the surface" on the reader's part.

In a subsequent section of *The Liberties*, Howe extends her attention to William Shakespeare's Cordelia, surely attractive to Howe for her refusal to accede to the patriarchal demand to accord with the picture of herself her father wished to perpetuate. This section, titled "White Foolscap," puns on "fool's cap" and thus reminds the reader that Cordelia is a dramatic character whose only "real" context is the play *King Lear*, complete with Fool. Yet the title also refers to the blank page that the writer addresses: metaphorically, the nothingness into which she throws herself, composing. In the next section, "God's Spies," a playlet, Stella and Cordelia meet, together with the ghost of Jonathan Swift; the women are dressed as boys in their early teens. The action is fragmented, the dialogue sparse, truncated, enigmatic. The longest speech is Stella's, a poem the historical Stella wrote, very much in the manner of Swift: When it is done, Stella shoots herself. To so sink herself in the style of another, Howe is saying, is tantamount to suicide.

The third and final section of *The Liberties*, "Formation of a Separatist, I," is prospective, as the previous sections were retrospective. Howe has composed these poems of isolated words—single words with white space between each, arranged in blocks—and celebrates their individual tones, rather than their syntactic possibilities. There are, however, other poems in this section which depend upon phrases and sentences; in fact, the book ends with these lines: "Tear pages from a calendar/ scatter them into sunshine and snow." The nightmare of history disperses into a present which is subject to elements in their own nature.

Pythagorean Silence is also divided into three sections: The first, "Pearl Harbor," opens with a poem titled "Buffalo, 12.7.41" and the announcement of the cataclysm that has unleashed such terrible forces upon the second half of the century, the cataclysm that has so thoroughly trammeled survivors and inheritors in an ethical dilemma that becomes, for the artist, an aesthetic dilemma as well. Theodor Adorno, the German theoretician of art and society, averred that it has become impossible, since Auschwitz, to write poetry; the tens of millions murdered since 1941 cry out whenever Being is addressed. A character in Howe's poem, who is called TALKATIVE, "says we are all in Hell": Howe suggests that a truer use of language, one less suspect (in Howe's world and work, all talking *about* things is seen as vitiated by its own remove), can be found in biblical Rachel's inconsolable cry: "her cry/ silences/ whole/ vocabularies/ of *names*/ for/ *things*." The problem with the declaration that we are all in Hell arises from the clichéd nature of the phrase, which works against an experience of its meaning. Howe's "negative poetry" would undo prior namings where these have become impenetrably familiar. This is why she nudges her poems along through puns: In the pun, other meanings break through the intended singularity of usage, the law of logical syntax is transgressed by the play of several possibilities. "Connections between unconnected things are the unreal reality of Poetry," she asserts in *My Emily Dickinson*.

In section 2, the title section of *Pythagorean Silence*, the initial poem opens with a pun arising from the fracturing of a single word: "He plodded away through drifts of i/ ce." "Drifts of i" suggests the accumulation of personal, even egocentric, experience, with "drifts" implying the contingent nature of such accumulations, accrued as "the wind listeth." The line's extension equates "i" with "ice"—a frozen lump of such subjectivity. Yet Pythagoras broke through the amassed subjectivity of his experience to accomplish, with his theorem, the objective; to the extent that he is the hero of this sequence and this book, Howe implicitly urges emulation of his persistence. The "silence" of her title—which Howe discovered in a footnote in E. R. Dodd's *The Greeks and the Irrational*—refers to the silence maintained by initiates of the Pythagorean rites prior to their more active worship, a form of meditation. Indeed, the impression of her poetry is of (to echo William Butler Yeats) "speech after long silence," a use of language directly opposed to unthinking, unfeeling chatter.

Notice should be taken, however, of Howe's statement in *My Emily Dickinson*:

> at the center of Indifference I feel my own freedom . . . the Liberty in wavering. Compression of possibilities tensing to spring. Might and might . . . mystic illumination of analogies . . . instinctive human supposition that any word may mean its opposite. Occult tendency of opposites to attract and merge.

Taking this as a rule of thumb and applying it to the claim that Pythagoras is the hero in her book, the reader will consider the possibility that he is also the villain, capable of leading the unsuspecting into frozen wastes of abstruse speculation. Nor will this afterthought annul the previous reading, but rather coexist with it. Howe's greatest clarity lies in her ability to imply and exemplify the insupportable partiality of any single answer.

Inescapably, Howe is, by birth and gender, both American and a woman, subject to the assumptions of those categories, and at once in revolt against such predications and eager to discover their underlying realities. In *My Emily Dickinson*, she would rescue the Dickinson of her particular vision from the several inadequate characterizations which prevent, to Howe's view, a full experience of the poetry. To this end, Howe, in a work that is cousin both to William Carlos Williams' *In the American Grain* (1925) and Charles Olson's *Call Me Ishmael* (1947), rereads the contribution of figures vital to Dickinson's production: Elizabeth Barrett Browning and Robert Browning, James Fenimore Cooper, Emily Brontë, Charles Dickens, Jonathan Edwards, Ralph Waldo Emerson, Cotton Mather, Mary Rowlandson, William Shakespeare, Henry David Thoreau, and Thomas Wentworth Higginson. Howe finds that, approached from this rich assortment of angles, Dickinson's poetry yields a wealth of information about Being in general, but also about being American and being a woman, and about how a poetry grows consanguineously. Howe is severe with certain feminist critics who, while lauding Dickinson, laud a Dickinson who is essentially the creation of patriarchal vision, swallowing whole this distortion. Toward the end of *My Emily Dickinson*, Howe observes: "Victorian scientists, philosophers, historians, intellectuals, poets, like most contemporary feminist literary critics—eager to discuss the shattering of all hierarchies of Being—didn't want the form they discussed this in to be shattering." Howe's poetic practice is the negation of this widespread and persistent error.

Other major works
  NONFICTION: *Religious Literature of the West*, 1971 (with John Raymond Whitney); *My Emily Dickinson*, 1985.

Bibliography
American Book Review. Review of *Defenestration of Prague*. VI (July, 1984), p. 18.
Armantrout, Rae. Commentary on *Pythagorean Silence* in *Poetics Journal*. II (September, 1982).
Butterick, George. Commentary on *Defenestration of Prague* in *Hambone*. III (1983).
Chamberlain, Lori. Commentary on *Defenestration of Prague* in *Sulfur*. IX (1984).
Library Journal. Review of *Defenestration of Prague*. CVIII (December 15, 1983), p. 230.
Perloff, Marjorie. "Recharging the Canon: Some Thoughts on Feminist

Poetics in the Avant-garde," in *American Poetry Review*. XV (July/
August, 1986), pp. 12-20.

Taggart, John. Commentary on *Pythagorean in Silence* in *Tamerisk*. V, nos.
3/4 (1983).

The Village Voice Literary Supplement. Review of *Defenestration of Prague*.
April, 1984, p. 8.

―――――――. Review of *My Emily Dickinson*. February, 1986, p. 16.

David Bromige

ISSA
Kobayashi Yatarō

Born: Kashiwabara, Japan; May 5, 1763
Died: Kashiwabara, Japan; November 19, 1827

Principal collections
Kansei kuchō, 1794; *Kansei kikō*, 1795; *Kyōwa kuchō*, 1803; *Bunka kuchō*, 1804-1808; *Shichiban nikki*, 1810-1818; *Hachiban nikki*, 1819-1821; *Kuban nikki*, 1822-1824; *The Autumn Wind*, 1957; *A Few Flies and I*, 1969.

Other literary forms
Although Issa is known primarily as one of the three great haiku poets, he also wrote prose—in *Chichi no shūen nikki* (1803; my father's last days), a response to his father's death—and mixed prose and verse, or *haibun*, in *Oragu haru* (1819; *The Year of My Life*, 1960), an autobiographical account of his most memorable year.

Achievements
Ezra Pound's recognition of the power of a single image which concentrates poetic attention with enormous force and his examination of the complexity of the Japanese written character led to an increasing awareness of the possibilities of haiku poetry for Western readers in the early part of the twentieth century. Combined with a growing interest in Oriental studies and philosophy, haiku offered an entrance into Japanese concepts of existence concerning the relationship of man and the natural world. Because the brevity of haiku is in such contrast to conventional ideas of a complete poem in the Western tradition, however, only the most accomplished haiku poets have been able to reach beyond the boundaries of their culture.

The most prominent among these are Bashō (1644-1694), Buson (1715-1783), and Issa. As William Cohen describes him, "in humor and sympathy for all that lives, Issa is unsurpassed in the history of Japanese literature and perhaps even in world literature." A perpetual underdog who employed humor as an instrument of endurance, who was exceptionally sensitive to the infinite subtlety of the natural world, and who was incapable of acting with anything but extraordinary decency, Issa wrote poetry that moves across the barriers of language and time to capture the "wordless moment" when revelation is imminent. More accessible than the magisterial Buson, less confident than the brilliant Bashō, Issa expresses in his work the genius that is often hidden in the commonplace. The definition of haiku as "simply what is happening in this place at this moment" is an apt emblem for a poet who saw man forever poised between the timely and the timeless.

Biography

The poet known as Issa was born Kobayashi Yatarō in 1763 in the village
of Kashiwabara, a settlement of approximately one hundred houses in the
highlands of the province of Shinano. The rugged beauty of the region, especially the gemlike Lake Nojiri two miles east of the town, led to the development of a tourist community in the twentieth century, but the harsh winter
climate, with snowdrifts of more than ten feet not uncommon, restricted
growth in Issa's time. The area was still moderately prosperous, however, because there was a central post office on the main highway from the northwestern provinces to the capital city of Edo (now Tokyo). The lord of the
powerful Kaga clan maintained an official residence which he used on his
semiannual visits to the shogun in Edo, and a cultural center developed
around a theater which featured dramatic performances, wrestling exhibi-
tions, and poetry readings.

Issa was the son of a fairly prosperous farmer who supplemented his
income by providing horse-pack transportation for passengers and freight.
His composition of a "death-verse" suggests a high degree of literary awareness. In the first of a series of domestic tragedies, Issa's mother died when he
was three, but his grandmother reared him with deep affection until Issa's father remarried. Although his stepmother treated him well for two years,
upon the birth of her first child, she relegated Issa to a role as a subordinate.
When she suggested that a farmer's son did not need formal schooling, Issa
was forced to discontinue his study of reading and writing under a local master. When her baby cried, she accused Issa of causing its pain and beat him
so that he was frequently marked with bruises.

According to legend, these unhappy circumstances inspired Issa's first
poem. At the age of nine or so, Issa was unable to join the local children at
a village festival because he did not have the new clothes the occasion required. Playing by himself, he noticed a fledgling sparrow fallen from its
nest. Observing it with what would become a characteristic sympathy for nature's outcasts, he declared:

> Come and play,
> little orphan sparrow—
> play with me!

The poem was probably written years later in reflection on the incident, but
Issa displayed enough literary ability in his youth to attract the attention of
the proprietor of the lord's residence, a man skilled in calligraphy and haiku
poetry, who believed that Issa would be a good companion for his own son.
He invited Issa to attend a school he operated in partnership with a scholar
in Chinese studies who was also a haiku poet. Issa could attend the school
only at night and on holidays—sometimes carrying his stepbrother on his
back—when he was not compelled to assist with farm chores, but this did

not prevent him from cultivating his literary inclinations. On one of the occasions when he was assisting his father by leading a passenger on a packhorse, the traveler ruminated on the name of a mountain that they were passing. "Black Princess! O Black Princess!" he repeated, looking at the snow-topped peak of Mount Kurohime. When Issa asked the man what he was doing, he replied that he was trying to compose an appropriate haiku for the setting. To the astonishment of the traveler, Issa proclaimed: "Black·Princess is a bride—/ see her veiled in white."

Issa's studies were completely terminated when his grandmother died in 1776. At his stepmother's urgings, Issa was sent to Edo, thrown into a kind of exile in which he was expected to survive on his own. His life in the capital in his teenage years is a mystery, but in 1790 he was elected to a position at an academy of poetics, the Katsushika school. The school had been founded by a friend and admirer of Bashō who named it for Bashō's home, and although Issa undoubtedly had the ability to fulfill the expectations of his appointment, his innovative instincts clashed with the more traditional curriculum already in place at the school. In 1792, Issa voluntarily withdrew from the school, proclaiming himself Haikaiji Issa in a declaration of poetic independence. His literary signature literally translates as "Haikai Temple One-Tea." The title "Haikai Temple" signifies that he was a priest of haiku poetry (anticipating Allen Ginsberg's assertion "Poet is Priest!"), and as he wrote, "In as much as life is empty as a bubble which vanishes instantly, I will henceforth call myself *Issa*, or One Tea." In this way, he was likening his existence to the bubbles rising in a cup of tea—an appropriate image, considering the importance of the tea ceremony in Japanese cultural life.

During the next ten years, Issa traveled extensively, making pilgrimages to famous religious sites and prominent artistic seminars, staying with friends who shared his interest in poetry. His primary residence was in Fukagawa, where he earned a modest living by giving lessons in haikai, possibly assisted by enlightened patrons who appreciated his abilities. By the turn of the century, he had begun to establish a wider reputation and his prospects for artistic recognition were improving, but his father's final illness drew him home to offer comfort and support. His father died in 1801 and divided his estate equally between Issa and his half brother. When his stepmother contested the will, Issa was obliged to leave once again, and he spent the next thirteen years living in Edo while he attempted to convince the local authorities to carry out the provisions of his father's legacy. His frustrations are reflected in a poem he wrote during this time: "My old village calls—/ each time I come near,/ thorns in the blossom."

Finally, in 1813, Issa was able to take possession of his half of the property, and in April, 1814, he married a twenty-eight-year-old woman named Kiku, the daughter of a farmer in a neighboring village. Completely white-haired and nearly toothless, he still proclaimed that he "became a new man" in his fifties, and during the next few years, his wife gave birth to five children. Unfortunately, all of them died while still quite young. Using a familiar line of scripture that compares the evanescence of life to the morning dew as a point of origin, Issa expressed his sense of loss in one of his most famous and least translatable poems:

> This dewdrop world—
> yet for dew drops . . .
> still, a dewdrop world ·

In May, 1823, Issa's wife died, but he remarried almost immediately. This marriage was not harmonious, and when the woman returned to her parent's home, Issa sent her a humorous verse as a declaration of divorce and as a statement of forgiveness. Perhaps for purposes of continuing his family, Issa married one more time in 1825, his bride this time a forty-six-year-old farmer's daughter. His wife was pregnant when Issa died in the autumn of 1828, and his only surviving child, Yata, was born after his death. Her survival enabled Issa's descendants to retain the property in his home village for which he had struggled during many of the years of his life.

In his last years, while he was settled in his old home, he achieved national fame as a haikai poet. His thoughts as a Master were valued, and he held readings and seminars with pupils and colleagues. After recovering from a fairly serious illness in 1820, he adopted the additional title Soseibo, or "Revived Priest," indicating not only his position of respect as an artist and seer but also his resiliency and somewhat sardonic optimism. As a kind of summary of his career, he wrote a poem which legend attributes to his deathbed but which was probably given to a student to be published after his death. It describes the journey of a man from the washing bowl in which a new baby is cleansed to the ritual bath in which the body is prepared for burial: "Slippery words/ from bathtub to bathtub—/ just slippery words." The last poem Issa actually wrote was found under the pillow on the bed where he died. After his house had burned down in 1827, he and his wife lived in an adjoining storehouse with no windows and a leaky roof: "Gratitude for the snow/ on the bed quilt—/ it too is from Heaven." Issa used the word *Jodo* (Pure Land) for Heaven, a term which describes the Heaven of the Buddha Amida. Issa was a member of the largest Pure Land sect, the Shin, and he shared the sect's faith in the boundless love of the Buddha to redeem a world in which suffering and pain are frequent. His final poem is an assertion of that faith in typically bleak circumstances, and a final declaration of his capacity for finding beauty in the most unlikely situations.

Analysis

The haiku is a part of Japanese cultural life, aesthetic experience and philosophical expression. As Lafcadio Hearn noted, "Poetry in Japan is

universal as air. It is felt by everybody." The haiku poem traditionally consists
of three lines, arranged so that there are five, seven, and five syllables in the
triplet. Although the "rules" governing its construction are not absolute, it
has many conventions that contribute to its effectiveness. Generally, it has a
central image, often from the natural world, frequently expressed as a part of
a seasonal reference, and a "cutting word," or exclamation that states or implies the poet's reaction to what he sees. It is the ultimate compression of
poetic energy and often draws its strength from the unusual juxtaposition of
image and idea.

It is very difficult to translate haiku into English without losing or distorting some of the qualities which make it so uniquely interesting. English syllables are longer than Japanese *jion* (symbol sounds); some Japanese characters have no English equivalent, particularly since each separate "syllable"
of a Japanese "word" may have additional levels of meaning; a literal rendering may miss the point while a more creative one may remake the poem so
that the translator is a traitor to the original. As an example of the problems
involved, one might consider the haiku Issa wrote about the temptations and
disappointments of his visits to his hometown. The Japanese characters can
be literally transcribed as follows:

Furosato	ya	*yoru*	*mo*	*sawaru*	*mo*	*bara-no-hana*
Old village	:	come-near	also	touch	also	thorn's-flowers

The poem has been translated in at least four versions:

> At my home everything
> I touch is a bramble.
>
> > (Asataro Miyamori)

> Everything I touch
> with tenderness alas
> pricks like a bramble.
>
> > (Peter Beilenson)

> The place where I was born:
> all I come to—all I touch—
> blossoms of the thorn.
>
> > (Harold Henderson)

> My old village calls—
> each time I come near,
> thorns in the blossom.
>
> > (Leon Lewis)

Bashō's almost prophetic power and Buson's exceptional craftsmanship
and control may be captured fairly effectively in English, but it is Issa's at-

titude toward his own life and the world that makes him perhaps the most completely understandable of the great Japanese poets. His rueful, gentle irony, turning on his own experiences, is his vehicle for conveying a warmly human outlook which is no less profound for its inclusive humor. Like his fellow masters of the haiku form, Issa was very closely attuned to the natural world, but for him, it had an immediacy and familiarity that balanced the cosmic dimensions of the universal phenomena which he observed. Recognizing human fragility, he developed a strong sense of identification with the smaller, weaker creatures of the world. His sympathetic response is combined with a sharp eye for their individual attributes and for subtle demonstrations of virtue and strength amid trying circumstances. Although Issa was interested in most of the standard measures of social success (family, property, recognition), his inability to accept dogma (religious or philosophical) or to overlook economic inequity led him to a position as a semipermanent outsider no matter how successful he might be.

Typically, Issa depicts himself as an observer in the midst of an extraordinary field of natural phenomena. Like the Western Romantic poets of the nineteenth century, he uses his own reactions as a measuring device and records the instinctive responses of his poetic sensibility. There is a fusion of stance and subject, and the man-made world of business and commerce occurs only as an intrusion, spoiling the landscape. What matters is an eternal realm of continuing artistic revelation, the permanent focus of man's contemplation: "From my tiny roof/ smooth . . . soft . . . / still-white snow/ melts in melody." The poet is involved in the natural world through the action of a poetic intelligence which re-creates the world in words and images, and, more concretely, through the direct action of his participation in its substance and shape: "Sun-melted snow. . . / with my stick I guide/ this great dangerous river." Here, the perspective ranges from the local and the minimal to the massively consequential, but in his usual fashion, Issa's wry overestimation of his actions serves to illustrate his realization of their limits. Similarly, he notes the magnified ambition of another tiny figure: "An April shower. . . / see that thirsty mouse/ lapping river Sumida." Amid the vast universe, man is much like a slight animal. This perception is no cause for despair, though. An acceptance of limitations with characteristic humor enables him to enjoy his minuscule place among the infinities: "Now take this flea:/ He simply cannot jump . . . / and I love him for it."

Because he is aware of how insignificant and vulnerable all living creatures are, Issa is able to invest their apparently comic antics with dignity: "The night was hot . . . / stripped to the waist/ the snail enjoyed the moonlight." The strength of Issa's identification of the correspondence between the actions of human beings and animals enables him to use familiar images of animal behavior to comment on the pomposity and vanity of much human behavior. In this fashion, his poems have some of the satirical edge of eighteenth century wit, but Issa is much more amused than angry: "Elegant singer/ would you further favor us/ with a dance, O Frog?" Or if anger is suggested, it is a sham to feign control over something, because the underlying idea is essentially one of delighted acceptance of common concerns: "Listen, all you fleas . . . / you can come on pilgrimage, o.k. . . . / but then, off you git!" Beyond mock anger and low comedy, Issa's poems about his participation in the way of the world often express a spirit of contemplation leading to a feeling of awe. Even if the workings of the natural world remain elusive, defying all real comprehension, there is still a fascination in considering its mysterious complexity: "Rainy afternoon . . . / little daughter you will/ never teach that cat to dance."

At other times, however, the landscape is more forbidding, devoid of the comfort provided by other creatures. Issa knew so many moments of disappointment that he could not restrain a projection of his sadness into the world: "Poor thin crescent/ shivering and twisted high/ in the bitter dark." For a man so closely attuned to nature's nuances, it is not surprising that nature would appear to echo his own concerns. When Issa felt the harsh facts of existence bearing heavily on him, he might have found some solace in seeing a reflection of his pain in the sky: "A three-day-old moon/ already warped and twisted/ by the bitter cold." Images of winter are frequent in Issa's poetry, an outgrowth of the geographical reality of his homeland but also an indication of his continuing consciousness of loss and discouragement. Without the abundant growth of the summer to provide pleasant if temporary distraction, the poet cannot escape from his condition: "In winter moonlight/ a clear look/ at my old hut . . . dilapidated." The view may be depressing but the "clear look" afforded by the light is valuable, and in some ways, reassuringly familiar, reminding the poet of his real legacy: "My old father too/ looked long on these white mountains/ through lonely winters."

Issa spent much time trying to establish a true home in the land in which he was born because he had a strong sense of the importance of family continuity. He regarded the family as a source of strength in a contentious and competitive environment and wrote many poems about the misfortune of his own family situation. Some of his poems on this subject tend to be extremely sentimental, lacking his characteristic comic stance. The depth of his emotional involvement is emphasized by the stark pronouncement of his query: "Wild geese O wild geese/ were you little fellows too . . . / when you flew from home?" These poems, however, are balanced by Issa's capacity for finding some unexpected reassurance that the struggle to be "home" is worthwhile: "Home again! What's this?/ My hesitant cherry tree/ deciding to bloom?" Although nothing spectacular happens, on his home ground, even the apparently mundane is dressed in glory: "In my native place/ there's this plant:/ As plain as grass but blooms like heaven." In an understated plea for placing something where it belongs, recalling his ten-year struggle to win a share of his father's property, he declares how he would dispense justice: "Hereby I assign in perpetuity to wit:/ To this wren/ this fence." For Issa, the natural order of things is superior to that of society.

The uncertainty of his position with respect to his family (and his ancestors) made the concept of home ground especially important for Issa as a fixed coordinate in a chaotic universe. His early rejection by his stepmother was an important event in the development of an outlook that counted uncertainty as a given, but his sense of the transitory nature of existence is a part of a very basic strain of Japanese philosophy. The tangible transmixed with the intangible is the subject of many of his poems: "The first firefly. . ./ but he got away and I—/ air in my fingers." A small airborne creature, a figure for both light and flight, is glimpsed but not caught and held. What is seen, discernible, is rarely seen for long and never permanently fixed. The man who reaches for the elusive particle of energy is like the artist who reaches for the stuff of inspiration, like any man trying to grasp the animating fire of the cosmos. The discrepancy between the immutable facts of existence and the momentary, incredible beauty of life at its most moving is a familiar feature of Issa's work: "Autumn breezes shake/ the scarlet flowers my poor child/ could not wait to pick." Issa's famous "Dewdrop" haiku was also the result of the loss of one of his children, but in this poem too, it is the moment of special feeling that is as celebrated—a mixture of sadness and extraordinary perception.

The consolation of poetry could not be entirely sufficient to compensate for the terrible sense of loss in Issa's life, but he could not accept standard religious precepts easily either. He was drawn to the fundamental philosophical positions of Buddhist thought, but his natural skepticism and clear eye for sham prevented him from entering into any dogma without reservation. Typically, he tried to undermine the pomposity of religious institutions while combining the simplicity of understated spiritualism with his usual humor to express reverence for what he found genuinely sacred: "Chanting at the altar/ of the inner sanctuary. . ./ a cricket priest." Insisting on a personal relationship with everything, Issa venerated what he saw as the true manifestation of the great spirits of the universe: "Ah sacred swallow. . ./ twittering out from your nest in/ Great Buddha's nostril." The humanity of his position, paradoxically, is much more like real religious consciousness than the chanting of orthodox believers who mouth mindless slogans although unable to understand anything of Amida Buddha's message to mankind: "For each single fly/ that's swatted, *"Namu Amida/ Butsu"* is the cry." Above all, Issa was able to keep his priorities clear. One is reminded of the famous Zen description of the universe, "No holiness, vast emptiness," by Issa's determination to keep Buddha from freezing into an icon: "Polishing the Buddha . . ./ and why not my pipe as well/ for the holidays?" As Harold Henderson points out, "the boundless love attributed to Amida Buddha coalesced with his own tenderness toward all weak things—children and animals and insects." Even in those poems of a religious nature which do not have a humorous slant there is a feeling of humility that is piety's best side: "Before the sacred/ mountain shrine of Kamiji . . . / my head bent itself." In this poem, too, there is an instinctive response that does not depend on a considered position or careful analysis, thus paralleling Issa's reaction to the phenomena of the natural world, the true focus of his worship.

While most of Issa's haiku are like the *satori* of Zen awareness, a moment of sudden enlightenment expressed in a "charged image," Issa's "voice" also has a reflective quality that develops from a rueful realization of the profound sadness of existence. What makes Issa's voice so appealing in his more thoughtful poems is his expression of a kind of faith in the value of enduring. He can begin the new year by saying: "Felicitations!/ Still . . . I guess this year too/ will prove only so-so." Or he can draw satisfaction from triumphs of a very small scale: "Congratulations Issa!/ You have survived to feed/ this year's mosquitos." The loss of five children and his wife's early death somehow did not lead to paralysis by depression: "If my grumbling wife/ were still alive I just/ might enjoy tonight's moon." When his life seemed to be reduced almost to a kind of existential nothingness, he could see its apparent futility and still find a way to feel some amusement: "One man and one fly/ buzzing together in one/ big bare empty room." Or he could calculate the rewards of trying to act charitably, his humor mocking his efforts but not obscuring the fact that the real reward he obtained was in his singular way of seeing: "Yes . . . the young sparrows/ if you treat them tenderly—/ thank you with droppings."

There were moments when the sadness became more than his humor could bear. How close to tragic pessimism is this poem, for example: "The people we know . . ./ but these days even scarecrows/ do not stand upright." And how close to despair is this heartfelt lament: "Mother lost, long gone . . . / at the deep dark sea I stare—/ at the deep dark sea." Issa is one of those artists whose work must be viewed as a connected body of creation with reciprocal elements. Poems such as these somber ones must be seen as dark seasoning, for the defining credo at the crux of his work is that his effort has been worthwhile. In another attempt at a death song, Issa declared: "Full-moon and flowers/ solacing my forty-nine/ foolish years of song." Since death was regarded as another transitory stage in a larger vision of existence, Issa could dream of a less troubled life in which his true nature emerged: "Gay . . . affectionate . . . / when I'm reborn I pray to be/ a white-wing butterfly." He, knew, however, that this was wishful thinking. In his poetry, he was already a "white-wing butterfly," and the tension between the man and the poem, between the tenuousness of life and the eternity of art, energized his soul. As he put it himself, summarizing his life and art: "Floating butterfly/ when you dance before my eyes . . . / Issa, man of mud."

Other major works

NONFICTION: *Chichi no shūen nikki*, 1803.

MISCELLANEOUS: *Oragu haru*, 1819 (*The Year of My Life*, 1960); *Issa zenshū*, 1929; *Issa zenshū*, 1979 (nine volumes).

Bibliography

Beilenson, Peter, and Harry Behn. *Japanese Haiku: Series I-IV*, 1958-1962.

Blyth, R. H. *History of Haiku*, 1963-1964.

Cohen, William Howard. *To Walk in Seasons*, 1972.

Henderson, Harold O. *An Introduction to Haiku*, 1958.

MacKenzie, Lewis. Introduction to *The Autumn Wind*, 1957.

Leon Lewis

RONALD JOHNSON

Born: Ashland, Kansas; November 25, 1935

Principal poems and collections

A Line of Poetry, A Row of Trees, 1964; *Assorted Jungles: Rousseau*, 1966; *Gorse/Goose/Rose and Other Poems*, 1966; *Sunflowers*, 1966; *Io and the Ox-eye Daisy*, 1966; *The Book of the Green Man*, 1967; *The Round Earth on Flat Paper*, 1968; *Reading 1 and 2*, 1968 (two volumes); *Valley of the Many-colored Grasses*, 1969; *Balloons for Moonless Nights*, 1969; *The Spirit Walks, The Rocks Will Talk*, 1969; *Songs of the Earth*, 1970; *Maze/Mane/Wane*, 1973; *Eyes and Objects*, 1976; *RADI OS I-IV*, 1977; *Ark: The Foundations 1-33*, 1980; *Ark 50: Spires 34-50*, 1984.

Other literary forms

In addition to his poetry, Ronald Johnson has published the cookbooks *The Aficionado's Southwestern Cooking* (1968), *Southwestern Cooking, New and Old* (1985), and *The American Table* (1984), the last-named being his culinary magnum opus.

Achievements

A disciple of Charles Olson, Johnson has followed Olson's intuition that a poem must find the form necessary to its fullest expression. For Johnson, this has meant the writing of poems which by conventional measures of poetry do not seem to be poems at all. As well, under the pull of energies initially mobilized during the concrete poetry movement in the early 1960's, Johnson has explored the poetic possibilities of typography and the visual presence of a poem as a kind of sign. At the root of his attention is the natural world, its sounds and sights. Out of his deference to this phenomenal world, Johnson has devised techniques to register it in a new way. In some of his poems, where his manipulation of typography and instinct for the suggestibility of individual letters is working, the poem becomes a wholly novel visual experience.

From his early concrete poems to his recent Ark series, Johnson has sought to bind the world of poetry to the world of made things. Thus, his work is a rare and refreshing turn-away from the hypersubjectivity typical of much postmodern poetry. Against the ramblings of selfhood he erects a bright vision, directing one toward the complex and beautiful universe.

Prizes awarded to Johnson for his poetry include the Boar's Head Prize for Poetry, in 1960; the *Poetry*'s Inez Boulton Award, in 1964; National Endowment for the Arts awards, in 1969 and 1974; and the National Poetry Series Award, in 1983.

Biography

Ronald Johnson was born and grew up in Ashland, Kansas. He briefly attended the University of Kansas before spending two years in the United States Army, earning as a result the post-Korea veterans' benefits which allowed him to attend and be graduated from Columbia University, New York, in 1960. During the years in New York, he became acquainted with many other artists, poets, and scholars, including the people associated with Black Mountain College in North Carolina. In the early 1960's, Johnson traveled in England with the poet and publisher Jonathan Williams, and he received inspiration from the country for many of his most memorable poems. During this time he participated in the concrete poetry movement and became a close friend of Ian Hamilton Finlay, one of the best-known poets in the movement.

In 1968, Johnson moved to San Francisco, where, with the exception of two teaching jobs, he was to make his permanent home. In 1971, he taught creative writing at the University of Kentucky, and in 1973 he held the Roethke Chair for Poetry at the University of Washington.

Analysis

In his book *Valley of the Many-colored Grasses*, Ronald Johnson quotes Ralph Waldo Emerson in an epigraph to one of his poems. The quotation attributes to Nature the power to use creation as a means of expressing itself: "The air is full of sounds; the sky, of tokens; the ground is all memoranda & signatures." These signs speak to "the intelligent," or human beings with eyes and ears. If "the intelligent" are not suitably articulate to pass on the language Nature speaks, it "waits & works, until, at last, it moulds them to its perfect will & is articulated." Reading the poem following the epigraph, one discovers that it is simply the words of the epigraph "aired out" in free-verse lines, Johnson's spacial arrangement of the words serving to arrest the flow of Emerson's prose and emphasize key perceptions. A poem has been found in Emerson's text.

This poem, titled "Emerson, on Goethe," exemplifies two characteristics of Johnson's thought and writing. The first is his preoccupation with nature, or everything that makes up the cosmos, from ants to stars and not exclusive of what an architect designs or a composer composes. A man is subservient to nature, inhabiting nature, dependent upon nature. Nature produces patterns of order and sentient secretaries, artists of various kinds, who are not justified in feeling alienated from a world so animated and willful. Pervading Johnson's poetry is the idea that a poet is someone who brings nature to the ears and eyes of nonpoets under the command of nature itself. This mission puts Johnson as a poet outside the trend of contemporary poetry, where the poet seems more often the secretary of himself, that subjective complex which utters forth from deep within its private and often obscure consciousness. Johnson's heritage as a writer is much more old-fashioned. His poems frequently refer to writers and painters, for whom the real show is the world outside the self. The Johnson heritage includes, along with the transcendentalist Emerson, the poet William Blake, who saw everything in a grain of sand. It embraces the records Henry Thoreau left of his daily eyework along Walden Pond and the paintings of Joseph Turner, who had himself roped to a ship's mast during a storm, the better to know what he was painting. It welcomes the visionary eye of the painter Samuel Palmer, as in Johnson's poem on Palmer, in which the eye is "covered with fire after every immersion/ in the air" and is taken by nature's leading beyond the horizon, where "it gathers to itself all light/ in visionary harvest." It is the same heritage which guided the poet Ezra Pound, in his World War II prison cage, to find in the wasps and midges in the grass a vision of the highest order, an order uncreated by humans but requiring gifts of sensitivity and vision to recognize.

The second characteristic that Johnson's Emerson "poem" demonstrates is Johnson's unconcern about what is actually a poem. None of its words is Johnson's, but the perception of the words is Johnson's. Perception, attention, and observation are of more value to the poet than so-called originality, not that Johnson as a writer is simply copying down what others have written. His attention is arrested by nature and by other writers who testify to similar devotion, so, if in the course of writing a poem Johnson remembers that "to Coleridge, the Marigold,/ Monk's-hood,/ Orange-lily & Indian pink/ flash with light—" the poem is not spoiled by borrowing. On this poet's mind, Johnson's, happened to be the working of another poet's mind, Samuel Taylor Coleridge's. Appropriately, then, the line that follows the one just quoted tells about Charles Darwin's ability to see phosphorus in a horse's eyes. The poetic spell has surely been ruined by telling about what a scientist can do, but Johnson is simply not concerned about "the poem" but about evoking dazzling examples of human eyesight working in the real world.

Johnson is also concerned about "the poem." He wants his poems to be new, bright, as dazzling as the source of inspiration. To readers familiar with what T. S. Eliot and Ezra Pound did to the form of a poem, Johnson's poetry does not seem unpoetic at all. What does seem uncommon is Johnson's persistent belief in a nature which speaks to human beings. Johnson is not interested merely in objectivity, but in seeing through the objectivity. He pursues the calling of seer, or hearer: A tree and its leaves are never ordinary; commonplace objects speak and establish intimacy, an intimacy which is the vision. Thus, a suite of Johnson's poems in his other early book, *The Book of the Green Man*, have sweetly innocent titles: "What the Earth Told Me," "What the Air Told Me," and "What the Leaf Told Me." In this book, Johnson mentions the "skiey influences" which entered into the poet William Wordsworth's pores, sustaining his poetic vision of countryside and lakes. Johnson desires such a relationship. He longs to hear the earth speak, to "issue some dark, meditated/ syllable perhaps—/ something more/ than this inarticulate warble and seething." The earth writes to the poet instead: "Today I saw the word written on the poplar leaves./ It was 'dazzle.'/ As a leaf startles out/ from an undifferentiated mass of foliage,/ so the word did from a leaf—." The poet is Adam in a garden which has not yet been seen with language. Nature continues to educate Adam in this garden, beyond declaring the adjectives through which it is known, with basic scientific facts: "For the tree forms sun into leaves, & its branches & saps/ are solid & liquid states of sun." Johnson would have his reader respond to photosynthesis as a visionary entity, while still bringing along his knowledge of electrochemical force and the laws of physics. When the earth tells the poet "nothing is allowed to stand still," the commonplace law becomes marvelous in its numberless examples, poplar leaves in the wind being only one in the countless manifold. "In the homage of attentions 'all things/ are in flux,'" Johnson writes, and, throwing a stone into a pond, observes "its circles interlacing/ & radiating out to the most ephemeral edge." Again, the high school physics experiment becomes an occasion for religious meditation.

Writing of Johnson's poetry, Guy Davenport notes that "his every poem has been to trace the intricate and subtle lines of force wherein man can discern the order of his relation to the natural world." Thus, Johnson's desire to make nature have a voice is to regather the modern ear to a hearing of what it has been taught is dead. In his poems, the goal of registering the voice of phenomena is reached by pruning away conventional poetic rhetoric and extruding lines of gnomic brevity. In *The Book of the Green Man*, the theme is that a man desires to enter the green world and be taught by it. The man of the title is that mythical figure from England who, in one of his guises, has leaves growing on his face like a beard and foliage for hair. This man bespeaks that intimacy of botany and humanity which for Johnson is the substratum of his art of writing a poem: "Poems beginning germinal in the instant/ —reeling out, unravelling, tendril & silken, into the air—/ ethereal growths,/ sudden, & peculiar as mushrooms?/ Uncrumpling/ as moths from cocoons—." The poet marvels at the relationship between the world and the mind and understands the relationship as something ethereally botanical, biological. In this light, Johnson assembles a corps of writers, from Alexander Pope to Wordsworth to William Klivert, who sensed the heavenly abode which nature suggested. Pope dreamed of planting a cathedral from poplar trees; Johnson dreams in a poem of entering "the architecture of bees" and the mole's passages and the lizard's route through "scrolls of leaves." Dominant in all Johnson's work is this urging to go *into* nature, and to recall those writers who attempted the same kind of entry and union.

In a slender volume published in 1970 titled *Songs of the Earth*, Johnson continued his efforts to listen to the world. He said of the poems: "These songs are listenings, as poems must listen and sing simultaneously." One of the poems is simply the word "earth" repeated without spacing three times in one line, this one line repeated seven times: "earthearthearth." The eye picks out significant terms hiding in the bushes: art, ear, hear, heart, hearth. Another poem spaces out the first and last "s" in the word "stones" to reveal "tone." Yet another places the word "wane" in a square grid, the word printed with spaces between the letters and the lines. Within the square thus formed of capital letters the word "anew" appears in lowercase letters. As in nature, there is no waning that leads to nothing; all waning is, rather, a kind of reprocessing, so in the poem the recycling of letters displays new meaning. Such a poem cannot be spoken, and such poetry to Johnson is "a magical world where all is possible and an 'o' can rise, like the real moon, over the word *moon*." Such writing is sign-making and emphasizes the dominance of the eye as the ruling mode of perception for Johnson. His *Songs of the Earth* was written in response to Gustav Mahler's symphony of the same name. The concrete poems which resulted may have been the product of the poet's listening, but they exist for the reader solely as mute visual patterns, for the eye alone. Johnson considers this not a drawback but a revolution: "We can now make a line of poetry as visible as a row of trees." In a later volume of poetry, titled *Eyes and Objects*, Johnson defines a self as the things it sees: "You are what you look for/ zeroing out on the light-and-dark,/ the X of eyes." His need and intuition as a poet have been to make visible objects for pairs of eyes to converge upon and see.

His latest work shows Johnson continuing to marvel at the products of the universe and continuing to erect structures to hold his marvellings. A book titled *RADI OS I-IV* is a rewriting by excision of John Milton's *Paradise Lost* (1667, 1674). Milton's text, like his title, undergoes a rereading by Johnson, and what is left after the cutting is a modern poem, both in appearance and in ideas. One theme is energy, a familiar twentieth century concern. The radii of the sun energize men and also enable them to see. A fragment of the poem reads: "Too well I see/ :for the mind/ swallowed up/ entire, in the heart/ to work in fire,/ words The Arch." The poet takes his vocation, a commitment not without risk, from the energy mysteriously generated by his capacity to be impassioned by the world. *RADI OS I-IV* is one part of a longer work titled *Ark: The Foundations 1-33*, in which the analogy between writing poetry and creating physical structures is declared in the subsection's titles: "The Foundations," "The Spires," and "The Outworks." In a note on *Ark*, Johnson says that he wrote the poem "with stones of words and mortar of song." Individual poems in the work are "Spires," and the reader is impressed by Johnson's unique ability to *arrest* language, whether single words or phrases:

> to say then head wedded nail and hammer to the
> work of vision

of the word
at hand
that is paradise

"Ark" is that structure so literally prescribed for Noah by God in which he would leave behind the old world and find a new, a terrestrial paradise. It, the ark, is also the arc, the curve of the globe, one segment of which is America, the last promised land humanity was vouchsafed and from which humanity managed to fall, ignoring and persecuting the original inhabitants. Artificers, builders, poets, remain, however, Johnson a member of the host, and they project their various visions. The vision is work, Johnson reminds the reader: "for if hell indeed rein time stood still/ and paradise thus daily fall/ unlikely wings/ on usual shoulders." Johnson clearly views writing poetry as a religious quest, as the establishment of a testimonial edifice which will inspire belief in the hearts of nonartificers. Behind this poem stand Johnson's predecessors for whom nature was the first place to look for inspiration—William Blake, Walt Whitman, Henry David Thoreau, and Samuel Palmer. It is a vision which sees swarms of mayflies as bands of angels and an ear for which "even the humble fly/ buzz anthem/ Christ:".

The poetry of Ronald Johnson is inimical to despair and gloom. It derives from a mandate, clearly religious, to make the world seen and heard. In vain a reader will search for confirmations or investigations of the popular twentieth century focus: the self. In abundance, however, the reader will find things for that self to study and see, and constant reminders of what powers of perception a human possesses, and what he or she is supposed to do with them:

Let us grasp at
the gate, unhinge the dark

clear lake

(moon to sky's edge)

awake! awake!

Other major works

NONFICTION: *The Aficionado's Southwestern Cooking*, 1968; *The American Table*, 1984; *Southwestern Cooking, New and Old*, 1985.

TRANSLATION: *Sports and Divertissments*, 1965 (of notes by Erik Satie to his piano pieces under the same title).

Bibliography

Davenport, Guy. *The Geography of the Imagination*, 1981.
Jaffe, Dan. Review of *Valley of the Many-colored Grasses* in *Saturday*

Review. LII (September 6, 1969), p. 29.
Library Journal. Review of *The American Table*. CIX (August, 1984), p. 1448.
_____. Review of *RADI OS*. CII (December 15, 1977), p. 2469.

Bruce Wiebe

ROBERT KELLY

Born: Brooklyn, New York; September 24, 1935

Principal poems and collections
Armed Descent, 1961; *Her Body Against Time*, 1963; *Twenty Poems*, 1967; *Axon Dendron Tree*, 1967; *Finding the Measure*, 1968; *Songs I-XXX*, 1968; *The Common Shore, Books I-V: A Long Poem About America in Time*, 1969; *Kali Yuga*, 1970; *Flesh Dream Book*, 1971; *The Mill of Particulars*, 1973; *The Loom*, 1975; *The Convections*, 1978; *The Book of Persephone*, 1978; *The Cruise of the Pnyx*, 1979; *Kill the Messenger Who Brings Bad News*, 1979; *Spiritual Exercises*, 1981; *The Alchemist to Mercury*, 1981; *Under Words*, 1983.

Other literary forms
Although Robert Kelly is known primarily for his poetry, it is his fiction that has generated the most enthusiastic reviews. The fiction consists of one novel, *The Scorpions* (1967), a fanciful travelogue, *Cities* (1971), and a collection of stories, *A Transparent Tree* (1985). Kelly has consented to more than half a dozen published interviews, has written prefaces for eight books by other authors, and has contributed occasional statements on film, poetry, and related topics to numerous periodicals since the early 1960's. One collection of such writings was published in 1971, *In Time*, and this book has taken its place as the most significant summation of Kelly's poetics.

Achievements
Kelly has written and published abundantly since his first book appeared in 1961. Recognized at once as one of the most gifted poets of his generation, he has subsequently lived up to his potential by deviating from his original promise over and over again. The first twenty-five years of Kelly's career saw the publication of more than three thousand pages of poetry and nearly one thousand pages of prose. What is remarkable is the consistency of the work and the variety of its forms. It seems certain that Kelly's contribution to the long poem will itself command respect for some time to come. At the same time, he is an adroit miniaturist, a most elegant prose stylist, and a discerning commentator on the work of other poets.

Kelly's prolific body of work is predicated on the fundamental commitment to poetry as a grand project, shared among all of its practitioners. His work is keenly motivated by a sense of poetry as a monumental structure, like a cathedral, arising through centuries of sustained craftsmanship—involving generations and entire communities. The sense of the poem as an addressing of communal concerns is evident throughout Kelly's collections.

On a more private level, Kelly's work is of considerable interest as the daily registration of poetry as process. Because there has been no slackening of energy as the decades have gone by, Kelly's poetry is an invaluable testimony to a demystification of the Romantic legacy of inspiration and divine election. The Kelly poem is a distinct engagement with vision and plenitude as daily obligations. Failure is as inextricably written into the work as success, given the improvisatory legacy of sheer dailiness as a modus operandi.

As several critics noted in a special issue of *Vort* devoted to Kelly in 1974, he is possessed of a rare gift of prosody. This has helped make even his minor efforts seems virtuous in comparison with the preponderance of bad habits prevalent in contemporary free-verse practice. This is all the more astonishing considering Kelly's staggering productivity. The size of his oeuvre has, almost from the beginning, kept his work from being as widely read as that of some of his parsimonious contemporaries. Read even in patches, however, it leaves a lasting impression of energy and eloquence, colloquial ease, and formal grace—a combination rare in the poetry of any period.

Biography

Robert Kelly was born and reared in Brooklyn, in a stimulating urban environment that nourished much of his early poetry. Quite precocious, Kelly entered the City College of New York at age fifteen and entered Columbia at nineteen as a graduate student of medieval studies. The stability of his life as a professor at Bard College since 1962 has afforded Kelly a reliability of circumstance to devote himself to poetry on a prodigious scale. Furthermore, the professorial role at a small college has meant that his daunting intellectual fortitude has been at the service of his poetry rather than diverted into formal scholarship as such.

At the beginning of his carrier, in the late 1950's and early 1960's, Kelly was associated with a circle of poets that included Paul Blackburn, David Antin, Jerome Rothenberg, Armand Schwerner, George Economou, Diane Wakoski, and Clayton Eshleman. Kelly and Rothenberg in particular rose to some prominence as exponents of "deep image," a short-lived but effective stance for young unknown poets to take, insofar as their manifestos commanded respect and their poetry was taken to be a rich demonstration of the theory. Kelly edited two ephemeral magazines in the early 1960's—*Trobar* and *Matter*—which helped establish him as a proponent of the free-verse line of poetry indebted to Charles Olson, Robert Duncan, and Louis Zukofsky among then-living masters.

From 1967 to 1973, Kelly served as associate editor for Clayton Eshleman's widely influential magazine *Caterpillar*. Kelly's involvement ensured that such contemporaries as Kenneth Irby and Gerrit Lansing were regularly featured in the magazine, as well as students and young protégés such as Thomas Meyer, Charles Stein, Richard Grossinger, Harvey Bialy, and Bruce McClelland. This was a period of extraordinary productivity for Kelly himself, making *Caterpillar* a showcase for his many forays into the long poem, culminating in the magazine's final issues with glimpses of the masterwork *The Loom*.

The demise of *Caterpillar* marked the end of a certain burgeoning of public poetry in the United States, not only for Kelly but also for his generation. Kelly subsequently became more involved at Bard College on administrative levels, continuing to teach but also becoming director of the writing program of the Avery Graduate School of the Arts. Kelly has been a recipient of a fellowship from the National Endowment of the Arts. His collection *Kill the Messenger Who Brings Bad News* was awarded the first annual prize in poetry at the Los Angeles Times Book Awards in 1980. In 1981, his archives were acquired by the Poetry/Rare Books Collection of the University Libraries, State University of New York at Buffalo.

Analysis

Robert Kelly's first book, *Armed Descent*, showed some indebtedness to Ezra Pound's balance of line, presentation of a numinous world through direct images, and a rhythmically modulated musicality. Most striking, however, was not the debt but the originality and the confidence. It was a sensuous poetry, a demonstration of Kelly's proclamation that the fundamental rhythm of a poem was the rhythm of images. Each poem contended in its own way for the proposition that visible realities be read as spiritual clarities. The spirit made flesh was the manifest mystery, but there was a practical injunction as well: "The gateway is the visible; but we must go in."

Kelly's imagistic skills might have easily been directed toward the production of autonomous free association. It was within his means to become a giant among American surrealist poets. He was engaged in a quest which could not rest comfortably on surfaces, however, nor reside in a simple succession of images. In his 1968 retrospective pamphlet *Statement*, Kelly stressed that the significant term in "deep image" had been the word *deep*: It was depth that was striven for in poems. Images were simply material agencies and were to be regarded as cues, clues, tangible signs of spiritual intensity.

The sense of depth, in conjunction with the concept of the image, led Kelly to postulate a location "behind the brain" where human lives as experienced through sense and image are "slain/ minute by minute." The Catholicism of Kelly's childhood has persisted in his poetry in the form of guiding images. This epiphany of "the place of the death of Images" is, suitably, from the poem "In Commentary on the Gospel According to Thomas" (in *The Alchemist to Mercury*), and it should be noted that the epigraphs to *Armed Descent* are also drawn from that apocryphal gospel. Kelly was fascinated with the image as something that is born or appears (is a *phenomenon*, from the Greek word for "to appear," *phaino*), dies or lapses, and then reappears or is resurrected. Kelly's Christian roots go deep in this image cycle, of which Christ and the grail chalice that holds his life's blood are the sustaining images. Kelly's is a patently antiauthoritarian Christian vision, however, informed by pagan rites, gnostic and neoplatonist philosophy, heretical sects, and alchemy.

The sense of depth for which Kelly was striving in his early poetry soon became associated with what he called "The Dream Work" (in *In Time*). By linking the production of images in a poem with that productive energy of the dream world, Kelly was able to ground his poetics in a mode of psychic creation going on all the time. This certainly facilitated his orientation to poetry as daily practice. Unlike such previous poetics as that of the French Surrealists, who were fascinated with dream imagery, Kelly's was concerned with drawing psychic energy from the depths from which dreams speak, *not* using the poem as a means of reporting on or approximating dream states. Kelly's success is most evident in the narrative passages of *The Loom*, where such dreamlike images as the detached skull or a notch of coffin-shaped sunlight seen through a keyhole become the stimulus for meditations which are somnambulistic yet acutely conscious at the same time.

Given Kelly's training as a medieval scholar, it is no surprise that his poems evoke the world of the books of hours, the body as a zone of astrological inscriptions and humours, and the spirit as a vehicle for ascent through the plectrum of the harmoniously organized stars and planets. "Finding the measure" (the title of his most acclaimed book), in its literal sense, refers to the process of modulating the rhythms of attention to the shape of the language in its shapely apparition as a poem. Finding the measure for Kelly has all the force of a cosmological prescription as well: "Finding the measure is finding the/ specific music of the hour,/ the synchronous/ consequence of the motion of the whole world." At this level, finding the measure is a mode of tuning or attunement, a means of "keeping in touch" with a cosmos that is intimate (a microcosm) despite its infinitude (a macrocosm). "In the burgeoning optimism of unlimited desire, I reach out for universal intimacy" wrote Kelly in "An Alchemical Journal" (in *The Alchemist to Mercury*). In various ways, the poetry has clearly manifested such unlimited desire in the forms of both sacred and profane yearning. Much of the best work of the late 1960's and early 1970's chronicles this reaching out for universal intimacy in the images provided by alchemy.

Because alchemy is a lapsed language of science, there have been complaints of esotericism directed at Kelly. It is true that much of the work of *Songs I-XXX* and *Flesh Dream Book* is densely allusive. Some simple reminders, however, are in order. Kelly's skills as an image maker have always been prodigious. Even the poems most saturated with arcane lore are guided by the familiar Christian cycle of personal redemption. For Kelly, alchemy was of use in clarifying the concept of the grail. Alchemy was an allegorical presentation of quest motifs intrinsic to the grail legend; in fact, the fundamental concept in alchemy is that of the *vessel*.

In Kelly's work, the experience of being *embodied*—being subjected to growth and decay—is the essence of the alchemical work. The body is the vessel, and the experience is oracular: "Every orifice is a sybil's cave." Every vessel is a chalice or grail, a body that fills, overflows, spills, and is emptied out. This is the cycle of redemption written into Kelly's work from his earliest long poem "The Exchanges" (in *The Alchemist to Mercury*) to "The Emptying" (in *Spiritual Exercises*), passing through such large mediating epiphanies as "Arnolfini's Wedding" and "The World" in *The Mill of Particulars* and *The Loom*.

There are not so much difficulties in Kelly's work as there are mysteries, because Mystery is at the heart of it. Kelly's is the *mysterium tremendum* of sanctity and grace; his single most abiding theme (and the most exacting single pronouncement of his poetics) is the "nonstop imagery of making love salvation." It is Christian in its overall motivation, while allowing for the non-stop profanity of image making and of "making love." In one of his poems, in fact, Kelly toys with the notion that images are to the eyes what sex is to the body. Both are engaged in a quest for depth, an inkling of that place where images and bodily energies are quelled.

It seems plausible that, in the long run, Kelly's most acclaimed book will be the four-hundred-page poem *The Loom*. This poem oscillates between meditations and narrative, coiling images and insights around the slender axis of the very short line, often consisting of only three or four words. In *The Loom*, Kelly has not so much found his measure as returned to it, in that one of his most compelling early poems was the short-lined, book-length *Axon Dendron Tree*. *The Loom* is a book in which all of Kelly's obsessions (sex, death, pain, revelation, transfiguration) are ceaselessly recycled toward a resolution of metabolism, a quieting in which a "sacred language" can be "known best/ when you're hardly listening." Readers of *The Loom*, in fact, can come to know the specific cycle of the alchemical Great Work through the poem, for it duplicates the prescribed stages of alchemical transmutation of base metal into gold without drawing any attention to this as such. The reader not privy to alchemical lore can be satisfied by *The Loom* without even knowing that an immense catalog of occult data is circulating through the text, in the form of narratives and precise images, all of which seem "natural" and not imposed. This is a singular achievement, to transmit secret information in the form of a transparent, lucid text which can be comprehended on an initial (aesthetic, psychological, and philosophic) level without reference to the underlying allegory.

Kelly's work enacts a quest for attaining spiritual intensities in the world of physical forms and forces. It is continually resourceful at generating images that aid the contemplation of this enduring contradiction. The reader's grati-

tude and perplexity are registered in the image of the poet going into a hard-
ware store to buy a pair of needle-nosed pliers and spark plugs, "as if I were
a man on earth": One is moved or unsettled or both, according to one's
lights, by the stubborn grace of Kelly's *as if*.

Other major works
NOVEL: *The Scorpions*, 1967.
SHORT FICTION: *A Transparent Tree*, 1985.
NONFICTION: *Cities*, 1971; *In Time*, 1971.

Bibliography
Ossman, David. Interview in *The Sullen Art*, 1963.
Rasula, Jed. "Robert Kelly: A Checklist," in *Credences*. III, no. 1 (1984), pp.
	91-124.
_____. "Ten Different Fruits on One Different Tree: Reading Robert
	Kelly," in *Credences*. III, no. 1 (1984), pp. 127-175.
_____. *Vort*. No. 5 (1974). Special Kelly issue.

								Jed Rasula

VLADISLAV KHODASEVICH

Born: Moscow, Russia; May 28, 1886
Died: Paris, France; June 14, 1939

Principal collections
Molodost', 1908; *Shchastlivy domik*, 1914; *Putem zerna*, 1920; *Tyazhelaya lira*, 1922; *Evropeiskaya noch'*, 1927; *Sobranie stikhov*, 1927.

Other literary forms
In addition to his poetry, Vladislav Khodasevich published many critical essays and memoirs. The most important of these are collected in *Nekropol'* (1939), *Literaturnye stat'i i vospominaniia* (1954), and *Belyi koridor: Izbrannaia proza v dvukh tomakh* (1982). His biography of the eighteenth century poet Gavrila Derzhavin (*Derzhavin*, 1931) is also notable. As is the case with Khodasevich's poetry, very little of his prose is available in English translation.

Achievements
Khodasevich was one of the most highly regarded Russian poets of his own time and is one of the least known of ours. Twelve years of poetic silence before his death contributed to that obscurity, and a virtual ban on publishing his work in the Soviet Union as well as difficult relations within the Russian émigré community in Western Europe negatively affected his reputation for years. He has reemerged only recently, and there is growing interest in him both in the Soviet Union and in the West.

A pupil of the Symbolists who soon freed himself from their poetics if not their perceptions, a contemporary of Boris Pasternak, Anna Akhmatova, Marina Tsvetayeva, and Osip Mandelstam but resembling none of them, Khodasevich is a poet not easily classified. He is often described as a classicist because of his loyalty to Alexander Pushkin and Russian verse tradition, yet his always ironic and sometimes bleak vision of the world is no less a product of the twentieth century. His poetic output was small and his demands on himself severe, but his mature verse, with its paradoxical combination of domesticity and exile, banality and beauty, harmony and grotesquerie, places him among the finest Russian poets of the century.

Biography
Vladislav Felitsianovich Khodasevich was born in Moscow on May 28 (May 16, Old Style), 1886. Neither his father nor his mother was a native Russian (Felitsian Khodasevich was Polish, Sophie Brafman a Jewish convert to Catholicism and a fervent Polish nationalist), but perhaps as much because of his background as despite it, young Khodasevich considered himself thor-

oughly Russian in both allegiance and sensibility. The youngest of six children, he was educated at Moscow's Third Classical Gimnazium. Even before he left school, his ambitions turned to writing, and it was through a schoolmate that he made his first shy forays into the febrile world of *fin de siècle* Moscow literary life—the world of Valery Bryusov, Andrey Bely, and Aleksandr Blok. After graduation, Khodasevich began writing and publishing, and except for an almost comic bureaucratic interlude immediately after the revolution, he practiced no other profession.

Chronic ill health aggravated by hardship and privation kept Khodasevich out of military service during World War I and the Russian Revolution. In April of 1921, Khodasevich moved with his second wife, Anna Chulkova, and her son Garik to St. Petersburg, the abandoned capital, to work and live in the subsidized House of the Arts. It was there that Khodasevich, in a concentrated burst of energy, wrote many of his finest poems. Roughly one year later, however, spurred by private difficulties and by doubts about the future for writers in the new Soviet state, he and young poet Nina Berberova left for Western Europe. Khodasevich, like many other artists and intellectuals who left at the same time, did not expect his sojourn there to be a permanent one, and he maintained literary and personal ties with his homeland. Yet Khodasevich soon found himself on the list of those who were to be barred from returning, and his skepticism about the Soviet Union began to harden into conviction.

Khodasevich was not of like mind with much of the émigré community, and although he settled permanently in Paris in 1927, he—like Marina Tsvetayeva—found that their aesthetic isolation in Russian letters, their lack of a convenient niche, was to become an oppressive physical and spiritual isolation as well. Khodasevich, unlike Tsvetayeva, was never ostracized by fellow émigrés, and was able to earn a meager living writing criticism for Russian periodicals, but there were few kindred spirits to be found among his own countrymen, let alone among the left-leaning French intellectual community of 1930's Paris. Khodasevich believed that he was witnessing the final eclipse of Russian letters and, ironically, continued to insist on the primacy of tradition even as his own poetics were discarding their much-vaunted classical proportions.

Khodasevich's last years were difficult ones: He wrote practically no poetry after 1927, and a final break with Berberova in 1932, financial straits, and failing health all contributed to depression. He did remarry and continue to write remarkable prose, and he was at work on a Pushkin study when he was fatally sticken with cancer in 1939. He died in the spring of that year.

Analysis

Vladislav Khodasevich made his poetic debut in the heyday of Russian Symbolism. For the Symbolists, passion was the quickest way to reach the limits of experience necessary for artistic creation, and so all the motifs which accompany the Symbolist/Decadent notion of love—pain, intoxication, hopelessness—are explored by Khodasevich, diligent student of decadence, in his first collection. In *Molodost'* (youth), he treats the transcendent themes of death, love, art, and eternity (so dear to the Symbolist canon) to both facile versifying and facile dramatization. His lyric voice is that of the seer, the magus, the seeker—a pale youth with burning eyes, a self-conscious poet risking all for revelation and encounters with mystic dread.

Molodost' is the work of a talented beginner, but no more. The poems are infused with vague mystery and vague premonitions, full of hints of midnight trysts at crypts, of confounding of realities, of fashionable madness and jaded melancholy. Khodasevich's problem is the problem of Symbolism in general: Its claim to universality of experience was undercut by the lack of any universal, or even coherent, symbolic system. In seeking to create a language of those "Chosen by Art" they plumbed for the emblematic, "creative" meaning of words, but the choosing and the chosen—hence the meaning—might vary from salon to salon. No word or deed was safe from symbolic interpretation, but the poet's own self-absorbed consciousness was the sole arbiter of meaning. Indeed, at times it seemed that literature itself was secondary to the attempt to divine hidden meaning in everyday events, thereby creating a life which itself was art enough.

Khodasevich's poetics would begin to change with the advent of his next book, but his apprenticeship among the Symbolists would affect him for the rest of his life. From them, he learned to perceive human existence as the tragic incompatibility of two separate realities, and all of his poetic life would be an attempt to reconcile them.

His second volume of verse, *Shchastlivy domik* (the happy little house), shows Khodasevich replacing his early mentors—Bely, Blok, Bryusov, Innokenty Annensky—with eighteenth and nineteenth century classics—Pushkin, Evgeny Baratynsky, Derzhavin. His new persona is both more accessible and more distant than the pale pre-Raphaelite youth of the first book: He is more personal and biographical, surrounded by more concrete visual imagery and fewer abstractions, although the stylization, the deliberate archaisms, and the traditional meter in which those details are given serve to keep the poet's mask a generalized one—one poet among many, the latest heir to an elegiac tradition. *Shchastlivy domik* is still a diary of the emotions, kept by a self-absorbed "I," but here the spheres of emotion and art begin to separate. This poet belongs to a guild of craftsmen, not a hieratic brotherhood intent on perceiving life as a work in progress. A sense of history and linear time replaces the boundless "I" of the Symbolist/Decadent, defining both past and present and imposing different sorts of limits on the power of language to conjure, transform, or even affect reality. In this context, death becomes an even rather than a sensuous state of mind, and art becomes a means of overcoming death by very virtue of its formality and conventionality. These characteristics, not sibylline utterances, will carry the work beyond its creator's physical end.

Gone, then, are sadness and frustration at the utter futility of words, replaced by a less literal quietism—elegiac contemplation, meditation, and pride not in one's own oracular powers but in a tradition. Dignified humility replaces bombast, domesticity replaces exotica, and Pushkin is the chief guide. Although Khodasevich never lost his sense of the split between the world of appearance and the higher reality, in this collection he discovered inspiration in everydayness, in ordinary, prosaic, humble moments. In his next collection, his first book of truly mature work, he worked out the poetics appropriate to that discovery.

Most of the major poems in *Putem zerna* (the way of grain) were finished by 1918, but the book itself did not see print until 1920. In lexicon, choice of themes, and lyric voice, it is a testament to a sober but still joyful everyday life; the poet is an ordinary human, subject to the laws of time and space, vulnerable to cold, hunger, illness, and death, no more and no less significant than any other man on the street. Like his fellow Muscovites in times of war and revolution, he observes history, participates in it "like a salamander in flame," but possesses no Symbolist second sight and no power to guess, let alone prophesy, the future. Although the poet, unlike his fellows, does have occasion to transcend his human limits, his small epiphanies, too, depend on the physical world. Their source is earthly. They derive from moments in which the poet experiences an acute awareness of things heard, felt, seen, smelled, and tasted.

Straightforward syntax, simplicity of lexicon, an intimate, slightly ironic, conversational tone, and the unrhymed iambic pentameter of the longer poems all make *Putem zerna* a deliberately prosaic book of poetry. Its persona is both public and private—public in his identification with the lives and deaths of his fellow creatures, private in facing his own mortality. The two are linked by the central metaphors of the book; the biblical seed which dies to be born again and the life-giving bread baked from buried grain—the eternal cycle of being.

Many of the book's poems have an identifiable setting in both space and time, coordinates usually lacking in Khodasevich's earlier works. The homely images of Moscow neighborhoods lead to meditations on the passing of time, nations, generations, and the poet himself as he feels the onset of physical weakness, illness, and old age. The poems chronicle what Khodasevich called "holy banality": common, collective experiences such as hauling wood, selling herring rations to buy lamp oil, and watching the local coffin maker finish his latest order. Moments of transcendence come unrequested and unexpected, with the thump of a seamstress's treadle or the sight of an all-too-ordinary suicide in a local park. The thump of the poet's own rocking chair, for example, marking time, sparks this moment in "Epizod" ("Episode"). In this poem, the observer of others leaves his own body and instead observes himself—thin, pale, dying, cigarette in hand. He also observes all the objects surrounding him—a bookcase, the ubiquitous yellow wallpaper of modest, older apartments, Pushkin's death mask, the children, and their sleds. As the soul returns to its body, it journeys over water—a crossing of Lethe described in painstakingly physical terms.

The balance achieved in *Putem zerna* is both an acrobatic and a poetic feat, as Khodasevich points out in one of his short poems. It requires both muscle and brain. In his incarnation as ordinary man, Khodasevich has to balance life against death; in his role as poet, he has to balance creativity and the everyday world. For the moment, poetry makes that reconciliation possible by imposing order on the chaos and disarray of everyday life. Yet just as the poet cannot exist without the man, the poetry cannot exist without the chaos.

If earthly and divine principles complement each other in *Putem zerna*, they come into conflict in Khodasevich's 1922 collection, *Tyazhelaya lira* (the heavy lyre). Here the divine side of the poet's nature turns dominant, becomes a condition for the existence of all else. Poetic order is no longer simply one possible means of reconciliation but the only order possible if the "I" is to survive in any way. Equilibrium shifted, the prosy external world lends itself less and less to ordering. Unlike the poet in the previous collection (an ordinary man save for his flashes of kinship with "child, flower, beast"), the poet of *Tyazhelaya lira* is unmistakably a creature different from his fellows, one for whom the creative moment has expanded to fill his entire consciousness. His state is one of constant awareness of human limitations and his own duality, of constant service to his craft. This awareness reveals not affinities but differences, not community but isolation.

Exalted, yes, but smug—never. Khodasevich's version of the conventional antagonism between the two worlds of the poet is not at all simple and clear-cut. The two realities are mutually exclusive yet do, paradoxically, overlap. Each seeks to free itself of the other, but only in their uncomfortable union does the lyric "I" of this collection exist. This voice may be much more ironic and self-deprecating than that of the high priests of Symbolism, but the poet's gifts—vision and "secret hearing"—allow him to see and hear, not over, but through physical existence. They allow him to escape, however briefly, from his captivity in an aging, unattractive, bodily prison. Indeed, the collection is dominated by a set of images which provide that escape to the soul's true homeland: Eyes, windows, mirrors, and reflections all open onto another reality, an escape route for the spirit. Wings, wounds (sometimes mortal, death being the ultimate flight), verbs with transitional prefixes, and negative definitions also belong to a poetics whereby the word, the soul, and the spirit break out of the enclosed cell of body or world. Angels, Psyche,

Lucifer, an automobile winged by headlights, and acid consuming a photographic negative move across and through the tissue of existence.

One of the most striking poems of the collection, "Ballada" ("Ballad"), describes another journey out of the body. Here, as in "Episode," the poet is transformed into a creature with knowledge of the realms of both life and death. In both cases, the journey to the underworld begins with the speaker of the poem alone in his room, surrounded by familiar objects; the room has a window, and time passes strangely. Yet while "Episode" ends with a return to the mortal body and an understanding of life and death as kindred states, "Ballad" ends with the man transfigured, changed into Orpheus, and that transformation takes place because of poetry. Cut by the sharp blade of music, the man grows up and out of himself, setting dead matter into motion with him, re-creating both himself and the world around him. His instrument, his blade, is the heavy lyre handed him through the wind.

Khodasevich's last book, *Evropeiskaya noch'* (European night), did not appear separately but came out as part of his *Sobranie stikhov* (collected verse) of 1927. Like his two earlier books, *Evropeiskaya noch'* treats of both spiritual and material worlds. The epiphanies of *Putem zerna*, however, are long gone, as are the neat oxymorons and epigrammatic resolutions of *Tyazhelaya lira*. There are no escape routes here. Instead, there is the Gnostic's anti-Paradise, a grotesque Gogolian world of inferior time and space, demoniac in its unrelenting banality and tawdry stupidity. The poet is doubly exiled, for even language seems to have lost its ability to transform either the self or what surrounds it. Now the physical world shapes both the language and the voice, distorting them and depriving them of their fragile unity and identity. The possibility—or rather impossibility—of creativity involves three things: the victory of matter over spirit and the distortion of both; the confusion of masks, or the poet's inability to recognize even himself; and the dismemberment of the once coherent lyric "I," as in a poem which ends with the poet exploding, flying apart "Like mud, sprayed out by a tire/ To alien spheres of being."

Savagely funny, *Evropeiskaya noch'* covers a world densely populated by humans, animals, and objects as well as the trappings, gadgetry, and attitudes of the modern century. Animate and inanimate objects obey the same laws, are objects of the same verbs, undergo the same processes. The natural world is at best askew, at worst hostile. The luminous, sanctified domesticity of *Putem zerna* has turned paltry and pitiful, the entire universe reduced to a collection of "poor utensils." The lyric hero, a petty Cain, is exiled from his age and from himself: "Like a fly on sticky paper/ He trembles in our time." Too inarticulate to give voice, he merely groans in mute despair.

The breakup of coherent vision and the loss of sense of self and genuine creativity take poetic form in the breakup of a once smooth line, disjointed stanzaic structure, abrupt changes of rhythm, and incongruous rhyme. Imagery, too, disintegrates: The poet looks in mirrors and cannot recognize his past selves in the aging face confronting him, gazes at a shiny tabletop and sees his own severed head reflected in the window of a passing streetcar, looks at the "asphalt mirror" of a Berlin street at night and sees himself and his friends as monsters, mutants, and human bodies topped by dogs' heads. The creation of art, so closely tied to the re-creation of self, seems impossible in a world of dusty galleries and cheap cinemas. Appropriately enough, *Evropeiskaya noch'* ends with a counterfeit act of creation, a parody of Jehovah's Fourth Day and of the poet's ability to bring dead matter to life. In this last poem, called "Zvezdi" ("Stars"), the cosmos emerges at the wave of a seedy conductor's baton. The show begins, and light comes forth from darkness in the form of prostitutes: the chorus line as the Big Dipper and the soloists as the North Star and "l'Étoile d'Amour." In Khodasevich's earlier works, the poet had been able to create or re-create an earlier, truer existence, a cosmos of his own. He came to doubt his ability to perform such a task. In Khodasevich's later poems, it appears that corrupt and perverted forms—vaudeville comedians and down-and-out dancing girls—may be the only artistic order left to the modern world.

Other major works
NONFICTION: *Derzhavin*, 1931; *Nekropol'*, 1939; *Literaturnye stat'i i vospominaniia*, 1954; *Belyi koridor: Isbrannaia proza v dvukh tomakh*, 1982.
MISCELLANEOUS: *Sobranie stikhov*, 1927.

Bibliography
Bethea, David. *Khodasevich: His Life and Art*, 1983.
_____. "Sorrento Photographs: Khodasevich's Memory Speaks," in *Slavic Review*. XXXIX (March, 1980), pp. 56-69.
Malmstad, John E. "The Historical Sense and Xodasevič's *Deržavin*," in *Derzhavin*, 1975 (revised edition).
Miller, J. "Xodasevič's Gnostic Exile," in *Slavic and East European Journal*. XXVIII (Summer, 1984).
Nabokov, Vladimir. "On Khodasevich," in *The Bitter Air of Exile: Russian Writers in the West, 1922-1972*, 1977 (revised edition). Edited by Simon Karlinsky and Alfred Appel, Jr.

Jane Ann Miller

THOMAS KINSELLA

Born: Dublin, Ireland; May 4, 1928

Principal poems and collections

The Starlit Eye, 1952; *Three Legendary Sonnets*, 1952; *The Death of a Queen*, 1956; *Poems*, 1956; *Another September*, 1958, revised 1962; *Moralities*, 1960; *Downstream*, 1962; *Six Irish Poets*, 1962; *Wormwood*, 1966; *Nightwalker and Other Poems*, 1968; *Poems*, 1968 (with Douglas Livingstone and Anne Sexton); *Tear*, 1969; *Butcher's Dozen*, 1972; *A Selected Life*, 1972; *Finistere*, 1972; *Notes from the Land of the Dead and Other Poems*, 1972; *New Poems*, 1973; *Selected Poems, 1956-1968*, 1973; *Vertical Man*, 1973; *The Good Fight: A Poem for the Tenth Anniversary of the Death of John F. Kennedy*, 1973; *One*, 1974; *A Technical Supplement*, 1976; *Song of the Night and Other Poems*, 1978; *The Messenger*, 1978; *Fifteen Dead*, 1979; *One and Other Poems*, 1979; *Peppercanister Poems, 1972-1978*, 1979; *Poems, 1956-1973*, 1979; *One Fond Embrace*, 1981.

Other literary forms

In addition to his own poetry, Thomas Kinsella has published a large body of verse translated from the Irish. This work, which has been going on throughout his career, is most notably embodied in his celebrated version of the eighth century Irish epic *Tain bo Cuailnge* (*The Tain*, 1969) and in *An Duanaire: An Irish Anthology, 1600-1900, Poems of the Dispossessed* (1981; with Sean O Tuama). ("An duanaire," literally translated, means "the poemery.") An appreciation of the significance which Kinsella attaches to the Irish-language tradition of Irish poetry, and the magnitude of his commitment to it, is crucial to an overall sense of his achievement. His introduction to *The New Oxford Book of Irish Verse* (1986), which he edited, provides convenient access to Kinsella's thinking on the subject of the Irish-language poetic tradition. The attitude expressed in that introduction recapitulates earlier statements contained in the poet's small but influential body of cultural criticism.

Achievements

Kinsella is the most important Irish poet to emerge since the end of World War II. By means of a restlessly experimental formal and aesthetic sense, broadly conceived themes, and relentless self-scrutiny and self-exposure, his work has raised him above all of his Irish contemporaries and placed him in the forefront of his generation of poets writing in English.

In the context of contemporary Irish poetry, his work has an unwonted syntactical density, complexity of imagery, and dramatic intensity. Since modern Irish poetry in English is noted more for lyric grace than for tough-minded plumbing of existential depths, Kinsella's poetry gains in importance because of its originality. Its essential inimitability, in turn, commands respect by virtue of the tenacity of vision it embodies.

In recognition of his uniqueness and commitment, Kinsella has received widespread critical acclaim and has won numerous prestigious prizes and two Guggenheim Fellowships.

Biography

Thomas Kinsella was born in Dublin on May 4, 1928. His family background is typical of the vast majority of native Dubliners—Catholic in religious affiliation, left-tending Nationalist in politics and lower-middle/upper-working-class in social standing: the kind of background detailed with such loving despair by one of Kinsella's favorite authors, James Joyce, in the stories of *Dubliners* (1914). Thomas Kinsella's father worked at the Guinness brewery and was active in labor union matters.

Educated at local day schools, Kinsella received a scholarship to attend University College, Dublin, to read for a science degree. Before graduation, however, he left to become a member of the Irish Civil Service, in which he had a successful career as a bureaucrat, rising to the rank of Assistant Principal Officer in the Department of Finance.

Kinsella left the Civil Service in 1965 to become artist-in-residence at Southern Illinois University. In 1970, he was appointed to a professorship of English at Temple University. He eventually would teach for one semester a year at Temple, spending the rest of the year in Dublin running the Peppercanister Press.

Founded in 1972, Peppercanister is the poet's private press. It was established, in the poet's own words, "with the purpose of issuing occasional special items." As well as being a notable addition to the illustrious private and small tradition of Irish publishing, Peppercanister has allowed Thomas Kinsella to produce long poems on single themes and to carry out fascinating exercises in the area of the poetic sequence.

Analysis

From the outset of his career, Thomas Kinsella has shown an unremitting preoccupation with large themes. Love, death, time, and various ancillary imponderables are persistently at the forefront of Kinsella's poetic activity. Such concerns beset all poets, no doubt, as well as all thinking beings. More often than not, Kinsella grapples with these overwhelming subjects without the alleviating disguise of metaphor, and he confronts them without the consolations of philosophy. Their reality consists of the profundity of the poet's human—and hence, frequently baffled and outraged—experience of them.

Even in Kinsella's early love lyrics, it is impossible for the poet merely to celebrate the emotion. He cannot view his subject without being aware of its problematical character—its temporariness and changeability. Thus, to identify Kinsella's themes, while initially informative, may ultimately be misleading. It seems more illuminating to consider his preoccupations, which a reader may label time or death, as zones of the poet's psychic experience, and to recognize that a Kinsella poem is, typically, an anatomy of psychic experience, a rhetorical reexperiencing, rather than a particularly conclusive recounting. Such a view would seem to be borne out by the forms which his poems typically assume. Their fractured look and inconsistent verse patterns (unavoidably but not imitatively reproducing the prosody of T. S. Eliot and Ezra Pound) suggest an idea still developing. As Kinsella writes in "Worker in Mirror, at His Bench": "No, it has no practical application./ I am simply trying to understand something/ —states of peace nursed out of wreckage./ The peace of fullness, not emptiness."

An immediate implication of this approach to poetry is that it owes little or nothing to the poet's Irish heritage. His concerns are common to all humanity, and while the conspicuous modernism of his technique has, in point of historical fact, some Irish avatars (the unjustly neglected Denis Devlin comes to mind), these are of less significance for a sense of Kinsella's achievement and development than the manner in which he has availed himself of the whole canon of Anglo-American poetry. In fact, an interesting case could be made for Kinsella's poetry being an adventitious, promiscuous coalescence of the preoccupations of poets since the dawn of Romanticism. Such a case might well produce the judgment that one of the bases for Kinsella's general importance to the history of poetry in the postwar period is that his verse is a sustained attempt to inaugurate a post-Romantic poetic that would neither merely debunk its predecessor's fatal charms (as perhaps T. S. Eliot desired to do) nor provide them with a new repertoire of gestures and disguises (which seems to have been Ezra Pound's project). The effect of this judgment would be to place Kinsella in the company of the other great Irish anti-Romantic of twentieth century literature, Samuel Beckett.

A more far-reaching implication of Kinsella's technique is that it provides direct access to the metaphysical core of those preoccupations. Often the access is brutally direct. Throughout, Kinsella repeats the refrain articulated in the opening section of "Nightwalker": "I only know things seem and are not good." This line strikes a number of characteristic Kinsella notes. Its unrelieved, declarative immediacy is a feature which becomes increasingly pronounced as his verse matures. There is a sense of the unfitness of things, of evil, of times being out of joint. The speaker is strikingly committed to his subjective view. The line contains a representative Kinsella ambiguity, depending on whether the reader pauses heavily after "seem": Is "are not good" entailed by, or opposed to, "seem"? Readers familiar with Kinsella will hear the line announce a telltale air of threat and of brooding introspection. There is also, perhaps, a faint suggestion of meditative quest in "Nightwalker," which occurs in other important Kinsella poems from the 1960's (such as "Baggot Street Deserta," "A Country Walk," and *Downstream*). Such an undertaking, however, is hardly conceived in hope and does not seem to be a quest for which the persona freely and gladly volunteers. Rather, it seems a condition into which he has been haplessly born.

It is not difficult to understand Kinsella's confession that his vision of human existence is that of "an ordeal." In fact, given the prevalence in his verse of ignorance, darkness, death, and the unnervingly unpredictable tidal movements of the unconscious—all frequently presented by means of apocalyptic imagery—there is a strong indication that the poet is doing little more than indulging his idea of "ordeal," despite the prosodic virtuosity and furious verbal tension which make the indulgence seem an authentic act of soul-bearing. Such an evaluation, however, would be incomplete. Also evident is the poet's desire to believe in what he has called "the eliciting of order from experience." Kinsella's verse is a continuing experiment in the viability of the desire to retain such a belief and a commitment to negotiate the leap of artistic faith which alone is capable of overcoming the abyss of unjustifiable unknowing that is the mortal lot. The possibility of achieving that act of composed and graceful suspension is what keeps Kinsella's poetry alive and within the realm of the human enterprise.

Although Kinsella's oeuvre exemplifies, to a dauntingly impressive degree, persistence and commitment in the face of the virtually unspeakable abyss, it has gone through a number of adjustments and modifications. Taken as a whole, therefore, Kinsella's output may be considered an enlarged version of some of its most outstanding moments, a sophisticated system of themes and variations. In the words of the preface to *Wormwood*, "It is certain that maturity and peace are to be sought through ordeal after ordeal, and it seems that the search continues until we fail."

One of the most important adjustments to have occurred in the development of Kinsella's poetic career is its emergence from largely private, personal experience, primarily of love. His early poems, particularly those collected in *Another September* and *Downstream*, seem too often to conceive of experience as the struggle of the will against the force of immutable abstractions. While these poems respect the necessarily tense and tentative character of experience, they seem also to regard mere experience as a pretext for thought. These poems share with Kinsella's later work the desire to achieve distinctiveness through allegories of possibility. Yet their generally tight, conventional forms have the effect of limiting their range of possibilities. In addition, the typical persona of these poems seems himself an abstraction, a man with only a nominal context and without a culture.

By *Downstream*, such isolation was being questioned. The concluding line of this collection's title poem—"Searching the darkness for a landing place"—may be taken (albeit somewhat glibly) as a statement emblematic of much of Kinsella's early work. Yet the collection also contains poems which, while painfully acknowledging the darkness, consider it as an archaeological redoubt. One of the effects of this adjustment is that the poet's personal past begins to offer redemptive possibilities. In addition, and with more obvious if not necessarily more far-reaching effects, a generalized past, in the form of Irish history, becomes an area of exploration. It is not the case that Kinsella never examined the past prior to *Downstream* ("King John's Castle" in *Another September* is proof to the contrary). Now, however, to the powerful sense of the past's otherness which "King John's Castle" conveys is added a sense of personal identification.

The poem in *Downstream* which demonstrates this development in Kinsella's range (a development that occurred around the time that the poet was preparing *The Tain*, his translation of an eighth century Irish epic and a major work of cultural archaeology) is "A Country Walk." Here, the persona, typically tense and restless, finds himself alone, explicitly undomesticated, with nothing between him and the legacy of the past discernible in the landscape through which he walks. The poem does not merely testify to the influential gap between present and past (a crucial preoccupation in all modern Irish writing) but also enters into the past with a brisk openness and nonjudgmental tolerance. "A Country Walk" reads like a journey of discovery, all the more so since what is discovered is not subjected to facile glorification. The fact that the past is so securely embedded in the landscape of the poem suggests that history is in the nature of things and that there is as much point in attempting to deny its enduring presence as there is in trying to divert the river which is, throughout the course of the poem, never out of the poet's sight. The poem ends, appropriately, on a note of continuity: "The inert stirred. Heart and tongue were loosed:/ 'The waters hurtle throught the flooded night. . . .' "

If anything, the present is circumvented in "A Country Walk." To ensure that the reader is aware of this, Kinsella daringly uses echoes of Yeats's "Easter 1916" to show how counterheroic is contemporary Ireland and to emphasize that the country is still, to paraphrase a line from Yeats's "September 1913," fumbling in the greasy till. This moment in "A Country Walk" prefaces the understandable admission, "I turned away." The interlude, however, draws attention to a noteworthy feature of Kinsella's verse: its satire. From the outset, Kinsella's work was capable of excoriation. The addition of local, often contemporary, Irish subject matter has created the opportunity for some scalding satirical excursions.

Perhaps the most notorious of these sallies is to be found in the long title poem of *Nightwalker and Other Poems*, a poem which, in many ways, is an illuminating counterpart to "A Country Walk." Here, the setting is urban, contemporary Dublin, and the speaker, lacking the briskness of his opposite number in "A Country Walk," refers to himself as "a vagabond/ Tethered." The demoralizing spectacle of modern life is the poem's subject. Nothing is spared. In particular, Kinsella's years in the Civil Service are the basis for a damning portrait of national ideals stultified and betrayed. This portrait goes so far as to include figures from Irish public and political life who, although distorted by the poet's satirical fury, remain eminently recognizable and still occupy the highest positions in the land. Each of the poem's numerous scenarios is exposed as hollow social charades, and in direct contrast to the sense of release felt at the end of "A Country Walk," this poem concludes on a note of anticlimax: The speaker fails to find anything of redemptive value in current conditions.

While Kinsella has by no means forsaken the satirical mode (as *Butcher's Dozen*, Peppercanister's first publication, makes vividly clear), his career has developed more fruitfully through exploring the pretexts and presuppositions of his need that poetry be a salvage operation, acknowledging existence's many disasters and the intimacy of their wreckage, and through acknowledgment saving face. Thus, in *Notes from the Land of the Dead and Other Poems* and *New Poems* the past is personal and the poems seem like diagnoses of memory and origins. Just as the setting for many of these poems is the poet's childhood home, so the poems reveal what has to be internalized for the sake of comprehending one's native land. In these poems, the speaker is the absorbed witness of others' agony, not only the agony of the deathbed but also the equally unrelenting travail described in "Tear": "sad dullness and tedious pain/ and lives bitter with hard bondage."

The poems in *Notes from the Land of the Dead and Other Poems* are also noteworthy for their degree of interaction with one another. Earlier, in *Wormwood*, Kinsella produced a strict yet supple poetic sequence. Now, the idea of sequence reemerges and takes more fluid form, a technique which can be seen embryonically in the interrelated sections of "Nightwalker" and which finds mature embodiment in many of the Peppercanister poems. This greater access to range and flexibility has enabled the poet to be less dependent on the singular effects of the dramatic lyric, where, as noted, there seemed to be a considerable degree of pressure to will experience to denote purpose. As a result of an increasing commitment to formal and metrical variety, Kinsella's voice has become more authentically meditative, its brooding habit engendering a measure of containment rather than disenchantment. This voice is present not only in such important Peppercanister collections as *One*, *A Technical Supplement*, and *Song of the Night and Other Poems*, but in some of the superb individual poems these books contain, notably, *Finistere* (*One*) and "Tao and Unfitness at Inistiogue on the River Nore" (*Song of the Night and Other Poems*).

It is not clear, however, that Kinsella established Peppercanister with the expectation that such wonderful poems would result. On the contrary, the press came into being because of the need to publish an uncharacteristic Kinsella production, a poem written for a particular occasion. The poem in question, *Butcher's Dozen*, was written in response to the killing in the city of Derry, Northern Ireland, of thirteen civil rights demonstrators by British troops. This event took place on the afternoon of Sunday, January 30, 1972, a day which will live in infamy in the minds of Irish people. The poem's immediate occasion is the horrifying event, but its subtitle clarifies the line of attack taken by Kinsella. The subtitle, "A Lesson for the Octave of Widgery," names the Lord Chief Justice of the United Kingdom, Lord Widgery, chairman of the essentially whitewashing court of inquiry set up to examine the event. Thus, *Butcher's Dozen* is a critique not only of the troops' action but also of the mind-set such actions denote. The poem's incisive and abrasive couplets enact an alternative language and disposition to that of the Lord Chief Justice's report. While, from an aesthetic standpoint, *Butcher's Dozen* is hardly Kinsella's greatest poem, its significance as a cultural document is indisputable and is reinforced by the explanatory background notes which Kinsella wrote to accompany it.

The other occasional poems contained in the Peppercanister series also have to do with significant deaths. In order of appearance, the poems are *A Selected Life*, *Vertical Man*, *The Good Fight: A Poem for the Tenth Anniversary of the Death of John F. Kennedy*, and *The Messenger*. It has become standard practice to regard *A Selected Life* and *Vertical Man* together, two independent but intimately related treatments of the one event, the untimely death of the poet's friend, Seán Ó Riada. Again, the issue of cultural significance arises. Ó Riada, as well as being an accomplished composer of classical music (*Vertical Man* is the title of one of his compositions for orchestra), was also an extraordinary influence on Irish folk musicians. His conception of the rich tradition and important heritage of Irish folk music was the direct inspiration of the internationally acclaimed group The Chieftains. More relevant to the development of Kinsella's career, Ó Riada's scholarly, pleasure-giving rehabilitation of a dormant legacy is an important counterpart to the poet's explorations in Irish-language poetry. As the penultimate stanza of *Vertical Man* has it: "From palatal darkness a voice/ rose flickering, and checked/ in glottal silence. The song/ articulated and pierced."

In the light of the public demeanor assumed in *Butcher's Dozen* and the greater degree of interplay between textural openness and formal control contained in both the Ó Riada poems, Kinsella undertook his most ambitious public poem, *The Good Fight*. Not only is the poem's subject matter ambitious, in particular given how rare it is for Irish poets to seek subjects outside the ambit of their own culture and tradition (a rarity which younger Irish poets such as Derek Mahon are in the process of dismantling), but also, formally speaking, *The Good Fight* is one of Kinsella's more daring experiments.

As in the case of earlier Peppercanister poems on public themes, *The Good Fight* has an author's note attached, which begins with the remark, "With the death of Kennedy many things died, foolish expectations and assumptions, as it now seems." In a sense, the poem is a collage of contemporary desires, a view borne out by the numerous allusions to and quotations from Kennedy speeches and other sources from the period. Yet such a view is contradicted by two other features of the poem. The most obvious of these are the various quotations from Plato's *Republic* and *Laws*, which are used to counterpoint the poem's development. This classical reference has the effect of measuring Kennedy's fate against some nominal, yet conventionally uncontroversial, standard of age-old wisdom. This feature in turn is seen in terms of the pervasive sense of unfulfilled aftermath which pervades the poem. It seems remarkable that this achievement is so little known.

The significant death in *The Messenger* is not that of a well-known figure but of the poet's father. This immensely moving document testifies to Kinsella's growth as an artist. The poem's subject, death, has been a constant presence in his work since "A Lady of Quality," in *Poems*, and has been treated variously in such accomplished and representative poems as "Dick King" and "Cover Her Face." *The Messenger*, however, dwells more on celebrating the life that preceded its occasion than on the death, particularly on the public life, on the life of a man desiring to possess his culture: "The eggseed Goodness/ that is also called/ Decency." The poet's redemptive power, and his cultural as well as personal responsibility to discharge it, is seen to consummate effect in this powerful, moving work.

Kinsella's oeuvre, despite its unity and the persistence with which its central preoccupations are pursued, is open to various criticisms. It certainly is uneven. The tension and sense of barely suppressed exasperation present in some of even his most impressive early poems can prove an irritant to the reader, as can their complex, compressed imagery. In terms of intensity and commitment, however, as well as the fascinating odyssey of his development, Thomas Kinsella is clearly a poet worthy of the utmost respect. As to his honesty and artistic integrity, it seems appropriate to allow a verse from the preamble to *The Messenger* to speak for those qualities: "The hand conceives an impossible Possible/ and exhausts in mid-reach./ What could be more natural?"

Other major works

NONFICTION: *Davis, Mangan, Ferguson: Tradition and the Irish Writer*, 1970.

TRANSLATIONS: *The Breastplate of Saint Patrick*, 1954 (revised as *Faeth Fiadha: The Breastplate of Saint Patrick*, 1957); *Longes mac n-Usnig, Being the Exile and Death of the Sons of Usnech*, 1954; *Thirty-Three Triads, Translated from the XII Century Irish*, 1955; *The Tain*, 1969 (of *Tain bo Cuailnge*);

An Duanaire: An Irish Anthology, 1600-1900, Poems of the Dispossessed, 1981 (with Sean O Tuama).
ANTHOLOGY: *The New Oxford Book of Irish Verse*, 1986.

Bibliography

Harmon, Maurice. *The Poetry of Thomas Kinsella: "With Darkness for a Nest,"* 1974.
O'Hara, Daniel. "Appropriate Performance: Thomas Kinsella and the Ordeal of Understanding," in *Contemporary Irish Writing*, 1983. Edited by James D. Brophy and Raymond J. Porter.
_____. "An Interview with Thomas Kinsella," in *Contemporary Poetry*. IV, no.1 (1981), p. 14.

George O'Brien

STANLEY KUNITZ

Born: Worcester, Massachusetts; July 29, 1905

Principal poems and collections

Intellectual Things, 1930; *Passport to the War: A Selection of Poems*, 1944; *Selected Poems, 1928-1958*, 1958; *The Testing Tree: Poem*, 1971; *The Terrible Threshold: Selected Poems, 1940-1970*, 1974; *The Coat Without a Seam: Sixty Poems, 1930-1972*, 1974; *The Lincoln Relics*, 1978; *The Poems of Stanley Kunitz, 1928-1978*, 1979; *The Wellfleet Whale and Companion Poems*, 1983.

Other literary forms

Stanley Kunitz has published numerous essays, interviews, and reviews on poetry and art. These are collected in *A Kind of Order, a Kind of Folly: Essays and Conversations* (1975) and in *Next-to-Last Things: New Poems and Essays* (1985). In addition, he has made extensive translations of modern Russian poetry, most notably in *Poems of Akhmatova* (1973, with Max Hayward) and *Story Under Full Sail* by Andrei Voznesensky (1974) as well as editing and cotranslating Ivan Drach's *Orchard Lamps* (1978) from Ukrainian.

Achievements

In nearly sixty years of writing poetry, Kunitz has produced a corpus of work that is notable for its cohesiveness, its courageous explorations of the modern psyche, and its ever-broadening sympathies that adumbrate (with some fierce reservations and caveats) the unity of human experience. In language that has never failed to sustain a high degree of passionate dignity yet has never fallen prey to the hortatory or didactic, Kunitz has boldly knocked again and again upon the doors of his obsessions with family, love, memory, and identity to demand that they surrender their secret meanings.

From the start of his career, Kunitz has paid consummate attention to matters of form, as bespeaking—to use his borrowed phrase—"a conservation of energy." Indeed, Kunitz has on numerous occasions spoken of form as a constant in art, as opposed to techniques and materials, which vary according to time and cultural necessity. Nevertheless, for the last twenty years Kunitz's poems have surprised his readers with their fresh embodiments: journal poems, prose poems, and free verse. At the same time, the poems retain the characteristically impassioned, sometimes bardic, voice of the earlier work, a voice that constitutes an unbroken thread running through his six decades of poetry.

In many ways, Kunitz's work declares allegiance to the "flinty, maverick side" of American literature, the side inhabited by Henry David Thoreau and Walt Whitman, and holds to humanistic values, independent judgment, self-discipline, and a distrust of power in all of its modern manifestations, particularly in the hands of the state. At the same time, the poems bear witness to the individual's spiritual yearnings in an age of decreasing sanctity at all levels. While not explicitly a religious poet ("I'm an American freethinker, a damn stubborn one . . ."), Kunitz wrote poems that, nevertheless, remind readers of the tragic consequences that befall humans at the loss of that dimension. His achievement has been "to roam the wreckage" of his own humanity in a way that is both highly personal and representative and to ennoble that pursuit with the transformative powers of his art, an achievement which won for him the 1987 Bollingen Prize for Poetry.

Biography

The son of immigrants, Stanley Jasspon Kunitz was born July 29, 1905, in Worcester, Massachusetts. Kunitz's father, Solomon, descended from Russian Sephardic Jews, committed suicide shortly before Stanley was born—an event that was to haunt the poet and that stands behind some of his most important and best-known poems. His mother, Yetta Helen, of Lithuanian descent, opened a dry goods store to support herself, her son, and two older daughters and to repay accumulated debts. Reared principally by his sisters and a succession of nurses, Kunitz grew up with his father's book collection, into which, as he put it, he would "passionately burrow." Though his mother shortly remarried, his stepfather, of whom he was fond, died before Kunitz reached his teens.

Educated in Worcester public schools, Kunitz edited the high school magazine, played tennis, and was graduated valedictorian of his class. Winning a scholarship to Harvard, Kunitz majored in English and began to write poetry, subsequently winning the Lloyd McKim Garrison Medal for poetry. He was graduated summa cum laude in 1926 and the following year took his M.A. degree from Harvard. He worked briefly as a Sunday feature writer for the Worcester *Telegram*, where he had worked summers during college. He also completed a novel, which he later "heroically destroyed."

In 1927, Kunitz joined the H. W. Wilson Company as an editor. With Wilson's encouragement, he became editor of the *Wilson Bulletin*, a library publication (known now as the *Wilson Library Bulletin*). While at Wilson, he edited a series of reference books, including *Authors Today and Yesterday: A Companion Volume to "Living Authors"* (1933; with Howard Haycraft and Wilbur C. Hadden), *British Authors of the Nineteenth Century* (1936; with Haycraft), *American Authors, 1600-1900: A Biographical Dictionary of American Literature* (1938), and *Twentieth Century Authors: A Biographical Dictionary of Modern Literature* (1942; with Haycraft).

In 1930, Kunitz married Helen Pearse (they were divorced in 1937) and published his first collection of poems, *Intellectual Things*. The book was enthusiastically received by reviewers. Writing in *Saturday Review of Literature*, William Rose Benét observed, "Mr. Kunitz has gained the front rank of contemporary verse in a single stride." In 1939, Kunitz married a former actress, Eleanor Evans (from whom he was divorced in 1958), a union that produced his only child, Gretchen.

Kunitz's tenure with the H. W. Wilson Company was interrupted by World War II, during which he served as a noncommissioned officer in charge of information and education in the Air Transport Command. His second collection, *Passport to the War*, appeared in 1944. A reviewer of that volume for *The New York Times Book Review* noted, "Kunitz has now (it seems) every instrument necessary to the poetic analysis of modern experience." Kunitz was awarded a Guggenheim Fellowship in 1945 and began a second career as an itinerant teacher, first at Bennington College, at the behest of his friend, the poet Theodore Roethke, then at a succession of colleges and universities, including the State University of New York at Potsdam, the New School for Social Research, Queens College, Brandeis University, and the University of Washington.

In 1958, Kunitz married the artist Elise Asher, published *Selected Poems: 1928-1958*, which was awarded the Pulitzer Prize for Poetry in 1959, and received grants from the National Institute of Arts and Letters and the Ford Foundation.

During the 1960's, though based in New York City and Provincetown, Massachusetts, Kunitz was a Danforth Visiting Lecturer at colleges and universities throughout the United States. He also lectured in the Soviet Union, Poland, Senegal, and Ghana. In 1964, he edited a volume of the poems of John Keats and two years later translated selections from Russian poet Andrei Voznesensky's *Antiworlds and The Fifth Ace*. He continued to edit for the Wilson Company (with Vineta Colby, *European Authors: 1000-1900: A Biographical Dictionary*, 1967) and coedited a memorial volume of essays on the poet Randall Jarrell. In 1968, along with artist Robert Motherwell and novelist Norman Mailer, he helped found The Fine Arts Work Center in Provincetown, a resident community of young artists and writers, and in 1969 he assumed the general editorship of the Yale Series of Younger Poets.

The Testing Tree, a volume of poems and translations, appeared in 1971, prompting Robert Lowell to assert in *The New York Times Book Review*, "once again, Kunitz tops the crowd, the old iron brought to the white heat of simplicity." In 1974, Kunitz was awarded one of the nation's top official literary honors when he was appointed Consultant in Poetry to the Library of Congress. In addition to *The Testing Tree* and the collected volume *The Poems of Stanley Kunitz: 1928-1958*, a book of essays and conversations, *A Kind of Order, a Kind of Folly*, as well as three volumes of translations appeared during the 1970's.

Kunitz published a thematic volume of old and new poems, *The Wellfleet Whale and Companion Poems*, in a limited edition in 1983, with the new poems incorporated in *Next-to-Last Things: New Poems and Essays*, published in 1985. In recognition of his lifetime achievement, Kunitz was chosen as the first New York State Poet, for the term 1987-1989.

Analysis

Stanley Kunitz has constantly sought to achieve higher and higher ground, both in his thoughtful aesthetic and in his themes. Kunitz's first poems were composed after the initial wave of modernism, led, in poetry, by T. S. Eliot and Ezra Pound, had crested. They resemble, to some extent, the earlier, tightly organized, ironic poems of Eliot, though the influence of the seventeenth century Metaphysical poets, particularly George Herbert (again an indirect influence of Eliot, who was largely responsible for the resurgence of interest in the Metaphysicals), is probably more preponderant. Moreover, by the 1920's, the work of Sigmund Freud had successfully invaded American arts and provided the introspective poet with a powerful tool for the analysis of self and culture.

The poems of *Intellectual Things* sketch many of the themes that will later be subject to elaboration and enrichment: the figure of the regenerative wound that is both the fresh scar of loss and the font of the power to transform experience into art, man's willful capriciousness (the "blood's unreason") and the inevitable cargo of guilt, and the search for the father, which is ultimately the search for identity, authority, and tradition.

Eloquent and formally rigorous, the poems in this first collection show a poet already mature in his medium, writing of his "daily self that bled" to "Earth's absolute arithmetic/of being." Characterized by paradox and a wish for transcendence (though that wish is frequently denied or diverted to another object), the early poems often poise upon niceties of intellection— though they are also fully felt—and suggest transport by language rather than the transcendence to which they aspire. From the first, Kunitz's poems have typically employed the language and images of paradox. In "Change," the opening poem to his first collection, man is "neither here nor there/ Because the mind moves everywhere;/ And he is neither now nor then/ Because tomorrow comes again/ Foreshadowed. . . ." In more characteristically personal poems, such as "Postscript," the poet observes, in what will develop into one of his ongoing themes, the self's phoenixlike destruction and subsequent regeneration: "I lost by winning, and I shall not win/ Again, except by loss." The losses Kunitz traces in *Intellectual Things* are those of past life (or of a past one was denied), symbolized by the loss of his father, and the loss of love. In "For the Word Is Flesh" the poet admonishes his dead father: "O ruined father dead, long sweetly rotten/ Under the dial, the time-dissolving urn,/ Beware a second perishing. . . ." The second death is the doleful fate of being erased from the memories of the living. In a memorable passage that presages a later, more famous poem ("Father and Son"), Kunitz writes, "Let sons learn from their lipless fathers how/ Man enters Hell without a golden bough," that is to say, uninstructed.

Some of the finest effects attained in *Intellectual Things* can be attributed to a high degree of control over phrasing, combined with the use of rhyme as a tool of force reminiscent of Alexander Pope, as in "Lovers Relentlessly": "Lovers relentlessly contend to be/ Superior in their identity.// The compass of the ego is designed/ To circumscribe intact a lesser mind. . . ." Kunitz uses rhyme also as a vehicle of wit, as in the shorter, three-beat lines of "Benediction": "God banish from your house/ The fly, the roach/ the mouse// That riots in the walls/ Until the plaster falls. . . ."

Passport to the War retains much of the density and bardic resonance of *Intellectual Things*, but the range of subject matter is broader: The self must now take its transformations into account against the background of recent history, for which regeneration is entirely problematic: "One generation past, two days by plane away,/ My house is dispossessed, my friends dispersed,/ My teeth and pride knocked in, my people game/ For the hunters of manskins in the warrens of Europe." To the question "How shall we uncreate that lawless energy?" the poet can only defer to the determinisms of time: "I think of Pavlov and his dogs/ And the motto carved on the broad lintel of his brain:/ "Sequence, consequence, and again consequence." If the shadow of history casts the representative self in a darker hue, the poet, like Matthew Arnold before him, clings to what is most central to the life of the individual: "Lie down with me, dear girl, before/ My butcher-boys begin to rave./ 'No hope for persons any more,'/ They cry, 'on either side of the grave.'/ Tell them I say the heart forgives/ The World." The strange weapons of intimacy and charity would seem ill-suited as protection in a brutal world, but the sacramental element, the desire to raise the supposed commonplace, remains one of the bolts of a civilization unravaged by history. If history is the inevitable backdrop of our mortality, so do a representative mortal's most private strivings and sufferings themselves constitute a part of its fabric: "What the deep heart means,/ Its message of the big, round, childish hand,/ Its wonder, its simple lonely cry,/ The bloodied envelope addressed to you,/ Is history, that wide and mortal pang."

The visionary "Father and Son," perhaps Kunitz's best-known poem, establishes, in surrealistic images full of longing and regret, the poet's existential fate in the context of history. "Whirling between two wars," he follows "with skimming feet,/ The secret master of my blood . . . whose indomitable love/ Kept me in chains." Addressing his father "At the water's edge, where the smothering ferns lifted/ Their arms . . . ," the poet asks for his father's instruction: "For I would be a child to those who mourn/ And brother to the foundlings of the field . . ./ O teach me how to work and keep me kind." Yet the summons brings only a shocking specter of discontinuity: "Among the turtles and the lilies he turned to me/ The white ignorant hollow of his face." One senses that what the poet asks is already, in some way, self-provided, though minus the love so deeply rooted in biology that it has the status of a cultural given. As war and upheaval expose these roots, one senses the poet's implication that, in a metaphorical sense, all are orphans.

"Open the Gates," another well-known visionary lyric, delivered in a grave voice that eerily suggests posthumous utterance, finds the poet "Within the city of the burning cloud," standing "at the monumental door/ Carved with the curious legend of my youth." Striking the door with "the great bone of my death," the poet stands "on the terrible threshold," where he sees "the end and the beginning in each other's arms." The seamless and incestuous image suggests the allegorical figures of Sin and Death in John Milton's *Paradise Lost* (1667), and the allusion holds to the extent that both figures are determinants of human fate. At the same time, the emphasis is less on moral conditioning than on the endlessly reforming fate of the human, as felt from the inside, in contrast with the wholeness of a life, glimpsed, so to speak, from a vantage somehow apart from it. Our lives, as William Shakespeare said, are "rounded with a sleep," and it is a matter of indifference whether one attempts an artificial distinction between the two sleeps, except, of course, that one's only knowledge takes place as human, and forever from the vantage of one looking outward (even when he is looking inward). As for the question of inside versus outside, no other consciousness has yet much to contribute to the subject.

In 1958, after another long hiatus, Kunitz published his *Selected Poems, 1928-1958*, more than a third of which are new poems. The new poems take up the modern subject of otherness, as in "The Science of the Night," in which the speaker contemplates his sleeping beloved "Down the imploring roads I cannot take/ Into the arms of ghosts I never knew." Even if he could track her to her birth, he admits, "You would escape me." He concludes, "As through a glass that magnifies my loss/ I see the lines of your spectrum shifting red,/ The universe expanding, thinning out,/ Our worlds flying, oh flying, fast apart." Always a time-bewitched poet, Kunitz brings to this and other new poems in the volume an added sense of urgency, for they are imbued with a love and desire unintentionally but nevertheless increasingly rearranged by the shifting weight of years.

With amiable, if slow, regularity, Kunitz's fourth volume, *The Testing Tree*, marks a departure from the rhetorical shimmer and elevated diction displayed in the previous collections. Written in a less knotty, more transparent syntax and style, the poems confront the upheavals of the 1960's, the guilt of failed marriage and inadequate parenthood, the ravages of time past ("the deep litter of the years"), and the inexplicable urge to carry on in the face of public and private failures: "In a murderous time/ the heart breaks and breaks/ and lives by breaking." The consolations of this volume, though sparse, strike the reader as all the more authentic for their scrupulous lack of façade, which, however, in no way implies a lessening of charity on the part of the poet.

One of the most notable poems in *The Testing Tree* is "King of the River," a poem of the skewed hopes and unclear motives that disfigure and sometimes break a life, but which are finally overtaken, with individual life itself transcended and transfigured by the relentless biological urge to perpetuate the species. The poem, whose central symbol is the chinook salmon swimming upstream to spawn, seeks to rebut the materialist's claim that "there is no life, only living things." By addressing the fish throughout as "you," the poet clearly implicates the reader in an allegory of life: "If the water were clear enough,/ if the water were still,/ but the water is not clear... If the knowledge were given you,/ but it is not given,/ for the membrane is clouded/ with self-deceptions." The psychological phrase helps swing the pointed finger around to the reader. "If the power were granted you/ to break out of your cells,/ but the imagination fails... If the heart were pure enough, but it is not pure...," continues the litany of denial that underpins the allegory. The salmon ("Finned Ego") thrashes to a place of which it has no knowledge, for "the doors of the senses close/ on the child within." The blind, headlong rush to "the orgiastic pool" brings about dreadful change ("A dry fire eats you./ Fat drips from your bones") into something "beyond the merely human," where, despite the "fire on your tongue," promising that "The only music is time/ the only dance is love,/ you would admit/ that nothing compels you/ any more... but nostalgia and desire,/ the two-way ladder/ between heaven and hell." At the "brute absolute hour" when the salmon spawns only to die, when "The great clock of your life/ is slowing down,/ and the small clocks run wild" he ("you") stares into the face of his "creature self" and finds "he is not broken but endures," but at a price: he is "forever inheriting his salt kingdom,/ from which he is banished/ forever." The "forever" that rounds the conclusion like a little sleep, suggests that the victory of life's mission to perpetuate itself is ironically accomplished at the loss of the human's vaunted objectivity and understanding.

In "Robin Redbreast," Kunitz reveals a similar, but distinct, necessity. In "the room where I lived/ with an empty page" (a room identified in "River Road" from the same volume as one the poet inhabited after his second divorce), the poet hears the squawking of blue jays tormenting a robin, "the dingiest bird/ you ever saw." Going out to pick up the bird "after they knocked him down," in order to "toss him back into his element," he notices the bullet hole that "had tunneled out his wits." The hole, cut so clean it becomes a window, reveals "the cold flash of the blue/ unappeasable sky." The sky's indifference to the poet's sympathy for the bird ("Poor thing! Poor foolish life!) or his own condition (he lives "in a house marked 'For Sale'") provides the chilling backdrop for a revelation of the necessity for human charity toward all living things. The poem knowingly alludes to a passage in "Father and Son": "For I would be . . . brother to the foundlings of the field/ And friend of innocence and all bright eyes." As with that earlier poem, "Robin Redbreast" finds no consolation in received wisdom, either from a father's love or the heavens. What charity there is exists (as do humans) in what scientists dryly refer to as "terminal structure."

Memory is more directly the subject of "The Magic Curtain," a cultural tour of America during the 1920's. A paean to his nurse, Frieda, the poem affectionately recounts his happy childhood adventures with this blue-eyed, Bavarian maid, while his mother, "her mind already on her shop," unrolled "gingham by the yard,/ stitching dresses for the Boston trade." Frieda, identified as his "first love," in secret complicity with the knowing child, bestows "the kinds of kisses mother would not dream" and serves as his guide to the melodramatic, romantic world of the motion pictures where, during reels of *The Perils of Pauline* (1914), Keystone Cops, and Charlie Chaplin, "School faded out at every morning reel." The films are a hint of the glamorous world beyond for Frieda too, who takes her cue in a cinematic cliché and runs off "with somebody's husband, daddy to a brood." Although the poet's mother never forgives her this abandonment, the older poet, returning to her in the sanctuary of memory, eagerly does, for each has in a different way unknowingly conspired in fulfilling the dreams of the other.

The uneasy subject and situation of parents (and parent figures) weighs heavily, if somewhat obliquely, in the poems of *The Testing Tree*. In fact, the volume opens with "Journal for My Daughter," a poem in which the poet, in nine free-verse sections, confronts his own hesitations and guilt in the upbringing of his only child. He imagines himself through her eyes as beckoning "down corridors,/ secret, elusive, saturnine." Now that, he hopes, the smoke of these misgivings has cleared, he declares, "I propose/ that we gather our affections." Looking back over his role in her life, he recounts his absence ("his name was absence") but claims, "I think I'd rather sleep forever/ than wake up cold/ in a country without women." He recounts too, drunken nights of bonhomie with his friend, the poet Theodore Roethke, "slapping each other on the back,/ sweaty with genius," while she "crawled under the sofa." While he confesses that he is now "haggard with his thousand years," he declares his solidarity with her 1960's protests: "His heart is at home/ in your own generation," and to prove it he equates her misspelled slogan "*Don't tred on me*" with the "*Noli me tangere!*" he used "to cry in Latin once." Though it seems implausible that one would cry out in Latin anyplace outside the Vatican or a course in Tudor poets, the point is well made. Recalling "the summer I went away," he carries her outside "in a blitz of fireflies" to observe her first eclipse. To this image he adds Samuel Taylor Coleridge's carrying his crying son outside and catching the reflection of stars in each of his suspended tears. The heavens and the natural world are captured, comfortably diminished, and naturalized as a way of sanctioning human folly and love.

The reverse of this coin, is that it is an illusion, a pint-sized reflection of a placid cosmos that will momentarily evaporate.

The book's title poem, composed in four sections of unrhymed tercets, concerns a ritualistic childhood game of stone-throwing ("for keeps") at a specific oak tree able to confer magic gifts: one hit for love, two for poetry, three for eternal life. In the summers of his youth, searching for "perfect stones," he is master "over that stretch of road . . . the world's fastest human." Leaving the road that begins at school at one end and at the other that tries "to loop me home," he enters a field "riddled with rabbit-life/ where the bees sank sugar-wells/ in the trunks of the maples" to a clearing. There in the shadow of the "inexhaustible oak,/ tyrant and target," he calls to his father, *"wherever you are/ I have only three throws/ bless my good rightarm."* In the final section, he recalls a recurring dream of his mother "wearing an owl's face/ and making barking noises." As "her minatory finger points," he steps through a cardboard door and wonders if he should be blamed for the dirt sifting into a well where a gentle-eyed "albino walrus huffs." Suddenly the scene shifts, and the highway up which a Model A chugs becomes the road "where tanks maneuver,/ revolving their turrets." He concludes, "It is necessary to go/ through dark and deeper dark/ and not to turn." With the clear implication that the poet is mindful of his approaching mortal hour, and with or without his father's blessing, he cries, "Where is my testing-tree?/ Give me back my stones!"

The Testing Tree differs from the first three volumes in being composed of nearly a quarter translations, all from postrevolutionary Russian poetry. It was during the 1960's that Kunitz met and befriended two of the Soviet Union's best-known poets, Yevgeny Yevtushenko and Andrei Voznesensky, and, in collaboration with Max Hayward, translating a selection of poems by a third, Anna Akhmatova. Clearly, the poems enabled Kunitz, with the aid of this fortuitous ventriloquism, to take aim at the brutality and inhumanity of the modern political bureaucracy, whether Soviet or American. In Yevtushenko's "Hand-Rolled Cigarettes," for example, the common man's practice of rolling cigarettes in papers torn from *Pravda* and *Izvestia*, the two chief organs of state propaganda, gives rise to a dandy send-up of the bureaucrat's contempt for the common man: "Returning late, the tired fisherman/ enjoys his ladled kvass's tang,/ and sifts tobacco at his ease/ onto some bureaucrat's harangue."

Like *Selected Poems, 1928-1958, The Poems of Stanley Kunitz, 1928-1978* contains a section of new poems, entitled "The Layers." Here, the poet returns to the garden of his obsessions—father, family, time, the wounds of guilt, and memory—in poems of reconciliation and commemoration. In the opening poem, "The Knot," the poet imagines that the knot "scored in the lintel of my door" keeps "bleeding through/ into the world we share." Like a repressed thought, the knot wants more than anything to grow out again, to become a limb: "I hear it come/ with a rush of resin/ out of the trauma/ of its lopping-off." Characteristically, the poet associates the wound with a door, a threshold. It is as though something in nature has had to be tamed in order to effect the domestic tranquillity so delicately limned here, but its desire to return to its true nature is such that it "racks itself with shoots/ that crackle overhead." Identifying a part of his own nature with that of the knot, the poet completes the metaphor: "I shake my wings/ and fly into its boughs."

Kunitz returns to the theme of the lost father in "What of the Night?" and "Quinnapoxet." In the former, the poet wakes in the middle of the night "like a country doctor," having imagined, "with racing heart," the doorbell ringing. It is a messenger (Death) whose "gentle, insistent ring" finds the poet "not ready yet" and realizing "nobody stands on the stoop." Suddenly the poem switches focus from the grown son to the father: "When the messenger comes again/ I shall pretend/ in a childish voice/ my father is not home." His father has, in actuality, never been home, but in a deeper, metaphorical sense, he has never left home. In this light, just as the grown man must receive the messenger at the end of his life, so the son must protect the father in memory from the "second death," the oblivion of forgetting. The poet's task of remembering is obligatory, as his question earlier in the poem recognizes: "How could I afford/ to disobey that call?" "Quinnapoxet" takes place on a mysterious fishing trip where, on a dusty road similar to the one described in "Father and Son," the poet describes a hallucinatory vision of his mother and father "commingling with the dust/ they raised." His mother admonishes him for not writing, and the poet's response is simple: "I had nothing to say to her." Yet for his father who walks behind, "his face averted . . . deep in his other life," the poet, too awestruck to attempt speech, touches his forehead with his thumb, "in deaf-mute country/ the sign for father."

One of the most original of the new poems in this volume is "A Blessing of Women," a prose poem inspired by an exhibit of early American women painters and artisans mounted by the Whitney Museum. In the form of a litany, the poem briefly describes, in dignified understatement, the works and lives of five of the representative women: an embroiderer, a quilter, and three painters, "a rainbow-cloud of witnesses in a rising hubbub." He blesses them and greets them "as they pass from their long obscurity, through the gate that separates us from our history."

"Our history" is again the subject of "The Lincoln Relics," a meditation on Lincoln's passage from the "rawboned, warty" mortal "into his legend and his fame." Written not long after the Watergate trauma during Kunitz's tenure at the Library of Congress, the poem alludes to that episode by invoking the ancient struggle between idealism and materialism, no less fierce in Lincoln's day than in ours: "I saw the piranhas darting/ between the rose-veined columns,/ avid to strip the flesh/ from the Republic's bones." The source of

Lincoln's, the sacrificial redeemer's, strength is identified as his "secret wound," that is to say, "trusting the better angels of our nature." It is this trust, evoked by the humble but talismanic relics—a pocketknife, a handkerchief, a button—found on his person after the assassination that "make a noble, dissolving music/ out of homely fife and drum."

The title poem of the new section, "The Layers," looks forward to the possibilities of new art. The poet has "walked through many lives" and from the present vantage sees "milestones dwindling/ toward the horizon/ and the slow fires trailing/ from the abandoned camp-sites." To the question, "How shall the heart be reconciled/ to its feast of losses?" the answer comes "In my darkest night" from a "nimbus-cloud voice" that thunders, "Live in the layers,/ not on the litter." Though the poet admits, "I lack the art/ to decipher it," he concludes, "I am not done with my changes."

Kunitz's work *Next-to-Last Things: New Poems and Essays* makes at least three important additions to his poetic canon. A dream poem, "The Abduction," begins with the image of the beloved stumbling out of a wood, her blouse torn, her skirt bloodstained; she addresses the poet with the mysterious question, "Do you believe?" Through the years, he says, "from bits/ from broken clues/ we pieced enough together/ to make the story real." Led into the presence of "a royal stag,/ flaming in his chestnut coat," she was "borne/ aloft in triumph through the green,/ stretched on his rack of budding horn." In the next verse paragraph, the poet discloses that the episode was "a long time ago,/ almost another age" and muses on his sleeping wife (recalling, with the same image, the theme of otherness in "The Science of the Night"): "You lie in elegant repose,/ a hint of transport hovering on your lips." His attention shifts "to the harsh green flares," to which she is indifferent, that "swivel through the room/ controlled by unseen hands." The night world outside is "childhood country,/ bleached faces peering in/ with coals for eyes." His meditation leads him to realize that "the shapes of things/ are shifting in the wind," and concludes, "What do we know/ beyond the rapture and the dread?" echoing William Butler Yeats's famous question, "How can we know the dancer from the dance?" As a poem of transformation, "The Abduction" does not lend itself easily to interpretation—partly by design—for, at a very basic level, the preternatural images of transformation are rooted in undisclosed biographical events. As a poet of knowledge, however, Kunitz is poignant in his recognition that when people sleep, when they are most themselves, they are also most withdrawn and indifferent to their surroundings, even, or especially, from those they love. Yet by acknowledging, even honoring, the terms of this indifference, one most surely understands the unselfish nature of love.

"Days of Foreboding" begins with the announcement, "Great events are about to happen." The poet has seen migratory birds "in unprecedented numbers" picking the coastal margin clean. Turning to himself, he observes,

"My bones are a family in their tent/ huddled over a small fire/ waiting for the uncertain signal/ to resume the long march." He too is migratory, warmed by the small fire of his heart. Presumably, the "uncertain signal" is in some way keyed to the signal by which the migratory birds decide to move on, that is, it is keyed to nature. Moreover, while the signal is uncertain in terms of time and origin, it is nevertheless inevitable. The ultimate phrase, "the long march," sings with historical resonance and the promise of an irreversible transformation at the end. In this poem and in others, Kunitz accepts the awful (literally) fact of mortality, not by making an abstraction of it, but by naturalizing both it and the patch of history that is the bolt of time and circumstance given for its completion. Avoiding the need for consolation, it is a brave and existential view.

Certainly the centerpiece of *Next-to-Last Things* is the five-part meditative elegy, "The Wellfleet Whale," composed, like "The Testing-Tree," in tercets. Kunitz has noted that much of contemporary meditative poetry suffers from "the poverty of what it is meditating on," but this poem, occasioned by the beaching of a finback whale near the poet's home on Cape Cod, is rich in its suggestion that life's secret origins can be, if not revealed, then somehow embodied by the evocativeness of language, which is itself, as the poet notes elsewhere, "anciently deep in mysteries." The poem begins by ascribing to the whale, both Leviathan and deliverer of Jonah, Christ's precursor, the gift of language: "You have your language too,/ an eerie medley of clicks/ and hoots and trills. . . ." That language, to which humans are denied access (just as historical man, exiled from Eden, can no longer hear the Music of the Spheres), becomes only "sounds that all melt/ . . . with endless variations,/ as if to compensate/ for the vast loneliness of the sea." In the second section of the poem, the whale's arrival in the harbor is greeted with cheers "at the sign of your greatness." Unlike man, the whale in its element seems "like something poured,/ not driven," his presence asking "not sympathy, or love,/ or understanding,/ but awe and wonder," responses appropriate to deity. Yet by dawn, the whale is stranded on the rocks, and the curious gather in: "schoolgirls in yellow halters/ and a housewife bedecked/ with curlers, and whole families in beach/ buggies. . . ." As the great body is slowly crushed by its own weight, the Curator of Mammals arrives to draw the requisite vial of blood, someone carves his initials on the blistered flanks, and sea gulls peck at the skin. The poet asks, "What drew us, like a magnet, to your dying?" and answers, "You made a bond between us." This unlikely company, "boozing in the bonfire night," stands watch during the night as the whale enters its final agony and swings its head around to open "a bloodshot, glistening eye/ in which we swam with terror and recognition." The terror is that of witnessing "an exiled god" and the recognition that the creature, bringing with it "the myth/ of another country, dimly remembered" is "like us,/ disgraced and mortal," like all beings, and "delivered to the mercy of time." Despite the desecrations visited upon the creature, it remains an emissary from that other "country," the country of myth and inspired origin that stands at the beginning of human memory—and thus of identity—and so supervenes upon the noble disenchantment of the poem.

The tension that is everywhere apparent between noble disenchantment and hard-won acceptance demonstrates the ruling dialectic in Kunitz's poems. At the very least, it reveals the long trail of a poetic career (poetic careers have been built on much less); at its most resplendent, this dialectic embodies, through its variously charted interests, experiences, and investigations, a reason for the mind's commitment to the things of this world. Standing simultaneously in their singular and typical natures, they suggest the duality that is both our curse and triumph and lead us to an appreciation and understanding, as we rebound endlessly between the two, of the transformations we must endure to ensure our survival.

Other major works

NONFICTION: *A Kind of Order, a Kind of Folly: Essays and Conversations*, 1975.

TRANSLATIONS: *Stolen Apples*, 1972 (with others, of Yevgeny Yevtushenko's poetry); *Poems of Akhmatova*, 1973 (with Max Hayward); *Story Under Full Sail*, 1974 (of Andrei Voznesensky's poetry); *Orchard Lamps*, 1978 (of Ivan Drach's poetry).

MISCELLANEOUS: *Next-to-Last Things: New Poems and Essays*, 1985.

Bibliography

Hénault, Marie. *Stanley Kunitz*, 1980.
Mills, Ralph J. "Stanley Kunitz," in *Contemporary American Poetry*, 1966.
Orr, Gregory. *Stanley Kunitz: An Introduction to the Poetry*, 1985.

David Rigsbee

JANET LEWIS

Born: Chicago, Illinois; August 17, 1899

Principal collections
The Indians in the Woods, 1922; *The Wheel in Midsummer*, 1927; *The Earth-Bound, 1924-1944*, 1946; *The Ancient Ones*, 1979; *The Birthday of the Infanta*, 1979; *Poems Old and New, 1918-1978*, 1981.

Other literary forms
Janet Lewis is best known for her four historical novels, critical and popular successes published between 1932 and 1959. The first and least acclaimed, *The Invasion: A Narrative of Events Concerning the Johnston Family of St. Mary's* (1932), shared with her early poems an interest in Native American life and the American wilderness. Three others, of which *The Wife of Martin Guerre* (1941) and *The Trial of Soren Qvist* (1947) are probably the best known, deal in a lucid, documentary style with historic cases of circumstantial evidence. Lewis' fictional prose reflects her apprenticeship in Imagistic poetry—a narrative style that, in her own words, is "supposed to be transparent."

Lewis also published a novel with a contemporary setting, *Against a Darkening Sky* (1943), and a collection of contemporary short stories, *Good-Bye, Son, and Other Stories* (1946), as well as children's books. She has adapted *The Wife of Martin Guerre* as an opera, produced in 1956 by the Juilliard School of Music and subsequently at other schools.

Achievements
Lewis' poetic output is slight but distinguished. The ninety-four lyrics in her collected poems, many of them brief, show a remarkable stylistic evolution through her career of more than sixty years. A reviewer of the volume for *Poetry* described Lewis' poetic gift as "slight—I mean, both delicate and minor." Her husband, poet-critic Yvor Winters, praised her as a "stylist of remarkable native gift" but regretted her penchant for "domestic sentiment, which sometimes goes all the way to sentimentality."

Whatever the merits of these limiting remarks, Lewis remains important as a verse stylist and as a participant in—and transcender of—modern literary quarrels regarding the use of traditional forms. Her first book of poems, perhaps one of the best collections in the strict Imagist mode, was published in 1922 in a series which included William Carlos Williams and Marianne Moore. Two books later, in 1946, she had evolved into openly philosophical verse in traditional forms, and she won the Shelley Memorial Award for poetry in 1948. Her newer poems, a group begun when she was seventy-two years old, expand her reputation and answer the complaints of sentimentality and dry formalism sometimes lodged against her work of the 1930's and 1940's.

Lewis' collected poems appeared at a time when fashion had caught up with her lifelong interests. The American Indian, the Sun Belt, and the life of women had become, in the words of a *Parnassus* reviewer, "radical chic." In her eighties, Lewis achieved long-postponed recognition for decades of lyrical vision and craftsmanship.

Biography

Janet Lewis was born on August 17, 1899, in Chicago, Illinois, the daughter of Edwin Herbert Lewis, a poet, novelist, and English teacher. In the summer, the family lived in northern Michigan, where Lewis came to know the Ojibwa Indians, the subjects of her first book. She published her first poem in *Poetry* when she was twenty-one, a book when she was twenty-three. Earning an A.A. at the Lewis Institute in 1918 and a Ph.B. at the University of Chicago in 1920, Lewis worked for the American consulate in Paris, for *Redbook* magazine in Chicago, and finally, for the Lewis Institute in Chicago, where she taught until stricken with tuberculosis in 1922. She moved for her health to Santa Fe, New Mexico, and became a friend of Yvor Winters, another Chicago poet convalescing in the West. On June 22, 1926, when Lewis was still in frail health, they were married and in 1927 moved to Stanford University in California, where her husband pursued his doctorate and began teaching in 1928.

The direct effect of Winters, Janet Lewis' famous husband, on her career is not easy to assess. They remained devoted to each other until his death in 1968, and her poetic style evolved in a way harmonious with his published critical stance. Both strict Imagists in the 1920's, Winters and Lewis began, in the 1930's, to work in traditional verse forms and with paraphrasable morals—a position hostile to the high modernist mode of T. S. Eliot and Ezra Pound and closer to the writing of Thomas Hardy than to any other major modern poet.

Meanwhile, writing in the mornings when the family was "off to school," Lewis established a national reputation as a novelist and published in 1946 what was to be for more than thirty years her last volume of poetry. It won for her the Shelley Memorial Award for poetry in 1948. Writing her books and assuming the public role of housewife in Los Altos, California, near Stanford University, Lewis apparently settled into a peaceful uniformity of life suggested in her poem "No-Winter Country." A Guggenheim Fellowship in 1950-1951 to research in Paris her novel *The Ghost of Monsieur Scarron* (1959) was perhaps the most significant interruption in her routine until her husband died of cancer in 1968.

In 1971, still living in Los Altos, Lewis began writing poetry again, and her style again differed from what had gone before. The new work, in a more expansive and intimate voice, reestablished her reputation as a poet. For some years before and after her husband's death, Lewis taught writing at Stanford University. In 1976, she visited Indian ruins in northern Arizona, making the last part of the journey on horseback and by foot, and her experiences on this pilgrimage back toward the Indian themes of her earlier work resulted in some of her strongest new poems, a thin volume entitled *The Ancient Ones*. In the 1980's, she has continued to write poetry.

Analysis

During a literary career spanning more than sixty years, Janet Lewis has produced a small body of well-crafted poetry in styles evolving through three distinct stages: compact Imagism in the 1920's, formal lyricism in the 1930's and 1940's, and after a twenty-five-year hiatus, a free incantatory style in the 1970's and 1980's. The first two stages paralleled the career of Winters, who began as a strict and respected Imagist and became in the 1930's the leader of a self-styled "reactionary" return to traditional rhyme and accentual meter. Opinion is divided as to whether Lewis' formalist turn was well advised, whether her middle poems moved toward sentimentality and dryness or whether she wrote rich and finely crafted work in the tradition of Thomas Hardy and earlier English verse.

Her collected volume, *Poems Old and New, 1918-1978*, has been received with almost universal praise, critics differing only about which poems to single out. In this book, Lewis collects her best poems in a wide range of styles, including the 1918 poem which won for her entrance into the Poetry Club at the University of Chicago. The most recent works in the volume, written after 1971, are a synthesis and extension of the styles which preceded them—a return to the free verse and Indian subjects of her Imagistic period but exploring the powers of a complex, discursive long line. Without the Imagistic restrictions against abstract statement and paraphrasable content, Lewis displays more freely her feeling for nature, her lyricism, and her sense of history.

The lyrics in her 1922 volume, *The Indians in the Woods*, average less than twelve lines and, with haikulike compression, suggest the closeness between the lives of the Ojibwa Indians and the processes of nature, particularly the cycle of the harsh northern seasons. The poems are rigorously Imagistic, expunged of nearly all general statement or transition—each a sequence of evoked sensations and elemental feelings. Central to the sequence is the god whose return is celebrated in the spring; even without this underpinning of myth, however, the poems function individually as icons of time's destructive passage, the promise of rebirth, and the muted joy of participation in natural process. The narrator is repeatedly identified as female, at times a wife, at times a grandmother, so that the poems are genuinely feminocentric, with a male god playing the role of mysterious natural Other. In most of the poems, the god could as well be a mortal lover, the seasons as well figurative as literal, and the forest as well suburban as primeval. The reversal of literary gender roles—particularly in 1922—is reason alone to reread these poems. If stripped of their bibliographic history, they might as readily be attributed to the 1970's as to the 1920's. Like William Carlos Williams' poems in *Spring and All* (1922), which they antedate and resemble, the lyrics are spare and evocative, short lines that play occasional run-ons against the expected pause at line's end. What the Ojibwa poems lack in range, they make up for in polished intensity.

Actually, though Imagism stands at the beginning of Lewis' collected poems, it was not her first style. "The Freighters," her earliest published poem, uses traditional accent and meter and describes trees along a bank as singing "with moving branches/ Songs of eternity." This is the sort of generalization which Lewis, as an Imagist, excluded from the 1922 volume, but to which she would return in her post-Imagist work after 1930. Between 1922 and 1927, the years of her convalescence, Lewis was evolving toward a softer, more traditional style without sacrificing the Imagistic virtues of sensation and compression. Some of her most memorable short poems are from this transitional period. Generally domestic in subject, the poems often use traditional lyric forms but with compact images in the foreground. Some, like the title poem to her second book, "The Wheel in Midsummer," are stylistically similar to the Ojibwa poems. Among the best works from her convalescent period are "The Reader," "Girl Help," and "Remembered Morning," which chart the direction in which her art was to evolve. "The Reader" is a delicately descriptive poem about a reader lost in a book, as the sun, the fire, and the leaves clamor ineffectually to recall him to sensory reality—all this shown with Imagistic directness. Then a newborn "creature"—presumably a moth—is at the screen door "heaving damp heavy wings." Lewis' readers are left with the nascent symbol, no explanation. Less cryptic but equally delicate is "Girl Help," a three-quatrain rhyming poem in which a servant is shown to pause and smell lilacs scented with promise. "Remembered Morning" succeeds with perhaps an even less promising subject, the remembrance of a happy summer's day in childhood. Yet Lewis' spare, evocative description rescues the poem from its conventional versification and a line such as "O happy early stir!" Less successful experiments with traditional verse include "Love Poem," "The Candle Flame," "The Manger," and "The Tennis Players," which fall into the mannerisms of turn-of-the-century magazine verse.

After her marriage and move to California, Lewis' style changed decisively, probably encouraged by her husband, who had recently made a sharp theoretical turn against "experimental" modern poetry and was already developing the position he would expound in his controversial critical books. Lewis' poems between 1927 and 1944 were in a style that adapted traditional prosody and direct paraphrasable purpose to the needs of twentieth century life. Some are flawed, at least from the mainstream perspective, by archaisms, inversions, predictable rhymes, and hackneyed similes—dangers deliberately courted by a reformed Imagist who knew what she was doing. The best are effective as beautifully crafted antiques newly made, and that was clearly Lewis' intention. Among the best is "Time and Music," a philosophical poem in octameter couplets which uses its very formality as an extension of its content: the suggestion that willed form is life; its absence, death. "Country Burial" works in a more emotional mode, describing vividly a funeral procession across a flowery field, then turning away from the numbing, discomforting vision of a Heaven without the wetness and color of earth. In this, and in "Baby Goat"—a poem saved from preciousness by the visual exactness of Lewis' descriptions—she contrasts the world of changing doomed colors with the mysterious colorless world of Heaven or unchanging form. This theme was implicit even in the "The Freighters" and the Ojibwa poems, but the best of the middle poems gain intellectual and moral density by making it explicit.

In the poems written between 1930 and 1944, Lewis has clearly accepted the aim expressed in her husband's criticism and adopted by a school of California poets: to fuse fully realized descriptive detail with expressed abstract meaning through exertion of the conscious will in traditional verse. "Lines with a Gift of Herbs," "The Hanger at Sunnydale," "In the Egyptian Museum," and "Helen Grown Old" are successes in this effort, all reflecting on the contrast between particulars which change and universals which inhere through this change—the scent in dry herbs, the steel hanger of a lost dirigible, the jewelry of a dead civilization, and the mystery of Helen of Troy's unmemorialized old age. Though the verse, again, is sometimes too dry, too mannered for some modern tastes, these poems do seem to work through the willed fusion of image and explicit moral called for by Winters' theory. Nevertheless, despite the critical success of these poems, Lewis ceased writing poetry altogether between 1944 and 1971.

When she took up verse again, it was free verse without rhyme or with casual rhyme in the manner of Ezra Pound or William Butler Yeats, and her lines set up biblical narrative cadence not as free as Walt Whitman's but clearly in the same tradition. This was a clear break from the formalism of the middle years, though it is not a return to Imagism, for abstract statement and reasoning mix freely with description. Also, Lewis returns to the domestic and Indian subjects of her pre-California lyrics. Here the interplay between the transient and the eternal receives its most serene and poignant treatment in poems such as "For the Father of Sandro Gullota," "The Anasozi Woman," "The Ancient Ones: Betákin," "In a Convalescent Hospital," and "Geometries." Though Lewis maintains a recognizable voice through all of her changes, in the later poems she seems to draw the reader closer, sharing her empathy with a child dying of leukemia, with the mummy of an Indian woman, with a ruins of pre-Navajo people moved by universals of water and beauty, with a once-vital woman dying alone, and with geometric shapes replicated eternally in nature. The later poems in her collected volume are not all the best, but they are a triumphant summation, suggesting or incorporating the best of what came before.

Other major works

NOVELS: *The Invasion: A Narrative of Events Concerning the Johnston Family of St. Mary's*, 1932; *The Wife of Martin Guerre*, 1941; *Against a Darkening Sky*, 1943; *The Trial of Soren Qvist*, 1947; *The Ghost of Monsieur Scarron*, 1959.

SHORT FICTION: *Good-Bye, Son, and Other Stories*, 1946.

OPERA: *The Wife of Martin Guerre*, 1956 (adaptation of her novel).

Bibliography

Doyle, Suzanne J. "Janet Lewis's *The Ancient Ones*," in *The Southern Review*. XVI, no. 2 (1980), p. 531.
Gioia, Dana. "Poetry Chronicle," in *The Hudson Review*. XXXIV, no. 4 (1981/1982), p. 579.
Hofheins, Roger, and Dan Tooker. "A Conversation with Janet Lewis," in *The Southern Review*. X, no. 2 (1974), pp. 329-341.
Trimpi, Helen P. "The Poetry of Janet Lewis," in *The Southern Review*. XVIII, no. 2 (1982), pp. 251-258.
Winters, Yvor. *Forms of Discovery*, 1967.

William H. Green

HUGH MacDIARMID
Christopher Murray Grieve

Born: Langholm, Scotland; August 11, 1892
Died: Edinburgh, Scotland; September 9, 1978

Principal poems and collections

A Moment in Eternity, 1922; *Sangschaw*, 1925; *Penny Wheep*, 1926; *A Drunk Man Looks at the Thistle*, 1926; *The Lucky Bag*, 1927; *To Circumjack Cencrastus: Or, The Curly Snake*, 1930; *First Hymn to Lenin and Other Poems*, 1931; *Scots Unbound and Other Poems*, 1932; *Selected Poems*, 1934; *Stony Limits and Other Poems*, 1934; *Second Hymn to Lenin and Other Poems*, 1935; *A Kist of Whistles*, 1947; *In Memoriam James Joyce*, 1955; *The Battle Continues*, 1957; *Three Hymns to Lenin*, 1957; *Collected Poems of Hugh MacDiarmid*, 1962; *A Lap of Honour*, 1967; *Complete Poems, 1920-1976*, 1978 (two volumes).

Other literary forms

Hugh MacDiarmid wrote prolifically through most of his long life. His more than seventy books include social criticism, political polemics, autobiography, and literary criticism. He edited earlier Scottish poets such as William Dunbar and Robert Burns and several poetry anthologies, and he founded and edited a number of Scottish periodicals.

Achievements

Only slowly has MacDiarmid come to be recognized as a major twentieth century poet. He spent most of his life laboring in one way or another for Scotland and won his earliest acclaim there. He was a founder, in 1927, of the Scottish Center of PEN, the international writers' organization, and of the National Party of Scotland the following year, although his always radical political views led him into the Communist Party in the 1930's. Despite his extreme social and political views, his friends were legion. He once observed that few other people could boast of friendships with William Butler Yeats, T. S. Eliot, *and* Dylan Thomas, and the circle of his admirers extended worldwide. After many years of promoting, usually undiplomatically, Scotland and Scottish culture, he was awarded a Civil List pension in 1950, and although his criticism of Scottish education continued unabated, Edinburgh University awarded him an honorory Doctor of Laws degree in 1957.

Not until the 1960's, however, did MacDiarmid's poetry begin to appear in British and modern poetry anthologies. Despite a general awakening to his greatness since that time, reliable commentary on his work remains largely in the hands of Scottish critics. It is safe to say that the study of his poetry to date represents a tiny portion of what will emerge in the years and decades to come. As an innovator in modern literature, MacDiarmid deserves to be ranked with Eliot, James Joyce, and Samuel Beckett.

Biography

Christopher Murray Grieve was born on August 11, 1892, in Langholm, Scotland, near the English border. His father's side of the family worked mostly in tweed mills, while his mother's people were farmers; throughout his life, Hugh MacDiarmid championed the working class. His father, who was a rural postman, died while Christopher was still a teenager. Educated at Langholm Academy and Broughton Junior Student Center, Edinburgh, the young man worked thereafter as a journalist and became active in politics. In World War I, he served in the Royal Army Medical Corps in Salonika, Italy, and France.

In 1918, MacDiarmid was married, and he settled after the war in Montrose, Angus, where he continued as a reporter, local politician, and contributor to the Scottish Renaissance and Nationalist movements. Adopting the pen name Hugh MacDiarmid in the early 1920's, he continued to write prose under his given name for years afterward. He lived in England most of the time between the years 1929 and 1932, working at temporary jobs, perfecting his antipathy to the English, and suffering the breakup of his marriage.

After being married in 1932, MacDiarmid returned to Scotland, worked briefly in Edinburgh, and from 1933 to 1941 lived in Whalsay in the Shetland Islands, where he developed the geological interest which permeates his poems of this period. He performed factory and merchant tasks during World War II, after which he traveled considerably, including trips to Communist nations. As late as 1964, when he was seventy-two, he stood as Communist candidate for Parliament in the district of Kinross and West Perthshire, insisting as always that his Communist and Nationalist commitments in no way conflicted. The publication of *Collected Poems of Hugh MacDiarmid* in the United States in 1962, while omitting many good poems, brought him to the attention of a wider reading public, and in his final years, he was acknowledged as one of Scotland's greatest poets. He died at the age of eighty-six on September 9, 1978.

Analysis

When Hugh MacDiarmid began writing poetry seriously after serving in World War I, the Scots literary tradition had reached one of its lowest points. In the century following the deaths of Robert Burns, Sir Walter Scott, and Lord Byron, Scottish poetry consisted largely of enervated and sentimental effusions which imitated the surface mannerisms of Burns's lyrics. Under the circumstances, it is hardly surprising that MacDiarmid wrote his earliest poems in standard English. Although his style was reminiscent of English

Romanticism, it had from the start more vigor and individuality than the work of most of his contemporaries. The best of these early poems, *A Moment in Eternity*, first appeared in MacDiarmid's *Annals of the Five Senses* (1923), which contained chiefly experimental prose. This poem establishes his essentially Romantic disposition, "searching the unsearchable" in quest of God and immortality. Although his style and technique were to change radically, these ambitions remained with him, and "eternity" remained to the end of his career one of the most frequent words in his poetic vocabulary. His rhythms in this early poem are supple, varied, but basically iambic; his diction, pleasant but rather conventional.

It was not long, however, before he began to write under his pseudonymn in a vocabulary forged from various local Scottish dialects and words from literary Scots dating as far back as the late medieval period of Scottish literary glory, when Robert Henryson, William Dunbar, Gavin Douglas, and others overshadowed the best English poets. He charged this "synthetic Scots" with a surprising vitality in two early books of lyrics, *Sangschaw* and *Penny Wheep*. The poems were about God, eternity, the Scottish countryside, love, and other subjects. Because he broke with the stereotypes of recent Scottish poetry and because he challenged his traditionally literate countrymen with a diction reaching back to a time of Scottish literary ascendancy, MacDiarmid was basing his strategy on an appeal to the best in his readers.

Before the publication of the second of these works, he was already shaping another book. *A Drunk Man Looks at the Thistle*, also issued in 1926, proved a much more ambitious work: a sequence of lyrics and meditative poems making up one long, symbolically unified poem. Although MacDiarmid was to write many long poems, he would never find a structural principle more effective than the one he used here. While some critics have objected to the titles of the fifty-nine poems as interfering with the unity of the book, anyone reading through the sequence will have no trouble perceiving its integrity. The first title, "Sic Transit Gloria Scotia," signals the poet's concern with the cultural and literary decline of his native land and suggests his intention of arresting that decline personally. *A Drunk Man Looks at the Thistle* has come to be recognized as more than a regional achievement, though MacDiarmid took several risks which probably delayed recognition of the scope of his achievement.

In the first place, the title, while accurate, is an odd one for an ambitious literary work, as it seems to lack seriousness and in fact to cater to the common perception of the Scottish peasantry as whiskey-guzzling ne'er-do-wells. His employment of a Scots vocabulary also posed problems. The vocabulary threatened to repel English readers, who expected poets to clothe respectable verse in literary English. The numerous dialect words required heavy use of a specialized dictionary. Even if willing to wrestle with the words, however, such readers were likely to associate Scots with feeble imitations of

Burns. MacDiarmid appeared unconventional and frivolous not only in choosing a drunkard as the poem's speaker but also in choosing the lowly thistle, rather than a more "worthy" flower such as a rose, as his central symbol. Who else had made anything of such a homely weed since the rhetorical question of Matthew 7:16: "Do men gather grapes of thorns, or figs of thistles?"

Nevertheless, MacDiarmid had reasons to hope for a harvest. His format permitted him a series of lyrical, comical, and satirical reflections in a variety of meters and stanzas, both rhymed and unrhymed, with the concomitant advantage of showing off his technical versatility. He could also expect that his more extravagant poetic flights, being merely the dreams of a drunken man, would not reflect on him. Apparent digressions were no problem, either, for everyone expects a drunken man to meander. Therefore, while his character indulged in a leisurely display of reactions to all that ailed him and Scotland, the poet could carefully guide his inebriated speaker along a purposeful path.

The drunkard begins by complaining of the difficulty of keeping up with his drinking partners, especially since the Scotch does not compare with the old-time variety, thereby establishing that everything Scottish now seems to be "destitute o'speerit," including the appalling poetry now produced by supposed devotees of Burns. An immediate dilemma presents itself: How can one be a good Scot yet shake off the Scottish lethargy and mediocrity? Interestingly, MacDiarmid's method involves the occasional incorporation of translations and adaptations from French, Belgian, German, and Russian poets, and two original lyrics addressed to Fyodor Dostoevski. MacDiarmid obviously considered the great Russian novelist a kindred spirit in the struggle to repossess imaginatively a stubbornly recalcitrant homeland. To be a good Scot meant, among other things, to accept competent assistance wherever available.

In a poem called "Poet's Pub," based on a poem by Alexander Blok, the drunkard resists the idea of going home to his wife, Jean, who is sure to nag him. Instead, he hopes to discover the truth said to be in wine, especially those truths ordinarily dark to him and to his cronies. He catches sight of a "silken leddy" in the pub, but she soon fades from sight, and eventually he stumbles outside to begin his homeward trek. The fourth poem of the sequence introduces the thistle and the image with which MacDiarmid customarily pairs it, the moonlight: "The munelicht's like a lookin'-glass,/ The thistle's like mysel'," he observes, one of the resemblances being that he needs a shave.

In the poems that follow, the symbolic values of thistle and moonlight proliferate. A poem addressed to "The Unknown Goddess"—again adapted from Blok—presumably refers to the mysterious lady of the pub, who may represent his muse but is certainly the opposite of Jean. The drunkard's attention alternates between depressing reality ("Our Educational System," "The Barren Fig," "Tussle with the Philistines") and inspired visions ("Man and the Infinite," "Outward Bound," "The Spur of Love"). The drunken man is not sure of much: "And yet I feel this muckle thistle's staun'in'/ Atween me and the mune as pairt o' a Plan." He regards himself as his nation's "soul" and thus free to appropriate the humble thistle: In one of his flights he compares his homeward course to the wanderings of Ulysses; in another he sees himself "ootward boond" toward eternity. The thistle may serve to unite man and the infinite, or it may simply take off on its own and leave man nothing but the hole in which it was once rooted. Periodically his thoughts return to Jean, who "ud no' be long/ In finding whence this thistle sprang," for it is in her absence that the plant has grown for him.

The man's thoughts oscillate between Scotland—materialistic, Philistine, ill-educated, yet worth redemption—and himself as representative of the more general human condition—earthbound and mortal yet aspiring to eternity. The thistle has, despite its general ugliness, the capacity to flower, to put out at its tip a "rose" that permits MacDiarmid the traditional associations of that flower in a different context. In "The Form and Purpose of the Thistle," the speaker reflects on the "craft" that produced the odd, prickly stalk capable of breaking into flowers "like sudden lauchter," a craft of puzzling contrarieties. In "The Thistle's Characteristics," the poet ranges over man's illusions and presumptions, "For wha o's ha'e the thistle's poo'er/ To see we're worthless and believe 't?" Later he employs the Norse myth of Yggdrasill, the ash tree which binds together Earth, Heaven, and Hell; in this case, however, man is a "twig" on a giant thistle that, far from uniting creation, "braks his warlds abreid and rives/ His heavens to tatters on its horns." The Yggdrasill poem insists on man's suffering and ends by seeing humans as so many Christs, carrying their crosses "frae the seed," although as the drunkard slyly puts it, most feel it far less than he "thro' bein' mair wudden frae the stert!" Such satiric thrusts at his countrymen occur frequently in the work as a whole. However painful the life, the soul will soar in its "divine inebriety." Intoxication, then, is also a metaphor in this poem, standing for the poetic imagination that can rise above, and gain solace by reflecting on, mankind's common "Calvary."

The drunken man contemplates the oppressive English rule over an exhausted and often foolish Scotland, but even more often, his thoughts wind between Heaven and Earth, between the aspirations of the rose and the limitations of the rooted stalk. He longs for the mysterious lady, then is gripped by the recollection of practical Jean at home. Near the end of the work, he sees himself, God, the Devil, and Scotland all on a great cosmic wheel which sums up Scotland's and man's slow journeys through history. Pondering Scottish resistance to change and new ideas, he wonders if he must "assume/ The burden o' his people's doom" by dying heroically for his recalcitrant fellows.

He falters over the decision, not exactly rejecting heroism but choosing to return to Jean's arms. The last lyric of the poem pays eloquent tribute to what he has left of his vision: silence. The conclusion is a joke, for he imagines what Jean will say to that: "And weel ye micht,/ . . . efter sic a nicht!"

The final lines of the poem are consistent with the whole work: Despite his insistence on the dignity of human imagination, the drunken man is always aware of the indignity of human circumstances and his inability to grasp the meaning of life. Only a drunk—that is, only a person intoxicated by life generally and the life of the mind particularly—would bother with such a spiritual quest.

MacDiarmid's next book of poetry, *To Circumjack Cencrastus*, is more of a miscellany, but one stanza of the poem aptly titled "MacDiarmid's Curses" holds a particular irony:

> Speakin' o' Scotland in English words
> As it were Beethoven chirpt by birds;
> Or as if a Board school teacher
> Tried to teach Rimbaud and Nietzsche.

Although these lines do not precisely deny the possibility of a shift to "English words," they scarcely foretell the fact that within a few years MacDiarmid would virtually cease to write in his Scottish amalgam, even when "speakin' o' Scotland." By the middle 1930's, he would be creating a very different sort of poetry using standard English.

In the meantime, MacDiarmid continued to employ Scots for his first two "hymns to Lenin." Many intellectuals of the time shared his hope, but few his enduring faith, in the efficacy of Communism. It remains difficult to read objectively the "First Hymn to Lenin," in which the Soviet leader is hailed as a successor to Christ, or to appreciate it as poetry. MacDiarmid seems to have traded metaphysical doubts for political assurance, and the exchange does not enhance his poetry. He was always extreme in his enthusiasms, but from this point on his polemical voice invaded his poetry more frequently. Within *First Hymn to Lenin and Other Poems*, however, is found "At My Father's Grave," with its eight lines of flexible blank verse meditating hauntingly on his father, as if from "across a valley."

With *Stony Limits and Other Poems*, MacDiarmid moved into a new phase of his poetic career. He still included poems in Scots, notably a group called "Shetland Lyrics," but he was now working in a literary English that differed markedly from that of his very early poetry. The English poems were at this point more discursive, somewhat less concrete, and considerably more formal. The title poem, in nine ten-line stanzas, pays tribute to Charles Doughty, a poet, geologist, and travel writer who delighted in the lonely occupation of studying the soil and rock formations of remote regions, his most famous book being about the Arabian desert. Gregarious himself, Mac-

Diarmid could respond enthusiastically to Doughty's serenity, his indifference to the crowd, and his capacity for appreciating realms of silence. When this book appeared, MacDiarmid had retreated to the Shetland Islands, where, without ceasing his political involvements, he had begun to study the geology of this northern outpost. He created a new difficulty for his readers, for "Stony Limits" is peppered with terms such as "xenoliths," "orthopinacoid," "striae," and "microline." The geological terminology signals his camaraderie with Doughty and also a growing love of precision quite distinct from the passion for suggestiveness which created the thistle and moonlight images in *A Drunk Man Looks at the Thistle*. This elegy is quiet, almost reverent, but without the defiant tone of his hymns to Lenin.

He carries his scientific enthusiasm further in a longer poem in the same collection, "On a Raised Beach." The poem begins "All is lithogenesis—or lochia," a line hardly calculated to appeal immediately to the laity, but since the first term signifies rock formation and the second the discharge from the womb after childbirth, the line immediately juxtaposes the contrasting elements of the poem, stones and human life. Actually, the first twenty-four of the poem's more than four hundred lines teem with technical geological terms, most of which cannot be found in an ordinary desk dictionary. Anyone who braves this formidable initial barrier, however, discovers an arresting meditation on the human situation vis-à-vis that of the stones, which "are one with the stars."

MacDiarmid points out that specific terms can be given to scientific phenomena, but man finds more difficulty in expressing his own convictions and preferences. The permanence of stone emphasizes the transience and impatience of man. Early in the poem, he compares man unfavorably to the one other creature stirring on the beach, a bird whose "inward gates" are, unlike man's, "always open." MacDiarmid argues that the gates of stones stand open even longer. The poet's admiration for these enduring veterans of a world older than man can easily imagine resembles Henry David Thoreau's for living nature, and a number of the lines have a Thoreauvian ring to them—for example, "Let men find the faith that builds mountains/ Before they seek the faith that moves them." As in Thoreau, nature teaches the perceptive person humility. Life is redundant, says MacDiarmid, but not stones. Human culture pales before the bleak but beautiful sentinels of time on a scale beyond man's ordinary comprehension.

As the stately free verse moves on, MacDiarmid alludes to various stones with human associations: the missile that David hurled at Goliath, pebbles with which Demosthenes filled his mouth, the rock that guarded Christ's tomb. Human culture is like Goliath, doomed to fall, and no orator can hope to rival the lithic earth in eloquence. Stones not only draw men back to their beginnings but also lead them on to their end. No stone can be rolled aside like the "Christophanic" one to release death, but death is not on that account to be feared, because dying is less difficult than living a worthwhile life.

Despite the weightiness of "On a Raised Beach," despite its rather sepulchral tone, the poem does not oppress but conveys a breath of caution, a salutary deflation of human arrogance. The poem might have benefited from a beach more specifically evoked, like Matthew Arnold's Dover Beach, but it nevertheless communicates effectively the "capacity for solitude" by which MacDiarmid strives to imitate the great stones.

The virtual disappearance of Scots lyrics after *Stony Limits and Other Poems* seems to be not a repudiation of the poet's earlier theory but an acknowledgment that after several hundred poems in that medium he needed to test the linguistic possibilities of English. Like Burns before him, MacDiarmid could sing best in Scots and create more comedy and humor than he ever seemed to have tried in literary English. Advocates of his poetry (many of whom are Scottish) have tended to prefer the Scots poems, but the best of his English poems have their own excellence, and it is of a sort appropriate to an older man. They are sober, thought-provoking, and reflective of the intensity of a poet deeply committed to his art and alert to the world about him. Like Yeats and Eliot, he changed his style in middle age to produce a kind of verse in sharp contrast to that which gained for him his initial audience.

Not until the publication of his autobiography, *Lucky Poet*, in 1943 did MacDiarmid formulate in detail his prescription for the poetry he had been attempting to practice for a decade. This book contains several previously unpublished poems, one of which, "The Kind of Poetry I Want," sets forth vigorously the theory that he had been developing. The diction and rhythms of this long poem are prosaic, and its topical allusions date it severely, but it rings with conviction. Probably no poem ever written realizes all of its specifications. According to MacDiarmid, the poet must be a polymath who can base his or her work on "difficult knowledge" in many fields, including the sciences, and must be technically accomplished and equipped with "ecstasy." Poetry must reflect closeness to and knowledge of nature. The poet must know the countryside and the technological order and must deploy linguistic and historical learning. Poetry must be factual and still illuminate values, argues MacDiarmid; it must integrate the knowledge of its various sources and—as a crowning touch—must reflect a poet uninterested in personal success. At one point, MacDiarmid concedes that such poetry must await social reorganization, presumably along communistic lines.

MacDiarmid was better equipped than most to pursue his poetic ideal. By mid-career, his poetry bristled with learned allusions to Russian, Hebrew, Turkish, Chinese, Greek, and Gaelic poetry, to name a few. Not all the poems in *Lucky Poet* are learned, but they are all provoking. Two of them excoriate the cities of Edinburgh and Glasgow for their bourgeois sins, and the good humor of his earlier social criticism has vanished. Clearly, he is less willing than ever to cater to merely conventional taste and expectations.

By the time of *In Memoriam James Joyce*, MacDiarmid was brewing a poetry in some ways like Joyce's prose, packed with recondite allusions, quotations in many languages, puns, technical vocabulary, and an often tortuous syntax. The tone was more likely to be oracular and insistent. How many of his poetic tenets he was then fulfilling is disputable, but he clearly was not integrating knowledge, and perhaps he was inadvertently demonstrating the impossibility of such integration in the second half of the twentieth century, with its myriad specialists. Reminiscent of his previous work is the poem "We Must Look at the Harebell." MacDiarmid is at his best when "looking" rather than persuading, and this poem has fresh observations not only of the harebell but also of the pinguicula or butterwort (a small herb), the asphodel, the parsley fern, and other flora to be found by a person willing to climb rocks and descend into bogs. The plants he observes are interesting, but even more interesting is his determination to reveal the prospects of nature.

MacDiarmid appears to have written relatively little new poetry after the publication of *In Memoriam James Joyce*, but because *Collected Poems of Hugh MacDiarmid* omitted a number of his earlier poems, the volume *A Lap of Honour*, which appeared five years later, when the poet turned seventy-five, was an important addition. It contained some poems that had appeared only in periodicals and others from books difficult to obtain in 1967. One of the most important inclusions was "On a Raised Beach," only a short extract of which had appeared in the 1962 collection. There were several, by then welcome, Scots poems from an earlier day. Thus, this volume made accessible to many readers for the first time a sampling of MacDiarmid's work over the decades of his greatest vitality, the 1920's, 1930's, and 1940's.

The innovations of his later poetry have an importance beyond the success of individual poems. In an age when many poets knew little about science and even affected to despise it, MacDiarmid was trying to widen the range of the poet's expertise. While the scientific knowledge of even an amateur such as MacDiarmid is bound to seem inadequate to a well-trained scientist, he was often able to enhance his subjects with metaphors drawn from science. Thus, in "Stony Limits," he compared his projected poem in praise of Doughty to the process of crystallization in rocks and to the growth of lunar formations, and in "Crystals Like Blood," he could liken the memory to the extraction of mercury from cinnabar. Such metaphors doubtless have very little effect on a scientifically illiterate reader, but his fear was of a poetry that failed by appealing only to the badly educated. His aspiration to the precision of the exact sciences was probably unrealistic, but he was doing his part to integrate the "two cultures" at a time when many intellectuals were dividing into mutually antagonistic and uncomprehending camps. His efforts to apply the discoveries of modern linguistics to poetry were unsuccessful, but there is no telling what they may have suggested to younger poets. He carried allusion and quotation beyond what many readers would consider tolerable limits, but he did not shrink from challenging those who were able and willing to follow him. Like Eliot, MacDiarmid was trying to use tradition creatively, and like Ezra Pound, he often moved outside the Western tradition favored by Eliot. Few poets have worked so diligently for so long to widen the possibilities of poetry.

By a curious irony, MacDiarmid's poems in English, because of their high density of technical words and obscure quotations and allusions, present greater difficulties than his earlier ones in Scots. Lacking the humor and lyricism of the early poems, his English poems often repay the reader's careful attention with their insight into the natural world and their challenge to conventional ways of looking at the world and of expressing the results of such observations. Nevertheless, his early mission to rescue Scottish poetry by creating a composite dialect out of folk and literary sources and to speak to a materialistic generation of the possibilities of a richer culture and authentic spiritual life was doubtless his greatest accomplishment. Even without consulting the glossary of *Collected Poems of Hugh MacDiarmid*, the English-speaking reader can take pleasure in the energy and lyrical buoyancy of *A Drunk Man Looks at the Thistle*, and with very little trouble the full meaning is available to all. It has been suggested that this poem is the modern equivalent of the medieval dream vision. Undoubtedly, only a poet steeped in literary tradition could have written it. Taking advantage of a form that allows a comprehensive and uninhibited vision, MacDiarmid fashions a poem that is highly original because it reflects a modern, skeptical sensibility, and is readily understandable because it is made from the materials of everyday life. While aiming at universality in his later poetry, he achieved it most fully in his odyssey of a drunken cottager beneath the Scottish "mune."

Other major works

NONFICTION: *Albyn: Or, Scotland and the Future*, 1927; *The Present Condition of Scottish Music*, 1927; *At the Sign of the Thistle: A Collection of Essays*, 1934; *Scottish Eccentrics*, 1936; *The Islands of Scotland*, 1939; *Lucky Poet*, 1943; *Burns Today and Tomorrow*, 1959; *David Hume: Scotland's Greatest Son*, 1961; *The Company I've Kept*, 1967; *Scotland, 1968: Selected Essays of Hugh MacDiarmid*, 1969 (edited by Duncan Glen).

ANTHOLOGIES: *Northern Numbers, Being Representative Selections from Certain Living Scottish Poets*, 1920-1922 (three volumes); *The Golden Treasury of Scottish Poetry*, 1940.

MISCELLANEOUS: *Annals of the Five Senses*, 1923.

Bibliography
Buthlay, Kenneth. *Hugh MacDiarmid*, 1964.
_____. *Hugh MacDiarmid*, 1982.
Daiches, David. "Hugh MacDiarmid and Scottish Poetry," in *Poetry*. LXXII (July, 1948), pp. 202-218.
Duval, K. D., and Sydney Goodsir Smith, eds. *Hugh MacDiarmid: A Festschrift*, 1962.
Glen, Duncan. *Hugh MacDiarmid and the Scottish Renaissance*, 1964.
_____, ed. *Hugh MacDiarmid: A Critical Survey*, 1972.
Morgan, Edwin. *Hugh MacDiarmid*, 1976.
Scottish Literary Journal. V (December, 1978). Special MacDiarmid issue.

Robert P. Ellis

HARRY MARTINSON

Born: Jämshög, Sweden; May 6, 1904
Died: Stockholm, Sweden; February 11, 1978

Principal poems and collections
Spökskepp, 1929; *Nomad*, 1931; *Natur*, 1934; *Passad*, 1945; *Cikada*, 1953; *Aniara: En revy om människan i tid och rum*, 1956 (*Aniara: A Review of Man in Time and Space*, 1963); *Gräsen i Thule*, 1958; *Vagnen*, 1960; *Dikter om ljus och mörker*, 1971; *Tuvor*, 1973; *Wild Bouquet*, 1985.

Other literary forms
In addition to his poetry, Harry Martinson has published impressionistic travelogues as well as two autobiographical childhood recollections and a novel. They are all centered on the major symbol in his work, the "world nomad," the restless traveler, and form one coherent poetic *Bildungsroman* in which initial bitterness over strong social handicaps and anguish at a world without love are superseded by the protagonist's, that is, the poet's, search for tenderness and acceptance. Martinson's later essay collections—sketches, meditations, and prose poems—in which concrete nature observation is blended with philosophical speculation, mark a departure from the autobiographical realm. Yet Martinson insists on drawing parallels between life in nature and human life. This approach leads him to a scathing criticism of modern civilization in the Rousseauean tradition, climaxing in his reports from Finland's Winter War of 1939-1940 against Russia.

Achievements
The immediate and acclaimed breakthrough which Martinson experienced with his collection *Nomad* was rather unique in Swedish literature. The critics unanimously agreed in acknowledging an unusually gifted writer who combined sharp intellect and concise power of observation with an almost visionary ability to perceive a cosmic unity behind the fragmentation of modern thought, qualities which Martinson's later writings have confirmed.

In Swedish literary history, Martinson belongs chronologically to the 1930's. For a time, he joined the group of young radical poets who rejected morality and modern civilization as too inhibiting in favor of an unrestricted worship of spontaneity and instinctive forces in life. Yet, in spite of his contributions to the anthology *Fem unga* (1929), Martinson is only in part related to the decade's D. H. Lawrence–inspired vitalism and primitivism. Nor does he belong to the exclusive and self-centered school of T. S. Eliot–inspired modernists of the 1940's. Already during his lifetime, he was accepted as a classicist, a classicist distinguished through linguistic imagination and a highly developed associative and myth-creating imagination. Also notable is his continuous endeavor to search for coherence in a chaotic world and—for the sake of troubled humanity—to warn against abusing the achievements of modern technology.

It is, however, impossible to place Martinson in a specific school or trend. Indeed, after his epic poem *Aniara*, a tremendous critical and public success, he emerged as one of the most independent yet compassionate humanists in twentieth century Scandinavian literature. In 1959, when *Aniara* premiered as an opera, with libretto by another prolific Swedish poet, Erik Lindegren, and music by Karl-Birger Blomdahl, it received international recognition. In 1949, Martinson was elected to the Swedish Academy as its first self-taught proletarian writer; in 1954, he received an honorary doctorate from the University of Gothenburg; and, in 1974, he shared, together with Eyvind Johnson, the Nobel Prize for Literature.

Biography

Harry Edmund Martinson was born on May 6, 1904, in Jämshög in the southeastern province of Blekinge, Sweden. His father, a captain in the merchant marines and later an unsuccessful businessman, died when Martinson was five. One year later, his mother emigrated to the United States, leaving her seven children to be cared for by the local parish. As a child, Martinson escaped from harsh reality into nature and into a fantasy world nourished by his reading (in particular the works of Jack London), and he dreamed of going to sea. He spent two years as a vagabond throughout Sweden and Norway before going to sea as a stoker and deckhand. He spent the next six years on fourteen different vessels, with extended periods in India and South America, before he finally returned to Sweden, having contracted tuberculosis.

The year 1929 proved to be a turning point in Martinson's life. He made his literary debut and also married the writer Moa Martinson, beginning a stimulating partnership which lasted until 1940. During the early 1930's, Martinson was tempted to pursue a career as a professional artist. His favorite subjects were factory workers, the jungle, and underwater scenes executed in a colorful and naïve style. In August, 1934, he participated in the Soviet Writers' Congress in Moscow, an experience which disillusioned the former Communist sympathizer. The outbreak of World War II was seen by him as the result of the "civilization of violence." In 1939, after Finland was attacked by the Soviet Union, Martinson joined the Finnish side as a volunteer. He wrote a book about his experiences, partly a glorification of rural Finland and its deep-rooted traditions as well as the country's courageous battle against the war machine from the east, partly direct reportage from the front, the "unequivocal idiot-roaring grenade reality." In 1942, Martinson married Ingrid Lindcrantz and settled in Stockholm, where he died on February 11, 1978.

Analysis

From the very outset, it was Harry Martinson's intention to change the world. He embodied this intention in his utopian figure of the altruistic "world nomad," who represents humanity's search for a better world. The nomadic concept must be understood both concretely, in a geographical sense, and symbolically, as a journey into the realms of fantasy, dream, and the ideal future. Thus, dynamism and a moral intent emerged as the two basic qualities which were to characterize everything he wrote.

Martinson's own life as a sailor was the obvious point of departure for this expansion, which in his earliest poems is mainly depicted as daydreaming without specific direction: "Our thoughts are seabirds and they always fly away from us." They were written at sea on paper bags, Rudyard Kipling and Robert Burns being their models. Nevertheless, these texts, in particular those written with a free rhythmical and rhymeless structure, are characterized by a unique melodious softness and a balladelike flow hitherto unknown in Swedish literature. In addition, Martinson's own experiences abroad add a quality of reliability and concreteness, which also became a personal trademark of his later writing.

Other literary models, Walt Whitman and Edgar Lee Masters, are noticeable in Martinson's contributions to the anthology *Fem unga*. Yet his poetry increasingly relies on memories from his childhood and impressions from the world of nature and of the sea, guided by the poet's vivid associative power: "Out at sea you feel a spring or summer only like a breeze./ The drifting Florida seaweed sometimes blossoms in the summer,/ and on a spring night a spoonbill stork flies towards Holland." Yet a simultaneous striving for brevity and concentration, influenced by the Old Norse Eddic poetry, occasionally leads to a syntactic complexity and obscurity of thought. These characteristics are particularly present in his third collection, *Natur*, in which some of his most successful texts take on a surrealist quality inspired by Vladimir Mayakovski and contemporary art.

Martinson, in his progression from concrete detail to an almost mystical experience of a pantheistic unity, never loses sight of mankind in his writing. Satire can be found in "Rhapsody," the portrayal of a scientist who hunts for birds with a machine gun while at the same time recording bird songs. Usually—and in particular in the volumes *Passad* and *Aniara*—Martinson focuses on humanity in general, treating it in conjunction with the travel motif. In *Passad*, he creates a grandiose vision of the fundamental division of Western civilization pictured in the two travelers, Ulysses and Robinson Crusoe. One is the humanist and poet, the other the empiricist and scientist, and Martinson sees modern man's tragedy in the fact that these two personalities have not been synthesized. The trade wind, the "passad," becomes the symbol of the search for such a unity and harmony, which can only be discovered within oneself: "But new and wise explorers I have met/ have pointed inward . . . and I have listened to them/ and sensed/ a new trade wind." A fictional representative of Martinson's worldview is the persona of Li Kan, introduced in *Passad*, evincing Martinson's preoccupation with Chinese poetry and Oriental philosophy, Taoism in particular. Li Kan's media are terse, almost aphoristic maxims, in which a tone of resignation and melancholy counterbalances Martinson's otherwise optimistic message of universal harmony.

Achieving this harmony becomes increasingly problematic in Martinson's works in the period after 1950. This was a time in which his cosmic expansion and escaping dreams offered little consolation, a time overshadowed by nuclear bombs, wars, and political uprisings. Initially expressed in twenty-nine poems or songs, included in the collection *Cikada*, this misanthropy comes to its full expression in the verse epic *Aniara*, expanded to 103 songs. For years, Martinson had taken a keen interest in mathematics, physics, and astronomy. This expertise now formed the background for his account of the giant spaceship *Aniara*, which in the year 9000 takes off with eight thousand evacuees from planet Earth following a nuclear catastrophe. The passengers seek consolation from the Mima, a supercomputer, which shows pictures from the earth and from other planets. Soon, however, the journey is no longer one of discovery but of horrible certainty, a travel toward ultimate extinction. After twenty-four years in space, the passengers die and the *Aniara*, now a giant sarcophagus, continues on its way out of the galaxy. The *Aniara* is meant to be an image of civilization, and the characters aboard, prisoners indeed, represent a world steadily departing further from humanity toward still greater technological, impersonal sterility. Life aboard the spaceship offers a cross section of contemporary society, its different aspects and attitudes. Yet Martinson goes beyond the social and political realm to an analysis of man's moral and spiritual decay. Thus, the *Aniara* becomes an image of man and his doomed situation as he desperately attempts to avert catastrophe through artistic expression, rituals, and idolatry. Against this ship of fools, Martinson contrasts an ideal life of simplicity and harmony with nature as portrayed in an exquisite scene from the forests of Finnish Karelia. A beam of hope is lit through the various female characters, who together strive for nothing less than the Platonic ideals of truth, beauty, and goodness: "The eternal mystery of the firmament/ and the miracle of the celestial mechanics/ are laws but not the Gospel. Charity sprouts in the ground of life."

The style of *Aniara* is remarkable. Martinson's associative technique allows him to create a futuristic language composed of a flow of literary allusions ranging from the Bible to contemporary popular songs, hidden quotes, as well as a unique terminology based on self-coined technical words. With *Aniara*, Martinson created the only epic in Swedish literature of any significant artistic value.

Subsequently, Martinson returned to a simpler poetic form closer to that of his earlier works. In collections of lucid and artless poetry, he protests the exploitation and destruction of nature and continues to reject today's life-style marred by commercialism, superficiality, and rootlessness.

It is important to remember that Martinson's view of nature is strictly unsentimental and anti-idyllic. His skepticism is not aimed at technology per se but at mankind's inability to cope with its advances and to make it subservient to humanity. Instead, the products of civilization are threatening mankind's dreams and imagination—the airplane is being used to drop bombs on civilians, and the radio has become an instrument for political propaganda. Hence also Martinson's prevailing hope that mankind can avoid the fate of the *Aniara* and its passengers, a hope that in some poems takes on a metaphysical dimension: "We have a foreboding that what we call space . . ./ is spirit, eternal spirit, untouchable,/ that we have lost ourselves in the sea of the spirit."

Martinson's vision is wider than that of any modern Swedish poet. His visionary and mystical approach is counterbalanced by the clarity and simplicity of his poems about childhood and nature; his sophisticated analyses of modern technology are counterbalanced by an intuitive delving into the fantasies and hopes of the human mind. He has created an entirely new poetic language and imagery, inspired by modern technology and the pictorial arts, the boldness of which makes him a modernist in the forefront of his art. At the same time, his humanist message establishes bonds that reach back to a long historical tradition.

Other major works

NOVEL: *Vägen till Klockrike*, 1948 (*The Road*, 1955).

PLAYS: *Lotsen fran Moluckas*, 1938; *Tre knivar från Wei*, 1964.

NONFICTION: *Det enkla och det svåra*, 1930; *Resor utan mål*, 1932; *Kap Farväl*, 1933 (*Cape Farewell*, 1934); *Nässlorna blomma*, 1935 (*Flowering Nettle*, 1936, autobiography); *Vägen ut*, 1936 (autobiography); *Svärmare och harkrank*, 1937; *Midsommardalen*, 1938; *Verklighet till döds*, 1940; *Utsikt från en grästuva*, 1963.

Bibliography

Johannesson, Eric O. "*Aniara*: Poetry and the Poet in the Modern World," in *Scandinavian Studies*. XXXII (1960), pp. 185-202.

Rossel, Sven H. *A History of Scandinavian Literature, 1870-1980*, 1982.

Sjöberg, Leif. "Harry Martinson: From Vagabond to Space Explorer," in *Books Abroad*. XLVIII (1974), pp. 476-485.

——————. "Harry Martinson: Writer in Quest of Harmony," in *The American-Scandinavian Review*. LX (1960), pp. 360-371.

Steene, Birgitta. "The Role of the Mima: A Note on Martinson's *Aniara*," in *Scandinavian Studies: Essays Presented to Dr. Henry G. Leach*, 1965.

Tideström, Gunnar. "Harry Martinson's *Aniara*, in *Scandinavica*. XIII (1974), pp. 1-17.

Vowles, Richard B. "Harry Martinson: Sweden's Seaman-Poet," in *Books Abroad*. XXV (1951), pp. 332-335.

Sven H. Rossel

JOSEPHINE MILES

Born: Chicago, Illinois; June 11, 1911
Died: Berkeley, California; May 12, 1985

Principal poems and collections
Lines at Intersection, 1939; *Poems on Several Occasions*, 1941; *Local Measures*, 1946; *Prefabrications*, 1955; *Poems, 1930-1960*, 1960; *Civil Poems*, 1966; *Kinds of Affection*, 1967; *Saving the Bay*, 1967; *Fields of Learning*, 1968; *To All Appearances: Poems New and Selected*, 1974; *Coming to Terms: Poems*, 1979; *Collected Poems, 1930-1983*, 1983.

Other literary forms
In addition to her many volumes of poetry, Josephine Miles wrote more than a dozen books developing her theories of poetry and applying these theories to particular poets and eras. Among the most widely read of these works are *Eras and Modes in English Poetry* (1957, revised 1964) and *Style and Proportion: The Language of Prose and Poetry* (1967, revised 1984). These books are detailed structural analyses of English poetry and prose; all of Miles's criticism expounds her theory that the structure of language changes to reflect the time spirit that the language expresses. Her one play, *House and Home*, was first performed in 1960 and was published in *First Stage* in 1965.

Achievements
Miles's contribution to American poetry is valuable and unusual. She combined poetry of political commitment with sound scholarship and theory to produce a body of work that is at the same time of the tower and of the streets. Her work is a challenge both to the poet/propagandist and to the "art for art's sake" poet.

Miles's many awards and honors include a Guggenheim award in 1948, the Oscar Blumenthal Prize in 1959, an American Council of Learned Societies Fellowship in 1965, a National Endowment for the Arts grant in 1967, and an American Academy of Poets Fellowship in 1978. Although her critical works have been to some extent superseded, Miles's poetry has guaranteed for her a lasting place in twentieth century American literature.

Biography
Josephine Louise Miles was born on June 11, 1911, to Reginald and Josephine Miles, a Chicago couple. When she was still an infant, Miles was diagnosed as having rheumatoid arthritis, a disease which plagued her all of her life. When she was five, her father, who was in the insurance business, moved the family to Southern California, hoping that the climate there would

be beneficial to his daughter's condition. The family moved back to Evanston, Illinois, for a time, but Miles had identified California as her spiritual home. The family eventually settled down in Los Angeles, and Miles, after finishing at Los Angeles High School, attended the University of California, Los Angeles. After receiving her B.A. in 1932, she enrolled in graduate school at the University of California at Berkeley. She completed her M.A. in 1934 and her Ph.D. in 1938.

Although she had written poems since childhood, it was during her graduate school years that she first began to publish seriously and to gain recognition. Her first poems were published in an anthology, *Trial Balances* (1935), and this work earned for her two awards. Her first book, *Lines at Intersection*, appeared in 1939 and contains the best poems of her graduate school period.

In 1940, Miles began teaching at Berkeley as an instructor, and she remained there for the rest of her life. In 1947, she was the first woman to be tenured by Berkeley's English department, and in 1952 she was made a full professor. Miles never married, devoting her life to teaching, research, and poetry; during her years at Berkeley, she published more than two dozen books, in addition to numerous articles and reviews. She retired in 1978 and was given the status of Distinguished Professor Emerita. She died in Berkeley of pneumonia on May 12, 1985.

Analysis

Josephine Miles's poetry reflects both her political involvement in liberal causes and her intense concern with the sounds and structures of English. Over the decades of her writing, the poems became less formal and closed as their political content increased. Her topics shifted from minute observations of daily activities to analysis of the poet's role in the chaotic contemporary world. Nevertheless, even her most strident political poems show careful craftsmanship and attention to sound.

Miles's first published poems are tightly structured and intellectually dense. Her often-anthologized "On Inhabiting an Orange," published in the anthology *Trial Balances* in 1935, precedes her first collection. "All our roads go nowhere," the poem begins. "Maps are curled/ To keep the pavement definitely/ On the world." Because of these conditions, people's plans for "metric advance" must "lapse into arcs in deference/ To circumstance." The poem develops its single metaphor with clarity and sureness, using common metaphysical geometric images to provide the pleasure afforded by this kind of poetry. It is not surprising that her first work received two awards, the Shelley Memorial Award (1936) and the Phelan Memorial Award (1937).

Her first collection, *Lines at Intersection*, is a series of poems of everyday events arranged by time of day—morning poems, noon poems, evening poems. The individual works are mostly formal in structure, but they are more impressionistic than the early poems, and their music is more subtle. These poems incorporate such devices as internal rhymes, unusual metrical patterns, Dickinsonian slant rhymes, and incremental repetition. The poems are personal but not intimate, providing new perspective on such familiar things as the morning paper, the door-to-door salesman, baseball games, and theater performances. A few of the poems still show her preoccupation with mathematics and geometry, while others foretell one of her future concerns: the world of business, which was to become a major metaphor for the contemporary world. *Lines at Intersection* was well received, with favorable reviews in *Poetry* and elsewhere.

Miles's second collection, *Poems on Several Occasions*, shows a marked divergence from her earlier work in content. These poems, too, are arranged by time of day, and they also represent the life cycle from birth to death; moreover, these poems use the same stylistic devices as those of her earlier collection. This group, however, begins to define Miles's social commitments. By this time, Miles was becoming more aware of the inequalities, injustices, and false promises of contemporary America. Her titles show her new perspective: "Market Report on Cotton Gray Goods," "Committee Report on Smoke Abatement in Residential Area," "Committee Decision on Pecans for Asylum." The America in these poems is as unattractive as that of Allen Ginsberg in the 1950's and 1960's, and often for the same reasons. Business transactions take the place of personal contact, and there is a vast gap between what society would provide and what people want and need. Yet the poems are by and large wistful and do not actively suggest interference with the processes of oppression.

Local Measures marks a change in style: These poems are more conversational and irregular than Miles's earlier works. Their subjects include daily observations, social topics, and the relation of art to life. More of these poems are free verse or highly individualized forms. Dancing and motion pictures are analogues to poetry; the collection, written while Miles was working on her analysis of poetic forms in different periods of history, reflects her own search for a form appropriate to herself and her time. The mutual reflection of art and life is a theme approached again and again, as in "Redemption." Films, dances, even the jewelry that appears in these poems show Miles's attempts to define and thus master the process of creation.

Prefabrications combines her concerns for art and the social world. This rich and varied collection of sixty poems demonstrates the sense of community and continuity she was developing in the poetic theory on which she was working at the same time. Some of these poems, such as "The Plastic Glass," express the belief that the essentially human transcends the shabbiness and emptiness of life's surfaces. Others, such as "The Student," seek a source or definition of that humanness, often using metaphors and images that are accessible to all but particularly compelling to academics. Indeed, in this and

(none)

other poems in the collection, the academic life itself becomes a metaphor of the teaching-learning dialogue with the world. Some of the poems are about art. "Two Kinds of Trouble," a long poem, compares the social structures that made it hard for Michelangelo to communicate his vision with the problems of contemporary artists—a different kind of trouble.

Miles's *Poems, 1930-1960* included selections from all of her earlier books and a new group of poems, "Neighbors and Constellations," for the most part negative assessments of the possibility of meaningful intercourse among members of the human community. These poems, however, marked a turning point in her attitude, and the next collections showed a more active involvement in causes combined with a belief in the possibility of success.

Civil Poems and *Kinds of Affection* show that Miles was in and of Berkeley in the 1960's. These two collections center on pollution, poverty, destruction of beauty for purposes of greed, experimentation with animals, gun control, the war, the bomb, technology. An index to these poems would please nostalgia buffs, but the poems are less calls to action than expressions of the notion that social involvements are in fact ways of loving, or "kinds of affection." Among references to Dag Hammarskjöld, Molotov cocktails, and other hallmarks of the time, Miles returns again and again to the subject of commonality, the sharing underneath that survives all divisions. *Fields of Learning* does not diverge greatly from the previous two collections, but includes more science and slightly less politics. The world of these poems is filled with deoxyribonucleic acid, AMPAC, free neutrons, and gravitational electromagnetic fields. Yet despite their heavy freight of theoretical physics and technology, these poems are not inaccessible. They communicate a sense of human potential that exists not because of, but in spite of, technological advancement.

To All Appearances, while still political, is in many respects a return to earlier themes. Many of these are quiet poems of family and friendship. Their form is (usually) free verse, but in content the work is often reminiscent of *Local Measures*. One of the most memorable of the group is "Conception," which begins:

> Death did not come to my mother
> Like an old friend.
> She was a mother, and she must
> Conceive him.

The poem elaborates on its controlling metaphor, as do some of Miles's earliest poems, but here the appeal is as much emotional as it is intellectual. In general, these poems seem more direct than her earlier work. She uses "I" often in poems of reflection on her experiences inside and outside the university community.

Miles's last major collection (exclusive of her *Collected Poems, 1930-1983*) was *Coming to Terms* in 1979. This powerful collection gathers together the many strands of her lifelong preoccupations and weaves them into a single fabric. These are poems of social and aesthetic interest, asking the broadest questions and providing penetrating answers. The critics received the work with highest praise; Miles's last years were filled with honors and awards. More than one reviewer found the long poem "Center" to be Miles's strongest work. The poem poses the question "What are we here for?"—"we" being poets, creators, and humane visionaries. Her answer, not unlike that of the God in Johann Wolfgang von Goethe's *Faust*, is that we are here to make the best mistakes:

> Give us to err
> Grandly as possible in this complete
> Complex of structure, risk a soul
> Nobly in north light, in cello tone . . .

The result of such risk and error is a re-vision, a new perspective from which to view the possible. Human creativity in all of its forms becomes a medium "To take, as a building, as a fiction, takes us,/ Into another frame of space/ Where we can ponder, celebrate, and reshape." Miles's late view of poetry as process, or becoming, is similar to Wallace Stevens' final aesthetic. In this poem, Miles shows her own adjustment of vision, from the downward glance at the fatal curve of Earth in "On Inhabiting an Orange" to the upward and outward vistas of the possible from "the center."

Collected Poems, 1930-1983 gives an overall view of Miles's development and includes her last poems, for the most part scenes of Berkeley and of the university. (She lived only about a year after the appearance of this volume, which was popular as well as critically acclaimed, and she was awarded *The Nation's* Leonore Marshall Poetry Prize in 1983.) Her careful craftsmanship and metrical felicity can be appreciated in this final publication, a well-edited work which illustrates the range of her poetic gift. Her "search for a common language" antedated Adrienne Rich's better-known one and combined some of the same ingredients. This collection shows how her hopes for community within human society paralleled her search for what she called "commonality" in language. Her intellectually and emotionally persuasive metaphors, her subtle music, and the potency and optimism of her later work make Miles a significant contributor to twentieth century American poetry.

Other major works

PLAY: *House and Home*, 1960.

NONFICTION: *Wordsworth and the Vocabulary of Emotion*, 1942; *Pathetic Fallacy in the Nineteenth Century: A Study of a Changing Relationship Between Object and Emotion*, 1942; *Major Adjectives in English Poetry from Wyatt to Auden*, 1946; *The Primary Language of Poetry in the 1640's*, 1948; *The Primary Language of Poetry in the 1740's and 1840's*, 1950; *The Primary*

Language of Poetry in the 1940's, 1951; *The Continuity of Poetic Language: Studies in English Poetry from the 1540's to the 1940's*, 1951 (includes preceding three volumes); *Eras and Modes in English Poetry*, 1957, revised 1964; *Renaissance, Eighteenth-Century, and Modern Language in English Poetry: A Tabular View*, 1960; *Ralph Waldo Emerson*, 1964; *Style and Proportion: The Language of Prose and Poetry*, 1967, revised 1984; *Poetry and Change: Donne, Milton, Wordsworth, and the Equilibrium of the Present*, 1974; *Working Out Ideas: Predication and Other Uses of Language*, 1979.

Bibliography

Beloof, Robert. "Distances and Surfaces: The Poetry of Josephine Miles," in *Prairie Schooner*. XXXII (Winter, 1958), pp. 276-284.

Hammond, Karla M. "An Interview with Josephine Miles," in *Southern Review*. XIX (Summer, 1983), pp. 606-631.

Smith, Lawrence R. "Josephine Miles: Metaphysician of the Irrational," in *Pebble*. Nos. 18-20 (1979), pp. 22-35.

Janet McCann

KENJI MIYAZAWA

Born: Hanamaki, Japan; August 27, 1896
Died: Hanamaki, Japan; September 21, 1933

Principal poems and collections
Haru to shura, 1924 (*Spring and Asura*, 1973); *The Back Country*, 1957.

Other literary forms
In addition to a substantial body of free verse and many tanka poems (the tanka is a fixed form of thirty-one syllables in five lines), Kenji Miyazawa wrote children's stories, often in a fantastic vein. He also wrote a limited number of essays, the most important one of which outlines his ideas for an agrarian art. The children's stories have proved popular in Japan, and some of them are available along with the major poems in English translation. It should also be noted that Miyazawa drafted and reworked his poems in a series of workbooks over the course of his creative life; while the notebooks are not publications in a formal sense, they might be considered part of the Miyazawa canon. In any case, they are commonly utilized by scholars investigating the sources of the poet's art.

Achievements
A poet of unique gifts, Miyazawa spent his relatively brief life in almost total obscurity. Living in a primitive rural area, writing virtually as a form of religious practice, Miyazawa published only one volume of stories and one of poetry during his life. Neither work attracted attention at the time of its publication.

Shortly after Miyazawa's death, however, his work began to be noticed. His utilization of scientific, religious, and foreign terms became familiar, and the striking images and energy of his verses seemed exciting alongside the generally restrained modes of Japanese poetic expression.

Most surprising of all, Miyazawa started to attain the prominence and affection he still enjoys among the general public. Almost any literate Japanese would know one poem that he jotted down in his notebook late in life. Sketching the portrait of Miyazawa's ideal selfless person, the poem begins with the lines, "Neither to wind yielding/ Nor to rain."

Miyazawa began composing tanka poems while still a middle school student. His principal works are in free verse, however, and these he composed mostly during the decade of the 1920's. Throughout these years, various forms of modernism—Futurism and Surrealism, for example—were being introduced to Japan, and certain native poets experimented with these new styles of writing. Miyazawa, however, worked in total isolation from such developments. This is not to say that his work is *sui generis* in any absolute sense. Assuredly a religious poet, Miyazawa worked out a cosmology for certain of his poems which, according to one Western scholar, resembles in a general way the private cosmologies of such poets as William Blake and William Butler Yeats.

Biography

Kenji Miyazawa was born on August 27, 1896, in the town of Hanamaki in the northern prefecture of Iwate. Iwate has a cool climate, and the farmers of the region led a precarious existence. Miyazawa's father ran a pawnshop, a business which prospered in part because of the poverty of the local farmers.

As the oldest son, Miyazawa would normally have succeeded his father as head of the family business. Uneasy at the thought of living off the poverty of others, however, Miyazawa neglected the task of preparing himself to succeed his father in the family business. Instead, he immersed himself in the study of philosophy and religion. An exemplary student in grade school, Miyazawa's record became worse from year to year in middle school as he pursued his own intellectual interests. Some of this independence is also discernible in occasional escapades during his youth, one of which led to his expulsion from the school dormitory.

By 1915, Miyazawa had decided to find work outside the family business. In this year, he entered the Morioka College of Agriculture and Forestry. Along with his studies in such areas as chemistry and soils, Kenji formulated various plans for his future, plans whereby he could utilize his knowledge to contribute to the amelioration of the harsh conditions of rural life. For a time he even hoped to turn the resources of the family business to some new venture that might be of general economic benefit—producing industrial chemicals from the soil of the area, for example.

A new dimension was added to Miyazawa's differences with his father during these years. Initially he had followed his father's religious preference as a believer in the Jōdo Shin sect of Buddhism. Eventually, however, Kenji decided that ultimate truth resided in the militant Nichiren sect, especially in its intense devotion to the Lotus Sutra. In January, 1921, he took the extraordinary step of fleeing the family home in Hanamaki in order to join a Buddhist organization in Tokyo known as the State Pillar Society. Miyazawa returned home late that same year, partly because of the serious illness of his younger sister Toshiko, partly to take a teaching position at the two-year Hienuki Agricultural School.

Toshiko died in November, 1922, an event which the poet commemorated in a number of impressive elegies. Miyazawa continued to teach until March, 1926. In his spare time, he took his students for long treks in the countryside, writing incessantly in the notebooks which he took on these excursions. The poet made his first and only attempt at publishing his work in 1924. In addition to a volume of children's stories, he brought out at his own expense a volume of sketches in free verse, *Spring and Asura*.

Miyazawa gave up teaching from a sense of guilt. How could he accept a regular wage, no matter how small, when the average farmer was often destitute? Miyazawa decided, thus, to become a farmer himself. A bachelor his entire life, he lived by himself raising vegetables for his own table and several small cash crops in addition. Using the knowledge he had learned over the years, he attempted to serve as an informal adviser to the farm community. In addition, he tried to instill in the rural populace a desire for culture.

Miyazawa had never possessed a strong constitution. He was ill on a number of occasions, and around 1928 unmistakable signs of tuberculosis began to appear. During the final years of his life, Miyazawa seems to have lost his creative urge—or, perhaps, sensing the imminence of death, he simply tried to rework the poems he had already written. The poet spent his last two years, from 1931 to 1933, as an invalid at the family home in Hanamaki. He and his father put aside their religious differences as death came closer for the son. Just before he died, on September 21, 1933, Miyazawa pointed toward a bookshelf and remarked that his unpublished manuscripts lying there had been produced out of a delusion.

Analysis

Like the American poet and physician William Carlos Williams, Kenji Miyazawa absorbed himself in ceaseless service to other people, whether his students or the local farmers. Like the American, Miyazawa, too, would jot down poems in the spare moments available to him. Unlike Williams, however, Miyazawa never seems to have considered a poem finished. With only one volume of poems published in his lifetime, Miyazawa worked steadily at revising and reworking his drafts. Three different sets of poems are titled *Spring and Asura*, a fact which suggests a common ground for a number of seemingly disparate works.

The first volume of *Spring and Asura* contains a poem similarly titled, a crucial poem which describes the poet caught up in intense visions of his own making. The persona narrates the vision from the viewpoint of an asura, that is, a being which ranks between humans and beasts in the six realms of existence in the Buddhist cosmology. (The six realms are devas, humans, asuras or demons, beasts, hungry ghosts, and dwellers in hell.) Despite the Buddhist references, the world of this asura is one of the poet's own making. A close study of Miyazawa's visionary poems by the American scholar Sarah Strong has uncovered a structure of levels—from a kind of Vacuum at the highest level (with the possibility of other worlds beyond) to the realm of the Western Marshes at the lowest. In between are various levels, with the Radiant Sea of Sky being the most complicated. The asura of Miyazawa's poems rushes about in this universe, finding "ecstasy" and "brightness" at the upper levels while encountering "unpleasantness" and "darkness" toward the bottom. This "structure," it must be noted, is not an immediately obvious feature of the poem. Indeed, to the untutored reader, many of Miyazawa's poems will seem mystifying and kaleidoscopic. For many, the effect of reading such works will surely be dizzying.

Miyazawa's visionary poems are difficult, but the poet has inserted passages which point the way to understanding. Preceding the Japanese text of "Spring and Asura," for example, he has entered these words in English which indicate the nature of the work to follow: "mental sketch modified." The initial volume of *Spring and Asura* also has an introductory poem or "Proem" preceding the title poem of the collection. In "Proem," Miyazawa includes lines and phrases that appear to point quite definitely at his intentions. For example, the poet says that the sketch to follow represents the workings of his imagination over the past twenty-two months. His way of putting the matter may be unusual (each piece on paper is a "chain of shadow and light," linked together "with mineral ink"), but the difficulty is more with the oddity of expression than with the meaning.

Another set of poems by Miyazawa, the famous elegies composed upon the death of his sister Toshiko, also shows the imaginative energy of the poet. In this instance, however, the persona tends to stay within the normal and identifiable bounds of nature. The poet races outdoors to collect snow for comforting his dying sister or, after her death, wanders far beyond the region of the home in search of her whereabouts. The reader, however, knows exactly where the action is occurring. Bound to a specific and easily identifiable situation, these works seem more accessible than the aforementioned works from *Spring and Asura*.

Miyazawa's elegies on Toshiko exhibit an idiosyncrasy of vocabulary and image equal to that of *Spring and Asura*. In contrast to the thematic uniqueness of this visionary poem, however, the elegies actually fit into a venerable tradition of Japanese poetry. Indeed, the elegy goes back to almost the beginnings of Japanese poetry in the eighth century collection known as the *Manyōshū* (collection of myriad leaves; English translation, 1940). Admittedly, the grief expressed by Miyazawa over the death of his sister seems more private and concentrated than the emotion found in certain *Manyōshū* elegies—in the partly ritualistic works by Kakinomoto no Hitomaro, which mourn the deaths of the high nobility, to mention a celebrated example. At the same time, Miyazawa follows Hitomaro and other elegists of the *Manyōshū* in his search for a trace of the deceased in nature and in his refusal to be satisfied with encountering anything less than the actual person.

If Miyazawa had written only visionary and elegiac poems, he probably would not have attained popularity except as a writer of children's tales. At the very least, his frequent use of foreign terms, whether Chinese or Sanskrit, German or Esperanto, would have made the poetry difficult for the average reader. Aside from the above kinds of poems in which Miyazawa addresses his private concerns, however, there are certain works which reflect the desire to instruct the common people. In the most celebrated of these didactic works—invariably printed as recorded in a notebook, that is, in the *katakana* syllabary understandable even to a beginning schoolchild—the poet sketches a portrait of the ideal person he wishes to be. That person lives a life of extreme frugality and of selfless devotion to others. Like the bodhissattva of Buddhist doctrine, Miyazawa's ideal person is totally compassionate—caring for the sick, alleviating hunger, patching up quarrels, and carrying out other works of charity.

Miyazawa was very much involved in the everyday life of the common people. This, in conjunction with his high ideals, occasionally elicited from him at least a partly satiric response. A work in this vein, entitled "Kanbatsu to zazen" ("Drought and Zazen"), seems to belittle the Zen practice of meditation—either for ignoring a pressing practical problem or for deluding its adherents into a false sense of religion's sphere of efficacy. The poem begins by describing some frogs as a Zen chorus anxiously trying to solve those perplexing puzzles known as koans. After this comic opening, Miyazawa depicts himself intently calculating the sequential phases through which the rice seedlings must pass before ripening. The contrast between religious petition on the one hand and this primitive sort of scientific calculation on the other is very striking.

To claim that Miyazawa is satirizing Zen or Zazen in this poem might well be an overstatement. If satire is at work, it is certainly good-humored. In fact, the lighthearted side of the poet needs special emphasis in view of the fact that his central works, especially a poem such as "Spring and Asura" and the elegies on Toshiko, are so somber and brooding.

On occasion, the poet will enjoy a lighter moment by himself—when, for example, in a poem entitled "Shigoto" ("Work") he momentarily worries about the manure he threw from a cart and left on a hillside. More often, he will jest with the farmers and peasants of the region. In one poem, he pokes fun at a farmer named Hosuke for getting upset when a manure-carrying horse proves unruly; in another instance, he counsels a hardworking farmer to leave off bundling rice at midnight for the sake of the weary wife who is doing her best to assist him. In most of these works, the poet seems a carefree observer and counselor. Since Miyazawa is normally a somber poet, though, and the farmers, even in his lighthearted poems, are always hard at work, one might surmise that the poet regarded humor principally as a way for the farmer to cope with his burdens.

In any event, this playful side of Miyazawa is present in many different poems. Sometimes, the poet simply observes an appealing scene. His poem on an Ayrshire bull is a good example. The animal, seen at night against the light of a pulp factory, enjoys itself by rubbing its horns in the grass and butting a fence. At other times, Miyazawa seems to play with language in an extravagant manner. A certain horse in another poem is said to "rot like a potato" and "feel the bright sun's juice." A second horse meets a dire fate by running into a high-voltage wire in its stable, the funeral taking place with the human mourners shedding "clods of tears" upon the "lolling head" of the dead animal. Hosuke's manure horse engages in some impressive acrobatics, rearing up with "scarlet eyes" on one occasion as if to "rake in blue velvet, the spring sky."

The poem on the Ayrshire bull depicts a casual encounter, the sort of event that happens often in Miyazawa's playful poems about people. Running into an acquaintance, the poet engages this other in a little drama. These poems, most of them brief, present simple emotions and often contain some deft humor. Certain works employ the same techniques but pursue more ambitious aims. Among them is a fascinating piece entitled "Shita de wakareta sakki no hito" ("The Man I Parted from, Below"). The man in question is a somewhat disembodied image which remains in the memory of the poet after the meeting to which the title alludes has taken place. Defined mainly as a smoker, the man has been leading a horse somewhere, possibly to another group of horses visible in the distance. At least this thought occurs to the poet as he surveys the scene before him and composes his appreciation of it. Certain of Miyazawa's typical concerns manifest themselves in the course of the work—the identification and naming of places, for example, or the sense of things happening in a kind of space-time continuum. Occasionally, an odd turn of phrase, too, reminds the reader of the poet's identity— the "aquamarine legs of winds," for example, or the highlands spread out "like ten or more playing cards." The horses on those highlands originally looked to the poet like "shining red ants." Such language, hardly startling to the Miyazawa aficionado, helps to elevate parts of the poem above mere plain description.

Indeed, "The Man I Parted from, Below" might seem tame alongside the coruscating images of "Spring and Asura" and the vibrating language of "Proem." The poem has certain compensations, however, even as a somewhat atypical work of Miyazawa. It shows that the poet could be at home in the calmer modes of Japanese lyricism, that he could deftly lay out a pattern of relationships involving himself, nature, and his fellowmen.

Having parted from the poet, the smoker is now observed together with his horse moving off toward the distant herd. Though abandoned by the smoker as surely as he had once been by Toshiko, Miyazawa does not seem bereft in this poem. All about him are the familiar mountains and valleys for which, at this moment, he feels an "oddly helpless love." All the men in the poem—the keeper of the distant herd, the man with his sole horse, and the poet, too—seem related to one another, and to the animals as well, by their mere presence in the scene. Slightly idiosyncratic, moderately optimistic, entirely understandable, "The Man I Parted from, Below" shows the poet submitting his vision to the requirements of realism on a human scale.

Other major works

SHORT FICTION: *Chūmon no ōi ryōriten*, 1924; *Winds from Afar*, 1972 (juvenile; translated by John Bester).

MISCELLANEOUS: *Miyazawa Kenji zenshū*, 1968.

Bibliography
Bester, John. Foreword to *Winds from Afar*, 1972.
_____. "To the Reader," in *Winds and Wildcast Places*, 1967.
Sato, Hiroaki. Introduction to *Spring and Asura*, 1973.
Ueda, Makoto. *Modern Japanese Poets and the Nature of Literature*, 1983.

James O'Brien

LES A. MURRAY

Born: Nabiac, Australia; October 17, 1938

Principal poem and collections

The Ilex Tree, 1965 (with Geoffrey Lehmann); *The Weatherboard Cathedral*, 1969; *Poems Against Economics*, 1972; *Lunch and Counter Lunch*, 1974; *Selected Poems: The Vernacular Republic*, 1976; *Ethnic Radio*, 1977; *The Boys Who Stole the Funeral*, 1980; *The Vernacular Republic: Poems 1961-1981*, 1982; *The People's Otherworld*, 1983; *Selected Poems*, 1986.

Other literary forms

Les A. Murray has collected two volumes of prose pieces (primarily reviews and articles): *The Peasant Mandarin: Prose Pieces* (1978) and *Persistence in Folly* (1984). Of particular interest in the latter book is the essay "The Human Hair-Thread," in which Murray discusses his own work and thought and the influence aboriginal culture has had on it.

Achievements

Increasingly, Murray is considered not only a major Australian poet but also one of the finest poets of his generation writing in English. His books appear in Great Britain and the United States, and his following is an international one. Moreover, the uniqueness and power of his poetic voice have caught the ear of many of his fellow poets throughout the world, for he has been hailed by Joseph Brodsky, Peter Porter, Mark Strand, and others. He is a prolific and ambitious writer, always willing to try new and unusual techniques but equally at home in the traditional forms of verse, of which he seems to have an easy and lively mastery. Murray is largely admired in Australia, where even his detractors acknowledge his accomplishments. He has received numerous awards and prizes, including the Australian Literature Society Gold Medal (1984) and the New South Wales Premier's Prize for the best book of verse in 1983-1984. He is also a frequent recipient of grants from the Literature Board of the Australia Council.

Biography

Leslie Allan Murray was born at Nabiac, on the rural north coast of New South Wales, and brought up on a dairy farm in nearby Bunyah, a locale that often figures as the subject or backdrop for his poems. He attended school in the town of Taree and then, in 1957, went to the University of Sydney, where he stayed until 1962, spending an intervening year serving in the Royal Australian Naval Reserve (1960-1961). At the time, he left without a degree, but he did return and was graduated in 1969. He married Valerie Morelli in 1962 (they have several children) and worked as a translator at the Australian National University in Canberra from 1963 to 1967. After a year in Europe, he returned to Sydney in 1968 and worked at a number of transient jobs before going to Canberra again, where he took a position in the Labour government's Department of Economic Development. Moving back to Sydney and refusing to work any longer in, for him, meaningless employment, Murray, in his own words, "Came Out as a flagrant full-time poet in 1971." He has since supported himself solely on the basis of his literary work. In addition to the books he has published and those he has edited, Murray writes book reviews, contributes to newspapers and magazines, advises Angus and Robertson publishers, and gives poetry readings throughout Australia and abroad. Between 1973 and 1979, he served as editor of *Poetry Australia*.

Murray published his first book, *The Ilex Tree*, jointly with another young poet, Geoffrey Lehmann, in 1965, and quickly became known as a poet of real promise. His many subsequent volumes confirmed his status as a major voice in Australian literature.

Analysis

Readers of Les A. Murray's poetry are often attracted by the coherence of the thematic concerns that reappear consistently in his work and which are presented lucidly and imaginatively. Moreover, the stylistic features of his verse, though varied, have themselves cohered into an identifiable style uniquely his own and flexible enough to allow for the wide range of his poetic interests. Broadly, these interests may be grouped under categories of the religious and spiritual, the societal and cultural, the historical and familial, the linguistic and poetic. Murray has strong opinions about many issues facing contemporary society, and his poetry often bespeaks them. In their most reductive form, these issues would require consideration of such propositions as: Western man must rediscover a core of religious values and recover certain traditional modes of being; society should embrace a more democratic egalitarianism, avoiding the twin perils of elitism and false ideology; aboriginal attitudes regarding nature and the environment need to be better understood by white Australians and to some extent adopted; Australia itself represents an island of hope in the world, as a place where many of the divisive features undermining modern society might be finally reconciled. While such statements are virtually caricatures or distortions and far too coarse to do justice to the subtlety and rigor of Murray's poetry, they do indicate some of the general areas of his thinking. His is very often a poetry of statement, for he does not shy away from taking clear positions on matters he considers crucial, and he has none of the horror of didacticism that seems to restrain much contemporary writing. It is not, however, for his opinions or ideas that Murray is chiefly valued; rather, it is the fineness of his poetry that speaks most clearly to his readers.

In an early poem, "Driving Through Sawmill Towns," Murray renders the remoteness and tedium of life in the rural towns, those "bare hamlets built of boards," where "nothing happens" and "the houses watch each other." The evocative detail, the careful diction, the sense of quiet control convey both an appreciation of this as a way of life and an acknowledgment that it is a lonely and even desperate existence. A woman gazes at a mountain "in wonderment,/ looking for a city," and men sit by the stove after tea, "rolling a dead match/ between their fingers/ thinking of the future." It is a place one only drives through, not a place in which one wishes to live. In that sense, this poem contrasts with others in which the country life appears more salubrious, as in "Noonday Axeman" or "Spring Hail," where isolation is not necessarily loneliness.

Murray's most famous poem of rural Australia is also the one most indebted to aboriginal sources, "The Buladelah-Taree Holiday Song Cycle." It is a long poem, in thirteen sections, based in part on a translation by R. M. Berndt of "The Moon-Bone Song," a ritual poem of Arnhem Land aborigines which Murray claims "may well be the greatest poem ever composed in Australia." His poem is an attempt to use an aboriginal mode and structure to "celebrate my own spirit country," a stretch of land on the north coast between the two towns of Buladelah and Taree, where he grew up and lives as an adult and where many holiday vacationers go in the summer to enjoy the beaches and the countryside. In the same way that the aborigines celebrate their unity as a people and their harmony with the land, so Murray sees the returning vacationers, many of whom have family ties to the area, as a cyclic affirmation of ancestral values and a joyous communing with nature. In his vision, each new generation rediscovers the spiritual significance of commonplace things, as people come to possess the land imaginatively. Each section of the poem presents an aspect of this summer ritual, from the preparations made by the local inhabitants to the journey from Sydney along the Pacific Highway (represented as a glowing snake) to all the adventures, experiences, and tensions that go with a summer holiday. The poem ends with a linking of the region with the heavens above, as the Southern Cross constellation looks down upon "the Holiday." The poem is unique in its successful wedding of an aboriginal poetic structure with the matter of white Australian culture; in particular, Murray's use of place names and capitalization seems to give mythic status to the events and locations of the poem, analogous to the aborigine's sense of a "spirit of place."

In 1980, Murray published *The Boys Who Stole the Funeral*, a verse novel consisting of 140 sonnets of considerable variety. This unusual poem picked up many of the concerns and opinions prevalent in the earlier work and fashioned them into a narrative, both effective as poetry and affective as a story. In this novel sequence, two young Sydney men, Kevin Forbutt and Cameron Reeby, steal from a funeral parlor the body of Kevin's great-uncle,

Clarrie Dunn (a "digger," or World War I veteran), in order to take him back home to the country where the old man had asked to be buried. Clarrie's relations having refused to pay for or honor this request, the boys have taken it upon themselves. In doing this, they set out on a journey of self-discovery as well. Such familiar Murray themes as the value of community and respect for the ordinary man are underscored repeatedly in the poem, as when the two boys get to Dark's Plain, Clarrie's old home, and are assisted by people there with the burial and with evading the police who have come to arrest them. The novel later culminates with the shooting of Cameron by a policeman. The shocked and distraught Kevin flees into the bush, falls ill, drops into a coma, and has a vision of two figures from aboriginal legend, Njimbin and Birroogun. In this vision, the central event of the novel, Kevin is put through an initiation where his soul is healed by the symbolic "crystal of Crystals" and where he is instructed by Njimbin and Birroogun (whose name modulates to Berrigan, connoting a blend of white and black Australians) in the mysteries of the spirit. Kevin is offered the Common Dish from which to eat, the vessel of common human joys and sufferings by which most people in the world are nourished. As an act of solidarity with common humanity, Kevin takes it and eats and then wakes from his comatose vision. Having been in effect reborn, he returns to live at Dark's Plain, to "keep faith" with the rural "battlers" who are the spiritual inheritors of the land. The poem as a whole is a virtuoso performance, displaying Murray's ability to handle the complex interplay of form, narrative, and character. He holds the reader's attention and, once again, interweaves aboriginal material in a convincing way.

One of Murray's preoccupations is with the notion of the vernacular; indeed, when he calls his selected poems *The Vernacular Republic*, he is reflecting upon the colloquial nature of his language and simultaneously reflecting a passionate concern which the world of his poems addresses: the need for Australia to fuse its three cultures, urban, rural, and aboriginal. Murray's vision for Australia is for a culture of convergence, where the sophisticated city dwellers, the more traditional rural folk, and the indigenous blacks can all come together to forge a society in harmony with the continent. In this, he is close to the position of the Jindyworobaks, a literary movement of the 1930's and 1940's which emphasized the uniqueness of the Australian environment and sought to align itself with aboriginal culture. Although not as narrowly nationalistic as that earlier group, Murray does see a need to avoid repeating the mistakes of Europe and America and to develop in accordance with the character and values of Australia itself, not in submission to alien and imported fashions or ideologies. For him, Australia has the possibility of becoming truly egalitarian, a place of justice and virtue for the common man, a place where what is traditional is recognizably Australian. This, for Murray, includes a certain dry sense of humor and an appreciation of an unhurried mode of living, which may be primarily a rural manner but nevertheless seems a national characteristic. His poem "The Quality of Sprawl" is a good example.

"Sprawl," in this poem, is defined through the course of eight stanzas as a way of being, at once nonchalant ("the rococo of being your own still centre"), laid-back ("Sprawl leans on things"), generous ("driving a hitchhiker that extra hundred miles home"), unpretentious ("the quality/ of the man who cut down his Rolls-Royce/ into a farm utility truck"), classless (someone "asleep in his neighbours' best bed in spurs and oilskins"), unflappable ("Reprimanded and dismissed/ it listens with a grin and one boot up on the rail/ of possibility"), and so on. It is also defined by what it is not: "It is never lighting cigars with ten-dollar notes"; "Sprawl almost never says Why not? with palms comically raised"; "nor can it be dressed for." Murray presents it as a very attractive quality indeed, but, characteristically, he is aware of the negative element, the price one sometimes has to pay for independence of mind. "It may have to leave the Earth," he says, but then he gently undercuts his own hyperbole: "Being roughly Christian, it scratches the other cheek/ and thinks it unlikely." While not exactly turning the other cheek in Christian fashion, he does conclude with the mild warning, "Though people have been shot for sprawl." Sprawl, then, is the opposite of the uptight, aggressive, overly sophisticated self-consciousness that Murray sees around him and that he considers foreign and inappropriate for Australia—a place, perhaps, where Mark Twain's Huck Finn might have been at home. While "sprawl" may appear a public attitude and manner, it rests upon a more essential inward feature, which Murray terms "equanimity," in a poem of that title.

"Equanimity" is a poem that draws together several strands of Murray's work: His populist, bardic stance mingles with a more purely prophetic strain. Here, his democratic vistas are underwritten by a transcendental authority, based upon a personal and even sacramental experience. That experience, which he calls "equanimity," is like an influx of quiet power, an exaltation of the spirit grounded in love. "There is only love," he says; "human order has at heart/ an equanimity. Quite different from inertia," a place "where all are, in short, off the high comparative horse/ of their identity." This is the place at which people join together in a "people's otherworld," a vernacular republic of the spirit that allows for a "continuous recovering moment." It is an effortless effort, reminiscent of a Buddhist or Kantian disinterestedness: "Through the peace beneath effort/ (even within effort: quiet air between the bars of our attention)/ comes unpurchased lifelong plenishment." Yet, foremost for Murray, this is a Christian quality; it is at the very heart of Christ's teachings and is the place from which he taught: "Christ spoke to people most often on this level/ especially when they chattered about kingship and the Romans;/ all holiness speaks from it." To experience such equanimity would be tantamount to experiencing holiness itself, and that is precisely the sort of graceful redemption Murray seeks to convey. There can be nothing programmatic about such an attitude, but no program of reform, be it social, political, or cultural, can possibly succeed without it. That, for Murray, is the basis upon which all else proceeds, including his own poetry.

Writing poetry, for Murray, is like playing upon an instrument, finding out just what it can do and learning how to do it. His poems have an energy and inventiveness that reveal a delight in the resources of language and a conviction that what needs to be said can be communicated through the adequacies of poetry.

Other major works

NONFICTION: *The Peasant Mandarin: Prose Pieces*, 1978; *Persistence in Folly*, 1984.

Bibliography

Barnie, John. "The Poetry of Les Murray," in *Australian Literary Studies*. XII, no. 1 (May, 1985).

Gray, Robert. "An Interview with Les Murray," in *Quadrant*. XX, no. 12 (1976).

Oles, Carole. "An Interview with Les Murray," in *The American Poetry Review*. XV (March/April, 1986).

Pollnitz, Christopher. "The Bardic Pose: A Survey of Les A. Murray's Poetry," in *Southerly*. XLI, no. 2 (1981).

Trigg, Stephanie. "Les A. Murray: Boeotian Count," in *Scripsi*. II, no. 4 (1984).

Paul Kane

LORINE NIEDECKER

Born: Near Fort Atkinson, Wisconsin; May 12, 1903
Died: Near Fort Atkinson, Wisconsin; December 31, 1970

Principal poems and collections

New Goose, 1946; *My Friend Tree*, 1961; *North Central*, 1968; *T&G: The Collected Poems, 1936-1966*, 1969; *My Life by Water: Collected Poems, 1936-1968*, 1970; *Blue Chicory*, 1976; *The Granite Pail: The Selected Poems of Lorine Niedecker*, 1985; *From This Condensery: The Complete Writing of Lorine Niedecker*, 1985.

Other literary forms

Although known primarily for her poetry, Lorine Niedecker also wrote radio plays, creative prose, and reviews. "As I Lay Dying" condenses and adapts William Faulkner's novel of the same title, and "Taste and Tenderness" centers on William, Henry, and Alice James. "Uncle," "Untitled," and "Switchboard Girl," local-color sketches, provide insight into Niedecker's family background, work experiences, and philosophy, and her reviews of the poetry of Louis Zukofsky and Cid Corman reveal Niedecker's poetics. Of her letters, which Zukofsky early praised as her best writing, her ten-year correspondence with Corman has been published, and her thirty-year correspondence with Zukofsky rests at the Humanities Research Center at the University of Texas, Austin.

Achievements

Niedecker has proved that a twentieth century American writer does not have to travel far or have exotic experiences to be able to present her culture objectively and honestly. Although in her poetry, spring floods buckle her floors and breed water bugs under her hooked rugs, the waters also reminded her of life's constant flux and helped her avoid becoming static and rootbound. Relying primarily on the past, nature, and long-distance support from a few fellow poets, she overcame the fragmentation and materialism of which so many twentieth century artists complain and to which they often succumb. Sincerity, hard work, and isolation from fame have helped earn for her a reputation as the twentieth century's Emily Dickinson. In 1978, her home state recognized her achievements by awarding her the Notable Wisconsin Writers Award.

Biography

Born on May 12, 1903, on Blackhawk Island, near the Rock River and Lake Koshkonong, three miles from Fort Atkinson, Wisconsin, Lorine Niedecker, the only child of commercial fisherman Henry E. Niedecker and his swamp-bound housewife Theresa Daisy Kunz Niedecker, never grew far from her roots. Niedecker was educated in Fort Atkinson and Beloit, where she went to Beloit College to study literature from 1922 until 1924. Returning home because her mother was becoming increasingly deaf, Niedecker married Frank Hartwig in 1928, but the couple separated in 1930 when Hartwig defaulted on a loan and lost their house. Niedecker assisted in the Dwight Foster Public Library during this period. From 1928 until 1942, she worked in Madison for the Works Progress Administration's state guide as a writer and research editor, exploring the early history of her region. She began writing radio plays during the 1930's, her interest leading her in 1942 to a brief job as scriptwriter at station WHA in Madison. She returned that year to Black-hawk Island and in 1944 began work as a stenographer and proofreader at Hoard's Dairyman, publishers of a national journal, remaining there until 1950. Her mother, completely deaf, died in 1951, and her father, in 1954. Niedecker inherited two houses on Blackhawk Island and spent some time overseeing her property while living in a small cabin nearby, which she had built in 1947; then she scrubbed floors and cleaned the kitchen at the Fort Atkinson Memorial Hospital from 1957 until 1962. In mid-1960, she started keeping company with Harold Hein, a widowed dentist and amateur artist who spent his Christmas holidays in Florida and did not want to remarry. The couple spent most of their weekends together, driving north to Manitowish Waters in June, 1961, and reading together the Thomas Jefferson-John Adams correspondence. One of Niedecker's most valued gifts from Hein was a birdfeeder, which attracted so many birds that the poet said she would have to hire a birdsitter to keep it full of seeds while she was at work. During the fall of 1962, Hein visited Niedecker less often, and in spring, 1963, she met Albert Millen, a housepainter from Milwaukee, to whom she was married on May 24, 1963, and with whom she moved to a run-down part of that city. When her husband retired, they built a two-and-a-half-room cabin on Black-hawk Island and spent most of their time there, although they traveled briefly to South Dakota and around Lake Superior. Niedecker died, on December 31, 1970, where she was born.

Niedecker began writing early but published little until late in life. She mentions an ode to Lake Koshkonong written in high school, and her first published poem appeared in her high school annual, *The Tchogeerah*, in 1922. Her poems were printed in literary journals in 1928, and in 1933 several appeared in *Poetry*. In the early 1930's, she initiated correspondence with Louis Zukofsky, who would become one of her mentors and friends. She exchanged visits and gifts with the Zukofsky family and from Louis learned about condensation, reliance on folk dialogue, rejection slips, and publication procedures. Her first book eventually appeared in 1946. In 1960, she began to correspond with Cid Corman, who published many of her poems in his influential magazine *Origin* and who recorded her only known poetry reading a few weeks before she died. In the late 1950's and into the 1960's, she wrote many poems to Zukofsky's violinist son, Paul, and finally, in the late 1960's, when she published three volumes of poetry, she began to be recognized by a wide audience. She left three finished manuscripts, which were included in her complete writings in 1985. All of her poems, most brief and many untitled, have been arranged chronologically in *From This Condensery* and divided into seven major sections: "Early Poems," "For Paul and Other Poems," "The Years Go By," "In Exchange for Haiku," "Home/World," "North Central," and "Harpsichord and Salt Fish."

Analysis

In her review of the poetry of Louis Zukofsky, Lorine Niedecker quotes William Carlos Williams: "You cannot express anything unless you invent how to express it. A poem is not a freudian 'escape' (what childishness) but an adult release to knowledge, in the most practical, engineering manner." Niedecker used her poetry to invent herself, to discover her own wholeness. This quest for wholeness has been a persistent theme in the writing of American women since the time of Margaret Fuller. A glass cutter of words, Niedecker discards traditional poetic modes of expression *en masse*, yet selects those devices which best help her construct small stained-glass pieces, later combining some of these reflective objects into longer poems. She trims her glasslike achievements often, arranges them variously, and finally creates two outstanding large pieces: "Wintergreen Ridge" and "Paean to Place." Niedecker appropriates glass of many colors from several sources: the men and women whom she knew and read about, American society during her lifetime, nature, and art.

Of the men and women whom she knew, her father and mother engaged her most fully. In her early poems, she depicts her father building and losing houses, rocking in his chair, seining to finance his daughter's education, and wondering about the meaning of life. In "For Paul," she recalls her father's description of a warm Thanksgiving Day when he helped seine twenty thousand pounds of buffalo fish by moonlight. Other times, his "hands glazed/ to the nets." In "The Years Go By," she recalls "mild Henry" as "absent" and describes him as a catalpa tree, serene, refusing "to see/ that the other woman, the hummer he shaded/ hotly cared/ for his purse petals falling—/ his mind in the air." Niedecker also pictures her father planting trees and burying "carp/ beneath the rose" after he lost his wife. She continues that "he opened his wine tank" to "bankers on high land," wanted "his only daughter/ to work in the bank" but had left her a "source/ to sustain her—/ a weedy speech." In "North Central," she again writes of the trees her father planted, "evenly following/ the road." She walks beside them on New Year's Day and each one speaks to her: "Peace." Niedecker's father learned the "coiled celery," "duckweed," and "pickerelweeds" of the swamp but "could not/ —like water bugs—/ stride surface tension/ He netted/ loneliness." He sat rocking at night "beside his shoes," "Roped not 'looped/ in the loop/ of her hair.'" Hard work, serenity, unhappiness in marriage, planting, swamp, rocking: These scattered details kaleidoscope into Niedecker's benediction for her father: Peace.

Niedecker has more trouble coming to terms with her mother. The annual spring floods soak the floors, pump, washing machine, and lilacs of "the woman moored to this low shore by deafness," who has wasted her life in water. Niedecker's deaf mother contradicts herself, wishing she could hear, then complaining about "too much talk in the world." With "big blind ears" under "high" hair, a husband with "leaky boats," a writer daughter who "sits and floats," Niedecker's mother dies with "a thimble in her purse," her last words urging her daughter, "Wash the floors, Lorine!/ Wash clothes! Weed!" Daisy Niedecker parks uncharacteristically in "her burnished brown motor-less automobile," "She who wheeled dirt for flowers" waiting to be buried in ground in which "She could have grown a good rutabaga." Daisy grew up in marsh land, Niedecker later explains, "married mild Henry/ and then her life was sand." Daisy, tall and thin, "took cold on her nerves," built the fires with the wood she chopped, helped rebuild a burned house, gave "boat" instead of birth to her daughter in the flooding spring, and philosophized: "Hatch, patch and scratch,/ that's all a woman's for/ but I didn't sink, I sewed and saved/ and now I'm on second floor."

Snow on branches later reminds Niedecker of the cotton that her mother "wore in her aching ears," her hard work, and her protectiveness. She calls her mother a "distrait wife," a "thorn apple bush,/ armed against life's raw push." Niedecker tells Kenneth Cox, however, that her mother had a "rhym-ing, happy" father and spoke "whole chunks of down-to-earth (o very earthy) magic." In "Wintergreen Ridge," which she considers her best poem, Niedecker remembers how her mother loved "closed gentians/ she herself/ so closed" and identifies with her in "Paean to Place," saying they both were born "in swale and swamp and sworn/ to water." A wealth of autobiographi-cal material follows. Her father "sculled down" and saw her mother, who was playing the organ but who later stopped, turned "deaf/ and away." Daisy "knew boats/ and ropes," helped Henry "string out nets/ for tarring," and "could shoot." Niedecker mourns the fact that her mother could not hear canvasbacks take off and sora rails sing, and she wonders if she giggled when she was a girl. Her question underscores the somber light in which she sees her mother, the assonating *o*'s in "the woman moored to this low shore," and the following poem sustaining this sober mood:

> Hear
> where her snow-grave is
> the *You*

ah you
of mourning doves

Her father, from upcountry, contemplating the stars, drawing fish from water, plants from land, rocking, lonely, wants his daughter to move to high ground. Her mother, from the swamp, enduring floods, protecting her family, closing gradually into total silence, ridicules her husband's "bright new car," declaring, "A hummingbird/ can't haul." Niedecker alternates between swamp and upland, but resides primarily in the former.

From this fragmented relationship, Niedecker must wrest her wholeness, which she does partly by observing other men and women from the present and the past. Her early poems depict her male contemporaries as J. Alfred Prufrock-like: posturing, ineffectual, directionless, out of touch with reality. Some play cards instead of chopping wood; one "strolls pale among zinnias." She later describes a prospective employer as "Keen and lovely," graceful, cultured, kind, but he does not hire her. She mentions men who carefully build weapons to irradiate others; businessmen smoking cigarettes, leaving "droppings/ larger, whiter than owls'," wearing time on their wrists, wool on their bodies, making money unscrupulously and demanding to be "jazzed" for which they pay in "nylons." She dislikes a "clean man," prefers one who falls while fishing in muddy water, "dries his last pay-check/ in the sun, smooths it out/ in *Leaves of Grass*." Niedecker mentions few modern examples of complete men.

In the past she finds many men whom she admires: John James Audubon, Michel-Guillaume-Jean de Crèvecoeur, Thomas Jefferson, John Adams, Michelangelo, William Morris, Charles Darwin, Carolus Linnaeus, Vincent van Gogh. Men who value the earth, the arts, solitude, exploration, plants, creation, equality, and humanity appeal to her. Poems on great men are sprinkled through her writing, ranging from an early short poem written from van Gogh's point of view to a long, late poem on Darwin. She compares Aeneas and Frédéric Chopin, observing that Aeneas "closed his piano/ to dig a well thru hard clay," whereas "Chopin left notes like drops of water." She ends this brief poem with Aeneas' words to Chopin: "O Frederic, think of me digging below/ the surface—we are of one pitch and flow." The high/low dichotomy which separated her parents is erased by these great men, who cooperate to bring harmony to the world. The examples supplied by great men also help Niedecker choose a partner from among her contemporaries, a man she chooses for "warmth."

Lacking models of great women from both present and past, Niedecker must create herself from within. She first deals with the female models which surround her. In her early poetry, she ridicules a lady wearing a leopard coat for being directionless and scorns women who demand only money from men and become slaves to fashion. She describes a woman who "hooks men like rugs," "covets the gold in her husband's teeth," and would "sell your eyes fried in deep grief." She rhymingly itemizes the "needs" of women: "washers and dryers, . . . bodice uplift, . . . deep-well cookers, . . . power shift." She describes an office girl who "carries her nylon hard-pointed/ breast uplift/ like parachutes/ half-pulled" which "collapse" at night among all of her material possessions.

In contrast, she mentions in later poems famous women of the past. "Who was Mary Shelley?" she asks, who eloped, wrote her novel after Lord Byron and Percy Bysshe Shelley "talked the candle down," read Greek, Italian, and bore two children who died. Margaret Fuller "carried books/ and chrysanthemums/ to Boston/ into a cold storm." Abigail Smith, who according to her suitor John Adams had faults, such as hanging her head, reading, writing, thinking, and crossing her "Leggs/ while sitting," proved to be a faithful wife. Niedecker later writes that Abigail was an architect and artist, made cheese and raised chickens, talked as an equal with Jefferson, and wrote letters that both Adams and Jefferson appreciated.

In her early poems, Niedecker writes of refusing to admit excitement or pain, the former inconvenient and the latter too great. Writing to Zukofsky's son Paul, she tells how her feelings for the boy enable her to love more fully, and in "The Years Go By," she discusses, in a manner similar to Emily Dickinson's, the ebb and flow of sorrow. The central change in a woman's life, menopause, she describes as "hot fears" in "middle life" but says in "cool years . . . who'll remember/ flash to black?/ I gleamed?" Then she begins to look back at herself, examining a photograph and remembering her "young aloofness," her wish to stay "cool," the fact that she "couldn't bake." She also begins to express her discontent with her "black office," looking forward to her "three/ days of light: Saturday, Sunday,/ memory." In "Home/ World," she says her life is "a wave-blurred/ portrait" and depicts herself as a "swamp/ as against a large pine-spread—." She becomes self-conscious: Out of ten thousand women dancing on skates, she is the only one who wears boots, she remarks. Much earlier she had praised the energy of women who could work, keep a house and children, go to church, and bowl, wondering what they would think if they knew how much energy she spent on her poetry. At the time of her marriage, she visits her family cemetery, recognizing and accepting that her family line ends with her: "but sonless/ see no/ hop/ clover boy to stop/ before me." The assonating *o*'s, which she reserves for special occasions, underscore the momentous solemnity of her recognition, the rhyming *e*'s focusing attention on her as an individual. Now she can speak of the peace her father's trees bring her and compare love to a leaf, all parts relating. In "Paean to Place," about which she expressed excitement to Kenneth Cox in 1969 and stated that his questions about her background inspired the poem, she traces her life: a "solitary plover," a seven-year-old with only two dresses, a visitor to the grave of her grandfather who delighted

her with folk and nursery rhymes. She recalls her love for the boy who
played the violin and says,

> O my floating life
> Do not save love
>   for things
>   Throw *things*
> to the flood

She ends "Paean to Place" by describing the "sloughs and sluices" of her
mind "with the persons/ on the edge."

She also felt herself to be part of American society. She expressed her concern for the social ills of her day repeatedly, discussing such topics as poverty,
hunger, religion, electricity, consumerism, traffic speeding, commercialism,
hunting, plumbing, private property, war, and the atom bomb. She opposed
most modern conveniences and luxuries, pleased most with her "New-saved/
clean-smelling house/ sweet cedar pink/ flesh tint" with a "Popcorn-can
cover" over a hole in her wall "so the cold/ can't mouse in." She often
describes *things* in terms of people and animals, maybe trying to lessen their
otherness, and enjoyed such creative activities as hooking rugs, quilting, sew-
ing, and cooking. She stresses that becoming involved with the material
world leads one to wake up at night and say to oneself,

> I'm pillowed and padded, pale and puffing
> lifting household stuffing—
> carpets, dishes
> benches, fishes
> I've spent my life in nothing.

Rejecting materialism and those elements of society which thrive on it,
Niedecker is especially appalled at people's desecration of nature. The "ten
dead ducks' feathers/ on beer-can litter" will be covered by snow, but when
man exterminated the carrier pigeon without cause, he destroyed "cobalt/
and carnelian." One of her most vehement protests involves the quiet
muskrat who swims "as if already/ a woman's neck-piece." A second stanza
juxtaposes the image of "Nazi wildmen/ wearing women."

Most of her nature poetry, however, exudes harmony and peace. She writes
of wild swans, sandhill cranes, pheasants, pink flamingos, curlews, canvasbacks, mergansers, and warblers. Willows and poplars, cherry trees and
maples, pines and catalpas dot her work. Flowers from the wild sunflower to
the blue chicory to water lilies blossom, and she notes that "men are plants
whose goodness grows/ out of the soil." She is especially attuned to the seasons. In winter, she watches chunks of ice swim swanlike down the river and
in March notices her

                        Bird feeder's
                         snow-cap
                          sliding
                            off

April brings "little/ yellows" and frogs rattling in contrast to freight trains,
whereas June is hot and sticky, "a lush/ Marshmushing, frog bickering/ moon
pooling, green gripping." Waxwings stain berry branches red in July, while
autumn nights force her to pull her curtains because the leaves have fallen,
reminding Niedecker of tree toads and her starlight talks with a boy. October
she considers to be the head of spring, which is in turn the body of the year.
She notices small creatures: mites in rabbits' ears, dragonflies, gophers,
crickets, and frogs which stop sounding because they have turned out their
lights. Only occasionally does nature frighten her, as when she hears a
muskrat eat frogs and mice outside her door and when she describes a late
fall weed stalk as a rapist. Generally, Niedecker presents nature as a cherished friend and often uses nature images to describe people. She also talks
of multistratified rocks, lichens which can pulverize granite, and mosses and
horsetails which outlived dinosaurs. People are composed of and interrelated
with nature. The water lily exemplifies perfect order. In her longest poem,
"Wintergreen Ridge," she calls wintergreen by its Indian name, pipsissewa,
which literally means "breaks it into fragments." In no other part of life does
Niedecker see the absence of fragments as in nature. Parts combine to make
a whole, and her immersion in nature, evident throughout her poetry but
especially in "Wintergreen Ridge" and "Paean to Place," helps her to recognize and to remember her own wholeness. As she wrote to Corman in 1969,
"the lines of natural growth, of life, [were] unconsciously absorbed from foliage and flowers while growing up."

Niedecker drew on the life which surrounded her for her poetry, transforming life into art by filling her subconscious, leaving herself alone, then
pulling out material for her poetry. The "lava" flowed only while she wrote;
then came the discipline of forming and polishing her words. Her first collected poems show her awareness of the way her contemporaries have
debased language, have deified slang and narrowed their vocabularies. She
early recognizes her affinity for imagism and philosophy, describes her poetic
inspiration rising like feathers and gas, and realizes that wealth for her is
staying in one place and writing. She mentions several poets who have influenced her, showing what type of bird she would be if depicted by H. D.,
William Carlos Williams, Marianne Moore, Wallace Stevens, Louis Zukofsky, E. E. Cummings, and Charles Reznikoff. Bashō and Gerard Manley
Hopkins also helped form her poetry. Intellectual influences include Plato,
Marcus Aurelius, Gottfried Wilhelm Leibnitz, Emanuel Swedenborg, Ralph
Waldo Emerson, and Henry David Thoreau. From these thinkers, she dis-
tilled mental rigor and a belief in the soul.

Niedecker, who created her poems from familiar people and surroundings, commented that she did not want her neighbors to know she wrote because she would lose some of her finest sources of language. She used both traditional and contemporary poetic devices to shape her work: rhyme of all types, varying rhythms, alliteration, assonance, consonance, juxtaposition. She experimented with both line and stanza length, revising, arranging, and rearranging her poems into different sequences. She took seriously her mother's final words to wash, scrub, and weed, and did just that to her poems, polishing them until they gleamed with meaning and clarity, compressing them until they yielded their intrinsic forms. Her work is alive because she grounded it thoroughly in life and because she encouraged it to grow and change as she did. Filled with fragments and whole poems, the work of Lorine Niedecker reminds one that wholeness is possible even amid a chaotic world.

Other major works

NONFICTION: *Between Your House and Mine: The Letters of Lorine Niedecker to Cid Corman, 1960-1970*, 1986.

Bibliography

Dent, Peter, ed. *The Full Note: Lorine Niedecker*, 1983.
Heller, Michael. *Conviction's Net of Branches: Essays on the Objectivist Poets and Poetry*, 1985.
Truck. No. 16 (Summer, 1975). Special Niedecker issue.
Williams, Jonathan, ed. *Epitaphs for Lorine*, 1973.

Shelley Thrasher

CHARLES OLSON

Born: Worcester, Massachusetts; December 27, 1910
Died: New York, New York; January 10, 1970

Principal collections

Y & X, 1948; *Letter for Melville 1951*, 1951; *This*, 1952; *In Cold Hell, in Thicket*, 1953; *The Maximus Poems 1-10*, 1953; *The Maximus Poems 11-12*, 1956; *O'Ryan 2 4 6 8 10*, 1958 (expanded edition, *O'Ryan 12345678910*, 1965); *The Maximus Poems*, 1960; *The Distances*, 1960; *The Maximus Poems, IV, V, VI*, 1968; *Archaeologist of Morning: The Collected Poems Outside the Maximus Series*, 1970; *The Maximus Poems, Volume 3*, 1975; *The Maximus Poems*, 1983.

Other literary forms

Charles Olson was a prolific essayist, espousing the essay form in order to advance his poetic concerns to a wider audience. His prose style can present as many difficulties as his poetry, however, difficulties to a large extent deliberately sought by Olson, who was concerned that his literary production not be consumed too easily in an era of speed-reading. With *Call Me Ishmael*, a book-length study of Herman Melville, published in 1947, Olson announced his intention to define America for his day, even as Melville had, Olson believed, for *his* time, in *Moby-Dick: Or, The Whale* (1851). Key essays published within four years of *Call Me Ishmael* include "The Human Universe" and the celebrated "Projective Verse," which, together with many others, may be found in one of several collections, namely *Selected Writings of Charles Olson* (1966), *Human Universe and Other Essays* (1965), *Pleistocene Man* (1968), *Causal Mythology* (1969), *The Special View of History* (1970), *Poetry and Truth: The Beloit Lectures and Poems* (1971), and *Additional Prose: A Bibliography on America, Proprioception, and Other Notes and Essays* (1974).

Olson's letters have also proved of much interest, and many are collected in *Mayan Letters* (1953), *Letters for "Origin," 1950-1956* (1969), and the series of volumes issuing from Black Sparrow Press of his correspondence with the poet Robert Creeley.

Achievements

With his first poems and essays, Olson caught the attention of readers ready, like himself, for a profound renaming of a present grown extremely ambiguous with the destruction of traditional values during World War II. This audience continued to grow and, with the publication in 1960 of Don Allen's anthology *The New American Poetry, 1945-1960*, a year that also saw the publication in one book of the first volume of *The Maximus Poems* and another book of poems, *The Distances*, he was widely hailed as a leader of a revolution in poetry. Olson's section in the Allen anthology came first and was the largest; the poetry conference held at the University of British Columbia in 1963, and another, held at the University of California at Berkeley in 1965, were dominated by his presence. He remained "center-stage" until his death in 1970, and since then, his contribution has received steadily increasing attention from the scholarly community, while his influence on younger poets has continued to spread.

Olson spoke through his art to a historical moment that had come unhinged, and the cogency with which he advocated "screwing the hinges back on the door of civilization" inspired a fervor of response. Poets, editors, teachers, and lay readers formed a kind of "Olson underground," a network that disseminated the kinds of information which Olson's project favored, and these were various indeed: the founding and the decline of early civilizations (Sumer, Egypt, Greece, the Maya), the pre-Socratics, the Tarot, psychedelic drugs, non-Euclidean geometry, the philosophy of Alfred North Whitehead, and documents of the European settlement of New England—a far from exhaustive list. For the most part, Olson shunned publicity and was therefore less known to the counterculture of the 1960's than was his fellow poet Allen Ginsberg, but there can be no doubt that Olson, both in his own person and through this network, helped instigate and name the cultural revolution then attempted.

Olson's poetry instructs, deliberately, as do his essays. In this respect, it is noteworthy that his career as a teacher spanned four decades, starting at Clark University in the 1930's and resuming (after an interim during which he worked first for the American Civil Liberties Union and then in the Office of War Information) at Black Mountain College in the late 1940's. Olson continued to teach at Black Mountain until the college closed in 1956; he moved on to the State University of New York at Buffalo in 1963, where he worked for three years, and concluded his teaching career at the University of Connecticut. A partial list of his distinguished students includes John Wieners, Edward Dorn, Michael Rumaker, Fielding Dawson, Joel Oppenheimer, and Jonathan Williams. While serving as rector of Black Mountain College, from 1951 to 1956, Olson turned it into a center of the literary arts and was responsible for the publication of the *Black Mountain Review* (edited by Creeley), which gave its name to the group of writers most often published therein.

Olson was the recipient of two Guggenheim grants, in 1939 to continue his work on his dissertation on Herman Melville and in 1948 to write about the interaction of racial groups during the settling of the American West; in 1952, he received a grant from the Wenner-Gren Foundation to study Mayan hieroglyphics in the Yucatan. (It is characteristic of Olson that he completed none of these projects within the guidelines proposed but instead transmuted them into poetic essays and poetry.) In 1965, he was awarded the Oscar Blumenthal–Charles Leviton Prize by *Poetry* magazine, possibly the most prestigious award he received for his poetry. His poetry was too radical, and his life too short, for further such acknowledgment to come his way during his lifetime.

Biography

Charles John Olson was born on December 27, 1910, in the central Massachusetts town of Worcester. His mother, Mary Hines, was of Irish immigrant stock; his father, also named Charles, was of Swedish origin. Olson's giant proportions, (fully grown, he was to stand six feet, nine inches) obviously came from his father's side, the elder Olson having stood well over six feet tall himself, whereas the poet's mother was barely above five feet tall. Olson's father worked as a letter carrier, a career the poet was to take up at one point in his life. From 1915 until he left home, Olson spent part of each summer with his family in Gloucester, a small seaport of Massachusetts north of Boston; he would later live there and anchor his Maximus poems in this, to him, "root city." In 1928, he entered Wesleyan University, being graduated in 1932 and receiving his M.A. there the following year; his thesis, "The Growth of Herman Melville, Prose Writer and Poetic Thinker," led him to discover hitherto unknown portions of Melville's library, and this, in turn, led to his paper "Lear and Moby-Dick," written in the course of his doctoral studies at Harvard and published in *Twice-a-Year* in 1938. Between 1932 and 1939, Olson supported himself either by grants or by teaching: at Clark University from 1934 to 1936 and at Harvard from 1936 to 1939.

In 1939, awarded a Guggenheim Fellowship, Olson lived with his widowed mother in Gloucester, laying the groundwork for what was to become *Call Me Ishmael*. In 1940, he moved to New York City, working first as publicity director for the American Civil Liberties Union and then as chief of the Foreign Language Information Service of the Common Council for American Unity. During this period, Olson met and married Constance Wilcock. From 1942 to 1944, Olson served as associate chief of the Foreign Language Division of the Office of War Information, in Washington, D.C., and during Franklin D. Roosevelt's campaign for a fourth term in 1944, he served on the Democratic National Committee. The following year, he was offered high office in the new Democratic administration but chose instead to devote himself to writing, and, with the help of Ezra Pound, whom Olson often visited at St. Elizabeth's Hospital, he published *Call Me Ishmael* in 1947.

For the next ten years, Olson's life was to be closely associated with Black Mountain College, an experiment in education being carried on near Asheville, North Carolina, where he worked first as a lecturer and subsequently, starting in 1951, as rector. Olson during this period wrote his landmark essays on poetics and the poems that made up his book *The Distances*. Through

Vincent Ferrini, a Gloucester poet, Olson met Robert Creeley, and a correspondence ensued that was to prove seminal to the movement in poetry known as "Black Mountain poetry" or "projective verse" (the latter from the Olson essay so titled). In 1954, Creeley came to teach at the college and edited the *Black Mountain Review*. Another poet, Robert Duncan—association with whom was to prove vital to Olson—also taught at Black Mountain during this time. Olson, meanwhile, had ended his first marriage (which produced one child, Katherine, born in 1951) and embarked on a second, to Elizabeth Kaiser, whom he met and married in 1954; their son, Charles Peter, was born in May of the following year.

As Black Mountain College was no longer proving fiscally viable, Olson closed it in 1956, the year that saw the publication of *The Maximus Poems 11-22* (*The Maximus Poems 1-10* had been issued in 1953). In 1957, Olson journeyed to San Francisco to read at the Museum of Art and The Poetry Center and to deliver in five lectures his "special view of history." Olson then settled with his wife and son in Gloucester, working on another volume of Maximus poems. The year 1960 was his *annus mirabilis*: He was included in the anthology *The New American Poetry, 1945-1960*, his Maximus poems were reissued as a single book, and his other poems were collected into the volume *The Distances*. Thenceforth Olson's star, in the ascendant throughout the previous decade, was much more visibly so, and he met his quickly growing audience at a number of venues, among these the Vancouver Poetry Conference (1963), the Festival of the Two Worlds in Spoleto, Italy (1965), the Berkeley Poetry Conference (1965), the Literary Colloquim of the Academy of Art in Berlin (1966), the International Poetry Festival in London (1967), and Beloit College (1968), where he delivered the lectures subsequently published as *Poetry and Truth*. Several collections of his essays were issued during this decade also. From 1963 to 1965, Olson served as visiting professor of English at the State University of New York at Buffalo; in 1969, he accepted a similar post at the University of Connecticut.

These years were marked, however, by dissipation and heartbreak. His wife died in an automobile accident in 1964; Olson's health began to fail, and, in 1969, cancer of the liver was diagnosed; he died in a New York City hospital on January 10, 1970.

Analysis

Charles Olson's poetry is political in a profound, not superficial, sense; it does not spend time naming "current events," but rather, it devotes itself to defining "the dodges of discourse" which have enabled humanity (especially in the West) to withdraw from reality into increasingly abstract fictions of life. Olson came of age during the Great Depression and admired Roosevelt's New Deal, but with the death of the president in 1945 and the bombing of Hiroshima and Nagasaki, Olson lost faith in the possibilities for liberal democracy. It did not go wide enough or deep enough in the attempt to restore humanity's lost meaning. Nor did it provide enough checks and balances against the corporate takeover of the world. Olson encouraged a resistance based on knowledge from a range of sources which he endeavored, through his essays and his poems, to bring to common attention. "Resistance," in fact, is a key word here: One of his first essays bears that title, and often, Olson's stance reminds one of the Maquis and other "underground" pockets of resistance to the Fascists during World War II. His is a sort of intellectual commando operation bent on destroying, marshaling not yards or military arsenals but modes of thought (and, therefore of action) that are out of kilter with current realities and "fascistic" in their ability to crush individual senses of value that would struggle toward a coherence—where the merely subjective might transcend itself and establish a vital community. However sweeping Olson's proposals, in effect his program is reactive; such a reaction against the status quo was, as he saw it, the essential first step toward building a civilization that put people before profits. "When man is reduced to so much fat for soap, superphosphate for soil, fillings and shoes for sale," Olson wrote, the news of the Nazi death camps fresh in the minds of his audience as in his own, "he has, to begin again, one answer, one point of resistance only to such fragmentation, one organized ground. . . . It is his physiology he is forced to arrive at. . . . It is his body that is his answer." This answer led Olson to ground his poetics in the physical breathing of the poet, the vital activity that registers the smallest fluctuations of thought and feeling. Language had become separated from being over the centuries of Western civilization, so that, for example, it became more important to carry out orders than to consider their often terrible consequences. In the words of Paul Christensen, "The denotational core of words must be rescued from neglect; logical classification and the principles of syntax must be suppressed and a new, unruly seizure of phenomena put in their place." Civilization, to the extent that it alienates one from one's experience of the actual earth and the life that arises therefrom, has failed, and it supplants with "slick pictures" the actual conditions of human lives.

Therefore, it has become necessary, Olson argues, to deconstruct the accepted authorities of Western thought, while seeking to preserve the thought of such persons who, throughout history, have warned against systems of ideation that debase human beings. In Olson's vision, one of the great villains is Aristotle; one of the heroes, Apollonius of Tyana. With Aristotle, "the two great means appear: logic and classification. And it is they," Olson continues in the essay "Human Universe," "that have so fastened themselves on habits of thought that action is interfered with, absolutely interfered with, I should say." Olson in this same passage points out: "The harmony of the universe, and I include man, is not logical, or better, is post-logical, as is the order of any created thing." As for classification,

What makes most acts—of living and of writing—unsatisfactory, is that the person and/or the writer satisfy themselves that they can only make a form . . . by selecting from the full content some face of it, or plane, some part. And at just this point, by just this act, they fall back on the dodges of discourse, and immediately, they lose me, I am no longer engaged, this is not what I know is the going-on. . . . It comes out a demonstration, a separating out, an act of classification, and so, a stopping.

In "Apollonius of Tyana, A Dance, with Some Words, for Two Actors," Olson addresses the reader through the medium of a contemporary of Christ, Apollonius, and the play's one other character, Tyana, the place of his origin, as well as through himself, as narrator/commentator. This last tells how Apollonius "knows . . . that *his* job, at least, is to find out how to inform all people how best they can stick to the instant, which is both temporal and intense, which is both shape and law." Apollonius makes his way through the Mediterranean world of the first century A.D., which "is already the dispersed thing the West has been since," conducting "a wide investigation into the local, the occasional, what you might even call the ceremonial, but without . . . any assurance that he knows how to make objects firm, or how firm he is."

Apollonius, readers are told, learned from his journeyings

that two ills were coming on man: (1) unity was crowding out diversity (man was getting too multiplied to stay clear by way of the old vision of himself, the humanist one, was getting too distracted to abide in his own knowing with any of his old confidence); and (2) unity as a goal (making Rome an empire, say) had, as its intellectual pole an equally mischievous concept, that of the universal—of the 'universals' as Socrates and Christ equally had laid them down. Form . . . was suddenly swollen, was being taken as a thing larger a thing outside a thing above any particular, even any given man.

These descriptions of the confusions which beset Apollonius clearly apply to those Olson himself was encountering, and therefore readers look to find, in Apollonius' solutions, those of Olson. This part of the work, however, rings less convincingly: Olson makes some rhetorical flourishes, but in the end the reader is simply told that Apollonius has learned that he must "commit himself"; he has also learned that Tyana (surely a figure for Olson's Gloucester) is intimately connected with his endeavor.

Olson's brilliance when specifying the major ills, and his vagueness when speaking to their cure, his inability to resolve the inherent contradictions between the latter and the former (how shall the individual make himself responsible for many of the elements in a society in whose false unity and swollen forms he himself is caught and of which he is a part?), all so clearly to be seen in this piece, persist throughout his canon. It is the problem he recognizes in Melville, who finds splendid embodiment for his society's evils in Ahab but who can never create a convincing hero. Large answers, the sweeping solution, evade Olson by the very nature of his method, which is to focus on particulars, even on "the blessing/ that difficulties are once more." These difficulties include the obvious truth that Olson is trammeled at the outset by the very tricks of discourse he would overthrow: Witness, for example, his sweeping generalization, near the beginning of his essay "Human Universe": "We have lived long in a generalizing time, at least since 450 B.C." Again, and on the other hand, given that he is urgent about reeducating his contemporaries to eradicate society's evils before it is too late, his refusal to write in received forms was bound to delay dissemination of his message. Moreover, while he was embodying the difficulties and the particularities in highly difficult and particular forms, and thereby rendering these virtually inaccessible except by the slow "trickle-down" process which accompanies aesthetically responsible art, he was given, in both poem and essay, to assertion without supporting evidence—such is the nature of the intuitive perception he espoused, as against a stupefied insistence on proof—and thereby to alienating many more conventionally trained readers.

That Olson could not accomplish his project was a result of its inherent impossibility; this failure, however, in no way erases the spellbinding body of his poetry. His magnificent embodiment and evocation of the dilemma in which he found himself remains as both consolation and exhortation. He gave a rationale for free (or, to use his own term, Open) verse, of which his own work is the most telling demonstration; he gave a scale and a scope to poetry which inspired and continue to inspire other poets and which make his own among the most compelling of all time. If his more general prescriptions regarding society—true as they still ring, particularly in their diagnostics—have been largely ineffectual against the momentum of social change (surely, from Olson's point of view, for the worse), his speculations, conjecture, and assertions concerning the practice of poetry stay valid, viable, and vital. Moreover, his insistence that the poet (as Percy Bysshe Shelley thought, a century and more before) be lawgiver to those of his day must be a salutary thorn in the side of any practitioner of the art.

The power of Olson's finest poems stems from a double movement: The poet strives to fill his poem with the greatest variety of subject matter that he can; the poet strives to empty his poem of everything he has brought into it. The plethora of subject matter (information, often conflicting) is there to say that the world is absolutely fascinating—its details are fit matter for anyone's attention; the act of emptying these out is to say nothing is as important, as worthy of attention, as the moment about to come into being. A quick topic sentence ("What does not change/ is the will to change"; "As the dead prey upon us,/ they are the dead in ourselves"), broad enough in application, allows Olson to bring in all manner of materials by logical or intuitive association that somehow fit under its rubric: Meditation upon change (in his early poem "The Kingfishers") leads, first, to a recalled cocktail party conversation that touched upon the passing of the fashion for kingfishers' feathers;

this soon leads Olson to recall Mao Tse-tung's speech upon the success of his revolution; and, a dialectic having now been set up between West (tyrannized by its markets—"fashion"—and associated with a dying civilization) and East (Mao's revolution, source of the rising sun), the poem proceeds to "dance" (a favorite term of Olson's for the poetic act), its details representing East/novelty/uprising in among those representing West/stagnation/descent, in a vocabulary variously encyclopedic, colloquial, hortatory, cybernetic, lyrical, prosaic. It is a collage, then, but one filled with movement, bearing out Olson's dictum "ONE PERCEPTION MUST IMMEDIATELY AND DIRECTLY LEAD TO A FURTHER PERCEPTION." Yet the poem ends: "shall you uncover honey/ where maggots are?// I hunt among stones," and while to one reader this may suggest that the poet's weight is thrown on the side of those details which belong to the "East/novelty/ uprising" sequence, to a reader who bears in mind that *all* these details now are of the past, it suggests that the poet opts for the present/future, which, being as yet all potential, is blank—as a stony landscape.

Ends, however, are only tiny portions of their poems and cannot cancel the keen pleasure a reader may take in tracing meaning among such enigmatically juxtaposed blocks of constantly altering language, while being carried along at such various velocities. There are many striking formulations— often evidently stumbled on in the compositional process, which appears to unfold before the reader's very eyes (and ears); these often appear as good counsel ("In the midst of plenty, walk/ as close to/ bare// In the face of sweetness,/ piss"; "The nets of being/ are only eternal if you sleep as your hands/ ought to be busy"). Syntax—at times so filled with baffles and circumlocutions as to be more properly parataxis—brilliantly evokes the difficulties Olson would name, even court; nouns carry much of the freight, whereas adjectives are scarce (description Olson thought not projective, not able to break the circle of representation); verbs tend to be those of concealment and discovery and of social acts—talking, urging, hearing, permitting, obtaining, and the like. Because his notation favors the phrase over the sentence, in Olson's poetry words can appear to leap from the page, freed significantly of their usual subjections. Although on occasion Olson (an accomplished orator) segues into a Roman kind of rhetoric, for the most part he stays true to his aim, namely, to attack a universe of discourse with a poetry not only of particulars but also particulate in its construction. As indicated earlier, each of these elements helps constitute an intense dialectic whose synthesis occurs only as the abolition of its components: "It is undone business/ I speak of, this morning,/ with the sea/ stretching out/ from my feet."

While Olson's poetry appeared as a number of volumes during his lifetime, these are now contained in two texts: *Maximus Poems* and *Archaeologist of Morning* (containing all of his non-Maximus poems). "Maximus" is the poetic figure Olson created to "speak" poems (sometimes called letters) to the people of Gloucester and, by extension, to any who would be people of "a coherence not even yet new"—persons of that vivid and imminent future which is the Grail to Olson's search and labor. Maximus knows the history of the geography of this seaport and, by extension, of both pre- and post-settlement New England; of the migratory movements of Europe and the ancient world; of other civilizations which, at some (usually early) stage, discovered the will to cohere, which Olson praised. He is to some degree based upon Maximus of Tyre, a maverick sage akin to Apollonius of Tyana from the second century A.D., although Olson appears not to have investigated this historical personage with much thoroughness, preferring, no doubt, not to disturb the introjcctcd Maximus hc was finding so fruitful. The significance of the city of Gloucester in these poems is complex but has to do with a place loved so well that it repays its lover with a battery of guarantees and tokens, enabling him to withstand the greased slide of present culture, the suck of absentee ownership and built-in obsolescence. It is for Olson the place where, in William Wordsworth's terms, he first received those "intimations of immortality" that even in the beleaguered present can solace and hearten. In his attachment to its particulars, his heat for its physical reality, the reader is invited to discover feelings for some actual place or entity akin to that of the poet, thereby to be led to the commitment essential to an awakened sense of life and a practice of person equal "to the real itself."

Other major works

SHORT FICTION: *Stocking Cap: A Story*, 1966.

PLAYS: *The Fiery Hunt and Other Plays*, 1977.

NONFICTION: *Call Me Ishmael: A Study of Melville*, 1947; *Mayan Letters*, 1953; *Projective Verse*, 1959; *Human Universe and Other Essays*, 1965; *Proprioception*, 1965; *Pleistocene Man*, 1968; *Causal Mythology*, 1969; *Letters for "Origin," 1950-1956*, 1969; *The Special View of History*, 1970; *Additional Prose: A Bibliography on America, Proprioception, and Other Notes and Essays*, 1974; *Charles Olson and Ezra Pound: An Encounter at St. Elizabeth's*, 1975; *Charles Olson and Robert Creeley: The Complete Correspondence*, 1980-1983 (five volumes).

MISCELLANEOUS: *Selected Writings of Charles Olson*, 1966; *Poetry and Truth: The Beloit Lectures and Poems*, 1971.

Bibliography
Boer, Charles. *Charles Olson in Connecticut*, 1975.
Butterick, George F. *A Guide to the Maximus Poems of Charles Olson*, 1978.
Byrd, Don. *Charles Olson's Maximus*, 1980.
Charters, Ann. *Olson/Melville: A Study in Affinity*, 1968.
Christensen, Paul. *Charles Olson: Call Him Ishmael*, 1975.

Dawson, Fielding. *The Black Mountain Book*, 1970.
Duberman, Martin. *Black Mountain: An Exploration in Community*, 1972.
Kenner, Hugh. *A Homemade World: The American Modernist Writers*, 1975.
Merrill, Thomas. *The Poetry of Charles Olson: A Primer*, 1982.
Paul, Sherman. *Olson's Push: "Origin," Black Mountain, and Recent American Poetry*, 1978.
Sutton, Walter. *American Free Verse: The Modern Revolution on Poetry*, 1973.
Von Hallberg, Robert. *Charles Olson: The Scholar's Art*, 1978.

David Bromige

F. T. PRINCE

Born: Kimberley, South Africa: September 13, 1912

Principal collections

Poems, 1938; *The Stolen Heart*, 1951; *Soldiers Bathing and Other Poems*, 1954; *The Doors of Stone: Poems, 1938-1962*, 1963; *Memoirs in Oxford*, 1970; *Drypoints of the Hasidim*, 1975; *Afterword on Rupert Brooke*, 1976; *Collected Poems*, 1979 (includes *A Last Attachment*); *The Yüan Chên Variations*, 1981; *Later On*, 1983.

Other literary forms

F. T. Prince has written widely in addition to his poetry. Among his more important publications are *The Italian Element in Milton's Verse* (1954), *William Shakespeare: The Poems* (1963), and *The Study of Form and the Renewal of Poetry* (1964).

Achievements

Equally distinguished as poet and scholar, Prince brings to all of his work a formidable and wide-ranging intellect, an informed compassion, and a remarkable eloquence. In addition, his poetry demonstrates that he has a perfect ear. Never involved in "movements" in the politics of literature, he has sometimes seemed a lonely figure, yet other poets have always been aware of his quality and importance, and his dedication to his craft has been a signal influence on younger writers at times when contemporary work has seemed to have lost its way. A consummate craftsman, at home in free or fixed forms, he is almost unique in being able to place all of his learning at the service of his poetry.

His work has been recognized by the award of honorary doctorates in literature from both the University of Southampton and New York University, and in recent years he has been invited to visit many overseas universities.

Biography

Frank Templeton Prince was born in Kimberley, Cape Province, South Africa, where his father, Henry Prince, was a prosperous businessman in the diamond trade. His mother, Margaret Hetherington Prince, had been a teacher. Both parents were English. Prince was a sensitive and studious child. He already possessed keen powers of observation and an eye for detail which led to an early interest in painting. His mother's influence and the stories and poems she read to Prince and his sister encouraged the boy to write, and he was a poet from the age of fifteen.

After a short period in which he trained as an architect, Prince went to En-

gland in 1931 and entered Balliol College, Oxford. He took a first-class honors degree in English in 1934. It is apparent that the move to Oxford was
both important and inevitable, since the poet's sensibility and culture were almost from the start, strongly European. He went up to Oxford already fluent
in French and deeply read in French poetry. He supported this by reading
Dante in Italian and by making several visits to Italy. He found the whole
period of the Renaissance, and in particular its art, highly congenial.

A meeting with T. S. Eliot in 1934 probably led to the later inclusion of
Prince's first collection, *Poems*, in the Faber and Faber poetry list in 1938.
Eliot recognized Prince's ability as well by printing the younger poet's "An
Epistle to a Patron" in the *Criterion*, which Eliot edited.

During 1934-1935, Prince was a Visiting Fellow at Princeton University,
but he returned to London to work at the Royal Institute of International
Affairs, an unlikely office for so apolitical a man. He was, however, writing,
and a meeting with William Butler Yeats in 1937, when Prince traveled to
Dublin to meet the great man, suggests that poetry held pride of place in his
mind.

There is no acknowledgment in Prince's work at this point that Europe was
on the point of war, but the poet was soon to be personally involved. He was
commissioned into the Intelligence Corps of the British army in 1940, and
sent to Bletchley Park. This was the Government Communications Centre,
hardly a typical army environment. Men were allowed to wear civilian
clothes, discipline was relaxed, and among the creative people involved
there, many were not of the type to worry unduly about military correctness.
The poet Vernon Watkins served there, as did the composer Daniel Jones, a
friend of Dylan Thomas. Prince was at Bletchley Park until March, 1943,
when he was posted to Cairo. Before leaving, he married Elizabeth Bush.
There are two daughters of the marriage.

His time in Egypt, which lasted until 1944, gave Prince the experience
which resulted in the writing of his best-known poem, "Soldiers Bathing."
On his return, Prince spent several months as an interpreter in Italian
prisoner-of-war camps in England before his demobilization.

In 1946, Prince began his academic career, being appointed lecturer in English at the University of Southampton, at that time a small university in an
interesting city, which must have been a pleasant appointment for Prince. In
any event, he stayed there for nearly thirty years, becoming eventually
professor of English and, between 1962 and 1965, dean of the faculty of arts.
It was there, moreover, that he wrote the great bulk of his postwar poetry.
He was a Visiting Fellow of All Souls College, Oxford, in 1968, and Clark
Lecturer at Cambridge in 1972.

His retirement from Southampton was unexpectedly early, but he continued to teach at universities abroad, among them Brandeis University in Boston and Washington University in St. Louis. This period allowed his Ameri-

can admirers, among them John Ashbery, to show their respect for his work and to assist in its dissemination.

Prince continues to have a permanent home in Southampton and, if he travels less frequently, continues to write.

Analysis

The *Collected Poems* of 1979 brought together all the early work from *Poems* and *Soldiers Bathing and Other Poems* which F.T. Prince wanted to retain. He also included the whole of *The Doors of Stone* and four long, late poems, *Memoirs in Oxford*, *Drypoints of the Hasidim*, *Afterword on Rupert Brooke*, and *A Last Attachment*. These poems may be safely considered the work by which Prince would wish to be judged.

The first poem is "An Epistle to a Patron," so admired by Eliot. When one recalls that the great young poet of the day was W.H. Auden and that the most admired poetry then was political and very aware of the contemporary world, Prince's lines are startling.

> My lord, hearing lately of your opulence in promises and your house
> Busy with parasites, of your hands full of favours, your statutes
> Admirable as music, and no fear of your arms not prospering, I have
> Considered how to serve you . . .

The reader is at once in Renaissance Italy, a period much favored by Prince and one in which he is at home. Yet, although the poem is written in the first person, it must not be assumed that the voice is Prince's voice. Rather, the poem is a dramatic monologue. It is not in the manner of Robert Browning either, although it moves in an area Browning sometimes occupied. Its splendid opulence, its sonorous and bewitching periods, are not like Browning. Nor do they hide the slyness, the mockery behind the flattery with which this postulant addresses his hoped-for patron. Ben Jonson could have written it, but it is a strange invention for the late 1930's. And if Prince uses the first person voice, as he does often throughout his career, rarely does he speak as himself—then he is a more everyday speaker altogether—but rather as a real resident of those times and places into which his learning and his curiosity have led him. His manner is courtly and aristocratic. If he uses, as he does in the opening lines of "To a Man on His Horse," a poetic inversion, it is for the dance of the statement, because he wants the movement:

> Only the Arab stallion will I
> Envy you. Along the water
> You dance him with the morning on his flanks . . .

The early work is full of such lines, stately, strangely out of time, full, too, of references to painters such as Paolo Veronese or statesmen such as Edmund Burke. It is a paradox when one realizes that Prince's most famous poem, "Soldiers Bathing," is not at all like the rest of the early work, that it is written about ordinary men, poor, bare, forked animals of the twentieth century. It gave Prince an immediate fame and is known to many readers who know nothing else the poet has written.

"Soldiers Bathing" is a poem of sixty-six lines, organized in six irregular verse paragraphs. The lines are not of regular length, and they rhyme in couplets. In it, the poet, an army officer, watches his men as, forgetting momentarily the stress and mire of war, they swim and play in the sea. It is often a clumsy poem, the longer second line of some of the couplets occasionally dragging along without grace, the structure and movement absurdly prosaic for a poet of Prince's skill. Yet it is intensely moving. The extraordinary syntax of the last line of the first stanza, so written, surely, to accommodate the rhyme, has been noted by many critics, particularly by Vernon Scannell in *Not Without Glory*. "Their flesh worn by the trade of war, revives/ And my mind towards the meaning of it strives." It is also, however, full of marvelous compassion, as Prince, recalling Michelangelo's cartoon of soldiers bathing, is able to unite friend and foe, dead and living soldiers, through his insight into the continuing folly of wars. He does this through his knowledge of art, but his own comfort comes from his religion. Prince is a Catholic, and the reader's understanding of his poetry is incomplete without this knowledge. He arrives at a sad conclusion: "Because to love is frightening we prefer/ The freedom of our crimes." 'He began the poem under "a reddening sky"; he ends it "while in the west/ I watch a streak of blood that might have issued from Christ's breast." This is a typical movement in a poem by Prince, one in which the plain and dissimilar elements are united in an understanding brought about by the poet's belief.

The great popularity of that fine poem tended to overshadow a number of poems which might more surely have suggested the nature and direction of Prince's gift. There were, for example, some love poems of great beauty and passion. He was to develop this ability until, in July, 1963, an anonymous reviewer in *The Times Literary Supplement* could write of Prince that he is "one of the best love poets of the age, a lyricist of great charm and tenderness and emotion, counter-balanced by a subtlety of thought and metaphor which often reminds one of Donne. . . ." The reference to John Donne is felicitous, since there is an affinity in the work of these men, brought into even clearer focus by Prince's liking for and familiarity with the seventeenth century.

The Doors of Stone, then, contains poems of all the categories noted so far; monologues such as "Campanella" and "Strafford," love poems such as the eighteen sections of "Strombotti," poems suggested, like "Coeur de "Lion," by history. They demonstrate once again the curious, elusive quality of Prince's poetry; such dignity, such honesty, even such directness, yet the poet himself remains aloof, often behind masks.

Almost as a rebuff to that opinion, Prince's next book was a long autobiographical poem, *Memoirs in Oxford*. Written in a verse form suggested by the one Percy Bysshe Shelley used in *Peter Bell the Third* (1819), it is at once chatty, clever, and revealing. It is particularly helpful about the poet's early life. It is also a delightful and accomplished poem—and a very brave one. To write a long poem in these days is unusual; to abandon what seems to be one's natural gift for eloquence and adopt a different tone altogether in which to write a long poem might seem foolhardy. Yet it is a very successful poem, having the virtues of clarity, wit, and style as well as some of the attraction of a good novel.

Prince's father was of partly Jewish extraction, which might account for his interest in those "Dark hollow faces under caps/ In days and lands of exile . . . and among unlettered tribes" which figured so strongly in his next long poem, *Drypoints of the Hasidim*. Hasidism was a popular Jewish religious movement of the eighteenth and nineteenth centuries, and Prince's poem is a long meditation on the beliefs of this movement. Despite its learning, it is extremely clear, like all of Prince's poetry. Rarely can there have been a poet so scholarly and knowledgeable whose verse is so accessible.

As if to emphasize his virtuosity, Prince's next work is a verse reconstruction of the life and times of Rupert Brooke, the young and handsome poet whose early death in World War I assured him of fame. Using the information provided by Christopher Hassall in his biography of Brooke, Prince wrote from his own standpoint of "the damned successful poet" and also added, years after his own war, a commentary on youth and love and the ironies of war. The texture of these lines is far removed from the great splendors of the young Frank Prince:

> But Bryn quite blatantly prefers
> Walking alone on Exmoor to the drawing-room
> With the Ranee, and she finds all the girls so odd . . .

It does, however, contain a real feeling of the times, despite occasional prosiness.

Prince has never been afraid of the long poem; even as a young man, he wrote pieces of unusual length for modern times. *A Last Attachment* is based on Laurence Sterne's *Journal to Eliza* (1904). Shorter than the two poems previously noted, it once again considers the recurring problems which are central to Prince's preoccupations: love, the onset of age, an inability to settle and be content, jealousy, the triumphs and failures of the creative and artistic life—all great problems, glanced at, too, in *The Yüan Chên Variations*. They are problems that no doubt beset Prince himself, but he has chosen with dignity and objectivity to consider them most often through a series of characters taken from literature or history or art, rather than use direct personal experience. He has written of them all with elegance and seriousness and with great skill and honesty. His poetry is sometimes said to be unfashionable, and so it is if the word means that he belongs to no group, is determined to be his own man. He has always commanded the respect of his fellow poets, and that, very probably, is a guarantee of his importance and his growing stature.

Other major works

NONFICTION: *The Italian Element in Milton's Verse*, 1954; *William Shakespeare: The Poems*, 1963; *The Study of Form and the Renewal of Poetry*, 1964.

TRANSLATION: *Sir Thomas Wyatt*, 1961 (of Sergio Baldi's biography).

Bibliography

Nigam, Alka. *F. T. Prince: A Study of His Poetry*, 1983.
Scannell, Vernon. *Not Without Glory*, 1976.
The Times Literary Supplement. Review of *The Doors of Stone*. July 26, 1963, p. 557.

Leslie Norris

PIERRE REVERDY

Born: Narbonne, France; September 13, 1889
Died: Solesmes, France; June 17, 1960

Principal poems and collections

Poèmes en prose, 1915; *Quelques poèmes*, 1916; *La Lucarne ovale*, 1916; *Les Ardoises du toit*, 1918 (*Roof Slates*, 1981); *Les Jockeys camouflés*, 1918; *La Guitare endormie*, 1919; *Étoiles peintes*, 1921; *Cœur de chêne*, 1921; *Cravates de chanvre*, 1922; *Grande Nature*, 1925; *La Balle au bond*, 1928; *Sources du vent*, 1929; *Pierres blanches*, 1930; *Ferraille*, 1937; *Plein verre*, 1940; *Plupart du temps*, 1945 (collected volume, 1913-1922); *Le Chant des morts*, 1948; *Main d'œuvre: Poèmes, 1913-1949*, 1949; *Pierre Reverdy: Selected Poems*, 1969; *Roof Slates and Other Poems of Pierre Reverdy*, 1981.

Other literary forms

Pierre Reverdy worked extensively in other forms besides poetry. He wrote two novels and many stories and published collections of prose poems. Most of these are in a Surrealist vein, mixing experimentation in language with personal and unconscious reflection. As an editor of an avant-garde review, Reverdy also contributed important theoretical statements on cubism and avant-garde literary practice. Later in his career, he published several volumes of reminiscences, including sensitive reevaluations of the work of his near contemporaries, including Guillaume Apollinaire.

Achievements

Reverdy is one of the most central and influential writers in the tradition of twentieth century avant-garde poetry. Already well established in terms of both his work and his theoretical stance by the mid-1910's, Reverdy exerted considerable influence over the Dada and Surrealist movements, with which he was both officially and informally affiliated.

Reverdy's firm conviction was in a nonmimetic, nontraditional form of artistic expression. The art he championed and practiced would create a reality of its own rather than mirror a preexisting reality. In this way, the language of poetry would be cut loose from restraining conventions of meter, syntax, and punctuation in order to be able to explore the emotion generated by the poetic image.

In connection with the avant-garde artists of cubism, Dada, and Surrealism, Reverdy's formulations helped to break down the traditional models of artistic creation that then held firm sway in France. Reverdy's firm conviction was that artistic creation precedes aesthetic theory. All the concrete means at an artist's disposal constitute his aesthetic formation.

Along with Apollinaire, his slightly older contemporary, Reverdy became a central figure and example for a whole generation of French poets generally grouped under the Surrealist heading. His having been translated into English by a range of American poets from Kenneth Rexroth to John Ashbery shows the importance of his work to the modern and contemporary American tradition as well.

Biography

Pierre Reverdy was born on September 13, 1889, in Narbonne, France, a city in the Languedoc region. The son and grandson of sculptors and artisans in wood carving, he grew up with this practical skill in addition to his formal studies. The Languedoc region at the turn of the century was an especially volatile region, witnessing the last major peasant uprising in modern French history.

After completing his schooling in Narbonne and nearby Toulouse, Reverdy moved to Paris in 1910, where he lived on and off for the rest of his life. Although exempted from military service, he volunteered at the outbreak of World War I, saw combat service, and was discharged in 1916. By profession a typesetter, Reverdy also worked as the director of the review *Nord-Sud*, which he founded in 1917.

Reverdy worked during the years 1910 to 1926 in close contact with almost all the important artists of his time. He had especially close relationships with Pablo Picasso and Juan Gris, both of whom contributed illustrations to collections of his verse. As the editor of an influential review, he had close contact with and strong influence on the writers who were to form the Dada and Surrealist movements. Already an avant-garde poet and theorist of some prominence by the late 1910's, Reverdy was often invoked along with Apollinaire as one of the precursors of Surrealism. He collaborated with the early Surrealist efforts and continued his loose affiliation even after a formal break in 1926.

That year saw Reverdy's conversion to a mystic Catholicism. From then until his death in 1960, his life became more detached from the quotidian, and he spent much of his time at the Abbey of Solesmes, where he died.

Analysis

In an early statement on cubism, Pierre Reverdy declaimed that a new epoch was beginning, one in which "one creates works that, by detaching themselves from life, enter back into it because they have an existence of their own." In addition to attacking mimetic standards of reproduction, or representation of reality, he also called for a renunciation of punctuation and a freeing of syntax in the writing of poetry. Rather than being something fixed according to rules, for Reverdy, syntax was "a medium of literary creation." Changing the rules of literary expression carried with it a change in ideas of representation. For Reverdy, the poetic image was solely responsible to the discovery of emotional truth.

In the years 1915 to 1922, Reverdy produced many volumes of poetry. The avant-garde called for an overturning of literary conventions, and Reverdy contributed with his own explosion of creative activity. In addition to editing the influential review *Nord-Sud*, he used his experience as an engraver and typesetter to publish books, including his own. The list of artists who contributed the illustrations to these volumes of poetry by Reverdy reads like a Who's Who of the art world of the time: Juan Gris, Pablo Picasso, André Derain, Henri Matisse, Georges Braques, among others. Reverdy's work, along with that of Apollinaire, was cited as the guiding force for Surrealism by André Breton in the *Manifestes du surréalisme* (1962; *Manifestoes of Surrealism*, 1969).

Reverdy's early work achieves an extreme detachment from mimetic standards and literary conventions that allows for the images to stand forth as though seen shockingly for the first time. The last two lines from "Sur le Talus" (on the talus), published in 1918, show this extreme detachment: "L'eau monte comme une poussière/ Le silence ferme la nuit" (The water rises like dust/ Silence shuts the night). There can be no question here of establishing a realistic context for these images. Rather, one is cast back on the weight of emotion that they carry and which must thus guide their interpretation. Reflections off water may appear to rise in various settings, though perhaps particularly at twilight. The dust points to a particular kind of aridity that may be primarily an emotional state. The sudden transition from an (implied) twilight to an abrupt nightfall undercuts any kind of conventional emotional presentation. The quick cut is a measure perhaps of the individual's lack of control over external phenomena and, by extension, inner feelings as well.

Much of Reverdy's early work is based on just such an imagistic depiction of interior states, with a strong element of detachment from reality and a certain resulting confusion or overlapping. The force of emotion is clearly there, but to pin it down to a particular situation or persona proves difficult because any such certainty is constantly being undercut by the quick transitions between images. The complete suppression of punctuation as well as a certain freedom of syntax as one moves from line to line are clearly tools that Reverdy developed to increase the level of logical disjunction in his poetry. At times, however, this disjunction in the logical progression of word and image gives way to a resolution. The short poem "Carrefour" (crossroad) sets up a surrealizing image sequence:

> De l'air
> De la lumière
> Un rayon sur le bord du verre
> Ma main déçue n'attrape rien

(Air
                          Light
              A ray on the edge of the glass
              My disappointed hand holds nothing)

Here the elements are invoked, and then two images, one of an inanimate object and one the hand of the speaker. From this atmosphere of mystery and disjunction, the poem's conclusion moves to a fairly well-defined emotional statement:

> Enfin tout seul j'aurai vécu
> Jusqu'au dernier matin
>
> Sans qu'un mot m'indiquât quel fut le bon chemin
>
> (After all I will have lived all alone
> Until the last morning
>
> Without a single word that might have shown me
>   which was the right way)

Here, as in many of Reverdy's poems, the emotion evoked is a kind of diffused sadness. The solitary individual is probably meant to stand for an aspect of the human condition, alone in a confrontation with an unknown destiny.

It was Reverdy's fate to see actual military duty during World War I, and it may well be that the magnitude of human tragedy he witnessed at the front lines served to mute the youthful enthusiasm that pervades his earliest works. It may also be the case that Reverdy, while espousing radical measures in literary practice, still was caught in the kind of bittersweet ethos that characterizes *fin de siècle* writers generally. Whatever the case may be, there is no question that Reverdy wrote some of the most affecting war poems in the French language. One of the most direct is entitled simply "Guerre" (war). Running through a series of disjointed, if coherent, images, Reverdy toward the end of the poem approaches direct statement, when the speaker says:

> Et la figure attristée
> Visage des visages
> La mort passe sur le chemin
>
> (And the saddened figure
> Visage of visages
> Death passes along the road)

Close to a medieval allegorizing of death, this figure also incorporates a fascination with the effect of the gaze. One's face is revealing of one's emotion because of the way one looks—the distillation of the phenomenon into a general characteristic is a strong term to describe death. If this image is strong, the poem's ending is more forceful still:

> Mais quel autre poids que celui de ton corps
> as-tu jeté dans la balance
> Tout froid dans le fossé
> Il dort sans plus rêver

> (But what other weight than that of your body
> have you thrown in the balance
> All cold in the ditch
> He sleeps no longer to dream)

Philosophers have questioned whether the idea of death is properly an idea, since strictly speaking it has no content. Caught between viewing another's death from the outside and facing one's own death, which one can never know, death is a supreme mystery of human existence. Reverdy in these lines seems to cross the line between the exterior, objective view of another's death and the unknowable, subjective experience of the individual. This is what he means by the emotion communicated through the poetic image.

Despite a continued tendency toward the surrealizing image in Reverdy's work, these poems in *Sources du vent* (sources of the wind) also represent the first major collection of poems after Reverdy's conversion to a mystic Catholicism in 1926. Increasingly, his poetry of the post-conversion period tends toward an introjection of the conflicts raised through the poetic image. While a tone of lingering sadness had always been present from the earliest work, in these poems the atmosphere of sadness and loss moves to the center of the poet's concerns. Unlike the conservative Christian poets Charles Péguy and Paul Claudel, the content of the poems is never directly religious. Rather, a mood of quietism seems to become more prominent in the collections of poems after the conversion. A concurrent falling off in the level of production also takes place. After 1930, Reverdy publishes only two more individual collections of verse, along with two collected volumes and works in other forms. After 1949, for the last twelve years of his life, the heretofore prolific Reverdy apparently ceased to write altogether.

The poem "Mémoire" (memory) from *Pierres blanches* (white stones), shows this mood of increasing resignation in the face of worldly events. The poem invokes a "she," someone who has left or is going to leave, but then, in apparent reference to the title, says there will still be someone:

> Quand nous serons partis là-bas derrière
> Il y aura encore ici quelqu'un
> Pour nous attendre
> Et nous entendre

> (When we will have gone over there behind
> There will still be someone
> To wait for us
> And to understand us)

The positive mood of these lines, however, is undercut by the poem's ending: "Un seul ami/ L'ombre que nous avons laissée sous l'arbre et qui s'ennuie" (A single friend/ The shadow we have left beneath a tree and who's getting bored"). The impersonality tending toward a universal statement that was present in Reverdy's early work here seems to work toward an effacement of the individual personality. If memory can be imaged as a bored shadow left beneath a tree, the significance of the individual seems tenuous at best. The emotion generated through the poetic image here seems to be one of sadness and extreme resignation.

The interpretation of a poet's work through biography must always be a hazy enterprise, all the more so in a poet such as Reverdy, whose life directly enters into his work not at all. In a general sense, then, the course of his poetic life and production might be said to mirror the course of French literary life generally. The enthusiasm of the avant-garde literary and artistic movements in Europe generally in the early years of the twentieth century saw a counterswing in the post–World War I years toward an art that questioned societal assumptions. Dada and Surrealism can be seen in terms of this large movement, and Reverdy's work as an example. The coherence of the Surrealist movement in turn breaks down in the late 1920's and early 1930's with the split coming over what political allegiance the Surrealist artists should take, according to its leaders. Reverdy's personal religious convictions cause him to cease active involvement with the movement altogether. It is a measure of his status as a strong precursor to the movement that he is not attacked directly by the more politically motivated leaders of Surrealism.

With the extreme politization of the Surrealist movement in the late 1930's, even some of the most dedicated younger adherents to Surrealism cut their formalities with the movement. René Char is an example. The young Yves Bonnefoy is an example of a poet with early leanings toward Surrealism who in the late 1940's moved more in the direction of a poetry expressive of essential philosophical and human truths. It might be possible, in like manner, to trace Reverdy's increasing distance from Surrealism as a movement to some kind of similar feelings that have been more openly expressed by his younger contemporaries. His collection *Plein Verre* (full glass) does indeed move more toward the mode of longer, contemplative poems, still in the atmosphere of sadness and resignation to life. The end of "Main-Morte" (dead-hand) shows this well:

> Entre l'aveu confus et le lien du mystère
> Les mots silencieux qui tendent leur filet

Dans tous les coins de cette chambre noire
Où ton ombre ni moi n'aurons jamais dormi

(Between the confused vow and the tie of mystery
The silent words which offer their net
In every corner of this black room
Where your shadow nor I will have ever slept)

Even the highly suggestive early lyrics do not contain quite the level of hovering mystery and intricate emotional states offered in these lines. One may well wonder if the "you" invoked here even refers to a person or whether it might be a quasi-human interior presence such as that invoked in the later poems of Wallace Stevens (such as "Final Soliloquy of the Interior Paramour"). The weight of the images in the direction of silence lends to this whole utterance an aura of high seriousness.

The last poem of the same collection, entitled "Enfin" (at last), also ends with a statement hinting at a highly serious attitude. The speaker states:

À travers la poitrine nue
Là
Ma clarière
Avec tout ce qui descend du ciel
Devenir un autre
À ras de terre

(By means of the naked breast
There
My clearing
Along with all that descends from the sky
To become an other
At earth level)

More and more in the later poems, a level of ethical statement seems to emerge. Whereas the early poems introduce strange and startling images in an apparently almost random fashion, the images here seem to be coordinated by an overall hierarchy of values, personal and religious. The naked breast at the beginning of this passage thus could refer to the lone individual, perhaps alone with his or her conscience. This is in contrast to something which descends from the sky, an almost unavoidably religious image. The wish "To become an other/ At earth level" might then be interpreted as the fervent desire of an extremely devoted individual to attain a higher level of piety here on earth.

The extended sequence, *Le Chant des morts* (the song of the dead), composed in 1944-1948 and published in 1948 as part of the collected volume *Main d'œuvre* (work made by hand), presents an extended meditation on the emotional inner scene of war-devastated France. Like he did in his earlier poems on World War I that drew on his direct experience of the horrors of war, Reverdy in this sequence utilizes a diction stripped bare of rhetoric, preferring instead the direct, poignant images of death and suffering. Death in these poems is both inescapable and horrible, or as he calls it: "la mort entêtée/ La mort vorace" ("stubborn death/ Voracious death"). As a strong countermovement to the implacable march of death, there is also a tenacious clinging to life. As the poet says: "C'est la faim/ C'est l'ardeur de vivre qui dirigent/ La peur de perdre" ("It is hunger/ It is the ardor to live that guide/ The fear of losing"). The poet of the inner conscience in these poems confronts the essential subject of his deepest meditations: the conscious adoption of his authentic attitude toward death.

The ultimate renunciation of poetry that characterizes the last years of Reverdy's life is preceded by an exploration of the subject most suited to representing death (remembering Sigmund Freud): that is, silence. The poem that Reverdy seems to have chosen to come at the end of his collected poems, entitled "Et Maintenant" (and now), ends with a poignant image of silence: "Tous les fils dénoués au delà des saisons reprennent leur tour et leur ton sur le fond sombre du silence" ("All the unknotted threads beyond the seasons regain their trace and their tone against the somber background of silence"). Reverdy here seems to hint at what lies beyond poetic expression in several senses. His entire ethos of poetic creation has been consistently based on an act of communication with the reader. Thus, the threads he refers to here could well represent the threads of intention and emotion that his readers follow in his poetry in order to achieve an experience of that emotion themselves, or to discover an analogous emotional experience in their own memory or personal background. He might also be hinting at those threads of intention and emotion that led beyond the limitations of individual life in a reunification with a divine creator. In the former interpretation, the background of silence would be that silence which precedes the poetic utterance or act of communication, as well as the silence after the act of communication or once the poet has ceased to write. In the religious interpretation, the background of silence would be that nothingness or nonbeing out of which the divine creation takes place and which, in turn, has the capability of incorporating silence or nonbeing into self, a religious attitude of a return to the creator even in the face of one's own personal death.

Reverdy is a complex and fascinating figure in the history of French poetry in the first half of the twentieth century. He was a committed avant-garde artist in the years directly preceding, during, and following World War I; his outpouring of poetry and aesthetic statements made him one of the most significant precursors to the movements of Dada and Surrealism. Though his formal affiliation with the Surrealist movement was of brief duration, his example of using the poetic image to communicate emotion is central to everything for which Surrealism stood. The extreme respect shown to his work by other poets and artists confirms his importance as a creative innovator. Reverdy, in turn, paid respectful homage to his poet and artist contemporaries a stance that shows his ongoing intellectual commitment to the importance of art and literature in human terms, despite his personal isolation and quietism toward the end of his life. The poems from the end of his career that bear the weight of a continued meditation on death are a moving commentary on that from which language emerges and into which it returns: silence.

Other major works

NOVELS: *Le Voleur de Talan*, 1917; *La Peau de l'homme*, 1926.

SHORT FICTION: *Risques et périls*, 1930.

NONFICTION: *Self Defence*, 1919; *Le Gant de crin*, 1927; *Le Livre de mon bord*, 1948; *Note éternelle du présent*, 1975; *Nord-Sud, Self Defence, et autres écrits sur l'art et la poésie*, 1975; *Cette émotion appellée poésie: Écrits sur la poésie, 1932-1960*, 1975.

Bibliography

Greene, Robert W. *The Poetic Theory of Pierre Reverdy*, 1967.

Guiney, Mortimer. *La Poésie de Pierre Reverdy*, 1966.

Rizzuto, Anthony. *Style and Theme in Reverdy's "Les Ardoises du toit,"* 1971.

Schroeder, Jean. *Pierre Reverdy*, 1981.

Peter Baker

MURIEL RUKEYSER

Born: New York, New York; December 15, 1913
Died: New York, New York; February 12, 1980

Principal collections

Theory of Flight, 1935; *U.S. 1*, 1938; *A Turning Wind: Poems*, 1939; *Beast in View*, 1944; *The Green Wave*, 1948; *Elegies*, 1949; *Selected Poems*, 1951; *Body of Waking*, 1958; *Waterlily Fire: Poems 1935-1962*, 1962; *The Speed of Darkness*, 1968; *Twenty-nine Poems*, 1970; *Breaking Open*, 1973; *The Gates: Poems*, 1976; *The Collected Poems of Muriel Rukeyser*, 1979.

Other literary forms

In addition to her own poetry, Muriel Rukeyser published several volumes of translations (including work by the poets Octavio Paz and Gunnar Ekelöf), three biographies, two volumes of literary criticism, a number of book reviews, a novel, five juvenile books, and a play. She also worked on several documentary film scripts. The translations were exercises in writing during dry spells; the biographies, like her poetic sequence "Lives," combine her interests in the arts and sciences. The two volumes of literary criticism (along with her uncollected book reviews) are central for understanding her views concerning poetry and life.

Achievements

With the publication of *Theory of Flight* in the Yale Series of Younger Poets in 1935, Rukeyser began a long and productive career as a poet and author. Her work also earned for her the first Harriet Monroe Poetry Award (1941), a Guggenheim Fellowship (1943), the Copernicus Award and Shelley Memorial Award (1977), an honorary D.Litt. from Rutgers, and membership in the National Institute of Arts and Letters. She also won the Swedish Academy Translation Award (1967) and the Anglo-Swedish Literary Foundation Award (1978) for her translations.

While Rukeyser has been linked to W. H. Auden, Stephen Spender, and other political poets, her work more clearly evolves from that of Ralph Waldo Emerson, Herman Melville, and Walt Whitman. From Emerson and the Transcendental tradition, she developed her organic theory of poetry, from Melville, her poetry of outrage. From Whitman, however, she obtained perhaps her most distinguishing characteristics: her belief in possibility, her long, rhythmic lines, her need to embrace humanity, and her expression of the power and beauty of sexuality. Her feminist views link her also with Denise Levertov and Adrienne Rich, while her experimentation with the poetic line and the visual appearance of the poem on the page remind one at times of May Swenson.

Although Rukeyser's work has been relatively well regarded, she has received little critical attention. Yet the quality and quantity of her work and the integrity of her feminist and mythic vision suggest that she will come to be seen as a significant figure in modern American poetry.

Biography

Muriel Rukeyser was born on December 15, 1913, in New York City, the daughter of Lawrence B. Rukeyser, a cofounder of Colonial Sand and Stone, and Myra Lyons, a former bookkeeper. Her childhood was a quiet one, her protected, affluent life a source of her insistence on experience and communication in her poetry. In *The Life of Poetry* (1949), she tells of recognizing the sheltered nature of her life: "A teacher asks: 'How many of you know any other road in the city except the road between home and school?' I do not put up my hand. These are moments at which one begins to see."

Rukeyser's adult life was as eventful as her childhood was sheltered. In 1933, at age nineteen, she was arrested and caught typhoid fever while attending the Scottsboro trials in Alabama; three years later, she investigated at firsthand the mining tragedy at Gauley Bridge, West Virginia; and in 1936, she was sent by *Life and Letters Today* to cover the Anti-Fascist Olympics in Barcelona as the Spanish Civil War broke out around her. These crusades dramatize her intense conviction in the sanctity of human life and her desire to experience life actively, and they all served as inspiration for her poetry, fulfilling her declaration in "Poem out of Childhood" to "Breathe-in experience, breathe-out poetry."

Throughout the remainder of a life filled with traveling and speaking for causes in which she intensely believed, Rukeyser never stopped learning, teaching, and writing; she declared that she would never protest without making something in the process. The wide range of knowledge in her poetry and criticism and the large volume of poetry and prose she published testify to this fact. She attended the Ethical Culture School and Fieldston School, Vassar College, Columbia University, and the Roosevelt School of Aviation in New York City, and she learned film editing with Helen Van Dongen. Besides conducting poetry workshops at a number of different institutions, she taught at the California Labor School and Sarah Lawrence College and later served as a member of the board of directors of the Teachers-Writers Collaborative in New York.

Rukeyser made her home in New York City, except for the nine years she spent in California and the times she was traveling. She moved to California in 1945 and shortly afterward married painter Glynn Collins (although the marriage was soon annulled). Three years later, she had an illegitimate son and was disowned by her family, experiences which figure prominently in her poetry after this date. She moved back to New York in 1954 to teach at Sarah Lawrence College.

Rukeyser left Sarah Lawrence College in 1967. Although in failing health, she continued to write and protest. For the Committee for Solidarity, she flew to Hanoi in 1972 to demonstrate for peace, and later that year she was jailed in Washington, D.C., for protesting the Vietnam War on the steps of the Capitol. In 1974, as president of the American center for PEN, a society that supports the rights of writers throughout the world, she flew to Korea to plead for the life of imprisoned poet Kim Chi-Ha. Rukeyser died in New York City on February 12, 1980.

Analysis

"Look! Be : leap," Muriel Rukeyser writes in the preamble to the title poem of her first collection, *Theory of Flight*. These imperatives identify her emphasis on vision, her insistence on primary experience, and her belief in human potential. Focusing on this dictum, Rukeyser presents to her readers "the truths of outrage and the truths of possibility" in the world. To Rukeyser, poetry is a way to learn more about oneself and one's relations with others and to live more fully in an imperfect world.

The publication of *Theory of Flight* immediately marked Rukeyser as, in Stephen Vincent Benét's words, "a Left Winger and a revolutionary," an epithet she could never quite shake although the Marxists never fully accepted her for not becoming a Communist and for writing poems that tried to do more than simply support their cause. Indeed, Rukeyser did much more than write Marxist poems. She was a poet of liberty, recording "the truths of outrage" she saw around her, and a poet of love, writing "the truths of possibility" in intimate human relationships. With the conviction of Akiba (a Jewish teacher and martyr who fought to include the Song of Songs in the Bible and from whom, according to family tradition, Rukeyser's mother was descended), Rukeyser wrote with equal fervor about social and humane issues such as miners dying of silicosis, the rights of minorities, the lives of women and imprisoned poets, and about universals such as the need for love and communication among people and the sheer physical and emotional joy of loving.

Unlike many political poets, Rukeyser tried to do more than simply espouse: to protect, but also to build, to create. For Rukeyser, poetry's purpose is to sustain and heal, and the poet's responsibility is to recognize life as it is and encourage all people to their greatest potential through poetry.

Refusing to accept the negation of T. S. Eliot's *The Waste Land* (1922), Rukeyser uses images of technology and energy extensively in her early volumes to find, in a positive way, a place for the self in modern technological society, thus identifying herself with Hart Crane and with the poets of the Dynamo school. "Theory of Flight" centers on the airplane and the gyroscope. The dam and the power plant become the predominant symbols in "The Book of the Dead," in *U.S. 1*, her next collection.

U.S. 1 also contains a series of shorter, more lyrical poems entitled "Night-Music." While these poems are still strongly social in content, they are more personal and are based on what Rukeyser refers to as "unverifiable fact" (as opposed to the documentary evidence in "Theory of Flight" and "The Book of the Dead"). This change foreshadows the shifting emphasis throughout her career on the sources of power about which she writes—from machinery to poetry to the self. It is this change in conception that allowed Rukeyser to grow poetically, to use fewer of the abstractions for which many critics have faulted her, and to use instead more personal and concrete images on which to anchor her message.

This movement is evident in *A Turning Wind*. She begins to see the power and the accompanying fear of poetry, and her poetic voice becomes increasingly personal, increasingly founded in personal experience. Poetry becomes the means, the language, and the result of looking for connections or, in Jungian terms, a kind of collective unconscious. Rukeyser notices, however, that poetry is feared precisely because of its power: "They fear it. They turn away, hand up palm out/ fending off moment of proof, the straight look, poem." The fear of poetry is a fear of disclosure to oneself of what is inside, and this fear is "an indication that we are cut off from our own reality." Therefore, Rukeyser continually urges her readers to use poetry to look within themselves for a common ground on which they can stand as human beings.

The poetic sequence "Lives" (which extends through subsequent volumes as well) identifies another of Rukeyser's growing interests—"ways of getting past impossibilities by changing phase." Poetry thus becomes a meeting place of different ideas and disciplines. It is a place where the self meets the self, diving to confront unchallenged emotions in the search for truth, and a place where the self can face the world with newly discovered self-knowledge. Using the resources they discover both inside and outside themselves, people can grow to understand themselves and the world better. The subjects of the "Lives" exemplify values and traditions Rukeyser believes important to the search.

Rukeyser's growth as a person and as a poet, then, has been a growth of the self, realizing her capabilities and her potential and, in turn, the capabilities and potential of those around her. She becomes increasingly open in her later poems, discussing her failed marriage, her illegitimate son and subsequent disinheritance, her son's exile in Canada during the Vietnam War, and her feelings about age and death. Yet while these poems may seem confessional, she is not a confessional poet such as Robert Lowell or W. D. Snodgrass. The details of her life, she tells the reader, are events she must consider from various angles as she dives within herself as Adrienne Rich goes "Diving into the Wreck," looking for the essence of being. "The universe of poetry is the universe of emotional truth," Rukeyser writes in her

critical work *The Life of Poetry*, and it is the "breaking open" of her precon-
ceived emotions to discover emotional truth that allows her to become closer
to the humanity around her. "One writes in order to feel," she continues.
"That is the fundamental mover."

In "Ajanta," Rukeyser makes perhaps her first statement of inner emotional truth according to poet-critic Virginia R. Terris. In this mythic journey
within the self, Rukeyser realizes that self-knowledge is the prerequisite for
all other kinds of knowledge.

Yet behind her search for self-knowledge and expansion of the self into the
world is her belief in the necessity of communication. The silence she experienced at home as a child had a profound effect on her, and in many early poems, such as "Effort at Speech Between Two People," communication is ultimately impossible. This same silence appears to be at the root of many of the
world's problems, and Rukeyser's open outrage and inner searching are attempts to right the problem, to achieve communication. By the time she
wrote "Ajanta," silence had become a positive force, allowing her the opportunity to concentrate on her journey within.

Rukeyser has at times been criticized for combining disparate images
within the same poem, as in "Waterlily Fire," from her collection by the same
name, but this seems unjust. Far from being unrelated elements, her images
grow, change, and develop throughout a poem and throughout her poetic
canon. She puts the responsibility of making connections on the reader; she
gives clues but does not take all the work out of the poem: "Both artist and
audience create, and both do work on themselves in creating." Rukeyser is
not an easy poet, and one cannot read her poetry passively. Yet she is a re-
warding poet for those who take the time to look at and listen to what she is
doing.

Another distinguishing mark of Rukeyser's poetry is the numerous poetic
sequences (such as "Lives") which are connected by a common situation,
theme, or character.

"Waterlily Fire," for example, is a group of five poems about the burning
of Claude Monet's *Waterlilies* at the Museum of Modern Art in New York
City. "Elegies" is a collection of ten poems extending over three volumes.
"Poem out of Childhood" is a cluster of fifteen poems, of which one is also a
cluster of three, centered on Rukeyser's childhood—what she learns from it
and how she uses it poetically.

Rukeyser's interest in poetic sequences grew from her training as a film
editor:

> The work with film is a terribly good exercise for poetry . . . the concept of sequences, the
> cutting of sequences of varying length, the frame by frame composition, the use of a trav-
> eling image, traveling by the way the film is cut, shot, projected at a set speed, a sound
> track or a silent track, in conjunction with the visual track but can be brought into bad
> descriptive verbal things and brought into marvelous juxtapositions.

The sequence makes more apparent to readers the necessity of looking for connections among poems—recurring images, phrases, and sounds—than could separate poems.

In *The Speed of Darkness*, Rukeyser returns to her preoccupation with silence, expressing it both structurally in and as a subject. From her earliest poems, she used space within lines (often combined with a proliferation of colons) to act as a new type of punctuation—a metric rest—but in *The Speed of Darkness*, she places greater emphasis on the placement of the poem on the page to achieve this metric rest, for space on the page "can provide roughly for a relationship in emphasis through the eye's discernment of pattern."

Rukeyser's verse has often been characterized as half-poetry half-prose because of the long, sweeping, encompassing, Whitmanesque free-verse lines especially noticeable in her early poems. In *The Speed of Darkness* and later poems, however, she moves toward shorter lines and works with smaller units of meaning in order to compensate for breathing. At times, her arrangement of these poems ("The War Comes into My Room," "Mountain: One from Bryant," and "Rune," for example) approaches Swenson's iconographs in their experimentation with the visual and physical movement of the line.

Perhaps another reason for the new, shorter lines is that they are more suited for the introspective journeys of Rukeyser's later work than are the long, flowing, altruistic lines she used earlier. They also help her to control more effectively her penchant for verbosity and maintain the development of her images. Yet the length and conclusion of the later lines are not without precedent. Many of the most powerful passages in the early poems were journalistic or cinematic passages, not yet matured but still effective in their performance. "The Book of the Dead" is especially noteworthy in this respect, for it contains the seeds of the concrete image and colloquial diction fully realized later.

Rukeyser's diction also gives ample reason for labeling her poetry half-prose. Yet as startling as it may be to encounter words such as "eugenically," "silicosis," and "cantillations" in her poems, these words make the reader pay attention. She also employs words and even sounds as physical, musical, and thematic ties within and among poems in the same way other poets use rhyme and in the same way she uses image sequences.

With the variety of line length and placement evident in Rukeyser's work, it is not surprising that her canon is characterized by a rich variety of styles. Her experiments with language, line length, and rhythm easily lend themselves to experiments with different verse styles, including but extending beyond elegies, sonnets, odes, rounds, and rondels.

While she uses traditional as well as nontraditional verse patterns, she often treats even her most traditional subjects untraditionally. Because of her belief in the community of humankind, she has written many love poems, yet she approaches even the most personal subjects in an unexpected way. A notable example is "Letter, Unposted" from *Theory of Flight*, which is centered on the traditional theme of waiting for a lover. Yet it is distinguished from other such poems by the speaker's refusal to languish in love and to see nature languishing along with her. The letter remains unposted because the speaker cannot write all the traditional sentimental foolishness expected of her. Instead, as in even the bleakest situations about which Rukeyser writes, she sees the positive side: "But summer lives,/ and minds grow, and nerves are sensitized to power. . . and I receive them joyfully and live : but wait for you." The speaker rejoices in life rather than feeling sorry for herself.

Although a feminine consciousness is evident in every volume of Rukeyser's poetry, *The Speed of Darkness* also begins a new and more imperative feminist outlook. In the same way that she refused to be simply a Marxist poet, she is not simply a feminist poet. Rukeyser sees with a feminist point of view, but rather than rejecting the masculine, she retains valuable past information and revisualizes history and myth with female vitality. For example, in "Myth," one learns that Oedipus was not as smart as he thought he was; he did not answer the Sphinx's riddle correctly after all: " 'You didn't say anything about woman.'/ 'When you say Man,' said Oedipus, 'you include women/ too. Everyone knows that.' She said, 'That's what/ you think.' " "Ms. Lot" adds another perspective to the Biblical story of Lot and his wife, and in "Painters" (from *The Gates*) she envisions a woman among the primitive cave painters.

Other poems written throughout her career on more contemporary issues reveal the strength of women while upholding their nurturing role. The mother in "Absalom" (from "The Book of the Dead") will "give a mouth to my son" who died of silicosis, and Kim Chi-Ha's mother in "The Gates" is portrayed as a pitchfork, one of Rukeyser's few uses of simile or metaphor. She also refuses to let women take the easy way out as some have been trained to do: "More of a Corpse than a Woman" and "Gradus Ad Parnassum," for example, display the vapidity of the stereotypical passive rich woman.

Yet while women are strong in Rukeyser's verse, they are still human. Sex is one of the driving forces in her work, and she frequently expresses the joys of love and sex, especially in *Breaking Open*. Significant examples are the powerful eroticism of "Looking at Each Other," the honesty of "In Her Burning" and "Rondel," and the power of sexual renewal in "Welcome from War." Giving birth is also a powerful image in many of the poems.

"The Gates," a fifteen-poem sequence organized around Rukeyser's trip to Korea to plead for the release of imprisoned poet Kim Chi-Ha, synthesizes her recurring images and messages in a final, powerful poetic statement. Like "Night-Music," this sequence is at once social commentary and personal discovery, but it takes a much stronger stance in demanding freedom of speech and assessing Rukeyser's own development as a poet in the light of Kim Chi-Ha's life.

"Breathe-in experience, breathe-out poetry" begins "Poem out of Childhood," the first poem in Rukeyser's first collection. Muriel Rukeyser wrote a poetry developing organically from personal experience and self-discovery, a poetry bringing the anguishes, miseries, and misfortunes of human beings around the world to her readers' attention, a poetry demonstrating her exhilaration with life and love. Readers cannot hide from reality in her poetry, nor can they hide from themselves. There is always the journey, but possibility always lies at its end: "the green tree perishes and green trees grow." Rukeyser's challenge to the world she left behind is found near the end of "Then" (in "The Gates"): "When I am dead, even then,/ I will still love you, I will wait in these poems . . . I will still be making poems for you/ out of silence." The silence and passivity against which she fought throughout her life will not triumph if her readers are alive to her words and to the world around them.

Other major works

NOVEL: *The Orgy*, 1965.

PLAY: *The Color of the Day: A Celebration for the Vassar Centennial, June 10, 1961*, 1961.

NONFICTION: *Willard Gibbs*, 1942; *The Life of Poetry*, 1949; *One Life*, 1957; *Poetry and the Unverifiable Fact: The Clark Lectures*, 1968; *The Traces of Thomas Hariot*, 1971.

CHILDREN'S LITERATURE: *Come Back, Paul*, 1955; *I Go Out*, 1961; *Bubbles*, 1967; *Mayes*, 1970; *More Night*, 1981.

TRANSLATIONS: *Selected Poems of Octavio Paz*, 1963; *Sun Stone*, 1963 (of Paz's poems); *Selected Poems of Gunnar Ekelöf*, 1967; *Three Poems by Gunnar Ekelöf*, 1967; *Early Poems, 1935-1955*, 1973 (of Paz's poems); *Brecht's Uncle Eddie's Moustache*, 1974; *A Mölna Elegy*, 1984 (of Ekelöf's poem).

Bibliography

DuPlessis, Rachel Blau. "Lyric Documents: The Critique of Personal Consciousness in Levertov, Rich, and Rukeyser," in *Feminist Studies*. III (1975), pp. 65-80.

Kertesz, Louise. *The Poetic Vision of Muriel Rukeyser*, 1979.

Packard, William. "Craft Interview with Muriel Rukeyser," in *The Craft of Poetry*, 1974. Edited by William Packard.

Rosenthal, M. L. "Muriel Rukeyser: The Longer Poems," in *New Directions in Prose and Poetry*, 1953. Edited by James Laughlin.

Kenneth E. Gadomski

JALAL AL-DIN RUMI

Born: Balkh; c. September 30, 1207
Died: Konya, Asia Minor; December 17, 1273

Principal poems and collections

Masnavi-ye Ma'navi, early thirteenth century (*The Mathnavī of Jalālu'ddīn Rūmī*, 1925-1940); *Divan-e Shams-e Tabriz*, early thirteenth century (*Selected Poems from the Dīvanī Shamsi Tabrīz*, 1898); *Mystical Poems of Rūmī*, 1968.

Other literary forms

Among Jalal al-Din Rumi's prose works, a collection of transcribed talks entitled *Fīhi mā fīhi* (*Discourses of Rumi*, 1961) deserves special mention. While in its spiritual messages and reflections this book is not any less dense and subtle than the *Masnavi-ye Ma'navi*, its free and informal prose style— in its original Persian as well as in the English translation by A. J. Arberry (1961)—provides a suitable introduction to the poet's teachings. A book of correspondences (*Maktubāt*) and a collection of seven sermons (*Majāles-e Sab'a*) are also attributed to Rumi.

Achievements

Speaking of Rumi and his *Masnavi-ye Ma'navi*, the well-known fourteenth century Persian Sufi poet Jami said, "He is not a prophet and yet he has given us a Holy Book." The British Orientalist R. A. Nicholson, after having devoted much of his life to the study and translation of Rumi's works, wrote, "Today the words I applied to the author of the *Mathnawi* thirty-five years ago, 'the greatest mystical poet of any age,' seems to me no more than just. Where else shall we find such panorama of universal existence unrolling itself through Time and Eternity?" More recently, the American author and psychoanalyst Erich Fromm praised Rumi as "a man of profound insight into the nature of man."

These are but a few examples of countless tributes bestowed upon the venerated Persian poet, who is also well-known for having laid the foundations of what came to be known as the Order of Whirling Dervishes. All the same, Rumi himself made no claims to any poetic accomplishments. Of writing poetry he once said, "I do it for the sake of these people who come to see me and hope that I'd gladden their hearts a little bit. So I recite a poem or two for them. Otherwise what do I care for poetry?" (*Discourses of Rumi*). This was no false modesty but the expression of the genuine feeling of a man who wanted, first and foremost, to unburden his listeners and readers of the sorrow that comes with ignorance and to awaken them to what Søren Kierkegaard called "possibility of life." In the long run, Rumi's greatest achievement has been just that—at least in the case of those readers who have found him, in the words of the celebrated Urdu and Persian poet Muhammad Iqbal, an opener of the doors: "What do I need of logicians' long polemics or professors' tedious lectures/ When a couple of lines from Rumi or Jami open the closed doors?"

A Rumi revival seems to have started, even if on a small scale, in America, and poets such as Robert Bly, Jack Marshall, and W. S. Merwin have produced modern renditions of some of the Persian poet's works.

Biography

Jalal al-Din Rumi, also known as Maulānā (our master), was born on or near September 30, 1207, in the city of Balkh (in modern northern Afghanistan). When he was five years old and shortly before the onset of the Mongol invasion, his father, who was a religious scholar of renown, left his native land in the company of his family and, traveling westward, finally settled in Konya, a city of Asia Minor (modern Turkey). After his father's death, Jalal al-Din Rumi succeeded him as a religious leader and scholar and soon gathered a large following.

The arrival in Konya of the wandering dervish Shams-e Tabrizi was an event of radical consequence in Rumi's life. The details of the meeting between the two are rather sketchy and at times contradictory. The account which seems to be more reliable than others belongs to the chronicler Dowlatshāhi and can be summarized as follows. One day, the peripatetic Shams—who, in search of a kindred soul, had arrived in Konya and had taken lodgings in the Caravansarai of Sugar Merchants—saw a man riding on a mule while his disciples followed him on foot. The man was Rumi, who after the death of his father had become Konya's most distinguished religious scholar, enjoying a large following. Walking up to him, Shams said, "Tell me, what is the purpose of all the discipline and study of books and recitation of knowledge?" "To know the religious laws and precepts, of course," the scholar answered. "That is too superficial," the Sage of Tabriz countered. Taken aback, the man of learning asked, "What else is there beyond these?" "True knowledge is that which leads you to the real, to the source," Shams replied and quoted a line from the Sufi poet Sanā'i: "Ignorance is far superior to that knowledge which does not free you of you." So profound was the impact of the exchange that Rumi dismounted his mule and right there and then decided to turn his back on a life of secondhand knowledge and academic disputation.

The details of what followed are scanty, veiled in hagiographical embellishments. What is certain is that the result of the communion that took place between the two was nothing short of life-changing for the thirty-seven-year-old Rumi: Soon, the respectable professor of religious studies turned into a poet of love and wisdom, and he altogether abandoned sermons and the seminary.

Utterly perplexed by the change in their master, Rumi's disciples directed their ire at the stranger from Tabriz and plotted against him. Shams fled to Damascus. Rumi dispatched his son and passionate poems of entreaty, asking the dervish to return. Shams complied and returned to Konya only to find his enemies' anger and jealousy surge anew. Finally sensing that a plot against his life was imminent, Shams disappeared, in about 1247, never to be seen again.

Shams' disappearance caused further upheaval in the poet's consciousness and released torrents of rapturous ghazals (lyrics), whose themes ranged from the sorrow of separation and the longing to be reunited to the ecstasy of the perception of the unity of love. Soon Rumi was to realize that Shams was, like himself, a mind reflecting the Supreme. Mirrors have no "content," therefore no separate entities. "While there was you I turned around you/ Once I became you, around myself I turn."

Two of Rumi's later disciples became, in succession, the recipients of a similar proffering of love. The second, Husāmuddin Chalabi, who asked the Master to compose the *Masnavi-ye Ma'navi*, was the transcriber of most of that monumental work and, in a way, its very *raison d'être*.

Analysis

In one of the ghazals of *Divan-e Shams-e Tabriz*, Jalal-al-Din Rumi cries out, "I have had it with the canons of measure, meter, rhyme and ghazal/ May floods come and take them away/ Paper-crowns deserving of poets' heads./ A mirror am I and not a man of letters/ You read me if your ears become eyes." The lines are indicative of how "the greatest mystical poet of any age" was at odds with the artifices of poetry and, in fact, with the entrapments of language itself. "I banish the word and thought/ And, free of those intruders, commune with thee." *Khāmush* (Persian for "silent") was the poetic pen name he used for many of his ghazals.

In a similar way, Rumi the thinker was a persistent negator of philosophical speculations of every kind. In fact, a recurrent theme of some twenty-seven thousand couplets that make up his magnum opus, the *Masnavi-ye Ma'navi*, is the inadequacy of logic and reason. "The feet of logicians are of wood," and wooden legs cannot be trusted. To be sure, he attests the necessity of clear thinking and reasoning, but in the same breath he points to the paralyzing limitations of "partial intelligence" (*aql-e joz'i*) which, anchored in knowledge, is in conflict with the wholeness of life.

> Partial intelligence is not the intelligence of discovery.
> It yields skill, and no insight.
> It is clear, but it is a thing.
> Nothing it has never been.
> Caught between losing and gaining it totters.
> Total intelligence soars high and is safe—come what may.

As can be seen from this small sample, the *Masnavi-ye Ma'navi* is not an easy book to read. Even though it has been revered through the ages, few people have the patience to carry on a sustained reading of even two or three pages of it. In part, its difficulty can be attributed to the author's multifarious nature. The Rumi of the *Masnavi-ye Ma'navi* is at once a serious spiritual teacher, a love-intoxicated poet, an entertaining raconteur, a learned man familiar with most of the current knowledge of his time, and a *Menschen-kenner* of profound psychological insights. To give an example of the inter-play of all these facets would not be possible in a limited space. To illustrate the point, however, here is how, in the middle of a moral discourse, one word leads by association to another, and the poet continues: "Once again I have become a madman. . . . And I have not a speck of reason left in me, see?/ So don't expect ceremonies and polite words, for/ Heaven's sake. Once again I have become a madman. . . ./ Otherwise, how do you account for this erratic/ Babble, O sober ones?"

On another occasion, when he is telling the story of Ayaz—the beautiful, pure-hearted, righteous serf of Sultan Mahmoud—the poet suddenly aban-dons the ongoing narrative. "O Ayaz! The tale of your anguish and ecstasy made me so weak./ I stop. *You* tell *my* story." In the course of another dis-course, having used the analogy of the sun, the word reminds him of its syn-onym *Shams*, and that in turn unleashes feelings about the vanished "king of love" Shams-e Tabriz.

Such stream-of-consciousness interruptions and interpolations, which are found throughout the *Masnavi-ye Ma'navi*, are responsible for its difficulty and for its unparalleled richness and density, as well as its unique stylistic fea-tures. It should be mentioned, however, that in no way is Rumi composing self-conscious literary work, much less giving discourses according to any design or for any motive such as self-expression. Rather, he creates as he goes along, with the utter freedom and felicity of love. When at the end of the sixth and final book of the *Masnavi-ye Ma'navi* he stops, even the promptings of his son Bahā'uddin Valad are of no avail, because as the latter quotes his father, "The camel of my speech is now laid to rest and not until doomsday will it raise its head."

Like any book of and on truth, the *Masnavi-ye Ma'navi* is full of seemingly contradictory statements: "Don't strive after water, seek thirst/ Waters will then spring aplenty, head to toe"; "So long as you haven't died [to yourself] the agony of dying will go on"; "Let go of your ears, then be all ears!/ Aban-don your consciousness, then be conscious!" Paradoxes of this kind are scat-tered through the *Masnavi-ye Ma'navi*. Paradoxical also is the fact that the poet is consistently absent from and ubiquitously present in the book. Often, it is difficult to tell whether it is the character in a story who is speaking or it is Rumi with one of his innumerable interpolations or poetic flights.

Scattered throughout the book are stories, ranging from anecdotes a sentence or two in length (such as the story of the ugly Negrito who rejoiced because others, not himself, saw his face) to elaborate tales. Some of the longer stories (such as the moving "Umar and the Harp Player" and "The Prophet and the Gluttonous Arab") are literary masterpieces and, at the same time, moral allegories with "epiphanies" at once ripe and hard-hitting. Seldom are the stories governed by the conventional demands of artistic unity; rather, their form is determined by the spontaneity borne of love, which "like life comes, in timeless moments, afresh."

If love is the creative propeller of the *Masnavi-ye Ma'navi*, it is, for the most part, the substance and subject matter of *Divan-e Shams-e Tabriz*. Except for a limited number of *rubā'iyāt* (quatrains), the *Divan-e Shams-e Tabriz* is a collection of ghazals of mixed chronology (grouped alphabetically according to the last letters of end-rhymes). The word "ghazal," which etymologically is related to love, lovemaking, and courting, denotes a lyric consisting of between six and seventeen lines, the last line containing the poet's *takhallos* (pen name). (For his *takhallos*, in most of the ghazals of the *Divan-e Shams-e Tabriz*, Rumi uses Shams-e Tabrizi's name, a token of love's undoing of separateness.) Originally an amatory lyric of mainly aesthetic significance, the ghazal underwent a transformation of intent and import in the hands of such Sufi-inspired poets as Arāqi, Sanā'i, and Attār, who found in the form a vehicle for the expression of the ineffable feelings of transcendent love.

It is, however, in the pages of Rumi's *Divan-e Shams-e Tabriz* that the ghazal achieves an ecstatic quality unexampled by any other Persian poet, not even by such masters as Hāfiz or Sa'di (the two names well-known to Western readers, thanks in part to the efforts of such luminaries as Johann Wolfgang von Goethe and Ralph Waldo Emerson). What distinguishes Rumi's poems from those of other lyricists cannot be elaborated here. Suffice it to mention that at their best the poems of the *Divan-e Shams-e Tabriz* throb with the raptures of a religious self-abandonment—religion not in the conventional sense of organized religion or of dogma, sect, or ritual but, in Rumi's own words, a "religion beyond all religions" (the complete line is: "The lover's religion is beyond all religions"). It is primarily the religion of lovers and love that permeates the pages of the poem. Here, to try to define the nature of love—as sacred, profane, personal, universal, divine, mystical and so on—or to identify the object of the poet's love (Shams? God? an "earthly" beloved such as a woman?)—to try to circumscribe love with such distinctions would be the result of thought's projections about love, whereas, as Rumi tries to drive home again and again, not only can thought not fathom the mystery of love, it is in fact an obstacle to it:

> Thought says, I have measured; all sides end in walls.
> Love says, I have travelled beyond these walls many times.
> Thought says, Beware! Don't step! the unknown is full of thorns.

Love says, look better, you're the maker of those thorns. . . .
Love saw a corner market and erected its little shop
Love saw many a variegated bazaar beyond . . .

By now it may be fairly clear why in many poems of the *Divan-e Shams-e Tabriz* the poet speaks in praise of wine, of taverns and tavern dwellers.

The importance of the auditory aspect of the Rumi ghazal, and that which is responsible for the difficulty of translation into English, cannot be over-emphasized. The poet who was the founder of the Order of Whirling Dervishes is believed to have composed most of his lyrics during *samā'* (sessions of listening to music, mostly of primitive instruments such as the reed in the case of the *Masnavi-ye Ma'navi*, or the drum and tambourine in the case of the *Divan-e Shams-e Tabriz*; ambulatory dances were part of the latter). Often, the lyric so seems to ride on the tidal wave of ecstatic rhythms that the poet refuses to bother about words as carriers of meaning. In one of the poems of the *Divan-e Shams-e Tabriz*, for example, the repetition of the refrain "tananāhā yāhou" spills over into an entire couplet and becomes nothing more than a nonsense cluster of prosodic syllables: "Tatatantan tatatantan tatatatan tatatan/ Tatatantan tatatantan tatatantan tatatan." It is important to point out that there is not the slightest indication of poetic mannerism in ghazals of this kind; rather, the interplay of the sound with the sense comes naturally, as if inevitably, creating rare spiritual lyrics of rhapsodic beauty.

As was mentioned earlier, the matrix of the poetry of Rumi, in the *Masnavi-ye Ma'navi* and the *Divan-e Shams-e Tabriz* alike, is love, and love does not permit the extraneousness of the word. "I think of rhymes and the beloved taunts/ Don't ever think of aught but seeing me!" It may now be understood why the author of two hefty volumes of poetry spoke so often and so rapturously of silence: With the lifting of the veil of words and their mental associations, the face of the Real is revealed in all its splendor, and "The pen [that] was running so swift and smooth/ Shatters when it comes to love, and stops."

Other major work
NONFICTION: *Fīhi mā fīhi*, early thirteenth century (*Discourses of Rumi*, 1961).

Bibliography
Arasteh, A. Reza. *Rumi the Persian*, 1965.
Davis, F. Hadland. *The Persian Mystics: Jalalu-din Rumi*, 1907.
Iqbal, Afzal. *The Life and Thought of Mohammed Jalal-ud-Din Rumi*, 1955.
Nicholson, R. A. *Rūmī, Poet and Mystic*, 1950.

Massud Farzan

UMBERTO SABA
Umberto Poli

Born: Trieste; March 9, 1883
Died: Gorizia, Italy; August 25, 1957

Principal collections

Poesie, 1911 (originally published as *Il mio primo libro di poesie*, 1903); *Coi miei occhi: Il mio secondo libro di versi*, 1912; *Il canzoniere (1900-1921)*, 1921; *Figure e canti*, 1926; *Tre composizioni*, 1933; *Parole*, 1934; *Ultime cose*, 1944; *Il canzoniere (1900-1945)*, 1945; *Il Mediterranee*, 1946; *Il canzoniere (1900-1947)*, 1948; *Uccelli*, 1950; *Quasi un racconto*, 1951; *Il canzoniere*, 1961, revised 1965; *Umberto Saba: Thirty-one Poems*, 1978.

Other literary forms

Although remembered primarily for his poetry, particularly as assembled in the monumental editions of *Il canzoniere*, Umberto Saba also wrote several significant prose works, most of which have been collected by Saba's daughter Linuccia in *Prose* (1964). *Scorciatoie e raccontini* (1946; short cuts and vignettes) consists mainly of terse reflections on poetry and meditations on politics and postwar society. The collection *Ricordi-racconti, 1910-1947* (1956; remembrances-stories) contains stories and sketches, some directly autobiographical. Saba's prose style is usually rich and complex, though not particularly experimental. Like his poems, the prose works are reflective and benefit from a careful rereading. The pieces in *Scorciatoie e raccontini* are "shortcuts" because they cut through the twisting paths of conventional, logical thought to arrive at a conclusion which is often startling in its revelation and insight. In *Storia e cronistoria del canzoniere* (1948; history and chronicle of the canzoniere), Saba turns his critical eye to his own works, explaining the biographical background of the poems in *Il canzoniere* and giving interpretations. This autocriticism not only recalls the commentary of Dante on his own poems in the *La vita nuova* (c. 1292; *The New Life*) but also exemplifies the influence of Sigmund Freud and psychoanalysis on Saba's thought and technique. The incomplete novel *Ernesto*, published posthumously in 1975, is on the surface Saba's least typical work; set in Trieste and vividly capturing the dialect of that Mediterranean city, *Ernesto* depicts the love of a young boy for an older man. Still, while more realistic and explicit than Saba's other works, *Ernesto* develops the same themes—art, love, change, and loss—with an equal complexity and subtlety.

Achievements

Often considered one of the three great Italian poets of this century, along with Giuseppe Ungaretti and Eugenio Montale, Saba is also one of the most important poets to combine traditional verse forms with a modern restraint and to treat universal themes with an analytical and self-conscious approach typical of the twentieth century.

The clarity and reflectiveness of Saba's earlier poems reveal the influence of the nineteenth century poet Giacomo Leopardi, and the calm, melancholy atmosphere of many of Saba's poems has its roots in the poetry of the *crepuscolari* (twilight) poets such as Guido Gozzano and Sergio Corazzini, who described everyday objects and settings with a wistful nostalgia. Saba's later poems break more definitely with traditional meter and line length, reflecting the terse, ragged rhythms of Ungaretti.

Saba won several prizes and honors, including the Premio Viareggio in 1946 for *Scorciatoie e raccontini*, the Premio dell'Accademia dei Lincei in 1951, and the honorary degree in letters from the University of Rome in 1953; critics have generally appreciated Saba's works, particularly since the 1960's. While Saba's poetical works have been generally well received and studied in Italy, however, his place in modern world literature has not yet been established, perhaps in large part because of a scarcity of translations. As critics continue to construct an account of Saba's biography and his rich inner life, his significance should become increasingly apparent.

Biography
The life of Umberto Saba is reflected throughout his work, and this relationship is most evident in Saba's structuring of *Il canzoniere* around the three periods of his development, youth, maturity, and old age; for Saba, all literature is in a sense autobiographical. Still, the richness and complexity of the poems and prose works give no indication of the relatively simple life of the poet.

Saba was born Umberto Poli on March 9, 1883, in Trieste, then part of the Austro-Hungarian Empire. His father, Ugo Edoardo Poli, was the son of the contessa Teresa Arrivabene; Saba's mother, Felicita Rachele Coen, was the daughter of Jewish parents who had a fairly successful business in the ghetto of Trieste. The marriage did not last long, and Ugo Poli, who had converted to Judaism, abandoned his wife as soon as Umberto was born. Saba refers to his parental background in sonnets 2 and 3 from the chapter "Autobiografia" in *Il canzoniere*. In the second, "Quando nacqui mia madre ne piangeva" (when I was born my mother cried), Saba describes both his and his mother's sorrow at being abandoned by his father. The speaker's happy memories of his relatives in the ghetto shopping for him and his mother are tempered by his loneliness: "But I soon became an expert at melancholy;/ the only son with a distant father." The third sonnet, "Mio Padre è stato per me 'l'assassino'" (my father has been for me "the assassin"), recounts the meeting between Saba and his father when Saba was twenty, a meeting which surprises the speaker, for he realizes that he has much in common with his father, the man whom he had hated for so long: "His face had my azure stare,/ a smile, amid suffering, sweet and sly." The speaker remembers his mother's warning not to be like his father and then understands for himself what she meant, that "they were two races in an ancient strife." With this awareness, the poet also sees in himself the unreconciled opposition of two forces, Jewish and Christian, old and new, victim and assassin.

As a boy, Saba was sent to stay with a nursemaid, Giuseppina Sabaz, from whom he derived his pseudonym and whom he recalls as Peppa in the chapter "Il piccolo Berto" (little Berto) in *Il canzoniere*. In "Il figlio della Peppa" (the son of Peppa), Saba remembers the paradise of his stay with Peppa, who had found in Berto a replacement for her dead son. The speaker sees this time with his Catholic nurse as lighter and happier than the time with his mother; after three years, as Saba remembers, his mother took him away from Peppa.

Saba had formal schooling beyond high school, attending the Ginnasio Dante Alighieri in Trieste. Wanting to be a sailor, he took courses at a nautical academy but was not graduated, for his mother made him take a position as a clerk in a commercial firm. In 1902, he left this job, traveling in Northern Italy and reading widely such poets as Leopardi, Giosuè Carducci, and Giovanni Pascoli, major influences on Saba's first volume of poetry, which was originally published in a private edition as *Il mio primo libro di poesie* (my first book of poetry) in 1903 and republished in 1911 as *Poesie*.

In 1908, Saba was drafted into the infantry and was stationed at Salerno, an experience that he depicts in *Il canzoniere* in "Versi militari" (military verses) and an experience which gave him for the first time a sense of comradeship with others. The same year, after finishing his service, he married the seamstress Carolina Wölfler, the "Lina" of his love poetry, whom he had met in 1907. The couple settled near Trieste and had a daughter, Linuccia. Saba returned to the army during World War I as an airfield inspector but did not see combat. After the war, Saba opened an antiquarian bookstore in Trieste, which served as his chief source of income and which furnished a meeting place for numerous writers and artists; from his bookstore, Saba published the first edition of *Il canzoniere* in 1921.

Much of the rest of Saba's life was relatively uneventful, and he published little between the years 1934 and 1945. Just before World War II, the growing anti-Semitic atmosphere pressured Saba into fleeing to France; later, he returned to Italy, staying incognito in Rome and in Florence. After the Liberation, Saba returned to Trieste and published in 1944 the volume *Ultime cose* (last things). The title is somewhat misleading, though, for in 1945 Saba published the first definitive gathering and reworking of his poems in *Il canzoniere*. After this edition, Saba continued writing poetry and prose, including some of his most famous works, such as "Ulisse" ("Ulysses"). In 1956, Saba was confined to a clinic in Gorizia; his wife died in November, and nine months later, on August 25, 1957, Saba himself died.

Analysis

The connection between Umberto Saba's life and his poetry is nowhere more evident than in his organization of the 1945 edition of *Il canzoniere*, the collection and revision of all of his previous poems. *Il canzoniere* consists of chronologically arranged chapters (some of which had been published separately) and is divided into three sections or volumes, each of which corresponds to a phase of Saba's life—adolescence and youth (from 1900 to 1920), maturity (from 1921 to 1932), and old age (in the 1961 edition, this includes additional poems from 1933 to 1954). These three sections also correspond to stages of Saba's poetic development, although certain themes and techniques persist throughout his career. The most salient characteristics of Saba's poetry are his preoccupation with retrospection, his treatment of modern themes in traditional meter and form but with concrete, everyday language, and his development of the theme of love as a unifying force in a chaotic world.

The first section of *Il canzoniere* contains some very early verse, much of which is less interesting and innovative than later poems, but the section also contains several of Saba's best-known lyrics, including "A mia moglie ("To My Wife") and "La capra" ("The Goat"). This section contains the chapters "Versi militari" (written during Saba's experience as an infantryman in 1908) and "Casa e campagna" (home and countryside), from which come "To My Wife" and "The Goat," "Trieste e una donna" (Trieste and a lady), which treats Saba's love for his wife Lina and for his native city, and "L'amorosa spina" (the amorous thorn), thirteen poems which analyze Saba's passion for Chiarretta, a young assistant in his bookstore.

The second volume of *Il canzoniere* begins with a group of poems based on the failed love for Chiarretta, "Preludio e canzonette" (prelude and songs), but these poems, written a year or two after the affair, are more sober and reflective. In fact, the majority of the second volume is retrospective, including the fifteen sonnets which make up "Autobiografia"—poems describing events and perceptions from the poet's birth to the opening of his bookstore and the development of his poetic career. The last section, "Il piccolo Berto," is dedicated to Edoardo Weiss, an Italian psychoanalyst who introduced Saba to Freudian psychology and to an analysis of Saba's past. These poems concentrate on Saba's relationship with his mother and the various mother figures of his childhood.

The third volume begins with "Parole" ("Words"), which, written after Saba's experience with psychoanalysis, marks a new direction in his poetic diction and form. The dense, often elliptical poems in this chapter recall the hermetic style of Eugenio Montale, but Saba's sparse style often suggests a richness of emotion rather than a dryness; the purifying of language and avoidance of traditional forms and rhymes, as well as the minimalization of narrative, allow the reader to concentrate on and appreciate anew the sharp-

ness of the images and the resonance of the sounds. The chapter "Mediterranee" (Mediterranean) contains Saba's most famous poem and perhaps his
most successful synthesis of form and content—the poem "Ulysses," which
parallels the wandering of the Greek hero with the poet's sense of his own
age and homelessness.

The evolution of a poetic idiom should not obscure the unchanging features of Saba's artistry. Since *Il canzoniere* itself is not only a collection but
also a reworking of previous poems, this anthology presents the reader with a
consistent, retrospective view of the poet's career. This retrospection is clear,
for example, in the inclusion of the autobiographical poems of "Il piccolo
Berto" in the second volume—the volume of Saba's middle age; these poems
of childhood reflect not so much the child's perspective as that of the adult,
looking backward and seeking to understand or assimilate the past.

To an extent, the poet's use of traditional versification parallels his concern
for the past. The poem "Amai" ("I Loved"), from "Mediterranee," shows
that Saba views poetic tradition not as a series of principles to be slavishly
venerated or as a confining set of prescriptions but as a source of inspiration
for innovation: "I loved the trite words that no one/ dared to use. I was en-
chanted by the rhyme 'flower—love' [*fiore—amore*],/ the oldest and most
difficult in the world." The trite rhymes and everyday words are the most difficult because they have been used for so long, and yet, the poet implies,
these words and forms have a beauty and a truthfulness that endures. The
innovative use of tradition provides the poet with a common ground for communicating truth to the reader, and at the same time it requires that the poet
find a new and personal way of perceiving and shaping this truth.

For Saba, in fact, the role of the poet is to perceive the world—the world
of the everyday—as it is, not as custom or habit deforms it, and to convey
this childlike rediscovery to the reader. Since, however, the poet is also aware
of the individual's ability to overlook or forget this primal joy and to fall prey
to despair, he does not represent this rediscovery as a panacea for human suffering. This suffering, in fact, becomes as integral a part of the poem as is the
joy, and in many of Saba's poems, the speaker's confrontation with pain is
more significant than his apprehension of happiness. This awareness links the
speaker with others who have suffered; it is the highest form of love. The
poem "The Goat" illustrates this perception. At first, the speaker is intrigued
by a tethered goat, as if for a joke, but then the speaker hears in the goat's
bleating the eternal nature of suffering and sees in the goat's Semitic face
"the complaint of every other being at every other evil."

This love—the yearning that binds all living beings—is perhaps the central
theme of Saba's poetry. Love may be erotic, as in the love poems to Lina; or
it may be filial, as in the poem "A mia figlia" ("To My Daughter"); it may be
a love of one's city or society, as in "Città vecchia" ("Old town") and other
poems in "Trieste e una donna," or the poem "Ulysses"; or it may be a long-

ing for the past, whether the past of childhood or the tradition of poetry.

One of Saba's most frequent attempts to make contact through love is to find a sense of community with his fellow humans. In "Old town," the speaker discovers in the humblest, most squalid section of Trieste a kinship, a feeling of belonging, since in this section one finds the most characteristically human people (the most human because they are most suffering). Still, as the poem "Il borgo" (the hamlet) shows, Saba does not expect this love to bring universal happiness or harmony. The poet laments the fact that his goal to become one with the ordinary people can never be fully realized, since the poet, in his very yearning to unite with the people, places himself on a higher level, an unchanging intellectual unable to become part of a changing society.

The poet finds more success in his amatory relationships, especially that with Lina. The poem "La brama" (hunger, desire) reveals the influence of Freudian psychoanalysis. Desire, or the libido, impels people, often with painful or destructive results, yet it is still a positive and necessary force in the world; in fact, *eros* is the quintessential motive for human beings.

Another source of inspiration for Saba is the animal world, as in the poem "The Goat." In his most famous love poem, "To My Wife," Saba combines both the erotic and the animal, comparing his wife to various animals—a hen, a heifer, a dog, a rabbit, a swallow, an ant. The simple joy that Lina gives Saba parallels the beauty and contentment of the domestic and wild animals; unlike poets in the courtly love tradition, elevating the beloved above the physical world, the poet elevates the potential for human love by appreciating fully the bond between the animal and the human world. In an earlier poem to his wife, "A Lina" ("To Lina"), Saba describes how the hooting of an owl reminds him of his sorrows with Lina, sorrows that he had wanted to forget. The animal world, then, often acts as a stimulus, a reminder of the need to go beyond one's narrow view of the world.

The experience of fatherhood, described in "To My Daughter," provided Saba with another opportunity for going outside himself, as well as a way of understanding the natural process of growth and change: "I don't love you because you bloom again from my stock,/ but because you are so vulnerable/ and love has given you to me."

In his later poetry, Saba contemplates the processes of change and aging with a sense of resignation, but not with despair or cynicism. The early poem "Mezzogiorno d'inverno" ("Winter Noon"), published in 1920, hints at such a mood. The speaker describes a sudden fit of sadness amid a great happiness. The source of this melancholy is not a beautiful girl passing by but a turquoise balloon floating in the azure sky, the loss of which must be causing a boy to grieve. The boy's pain is in contrast, however, to the beauty of the balloon, subtly contrasted against the sky, passing gracefully over the city of Trieste. In the later poem "Ceneri" ("Ashes"), from "Words," the poet strips away all unessential adornment and rhetoric from his description of an approaching death: "your bright/ flames engulf me as/ from care to care I near the sill/ of sleep." The speaker feels no anxiety, but instead sees death as a natural stage: "And to sleep,/ with those impassioned and tender bonds/ that bind the baby and the mother, and with you, ashes, I merge." The tone is reserved but not pessimistic: "Mute/ I leave the shadows for the immense empire."

The poem that sums up Saba's poetic development is his "Ulysses," a compendium of his themes and a hallmark of the use of restrained, concrete language to convey a deep understanding of the eternal themes of isolation and community, love and loss. Actually, the second poem of this title, the "Ulysses" of "Mediterranee," conveys the poet's sense of age and decline, his feeling of displacement from his society, his love for his home, and his sadness after the events of World War II. Assuming the persona of the wanderer Ulysses (as many have noted, the Ulysses of canto 26 of Dante's *Inferno* c. 1320, the Ulysses who, imprisoned in Hell, had left behind home and family to sail in search of further knowledge of the world), Saba describes vividly and with nostalgia his past experiences and his present loneliness and sorrow. "In my youth I sailed/ along the Dalmatian coast. Islets/ emerged from the waves' surface, where rarely/ a bird intent on prey alit,/ algae-covered, skidding, sparkling in the sun like emeralds." The speaker recalls his present exile, in an allusion to Ulysses' tricking of Polyphemus: "Today my kingdom/ is No-man's land." In his old age, the speaker has become a no-man, cut off from the comforts of home; the harbor lights are for others now. "Again to the open sea/ I am impelled by my unconquered spirit/ and the sorrowful love of life." The journey of Ulysses and his indomitable spirit echo Saba's lifelong devotion to his artistry, his sense of never reaching a final destination, of never making a human contact free of pain, of feeling more sharply the sense of isolation caused by the very wish to know others, and yet at the same time of feeling the joy in recapturing through memory and poetry the bright images of the world.

Although overshadowed by the monumental achievements of Ungaretti and Montale, Saba has, since just before his death in 1957, begun to acquire the critical acclaim that his life's work in poetry and prose deserves. This appreciation is largely limited to Italy, although translations of Saba's poetry are increasingly common, including book-length selections in French, German, and English. As critics begin to evaluate the subtle innovations of Saba's style and the depth of his thematic development, Saba's position as a major early modern poet should become increasingly secure.

Other major works

NOVEL: *Ernesto*, 1975.

NONFICTION: *Scorciatoie e raccontini*, 1946; *Storia e cronistoria del canzoniere*, 1948; *Ricordi-racconti, 1910-1947*, 1956; *Prose*, 1964.

Bibliography

Cary, Joseph. *Three Modern Italian Poets: Saba, Ungaretti, Montale*, 1969.

Renzi, Lorenzo. "A Reading of Saba's 'A mia moglie,'" in *Modern Language Review*. LXVIII (1973), pp. 77-83.

Singh, G. "The Poetry of Umberto Saba," in *Italian Studies*. XXIII (1968), pp. 114-137.

Steven L. Hale

JAROSLAV SEIFERT

Born: Prague, Czechoslovakia; September 23, 1901
Died: Prague, Czechoslovakia; January 10, 1986

Principal collections

Město v slzách, 1921; *Sama láska*, 1923; *Svătební cesta*, 1925; *Na vlnách TSF*, 1925; *Slavík zpívá špatně*, 1926; *Poštovní holub*, 1929; *Jablko z klína*, 1933; *Ruce Venušiny*, 1936; *Zpíváno do rotačky*, 1936; *Osm dní*, 1937; *Jaro sbohem*, 1937, 1942; *Zhasněte světla*, 1938; *Světlem oděná*, 1940; *Kamenný most*, 1944; *Přilba hlíny*, 1945; *Koncert na ostrově*, 1965; *Halleyova kometa*, 1967; *Odlévání zvonů*, 1967 (*The Casting of Bells*, 1983); *Morový sloup*, 1978 (*The Plague Column*, 1979); *Deštník z Piccadilly*, 1979 (*An Umbrella from Piccadilly*, 1983); *Býti Básníkem*, 1983; *The Selected Poetry of Jaroslav Seifert*, 1986.

Other literary forms

For much of his life, Jaroslav Seifert worked as a journalist, and he wrote countless newspaper articles. During the decade after World War II, Seifert was under attack, vilified by the adherents of Socialist Realism, and withdrew from public life. His publications were limited to editing the works of various Czech authors, to translating—his translation of the biblical Song of Songs is outstanding—and to writing poetry for children.

Seifert's memoirs, entitled *Všecky krásy světa* (all the beauties of the world), were first published in Czech in Toronto in 1981; a parallel edition under the same title, with minor deletions and alterations, was published shortly afterward in Prague.

Achievements

The critic René Wellek once observed, "Lyrical poetry was always the center of Czech literature." One reason for this is that poets have probably expressed the concerns and aspirations of the Czech people better than writers in other genres.

Seifert was the author of nearly thirty volumes of poetry, and he won the Nobel Prize for Literature in 1984. He was a member of one of the most remarkable groups of poets in the history of Czech literature, along with Vítězslav Nezval, Konstantin Biebl, František Halas, and Vladimír Holan. They were all born around the turn of the century, began to write when Czechoslovakia gained its independence after World War I, and took part in the numerous literary movements that flourished during the next two decades. They also lived through World War II, which their work records in depth, as well as the imposition of Communism on Czechoslovakia. Seifert survived the period of Stalinism, participating in the "Prague Spring" of

1968. He was honored by the government in 1966 and was named a National Artist, and served as acting chairman of the Union of Czechoslovak writers in 1968; he was its chairman in 1969-1970. In addition, he received state prizes for his verse in 1936, 1955, and 1968. Holan, Halas, Biebl, and Nezval all died before Seifert; he was the last surviving member of this extremely talented group of poets, dying at the age of eighty-four.

Seifert was remarkably popular in Czechoslovakia, both as a poet and as a symbol of freedom of expression for writers under an oppressive regime. In 1968, he condemned the Soviet invasion of his country and was one of the original signers of the Charter 77 Civil Rights movement.

Biography

Jaroslav Seifert was born in 1901 in Prague, in a working-class neighborhood called Žižkov. Throughout his life, Seifert liked to recall his childhood in this part of Prague with its strong proletarian flavor, many tenements, railroad tracks, taverns, and its own dialect. Seifert's mother was Catholic, his father an atheist and Socialist. Although his parents were poor, Seifert was able to attend a *gymnasium*, an academic secondary school, from which, however, he was not graduated; he left the *gymnasium* early and started working as a journalist.

Seifert wrote his first poems during World War I, when the future Czechoslovakia was still a province of Austria-Hungary. Czechoslovakia became independent in October, 1918; Seifert was associated with the left wing of the Social Democratic Party, and became one of the first members of the Communist Party when it was organized in 1921. Although "workers' poetry" was fashionable at the time, Seifert was one of the few practitioners who actually came from a working-class background.

The evolution of Seifert's poetry in the 1920's and 1930's is almost identical to the general evolution of Czech poetry during the period, proceeding from one major movement to the next. Seifert's friends, especially Karel Teige and Stanislav Neumann, weaned him from his earlier "proletarian poetry" and brought him closer to avant-garde artistic circles. Seifert joined them in founding a group called Devětsil; the name comes from a medicinal herb and flower that means, literally, "nine strengths." The group was inspired both by the Russian Revolution and by the heady atmosphere of freedom and national independence at the end of World War I. Its aim was nothing short of the rebuilding of the world.

Seifert also took part in the important movement of "Poetism" that left its imprint on almost all the arts in Czechoslovakia after 1924. Poetism was influenced both by Franco-Swiss Dada and by Surrealism. It was an avant-garde movement oriented toward the future, considering all aspects of life as art forms—in the future, art would become life, and life would become art. For the Poetists, poetry became an imaginative game of chance associations of ideas, images, and words, often illogical and paradoxical. Sound effects were strongly emphasized in poetry, as well as fresh, startling rhymes; logical connections were loosened. The subject matter of poetry was broadened to include areas previously considered to be nonpoetic, such as science, technology, and exotic information. The poets drew on all the arts for their inspiration: film, music, the ballet, pantomime, the circus, and the music hall. The movement represented a sharp break with proletarian poetry. In morality, the poets tended to be skeptical; they were indulgent in sensual aspects of life and art, and often generalized their enthusiasms. They are sometimes accused of artistic insincerity, but they performed the great service of expanding the frontiers and technical devices of poetry.

In the early 1920's, Seifert wrote for a variety of newspapers and reviews. He was a reporter for a Communist newspaper in Prague, then in Brno, the Moravian capital; later, he worked for a Communist bookstore and publishing house in Prague, and edited a Communist illustrated magazine. During this time, Seifert also traveled; he went to northern Italy and France. He also went to the Soviet Union in 1925 and 1928.

By 1929, Seifert believed that the closely knit circle of Devětsil had outlived its purpose, and he became disenchanted with the new leadership of the Communist Party. With eight other Czech Communist writers, he signed a letter protesting the new party line and cultural program. He was expelled from Devětsil and the Party, which he never rejoined.

The 1930's saw a great shift of taste in Czech literature. The previous decade had sought liberation from tradition in theme, form, and style. The pendulum began to swing back, and there was a decline in free verse, a return to punctuation in poetry, and formerly avant-garde writers began to use classical forms such as the sonnet and rondel. Seifert, too, used regular, compact, stanzaic verse forms during the 1930's, with ingenious rhymes and frequent refrains. He showed an unsuspected gift for pure lyrical poetry, especially the poetry of love, with a new sense of spiritual or moral values. It was during this beleaguered decade that Seifert found and developed the two major themes that were to mark his poetic output and were to become the basis of his reputation: the theme of love for women and his stance as a national poet. He wrote his cycle of elegies on T. G. Masaryk, *Osm dní* (eight days), in 1937. Masaryk, the president-liberator, symbolized the independence of Czechoslovakia, and his somber funeral was an occasion for both nationalistic pomp and an outburst of lyric verse. Seifert's volume was reprinted six times before it satisfied popular demand. Seifert's next collections turned to children's poetry, and the writer Božena Němcová; during World War II, Seifert published three collections, and most of the poems are about Prague, which comes to symbolize the continuity of Czech history. *Přilba hlíny* (helmet of clay) celebrates the May, 1945, uprising in Prague and the subsequent liberation of the city.

After the liberation, Seifert again became active in journalism, but he was attacked by the new Communist regime; in an article entitled "Not Our Voice," one minor critic accused him of being alien, bourgeois, and even un-Communist. Seifert was forced to withdraw from public life. It was only after 1954, following the death of Joseph Stalin, that he was able to publish selections from his past works and some new poetry. In 1956, he spoke from the platform at the Second Congress of the Union of Czechoslovak writers, advocating that writers express ethical conscience, civic consciousness, and public commitment—in his words, "May we be truly the conscience of our people."

After a decade of serious illness, Seifert emerged with a surprising new poetic manner. In *Koncert na ostrově* (concert on the island), he gave up much of his songlike intonation, rhyme, and metaphor for the sake of simpler, declarative free verse. It was during the Prague Spring, the time of maximum liberalization when Alexander Dubček became leader of the Czech Communist Party, that Seifert was named a National Artist of Czechoslovakia. In August, 1968, after the invasion of the country by the Soviet Union, Seifert rose from his sickbed, called a taxi, and went to the building of the Union of Writers. Those present elected him acting chairman of the independent Union of Writers. A year later, the union was dissolved. Isolated and sick, Seifert continued to write; his poems were typed and distributed in copies by individual readers. He lived in a suburb of Prague, Břevnov, helping anyone who called on him and writing reminiscences of his long life as a poet. Between 1968 and 1975, only sections from his old works were published in Czechoslovakia, but some new poems were published in Czech in periodicals abroad. He became an original signer of Charter 77. Illness required him to be frequently hospitalized; in 1984, he received the Nobel Prize in his hospital bed, where television crews and reporters descended on him, asking for interviews. His son-in-law and secretary, Daribor Plichta, was to go to Stockholm to receive the Nobel Prize on behalf of the ailing Seifert, but the Czechoslovak government refused to give Plichta an exit permit. In 1985, Seifert was well enough to leave the hospital and return home, where he continued to write poetry. He died a year later.

Analysis

Jaroslav Seifert's life and poetry are closely interwoven, and it is a mistake to separate them. He took part in all the major poetic movements of his long life. During some of these phases, it is possible to say that he was surpassed by a friend and colleague. Perhaps Stanislav Neumann wrote superior poems of political commitment during the 1920's, and, in the 1930's, perhaps Josef Hora expressed the sense of attachment to the native land better than anyone else in his monumental poem, "Zpěv rodné zemi" ("Song of the Native Land"). Indignation at the violent excesses of Communism was the most powerfully rendered in František Halas' superb "Potopa" ("The Deluge"). Vladimír Holan's output of meditative lyrics, published during the decade after World War II, was especially impressive. Yet is is futile to contrast Seifert to these poets as if they were competitors—they were often remarkably close and engaged in similar endeavors. Seifert has written poems addressed to almost each of these poets. Seifert's own poems are consistently interesting, of remarkably high quality, and represent a unique body of work.

Seifert's main themes were the love of woman and the celebration of what is most positive in life. His finest collections were probably written after World War II, when these themes were increasingly associated with his defense of the individual conscience. Before the war, in the words of Arne Novák, Seifert was "a poet readily inspired by contemporary events and an unusually fluent improviser; he was a master of intimate, emotional, and highly musical verse." It should be added that he was able to express the feelings and aspirations of a remarkably broad audience. After the war, unable to publish regularly, his poems were to increase in depth and resonance until the end of his life.

In Western European countries and the United States, there has been some confusion about Seifert's emphasis on women, on the sensual love for them and their beauty, which he consistently expressed in his poems from 1930 onward. Sensuality, sexuality, love: These are often thought to be asocial, purely private concerns. In Eastern Europe, however, they assume a much greater importance. They are central to that domain where the individual man or woman still has freedom, where the state is unable to intrude, and where a human being is able to wrest a small, habitable space from a hostile environment. There he is able to express love, intimacy, and his most positive values. Love becomes a form of protest and of personal commitment, even of heroism. Seifert has been able to express this theme in language that is not abstract but very concrete and specific, not moralistic or sanctimonious but frequently erotic. This is the unique synthesis of Seifert: The poems appear to be about specific experiences, but at the same time they are always more than this. He could define heaven and hell in these concrete terms, from "Jen jednou" ("Once Only"):

> Hell we all know, it's everywhere
> and walks upon two legs.
>   But paradise?
> It may be that paradise is only
> a smile
>   we have long waited for,
> and lips
>   whispering our name.
> And then that brief vertiginous moment
> when we're allowed to forget
> that hell exists.

Although many of Seifert's poems about women may appear at first glance to be simply erotic, about his desire for an individual woman, he almost always manages to raise that desire to a higher degree of generality, simultaneously maintaining the utmost concreteness and specificity. He writes in his poem, entitled "Vlastní životopis" ("Autobiography"), "But when I first saw/ the picture of a nude woman/ I began to believe in miracles." This notion of a "miracle" stayed with him as a measure of what was most positive, of the highest value. Toward the close of his life in "Merry-Go-Round with White Swan," he wrote:

> Goodbye. In all my life I never committed
> any betrayal.
> That I am aware of,
> and you may believe me.
>
> But the most beautiful of all gods
> is love.

The notion of a principle, and fidelity to it, might be easily missed. The strength of Seifert's notion of love is that it is both a positive moral concept and concretely erotic (entirely un-Calvinistic) at the same time.

A skeptical reader might ask, Is this love singular or plural? Does Seifert write of one woman, or several, or many? Or all women? Seifert moves from the singular to the plural with great ease, and the answer is that love is both singular and plural, one woman and many, concrete and universal. In addition, the concept is expanded in Seifert's many poems about Prague, which becomes "her," a distinctly feminine presence.

The notion of love is often defined in terms of its opposite:

> Those who have left
> and hastily scattered to distant lands
> must realize it by now:
> The world is horrible!
>
> They don't love anyone and no one loves them.
> We at least love.
>
> So let her knees crush my head!

A passage such as this one might be misread by a Western reader, who lives in a democracy and assumes a sharp dividing line between private life and society; this dichotomy is upheld by democratic laws, rights, and institutions. In a totalitarian society, however, the division is abolished. The individual must create his freedom and positive values by his own efforts on a daily basis.

In another passage, love is again defined in terms of its opposite. Here it is opposed to war, presumably World War II; once again the love is not escapist, but raised to a higher level of generalization and affirmation:

> The many rondels and the songs I wrote!
> There was a war all over the world,
> and all over the world
> was grief.
> And yet I whispered into bejewelled ears
> verses of love.
> It makes me feel ashamed.
> But no, not really.

Although such a passage might seem, on a superficial level, to mock feats of armed resistance, it should be read carefully. The love here is raised to a principle, it is almost a weapon used against war. Seifert is modest and shies away from large claims or abstract words; usually he seems whimsical, his agile verse leaps from image to image, but the reader should not be fooled by the self-demeaning manner. The jeweled earrings do belong not only to a soft, attractive body (here unseen, carefully removed from the picture) but also to an object of intense devotion, menaced by the war but momentarily beyond its reach.

Love is also defined and contrasted to another opposite—death. Especially in his 1967 volume *The Casting of Bells*, Seifert looks forward to his own death, which serves as a foil for his theme of love. In his poem "Dvořákovo requiem" ("A Requiem for Dvořák"), he describes a place on the Vltava River where two lovers killed themselves by drowning. Most of the poem describes the efforts to drag for the couple with hooked poles, and the reactions of the men as they finally see the naked body of the girl. In the hands of another poet, this might easily degenerate into an exercise in necrophilia or voyeurism. Yet Seifert maintains—surely, deliberately—the contrast between death and the beauty of life throughout:

> The men in the boat called to the shore:
> "Drag it out, boys!"
> Well, you know, there were many of them.
> As if stuck to the ground in iced terror,
> not one of them moved.

The ending of the poem occurs not with the conclusion of this scene but the next day, "a peaceful, normal day" when "The grass-pillows smelled hot/ and invited lovers again/ to the old game." The entire volume of *Odlévání zvonů* is a sustained meditation on imminent death and on life. The notion of the "casting" of a bell is a metaphor for the body which is "cast" or formed by sexual desire. Paradoxically, some poems in the volume are among Seifert's most positive.

Seifert creates a similar structure of contrasts in his cycle of poems on the bombing of the town of Kralupy during World War II. He was forced to take cover in a cemetery, behind a low grave in "Uder" ("The Blow"). When the dead girl buried there "gave me her hand," Seifert "held" it and was able to resist the explosions coming from the town nearby. The gesture became an affirmation of life, and of Seifert's strong ties to what is most positive in life: Even the dead, through the feeling of love they once felt—human, sexual, and erotic—are able to participate in these ties.

Seifert most explicitly contrasts love to totalitarian politics in his volume *The Plague Column*. As in Albert Camus' novel *La Peste* (1947; *The Plague*, 1948), Seifert's concept of a plague is allegorical and refers to contemporary history. The plague goes on and on:

> Don't let them dupe you
> that the plague has come to an end:
> I've seen too many coffins hauled past.
>
> The plague still rages and it seems the doctors
> are giving different names to the disease
> to avoid panic.

The "plague" is the Communism of the 1970's; it is also a grisly time of burning corpses and "cynical drinking songs." Like the young Seifert, the older poet again has an oppositional politics "in the name of love," though his politics are now anti-Communist rather than pro-Communist. Love is given its maximal meaning not only as a foil to death, and to war, but also to the rampant "plague" of political terror.

This theme of love also has its special style. It closely resembles the alert and highly agile style that Seifert developed in his last three volumes. It is flexible, allusive, moves in unexpected directions, and is always surprising. Seifert is an extremely subtle poet. The translations of his work vary widely in quality; different translations of the same passage in Czech can give rise to totally different interpretations—what might seem whimsy to one reader may appear to be sharp irony to another, and the American or English reader relying on translations of Seifert should beware. The unique style of Seifert's last volumes is characterized above all by intimacy, also by freedom and sensuality. He harks back to his style during the period of Poetism, with its Surrealist and Dada overtones, but it has more depth and follows the contours of thought, the rhythms of intimate impulse and feeling, with far greater closeness and fidelity. As Seifert told a French interviewer near the end of his life:

> As one grows older, one discovers different values and different worlds. For me, this meant that I discovered sensuality. . . . All language can be thought of as an effort to achieve freedom, to feel the joy and the sensuality of freedom. What we seek in language is the freedom to be able to express one's most intimate thoughts. This is the basis of all freedom.

Style, too, can be a function of a principle of love, of those most positive values that Seifert opposes to political repression. Professor Eduard Gold-stücker, chairman of the Czech Writers' Union in 1968 and subsequently exiled, emphasized Seifert's consistent role as a poet of resistance when he wrote in 1985: "Seifert's poems were always in the front line of resistance. In those dark years [of occupation by the Germans] he became the poet of his people, and he has remained so until this day."

Other major work
NONFICTION: *Všecky krásy světa*, 1981 (autobiography).

Bibliography
Carpenter, John. "Jaroslav Seifert, Caster of Bells," in *Abraxas 34*. 1986, pp. 58-61.
Enright, D. J. "Unpolitical but Not Innocuous," in *The Times Literary Supplement*. October 31, 1986, p. 1222.
French, Alfred. *Czech Writers and Politics, 1945-1969*, 1982.
_____. *The Poets of Prague*, 1969.
Gibian, George. Introduction to *The Selected Poetry of Jaroslav Seifert*, 1986.
Harkins, William E. *Anthology of Czech Poetry*, 1953.
_____. Introduction to *The Plague Monument*, 1979.
Kundera, Milan. "A Little History Lesson," in *The New York Review of Books*. November 22, 1984.
Novák, Arne. *Czech Literature*, 1976.
Osers, Ewald. Introduction to *An Umbrella from Piccadilly*, 1983.
Scruton, Roger. "Prague Through Parisian Eyes," in *The Times Literary Supplement* (London). February 24, 1984.
Součková, Milada. *A Literature in Crisis: Czech Literature 1938-1950*, 1954.
Wellek, René. *Essays on Czech Literature*, 1963.

John Carpenter

EDITH SÖDERGRAN

Born: St. Petersburg, Russia; April 4, 1892
Died: Raivola, Finland; June 24, 1923

Principal poems and collections

Dikter, 1916 (*Poems*, 1980); *Septemberlyran*, 1918 (*The September Lyre*, 1980); *Rosenalteret*, 1919 (*The Rose Altar*, 1980); *Brokiga iakttagelser*, 1919 (*Motley Observations*, 1980); *Framtidens skugga*, 1920 (*The Shadow of the Future*, 1980); *Landet som icke är*, 1925; *Min lyra*, 1929; *Edith Södergrans dikter*, 1940 (*The Collected Poems of Edith Södergran*, 1980); *We Women: Selected Poems of Edith Södergran*, 1977; *Love and Solitude: Selected Poems, 1916-1923*, 1980, 1985; *Poems*, 1983; *Complete Poems*, 1984.

Other literary forms

Edith Södergran died of tuberculosis at the age of thirty-one, and fully half the titles listed above were published posthumously. She left behind her a remarkable collection of letters to Hagar Olsson, a critic and novelist whose favorable review of Södergran's *The September Lyre* led to a close friendship between the two young women. Södergran's correspondence with Olsson was published under the title *Ediths brev: Brev från Edith Södergran till Hagar Olsson* (Edith's letters: letters from Edith Södergran to Hagar Olsson) in 1955.

Achievements

Södergran's poetry met with a baffled and even hostile reception in her own day, with a few notable exceptions, and even caused a journalistic debate as to her sanity. Writing in a period when Nordic verse still supported traditional values of regular meter and rhyme, Södergran espoused free verse and arrived—apparently on her own initiative—at something like the "doctrine of the image" laid out by Ezra Pound in 1912, derived by him in part from his study of the first poems of H. D. Therefore, shortly before her death, Södergran was hailed in the Finno-Swedish journal *Ultra* as the pioneer of Finnish modernism.

By the 1930's, Södergran's home in Raivola had become an unofficial shrine for younger poets, and Södergran's work was revered by a number of successors, among these Gunnar Ekelöf, the Swedish poet, and Uuno Kailas, the Finnish writer. Her courageous rejection of verse conventions inspired later poets to do the same. Her canon makes clear the expressionistic elements in the modernist temper, and in granting to irrational forces pride of place, Södergran (wittingly or not) aligned herself with such contemporaries as D. H. Lawrence, James Joyce, and André Breton. In the words of George Schoolfield, "Her simple directness, enlivened by her genius for the unexpected in language, is seen to best advantage when [she] is overwhelmed by forces outside herself." This primordial and homespun receptivity has proved to be a highly prospective stance, and accounts for Södergran's continuing popularity, enhanced by the feminist movement's reexamination of women's writing, spreading far beyond the boundaries of Norden, and gaining momentum more than sixty years after her death.

Biography

Edith Södergran was born on April 4, 1892, in the cosmopolitan city of St. Petersburg (later Leningrad), the principal Baltic seaport and then capital of Russia. Her father, Mattias Södergran, came from a family of farmers who, while they lived in northwestern Finland, were of Swedish stock. Her mother, Helena Holmroos, Mattias' second wife, was the daughter of a prosperous industrialist, also of Finno-Swedish descent. When she was three months old, Södergran's family moved to Raivola (later Rodzino), a village in the Finnish province of Karelia, close to the Russian border. Thenceforth, the family divided their time between St. Petersburg, where they wintered, and Raivola. Södergran received a sound education at a German church school, studying the literature of France, Russia, and Germany. Her apprentice verse was written in German, which she learned not only in school but also at the sanatorium in Davos, Switzerland; she was a patient there from 1912 to 1913 and again from 1913 to 1914. Heinrich Heine provided the model for much of Södergran's early writing.

Södergran's father died of tuberculosis in 1907, after which his family ceased to reside in St. Petersburg. In 1908, Södergran was discovered to be tubercular, and between 1909 and 1911, she was on several occasions confined to a sanatorium at Nummela, in Finland. Nummela was the only place she lived where Swedish was the primary language; otherwise, Södergran spoke Swedish mainly with her mother.

It is believed that the philologist Hugo Bergroth was instrumental in persuading Södergran to write in Swedish. Nevertheless, she had very little knowledge of the literature of that language, beyond the work of two nineteenth century authors, C. J. L. Almqvist, whose novel *Drottningens juvelsmycke* (1833; the queen's jewelry) she found fascinating, and Johan Ludvig Runeberg, with his aphoristic lyrical poems. Her interest, rather, lay elsewhere—in such German expressionists as Else Lasker-Schüler and Alfred Mombert, in Victor Hugo (whose *Les Misérables*, 1862, captured her attention), in Rudyard Kipling (particularly his *Jungle Book*, 1894), in Maurice Maeterlinck, in Walt Whitman, and in the Russians Konstantin Dmitrievich Balmont and Igor Severyanin.

A turning point in her life was her love affair, during her early twenties, with a married man, an affair of the kind customarily known as "unhappy." Presumably it was not consistently so. For a poet so able to live with paradox, the relationship may have been, after all, deeply inspirational. Certainly, the affair virtually coincided with an intense period of production, during which she wrote the first of her mature works. Södergran's sense of her own poetic powers had been waxing throughout these two years, 1915 and 1916, and had given her the impetus to visit Helsinki to show her manuscripts to Arvid Mörne, the poet, and Gunnar Castrén, the critic. Yet the literary world of Helsinki was unreceptive to her work; her first book, *Poems*, prompted one reviewer to wonder whether her publisher had wanted to give Swedish Finland a good laugh, and in general, reactions ranged from amused bewilderment to open ridicule. Södergran appears to have been taken completely aback by such uncomprehending hostility; her naïveté, one of the strengths of her poetry, was in this respect a major weakness of her person, and it caused her many painful passages.

Yet resilience was hers in equal measure, and before long, she regained equilibrium, coming to think of herself (indeed, quite properly) as a literary pioneer. Her sense of mission grew with her reading of Friedrich Wilhelm Nietzsche, whose influence may be traced throughout her subsequent work. Will in the sense of libido becomes a fundamental drive which her poetry not only acknowledges but also would advance. In a poem composed in 1919, Södergran writes:

> I am nothing but a boundless will,
> a boundless will, but for what, for what?
> Everything is darkness around me.
> I cannot lift a straw.
> My will wants but one thing, but this thing I don't know.
> When my will breaks from me, then shall I die:
> All hail my life, my death and my fate!

She praises the moment when these three abstract, powerful forces unite into the one action, the moment of discovery ("Ah, this is what I want, was wanting!"), when the alienation of categories is banished by the wholeness, the good health, of choice, when the will to choose and the will to be chosen fuse, banishing both subjective and objective, to disclose the truth: that life, death, and one's fate are all of a piece, compose one single motion. The "I" one was until that moment "dies" and is replaced by the "I" who has chosen, having discovered that "thing" which until then one had not known.

Resilient though she was, however, Södergran was increasingly ill, and it might have been literally the case that, on certain days, she could not "lift a straw." More than her personal world was in turmoil. World War I, in which Russia was then engaged, led to the Russian Revolution of 1917. Raivola, astride a trunk line of the railroad from St. Petersburg, witnessed both troop transports and refugee trains passing through, and, with the revolution, Södergran and her mother found themselves destitute, for St. Petersburg had been their source of funds. In this same year, 1917, Finland declared its independence from Russia, and the ensuing civil war resulted in near starvation for the poet and her family. Yet at the same time, to behold so many other substantially afflicted persons helped Södergran place her own hardships in perspective. She learned quickly from her experiences. Huge, irrational forces had been unleashed, yet Södergran had the grace to recognize her world. In her introduction to her next book, *The September Lyre*, she observes:

> My poems are to be taken as careless sketches. As to the contents, I let my instincts build while my intellect watches. My self-confidence comes from the fact that I have discovered my dimensions. It does not behoove me to make myself smaller than I am.

To some extent, this was surely a whistling in the dark. Two further books of poetry were met with tremendous hostility. There was one favorable review, however, by Hagar Olsson, and to this Södergran responded with incredulous joy. The two became fast friends, albeit mainly through correspondence. (Invited to visit Olsson in Helsinki, Södergran declined: "Insomnia, tuberculosis, no money. We live by selling our furniture.") They met only a few times, but their correspondence flourished.

Now Södergran became a convert to anthroposophy, the belief of Rudolf Steiner, and thence to a primitive Christianity, which replaced for her the writing of poetry. She returned to poetry however, shortly before her death, on June 24, 1923, at Raivola. The posthumous publication of her previously uncollected poems from 1915, under the title *Landet som icke är* (the land which is not), established her as a major poet. Subsequent collections and volumes of selected poems continue to appear, enhancing Södergran's reputation and securing for her an ever-widening audience.

Analysis

The power of Edith Södergran's poetry stems from the complex mixture of its elements. She gives the impression of being very straight-spoken, yet for all that, most of her poems are deeply enigmatic. Her choice of subjects is usually appropriate to this technique. One is reminded of a child just at that stage where puberty startles it out of one kind of consciousness into another. This is the age when the "big" questions come up: What is outside the universe? What was before time began? What is death? What shall be my destiny? And love—what is love?

Somehow, Södergran survived the subsequent stages of her life to produce virtually intact poems of a childlike naïveté wedded to a maturity that feels precocious—the precocious intelligence of the thirteen-year-old who has recently realized that she is more far-seeing than her elders and that she sees more clearly into the heart of adult life because she is so new to it. This image, subliminal in so many of her poems, of a gravely joyous child gazing directly into adulthood and finding it at once wanting and yet (wisely) sufficient, wreathes her poetry in an aura of heartbreak. All the mysterious grand abstractions—death, life, love, pain, happiness, grief, instinct, hell—framed by the pubescent as essential questions to be answered are answered in Södergran's poetry, as in life, with an image that may at first appear as basically haphazard but which one then comes to apprehend as intuitively adequate. Life proves to be not the wondrous thing one had at thirteen thought it to be; it turns out, however, in its difference from the ideal, to be *something* (a state of affairs that is recognized, by a sudden twist of maturity, to be in itself wondrous).

Södergran does not incorporate undigested personal experience into her work. Her experience is nearly always universalized, through either a symbol or (more interestingly) some less predicated distancing technique—or a combination of both, as at the end of part 2 of "The Day Cools . . .":

> You cast your love's red rose
> into my white womb—
> I hold it tight in my hot hands,
> your love's red rose that will shortly wilt . . .
> O thou master, with the icy eyes,
> I accept the crown you give me,
> that bends my head towards my heart.

This passage demonstrates Södergran's ability to qualify the symbol with realism and realism with its own stylization: "head" being a symbol for thought, rationality, as distinct from feeling, impulse, symbolized by heart, yet at the same time as she is using this symbolic language to imply that, in love, the head is brought nearer to the heart, she is also stating the fact that, in the act of love, the neck can bend the head forward, bringing it literally closer to the heart, but perhaps *only* literally. The physical undoes the symbolic, even as the latter transcends the physical. The same double movement is present throughout this poem: The presence of the physical both renders the symbolism ironic ("red rose" is so obviously a penis) and accounts for it, explains away its symbolism, even while the symbolic is raising the sad physical facts to a transcendent plane, as though from lust to love.

In this technique, the essential ambiguity of such a situation is preserved intact, preserved from the poet's intentions upon it, and from the reader's everlasting demand for assurance. Is the "master" subject only to "higher" motives? That one may doubt this is suggested in a subsequent poem, "Discovery":

> Your love darkens my star—
> the moon rises in my life.
> My hand is not at home in yours.
> Your hand is lust—
> my hand is longing.

Here, Södergran lays out neatly the two halves of the picture, the "fifty-fifty" of the heterosexual fix. His love, although desired (in fact, "longed for"), threatens to overwhelm the woman, who senses that her own "star" (her own sense of self and particular destiny) is being obscured by the male presence, no doubt filled with assumptions and demands, obscured in the way that the light of a star is blocked when the full moon rises. Panicked, she retreats: "My hand is not at home in yours." Presumably she had felt otherwise about this man. Thus she leads herself to her "discovery": He lusts, while she longs. He also longs, as no doubt she also lusts; it is a question of which emotion is primary. Enlightened, however sadly, the poet, through observing this dynamic, gives herself back to herself and finds her star. Able to describe the process, she finds a power within herself to withstand it. It is noteworthy that Södergran is not deterred from her use of natural imagery by preexisting symbolic meaning: that the moon, for example, is customarily a symbol of the female.

Such nature imagery permeates Södergran's work from start to finish. Whole poems are built from observations of the landscape and weather of Raivola. "Forest Lake" is a striking example of this:

> I was alone on the sunny strand
> by the forest's pale blue lake,
> in the heavens floated a single cloud
> and on the water a single isle.
> The ripening summer's sweetness dripped
> in beads from every tree
> and into my opened heart ran
> down one little drop.

Nature burgeons on all sides in supernumerous abundance, while in the felt middle of it all, the human singularity (which remarks not only the various signs of its own condition—cloud, island, lake, each one a singular—but also, the signs of its opposite state—the "beads" that drip from "every tree") inevitably, inescapably one feels, selects for itself that which most speaks to it of itself from out of the swarming possibilities. One senses at once the rightness of this as well as the sadness. In the phrase "one little drop" a pathos inheres: Why so little, when one is offered so much? Yet the poem offers also a sense of this as sufficient; it is characteristic of Södergran's poetry to play between senses of pathetic inadequacy and grateful, if humble, plenitude. Sometimes the speaker senses herself as the source of the inadequacy, as in part 4 of "The Day Cools . . .":

> You sought a flower
> and found a fruit.
> You sought a well
> and found a sea.

You sought a woman
and found a soul—
you are disappointed.

The irony of the situation, which she sees and names so clearly, does not completely expunge the guilt of the speaker. Somehow, one feels, she holds herself to blame for being so much more than the seeker expected to find. She is caught in the patriarchal trap, even as she would, with her vision and fluency, transcend it. Indeed, for her to testify otherwise would be an impossible distortion of reality, one which would demean her import and that of her fellow sufferers.

The simple symmetry of this poem reminds one of Södergran's courage in discarding so many of the conventional signs of verse. Perhaps it was as much a blind plunge forward as a reasoned decision; no matter, the result is the same. Whether the reader indeed interprets her poems, as she advised, as "careless sketches," or, disregarding that phrase as one born of a strictly temporary bravado, one views them as finished pieces is irrelevant. Certainly, she did not abjure regular meter and rhyme out of inability; while still a schoolgirl, she composed hundreds of verses in the manner typical of Heinrich Heine.

While at Davos, Södergran learned something of the current furor and ferment at work in European art and letters, and possibly of free verse. Above all, however, her writing is instinct with craft; Södergran has no need to make a display of her talent in more conventional terms because so many of her poems bear this out at the microcellular level.

If there are infelicities in Södergran's poetry, they are those inherent in writing poetry whose rhythms are at times those of prose. One notes the occasional deafness to the echoes of what is being said. "Have you looked your dreams in the eye?" she inquires, her own eye on the object of her poem, distracting her from the faintly ridiculous literal picture presented. Because both "dreams" and "look in the eye" are clichés, it is not easy to remember that they allude to specifics. Her practice of personifying abstractions gets her into trouble sometimes: "My soul can only cry and laugh and wring its hands," for example, or "Will fate throw snowballs at me?" Yet there is a charm of sorts in these minor ineptitudes, some echo of the child just learning to put words together; surely this is one with her ingenuousness and directness. The person who senses her soul as real, as real as her body, is blind to the unintended image offered of a pair of bodiless hands "wringing" each other; this is the same person who can write (of the abstraction "Nothing" in the poem of that name)

We should love life's long hours of illness
and narrow years of longing
as we do the brief instants when the desert flowers.

In this poem, Södergran is reminiscent of John Keats in "To Autumn"— the spiritual definition of "iron" circumstance which allows one room to live. It is a wonderful benignity, won at what cost from malign condition, and not at all ironic. There are certainly poems of less mitigated bitterness, but even with these, one feels that in the act of naming the enemy, Södergran has won the only release truly possible from the shadow of death and death-in-life. Through the storms within her own organism, as through the storms without (war, revolution, poverty, and hunger) she looked steadily into the heart of things. In a very late and striking poem, she wrote

> I long for the land that is not,
> because everything that is, I'm too weary to want.
> The moon tells me in silvery runes
> of the land that is not.
> The land where all our wishes shall be wondrously fulfilled,
> the land where our shackles drop off,
> the land where we cool our bleeding forehead
> in moon-dew.
> My life was a feverish illusion.
> But one thing I have found and one I have really won—
> the way to the land that is not.

The poem has a further stanza but should have ended here. Södergran's gift for discerning the positive in the negative has seldom been more strongly realized. Through her genius, the reader comes to understand how the negative is so qualified, somewhat as "faery lands forlorn" in Keats's "Ode to a Nightingale," and that a simple act of the imagination may transform nothingness into a vision more sustaining than anything which blank materialism affords.

Other major work

NONFICTION: *Ediths brev: Brev från Edith Södergran till Hagar Olsson*, 1955.

Bibliography

Boyer, Régis. "Les Structures de l'imaginaire chez Edith Södergran," in *Études germaniques*. XXVI (1971), pp. 526-549.

de Fages, Loup. *Edith Södergran*, 1970.

Espmark, Kjell. "The Translation of the Soul: A Principal Feature in Finland-Swedish Modernism," in *Scandinavica*. XV, no. 1 (1976), pp. 5-27.

Hird, Gladys. "Edith Södergran: A Pioneer of Finland-Swedish Modernism," in *Books from Finland*. XII (1978), pp. 5-7.

Katchadourian, Stina. Introduction to *Love and Solitude*, 1985 (second edition).

Mossberg, Christer Lennart. "I'll Bake Cathedrals: An Introduction to the

Poetry of Edith Södergran," in *Folio: Papers on Foreign Language and Literature*. XI (1978), pp. 116-126.
Schoolfield, George C. *Edith Södergran: Modernist Poet in Finland*, 1984.
_____. "Edith Södergran's 'Wallenstein-profil,'" in *Scandinavian Studies: Essays Presented to Henry Goddard Leach*, 1965. Edited by C. F. Bayerschmidt and E. Friis.

David Bromige

GERALD STERN

Born: Pittsburgh, Pennsylvania; Febraury 22, 1925

Principal poems and collections

The Pineys, 1969; *The Naming of Beasts and Other Poems*, 1973; *Rejoicings*, 1973; *Lucky Life*, 1977; *The Red Coal*, 1981; *Father Guzman*, 1982; *Paradise Poems*, 1984; *Lovesick: Poems*, 1987.

Other literary forms

Gerald Stern is known only for his poetry.

Achievements

Unlike the poems of many of his contemporaries, those of Stern explode upon the reader's attention with a high and impassioned rhetoric. The poems seem to tumble forward like trees in a flood, snaring, collecting, and finally sweeping subject matter one would have thought only peripherally connected to the main thrust. By using an engaging conversational tone, combined with the frequent use of repetition to sweep together myriad details, Stern's poems display a direct link to the poetics of Walt Whitman. Moreover, a psalmist's zest for parallelism and anaphora disclose a debt to biblical poetry and reinforce the pervasively spiritual, specifically Jewish, sensibility of Stern's work. His frequent use of surrealistic images, meanwhile, reveals a debt to twentieth century Spanish poets, and his love of humble specifics shows him to be a descendant of Ezra Pound and William Carlos Williams. The poems are, among other things, evidence of an immense curiosity about life set against the depersonalizing matrix of twentieth century history.

Eschewing the drift toward, on the one hand, hermeticism, and, on the other, the poetry of confession, Stern's poems, by capitalizing on many of the features of "open" poetry (in various of its historical incarnations), have shown a way for poetry to become equal to the task of transforming both memory and modern history into art. Although it is but one way, Stern's poetic is both stimulating and eminently suitable for representing and interpreting the variousness of American life in a way that encompasses both the tragic and the humorous into its fabric.

Biography

Born in 1925, Gerald Stern grew up in Pittsburgh. He attended the University of Pittsburgh and Columbia University and began his working career as an English teacher and a principal. After spending a number of years in Europe, mainly Paris and London, during the 1950's (though with a stint as an English teacher in Glasgow, Scotland), he returned to the United States and began teaching at Temple University in 1957. He also taught at the University of Pennsylvania, Indiana University of Pennsylvania, and Somerset County College in New Jersey. Stern has divided his time between his home in eastern Pennsylvania and the Writers' Workshop of the University of Iowa as a professor of English. Among his awards are a fellowship in creative writing from the National Endowment for the Arts (1976) and the Lamont Award (1977).

Analysis

Rejoicings announces most of the themes and much of the style of Gerald Stern's subsequent, better-known work. Already present are the tutelary spirits who people his later poems and the tension between his love of "high" culture as represented by various philosophers and poets, all heroes of the intellect and art, and his yearning for spontaneity and the "natural," represented by home-grown resources, as in "Immanuel Kant and the Hopi":

> I am going to write twenty poems about my ruined country,
>> Please forgive me, my old friends,
> I am walking in the direction of the Hopi!
> I am walking in the direction of Immanuel Kant!
> I am learning to save my thoughts—like
> one of the Dravidians—so that nothing will
> be lost, nothing I tramp upon, nothing I
> chew, nothing I remember.

While holding most of the Western intellectual tradition in high respect, Stern equally holds its neglect of emotion, intuition, and experience to be responsible for much of the misery to which human beings are taught to accommodate themselves. Thus, many of the poems in the collection have an aspect of unlearning about them, even as they continue to extol the finer mentors of Western tradition. Others look for a "third" way somehow to be negotiated between the mind/body dichotomy, as in "By Coming to New Jersey":

> By coming to New Jersey I have discovered the third world
> that hangs between Woodbridge Avenue and Victory Bridge.
> It is a temporary world,
> full of construction and water holes,
> full of barriers and isolated hydrants . . .

The "third world" of experience is one to which he will return again and again, finding it populated with all the things that are of little consequence to the heave of civilization: birds, flowers, weeds, bugs, and the like, as well as human detritus—the junkyards of America, superseded and yet everywhere visible as testimonials to other dimensions of life.

Although Stern had been publishing steadily for many years, the publication in 1977 of *Lucky Life* proved to be a watershed in his career. Expansive and ebullient, slyly melodramatic and hyperbolic (whether depicting the tragic, the nostalgic, or the mundane) but always wonderfully readable, the poems appeared during a period when the 1960's loose aesthetic had been exhausted, and the predictable return to formalism was just getting under way. The book seemed in some ways to partake of neither, though this is only a partial truth, for the poems are certainly more informed by the openness of the 1960's than by the subsequent swing the other way. By reaching back, through Whitman, to the psalmists, and imbuing the various techniques of poetic repetition with a dizzying parade of disjunctive images, emotional outbursts, jeremiads, and tender soliloquies, *Lucky Life* seemed to point the way to a new kind of democratic poetry, a kind of Whitman modernized and extended: "I am going to carry my bed into New York City tonight/ complete with dangling sheets and ripped blankets;/ I am going to push it across three dark highways/ or coast along under 600,000 faint stars."

Just as Whitman found American possibility teeming in New York, Stern, a century and a half later, locates it in the moral imperative to preserve its authentic and unrepeatable artifacts (as well as the national character that went into making them), as in "Straus Park":

> . . . if you yourself go crazy when you walk through the old shell
> on Stout's Valley Road,
> then you must know how I felt when I saw Stanley's Cafeteria
> boarded up and the sale sign out . . .

To this he opposes "California," that state of mind "with its big rotting sun": "—Don't go to California yet!/ Come with me to Stanley's and spend your life/ weeping in the small park on 106th Street." California is not a state of mind but a fact of life—to some, an ideal (to the poet, the wrong one). Still, it is possible to carry some of Stanley's memories even to California: "Take the iron fence with you/ when you go into the desert./ . . . Do not burn again for nothing./ Do not cry out again in clumsiness and shame."

The feeling for nostalgic way stations, for what, in a more somber locution, is sometimes called tradition, informs the poet's subject matter in a personal but dynamic way that is nevertheless always under threat by the rise of anonymity, conformity, and the pervasiveness of substitutes. These poems, then, are atavistic expressions of grief and longing for the return of authentic: "What would you give for your dream/ to be as clear and simple as it was then/ in the dark afternoons, at the old scarred tables?" Characteristically, the poet often identifies this longing and grief with his Jewishness, as when he stops to examine a road kill in "Behaving Like a Jew": "—I am going to be unappeased at the opossum's death./ I am going to behave like a Jew/ and touch his face, and stare into his eyes,/ and pull him off the road." Led by a detour to a dilapidated coffeehouse called (the poem's title) "This Is It" ("the first condemned building in the United States"), the poet talks to its owner, a "coughing lady," and commiserates with her over the collapse of the neighborhood. He listens to the stories of her youth, about her dog "and its monotonous existence," and proclaims, "Everyone is into my myth! The whole countryside/ is studying weeds, collecting sadness, dreaming/ of odd connections. . . ."

Sometimes, Stern begins his nostalgia on an ironic note before devolving into seriousness, as in "If You Forget the Germans":

> If you forget the Germans climbing up and down the Acropolis,
> then I will forget the poet falling through his rotten floor in New Brunswick;
> and if you stop telling me about your civilization in 1400 B.C.,
> then I will stop telling you about mine in 1750 and 1820 and 1935 . . .

After a list of such playful give-and-take, the poet shifts key: "Here are the thoughts I have had;/ here are the people I have talked to and worn out;/ here are the stops in my throat." The real theme—the search for happiness amid the ubiquity of details and through the murderous lurch of time—is discovered in a journey into the poet's own typically broken past, narrated in a mock travelogue ("If you go by bus . . ."). Yet after a series of perplexing directions, he admonishes, "Do not bury yourself outright in the litter." Instead, he says, in an ending that finds echoes in Christian liturgy:

> Sing and cry and kiss in the ruined dining room
> in front of the mirror, in the plush car seat,
> a 1949 or '50, still clean and perfect
> under the black dust and the newspapers,
> as it was when we cruised back and forth all night looking for happiness;
> as it was when we lay down and loved in the old darkness.

Happiness is the subject of the title poem: "Lucky life isn't one long string of horrors/ and there are moments of peace, and pleasure, as I lie in between the blows." With age and the accretions of scars and memories, happiness becomes more problematical: "Each year I go down to the island I add/ one more year to the darkness;/ and though I sit up with my dear friends . . ./ after a while they all get lumped together." Announcing that "This year was a crisis," the poet lumbers through memories of past vacations, through dreams of getting lost on South Main Street in a town in New Jersey, of looking for a particular statue of Christopher Columbus, of sitting at a bar listening to World War II veterans, then dreams of himself sitting on a porch "with a whole new set of friends, mostly old and humorless." There follows a burst of apostrophes: "Dear Waves, what will you do for me this year?/ Will you drown out my scream?/ Will you let me rise through the fog?" The poem ends on a note of provisional affirmation:

Lucky life is like this. Lucky there is an ocean to come to.
Lucky you can judge yourself in this water.
Lucky the waves are cold enough to wash out the meanness.
Lucky you can be purified over and over again.

With the publication of *The Red Coal* in 1981, some critics believed that
Stern had fallen into self-imitation and saw the poems as mannered in their
style and sometimes bombastic in their treatment of subject matter. For
example, the critic for *The New York Times Book Review* asserted, "In poem
after poem he sets up for himself some temptation over which he wins a lyrical triumph. The invariability with which he clears those hurdles makes one
suspect that the fences have been lowered." A dissenting view, however,
would simply note that, in a poem, all triumphs are "lyrical," for in what
sense could they be "actual"? Perhaps the insinuation of repetition is the
more damaging. While it is true that Stern's poems offer little in the way of
stylistic variation, their range is impressive.

Simply to list the place-names and people who gather to Stern's poems like
flocking birds is to suggest the presence of a poet with wide cultural affinities
and concerns. While all the figures and places could, with skepticism, be
seen as a form of name-dropping, it is more likely that they play a totemic
role, suggesting whole ranges of other experience anterior to the specific subject matter. Nicolaus Copernicus, Isaac Stern, Yascha Heifeitz, Emma Goldman, Eugene V. Debs, Pablo Picasso, Vincent van Gogh, Casimir Pulaski,
Galileo, Albert Einstein, Fyodor Dostoevski, Guillaume Apollinaire, Hart
Crane, Ezra Pound, Thomas Jefferson, Gustave Flaubert, Wyndham Lewis,
Maurice Ravel, Aleksandr Nikayevich Scriabin, Antonio Vivaldi, Eugene
O'Neill, Johann Wolfgang von Goethe—all these and many more haunt the
poems like figures in a pantheon.

As for the kind of mind necessary for the poet's—and, by extrapolation,
modern man's—survival, Stern compares a model of Galileo's to one of his
own in a poem intriguingly titled "I Remember Galileo": "I remember
Galileo describing the mind/ as a piece of paper blown around by the wind,/
and I loved the sight of it sticking to a tree/ or jumping into the back seat of a
car." At first, he says he watched paper "for years," as if to test the adequacy
of the metaphor, but "yesterday I saw the mind was a squirrel caught cross-
ing/ Route 60 between the wheels of a giant truck." The squirrel escapes, but
not before "his life [was] shortened by all that terror." The poet decides that
"Paper will do in theory," but the alert, capable squirrel, "his whole soul
quivering," finishes his mad scramble across the highway and escapes up his
"green ungoverned hillside."

Such seizures and terror, often encountered in retrospect, are usually
made over to the poet's advantage, as in "The Red Coal," the title poem,
whose central image (most likely derived from the biblical story of the infant
Moses, who chose Pharaoh's tray of burning embers over a tray of rubies)

presides like a second sun over the poet's difficult but intellectually and spiritually formative years traveling with his friend, the poet Jack Gilbert:

> I didn't live in Paris for nothing and walk
> with Jack Gilbert down the wide sidewalks
> thinking of Hart Crane and Apollinaire
>
> and I didn't save the picture of the two of us
> moving through a crowd of stiff Frenchmen
> and put it beside the one of Pound and Williams
>
> unless I wanted to see what coals had done
> to their lives too . . .

The incandescent coal represents the yearning for knowledge, "as if knowledge is what we needed and now/ we have that knowledge." On the other
hand, the coal almost certainly guarantees pain for those who would be its
avatars: "The tears are . . . what, all along, the red coal had/ in store for us."
Yet the tears are not the result of futility or disappointment; they are the liquid registers of experience as it imposes itself upon time, the baffling sea
change of the body and mind that puts even the most familiar past at a
strange remove: "Sometimes I sit in my blue chair trying to remember/ what
it was like in the spring of 1950/ before the burning coal entered my life."

Many of the poems in *The Red Coal* cast a backward look over the poet's
life, coming to terms with the effects of his commitment, "getting rid of bag-
gage,/ finding a way to change, or sweeten, my clumsy life." That clumsiness,
that self-estrangement, appropriately finds an equivalence, and hence an inward dialogue, with the lowly and dishonored things of the world, from
weeds and animals (including insects and spiders) to Emma Goldman in-
veighing against the tyranny of property and the injustice toward winos
whose lives the bright and aggressive world has cast aside. Such pity and
commiseration are particularly strong in Stern and at times take on a marked
spiritual coloring. In "The Poem of Liberation," the poet observes a large
"vegetable garden planted in the rubble/ of a wrecked apartment house, as if
to claim/ the spirit back before it could be buried/ in another investment of
glass and cement." In "Dear Mole," the title animal is compared to John Ruskin, "always cramming and ramming, spluttering in disgust/ . . . always starting over,/ his head down, his poor soul warbling and wailing." A monkey appears in "For Night to Come":

> All morning we lie
> on our backs, holding hands, listening to birds,
> and making little ant hills in the sand.
> He shakes a little, maybe from the cold,
> maybe a little from memory,
> maybe from dread.

As the day passes, they "watch the stars together/ like the good souls we are,/ a hairy man and a beast/ hugging each other in the white grass."

Between the 1981 collection, *The Red Coal*, and the 1984 *Paradise Poems*, Stern published a book-length dramatic poem, *Father Guzman*. Cast in the form of a half-demented conversation between a savvy fifteen-year-old street urchin and a Maryknoll priest—both prisoners in a South American jail— the poem is an energetic, if at times prosy, political dialogue that touches on the likes of Christopher Columbus, Simón Bolívar, and Abraham Lincoln, and by way of Plato, Ovid, Campanella, Goethe and Dante. Father Guzman, whose head has just been cracked by rifle-butts of the National Guard, sits in his cell and confronts the taunts of the Boy, a native; from the initial exchange extends an impassioned conversation of forty pages. Foulmouthed and in-the-know, the Boy begins the poem by extolling his hero (Bolívar) and his affiliation (anarchist). Father Guzman replies that in the room where he was beaten were two American policemen carrying looseleaf notebooks. He compares them with flies and suggests that their incarceration is the result of the same oppression:

> You know the common fly
> has 33 million microorganisms
> flourishing in its gut and a half billion more
> swarming over its body and legs? You know
> that Bolivar left to his vice-presidents
> the tasks of pity?

Father Guzman concludes that Bolívar was "a Caesar" and "that the Mellons plan to betray the universe/ that Nelson Rockefeller was an ichneumon and/ David Rockefeller is a house fly." This makes the Boy sit up, and, weakly suggesting that his admiration of Bolívar results from the fact that both were orphans, changes the subject to "Venus, Bolívar's favorite goddess." Father Guzman understands how the mythology of heroes is such that even tyrants and demagogues can appeal to the masses through the lens of "love," a lens capable of distorting everyone equally:

> but I have seen enough
> of what you call love to last me a lifetime;
> and I have read de Rougement and Goethe,
> but I prefer to talk about this slum
> and the nature of oil capitalism . . .

The Boy, buoyed on the crest of his own postpuberty, continues unconcerned, by listing his "favorites": Plato, the Ovid of *Amores*, the author of the *Kama Sutra* ("The section on plural intercourse/ really turns me on"), and other *maestros* of love. Father Guzman responds that he would like the Boy to experience the pornographic trenches of New York ("you would love

New York City"). He admits that he, too, "wanted to burn [his] seed . . . to die!": "What Raleigh fought for, what the insane Spaniards/ dreamed of for a lifetime. I saw the/ issue of their violent quest." The Boy shifts again ("There is true love in the universe, you know that!/ Think of Dante! Think of the Duke of Windsor") but demurs and admits, "you I love more than my own flesh and blood."

In the second section, Father Guzman asks the Boy, "Why is life/ a joke to you?" The Boy replies that he would simply like to go for a swim and forget about history. Father Guzman interjects: "Listen to me! Without a dream you'd die!/ This slime of ours would fill/ the whole world!" The Boy says that his dream is to live "without misery and sickness and hunger." Father Guzman turns the talk to Utopias and Tommaso Campanella's *La cittá del sole* (1602; *The City of the Sun*, 1637), saying that he "worship[s] his spirit," but concedes that he does not like "the Caesar Complex . . ./ and all that control, in industry, education, and art,/ control of the mind, even of the heart." The Boy characteristically focuses on the control of the heart and exclaims, "I hate policemen! I can't stand them/ looking at you as if they knew/ what you already had in your pockets." Father Guzman wonders why, "in the whole history of the world/ there have never been two months of kindness?" and steers the talk to his admiration of Charles Fourier, "one of the true madmen of love/ and one of the great enemies of repression." The Boy asks Father Guzman what he believes in, and Guzman replies, "my heart is still old-fashioned and I want/ people to be happy in a world I recognize . . ./ . . . where souls can manage a little . . ./ without shaming themselves in front of the rats and weasels."

In section 3, the Boy puts on a dress and convincingly impersonates Father Guzman's former lover, who explains that she left him "when I saw your sadness and confusion." Dramatizing the ritual in painful detail, the Boy concludes, "There's nothing sadder than talking to the dress." They then act out an exchange between the American ambassador (Guzman) and the president (the Boy). The talk then turns to El Dorado. "Gomez" admits that there is no El Dorado but asserts that the dream is nevertheless a good one because it is idealistic, a kind of Grail. The "Ambassador" explains that in North America there is no such dream and consequently the jails are "like hotels": ". . . They sit there,/ all those priests and rabbis, weeping/ in the hallways, lecturing the police."

"Gomez" shows his machismo by describing tortures that he has invented and tries to justify the graft and nepotism he has installed in his country when the Boy breaks through: "I can't do it! I quit!" Guzman concurs, "I don't know how we started in the first place." Yet the pair play one more charade, with Father Guzman playing the part of Columbus: "I challenge anyone on horseback or foot/ to deny my rights to take this place by force." "Columbus" tells the Boy that he can bring him more than he has ever

dreamed. The Boy claims not to understand the meaning of Columbus and
wonders if in his cynicism he has been too hard on his country: "After all,/
we've changed, haven't we?" Exhausted by the heat of their encounter, the
Boy begins to think of exile, and Father Guzman recommends New York:
"Brooklyn's the place for you! I understand/ Flatbush is having a comeback.
You could go/ either to Brooklyn College or N.Y.U." The poem ends with
both prisoners looking at a star, and Father Guzman makes the comment,
"Campanella is probably washing himself/ in the flames. Dante is probably/
explaining the sweetness to Virgil." The Boy replies, "It is a beautiful night.
Life is still good./ And full of pleasure—and hope—"

Despite the unconvincing precocity of the Boy and Father Guzman's
pervasive profanity, both in thought and in speech, the poem manages to
dramatize most of Stern's previous themes: love of pleasure and exploration
(as symbolized by poets and philosophers), the striving for justice, sympathy
for the downtrodden, and hatred of exploitation and greed, especially that
which is institutionalized by politics. It is a bold essay into history, poetry,
and psychology, and though one can hear the poet's private voice coming
through at times, it marks a welcome change from the Whitman-like first-
person poems that so markedly characterize the earlier work.

In *Paradise Poems*, Stern works to bring his poems to a higher rhetorical
pitch and, frequently, a longer format. A deeper, more elegiac strain runs
through the poems, and the most notable poems are formal elegies for poets
W. H. Auden ("In Memory of W. H. Auden") and Gil Orlovitz ("At
Jane's"), the Yiddish actor Luther Adler ("Adler"), the photographer Alfred
Stieglitz ("Kissing Stieglitz Goodbye"), and the poet's father, ("The Expulsion"). In the elegy for Auden, the younger Stern plays Caliban to Auden's
Prospero, as he waits outside for Auden's "carved face to let me in," hoping,
like all young poets, to get the master's nod but realizing, "that I would have
to wait for ten more years/ or maybe twenty more years for the first riches/
to come my way, and knowing that the stick/ of that old Prospero would
never rest/ on my poor head . . ." Though Auden is "dear. . . with his robes/
and his books of magic," Stern understands that "I had to find my own way
back, I had to/ free myself, I had to find my own pleasure/ in my own sweet
cave, with my own sweet music."

By contrast, "At Jane's" sets the death of the impoverished and neglected
poet Orlovitz against Stern's rising success. Orlovitz's death in a New York
City street is portrayed as a stylish exit, adding a note of poignancy to his
loss: "He fell in the street/ in front of a doorman; oh his death was superb,/
the doorman blew his whistle, Orlovitz climbed/ into a yellow cab, he'd never
disappoint/ a doorman."

Stern, meanwhile, finds himself "brooding a little . . ./ saying inside/ one of
Orlovitz's poems/ going back again/ into the cave." Later, in a contrapuntal
image of American-style safety and success, Stern finds himself among the

tea-and-chatter of inconsequential, provincial literary life: "I wore my black suit for the reading, I roared/ and whispered through forty poems, I sat like a lamb/ in the mayor's living room, I sat like a dove/ eating cheese and smiling, talking and smiling . . ."

"The Expulsion" alludes to the expulsion from the Garden into history and memory. The paradise here is the "paradise of two," father and son. The expulsion also means coming to terms with the fact and significance of mortality. Stern's father has lived the exile of countless immigrants: memories of the old country, the myriad adjustments and new fittings needed for life in America, the striving for success, and then death—almost a cliché—in Florida. It is, in many ways, a typical life, yet it is horrifyingly disjunctive, with so many losses trailing after it, that death itself is somewhat anticlimactic: "He had/ fifty-eight suits, and a bronze coffin; he lay/ with his upper body showing, a foot of carpet." Yet this life partakes of a paradise that is only revealed with the father's passing: "My father/ and I are leaving Paradise, an angel/ is shouting, my hand is on my mouth." That paradise will now become a fixture of memory and art, a fertile and yet minatory place:

Our lives are merging, our shoes
are not that different. The angel is rushing by,
her lips are curled, there is a coldness, even
a madness to her, Adam and Eve are roaring,
the whole thing takes a minute, a few seconds,
and we are left on somebody's doorstep . . .

Already this paradise is becoming "the secret rooms, the long and brutal corridor/ down which we sometimes shuffle, and sometimes run."

The universality of exile is the theme of "The Same Moon Above Us," perhaps the most interesting poem in the collection. Here, the figure of Ovid, whose exile from Rome began a literary tradition that modern poets as different as Osip Mandelstam and Derek Walcott have found resonant with significance, is superimposed on the figure of a bum, "a man sleeping over the grilles" of New York. The point is to transform the exile into something triumphant, which these poets, to the greater glory of art, were able to do and which the bum, in his way, must also do: "The truth is he has become his own sad poem." When Stern writes "I think in his fifties he learned a new language/ to go with the freezing rain," one does not know whether this refers to the bum or to Ovid. Yet there is no confusion, for the harder one looks at the bum struggling among the garbage, the more Ovid comes into view, and vice versa. The poem is a haunting meditation on displacement and survival-by-transformation, no doubt the chief theme of this century's most valued poetry.

Stern's has been one of the more refreshing voices to emerge in American poetry since the 1960's, a voice neither too refined to proclaim its ecstasies nor too decorous to lament its sorrows. Sorrow and ecstasy are, after all, the two horizons of emotional exchange, but they are all too frequently bred or shouldered out of existence by the daily grind, and Stern, a historian of emotions, has clearly sought, throughout his career, to restore them. Because his poems are impatient with limitation, it is perhaps tempting to regard them as the enemies of restraint—restraint by which many believe the gears of civilized life are oiled. One must consider, however, that the battle between freedom and restraint is an ancient contest, and the struggle will doubtless persist as long as human beings exist. Stern's importance will not be decided on the basis of his beliefs but on the strength of his art. The son of Whitman, and yet his own man, Stern has produced an instrument capable of intimating, as perhaps no other contemporary American has, the sheer fullness of life in the twentieth century. That he has not substantially modulated this instrument may be a valid criticism. On the other hand, the persistence with which he repeats his enormous embrace of the world in poem after poem suggests a loyalty to his means that is equal to his loyalty to his vision.

Bibliography

Monroe, Johnathan. "Third Worlds: The Poetry of Gerald Stern," in *Northwest Review*. XVIII, no. 2 (1979), pp. 41-47.

Stern, Gerald. "Some Secrets," in *In Praise of What Persists*, 1983. Edited by Stephen Berg.

David Rigsbee

JOHN UPDIKE

Born: Shillington, Pennsylvania; March 18, 1932

Principal poems and collections

The Carpentered Hen and Other Tame Creatures, 1958; *Telephone Poles and Other Poems*, 1963; *Verse*, 1965; *Dog's Death*, 1965; *The Angels*, 1968; *Bath After Sailing*, 1968; *Midpoint and Other Poems*, 1969; *Seventy Poems*, 1972; *Six Poems*, 1973; *Query*, 1974; *Cunts (Upon Receiving the Swingers Life Club Membership Solicitation)*, 1974; *Tossing and Turning*, 1977; *Sixteen Sonnets*, 1979; *An Oddly Lovely Day Alone*, 1979; *Five Poems*, 1980; *Jester's Dozen*, 1984; *Facing Nature*, 1985.

Other literary forms

A prolific writer in all genres, John Updike is known chiefly as a novelist. His major works have been best-sellers and have won significant critical acclaim both from reviewers for highbrow publications and from academics. Among his most noted novels are *The Centaur* (1963), *Couples* (1968), and the trilogy depicting the life of Harry "Rabbit" Angstrom: *Rabbit, Run* (1960), *Rabbit Redux* (1971), and *Rabbit Is Rich* (1981). He is also an accomplished and respected writer of short stories, of which he has published several volumes, and a first-rate critic and essayist.

Achievements

Updike has achieved his fame largely through his novels. These works, and his growing collection of prose essays and reviews, have earned for him a reputation as one of America's leading literary voices. His poetry, on the other hand, has brought only modest acclaim. Many critics consider him only a dilettante in this genre, a show-off who is clearly skilled in handling poetic forms both traditional and modern. Since much of his work is gentle satire and light verse, he is often accused of lacking substance. Updike's record of publication for individual poems, however, belies that judgment to some degree. His poems have appeared in such journals as *The New Yorker* and *The Atlantic*, and even in *Scientific American*. As with much of his prose, Updike has shown an ability to deal in verse with a wide variety of experiences, making both the commonplace and the abstruse immediately accessible to his readers.

Biography

Born March 18, 1932, John Hoyer Updike grew up during the Depression in Shillington, Pennsylvania, and in the farming country outside this Northeastern town. His father was a mathematics teacher, his mother an intelligent, well-read woman who encouraged her son's reading. The Updikes lived with John's grandparents during the novelist's earliest years; many of the boy's memories of life in that household have found their way into his fiction and poetry. A good student in high school, Updike went to Harvard in 1950 on a full scholarship. There, while majoring in English, he edited the *Lampoon* and entertained visions of becoming a commercial cartoonist. While still a student at Harvard in 1953, Updike married Mary Pennington, an art student at Radcliffe. The following year, he was graduated summa cum laude.

Updike's own artistic talent was further fostered by a year's study at the Ruskin School of Drawing and Fine Art in Oxford, England, immediately following graduation. There, his first child, Elizabeth, was born. She was to be followed in the next six years by three others: David (1957), Michael (1959), and Miranda (1960).

Updike's desire to achieve fame through the visual arts was put aside in 1955, when he received an offer to join the staff of *The New Yorker*, to which he had sold his first story the year before. His full-time association with the magazine ended in 1957, however, when he took the daring step to become an independent writer, moving his family to Ipswich, Massachusetts, and establishing an office there. His first book, a collection of poems titled *The Carpentered Hen and Other Tame Creatures*, appeared in 1958.

The publication of two novels, *The Poorhouse Fair* (1959) and *Rabbit, Run*, brought Updike both critical and popular acclaim. For *The Centaur*, he received the National Book Award in 1964 and in the same year was elected to the National Institute of Arts and Letters. These were but the first of many honors.

Though a resident of New England continuously after 1957, Updike frequently traveled abroad. His first important trip was in 1964-1965, when he visited the Soviet Union, Romania, Bulgaria, and Czechoslovakia as a member of the U.S.S.R.–United States Cultural Exchange Program. In 1973, he served as a Fulbright lecturer in Africa. From his experiences in these countries, Updike brought back a wealth of materials that allowed him to expand his repertoire of characters beyond New England and Pennsylvania to include two of his most memorable creations: the middle-aged Jewish novelist Henry Bech and the African ruler Hakim Ellelou.

Updike and his family remained residents of Ipswich until 1974, when John and Mary were divorced. Shortly after the breakup of his marriage, Updike moved to Boston, then to Georgetown, Massachusetts. In 1977, he married Martha Bernhard, a divorcée whom he had known when both lived in Ipswich. Even during this period of personal difficulty, Updike's volume of writings poured forth unabated, and he went on to display both skill and versatility in a variety of literary genres.

Analysis

An appropriate starting point for an analysis of John Updike's poetry is Charles T. Samuels' summary remark in his brief study of the writer: "In verse," Samuels notes, Updike "frequently exploits the familiar," often simply "as an occasion to display his talent for comic rhyme." What strikes the reader immediately about Updike's poems is his heavy reliance on the everyday experience, whether autobiographical or generic, and the way he manipulates language to achieve distinctive, often unusual and amusing, rhyming and rhythmical patterns. Reviewers of individual volumes of Updike's work have not always been convinced, however, that this kind of rhetorical gamesmanship has offered sufficient compensation for a body of works that are, in fact, intellectually lightweight when compared to the serious fiction that Updike has produced during the past two decades. As a result, the serious student of Updike's poetry is faced with examining the work in a critical vacuum, or in the constant context of his fiction.

One can see, though, that Updike's poetry demonstrates his ability to work deftly within a variety of forms, turning them to his own purposes. His published poems include sonnets, free verse modeled on that of Walt Whitman and contemporary figures, Spenserian stanzas, elegiac quatrains, extended commentary in heroic couplets, and works that follow (at times almost slavishly) other poetic conventions. More often than not, the forms are used in parody, as are the manifold rhyme schemes that remind one of the cantos of Lord Byron's *Don Juan* (1819-1824) in their variety and in their reliance on sight rhyme or colloquial pronunciation for effect. For example, in "Agatha Christie and Beatrix Potter," Updike closes his short, humorous comparison of these authors (whose works he sees as essentially similar) with a couplet of praise for having given readers "cozy scares and chases/ That end with innocence acquitted—/ Except for Cotton-tail, who did it." Similarly, in a light limerick poking fun at young Swedish scholars, he opens with the couplet: "There was a young student of Lund/ Whose -erstanding was not always und."

Like many contemporary poets, Updike also relies on the appearance of the poem on the page for effect. In poems such as "Typical Optical," he prints various lines in different type styles and sizes to make his point: As one gets older, one's vision (literally) changes, and what one could see at close range as a child becomes blurred to more mature eyes. As a result, when Updike says that the novels of Marcel Proust and the poetry of John Donne "Recede from my ken in/ Their eight-point Granjon," he emphasizes the problem by printing the phrase "eight-point Granjon" in the type face and size to which it refers. Then, in his closing remark that his "old eyeballs" can now "enfold/ No print any finer/ Than sans-serif bold," he prints the final phrase in sans-serif type and has the final word in bold print. Similarly, the lines of the poem "Pendulum" are printed beneath the title at angles resembling the swinging of a pendulum on a clock, and individual words in the poem "Letter Slot" are arranged on the page to suggest letters falling through a mail slot onto the floor.

The reader often laughs at such tricks, but the poetry cannot be judged first-rate simply for the author's ability to manipulate both the language and the conventions of the tradition in which he works. As a consequence, Updike is too often dismissed as a dilettante in this field. A close examination of his published volumes, however, reveals that the author himself is careful to distinguish between "poetry" and "light verse." Much of what Updike calls "light verse" is simply poetic exercise, intended to highlight the wonderful ability of language to evoke amusement and thought in both reader and writer. Often the impetus for such poetry comes from the world around Updike: newspaper accounts, books that are popular best-sellers, visits he has made to various places where the benign incongruities of life manifest themselves to him. Poems such as "V. B. Nimble, V. B. Quick" may not offer substantial food for thought: The genesis of the poem—an entry in the British Broadcasting Corporation's *Radio Times* that "V. B. Wigglesworth, F.R.S., Quick Professor of Biology" will speak on an upcoming program—triggers in Updike's mind a humorous comparison with the hero of the nursery rhyme "Jack Be Nimble, Jack Be Quick," and the resultant verse about a frenetic scientist dashing off experiments and hurrying off to talk about them provides momentary pleasure to readers without trying to make a serious observation about the world of science. This poem, and many others like it in the Updike canon, are simply offered as tidbits to evoke humor and sympathy in an otherwise somber world.

Because Updike is so facile at handling the many demands facing the poet, it is easy to overlook the serious nature of much of his output. A substantial number of his poems are attempts to examine the significance of his own life's experiences and to explore questions of importance to contemporary society. As in his fiction, Updike is especially concerned with the place of religion in the modern world, and often, beneath the surface playfulness, one can see the poet grappling with complex moral and philosophical issues. He is also a careful student of the literary tradition he has inherited, and his attempts to examine the place of literature as an interpreter of experience often find their way into his poems.

The way in which Updike combines the comic and the serious is illustrated quite well in his poem "Love Sonnet." Its title suggests its subject, but the content is at first glance enigmatic. The opening line, "In Love's rubber armor I come to you," is followed by a string of letters printed down the page, as if they were the endings of lines which have been omitted: "b/ oo/ b./ c,/ d/ c/ d:/ e/ f—/ e/ f./ g/ g." The form of the sonnet has thus been preserved (the "oo" sound of the third line rhyming with the "you" at the end of the first line), but the content is absent. Adding simultaneously to the confusion and to the humor is the overt sexual implication of the only full line: One cannot mistake the literal meaning of the proposition. Nevertheless, a closer look at the poem, especially in the light of the literary tradition which it seems to parody, suggests that there may in fact be serious purpose here. Traditionally, sonnets have been poems about love. While their content has varied, the form itself has usually suggested to readers the kind of interpretation the poet expects. One looks for the words in a sonnet to be metaphors describing the way in which a speaker feels about his beloved. In this poem, however, the process is reversed. The overt reference to physical lovemaking is the metaphor: "Love's rubber armor" is the sonnet form itself, an elastic medium in which the lover, working within conventions—and protected by them—is able to "come to" his beloved and display both his wit and his devotion. In this way, then, Updike is making a comment on the literary tradition: The sonnet form has both strengths and weaknesses; its conventions provide a way to ensure that meaning is conveyed, but limit the extent to which the writer may put the form to use without risking misinterpretation. Appearing at first to be a risqué comic piece about a subject much talked of and trivialized in Updike's own society, "Love Sonnet" emerges as a serious statement about the nature of poetry itself.

The special strengths and weaknesses of Updike as a poet can be seen in those poems which he presents to the world as "poems" rather than verses. In these he is often franker in discussions of sex, and the explicit language may offend some readers. No subject seems sacred, yet it is precisely the concern Updike has for sacred things in human life that leads him to write graphically about human relationships. From his study of everyday occurrences, Updike tries to isolate that which is important for man, to show how man constructs meaning from the disparate events of his own life.

The most extended example of Updike's use of individual events to make statements about universals occurs in his long autobiographical poem "Midpoint." Published as the centerpiece of Updike's third volume of poetry in 1969, "Midpoint" is a collage of text, drawings, and photographs that traces the poet's life from infancy to its midpoint, as Updike reaches age thirty-six. Though the poem has been dismissed by some critics as "quirky," Updike himself insists that in it he demonstrates what is for him an artistic credo, a search for "the reality behind the immediately apparent." In "Midpoint," Updike reveals himself to be a believer in "pointillism" as both technique and philosophy: "Praise Pointillism, Calculus and all/ That turn the world infinitesimal." Like Whitman in *Leaves of Grass* (1855), Updike takes his own life as an example of the human condition, finding in it something of value to share with other men.

"Midpoint" consists of five cantos, four of which are modeled closely on writers of the past. Each is preceded by a short "argument" reminiscent of that provided by John Milton in *Paradise Lost* (1667), in which Updike provides the reader with clues to the action of the canto. In the first, in stanzas reminiscent of those in Dante's *The Divine Comedy* (c. 1320), Updike reviews his childhood and his growing awareness of himself as a discrete entity in the universe. An only child, he comes to see himself as the center of that universe, a point around which the world revolves. Though to sing of himself (an allusion to Whitman) is "all wrong," he has no choice since he has no other subject so appropriate or about which he knows so much. The second canto consists exclusively of photographs: Updike as baby and young child, his parents, himself as a teenager, himself and his wife, their first child. These are printed with varying degrees of sharpness: Some appear crisply defined, some are little more than a blur of dots on the page. This intentional shifting of focus carries out graphically the theme Updike expresses in the "argument" that he prints at the beginning of the canto: "Distance improves vision." In a sense, the action in this canto repeats that of the first, but from another perspective: The reader sees what he has just read about.

The third canto, composed in Spenserian stanzas, is titled "The Dance of the Solids." Based on Updike's readings in *Scientific American*, it presents in verse a view of the way the universe is constructed. The bonding of atomic particles into larger and larger structures eventually "yield[s],/ In Units growing visible, the World we wield!" It would be easy to lose sight of the poet's purpose in these most ingenious iambic pentameter lines. Updike uses the language of science, and even mathematical formulas, with exceptional precision to present his argument. For example, in explaining what happens when a solid is heated, he writes: "$T = 3Nk$ is much too neat." The stanzas are not simply virtuoso performances; in them, Updike provides an analogy for examining the human condition. Just as the visible world is composed of subatomic particles combined in meaningful ways, so are men's lives simply the ordered and meaningful arrangements of individual incidents. To understand the meaning, one must first isolate and describe the incident.

The fourth canto, "The Play of Memory," contains text, line drawings, and close-ups from the photographs that appear in canto 2. The text is modeled on Whitman's poetic technique of free verse. In this section of the poem, Updike explores his marriage and the role sex plays in shaping human lives. The final canto, written in couplets that suggest the method of Alexander Pope in *An Essay on Man* (1733-1734), is a review of the modern scene in which Updike the poet finds himself. In it, he offers advice, alternately serious and satiric, for living. In the fashion of Arthur Hugh Clough in "The Last Decalogue," a parody of the Ten Commandments, Updike admonishes his readers: "Don't kill; or if you must, while killing grieve"; "Doubt not; that is, until you can't believe"; "Don't covet Mrs. X; or if you do,/ Make sure, before you leap, she covets you." As in the third canto, readers may become so enraptured with the wise witticisms and the deft handling of poetic form that they lose the sense of the canto's place within the poem. In fact, the poem has prompted more than one reader to wonder, as did the reviewer for *Library Journal* in 1970, what Updike was "up to" in "Midpoint."

If, however, one accepts what Updike himself has said about "Midpoint," that in it he attempts to explain his own attitudes about his life and art, one can see the poem as a kind of poetic credo, a systematic statement about the poet's acceptance of his role as poet. The many references to other artists and the conscious use of recognizable forms associated with specific poets and poems suggests that Updike is using his own life to make a statement about the way art is created. In fact, in the closing lines of the fifth canto, he observes, "The time is gone, when *Pope* could ladle Wit/ In couplet droplets, and decanter it." No longer can "*Wordsworth's* sweet brooding" or "*Tennyson's* unease" be effective as vehicles for explaining the human condition. The world is now a sad and perhaps an absurd place, and art has followed suit by offering those who come to it only "blank explosions and a hostile smile." Updike, who has accepted the notion of the absurd from modern theologians who have pointed out that faith cannot be rational even if it is essential, offers this poem as an ironic, sometimes comic, and sometimes highly personal and hence prejudicial view of the world. For Updike, autobiography has become metaphor, because only by viewing the world through others' eyes can individuals hope to understand something of the significance of their own predicament. Similarly, as he has used the events of his own life to make a statement about life itself, Updike uses the forms of his predecessors to make a statement about the efficacy of art in the modern world.

Updike's art, especially his poetry, is thus intentionally enigmatic, because it contains a discoverable but not self-evident truth. The surface finish, whether comic, ironic, or sexually explicit, is often simply the bait to lure readers into the world of the poem. Once there, Updike asks his readers to look closely at their own lives, often challenging them to be as introspective about themselves as he is about his own experiences. In that way, he hopes to help others make sense of a world that he believes is essentially good and in which good men can prosper.

Other major works

NOVELS: *The Poorhouse Fair*, 1959; *Rabbit, Run*, 1960; *The Centaur*, 1963; *Of the Farm*, 1965; *Couples*, 1968; *Rabbit Redux*, 1971; *A Month of Sundays*, 1975; *Marry Me: A Romance*, 1976; *The Coup*, 1978; *Rabbit Is Rich*, 1981; *The Witches of Eastwick*, 1984; *Roger's Version*, 1986.

SHORT FICTION: *The Same Door*, 1959; *Pigeon Feathers*, 1962; *Olinger Stories: A Collection*, 1964; *The Music School*, 1966; *Bech: A Book*, 1970; *Museums and Women and Other Stories*, 1972; *Too Far to Go: The Maples Stories*, 1979; *Problems and Other Stories*, 1979; *Three Illuminations in the Life of an American Author*, 1979; *The Chaste Planet*, 1980; *The Beloved*, 1982; *Bech Is Back*, 1982.

PLAYS: *Three Texts from Early Ipswich: A Pageant*, 1964; *Buchanan Dying*, 1974.

NONFICTION: *Assorted Prose*, 1965; *Picked-Up Pieces*, 1975; *Hugging the Shore: Essays and Criticism*, 1983.

Bibliography

Detweiler, John. *John Updike*, 1984.

Greiner, Donald J. *The Other Updike: Poems, Short Stories, Prose, Play*, 1981.

Hamilton, Alice, and Kenneth Hamilton. "Theme and Techniques in John Updike's *Midpoint*," in *Mosaic*. IV, no. 1 (1970), pp. 79-106.

MacNaughton, William R., ed. *Critical Essays on John Updike*, 1982.

Samuels, Charles T. *John Updike*, 1969.

Vargo, Edward P. *Rainstorms and Fire: Ritual in the Novels of John Updike*, 1973.

Laurence W. Mazzeno

C. K. WILLIAMS

Born: Newark, New Jersey; November 4, 1936

Principal poem and collections

A Day for Anne Frank, 1968; *Lies*, 1969; *I Am the Bitter Name*, 1972; *With Ignorance*, 1977; *Tar*, 1983; *Flesh and Blood*, 1987.

Other literary forms

In collaboration with classical scholars, C. K. Williams has written verse translations of two Greek tragedies: one, in 1978, of Sophocles' *Trachinai* (435-429 B.C.; *The Women of Trachis*), and the other, in 1985, of Euripides' *Bakchai* (405 B.C.; *The Bacchae*). The translations, as their notes indicate, are for the modern stage as well as for modern readers. Williams hopes for a flowering of the "kernel" of Sophocles' tragedy within the translator's historical moment, "a clearing away of some of the accumulations of reverence that confuse the work and the genius who made them." The translations are thus not staid or literal but do aim for thematic accuracy and life. Williams also translated poems from Issa under the title *The Lark. the Thrush. the Starling* (1983).

Achievements

Williams achieved early success in the era of cynicism and protest surrounding the Vietnam War. His early work sketches in a tough, cryptic style the nightmare visions of a God-forsaken world. *I Am the Bitter Name* is a howl of protest against the various corruptions of the world, lacking even the tonal variety and scant hope of his earlier work. Though powerful, Williams' protest poetry was seen by critics as an artistic dead end.

During the five-year interim between the publication of *I Am the Bitter Name* and *With Ignorance*, Williams remade his style, writing in long lines which fold back from the margin of the page and tell stories with proselike lucidity. The sense of human suffering and isolation common in the earlier poems remains, but the long-line poems narrate dramatic tales set in American cities: scenes of family life, recollections of childhood, and views from the windows of urban apartments. Exact description and conventional punctuation replace the blurred grammar and dreamlike flow of the earlier verse. The later Williams poses in his poems as a sympathetic survivor who, seeing clearly the complexities and disillusionment of contemporary life, shares astonishing personal associations with the reader.

Biography

Born November 4, 1936, in Newark, New Jersey, the son of Paul B. and

Dossie (née Kasdin) Williams, Charles Kenneth Williams was educated at
Bucknell University and at the University of Pennsylvania, where he was
graduated with a B.A. in 1959. In 1965, he married Sarah Jones, and they
had one daughter, Jessica Anne, who figures in Williams' personal poems.
At the Pennsylvania Hospital in Philadelphia, he founded a program of poetry therapy and was a group therapist for disturbed adolescents.

A Day for Anne Frank led to the publication of two volumes of poetry in
1969 and 1972 which established Williams as a protest poet of the Nixon era.
He was a visiting professor at Franklin and Marshall College in 1977 and at
the University of California at Irvine in 1978, and he has taught creative writing at various workshops and colleges, including Boston University and
Columbia University.

A Guggenheim Fellowship in 1974 resulted in *With Ignorance*, the first
book in his new style. In 1975, Williams married Catherine Mauger, a jew-
eler. They have one son. He was awarded the Bernard F. Conner Prize for
the long poem by the *The Paris Review* in 1983. Professor of English at
George Mason University, he was on leave in 1987 when *Flesh and Blood* was
published.

Analysis

Stylistic originality distinguished C. K. Williams' earliest work, and he continued to evolve through five major collections. Consistent in all periods of
his work has been a "metaphysical" roughness and avoidance of merely literary polish. Meanwhile, he has treated frightening realities which are not
conventionally subjects of poetry. His experimental style began with dreamlike lyrics with short run-on lines, sporadic punctuation, and startling leaps of
image and diction. Strident in tone, sometimes shocking, the early poems
found quick acceptance in the Nixon years.

Lies includes the long poem *A Day for Anne Frank*, which was published
in a limited edition a year before it. In *Lies*, Williams anatomizes the horrors
of modern history and existential despair. The absence of divine order
grounds a series of nightmare visions with titles such as "Don't," "The Long
Naked Walk of the Dead," "Loss," "Trash," "Downward," "Our Grey," and
"It Is This Way with Men," which allegorizes men as spikes driven into the
ground, pounded each time they attempt to rise. Williams' universe is the
indifferent or hostile one of classic American naturalism, but it takes much
of its apocalyptic substance from the Holocaust and from the Vietnam War.
In spite of the negativity of his lyric outcries against suffering and waste, Williams' early poems burn, not only with terror but also with a passion that
things should be better. Optimism, authority, and poetic form are smashed
like atoms. Williams' complaint is that of the child-man against the parent-
universe in which he finds himself an unloved stepson.

There is monotony, even callowness, in this stance, in improbable metaphors and scatological language flaunted for shock value—expressing a gnostic rejection of his prison-body in the inhospitable universe. Nevertheless, *Lies* was critically acclaimed for its fusion of moral seriousness and verbal ingenuity. It concludes with the long poem about Anne Frank, the quintessential victim of history; to borrow a comparison from one of Williams' poems, she was like a little box turtle run over by a bus. "It's horrible," he says in that lyric. *A Day for Anne Frank* displays the horrible motto "God hates you!"

I Am the Bitter Name takes the technique of *Lies* one step further toward the abolition of technique—one step too far, most critics have argued. More homogeneous than *Lies*, this collection appears to try for and achieve self-portraits of apocalyptic incoherence. The poet displays, piled like monstrous fish, the products of his vigorous dredging of his nightmare unconscious. Critic Jascha Kessler, in one of the more positive reviews of Williams' work, catalogs his strengths and failings: "the simplicity, clarity of diction, haste and jumbling of his thought by the unremitting stroboscopic, kaleidoscopic pulsing of a voice from thought to speech to image to unvoiced thought." Impressed that the source of Williams' expression is valid, calling the book "real poems," Kessler is nevertheless disoriented by it. Other critics were less positive, charging that Williams' passionate flailings missed their targets or even dismissing the poems as sentimental and blurred.

As the tonal consistency of *I Am the Bitter Name* suggests, and as his later work confirms, Williams is a deliberate experimental stylist. Purged of commas, capitals, and periods, the poems sprout unpredictable question marks, exclamation points, and quotations. The sense spills over the ends of the short, jagged lines, so that it becomes almost a rule in these poems that a line end does *not* signal a break in sense. The effect is one of breathlessness, of a mind that, insofar as it is conscious at all, barely understands what it is saying. The reader seems to be hearing the raw emotive material of poetry at the moment of creation. Williams' vocabulary, too, suggests breathless, regressive speech, almost childishly simple but scatological—especially in the political poems. The voice again suggests a righteous man-child, outraged to surreal protest by the extent to which the real God and the real governments betray his standards.

Sometimes the words in *I Am the Bitter Name* are explicitly political, as in "A Poem for the Governments." This poem offers itself as an onion to make governments cry for the family of the imprisoned Miguel Hernandes, whose family has nothing but onions to eat. Reminding "mr old men" how they have eaten Miguel and "everything good in the world," the poem becomes "one onion/ your history" and concludes self-referentially, "eat this." Such explicit ordering of metaphor, common in *Lies*, is not the rule in *I Am the Bitter Name*, where even poems on political subjects dissolve into cryptic collisions of word and image. "The Admiral Fan," for example, begins with a "lady from the city" removing her girdle and baring her "white backside" in a barnyard and dissolves into a vision of her dismemberment, apparently not only by farm animals but also by a Washington lobbyist in a long car. She is emptied of "dolls." Her breasts become "dawn amity peace exaltation" in a vegetable field identified—as the grammar blurs—with nothingness, and flashing stoplights. Like the poems of André Breton, these let go even of grammatical structure in submission to the uprush of image and emotion.

Between 1972 and 1977, Williams was divorced, was remarried, and received grants and teaching appointments; during this time, he dramatically reinvented his poetic style. Except for its closing title poem, *With Ignorance* withdraws from the nightmare abyss and grounds its associations on human stories expressed in conventionally punctuated long lines with all the clarity of good prose. The change was presumably as much psychological as stylistic. The mature Williams, turned forty, tells his daughter that he has already had the bad dreams: "what comes now is calm and abstract." Later, in "Friends," he stands outside the terrors of his earlier poems to observe that "visions I had then were all death: they were hideous and absurd and had nothing to do with my life." The style of these self-possessed reflections is easy informal prose, the style of a personal letter refined in its very plainness, which sets the stage in the more effective poems for sudden outbreaks of metaphysical anguish or human pathos equal to the best of his earlier verse.

In "The Sanctity," Williams remembers going home with a married coworker from a construction site and seeing homicidal hostility between his friend's mother and wife, and the coworker's rage—a dark side of his character wholly masked by the ironic idyll of the workplace. The construction site is the only place, apparently, where the workmen feel joy, where they feel in power. Printed sources prompt some of the incantatory stories: an SS officer spitting into a rabbi's mouth to help him defile the Torah, until they are kissing like lovers; a girl paralyzed by a stray police bullet. Williams draws, however, usually from his experience: a veteran met in a bar, a friend in a mental hospital, an old bum seen after marital quarrel, a girl he "stabbed" with a piece of "broken-off car antenna" when he was eight. Here, in grotesque anecdotes, Williams again examines the irrational in human life, the inevitable discord and suffering, but with a sympathy for recognizable human faces and characters missing from most of his earlier work. Political concerns are implicit in the presence of veterans and police bullets, but there is no preaching. The one short poem not narrative is "Hog Heaven," which begins, "It stinks," and develops in biblical repetitions and variations an enveloping nausea for the flesh, a theme and method common in the protest poems but expanded here in limber, Whitmanesque lines.

Tar demonstrates greater mastery of the anecdotal long-line style, telling longer and more complex stories with more restraint and power and returning at times to openly political themes. The title poem recalls the day of the near-disaster at the Three Mile Island nuclear plant, which was also a day of roofing work on the narrator's apartment building. Without ceasing to be themselves, the workmen become both trolls from the underworld and representatives of vulnerable humanity, their black tar-pots associated with the nuclear threat to the north. Williams' old vision of the apocalypse is here, but the symbols are stronger because they move in a narrative with a persuasive surface of its own. Williams is reclaiming techniques many contemporary poets have abandoned to fiction. As he masters the long-line narrative style, the lines become less plain—not necessarily more ornate, but more susceptible to ornamentation without losing their naturalness and tone of the grotesque.

Some of the poems in *Tar* begin with nature imagery and are leavened by it, though the suffering face of the city still always shows. "From My Window," for example, begins with the first fragrances of spring, budding sycamore, crocus spikes, a pretty girl jogging—but this is only an overture to the movement outside the narrator's window of two alcoholic veterans, one of whom is in a wheelchair, and their tragicomic accident in the street, which reveals the unlovely, childlike nakedness of the crippled one. Like many of Williams' narratives, this one takes a sudden turn near the end, recalling the able-bodied veteran pacing wildly in a vacant lot in falling snow, struggling to leave his imprint while the buildings stare coldly down.

Tar is almost as much a book of short fictions as of poems; characters include a man falling in love with a black woman who walks her hideously ill dog outside his window, a boy awakening to night terrors in the city, a decaying luxury hotel taken over by drug users, mental patients, and old women. A pornographic tintype centers a fantasy on immigrant life; a welterweight fighter awakens memories of a German widow, a refugee following her husband's plot against Adolf Hitler, who encouraged her daughter's affair with the narrator—as if his Jewishness could expiate her guilt. Two of the most interesting poems, "Neglect" and "The Regulars," narrate no unusual events but are minimal narrative sketches of a bus layover in a faded coal town and old men in a neighborhood undergoing gentrification—short stories in their use of description and dialogue, but in the cadences of Williams' taut, long lines.

Some of the poems in *Tar* use quatrains, four long lines clustered and end-stopped. In *Flesh and Blood*, Williams invents and writes a sequence of lines in a form comparable to the sonnet in length and rhetorical structure, eight lines of about twenty syllables each, usually shifting direction after the fifth line. Moving away from the extended stories of earlier works, Williams does not lose focus on the pathos and character of the urban world, but, necessarily, his tales shrink into the frame—either to vignettes or to terse summaries like a gossiping conversation. Williams portrays victims of stroke and Alzheimer's disease, a poetry-loving bum, an unhappy wife, a sobbing child, a girlfriend who hates her body, and, in one subsequence, readers in a variety of places and poses.

There is always clarity in these portrait poems, usually wisdom and complexity, but little of the frenzy that burned in the earlier work. *Flesh and Blood* includes poems that develop allegorical subjects in abstract language, despite earlier critical disapproval of this method—particularly in "One of the Muses," the only poem in *Tar* which critics judged a failure. It is Williams' way, however, to take chances. His characteristic strength is his restlessness and formal creativity—his refusal to remain confined within a style after he has mastered it.

Other major works

TRANSLATIONS: *Women of Trachis*, 1978 (of Sophocles' play *Trachinai*; with Gregory Dickerson); *The Lark. the Thrush. the Starling*, 1983 (of poems by Issa); *The Bacchae*, 1985 (of Euripedes' play *Bakchai*; with H. Golder).

Bibliography

Berg, Stephen. "Paragraphs on the Poetry of C. K. Williams' Book *Lies*," in *December*. IX (1967), pp. 201-202.

Dickstein, Morris. "Politics and the Human Standard," in *Parnassus*. I (Fall, 1972), pp. 125-129.

Howard, Richard. Review of *Lies* in *American Poetry Review*. November/December, 1972, p. 45.

Kessler, Jascha. Review of *I Am the Bitter Name* in *Poetry*. February, 1973, p. 301.

William H. Green

YVOR WINTERS

Born: Chicago, Illinois; October 17, 1900
Died: Palo Alto, California; January 25, 1968

Principal collections

The Immobile Wind, 1921; *The Magpie's Shadow*, 1922; *The Bare Hills*, 1927; *The Proof*, 1930; *The Journey*, 1931; *Before Disaster*, 1934; *Poems*, 1940; *The Giant Weapon*, 1943; *To the Holy Spirit*, 1947; *Collected Poems*, 1952, revised 1960; *The Early Poems of Yvor Winters, 1920-1928*, 1966; *The Poetry of Yvor Winters*, 1978.

Other literary forms

Though Yvor Winters believed his poetry to be his principal work, he was, during his lifetime, better known as a critic. His criticism was virtually co-extensive with his poetry, the first published essays appearing in 1922 and the last volume in 1967. Controversial because of its wide-ranging and detailed revaluations of both major and minor writers in American, British, and French literature, the criticism indirectly but indisputably illuminates his own work as poet: by suggesting explanations for the changes it underwent, for the main styles he attempted, and even for details in individual poems.

His single short story, "The Brink of Darkness," is autobiographical. Its setting (the Southwestern United States) and subject matter (hypersensitivity in isolation, the advent of death, psychological obsession to the brink of madness, the recovery of identity) are those of many poems, especially early ones, in the Winters canon.

Achievements

Among his contemporaries, Winters was something of an anomaly. Instead of moving from traditional to experimental forms, he seemed to many readers to reverse that process. Before 1928, his published work was largely what is loosely called free verse, influenced by such diverse sources as the Imagists and French Symbolists, possibly Emily Dickinson, and certainly translations of Japanese and American Indian poetry. After 1930, Winters' published work used traditional metric and rhyme patterns exclusively. He appeared to stand against all the main poetic currents of his time.

At no time, however, early or late, did his poetry ignore modern influences. Among the poets he continued most to admire and emulate were Charles Baudelaire, Paul Valéry, Thomas Hardy, Robert Bridges, and Wallace Stevens. His effort consistently was to make use of the most fruitful traditions among all at his disposal, not merely those in fashion. Thus, many of his later poems are written in the great plain style of the Renaissance. In his most distinctive work, Winters tried to combine the sensitivity of perception which the recent associative and experimental methods had made pos-

sible with the rational structures characteristic of the older methods. The
result was something unique in modern poetry. Even before his death, his influence was beginning to be felt in such poets as Edgar Bowers, J. V. Cunningham, Catherine Davis, Thom Gunn, Janet Lewis, N. Scott Momaday,
Alan Stephens, and others.

In his criticism also, Winters went his own way, challenging accepted opinions and making enemies in the process. Not only did he define what he believed were mistaken and possibly dangerous directions in the thinking and
methods of many American poets, novelists, and prose writers; but also, in
his final volume, *Forms of Discovery: Critical and Historical Essays on the
Forms of the Short Poem in English* (1967), he offered new and for many
readers unpopular perspectives on the history of the short poem, both in
Great Britain and in the United States. His criticism, however, is not primarily destructive in bent. For one thing, he revised the reputations of many distinguished poets who had already begun to sink into oblivion, such as
George Gascoigne, Fulke Greville, and Charles Churchill from the older
periods; Bridges, T. Sturge Moore, and Frederick Goddard Tuckerman from
more recent times. For another, he found forgotten poems and qualities of
major writers that deserved attention—such poets as Ben Jonson, George
Herbert, and Henry Vaughan; Hardy, Stevens, and Edwin Arlington Robinson. Finally, he formulated coherent theories about poems, and in fact all literary forms, as works of art, theories to which his own work as a poet and his
evaluations of the work of others consistently subscribe. To ignore or dismiss
this copious and wide-ranging body of work is to overlook one of the clear-
est, most precisely analytical, and most disturbingly persuasive voices in
American criticism.

Of all the honors he received during his lifetime, Winters said he was
proudest of an issue of the Stanford undergraduates' magazine, *Sequoia*,
which paid tribute to him in 1961. In 1960, he received the Bollingen Award
from Yale University for his poetry, and in 1961, the Harriet Monroe Poetry
Award from the University of Chicago. Having served on the faculty of Stanford University since 1928, Winters was made full professor in 1949, and in
1962 he became the first holder of the Albert L. Guerard professorship in
English. In 1961-1962, a Guggenheim grant enabled Winters to complete the
work on his last volume of criticism. By the end of his life, he was beginning
to receive the acclaim that is due him. In 1981, *The Southern Review* honored
him with an entire issue devoted to studies of his life and work.

Biography

Born in the first year of the twentieth century, Arthur Yvor Winters spent
his earliest years in Chicago and in Eagle Rock (an area of Los Angeles),
California. The landscape of Southern California near Pasadena provides the
setting for two major poems in heroic couplets, "The Slow Pacific Swell" and

"On a View of Pasadena from the Hills." Later, he returned to Chicago, was graduated from high school, and for one year attended the University of Chicago, where, in 1917, he became a member of the Poetry Club, which, in his own words, "was a very intelligent group, worth more than most courses in literature." By then he had begun to study his contemporaries—Ezra Pound, William Carlos Williams, Stevens, William Butler Yeats—and the diverse poetic styles appearing in the little magazines.

In 1918, having contracted tuberculosis, he was forced to move to Santa Fe, New Mexico, confined to a sanatorium for three years. The debilitating fatigue and pain, the resultant hypersensitivity to sound and sight and touch, and the sense of death hovering were experiences indelibly etched in his poetry then and later. In 1921, Winters began teaching grade school—English, French, zoology, boxing, basketball—in a coal-mining camp called Madrid, and he taught high school the following year in Cerrillos. These five years in the Southwestern United States were a slow period of recovery in isolation, a time when his own study of poetry continued and his correspondence with many contemporary poets was active. It was also the time of his earliest publications. The landscape of New Mexico suffuses the poetry of his first four volumes.

In the summer of 1923, Winters began the academic study that would eventually bring him to Stanford for his doctorate, earning a B.A. and M.A. in romance languages, with a minor in Latin, from the University of Colorado. The skills he acquired enabled him to translate many poems from French and Spanish (including thirteenth century Galician) and, between 1925 and 1927, to teach French and Spanish at the University of Idaho at Moscow. During this period, he married Janet Lewis, later a distinguished novelist and poet, whom he had met in 1921 on a return visit to Chicago; their wedding was in 1926 in Santa Fe, where she, too, had gone to cure tuberculosis. Together now, they moved to Stanford in 1927, when Winters was twenty-six years old; then, under the tutelage of his admired mentor in Renaissance studies, William Dinsmore Briggs, he began the systematic study of poetry in English that occupied him for the rest of his life.

Winters' life in California as a teacher, husband, father, and involved citizen is reflected everywhere in his later poetry. He became a legend at Stanford. Depending on which students were reporting, he was dogmatic, shy, reasonable, surly, kind, hilarious, humorless, a petty tyrant, or an intellectual giant. His disciples and detractors felt intensely about him; few were indifferent. The marriage of Winters and Janet Lewis was a lasting and loving one, and it nurtured their independent careers as writers. His daughter Joanna was born in 1931 and his son Daniel in 1938. Hardly one to withdraw into an ivory tower, Winters liked to get his hands dirty. The raising and breeding of Airedale terriers was a lifelong activity. He kept goats and a garden. He became deeply involved with the trial of David Lamson, a friend unjustly accused of murdering his wife. During World War II, he served as a Citizens' Defense Corps zone warden for Los Altos. These experiences are the kinds of occasions he wrote about in his later work.

Before his retirement from Stanford in 1966, Winters had already endured the first of two operations for cancer, the disease that killed him in 1968. His final effort as a writer, amid acute pain, was to see his last book, *Forms of Discovery*, through to publication after the death of his publisher and old friend, Alan Swallow.

Analysis

The change in poetic forms from experimental to traditional—from Imagistic free verse to formalist poetry using the traditional plain style or post-Symbolist imagery—which Yvor Winters' poetry exhibits after 1930 is so dramatic that it is easy to overlook the continuity of certain stylistic features and thematic preoccupations throughout his career. From the very beginning of his poetic life, he abhorred an indulgent rhetoric in excess of subject matter; always he attempted an exact adjustment of feeling to intellectual content. He paid strict attention to the value of each word as an amalgam of denotative, connotative, rhythmic, and aural properties; to the integrity of the poetic line and the perfect placing of each word within it; and to the clarity and economy of a style that avoids cliché. A poem was for him a means of contemplating human experience in such a way that the meaning of that experience and the feelings appropriate to that meaning are precisely rendered.

Thematic continuity exists also. His first volume of poems, *The Immobile Wind*, whatever immaturities of style it may exhibit, contains themes that he worked and reworked in all of his poems thereafter. As a collection, it speaks of man alone in an empty universe whose end is death, whose choices are existence or creation. Man lives and observes. If this is all, life remains an unrealized potential, the experience of which may be beautiful or terror-ridden but will lack the possibility of meaning which the artist may be able to create. To do this, the artist must choose his reality, must will it; to create his own world, he must give over the things of this one, for this world is merely phenomenal, the raw material of vision, a means at best, not an end: "And all these things would take/ My life from me." The end for all is death, and, in addition for the artist, the possibility of awareness. Religion offers no solace. The subject of the book is the poet, his growth and mission and death. The images in *The Immobile Wind* are sharp and self-contained and their meanings elusive; as one reads through these poems, however, the subjects and images repeat themselves, interweaving, and patterns of meaning begin to emerge.

In its continual allusiveness to itself and to its own images and in its occasional obscurities, *The Immobile Wind* is an irritating book, but it is not impenetrable. More accessible is *The Magpie's Shadow*, which consists of a series of six-syllable poems (a few stretch to seven) grouped according to the season of the year. Each is intended to convey a sharp sense impression; each as an evocation of a season is evocative also of the passage of time and hence of change and death. "The Aspen's Song," from the summer section, is characteristic: "The summer holds me here." That is the poem. The aspen tree is celebrating its moment of being alive, a moment that creates an illusion of permanence and immobility, an illusion because the summer is transient and the motion of change is there in the tree at every moment. The motion/stasis paradox of this image—present also in the oxymoronic title *The Immobile Wind*—recurs through Winters' poetry. No doubt inspired by translations of American Indian and Japanese originals, it also may be seen as an early manifestation of what he later came to call the post-Symbolist method: the sharp sensory image of metaphysical import.

The Bare Hills is Winters' last and most successful book devoted entirely to experimental forms. It is divided into three sections. The first, called "Upper River Country: Rio Grande," consists of twelve poems, each describing a month of the year; together, they are emblematic of the poet's progress through life, the poet growing more sensitive to the beauty and brutality around him and more aware of the meaninglessness of life and the inevitability of death. The second, called "The Bare Hills," consists of seven groups of three, four, or five poems each; it tells of the poet surrounded by death and cruelty but trying to learn, feeling inadequate to his task of creation, lacking an audience: He has but "this cold eye for the fact; that keeps me/ quiet, walking toward a/ stinging end: I am alone. . . ." The third section, called "The Passing Night," consists of two prose poems describing a bleak landscape of endless cold, a minimal level of existence, almost void of hope; the poet waits and remembers and observes, and that is all.

In many of these poems, Winters is continuing to experiment with the evocative image. For example, here is the third of four stanzas from one of the finest poems in this collection, "The Upper Meadows":

> Apricots
> The clustered
> Fur of bees
> Above the gray rocks of the uplands.

Out of context, the images seem vivid, perhaps, but randomly juxtaposed; in context, which has been describing the dying leaves at the advent of autumn, the transience of these living beings—apricots and bees—is felt, reinforced by the final stanza, ending with this line: "But motion, aging." The landscape evoked in the poem is beautiful, vibrantly alive, and dying. In an early review of *The Bare Hills*, Agnes Lee Freer called it "a book inspiring in its absolute originality."

The Proof exhibits the transition from experimental to traditional forms. The first half of the volume consists of poems in the Imagistic/free verse manner of his early work; the second half contains several sonnets and a few poems in various traditional stanzaic patterns. Winters himself has said, "It was becoming increasingly obvious to me that the poets whom I most admired were Baudelaire and Valéry, and Hardy, Bridges, and Stevens in a few poems each, and that I could never hope to approach the quality of their work by the method which I was using." He had come to believe that, in poems of firm metrical pattern, more precise and hence more expressive rhythmical and aural effects were possible, the result being the communication of greater complexity of feeling. To this belief he adhered for the rest of his life.

"The Fable," originally a blank-verse sonnet but reduced to ten lines in the *Collected Poems*, is illustrative. After describing the sea, which "Gathers and washes and is gone," he writes:

> But the crossed rock braces the hills and makes
> A steady quiet of the steady music,
> Massive with peace.
>   And listen, now:
> The foam receding down the sand silvers
> Between the grains, thin, pure as virgin words,
> Lending a sheen to Nothing, whispering.

The sea is the wilderness surrounding us, emblematic of the empty universe and, in its ceaseless motion and ominous quiet, the process of dying. In the first line of this passage, the reversed feet in the first and third positions are metrical irregularities that, by contrast, emphasize the slow evenness of the next two lines, an evenness that recalls the quiet heaving of the sea itself. The sibilant sounds in the fourth line quoted are also descriptively accurate and metaphysically charged: The sound of the sea washing through the sand is the voice of the emptiness itself, of "Nothing, whispering."

His next volume, *The Journey*, consists of eight poems in heroic couplets. The first, "The Critiad," his longest poem, is an attempt to create satirical portraits in the manner of Alexander Pope; Winters chose to preserve neither it nor the last poem, "December Eclogue," in his collected works. The other six poems, most of them longer than his usual efforts, are among his most original, for they put the heroic couplet to new uses. "The Journey" through Snake River Country, for example, describes in forty-four lines a train trip at night through Wyoming and arrival at a destination in the morning. On a descriptive level, the poem is detailed and exact. On a symbolic level, it depicts a journey through hell, at the end of which the poet emerges intact from his spiritual trial. The following lines describe the poet's sudden awareness of the brutal and meaningless wilderness, the landscape of despair:

> Once when the train paused in an empty place,
> I met the unmoved landscape face to face;
> Smoothing abysses that no stream could slake,
> Deep in its black gulch crept the heavy Snake,
> The sound diffused, and so intently firm,
> It seemed the silence, having change nor term.

The poet has been describing the violence and squalor of life in the towns the train has passed through, and now he contemplates the empty landscape that harbors those towns. Descriptively, the language is very exact: The abysses are "Smoothing"—that is, being smoothed and stretching for endless distances—because of the river's ceaseless motion; the river's sound is diffused but also there, inevitably, forever, having neither change nor termination. One finds again the motion/stasis paradox which here is also a sound/silence paradox. In this quiet scene, decay is alive and busy; the river is the Snake, evil, eternal, obliterating all "Deep in its black gulch." Iambic pentameter couplets have not been used in this way before.

The next volume, *Before Disaster*, is a miscellaneous collection of poems in traditional forms: quatrains of three, four, or five feet; some sonnets; a few poems in rhymed couplets of varying line lengths. The subject matter is equally various: personal, as in "To My Infant Daughter" and "For My Father's Grave"; mythological, as in "Midas," "Orpheus," and "Chiron"; occasional, as in "Elegy on a Young Airedale Bitch Lost Some Years Since in the Salt-Marsh," "The Anniversary," "On the Death of Senator Thomas J. Walsh," "Dedication for a Book of Criticism," and so on. Here is the final stanza from a poem in the plain style called "To a Young Writer":

> Write little; do it well.
> Your knowledge will be such,
> At last, as to dispel
> What moves you overmuch.

Nothing could be plainer or seem simpler, but what is conveyed is a weighty sense of classical restraint and control, the power of realized truth.

All of the collections that follow are republications of old work, supplemented with either some new work or old work never before published in a book. The 1960 revision of his *Collected Poems*, however, represents something more than merely a new grouping. Even though it is a selection, hence incomplete, it arranges in chronological order the poetry he wished to keep, beginning with four poems from *The Immobile Wind* and ending with his last poems, "At the San Francisco Airport" and "Two Old-Fashioned Songs." Thus, it is a record of Winters' poetic life. The poems it contains are meditations on a wide variety of subjects: on the greatness of historical heroes, such as Socrates, Herman Melville, John Sutter, and John Day; on the greatness of legendary heroes, such as Theseus, Sir Gawaine, and Hercules; on the evil that people do, as in the poems that deal with World War II; on the vast beauty of the world, in such things as an orchard, a dirigible, California wine, the ancient manzanita, a Renaissance portrait, "summer grasses brown with heat," the "soft voice of the nesting dove," and so on; and on the ever-encroaching wilderness and our proximity to death: "Ceaseless, the dead leaves gather, mound on mound." The book is a reflection of a great mind, one at every moment intellectually alive as well as hypersensitive to physical reality. To read it is to partake of the richness, the depths of Winters' inner life. Because the poems exhibit the three very different methods Winters perfected—free verse, traditional plain style, and post-Symbolist imagery—to read the book is to understand something of poetry as an art. If Winters' belief in the power of literature to alter one's being is true, it is to change for the better as well.

Other major works

SHORT FICTION: "The Brink of Darkness," 1932, revised 1947.

NONFICTION: *Primitivism and Decadence: A Study of American Experimental Poetry*, 1937; *Maule's Curse: Seven Studies in the History of American Obscurantism*, 1938; *The Anatomy of Nonsense*, 1943; *Edwin Arlington Robinson*, 1946; *In Defense of Reason*, 1947; *The Function of Criticism: Problems and Exercises*, 1957; *Forms of Discovery: Critical and Historical Essays on the Forms of the Short Poem in English*, 1967; *The Uncollected Essays and Reviews of Yvor Winters*, 1973.

Bibliography
Davis, Dick. *Wisdom and Wilderness: The Achievement of Yvor Winters*, 1983.

Fields, Kenneth. "The Free Verse of Yvor Winters and William Carlos Williams," in *The Southern Review*. III (July, 1967), pp. 764-775.

Graff, Gerald. "Teaching: Yvor Winters of Stanford," in *American Scholar*. XLIV (Spring, 1975), pp. 291-298.

Kaye, Howard. "The Post-Symbolist Poetry of Yvor Winters," in *The Southern Review*. VII (Winter, 1971), pp. 176-197.

Peterson, Douglas L. Review of "By the Road to the Air-Base," in *The Southern Review*. XV (July, 1979), pp. 567-574.

Powell, Grosvenor. *Language as Being in the Poetry of Yvor Winters*, 1980.

The Southern Review. XVII (October, 1981). Special Winters issue.

Stanford, Donald E. "Classicism and the Modern Poet," in *The Southern Review*. V (April, 1969), pp. 475-500.

Winters, Yvor, and Hart Crane. *Hart Crane and Yvor Winters: Their Literary Correspondence*, 1978. Edited by Thomas Parkinson.

Joseph Maltby

UPDATES

UPDATES

Aleixandre, Vincente
BORN: Seville, Spain; April 26, 1898
DIED: Madrid, Spain; December 13,
 1984

Ashbery, John
BORN: Rochester, New York; July 28,
 1927
POETRY
A Wave, 1984
Selected Poems, 1985
ACHIEVEMENTS
Bollingen Prize for Poetry, 1985

Atwood, Margaret
BORN: Ottawa, Canada; November 18,
 1939
POETRY
True Stories, 1981
*Murder in the Dark: Short Fictions in
 Prose and Poems*, 1983

Beckett, Samuel
BORN: Foxrock, near Dublin, Ireland;
 April 13, 1906
POETRY
Collected Poems, 1930-1978, 1984
 (revised)

Beer, Patricia
BORN: Exmouth, Devon, England;
 November 4, 1924
POETRY
The Lie of the Land, 1983

Betjeman, John
BORN: London, England; 1906
DIED: Trebetherick, England; May 19,
 1984
POETRY
Archie and the Strict Baptists, 1977
Best of Betjeman, 1978
Church Poems, 1980
Uncollected Poems, 1982

Birney, Earle
BORN: Calgary, Canada; May 13, 1904
POETRY
The Mammoth Corridors, 1980
Copernican Fix, 1985

Bly, Robert
BORN: Madison, Minnesota; December
 23, 1926
POETRY
The Eight Stages of Translation, 1983
Four Ramages, 1983
*Out of the Rolling Ocean, and Other
 Love Poems*, 1984
A Love of Minute Particulars, 1985
Loving a Woman in Two Worlds, 1985
Selected Poems, 1986

Booth, Philip
BORN: Hanover, New Hampshire;
 October 8, 1925
POETRY
Relations: Selected Poems, 1950-1985,
 1986

Brathwaite, Edward Kamau
BORN: Bridgetown, Barbados; May 11,
 1930
POETRY
Sun Poem, 1982
Third World Poems, 1983

Bukowski, Charles
BORN: Andernach, Germany; August 16,
 1920
POETRY
*Horses Don't Bet on People and Neither
 Do I*, 1984
War All the Time: Poems, 1981-1984,
 1984
*You Get So Alone at Times That It Just
 Makes Sense*, 1986

Bunting, Basil
BORN: Scotswood-on-Tyne, England;
March 1, 1900
DIED: Hexham, England; April 17, 1985
POETRY
Selected Poems, 1971

Césaire, Aimé
BORN: Basse-Pointe, Martinique;
June 26, 1913
POETRY
Non-Vicious Circle, 1984

Char, René
BORN: L'Îsle-en-Sorgue, France;
June 14, 1907
POETRY
*No Siege Is Absolute: Versions of René
Char*, 1984 (includes *Fureur et mystère*,
Le Nu perdu, and *Aromates
Chasseurs*)

Ciardi, John
BORN: Boston, Massachusetts; June 24,
1916
DIED: Edison, New Jersey; March 30,
1986
POETRY
Selected Poems, 1984
The Birds of Pompeii, 1985

Corman, Cid
BORN: Boston, Massuchusetts; June 29,
1924
POETRY
Tu, 1983

Coxe, Louis Osborne
BORN: Manchester, New Hampshire;
April 15, 1918
POETRY
The North Well, 1985

Creeley, Robert
BORN: Arlington, Massachusetts;
May 21, 1926

POETRY
The Finger: Poems, 1966-1969, 1970
Mirrors, 1982
A Calender, 1983
*The Collected Poems of Robert Creeley:
1945-1975*, 1983
Memories, 1984
Memory Gardens, 1986

Dickey, James
BORN: Atlanta, Georgia; February 2,
1923
POETRY
The Early Motion, 1981
The Central Motion: Poems, 1968-1979,
1983
*Brownwen, the Traw, and the Shape-
Shifter: A Poem in Four Parts*, 1986

Dugan, Alan
BORN: Brooklyn, New York;
February 12, 1923
POETRY
New and Collected Poems: 1961-1983,
1983

Duncan, Robert
BORN: Oakland, California; January 7,
1919
POETRY
Veil, Turbine, Cord, and Bird, 1979
The Five Songs, 1981
Ground Work: Before the War, 1984

Durrell, Lawrence
BORN: Julundur, India; February 27,
1912
POETRY
*The Red Limbo Lingo: A Poetry
Notebook*, 1971
On the Suchness of the Old Boy, 1972
Vega and Other Poems, 1973
Lifelines, 1974
Collected Poems, 1931-1974

Eberhart, Richard
BORN: Austin, Texas; April 5, 1904

POETRY
Florida Poems, 1981
The Long Reach: New and Uncollected Poems, 1948-1983, 1984

Elýtis, Odysseus
BORN: Heraklion, Crete; November 2, 1911
POETRY
What I Love, 1986

Everson, William
BORN: Sacramento, California; September 10, 1912
POETRY
In Medias Res, 1984
Renegade Christmas, 1984

Ferlinghetti, Lawrence
BORN: Yonkers, New York; March 24, 1919?
POETRY
Endless Life: The Selected Poems, 1981
Over All the Obscene Boundaries: European Poems and Translations, 1984

Galvin, Brendan
BORN: Everett, Massachusetts; October 20, 1938
POETRY
Winter Oysters, 1983
A Birder's Dozen, 1984
Seals in the Inner Harbor, 1986

Ginsberg, Allen
BORN: Newark, New Jersey; June 3, 1926
POETRY
Collected Poems, 1947-1980, 1984
White Shroud: Poems, 1980-1985, 1986

Giovanni, Nikki
BORN: Knoxville, Tennessee; June 7, 1943
POETRY
Those Who Ride the Night Winds, 1983

Graves, Robert
BORN: Wimbledon, England; July 26, 1895
DIED: Deya, Majorca, Spain; December 7, 1985

Gunn, Thom
BORN: Gravesend, England; August 29, 1929
POETRY
Talbot Road, 1981
The Menace, 1982
The Passages of Joy, 1982

Hacker, Marilyn
BORN: New York, New York; November 27, 1942
POETRY
Assumptions, 1985
Love, Death, and the Changing of the Seasons, 1986

Hall, Donald
BORN: New Haven, Connecticut; September 20, 1928
POETRY
The Happy Man, 1986

Harrison, Jim
BORN: Grayling, Michigan; December 11, 1937
POETRY
The Theory and Practice of Rivers, 1986

Heaney, Seamus
BORN: Mossbawn, Ireland; April 13, 1939
POETRY
Station Island, 1984

Hecht, Anthony
BORN: New York, New York; January 16, 1923
POETRY
A Love for Four Voices: A Homage to Franz Joseph Haydn, 1983

ACHIEVEMENTS
Bollingen Prize for Poetry, 1983

Hein, Piet
BORN: Copenhagen, Denmark;
    December 16, 1905
POETRY
Viking Vistas, 1983 (with Jens Arup)

Herbert, Zbigniew
BORN: Lvov, Poland; October 29, 1924
POETRY
*Report from the Besieged City and Other
    Poems*, 1987

Heyen, William
BORN: Brooklyn, New York;
    November 1, 1940
POETRY
The Bees, 1981
The Trains, 1981
Erika: Poems of the Holocaust, 1984

Hill, Geoffrey
BORN: Bromsgrove, England; June 18,
    1932
POETRY
*The Mystery of the Charity of Charles
    Péguy*, 1983
Collected Poems, 1986

Hollander, John
BORN: New York, New York;
    October 28, 1929
POETRY
Powers of Thirteen, 1983
In Time and Place, 1986
ACHIEVEMENTS
Bollingen Prize for Poetry, 1983

Hughes, Ted
BORN: Mytholmroyd, England;
    August 17, 1930
POETRY
Primer of Birds, 1981
New Selected Poems, 1982
River, 1984

*Flowers and Insects: Some Birds and a
    Pair of Spiders*, 1986

Hugo, Richard
BORN: Seattle, Washington;
    December 21, 1923
POETRY
*Making Certain It Goes On: The
    Collected Poems of Richard Hugo*,
    1984

Ignatow, David
BORN: Brooklyn, New York; February 7,
    1914
POETRY
Whisper to the Earth: New Poems, 1982
Leaving the Door Open, 1984
New and Collected Poems, 1970-1985,
    1986

Kennedy, X. J.
BORN: Dover, New Jersey; August 21,
    1929
POETRY
Hangover Mass, 1984
Cross Ties: Selected Poems, 1985

Kinnell, Galway
BORN: Providence, Rhode Island;
    February 1, 1927
POETRY
The Fundamental Project of Technology,
    1983
The Past, 1985
ACHIEVEMENTS
Pulitzer Prize for Letters, 1983, for
    Selected Poems

Kizer, Carolyn
BORN: Spokane, Washington;
    December 10, 1925
POETRY
*Mermaids in the Basement: Poems for
    Women*, 1984
Yin: New Poems, 1984
ACHIEVEMENTS
Pulitzer Prize in Letters, 1985, for *Yin*

UPDATES

Koch, Kenneth
BORN: Cincinnati, Ohio; February 27, 1925
POETRY
Days and Nights, 1982
Selected Poems, 1950-1982, 1985
On the Edge, 1986

Larkin, Philip
BORN: Coventry, England; August 9, 1922
DIED: Hull, England; December 2, 1985
POETRY
Aubade, 1980

Levertov, Denise
BORN: Ilford, England; October 24, 1923
POETRY
Pig Dreams: Scenes from the Life of Sylvia, 1981
Candles in Babylon, 1982
El Salvador: Requiem and Invocation, 1983 (music by W. Newell-Hendricks)
Poems, 1960-1967, 1983
Oblique Prayers: New Poems with Fourteen Translations, 1984
The Menaced World, 1985
Selected Poems, 1986
Poems, 1968-1972, 1987

Levine, Philip
BORN: Detroit, Michigan; January 10, 1928
POETRY
Selected Poems, 1984
Sweet Will, 1985

Logan, John
BORN: Red Oak, Iowa; January 23, 1923
The Transformation: Poems January to March, 1981, 1983

MacBeth, George
BORN: Shotts, Scotland; January 19, 1932
POETRY
Prayers, 1973
Poems from Oby, 1983
The Long Darkness, 1984

McPherson, Sandra
BORN: San Jose, California; August 2, 1943
POETRY
Sensing, 1980
Patron Happiness, 1983
Floralia, 1985
Pheasant Flower, 1985

Matthews, William
BORN: Cincinnati, Ohio; November 11, 1942
POETRY
Flood: Poems, 1982
A Happy Childhood, 1984

Merrill, James
BORN: New York, New York; March 2, 1926
POETRY
Peter, 1982
The Changing Light at Sandover, 1983
From the First Nine: Poems, 1946-1976, 1983
Bronze, 1984
Souvenirs, 1984
Late Settings, 1985

Merwin, W. S.
BORN: New York, New York; September 30, 1927
POETRY
Finding the Islands, 1982
Opening the Hand, 1983

Michaux, Henri
BORN: Namur, Belgium; May 24, 1899
DIED: Paris, France; October 17, 1984
POETRY
Telegram from Dakal, 1986

Middleton, Christopher
BORN: Truro, England; June 10, 1926
POETRY
Woden Dog, 1982
III Poems, 1983
Serpentine, 1984

Milosz, Czeslaw
BORN: Šeteiniai, Lithuania; June 30, 1911
POETRY
The Separate Notebooks, 1984

Montague, John
BORN: New York, New York;
 February 28, 1929
POETRY
The Leap, 1979
Selected Poems, 1982
The Dead Kingdom, 1984

Moss, Howard
BORN: New York, New York;
 January 22, 1922
POETRY
New York, 1980
Rules of Sleep, 1984
New Selected Poems, 1986

Nemerov, Howard
BORN: New York, New York; March 1,
 1920
POETRY
Inside the Onion, 1984
ACHIEVEMENTS
Bollingen Prize for Poetry, 1981

Oates, Joyce Carol
BORN: Lockport, New York; June 16,
 1938
POETRY
Celestial Timepeace, 1980
Nightless Nights, 1981
*Invisible Woman: New and Selected
 Poems, 1970-1982*, 1982

Oppen, George
BORN: New Rochelle, New York;
 April 24, 1908
DIED: Sunnyvale, California; July 7, 1984

Oppenheimer, Joel
BORN: Yonkers, New York; February 18,
 1930

POETRY
At Fifty, 1982
Poetry: The Ecology of the Soul, 1983
New Spaces: Poems, 1975-1983, 1985

Orr, Gregory
BORN: Albany, New York; February 3,
 1947
POETRY
We Must Make a Kingdom, 1986

Parra, Nicanor
BORN: Chillán, Chile; September 5, 1914
POETRY
Sermones y prédicas del Cristo de Elqui,
 1977 (*Sermons and Homilies of the
 Christ of Elqui*, 1984)
Antipoems: New and Selected, 1985

Pastan, Linda
BORN: New York, New York; May 27,
 1932
POETRY
A Fraction of Darkness, 1985

Pavlović, Miodrag
BORN: Novi Sad, Voyvodina;
 November 28, 1928
POETRY
A Voice Locked in Stone, 1985

Paz, Octavio
BORN: Mexico City, Mexico; March 31,
 1914
POETRY
Selected Poems, 1984

Pinsky, Robert
BORN: Long Branch, New Jersey;
 October 20, 1940
POETRY
History of My Heart, 1984

Plath, Sylvia
BORN: Boston, Massachusetts; October
 27, 1932

DIED: London, England; February 11, 1963

ACHIEVEMENTS

Pulitzer Prize for Letters, 1982, for *The Collected Poems*

Plumly, Stanley
BORN: Barnesville, Ohio; May 23, 1939
POETRY
Summer Celestial, 1984

Randall, Dudley
BORN: Washington, D.C.; January 14, 1914
POETRY
A Litany of Friends: New and Selected Poems, 1981

Reed, Henry
BORN: Birmingham, England; February 22, 1914
POETRY
Lessons of the War, 1970

Rich, Adrienne
BORN: Baltimore, Maryland; May 16, 1929
POETRY
Sources, 1983
The Fact of a Doorframe: Poems Selected and New, 1950-1984, 1984
Your Native Land, Your Life, 1986

Różewicz, Tadeusz
BORN: Radom, Poland; October 9, 1921
POETRY
Zielona róza, 1961 (*Green Rose*, 1982)

Sarton, May
BORN: Wondelgem, Belgium; May 3, 1912
POETRY
Letter from Maine: New Poems, 1984

Schuyler, James
BORN: Chicago, Illinois; November 9, 1923

POETRY
A Few Days, 1985

Shapiro, Karl
BORN: Baltimore, Maryland; November 10, 1913
POETRY
Love and War, Art and God: The Poems of Karl Shapiro, 1984

Simic, Charles
BORN: Belgrade, Yugoslavia; May 9, 1938
POETRY
Austerities, 1982
Weather Forecast for Utopia and Vicinity, 1967-1982, 1983
Selected Poems, 1963-1983, 1985
Unending Blues, 1986

Simpson, Louis
BORN: Kingston, Jamaica; March 27, 1923
POETRY
People Live Here: Selected Poems, 1949-1983, 1983
The Best Hour of the Night, 1984

Smith, Dave
BORN: Portsmouth, Virginia; December 19, 1942
POETRY
Gray Soldiers, 1983
In the House of the Judge, 1983
Southern Delights, 1984 (poetry and prose)
The Roadhouse Voices, 1985

Snodgrass, W. D.
BORN: Wilkinsburg, Pennsylvania; January 5, 1926
POETRY
If Birds Build with Your Hair, 1979
Heinrich Himmler: Platoons and Flies, 1982
The Boy Made of Meat, 1983

D. D. Byrde Callying Jennie Wrenn, 1984

Snyder, Gary
BORN: San Francisco, California; May 8, 1930
POETRY
True Night, 1980
Axe Handles, 1983
Left Out in the Rain: New Poems, 1947-1985, 1986

Spender, Stephen
BORN: London, England; February 28, 1909
POETRY
Collected Poems: 1928-1985, 1985

Stafford, William
BORN: Hutchinson, Kansas; January 17, 1914
POETRY
A Glass Face in the Rain, 1982
Roving Across Fields: A Conversation and Uncollected Poems, 1942-1982, 1983
Segues: A Correspondence in Poetry, 1983 (with Marvin Bell)
Smoke's Way: Poems from Limited Editions, 1968-1981, 1983
Listening Deep, 1984

Still, James
BORN: Double Creek, Alabama; July 16, 1906
POETRY
The Wolfpen Poems, 1986

Swenson, May
BORN: Logan, Utah; May 28, 1919
ACHIEVEMENTS
Bollingen Prize for Poetry, 1981

Tate, James
BORN: Kansas City, Missouri; December 8, 1943
POETRY

Constant Defender, 1983
Reckoner, 1986

Tomlinson, Charles
BORN: Stoke-on-Trent, England; January 8, 1927
POETRY
Notes from New York and Other Poems, 1984
Collected Poems, 1985
Eden: Graphics and Poetry, 1985

Tranströmer, Tomas
BORN: Stockholm, Sweden; April 15, 1931
POETRY
Sanningsbarriären, 1978 (*Truth Barriers*, 1980)
Det vilda torget, 1983 (*The Wild Marketplace*, 1985)
Tomas Tranströmer: Selected Poems, 1987

Villa, José Garcia
BORN: Manila, Philippines; August 5, 1908
POETRY
Appassionata: Poems in Praise of Love, 1979

Wagoner, David
BORN: Massillon, Ohio; June 5, 1926
POETRY
First Light, 1983

Wakoski, Diane
BORN: Whittier, California; August 3, 1937
POETRY
Looking for Beethoven in Las Vegas, 1981
The Lady Who Drove Me to the Airport, 1982
The Collected Greed, Parts 1-13, 1984

UPDATES

Walcott, Derek A.
BORN: Castries, St. Lucia; January 23,
1930
POETRY
Midsummer, 1984
Collected Poems, 1948-1984, 1986
The Arkansas Testament, 1987

Warren, Robert Penn
BORN: Guthrie, Kentucky; April 24,
1905
POETRY
New and Selected Poems, 1923-1985,
1985

Whittemore, Reed
BORN: New Haven, Connecticut;
September 11, 1919
POETRY
*The Feel of Rock: Poems of Three
Decades*, 1982

Wilbur, Richard
BORN: New York, New York; March 1,
1921
POETRY
Verses on the Times, 1978

Advice from the Muse, 1981
Seven Poems, 1981

Wright, Charles
BORN: Pickwick Dam, Tennessee;
August 25, 1935
POETRY
Country Music: Selected Early Poems,
1982
Four Poems of Departure, 1983
The Other Side of the River, 1984

Yeats, William Butler
BORN: Sandymount, near Dublin,
Ireland; June 13, 1865
DIED: Cap Martin, France; January 28,
1939
POETRY
The Poems: A New Edition, 1984

Yevtushenko, Yevgeny
BORN: Zima Junction, U.S.S.R.; July 18,
1933
POETRY
Giolub v santiago, 1982 (*A Dove in
Santiago: A Novella in Verse*, 1982)

CRITICAL SURVEY
OF
POETRY

INDEX

II

"Essex" (Davie), 89.
"Et Maintenant" (Reverdy), 326.
Events and Wisdoms (Davie), 87.
Everson, William, 405.
Evropeiskaya noch' (Khodasevich), 228-229.
Exister (Follain), 126, 128.
"Expulsion, The" (Stern) 377.
Eyes and Objects (Johnson), 214.

"Fable, The" (Winters), 398.
"Fable from the Cayoosh Country" (Barnard), 29-30.
"Father and Son" (Kunitz), 243-244.
Father Guzman (Stern), 374-376.
"Faustus" (Hope), 191.
Fazendeiro do ar (Drummond de Andrade), 100.
Ferdowsi. *See* **Firdusi.**
Ferlinghetti, Lawrence, 405.
Fields of Learning (Miles), 278.
"Figlio della Peppa, Il" (Saba), 344.
Firdausi. *See* **Firdusi.**
Firdusi, 119-124; *Shahnamah*, 119-123.
First Hymn to Lenin and Other Poems (MacDiarmid), 263.
Firstborn (Glück), 134.
"Fitting, The" (Barnard), 24.
Flesh and Blood (Williams), 391-392.
Follain, Jean, 125-132; "L'Amirauté," 128-129; "L'Amitié," 128; "Apparition de la vieille," 131; "L'Appel du chevalier," 128; "La Brodeuse d'abeilles," 130; *Chants terrestres*, 126-128; "L'Enfant au tambour," 128; "Enfantement," 130; *Exister*, 126, 128; *La Main chaude*, 126-127; "Le Sapeur," 130-131; "Les Uns et les autres," 131.
"For My Mother" (Glück), 135.
"For the Word Is Flesh" (Kunitz), 242-243.
"Forest Lake" (Södergran), 364.
"Forests of Lithuania, The" (Davie), 88-89.
"Formation of a Separatist, I" (Howe), 196.
"Fragments of a Liquidation" (Howe), 195-196.
"Friends" (Williams), 390.
"From My Window" (Williams), 391.

Galvin, Brendan, 405.
"Garden, The" (Glück), 136.
"Gates, The" (Rukeyser), 334-335.
Gesammelte Werke in sieben Bänden (Ausländer), 18.
Ghazal, 149, 155-156, 340.
Ginsberg, Allen, 405.
Giovanni, Nikki, 405.
Glück, Louise, 133-139; "Autumnal," 137; "The Chicago Train," 134; *Descending Figure*, 136-137; "The Edge," 134-135; *Firstborn*, 134; "For My Mother," 135; "The Garden," 136; "Gretel in Darkness," 135; "Happiness," 137; *The House on Marshland*, 135-136; "Marathon," 138; "Metamorphosis," 137-138; "Mock Orange," 137; "The Racer's Widow," 135; "Thanksgiving," 134; *The Triumph of Achilles*, 137-138; "The Undertaking," 136.
"Goat, The" (Saba), 346.
"God's Spies" (Howe), 196.
Good Fight, The (Kinsella), 236-237.
Graves, Robert, 405.
"Gretel in Darkness" (Glück), 135.
Grieve, Christopher Murray. *See* **MacDiarmid, Hugh.**
"Guerre" (Reverdy), 322-323.
Gunn, Thom, 405.

Haavikko, Paavo, 140-148; *Kaksikymmentä ja yksi*, 146; *Neljätoista hallitsijaa*, 145-146; *Tiet etäisyyksiin*, 142-143; *The Winter Palace*, 144.
Hacker, Marilyn, 405.
"Haecceity" (Cunningham), 77.
Hafiz, 149-157; *Divan*, 149, 152-157.
Haiku, 203-204.
Hall, Donald, 405.
"Hand-Rolled Cigarettes" (Yevtushenko), 247.
"Happiness" (Glück), 137.
Harper, Michael S., 158-165; "American History," 162; "Brother John," 162; *Debridement*, 163; *Healing Song for the Inner Ear*, 164; "High Modes," 163; "History as Appletree," 163; "History as Personality," 163; *History Is Your Own Heartbeat*, 162; "The Militance of a Photograph in the Passbook of a Bantu Under Detention, 164; *Night-*